ENCYCLOPEDIA OF HOME
MAINTENANCE
AND
REPAIR

ENCYCLOPEDIA OF HOME MAINTENANCE AND REPAIR

William P. Spence

STERLING PUBLISHING COMPANY, INC.

Library of Congress Cataloging-in-Publication Data

Spence, William Perkins, 1925-
    The encyclopedia of home maintenance & repair/William P. Spence.
      p. cm.
    Includes index.
    ISBN 0-8069-8457-0
      1. Dwellings—Maintenance and repair—Amateurs' manuals. I. Title.

TH4817.3.S64 2000
643'.7-dc21

10 9 8 7 6 5 4 3 2 1

Published by Sterling Publishing Company, Inc.
387 Park Avenue South, New York, N.Y. 10016
©2000 by William Spence
Distributed in Canada by Sterling Publishing
℅ Canadian Manda Group, One Atlantic Avenue, Suite 105
Toronto, Ontario, Canada M6K 3E7
Distributed in Great Britain and Europe by Cassell PLC
Wellington House, 125 Strand, London WC2R 0BB, England
Distributed in Australia by Capricorn Link (Australia) Pty Ltd.
P.O. Box 6651, Baulkham Hills, Business Centre, NSW 2153, Australia
Manufactured in the United States of America
All rights reserved

Sterling ISBN 0-8069-8457-0

CONTENTS

CHAPTER THREE

Heating and Air-Conditioning 149

CHAPTER FOUR

Roof Repairs 199

CHAPTER FIVE

Exterior-Wall Maintenance and Repair 229

INTRODUCTION

This book is designed as a guide for those who want to do much of their own home maintenance and repairs. The topics covered include electricity, plumbing, heating, and air-conditioning; roofs and exterior and interior walls; furniture; painting and finishing techniques; and ways to set up the workshop to get the most from power tools. This information will also be helpful for those employing someone to do the work, because it can be used to evaluate the soundness of the job proposal and the actual work.

The selection of materials for particular jobs is described so that the best material for the job can be chosen. Safety is stressed throughout for all jobs, including those using ladders and scaffolding, power tools that are now available in many homes, and painting and finishing.

In chapters such as those describing plumbing and electrical repairs, the information is explained in a thorough manner that enables the reader to decide whether he or she wants to try doing the repair or will seek professional help.

Stressed throughout is the need to contact the local building inspector and verify if a special permit is needed and if the maintenance or repair work will satisfy the building codes.

Repeated references are made to reading materials provided by the manufacturers of materials and tools so that they are used properly and safely. Hardware and building-supply dealers can provide a great deal of helpful information in these areas. Other dealers of paint, wallpaper, carpeting, and flooring will also provide current helpful information.

Overall, the book will provide a wealth of information for helping you maintain and repair both the interior and exterior of your home.

William P. Spence

CHAPTER ONE

Plumbing Repairs

The plumbing system is a source of problems often due to poor control of the liquid discharged as waste. Many of the basic repair and maintenance problems can be handled if there is an understanding of how the system works and how to take corrective action. Some jobs are best left to the plumber; actually, building codes may require that a licensed plumber be employed for certain jobs such as replacing a toilet. This chapter will help you make basic repairs and have an understanding of those jobs if a plumber is employed.

The plumbing in a typical residence involves two systems: the potable water-supply system and the waste-disposal system. The **water-supply system** delivers potable hot and cold water to sinks, toilets,

and appliances. Potable water is water that is safe to drink. The **waste-disposal system** removes the liquid waste from fixtures and appliances and carries it to the house sewer.

THE POTABLE WATER SYSTEM

Water enters the home through a pipe from a water source. The source may be a well or a city water system. The pipe from a city water system that leads to the house is called the **water service entrance (1–1)**.

The water service entrance leads to a meter that measures the amount of water that flows into the house. This meter may be placed just inside the basement wall, or it may be located outside the

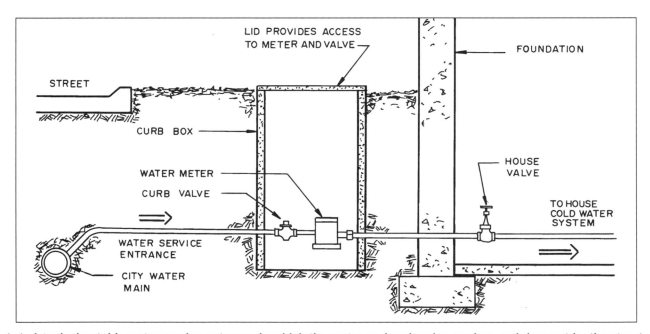

1–1. A typical potable water-service entrance in which the meter and curb valve are in a curb box out by the street.

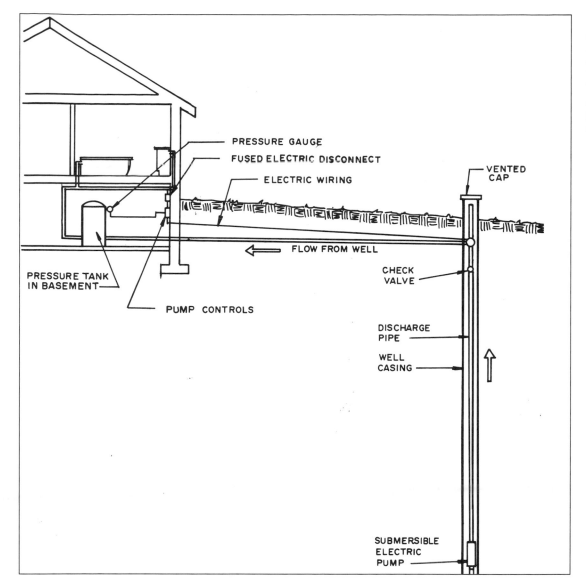

1–2. A simplified drawing showing the main features of a system securing potable water from a well. This system shows a submersible pump. Above-ground pumps are also used.

PRESSURE GAUGE

FUSED ELECTRIC DISCONNECT

ELECTRIC WIRING

VENTED CAP

FLOW FROM WELL

CHECK VALVE

PRESSURE TANK IN BASEMENT

PUMP CONTROLS

DISCHARGE PIPE

WELL CASING

SUBMERSIBLE ELECTRIC PUMP

house in a small underground box called a **stop box**. Inside the stop box and on the side of the meter away from the house, there is a shutoff valve called a **curb valve**. For houses with the meter located inside, the curb valve is usually located underground near the curb. It is often under a disk-shaped pipe cap labeled "water." The water company uses the curb valve to turn on and off the water supply to the house.

On the house side of the water meter, there is a valve called the **house valve**. This valve is used to turn off all the water to the building. If the water meter is inside the house, the shutoff valve will be a few inches away from the meter. If the water meter is in a stop box, the shutoff valve will typically be just inside the basement or utility room.

If the water comes from a well, it is delivered to the house by a pump driven by an electric motor. The pump moves water from the well to a storage tank in the house. The main shutoff valve is usually near the storage tank. The pump keeps the water system within the pressure needed for the system to operate (**1–2**).

In a city water system, the water pressure comes from the **water main**. The main is a large pipe in the ground that supplies the home and all the other homes on the block. The city must keep enough pressure in its system to supply all its customers with water. If the city water system loses pressure, the house loses pressure too.

The cold water that enters the house is run through a system of pipes supplying potable water

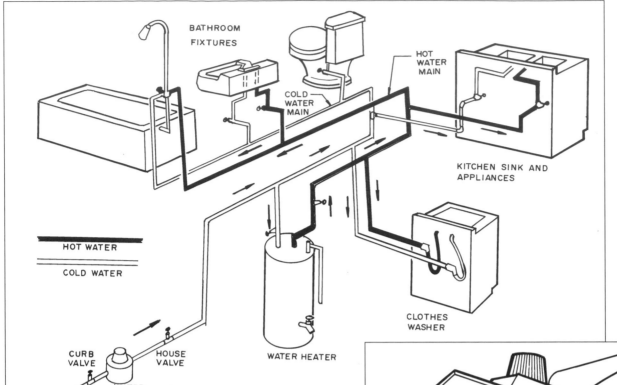

1–3. A typical piping system for supplying potable hot and cold water to fixtures, appliances, and the water heater.

to the various fixtures and appliances (**1–3**). **Fixtures** are sinks, lavatories (small sinks in bathrooms), toilets, and bathtubs. The most common appliances connected to the water-supply system are the washing machine and dishwasher. The cold water for fixtures and appliances first runs through a pipe called a **cold-water main**. Smaller-diameter pipes then branch off from the main pipe to feed the fixtures.

One branch pipe supplies water to the hot-water heater. Here, water is heated and sent out through the **hot-water main**. Smaller pipes branch off this main to feed the fixtures and appliances. There may be a shutoff valve on the cold-water pipe leading to the water heater. This valve is used to stop water from entering the heater when repairs have to be made. There may also be a shutoff valve on the hot-water pipe leaving the heater. This valve is used to shut off the hot water in the house from one point.

The actual connections to most fixtures are made by running a flexible riser connector from the

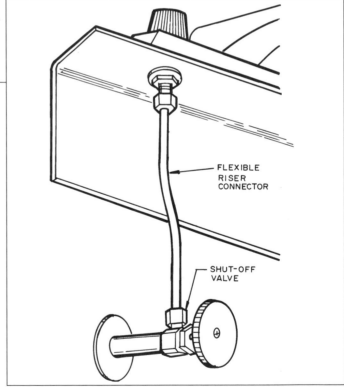

1–4. A flexible riser connector is used to connect the branch fixture pipe and the fixture.

branch pipe to the fixture connection, such as a faucet. Usually there is a shutoff valve at the end of the branch. The riser is attached to the shutoff valve (**1–4**). This valve allows the water to the fixture to be shut off. Some appliances, such as a washing machine, are connected to the branch circuit with

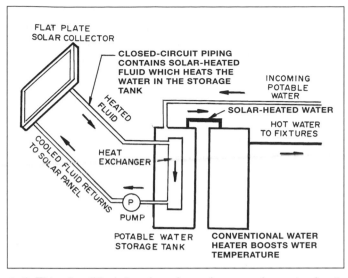

FLAT PLATE
SOLAR COLLECTOR

CLOSED-CIRCUIT PIPING
CONTAINS SOLAR-HEATED
FLUID WHICH HEATS THE
WATER IN THE STORAGE
TANK

INCOMING
POTABLE
WATER

HEATED
FLUID

SOLAR-HEATED WATER

HOT WATER
TO FIXTURES

COOLED FLUID RETURNS
TO SOLAR PANEL

HEAT
EXCHANGER

PUMP

POTABLE WATER
STORAGE TANK

CONVENTIONAL WATER
HEATER BOOSTS WTER
TEMPERATURE

1–5. This simplified drawing shows how a solar water-heating system operates. An actual system will have a pump and electronic controls to make it function.

high-pressure rubber hoses.

A solar water-heating system uses a solar panel to heat fluid in a closed piping circuit. The heat from the water in the closed piping circuit is transferred by convection to the water in a storage tank. The conventional water heater draws this preheated water from the tank and provides additional heat as needed. Solar water-heating systems are commercially available for installation on the hot-water system (**1–5**).

THE WASTE-DISPOSAL SYSTEM

The main parts of the waste-disposal system are the vents, waste pipes, soil pipe, soil stack, house drain, and house sewer (**1–6**). **Waste pipes** receive wastewater from sinks, tubs, lavatories, and appliances. The waste water flows through the waste pipes to

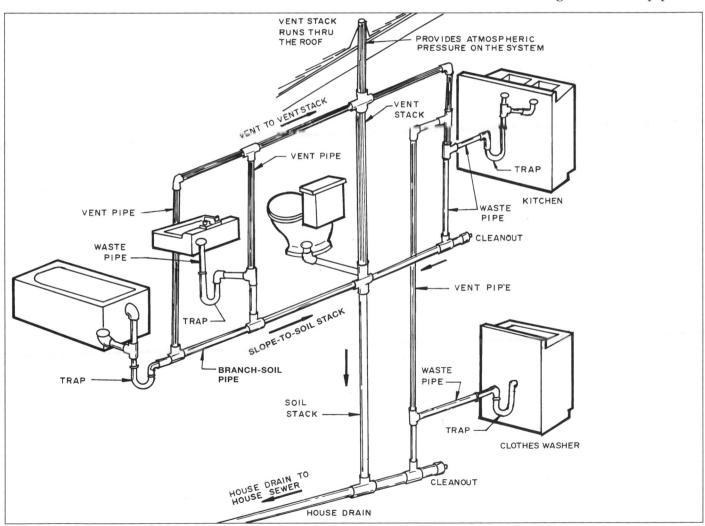

VENT STACK
RUNS THRU
THE ROOF

PROVIDES ATMOSPHERIC
PRESSURE ON THE SYSTEM

VENT TO VENT STACK

VENT
STACK

VENT PIPE

VENT PIPE

TRAP

KITCHEN

WASTE
PIPE

CLEANOUT

WASTE
PIPE

TRAP

VENT PIPE

SLOPE-TO-SOIL STACK

TRAP

BRANCH-SOIL
PIPE

WASTE
PIPE

SOIL
STACK

TRAP

CLOTHES WASHER

HOUSE DRAIN TO
HOUSE SEWER

CLEANOUT

HOUSE DRAIN

1–6. The major parts of a liquid-waste disposal system.

the **soil stack** or a branch soil pipe; they receive waste from water closets as well as from the waste pipes. The soil stack carries the waste to the **house drain**. The house drain carries the waste out of the house to the house sewer. The **house sewer** begins outside the foundation of the house. It carries the waste to the city sewer or to a septic tank.

The waste water in the disposal system flows by gravity, not by water pressure — as the water in the supply system does. However, to work properly, the waste-disposal system must be at the same pressure as the atmosphere. This means the system must be **vented** — that is, open to the outside air at some point. The **vent stack** is the main vent for the house. It is open to the outside air at the roof. Each waste pipe that leads from a fixture to the soil stack has a vent pipe connecting to the vent stack (refer to **1–6**). The vent pipes are all connected to the vent stack. A large house may have several vent stacks.

Each fixture connected to the waste-disposal system has a **trap**. A trap is a U-shaped pipe that is always full of water. The water seals the waste pipe and prevents sewer gases from entering the house. Because each trap is connected to a waste pipe, it is also connected to a vent pipe. This venting does two things: It prevents the water in the trap from being siphoned away, and it allows sewer gases to leave the house. Getting rid of the gases also helps reduce corrosion in the drain and sewer pipes.

PLUMBING CODES

Most communities have a **plumbing code**. A code is a series of regulations that must be followed when installing a plumbing system. The code sets standards so that all buildings in the community have plumbing that is proper and safe. The code usually specifies some plumbing jobs that must be performed by a licensed plumber. This means that home owners, unless they are a licensed plumber, cannot do those jobs. Before starting a major addition or remodeling job that includes plumbing, ask the local building-inspection department for information about the local plumbing code.

TOOLS USED WHEN PLUMBING

Most plumbing jobs require very few tools. Some tools are those that may already be owned for general repairs, while others are special for plumbing. The tools that may already be owned that could be useful in plumbing are the following:

1. Screwdrivers (flat and Phillips blade)

2. Pliers (slip-joint, multiple-joint, and locking)

3. Mallet

4. Hammer

5. Wrenches (adjustable and socket)

6. Files (metal-cutting)

7. Hacksaw

Some special tools that may be needed are the following:

1. Pipe wrench

2. Basin wrench

3. Rubber plunger

4. Auger (also called a **snake**)

5. Plastic joint-sealing tape

6. Pipe-joint compound

7. Tube cutter

8. Tube bender

9. Plumber's solder

10. Flux

11. Propane torch

12. Flaring tool

The use of some of these special tools will be described where they are needed to perform different plumbing jobs.

WATER PIPE AND TUBING

Perhaps a house is being enlarged — that is, one or more bedrooms or a bathroom are being added. Or maybe the house needs to be remodeled, and a half bath will be added. (A **half bath** contains only a toilet and lavatory.) Or maybe the kitchen is being remodeled and the sink has to be moved. These jobs require a knowledge about the types of pipes or tubing available.

On some repair jobs, a piece of pipe will need to be replaced. On most remodeling jobs, a new pipe will have to be installed. Regardless of the kind of pipe to be found in the house, the repair or addition can be made with copper or plastic tubing, or with galvanized steel pipe. Pipes of different materials can be joined together with special fittings. Be sure to check local plumbing codes to determine that the pipe chosen is approved for use in your locality. When selecting the type of pipe, be certain it is approved for the use intended.

Galvanized-Steel Pipe

Galvanized-steel pipe is very strong and is used where the pipe is not protected and could be damaged. It is joined by threading the ends, which screw into threaded galvanized-steel fittings. Threading takes special tools not available to the home owner. Often the company supplying the pipe will cut it to length and thread it.

Copper Tubing

Copper tubing is used for potable water- and waste-disposal systems. It is manufactured in 10- and 20-foot (3- and 6-meter) rigid lengths and in 30-, 60-, and 100-foot (9-, 18-, and 30-meter) coils. The rigid tubing is harder and tougher, but the softer coils are easier to install because they can be formed into curved shapes. Both types are installed by soldering, but the softer coil tubing can also be joined using flared connections.

Type K tubing is the heaviest and is used for exterior underground lines and interior lines. It is color-coded green. **Type L** is a medium-weight pipe used for interior applications. It

is color-coded blue. Both are available in straight lengths and coils. **Type M** is a lightweight tubing used for interior potable-water systems. Waste-disposal systems use **type DWV tubing**. It is coded yellow.

Plastic Pipe

Plastic pipe is lighter in weight and costs less than copper pipe. It is used for potable water and waste-disposal systems. Plastic pipe is manufactured as rigid sections and flexible lengths. Some types can be installed in the ground, while others are for interior aboveground applications. Since different types of plastic are used, you must be certain that the one chosen will do the job. Check the manufacturer's recommendations and the local building code.

Drain, waste, and vent (DWV) pipes and sewers are made from polyvinyl chloride (PVC) and acrylonitrile-butadiene-styrene resin (ABS). PVC is also used for cold-water lines, but not hot-water. Cold- and hot-water lines are made using chlorinated polyvinyl chloride (CPVC) and polybutylene (PB). Polyethylene (PE) is used for outdoor cold-water lines that are buried in the ground. Styrene is sometimes used for sewers and drainage piping. Sink and lavatory drains are made from polypropylene (PP). Each has limits on the amount of pressure and temperature it can carry.

When working with pipe, it is easiest if it can be measured and cut on the workbench. It is easier to cut and finish the ends at this height than to attempt it while you are on the floor or under the house. The first thing to do is cut the pipe to length. This distance, as shown in 1–7, is the sum of the distance between the end fittings plus the amount of pipe to be inserted into each fitting.

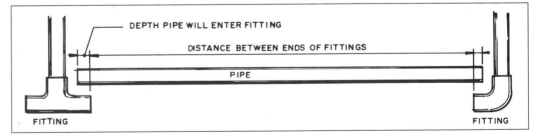

1–7. The length of a pipe between two fittings is the length between the ends of the fittings plus the amount the pipe will fit into each.

WATER-PIPE FITTINGS

Pipe fittings are used to join sections of pipe. The pipe may have the same or different diameters. Some fittings are used to change the direction of the pipe. These include the **Y, T,** and **elbow fittings.** Straight fittings, called **in-line fittings,** include couplings, reducers, nipples, unions, and caps. Generalized examples of these are shown in **1–8.** The specific design of each varies with the material.

The **coupling** is used to join, end to end, two lengths of pipe that are the same diameter. A **reducer** is used to join two lengths of pipe of different diameters end to end. A **nipple** is a short length of steel pipe threaded on both ends. It comes in lengths up to 12 inches (300 millimeters). A nipple is used to extend a length of pipe. A **union** is used to connect two lengths of pipe of the same diameter. It permits the two pieces to be taken apart easily when needed. A **cap** is used to close the end of a pipe.

If pipes made of different materials are being joined, special fittings are needed. A variety of such fittings are shown in **1–9.** To join copper pipe to steel pipe, use a **copper-to-steel fitting.** This fitting has threads on one end to attach to the steel pipe. The other end is smooth, in order to be soldered to the copper pipe. When using this fitting, wrap the threads with plastic joint tape before screwing the coupling to the pipe. The plastic tape will help prevent an electrochemical reaction between the two different kinds of metal. (This action eats away the pipe.)

The **plastic-to-steel fitting** (**1–9**) comes in two parts.

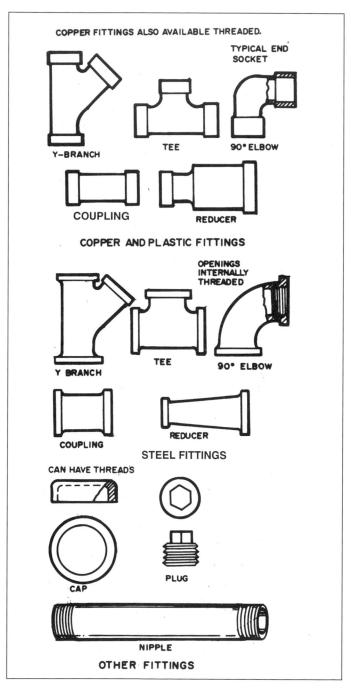

1–8. A few of the copper, plastic, and steel pipe fittings.

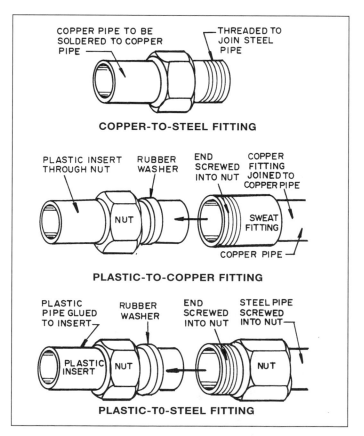

1–9. Typical fittings used to connect pipes made of different materials.

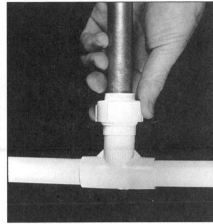

1–10. Copper-to-plastic and steel-to-plastic connections (courtesy of Genova Products, Inc.).

One part is a nut with a threaded extension on one end that is screwed onto the steel pipe. One end of the other part is a plastic insert that has a washer and plastic nut. The nut is tightened onto the threaded extension of the first part. The other end of the plastic insert is solvent cemented to the plastic pipe.

The **plastic-to-copper fitting** (1–9) also has two parts. One part is copper and has a threaded end and a smooth end. The smooth end is soldered to the copper pipe. The other piece is a plastic insert with a nut and washer. The nut is attached to the threaded end of the copper piece. The other end of the insert is cemented to the plastic pipe.

Two types of connections available from one manufacturer are shown in **1–10**.

DRAIN, WASTE, VENT, AND SEWER PIPE

Drain, waste, vent, and sewer pipe may be cast iron, copper, or plastic. Vitrified clay pipe can be used for the house sewer outside the building. Check the local building code to be sure which kinds are approved for use in your locality.

Cast-iron pipe is excellent for

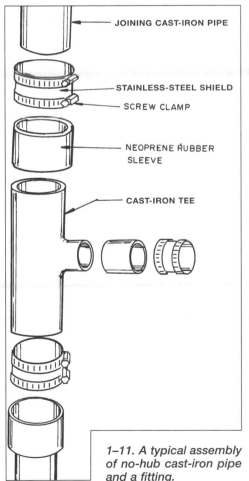

JOINING CAST-IRON PIPE

STAINLESS-STEEL SHIELD

SCREW CLAMP

NEOPRENE RUBBER SLEEVE

CAST-IRON TEE

1–11. A typical assembly of no-hub cast-iron pipe and a fitting.

waste-disposal lines, soil stacks, and vents inside and outside a house. It comes in two weights: **service** and **heavy**. Service weight is the one to use for the home. Cast-iron pipe usually comes in 5-foot (1.5-meter) lengths. **Copper pipe** is very good for all waste-disposal pipes. Copper DWV pipe is color-coded yellow. **Vitrified clay pipe** has a shiny glaze from a glass coating. This coating provides protection from acid and alkaline material in the soil and waste material. Use it for the house sewer, starting 5 feet *outside* the house foundation and leading to the city sewer or the septic tank. Do *not* use this kind of pipe for waste-disposal systems inside the house. PVC (polyvinyl chloride) and ABS (acrylonitrile-butadiene-styrene) plastic pipe are widely used on waste-disposal systems inside and outside the building. Again, check the local building code.

Plastic and copper waste pipes are joined in the same way as water pipe. These are discussed later in this chapter.

MAKING WASTE-LINE CONNECTIONS

Fittings for copper and plastic waste pipe are similar to those shown in **1–8**. The copper pipes are soldered and the plastic pipes are joined with a solvent cement. Cast-iron soil stacks are typically connected with no-hub connectors (**1–11**). This connector consists of a neoprene rubber sleeve and a stainless-steel shield that are slid over the joint. Screw clamps are tightened, securing the joint. Some cast-iron no-hub fittings are shown in **1–12**.

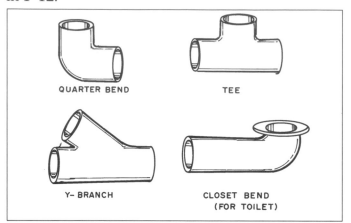

1–12. Typical cast-iron no-hub fittings.

JOINING RIGID COPPER TUBING

Rigid copper-tubing systems are joined by sweat-soldering, as discussed below. Sweat-soldered joints are less likely to leak than some types of mechanical connections.

Cutting the Tube

The tube is cut to length with a **tube** or **pipe cutter** as shown in **1–13**. The cutter is slid over the end of the tube. The knob is turned, pressing a cutter wheel against the tube, and then it is rotated around the tube, scoring the surface. Tighten the knob and rotate the cutter again. Repeat until the tube is cut through.

Copper tube can also be cut with a fine-toothed hacksaw, but it leaves a rough edge.

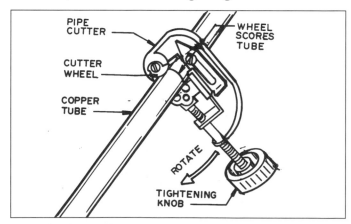

1–13. Cutting rigid copper tubing. The copper tube is cut by tightening and rotating the pipe cutter. It is tightened and rotated several times before the cut is complete.

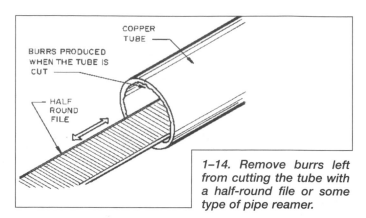

1–14. Remove burrs left from cutting the tube with a half-round file or some type of pipe reamer.

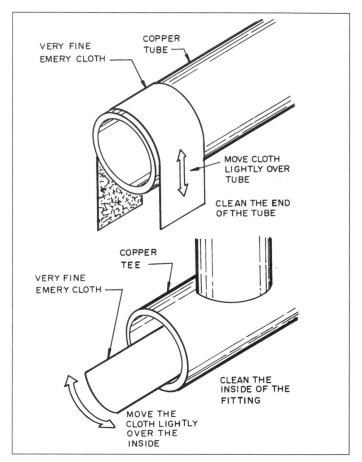

1–15. Clean the outside of the pipe and the inside of the fitting by rubbing them lightly with emery cloth.

SWEATING THE JOINT

To sweat the joint, do the following:

1. Ream the end of the tube, removing any burrs (**1–14**). A reamer or half-round file can be used.

2. Clean the outside end of the tube. Lightly clean the surface with a very fine emery cloth until it is

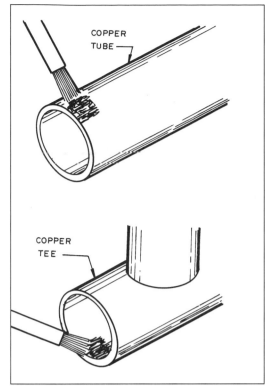

1-16. Apply a thin, even coating of flux to the tube and fitting with a brush. Do not use your fingers. Flux can be harmful to the eyes, mouth, and open cuts.

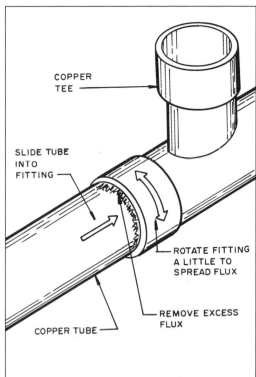

1-17. After the flux has been applied, slide the tube into the fitting and rotate the fitting a little to spread the flux in the joint. Wipe off excess flux.

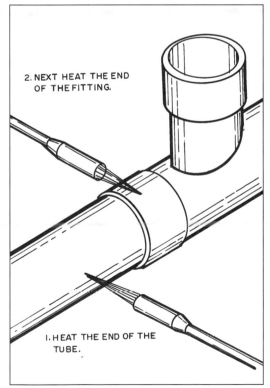

1-18. Heat the tube and the fitting until they are hot enough to melt the solder.

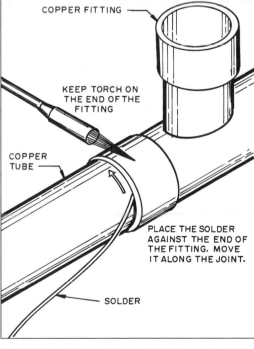

1-19. Place the solder against the end of the fitting and move it along the joint. It will melt and flow into the gap with the pipe. Keep the torch on the fitting to maintain the needed heat.

bright. Then clean the inside of the fitting with emery cloth. Special cleaning brushes are available. The surfaces must be very lightly cleaned. If too much material is removed, the joint may not solder properly (**1-15**).

3. Brush a thin layer of flux over the end of the pipe and inside the fitting (**1-16**). Be careful not to apply an excess of flux. This will cause corrosion problems later.

4. Slide the fitting onto the pipe until it butts the end of the pipe. Rotate it a little to spread out the flux (**1-17**). Wipe off any flux that drains out of the joint.

5. Move the flame of the propane torch over the tubes directly below the fitting. Then heat the end of the fitting. Move the flame back and forth (**1-18**).

6. When the solder is hot enough to melt, touch it to the edge where the two pieces meet. Move the solder around the joint in a continuous movement. When the joint is covered with no gaps, let it cool (**1-19**). Keep the torch on the fitting as the solder is applied.

How does the solder

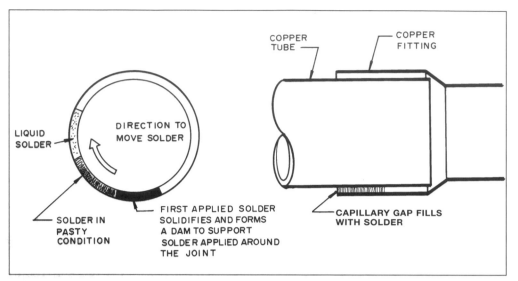

1–20. *This illustration shows how the solder fills the gap between the tube and a fitting.*

When using the torch, hold it in a nearly upright position. If it is tilted too far, the liquid propane will flow into the valve and block the vapors. The torch will then go out.

When finished with the torch, turn the valve to "off" and the flame will go out. If the tank is to be stored for a long time, remove the valve and nozzle from the tank.

enter the gap between the pipes? The solder is drawn into the gap between the tubing and fitting by capillary action. It will flow regardless of weather. The solder must flow horizontally, downward or upward (1–20).

The choice of solder depends upon the pressure of the liquid in the tube and its temperature. Solder and fluxes used in potable water systems must not have a lead content exceeding 0.2 percent.

Using a Propane Torch

A propane torch is used to sweat-solder joints in copper pipe. It is a relatively safe tool if properly used. The torch is a tank of fuel to which a valve and nozzle are attached (1–21). The valve controls the flow of fuel to the nozzle. The nozzle directs the flame.

To light a propane torch, follow these steps:

1. Hold the torch with the nozzle pointing away from you.

2. Strike a match and hold it near the nozzle.

3. Open the valve slightly, clockwise. The fuel will light.

4. Open the valve further until you have the flame needed. If the valve is opened too far, the flame may blow out. If this happens, turn off the torch and follow the lighting procedure again.

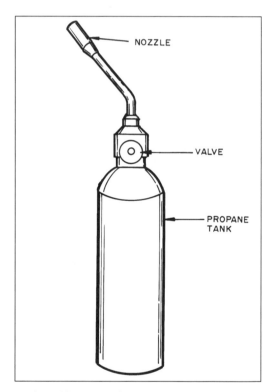

1–21. *Use caution when lighting the propane torch. Do not open the valve too much to light it. Follow the instructions given in the text.*

WORKING WITH SOFT COPPER TUBING

Gradual bends in soft copper tubing can be made by hand. However, a tube bender will lessen the chances that a kink will be put in the tube. A kink restricts the flow of water and may crack the tube. A

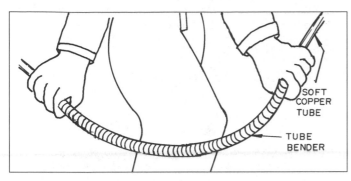

1–22. A flexible spring tube bender can be used to hand-bend soft copper tubing when large-diameter bends are needed. Overbend the tube slightly and then twist the spring off the tube.

tube bender is a flexible coil that is slid on the tube (**1–22**). Be certain the correct diameter of bender for the tube is being used. Lay the bender and pipe over your knee and apply enough pressure to get the bend needed. The larger the diameter of the bend, the less likely a kink will be put in the tubing.

Sharper bends can be made with a lever-type hand bender. The handles are at 180° F (82° C) when the tube is placed in the tool. Raise one handle, forming a right angle. The forming wheel has a mark used to locate the point of bend. Pull the handles toward each other until the desired angle is reached. Be certain the bender is the correct size for the tube (**1–23**).

Flared Tube Fittings

Soft copper tubing is frequently joined with flared tube fittings. They provide metal-to-metal contact and can be taken apart and reassembled. They are especially useful under conditions where a propane torch may cause a fire or when joining tubing in a remodeling job where the water cannot be removed from the old tubing.

To prepare a **flared joint**, place the flared nut over the pipe and then flare the end. The end of the tube is spread outward with a flaring die and a flaring tool (**1–24**). Use them to make the joint as follows:

1. Remove all burrs on the end of the tube.

2. Slide the flare nut on the tube.

3. Insert the tube in the flaring die and clamp it over the tube. Use the hole that is the same size as

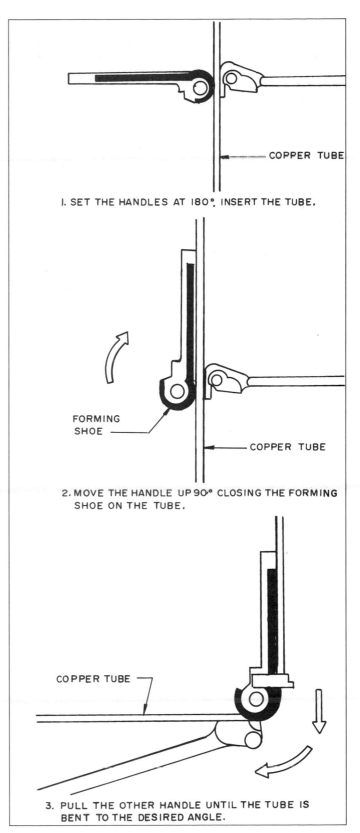

1. SET THE HANDLES AT 180°. INSERT THE TUBE.

2. MOVE THE HANDLE UP 90° CLOSING THE FORMING SHOE ON THE TUBE.

3. PULL THE OTHER HANDLE UNTIL THE TUBE IS BENT TO THE DESIRED ANGLE.

1–23. Copper tube can be bent with a lever-type hand bender. The minimum radius of the bend depends upon the diameter of the tube.

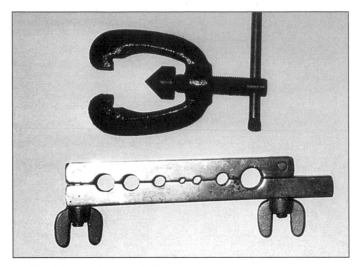

1–24. A flaring tool and die.

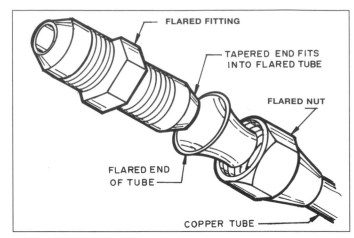

1–26. The flared end of the copper tube is joined to other tubing with a flare fitting.

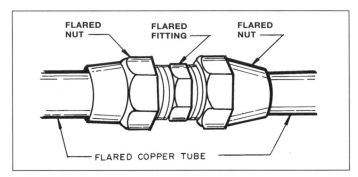

1–27. An assembled connection made with a flare fitting.

the tube. The end of the tube is set flush or slightly above the surface of the die.

4. Place the flaring tool over the copper tube, and turn it until the cone on the ram spreads the end of the tube to about 45 degrees (**1–25**).

5. Remove the pipe from the die. A flared joint connects to a flared fitting (**1–26**). Before securing the nut, wrap the threads with pipe-thread seal tape. An assembled connection is shown in **1–27**.

Some home owners like to cut the tube an inch or so longer than needed so that if the flaring fails it can be cut off and reflared, leaving enough tube to make the required connection.

Compression Fittings

Copper tubing can be joined to valves and fixtures with compression fittings. A **compression fitting** is made up of a compression ring and nut (**1–28**). The fitting is used when the connecting part is threaded. Join pipe using the compression fitting as follows:

1. Slide the nut and then the compression ring onto the tube.

2. Insert the tube into the valve or other fitting. Be sure the tube is exactly perpendicular to the opening in the fitting. The connection will leak if it is not perpendicular.

3. Slide the compression ring down the tube and push it against the fitting.

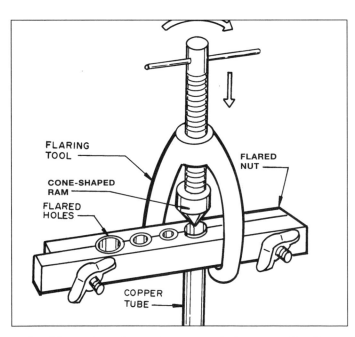

1–25. Clamp the tube to the correct hole in the die. Clamp the flaring tool to the die and turn the cone-shaped tip into the tube, causing it to spread into the flared opening in the die.

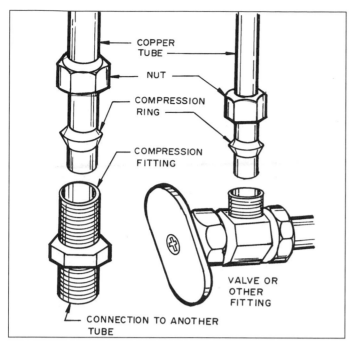

1–28. Compression fittings use a compression ring that fits snugly into a threaded compression fitting or threaded connector.

4. Fasten the nut on the valve. Tighten the nut only about a quarter-turn.

JOINING GALVANIZED-STEEL PIPE

Galvanized-steel pipe is not used often in new construction, but is found in many older homes. Some building-supply dealers no longer sell it. Often a dealer may sell it but not have the equipment to cut, ream, and thread it. Since it takes special equipment to thread the pipe, some telephone work may be needed to find where this can be done. Frequently

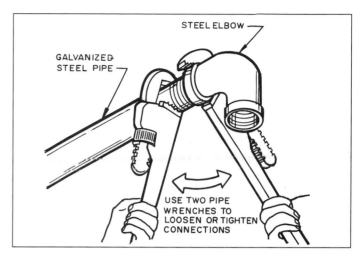

1–29. Use two pipe wrenches to tighten or loosen connections on galvanized-steel pipe.

the repair is made by splicing in copper or plastic pipe using special connections.

Steel pipe is galvanized (coated with zinc) to resist rust. It is strong, resists damage, and will last for years. Steel pipe is joined to fittings with threads. When steel pipe is joined or loosened at a fitting, two pipe wrenches must be used. One wrench holds the fitting and the other holds the pipe (1–29).

Steel pipe is typically cut to length, reamed, and threaded by the machine shown in 1–30, which is on the following page. The pipe is fed through the hole in the center of the machine, and jaws clamp it tight. It is then rotated and the cutting tool is held against it, cutting it to length. Then the reamer is placed in the end of the pipe and the rough edges are cut away. Finally, the threading dies are set on the end of the pipe. The threads are cut as the pipe is rotated.

There are hand tools used to cut and thread pipe.

1–30. Using an electric machine to cut steel pipe to length, ream out the burrs, and thread the end.
A: A close-up of the machine.
B: The cutting tool cuts the pipe as the machine rotates it.
C: The reamer clears rough edges on the inside of the pipe as the machine rotates it.
D: These four dies cut the threads as the machine rotates the pipe.
E: The threaded pipe after the dies have been removed.

A manual cutting tool is shown in **1–31**. A manual threading tool is shown in **1–32**.

Before steel pipe is installed, a joint sealer has to be applied to the threads. This prevents the joint from leaking. Three types are typically available. **Joint compound** is a paste that is brushed on the threads. **Wicking** resembles string and is wound around the threads. **Plastic joint tape** is wound over the threads 1½ turns clockwise. Pull it tight so that the threads show through (**1–33**).

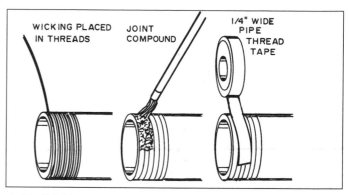

1–33. Wicking, joint compound, and pipe-thread tape are used to help prevent the joint from leaking.

WATER-LINE TAPS

By using a **tap-on fitting**, you can take a water line off an existing line without cutting it and inserting a fitting. To install a fitting (**1–34**), do the following:

1. Turn off the water in the line to be tapped and drain it.

1–34. A water-line tap yoke enables a new water line to be run off an existing line without cutting it and splicing in a tee.

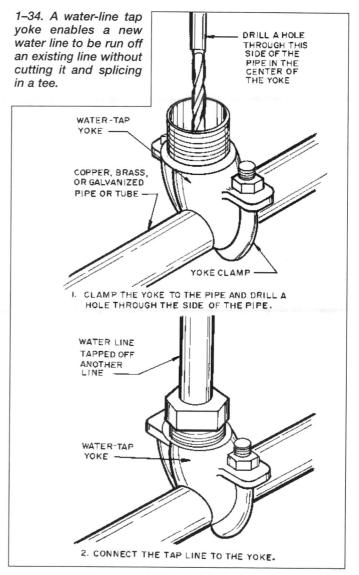

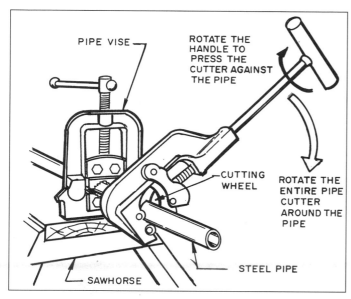

1–31. Galvanized-steel pipe is held in a pipe vise and cut with a wheeled cutter.

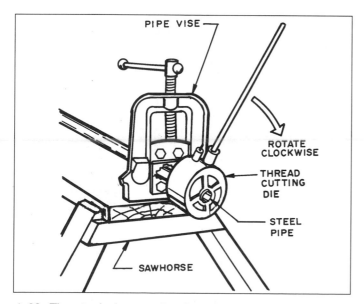

1–32. The steel pipe can be threaded manually with a die. Rotate the die clockwise. If it jams up a bit, rotate it counterclockwise to clear out any chips and return it to a clockwise rotation.

2. Clamp the tap-on fitting (referred to as the yoke in **1–34**) around the pipes.

3. Drill a hole in the front of the pipe through the opening in the fitting. Be careful you do not drill through the back of the pipe.

4. Connect the new water line to the yoke.

5. Turn on the water and check for leaks.

JOINING PLASTIC PIPE

Plastic pipe is easy to cut, low in cost, and easy to assemble. It is available in rigid and flexible types. **Rigid pipe** is joined to fittings by cementing. **Flexible pipe** is joined to fittings with mechanical connectors similar to the hose clamps used on automobile engines.

Rigid plastic pipe can be cut with a saw such as a hacksaw, backsaw, or crosscut saw. A miter box is especially useful because it gives a square cut. Flexible pipe can be cut with a saw or a knife.

Joining Rigid Plastic Pipe

Follow these steps to join rigid plastic pipe:

1. File the cut end smooth (**1–35**).

2. Remove any burrs from the end of the pipe with a knife, file, or reamer (**1–36**). Bevel (make slanted) the outside edge to allow the pipe to enter the fitting easily without scraping away any cement.

3. Before adding cement, try the pipe in the fitting to see that it fits properly. If it is too tight, the cement will be scraped away. If it is too loose, the joint will not seal properly.

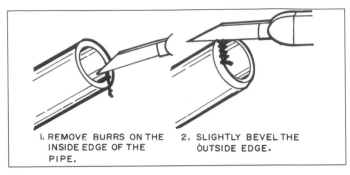

I. REMOVE BURRS ON THE INSIDE EDGE OF THE PIPE.

2. SLIGHTLY BEVEL THE OUTSIDE EDGE.

1–36. After cutting the plastic pipe, remove the burrs on the inside edge and smooth and slightly taper the outside edge.

4. With the pipe and fitting together, mark them both by scratching a line so that they can be put back in the same position when they are cemented together (**1–37**).

5. Separate the pipe and fitting.

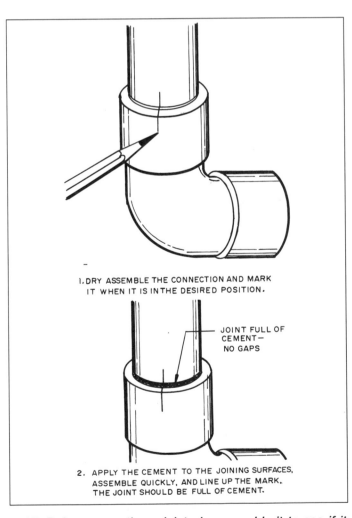

I. DRY ASSEMBLE THE CONNECTION AND MARK IT WHEN IT IS IN THE DESIRED POSITION.

JOINT FULL OF CEMENT— NO GAPS

2. APPLY THE CEMENT TO THE JOINING SURFACES, ASSEMBLE QUICKLY, AND LINE UP THE MARK. THE JOINT SHOULD BE FULL OF CEMENT.

1–37. Before cementing a joint, dry-assemble it to see if it closes properly, mark the position of the fitting, apply cement, and assemble the pipe and fitting quickly. The solvent cement sets in less than one minute.

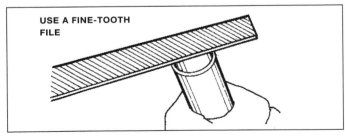

USE A FINE-TOOTH FILE

1–35. After cutting the plastic pipe, file the end smooth and square with a fine tooth file.

6. Lightly brush a coat of **primer** on the pipe and inside the fitting.

7. Wait 15 seconds for the **primer** to soften the plastic surface.

8. Immediately brush a coat of cement on the pipe and fitting. Use the type recommended by the pipe manufacturer for the type of plastic.

9. Slip the pipe into the fitting and align the marks (refer to **1–37**). Do not delay, because the cement sets rapidly. The joint should show a continuous bead of cement all the way around the fitting. Hold the joint together for a few seconds to allow the cement to bind the parts together.

10. Allow the joint to set for three or four minutes before handling it. Do not run water in the pipe for at least one hour. If the temperature is below 50° F (10° C), wait more than four minutes. Do not try to cement the pipe if the temperature is below 40° F (4.5° C). It works best at normal room temperature: 70° F (21° C).

Joining Flexible Plastic Pipe

Join flexible pipe to a fitting with hose clamps (**1–38**). The fittings usually have a rigid portion to fit inside the tubing. Set the clamp about 3/4 inch (19 millimeters) from the end of the pipe. If it is suspected that pressure may cause the joint to blow open, use two clamps on each side.

GAS PIPE AND TUBING

Natural and manufactured gas is widely used in residential construction, mainly for heating. Gas-fired logs in fireplaces are also popular. Gas is an explosive mixture, and the pipe and joints must be completely free of leaks. Local codes have specific requirements for gas pipes, including the type of

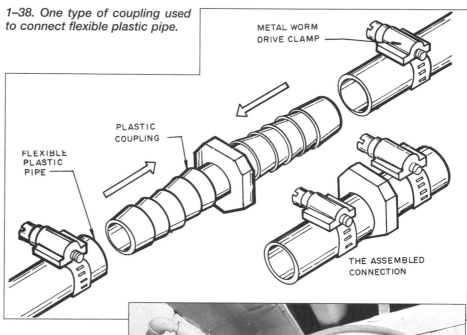

1–38. One type of coupling used to connect flexible plastic pipe.

1–39. This corrugated, semirigid stainless-steel tubing (CSST) is being taken directly off the gas meter (courtesy of Gas Research Institute).

pipe, pipe sizes, installation, and testing. A licensed plumbing contractor should handle the installation or repair.

The most common material used for gas pipes is black steel pipe that must meet ASTM A53 or ASTM A106. Some codes permit the use of copper or brass if the gas to be used is not corrosive to these materials. In some cases, polyethylene (PE) and polybutylene (PB) with heat-fused joints, and polyvinyl chloride (PVC) with solvent cement joints, are permitted for outdoor underground piping.

A relatively new pipe, corrugated, semi-rigid stainless-steel tubing (CSST), is finding increasing use. It is as strong as steel piping, yet has sufficient flexibility to make installation easier. In **1–39**, it has been connected to a gas meter. Since it is light and flexible, the number of connections is greatly reduced, which increases safety. CSST comes as a complete system, consisting of tubing in 250-foot (76-meter) coils, fittings, manifolds, valves, regulators, and protection devices (**1–40**).

1–40. These multiple CSST gas lines are taken from a regulator that reduces the pressure to be used within the building (courtesy Gas Research Institute).

ENERGY-SAVING TIPS

When planning and installing plumbing systems, consider taking energy-conservation measures. For example, insulate the water heater. Special insulation blankets are available and make insulating easy. Then set the water temperature to a lower setting than before. The water should still be as hot as needed.

Try to place all water pipes within the house to prevent them from freezing. If pipes must be in an unheated area, insulate them. Insulate the hot-water pipe as much as possible, regardless of location.

Heat loss from pipes inside a living space is not a total loss since it helps heat the air. However, during the summer the air conditioner might need to work a little harder, increasing air-conditioning costs slightly.

Replacing a Faucet

After many years of use, faucets become worn and tarnished. Perhaps there is an old faucet that needs frequent repair, or one with a leak that cannot be fixed with the usual simple repairs. In this instance, it is better to replace the old faucet with a new model. Leaking faucets waste hot water, increasing your electric or gas bill, and waste energy.

When buying a new faucet, be sure the distance between the centers of the pipes in the new faucet matches the distance and pattern of holes in the sink. Single-lever washer-less faucets typically need a three-hole pattern for a kitchen sink (**1–41**). Two-handle compression-type faucets need only two holes (**1–42**). Some kitchen sinks have a fourth hole located several inches to the right of the faucet. The fourth hole is for the spray hose (**1–43**). Bath lavatories usually have three holes. Two are for the faucets and the third is for the pop-up drain rod.

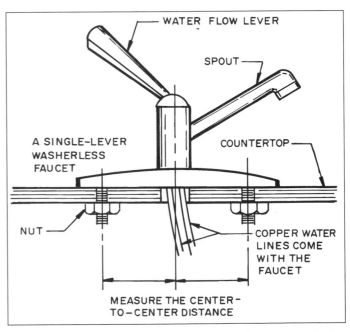

1–41. A single-lever washerless faucet requires three holes in the countertop. Measure to their centers before buying a replacement.

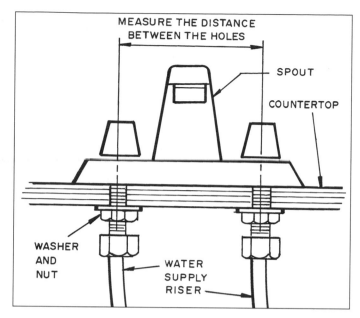

1–42. A compression faucet has two holes in the countertop. Replacement faucets may be made on different spacings, so check before buying one.

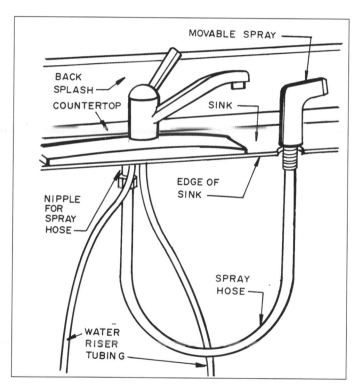

1–43. Some kitchen sinks have a hole to receive the spray hose, which connects to a nipple on the faucet.

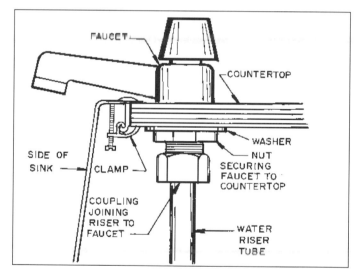

1–44. Shutoff valves are located below the sink on the hot- and cold-water riser tubes.

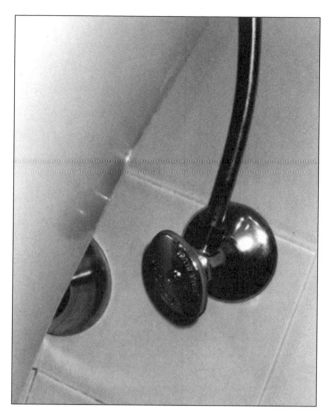

1–45. To begin replacing a faucet, remove the water-riser tube by unscrewing the coupling that connects it to the faucet. Use a basin wrench if one is available. Refer to 1–46.

Removing the Old Faucet

The first step in replacing a faucet is to remove the old one. Generally this can be done by following these steps:

1. Turn off the hot and cold water. Usually this can be done by turning the valves clockwise beneath the sink (1–44).

2. Open the faucet handles and let the water drain.

3. Unscrew the coupling nut that holds the water line to the faucet (1–45).

4. Loosen the locknuts that hold the faucet to the sink. These nuts are difficult to get at unless a basin wrench is used. However, some success is possible with an adjustable wrench (**1–46**).

5. If the sink has a pop-up drain, slide the control rod off the lever that controls the plug.

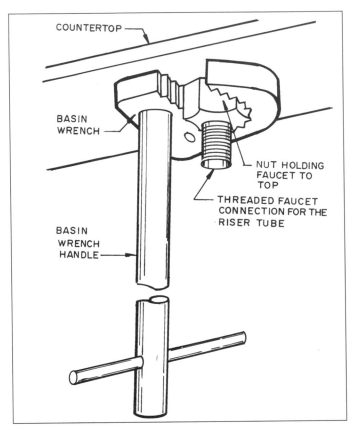

1–46. To remove the faucet from the countertop, remove the anchor nut. Use a basin wrench if one is available.

Installing the New Faucet

Install the new faucet as follows:

1. Place the new gasket on the sink and the new faucet on top of it (**1–47**).

2. Tighten the locknuts below the countertop to hold the fixture to the sink (**1–48**).

3. Attach the water lines. If the new fixture is very similar to the old faucet, the water lines may not have to be adjusted. Be sure the water lines align straight with the faucet when they are connected. Any slant will cause them to leak. A single-lever faucet has copper water lines leading to the water-control valve (refer to **1–48**). These lines must first

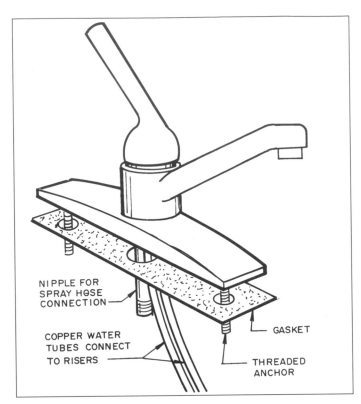

1–47. This single-lever faucet is ready to be set on the sink. The gasket seals the surface, preventing water from leaking into the cabinet below.

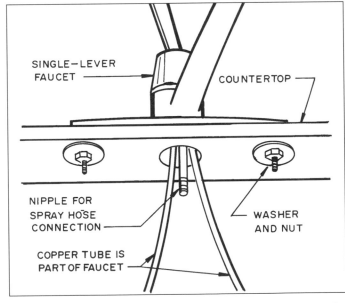

1–48. The single-level faucet is supplied with copper water tubing. It is bolted to the countertop.

be straightened to put them through the center hole in the sink. Then the faucet supply lines must be bent to meet the riser-tube water lines. Do so slowly and carefully. Do not put a kink in the line being bent. When the water lines align, put pipe-thread compound or plastic tape on the threads; then tighten the coupling nuts. It is easier if flexible plastic riser tubes are used for this connection. Detail for a compression faucet is shown in **1–49**.

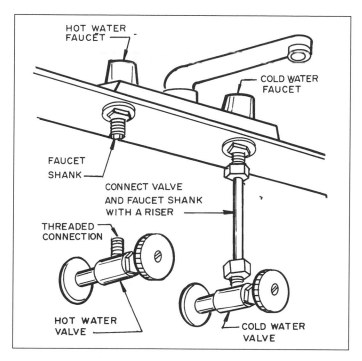

1–49. Compression faucets use a riser tube to connect the water to the faucet.

4. Turn on the water and test the faucet for leaks.

5. If a kitchen faucet is being replaced, connect the spray hose by tightening its connecting nut.

6. If the faucet has a pop-up plug, connect it as shown in **1–50**.

Replacing a Tub Spout That Has a Shower Diverter

Many tub spouts have a small knob on top that is raised to divert the water from the spout to the showerhead. When the mechanism becomes worn and leaks, it must be replaced as follows:

1. Remove the spout from the nipple that holds it (**1–51**). One way to do this is to insert a stick into the spout hole and turn it counterclockwise (**1–52**). If the spout is to be discarded, a pipe wrench can be used.

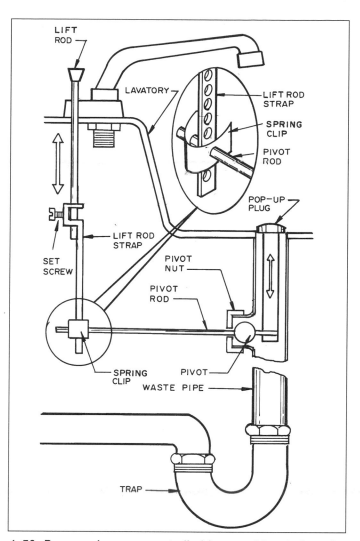

1–50. Pop-up plugs are controlled by a rod located on the faucet.

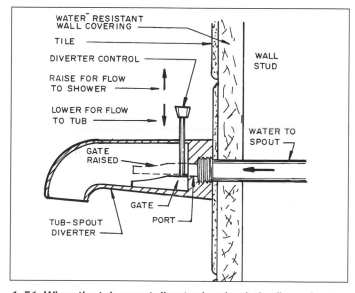

1–51. When the tub-spout diverter is raised, the flow of water is shut off to the spout and goes to a pipe that leads to the showerhead.

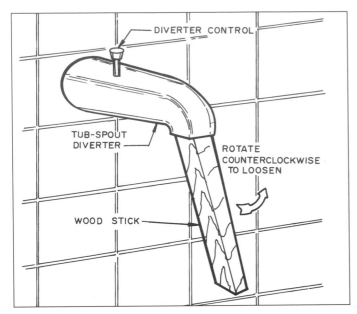

1–52. To remove the spout, put a stick in the end and turn it counterclockwise.

2. To install a new tub spout, put pipe compound or plastic tape on the threads.

3. Turn the new spout on the nipple by hand. (The **nipple** is the pipe that goes through the wall and upon which the spout is attached.) Use the wooden stick to gently turn and align the spout in the proper direction. Be careful. Tub spouts can be broken easily by using too much pressure to tighten them.

Tub-Shower Diverter Valve Systems

The piping for a tub-shower system with a diverter valve is shown in **1–53**. The diverter valve handle is turned clockwise to move the stem plunger forward, allowing water to flow to the showerhead pipe. If turned counterclockwise, it will shut off the shower and run water out the spout.

Another type of valve uses a single handle to regulate the flow of hot and cold water. It mixes the hot and cold water to the desired temperature and regulates the amount of water coming from the tub spout or showerhead. The diverter valve is controlled by a diverter control usually located below the water-flow handle (**1–54**). To open the valve for repairs, unscrew the knurled ring behind the handle as shown in **1–55**.

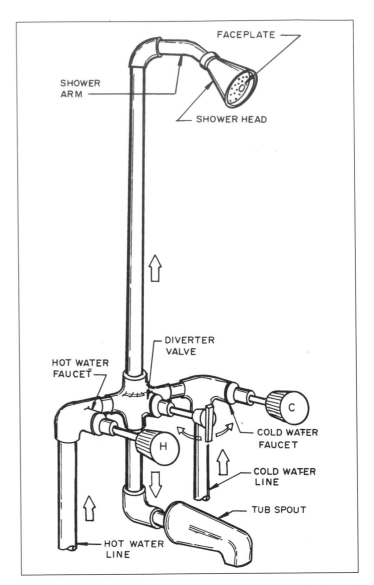

1–53. This tub-shower installation has separate hot- and cold-water faucets and uses a diverter valve to direct the flow to the showerhead or tub spout.

Replacing Showerheads

To replace a showerhead, follow these steps:

1. Unscrew the old showerhead from the pipe, called a **shower arm,** to which it is attached. Hold the arm with a pipe wrench or Vise-Grip pliers so that it does not become unscrewed from the connection inside the wall (**1–56**). Cover the wrench and pliers with thin cardboard to prevent damage to the surface.

2. Put pipe-joint compound or plastic tape on the threads.

3. Turn the new showerhead on the threads.

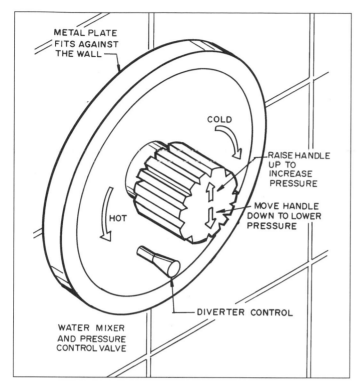

1–54. This is a typical pressure-balancing mixing valve with an integral diverter and volume control. One handle controls the mixing of hot and cold water and the pressure of the flow.

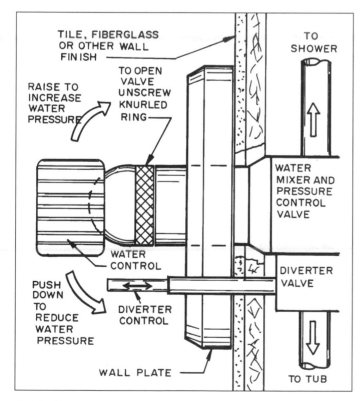

1–55. The single-handle pressure-balancing mixing valve with a diverter can be opened for repairs by unscrewing the knurled faucet ring. Remember to turn off the water before loosening the ring.

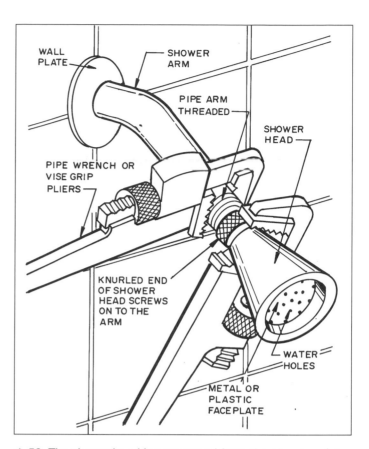

1–56. The showerhead is unscrewed from the pipe arm (also known as the shower arm) that extends from the wall. Be careful that the pipe arm is not unscrewed from the fitting inside the wall.

Hand-tighten and test it to see if it leaks at the threads. If it leaks slightly, tighten it gently with a wrench or pliers.

4. Showerheads may become clogged with mineral deposits in the water. After a few years, the small openings become smaller and some close up entirely. To clean metal faceplates, boil them in one-half cup vinegar and one quart water for 15 minutes. Plastic faceplates are less likely to clog, but if they do, soak them in a mixture of one-half cup vinegar and one-half cup hot water. Do not boil them. There are commercial mineral-dissolving cleaners available in grocery stores. Be certain they will not damage the metal faceplate. Plastic faceplates have a tendency not to clog with mineral deposits, so you may want to replace the metal plate with a plastic plate.

Replacing Traps

Traps are fittings placed on the waste pipe that hold some water blocking the passage of sewer gas that may flow up through the pipes to the fixture. The most commonly used trap is the P-trap (**1–57**). Building codes specify the acceptable traps. There are many traps in older houses, such as the full S-trap, which are no longer approved by some building codes (**1–58**). Metal traps tend to corrode over time. Usually they are replaced with plastic traps.

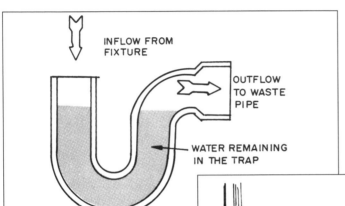

1–57 (above). A typical P-trap.

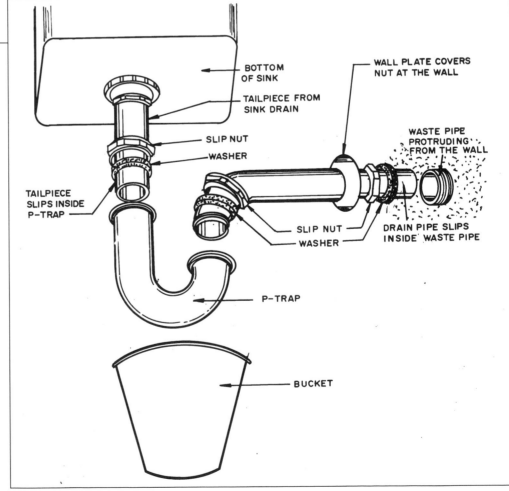

1–58. The S-trap is often not approved by the building code.

To replace a trap:

1. Place a bucket beneath the trap because its water will spill out when the trap is loosened.

2. Unscrew the slip nuts on both sides of the trap (**1–59**).

3. Slide the trap off the pipe connected to the sink, called the **tailpiece,** and off the drainpipe.

4. Install the new trap using the rubber washers that come with it.

5. Align the new trap in place.

6. Tighten the slip nuts.

1–59. A typical P-trap installation.

Often hand-tightening is enough. Be careful not to overtighten or the trap may break loose.

7. Fill the trap with water and check it for leaks.

Toilet Repairs

How a Flush Tank Works

There are several kinds of flushing mechanisms. The one shown in **1–60** is typical of those used for many years. When the flush handle is pressed, the **stopper ball** is lifted out of its **valve seat** and the water rushes out of the tank into the bowl. As the water leaves the tank, the stopper ball slowly settles until it reseats itself on the valve seat. This action stops the flow of water out of the tank.

Meanwhile, as the water leaves the tank the **float ball** drops. Its dropping opens the **inlet valve** on the top of the **ball cock**. This refills the tank through one line and puts water in the bowl through another line. As the tank fills, the water raises the float ball. When the float ball reaches a certain height, the incoming water is shut off.

The ball cock for a newer, more frequently used flushing mechanism is shown in **1–61**. This plastic mechanism has a **float cup** that replaces the float ball and its long arm. The float cup rides up and down on a vertical shaft. An inlet valve is on top of the shaft. When the water is let out of the tank, the float cup sinks and opens the valve. When the tank refills, the float cup rises and closes the valve. The flushing action raises a **flapper ball** that is seated on the **valve seat**.

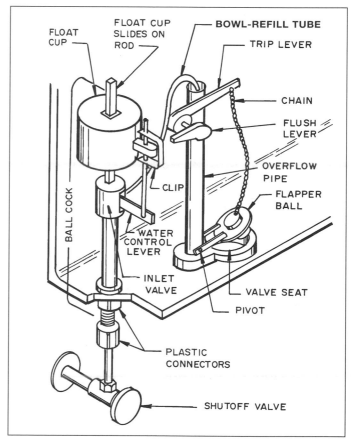

1–61. Typical mechanism for the newer type of flush mechanism using a float cup and a flapper ball. This is easier to install.

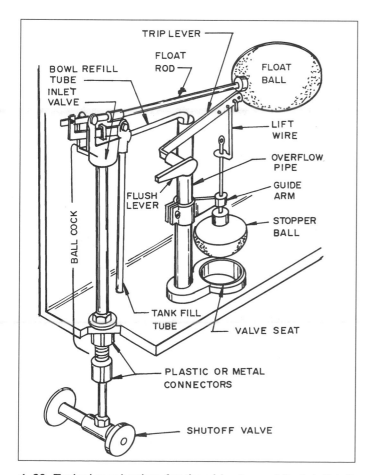

1–60. Typical mechanism for the older type of flush toilet. It uses a float ball to control the water level, and the flow is controlled by a stopper ball connected to the flush lever with a lift wire.

Replacing a Ball Cock

The old type of ball cock can be disassembled and washers replaced. However, it may be just as easy and not expensive to simply replace it with the newer type shown in **1–61**.

Remove the old ball cock and replace it as follows:

1. Shut off the water to the tank and drain the tank by flushing the toilet.

2. Unscrew the slip nut that holds the water line to the ball cock, as shown in **1–62**.

3. Loosen and remove the retaining nut from underneath the tank. Because the old ball cock will probably turn as the nut is turned, hold the pipe inside the tank with a wrench or locking pliers (**1–63**). Older types may have a nut on the inside of the tank. The new types usually do not. Look at **1–60** and **1–61** again.

4. Pull the ball cock out of the top of the tank.

5. Insert the new unit, placing the washers on the pipes as specified by the manufacturer.

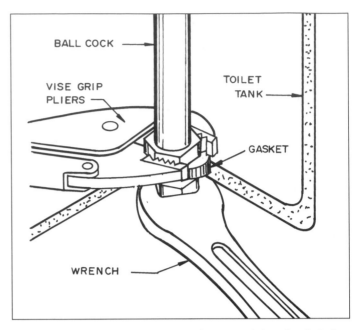

1–63. If the ball cock turns when the water-inlet pipe is being disconnected, grip it inside the tank with a wrench or Vise Grip pliers. Be careful that the vitreous china tank is not damaged.

6. Place plastic-joint tape on the threads. Tighten the retaining nut until firm, but do not over-tighten it.

7. Reconnect the water line.

8. Turn on the water and check for leaks.

9. Adjust the float to the water level desired.

On the older mechanisms, the water level is adjusted by bending the rod holding the **float ball** (**1–64**). On the newer mechanisms, the **float cup** is held on the **pull rod** by an **adjustment clip** (**1–65**). To raise or lower the float cup, squeeze the clip, slide the cup on the rod to the desired position, and release the clip (**1–65**). The water level should be such that a thorough disposal of the waste is accomplished yet excess water is not used.

When Water Flow in the Tank Will Not Stop

A common problem with toilets is that as they get older sometimes the water flow into the tank will not stop. If you listen carefully, a faint, continuous water flow can be heard. If not corrected, this will produce a large water bill. Following are reasons why the water flow is continuous, and the corrective measures that can be made:

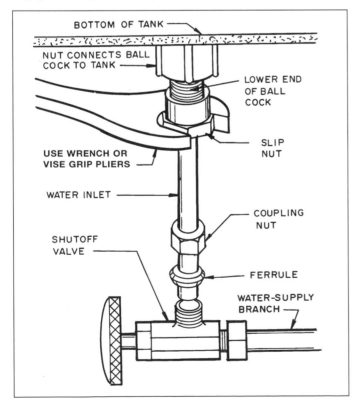

1–62. Unscrew the nut holding the water inlet pipe to the ball cock below the tank. Notice the connection used to secure the water-inlet pipe to the shutoff valve.

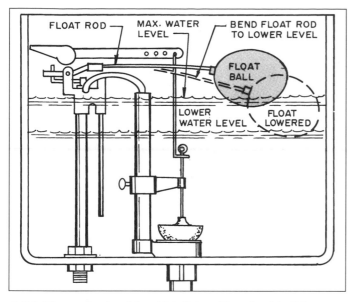

1-64. The water level in old toilets with a float ball is regulated by bending the float rod. Some prefer to put a brick or two in the tank to displace some of the volume of water.

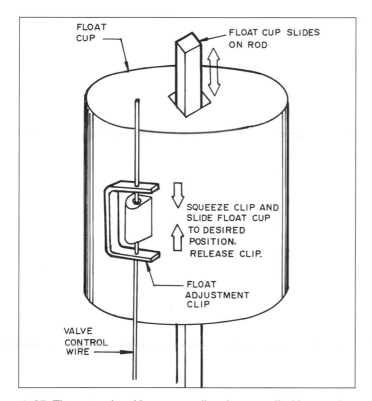

1-65. The water level in newer toilets is controlled by moving the float cup along the valve-control wire. Squeeze the clip, slide the float cup to the desired location, and release the clip.

1. The older type of float ball develops leaks, fills with water, and will not rise as the tank fills. Replace the ball. It is screwed on the end of the float rod (1-66).

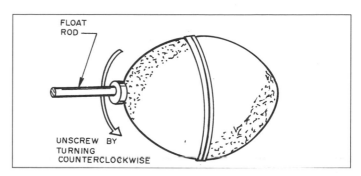

1-66. If the ball float feels soft or has water inside it, replace it. Unscrew it from the float rod by turning it counterclockwise.

2. The stopper or flapper ball may not be aligned with the valve seat. Shut off the water to the tank and flush it. Raise and drop the stopper ball to see if it falls squarely on the valve. Adjust as necessary until it seats properly (1-67).

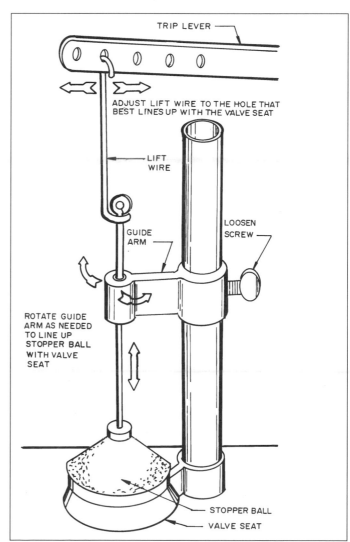

1-67. Adjust the lift wire on the trip lever and rotate the guide arm to get the stopper ball to seat securely on the valve seat.

3. The stopper or flapper ball may have deteriorated and should be replaced.

4. The valve seat may be covered with mineral deposits. Shut off the water, flush the tank, remove excess water on the bottom of the tank, and clean the valve surface. Use steel wool or a very fine abrasive pad. Commercial mineral-dissolving liquids are available from grocery stores and plumbing supply dealers. Be careful that the surface of the valve is not damaged (**1–68**). If the valve surface is worn, install a new valve seat.

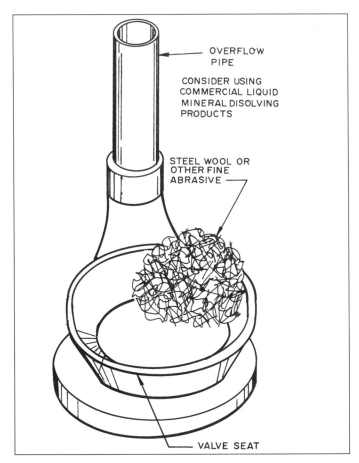

1–68. When the valve seat becomes encrusted with minerals, it will let the water in the tank constantly leak. The minerals can be removed, but be very careful that the edge of the valve seat is not damaged.

5. The ball-cock valve may be worn. To check, reach into the tank and manually raise the float ball or cup. If it does not shut off, replace the ball cock.

6. If there is difficulty getting the stopper ball on an older toilet to line up and seal on the valve seat,

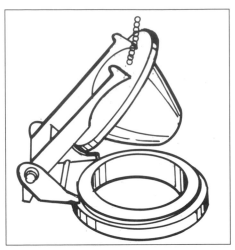

1–69. It is often best to replace the old stopper ball with a flapper valve. Special replacement valves are at the local hardware store.

consider replacing it with a flapper valve as shown in **1–69**. It does not require a lift wire or a guide arm and is therefore easier to install. It clamps onto the overflow pipe and is adjusted left or right until it seats properly.

Replacing a Toilet Seat

A toilet seat is held to the bowl with two bolts. On some, the top of the bolt is attached to the hinges for the seat and cover. The nuts on older toilet seats are

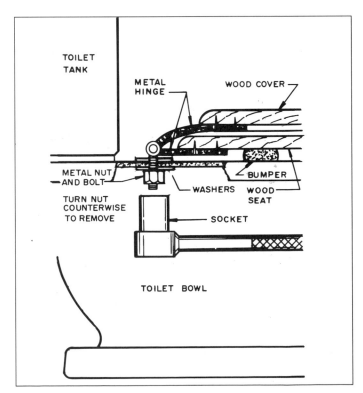

1–70. The old toilet seats have metal bolts and nuts connecting them to the bowl. A socket wrench is the best tool to use to remove them.

sometimes difficult to reach; a socket wrench usually works best (**1–70**). Sometimes pliers can grip the nut, but if it is corroded they may not be able to turn it. In this case, squirt penetrating oil on the bolt and let it sit for 20 or 30 minutes. This will sometimes loosen it. If this does not work, the bolt will have to be cut with a hacksaw. Cut it above the washer on the top of the bowl. Cover the ceramic bowl with cardboard or plywood so the surface is not damaged.

New toilet seats have plastic hinges. These have a plastic screw that can be easily reached from the top and a plastic nut. A screwdriver and pliers will tighten and loosen these easily (**1–71**). The new seat will come with all the parts necessary for installation. The bolts and nuts will probably be made of plastic — which eliminates the corrosion problem. Insert the bolts in the holes and tighten the nuts from underneath. Do not overtighten them.

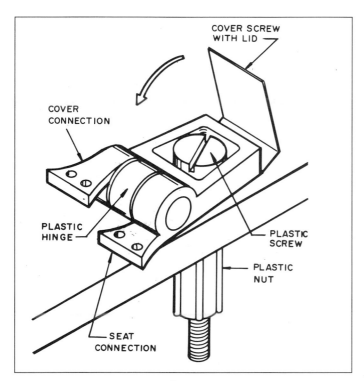

1–71. New toilet seats are installed with plastic hinges, bolts, and nuts. They are much easier to replace than the old seats with metal connections.

EMERGENCY REPAIRS

Once in a great while, there may be an actual plumbing emergency. A few simple steps will bring the emergency situation under control.

Stopping the Flow of Water

A pipe or fitting may have a leak from which water is gushing. This is a situation where the water must be turned off to stop the flow. Where is the water turned off? Depending on the plumbing in the house, the water may be turned off at the fixture or at the main valve near the water meter. Look for a valve on the water lines leading to a water closet, sink, or lavatory. Dishwashers and washing machines also should have a valve on their water lines.

When the valve leading to the problem is found, turn it clockwise to stop the flow of water (**1–72**). It should then be possible to make repairs on the leaking faucet or fixture.

If a valve cannot be found near a fixture or appliance, go to the main valve to shut down the water to the entire house. If the leak is in the valve or the pipe leading to the valve near a fixture, shut off the water at the main valve.

1–72. There is a shutoff valve on the water line leading to a toilet.

Draining the System

Once the flow of water is stopped, it may be necessary to drain the pipes before repairs can be made. To drain the pipes, follow these steps:

1. Turn the main valve to "off" to stop the flow of water through all the pipes in the house.

2. Open the faucets on the lowest level of the house.

3. Open faucets on higher levels of the house to let air into the pipes. Doing so will allow them to drain faster.

Making Temporary Repairs to a Leaking Pipe

Make a temporary repair to a leaking pipe as follows:

1. Drain the water from the pipe.

2. Place a piece of rubber or a small section of garden hose over the pipe at the point of the leak. Be sure the rubber extends a couple of inches beyond the leak on both sides.

3. Clamp the rubber or hose to the pipe using hose clamps or wire (**1–73**).

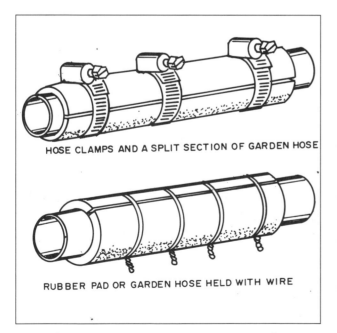

1–73. Two ways to make emergency repairs on a cracked water pipe.

4. An alternative solution is to buy and use a pipe clamp (**1–74**). A pipe clamp is more dependable than the garden-hose repair. However, eventually a permanent repair must be made.

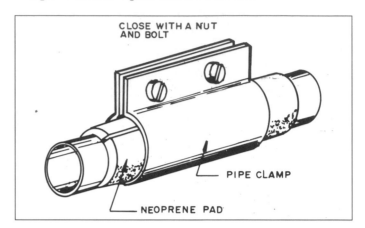

1–74. A cracked pipe can be temporarily repaired with a neoprene pad held around the pipe with pipe clamps.

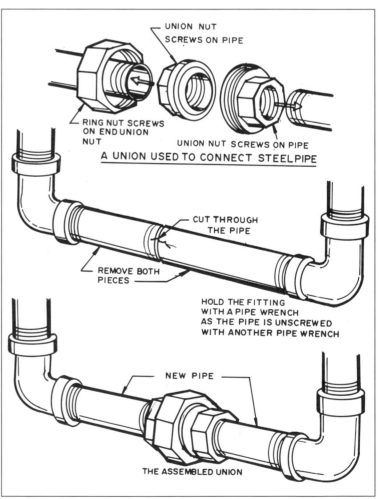

1–75. Leaking steel water pipe is permanently repaired by replacing the leaking section of pipe. A union is required to install the new pipe.

Permanent Repairs to Cracked Water Pipe

Cracked **steel water pipe** can be permanently repaired by removing the leaking section of pipe and replacing it with new pipe. This will require that a union be used (**1–75**).

Cracked **copper pipe** can be repaired by cutting out the damaged section and installing a coupling.

It may be necessary to remove and replace one end of the pipe if the damaged section is too long for a coupling to replace (**1–76**).

Since it is not possible to remove **plastic** pipe from a fitting, the repair is made by cutting out a section long enough to allow a new section of pipe with couplings on each end to be cemented into place (**1–77**).

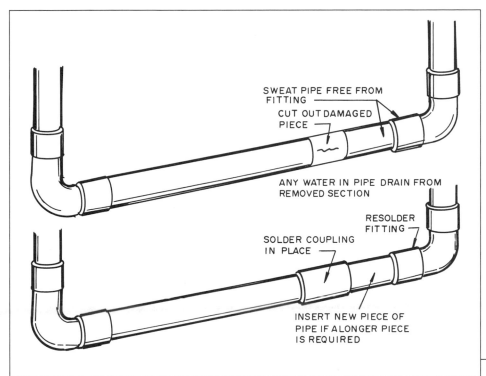

1–76. Cracked copper pipe can be permanently repaired by cutting out the damaged section and replacing it with a coupling.

1–77. Cracked plastic pipe can be permanently repaired by cutting away a section of the pipe and replacing it with a section of new pipe and two couplings.

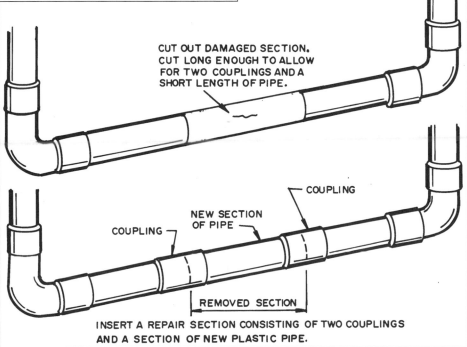

Thawing Frozen Pipes

Pipes that are full of water should be protected from freezing. If they are inside a heated house, they are safe unless the heat is off for a long time in freezing weather. However, if such a situation might exist, drain the pipes to prevent them from freezing. Since water expands as it freezes, it could split a pipe. Then, when the temperature rises and the ice melts, there is a water emergency.

Pipes should not be run in exterior walls. If there are pipes there, insulate them. Pipes are often run in unheated basements, crawl spaces, or in the attic. Insulate those pipes as well (**1–78**).

Should there be a frozen pipe, thaw it slowly.

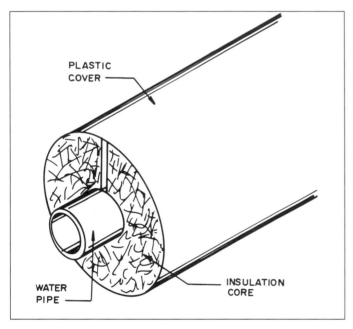

1–78. Preformed pipe insulation will give considerable protection from freezing. In extreme cold, additional protection may be needed. Insulate hot- and cold-water pipes.

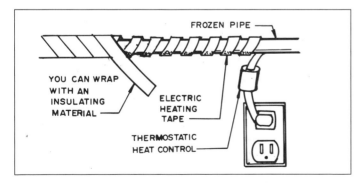

1–79. Frozen water pipes can be thawed by wrapping electric heating tape around them. It is more efficient if some form of insulating material is wrapped over the tape.

There are several ways of thawing a pipe. Before beginning, open the nearest faucet on the frozen line. *Begin thawing the pipe as close to the opened faucet as possible.* To begin thawing the pipe anywhere else is dangerous. If the water in the pipe is accidentally heated to a temperature great enough to cause steam to form, it could build up sufficient pressure to cause the pipe to explode. *Never* heat a pipe so hot that it cannot be touched with the hands. Thawing a pipe is a slow process that cannot be hurried without great risk. Have patience for the task and it will be performed safely.

The safest way to thaw frozen pipes that are inside a house is to turn on the heat and let the pipes thaw slowly as the house heats. If the pipes are not in the house, there are other ways to thaw them. Electric heating tape can be used. Wrap the pipe with the tape and plug it in. When one section of pipe is thawed, move the tape to the next section (**1–79**). Some tapes have a thermostatic control so the tape can be permanently left on a troublesome section of pipe. The tape will heat when the temperature drops to freezing. Wrap an electric heating pad around the pipe and put it on a medium or high setting. When a section thaws, move it to the next section (**1–80**).

Electric hair dryers or small portable electric heaters are effective and safe. Move them back and forth across a section of pipe and then move on (**1–81**).

A pipe can that is slightly frozen can sometimes be thawed by wrapping it with rags and continuously pouring hot water over it. This is messy and takes your constant attention.

Heat lamps are also effective and can be used to thaw pipes inside a wall or in the ceiling. Place the lamp six or eight inches from the wall or ceiling surface (**1–82**). The lamp can be installed in almost any fixture. The choice depends on the location of the pipe. If near combustible material, protect it with a noncombustible shield.

Finally, there is the propane torch that can be used to thaw frozen steel and copper pipes. *It is dangerous and if used requires great caution.* Use a flame-spreader nozzle (**1–83**). Place an asbestos sheet behind the pipe to prevent setting the house on fire. Have a fire extinguisher by your side. Make

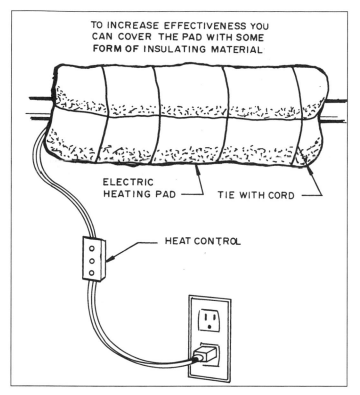

1–80. A frozen pipe can be thawed by wrapping an electric heating pad around it. While this is a bit slow, it does a good job, especially if some type of insulating material is wrapped around it to reduce heat loss to the atmosphere.

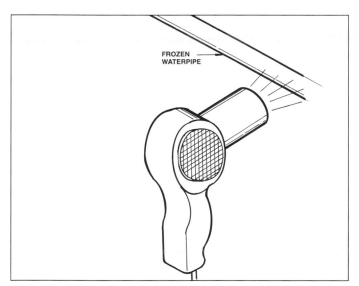

1–81. Frozen water pipes can be thawed with an electric hair dryer or electric heater.

sure there is at least one escape route from the place where the work is being done. Never leave a lit torch unattended. Be careful that the pipe does not get so hot that it cannot be touched. It might only be wise to use this method as a last resort because of the dangers involved.

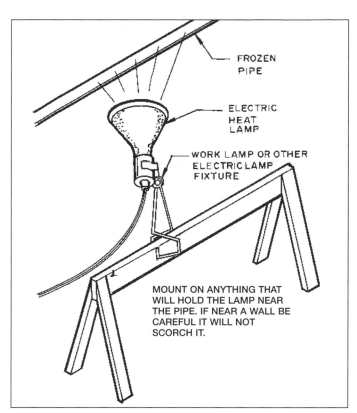

1–82. An electric heat lamp can be mounted in any electric fixture and positioned so it is near the frozen pipe. Be careful if it is near combustible materials.

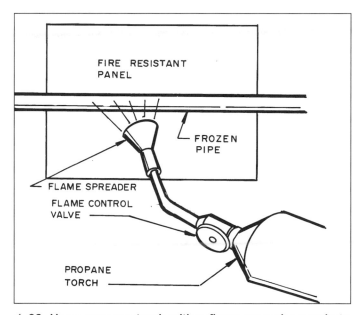

1–83. Use a propane torch with a flame-spreader nozzle to thaw a frozen pipe. Be sure to use an asbestos sheet behind the pipe to prevent a house fire.

When the water begins to drip out of the faucet, let it run. The flow will increase as the thaw progresses. The flowing water temperature is above freezing and will speed the thawing process.

1–84. A typical two-handle compression faucet that uses a washer at the end of the stem to control the flow of the water.

MISCELLANEOUS REPAIRS

Repairing a Compression Faucet

A typical two-handle compression faucet is shown in **1–84**. It has a threaded stem with a seat washer or an O-ring somewhere along the stem. When the faucet is off, the **seat washer** on the stem pushes against a part called the **seat**. This prevents the water from flowing. When the faucet handle is turned, the stem is revolved, causing the washer to move away from the seat and water to flow to and from the spout. The most usual problem is a dripping faucet. Usually this problem is fixed by changing the seat washer as follows (**1–85**):

1. Turn off the water to the faucet.

2. Remove the decorative cap, if any, to get to the screw that holds the handle on. The cap may unscrew or snap out.

3. Remove the handle by removing the screw. Some handles simply lift off the top of the stem, which has parallel grooves in it.

4. Slip off the bonnet if there is one.

5. With a wrench, remove the packing nut.

6. Remove the stem by placing the handle back on and turning counterclockwise for hot water and clockwise for cold water.

7. With a screwdriver, remove the brass screw on the end of the stem.

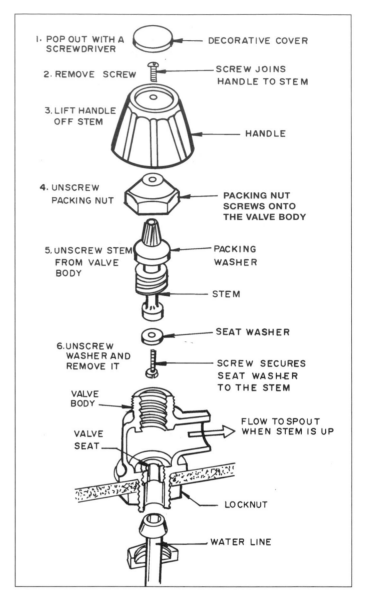

1–85. The parts of a typical compression faucet. The seat washer stops the flow when it is lowered against the valve seat.

8. Pry off the old washer.

9. Clean away any mineral deposits on the stem.

10. Put a new washer in place (**1–86**). Some washers are flat and some are beveled (slanted). Be sure to use the right kind and size. Emergency repairs can be made with a flat washer by turning it over and putting the worn side next to the stem.

11. Replace the brass screw (**1–86**).

12. Reassemble the faucet.

13. Turn on the water and check for leaks.

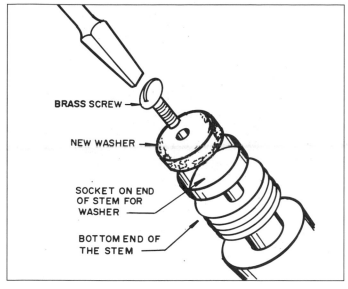

1–86. Install the new washer in the socket on the bottom of the stem.

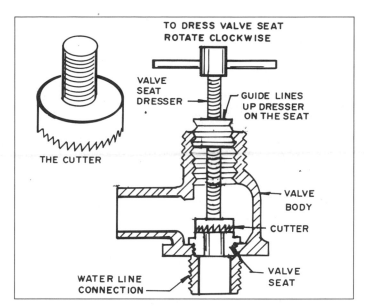

1–87. Worn valve-seat surfaces can be resurfaced by lightly dressing them with a valve seat dresser. Remove the stem, screw in the guide, and then rotate the dresser clockwise until it touches the valve-seat. Turn the handle clockwise carefully several times. Remove the dresser, flush the metal chips out of the faucet, and reassemble.

Refacing a Valve Seat

If the faucet still leaks, the valve seat may be worn. The seat can be resurfaced using a **valve seat dresser** (**1–87**). Use a dresser as follows:

1. Turn off the water.

2. Remove the valve stem.

3. Screw the dresser into the valve. There are a number of different valve dressers. Be certain to use one that is the same size as the valve seat.

4. Turn the dresser handle until the cutter touches the seat.

5. Turn the dresser handle a few turns clockwise to dress the seat. Be careful not to remove too much metal from the seat.

6. Remove the dressing tool.

7. Reassemble the valve.

8. Turn on the water and check for leaks.

Replacing a Valve Seat

Some faucets have replaceable valve seats. They can be removed with a special **valve–seat wrench** (**1–88**). The seat wrench is also used to install the

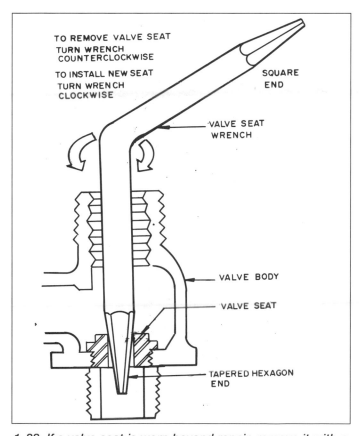

1–88. If a valve seat is worn beyond repair, remove it with a seat wrench and screw in a replacement seat. The wrench has a tapered hexagonal shape on one end and a square shape on the other. Use the one that best fits the opening in the seat. Before replacing the valve seat, put a little joint compound on the threads.

new valve seat. There are several types of seat wrenches available. Choose the one that fits the valve seat. To remove the old valve seat, force the end of the seat wrench into its opening and turn it counterclockwise. To install a new valve seat, place it on the end of the wrench, carefully lower it into the valve body, and turn it clockwise. This sometimes takes a little patience. Before installing the valve seat, put some pipe compound on the threads.

Fixing Leaks at the Stem

Often a faucet will leak around the stem. There are several different ways the stem may be sealed. Examine the stem to see which way it is sealed.

Some faucets have one or more preformed **packing washers** placed beneath the cap nut (**1–89**).

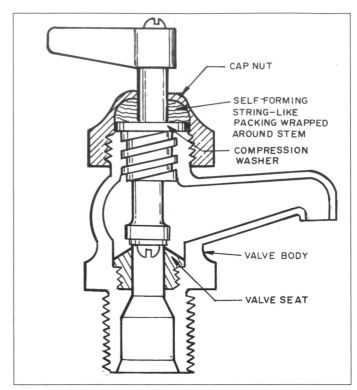

1–90. Some older faucets use a pliable string-like packing material under the cap nut to seal the stem. Remove the old hardened packing before adding new material.

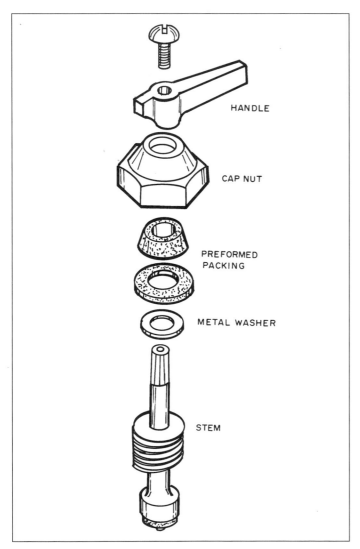

1–89. If the faucet is leaking at the stem and has a packing washer, replace the washer.

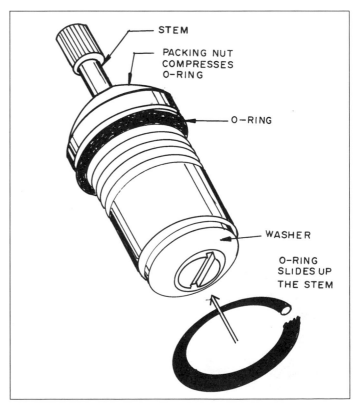

1–91. Many of the newer faucets use an O-ring to seal the stem. This is a typical example. The actual design of the stem will vary by the brand of faucet.

Replace them when they are worn. Some faucets use **self-forming packing** instead of a packing washer. Self-forming packing is made of a pliable material about 1/16 inch (1.5 millimeters) in diameter and several inches long. Cut away the old hardened packing and wrap new packing around the stem in about the same amount as the old packing (**1-90**). Then screw down the cap nut that compresses the pliable packing material. If the stem still leaks, add additional packing material.

Other faucets use one or two **O-rings** as a seal (**1–91**). When the O-ring is worn, slip it off the stem and replace it with another of the same size.

Cartridge Faucets

Quality faucets now available use a cartridge to control the flow of water. Most manufacturers claim these will never drip, so home maintenance is typically not a factor. Should they drip, the dealer should make repairs at little or no cost. One such two-handle lavatory faucet is shown in **1–92**. **Illus**. **1–93** is an exploded drawing showing the parts of this faucet.

The faucet cartridge has two O-rings. If they

1–92. This two-handle lavatory faucet uses a cartridge to control the flow of water. It is guaranteed to never leak or drip (courtesy Moen Incorporated).

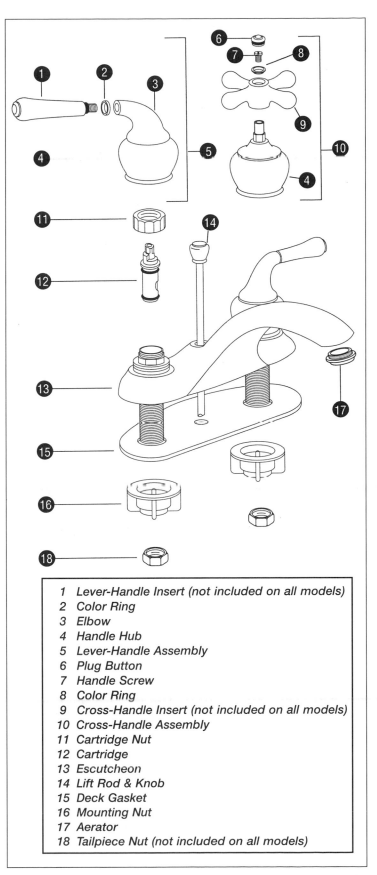

1	Lever-Handle Insert (not included on all models)
2	Color Ring
3	Elbow
4	Handle Hub
5	Lever-Handle Assembly
6	Plug Button
7	Handle Screw
8	Color Ring
9	Cross-Handle Insert (not included on all models)
10	Cross-Handle Assembly
11	Cartridge Nut
12	Cartridge
13	Escutcheon
14	Lift Rod & Knob
15	Deck Gasket
16	Mounting Nut
17	Aerator
18	Tailpiece Nut (not included on all models)

1–93. This exploded drawing shows the parts of a two-handle cartridge lavatory faucet (courtesy Moen Incorporated).

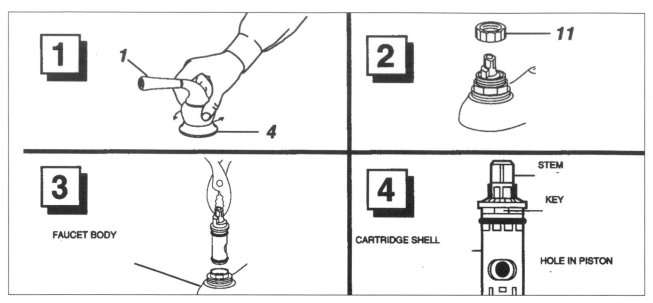

1–94. Should you need to replace the O-rings on a cartridge, remove the handle and cartridge nut and lift out the cartridge.

ever need replacing, remove the handle, unscrew the cartridge nut, and lift out the cartridge (**1–94**). Be certain to get the exact replacement O-rings.

Single-Lever Faucet

Single-lever faucets (**1–95**) control the water temperature and flow with one control. Moving the handle forward or backward increases or decreases the water flow. Moving the handle to the left provides hot water, while moving it right provides cold. Keeping the handle somewhere near the center provides warm water from a mix of hot and cold water.

1–95. This is a single-lever kitchen faucet that also offers a remote spray attachment (courtesy Kohler Company).

The most commonly used mechanisms are the rotating ball and the cartridge.

Repairing a Rotating-Ball Faucet

The **rotating ball** has three openings. One opening is the cold-water inlet, another the hot-water inlet, and the third is the opening to the spout. Moving the handle changes the size of the openings. In this way, water temperature and flow are controlled. It can also shut off all flow of water.

The construction of this type of faucet is shown in **1–96** and **1–97**. The valve body has two spring-loaded valve seats. It has two O-rings that seal it against the spout assembly (**1–96**). The flow of water is controlled by the brass ball inside the valve body. It rides on the valve seats and when turned lets hot or cold water flow to the spout (**1–97**).

To repair a rotating ball mechanism, follow these steps:

1. Turn off both the hot and cold water to the faucet.

2. Remove the lever. Look for a screw to loosen to allow the lever to be removed.

3. Unscrew the cap.

4. Remove the ball assembly.

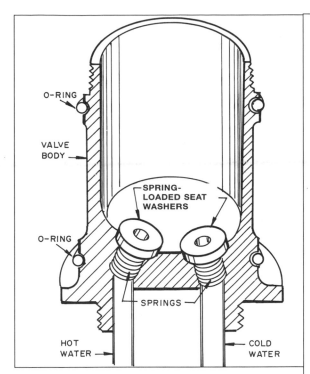

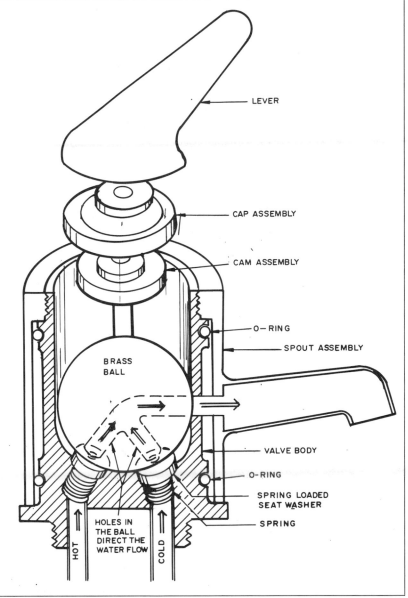

1–96 (above). This is a typical valve body and seat design for a rotating-ball faucet. Remember, the actual design will vary depending upon the brand of faucet purchased, but the basic idea is the same.

1–97 (right). A generalized example of an assembled rotating-ball faucet. As the ball is moved by the lever, the amount of hot and cold water is regulated to produce the desired temperature or the flow can be stopped. Notice the use of O-rings to seal the spout assembly with the valve body.

5. Replace the O-rings, valve seat, springs, and cam. These items are sold as a kit (**1–96**).

6. Reassemble the faucet.

7. Turn on the water and check for leaks. If the faucet still leaks, replace the ball. If the faucet leaks around the spout, replace the O-rings that are around the valve body.

Repairing a Single-Lever Cartridge Faucet

A single-lever cartridge faucet is shown in **1–98**. Cartridge faucets have a cartridge mechanism that has overlapping water-inlet holes much like those in the rotating-ball faucet. The hot and cold water enter through these holes and are mixed by adjust-

1–98. This single-lever cartridge faucet controls the temperature and flow by moving the lever up and down and left to right (courtesy Moen Incorporated).

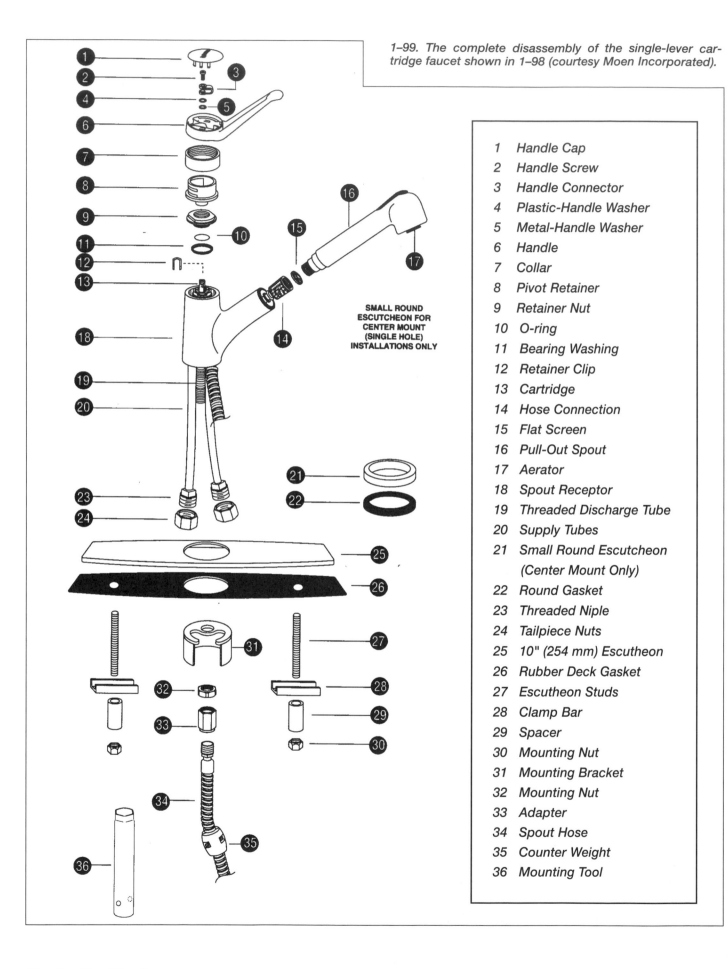

1–99. The complete disassembly of the single-lever cartridge faucet shown in 1–98 (courtesy Moen Incorporated).

SMALL ROUND
ESCUTCHEON FOR
CENTER MOUNT
(SINGLE HOLE)
INSTALLATIONS ONLY

1	Handle Cap
2	Handle Screw
3	Handle Connector
4	Plastic-Handle Washer
5	Metal-Handle Washer
6	Handle
7	Collar
8	Pivot Retainer
9	Retainer Nut
10	O-ring
11	Bearing Washing
12	Retainer Clip
13	Cartridge
14	Hose Connection
15	Flat Screen
16	Pull-Out Spout
17	Aerator
18	Spout Receptor
19	Threaded Discharge Tube
20	Supply Tubes
21	Small Round Escutcheon (Center Mount Only)
22	Round Gasket
23	Threaded Niple
24	Tailpiece Nuts
25	10" (254 mm) Escutheon
26	Rubber Deck Gasket
27	Escutheon Studs
28	Clamp Bar
29	Spacer
30	Mounting Nut
31	Mounting Bracket
32	Mounting Nut
33	Adapter
34	Spout Hose
35	Counter Weight
36	Mounting Tool

ing the cartridge to produce the desired water temperature. An exploded view of an entire installation is shown in **1–99** .

If the faucet eventually leaks, generally it is easiest to replace the cartridge. The exact process will vary depending upon the brand of faucet. Follow the manufacturer's replacement instructions when buying a new cartridge. Following are the steps to replace the Moen Incorporated cartridge faucet (**1–100**):

1. Turn off the water and open the faucet to reduce the pressure.

2. Remove the handle cap (step 1 in **1–100**) with a fine-point flat screwdriver. Tilt the handle (6) up and lift it off. Some brands hold the cap with a screw.

3. Unscrew the collar (7) and lift out the pivot retainer (8), unscrew the retainer nut (9), and remove the O-ring (10) and the bearing washer (11). Remove the washers (4) and (5) from the cartridge stem (step 2 in **1–100**). Be careful that the O-ring or washers are not damaged unless they will be replaced.

4. Pull the retainer clip (12) off the cartridge stem (step 3 in **1–100**).

5. Grip the cartridge stem with pliers (13) and lift it straight up out of the body (step 4 in **1–100**).

6. To install the new cartridge, follow the steps in reverse. Work carefully so that the O-rings on the new cartridge are not damaged. For this particular faucet, the installation requires that the following be observed:

A. The stem must be in the open position.

B. The ears should be positioned from front to back.

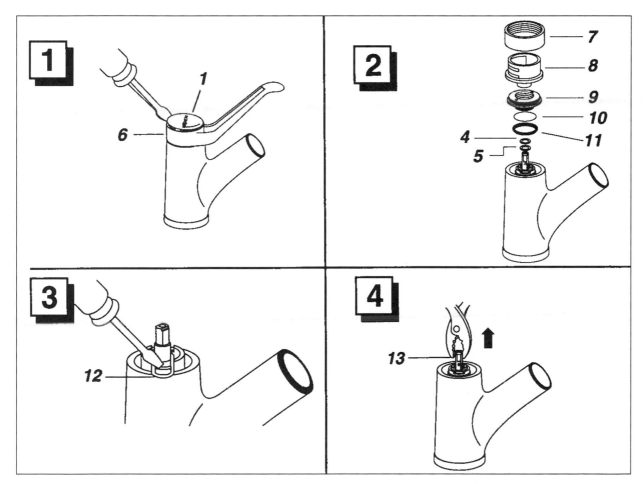

1–100. To replace a cartridge, remove the lever handle, unscrew the collar, lift out the parts below it, pull off the retainer clip, and lift out the cartridge (courtesy Moen Incorporated).

C. The notched flat on the stem should face forward.

D. The retainer clip should straddle the ears.

E. The pivot retainer groove should face the back.

F. Reinstall the lever handle by hooking the handle housing into the groove on the retainer pivot nut, tilting the handle assembly to the back while installing it.

These instructions for repairing one brand of faucet stress the importance of getting installation instructions with the new cartridge.

More expensive faucets use a **ceramic-disk cartridge mechanism**. Generally, they last for many years and seldom require replacement. Should they begin to leak, consult the dealer from which the faucet was bought. The manufacturer will often make repairs at no cost.

Faucets Mounted in a Wall

Some tub and shower faucets are mounted in a wall. They may be either compression-stem or cartridge faucets. Either kind is repaired as described earlier. The only difference between a tub or shower faucet and a sink faucet is the location. Because stem-type tub and shower faucets are mounted in a wall, they are difficult to get to and remove. To repair a leak in a wall-mounted stem faucet, follow these steps (**1–101**):

1. Turn off the water and open the faucet to release the pressure.

2. Remove the handle and any cover below it.

3. Use a **plumber's deep-socket wrench** to unscrew the bonnet nut, which removes the stem that's inside the wall. Small pieces of wallboard or plaster may have to be removed to get the socket in place.

4. Replace the washers, packing, or O-rings on a stem faucet.

5. Reassemble the faucet in reverse order.

6. Turn on the water and check for leaks.

The cartridge-type faucet (**1–102** and **1–103**) is

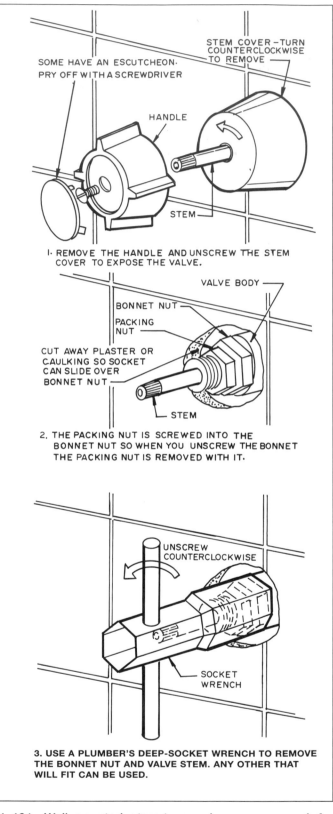

1. REMOVE THE HANDLE AND UNSCREW THE STEM COVER TO EXPOSE THE VALVE.

2. THE PACKING NUT IS SCREWED INTO THE BONNET NUT SO WHEN YOU UNSCREW THE BONNET THE PACKING NUT IS REMOVED WITH IT.

3. USE A PLUMBER'S DEEP-SOCKET WRENCH TO REMOVE THE BONNET NUT AND VALVE STEM. ANY OTHER THAT WILL FIT CAN BE USED.

1–101. Wall-mounted stem-type valves are opened for repairs by unscrewing the bonnet nut with a deep-socket wrench. The washer is replaced as discussed earlier for stem-type compression faucets.

1–102. This cartridge faucet is mounted on the wall of a fiberglass shower and controls the temperature and flow of the water.

sometimes mounted on the wall at a tub or shower. It operates in the same manner as already described for cartridge faucets. The one handle controls the flow and temperature. It is repaired by removing the handle and collar and pulling off the retainer clip with pliers. The cartridge can then be removed and replaced (**1–103**) as described earlier for cartridge faucets.

1–103 (below). A generalized example of the mechanism in a wall-mounted cartridge faucet. There are design differences in each of the brands available.

Stopping Water Hammer

If there is a pounding noise whenever a faucet is quickly closed (called **water hammer**), there is a situation present that could cause pipe-breaking pressure. To prevent this, an air chamber is installed between the water-supply pipe and the faucet. This can be done by adding a section of pipe (**1–104**) or

1–104. This is a typical use of a section of pipe at each valve connection. It uses the trapped air to reduce water hammer.

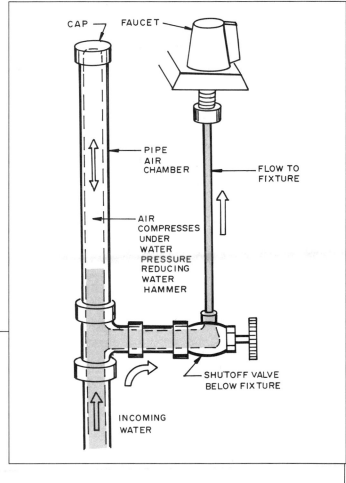

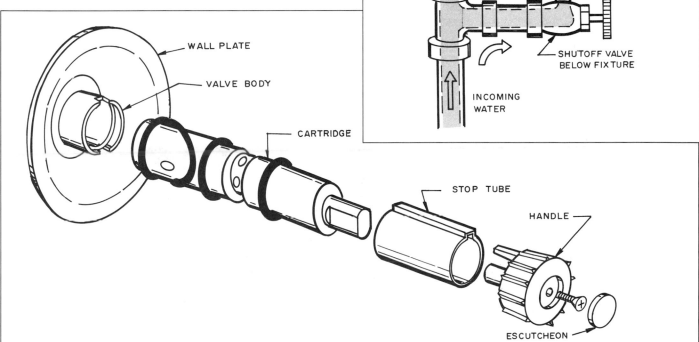

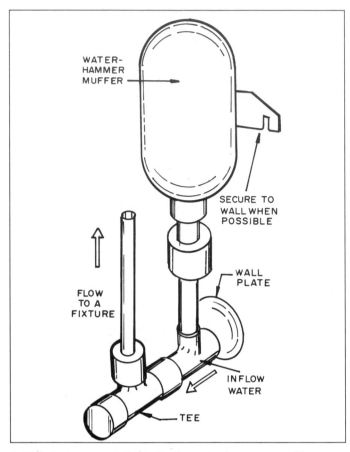

1–105. A commercially available water-hammer muffler connected between the line to the valve on the fixture and the incoming water (courtesy Genova Products, Inc.).

a commercial water-hammer muffler (**1–105**). The muffler manufactured by Genova Incorporated has a plastic air chamber with a flexible bladder inside. As the flow is suddenly stopped, the bladder fills with water, absorbing the shock (**1–106**). If the pipe system is used, it will gradually fill with water over a period of time and the system will need to be drained to empty it.

Cleaning an Aerator

Bath and kitchen spouts often have an **aerator** on their ends. The aerator mixes air with the water to produce a splashless stream (**1–107**). The older type has a perforated disk and a screen, which are metal and clog frequently. New types have plastic parts and use larger openings, which tend to clog less frequently. Clogs are caused by mineral deposits forming on the parts or by small trash particles in the water system. If you have the older type, it may be wise to replace it with the newer design.

To clean an aerator, follow these steps:

1. Remove the aerator by hand-turning it clockwise when looking down on it from above. If it will not turn by hand, wrap it with something to pro-

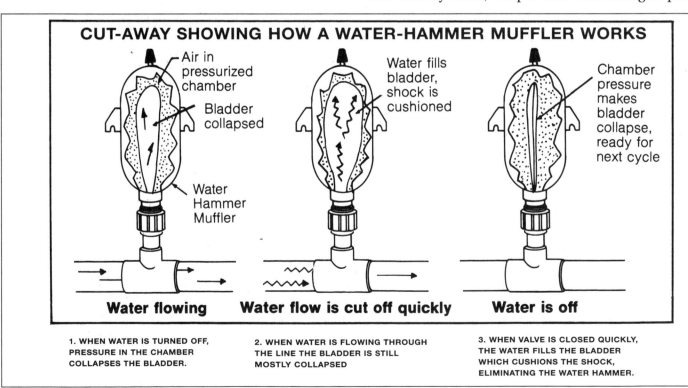

1–106. These steps show how a commercial water-hammer muffler controls water hammer (courtesy Genova Products, Inc.).

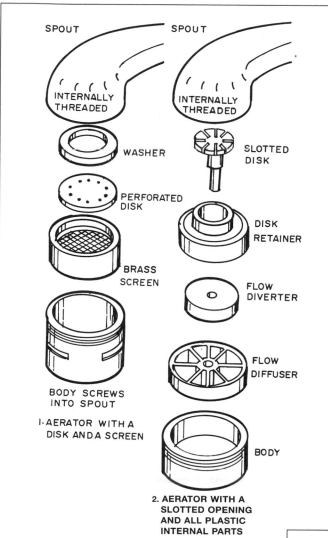

SPOUT

INTERNALLY THREADED

WASHER

PERFORATED DISK

BRASS SCREEN

BODY SCREWS INTO SPOUT

1. AERATOR WITH A DISK AND A SCREEN

SPOUT

INTERNALLY THREADED

SLOTTED DISK

DISK RETAINER

FLOW DIVERTER

FLOW DIFFUSER

BODY

2. AERATOR WITH A SLOTTED OPENING AND ALL PLASTIC INTERNAL PARTS

1–107 (above). Aerators can be disassembled for cleaning.

tect the finish and turn it with an adjustable wrench or pliers. A cloth or black electrician's tape will do.

2. Take the unit apart.

3. If it has a disk and screen, clear the holes with a pin or toothpick. If the disk and screen are badly clogged with mineral deposits, soak them in vinegar until they soften. The newer type of aerator seldom clogs, but if it does flush it out, soak it in vinegar, and clear away any deposits.

4. Put it back together and replace it on the faucet. Turn it hand-tight.

Cleaning a Spray Nozzle

A kitchen-sink spray nozzle is similar to an aerator (**1–108**). The perforated disk is cleared in a manner similar to the aerator. Sometimes the hose becomes clogged. Remove it from the faucet by loosening the locknut underneath the sink. If the hose is clogged with minerals, it may have to be replaced.

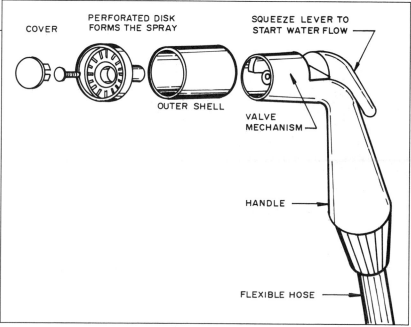

COVER

PERFORATED DISK FORMS THE SPRAY

SQUEEZE LEVER TO START WATER FLOW

OUTER SHELL

VALVE MECHANISM

HANDLE

FLEXIBLE HOSE

1–108. If the kitchen spray begins to clog the perforated disk, remove and clean it.

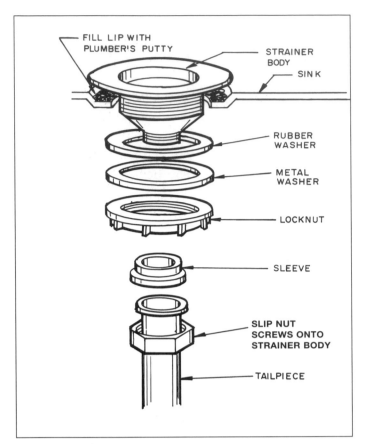

1–109. This type of sink strainer is held to the sink with a large-diameter locknut. Be certain to put a layer of plumber's putty below the rim of the strainer.

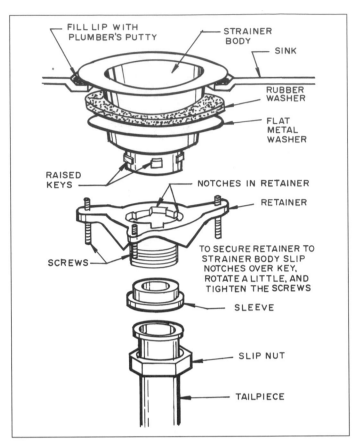

1–110. This older-style sink strainer uses a retainer and screws to secure the strainer to the sink. Notice the plumber's putty below the rim of the strainer.

Repairing or Replacing a Sink Strainer

There are several types of sink strainers. One uses a locknut to hold the strainer to the sink (**1–109**). It has been widely used and is found in many houses built a number of years ago. Another uses a retainer and screws to hold it in place (**1–110**). This is seldom used today, but can be found in some houses. The **clamp–cup sink strainer** is now widely used and makes a neat installation (**1–111**). It is easier to install and remove.

A common problem with a strainer is that after a number of years it begins to leak where it joins the sink. To fix the leak, follow these steps:

1. Loosen the tailpiece slip nut (**1–112** and **1–113**).

2. Loosen the locknut or retainer screws holding the strainer body to the sink. If the strainer has a **clamp cup,** use a monkey wrench, pipe wrench, or Vise Grip pliers to remove the locknut. If the strainer uses a rigid locknut, loosen it by placing a wood dowel or metal rod against one of the ridges and drive it around with a hammer (**1–113**). Rotate the locknut counterclockwise to loosen it.

3. If the strainer turns as the nut is being loosened, someone has to hold it in place. Insert a wood rod into the strainer from the top and press against one of the openings in the bottom. Push in the direction opposite the rotation of the locknut.

4. Drop the metal and rubber washers away from the sink.

5. Lift the strainer out of the sink from above.

6. Clean away the old plumber's putty from the sink and strainer.

7. Put a new ring of plumber's putty about ⅛ inch (3 millimeters) thick around the drain hole in the sink. Place the strainer in the drain hole and press it down against the putty (**1–111**).

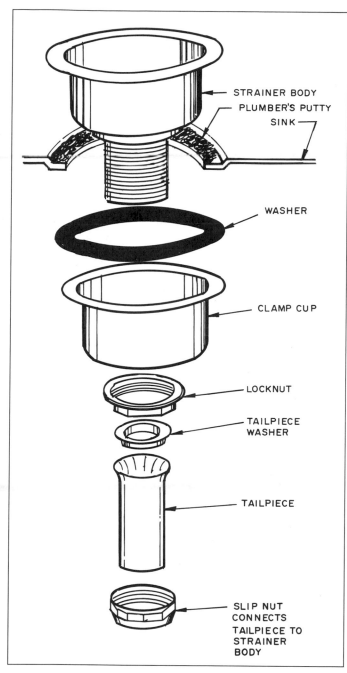

1–111. This widely used sink strainer is held to the sink with a clamp cup. It must have a layer of plumber's putty below its rim.

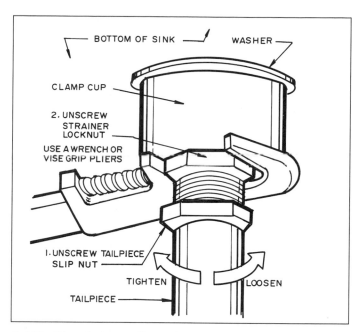

1–112. The strainer with a clamp cup can be removed by loosening the locknuts with a wrench or Vise Grip pliers.

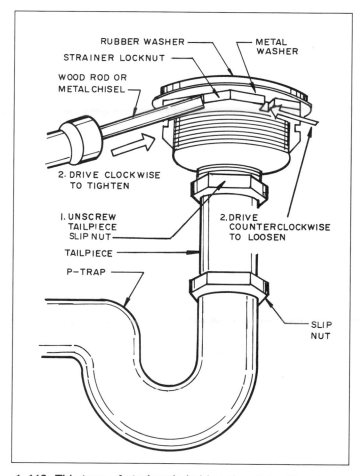

1–113. This type of strainer is held to the sink with a large-diameter locknut. Since it is large and difficult to reach, it is usually loosened and tightened by driving the locknut with a hammer and a rod.

8. Reassemble the rubber and metal washers from beneath the sink. Replace these if they are damaged.

9. Install the locknuts on the retainer.

10. Clean away the excess plumber's putty that is forced out around the edge of the strainer in the sink.

Adjusting and Cleaning a Lavatory Pop-Up Plug

A common way to hold water in a lavatory is with a pop-up plug. A **pop-up plug** is controlled by a lift rod found between the faucets (**1–114**; also refer to **1–50**).

Beneath the lavatory is the pop-up mechanism. The lift rod is connected to the lift-rod strap with a setscrew. The pivot rod is connected to the lift-rod strap with a spring clip. The pop-up plug is raised and lowered by the other end of the pivot rod. The amount the pop-up rises and lowers is adjusted with the setscrew connection on the lift rod. To adjust the mechanism, loosen the setscrew and slide the lift-rod strap up or down until the pop-up opens and closes as desired.

The pop-up plug may or may not be attached to the pivot rod (**1–115**). If it is not attached, simply pull it straight out for cleaning. Some pop-up plugs have a slot or hook built in. They are removed by turning and lifting them. Other pop-up plugs have a hole through which the pivot rod fits. To remove this kind for cleaning, loosen the pivot nut that holds the pivot rod to the drainpipe and slide the rod out of the hole in the pop-up plug. Be sure to use plastic tape or plumber's putty on the threads when reinstalling the pivot nut.

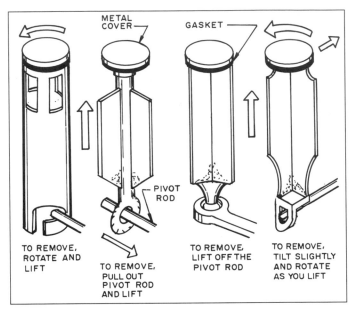

1–115. Some of the types of pop-up plugs commonly available.

Adjusting Tub Drains

Bathtub drains are controlled by a lever mounted on the overflow drain. Through a series of several rods or springs, the drain can be opened or closed. The two most common mechanisms use a plunger or a pop-up plug.

On a **plunger drain**, a lever pivots on a ball joint and moves the lift rod up or down. On one end of the lift rod is a plunger (**1–116**). When the plunger is down, the drain is closed.

If the drain lets water leak out of the tub, the plunger may be clogged. Clean it out as follows:

1. Remove the screws holding the overflow plate to the tub.

2. Pull the entire assembly out of the overflow tube (**1–117**).

3. Clean the plunger. Remove all corrosion by soaking it in vinegar and scrubbing it with a commercial cleaner.

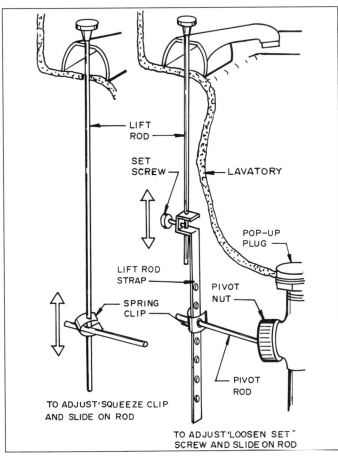

1–114. Two mechanisms for pop-up plugs. Both can be adjusted to regulate the amount the pop-up plug extends above the bottom of the lavatory. This controls the flow of water from the lavatory.

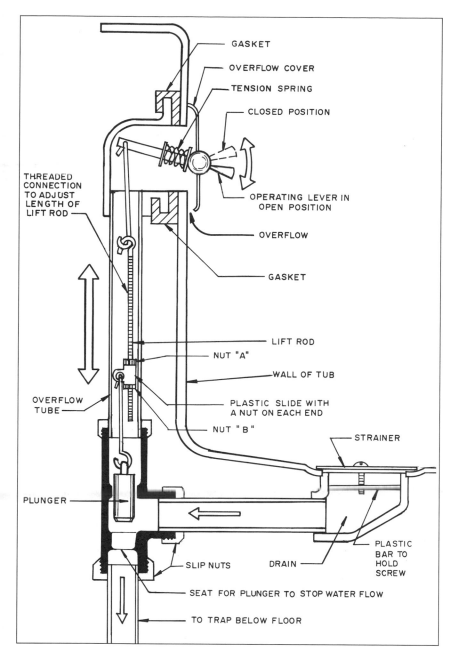

Labels in figure 1-116:
- GASKET
- OVERFLOW COVER
- TENSION SPRING
- CLOSED POSITION
- THREADED CONNECTION TO ADJUST LENGTH OF LIFT ROD
- OPERATING LEVER IN OPEN POSITION
- OVERFLOW
- GASKET
- LIFT ROD
- NUT "A"
- WALL OF TUB
- OVERFLOW TUBE
- PLASTIC SLIDE WITH A NUT ON EACH END
- NUT "B"
- STRAINER
- PLUNGER
- SLIP NUTS
- DRAIN
- PLASTIC BAR TO HOLD SCREW
- SEAT FOR PLUNGER TO STOP WATER FLOW
- TO TRAP BELOW FLOOR

1–116. This type of tub drain uses a plunger controlled by a lift rod to regulate the flow of water out of the bathtub.

4. Flush the drain with water.

5. Replace the plunger assembly in the overflow tube.

6. Reattach the overflow plate to the tub.

The drain may leak because the plunger does not go all the way down when closed. Lengthening the lift rod lowers the plunger. The lift rod has threads

1–117 (right). The plunger and lift rod are removed from the overflow opening in the tub so they can be cleaned.

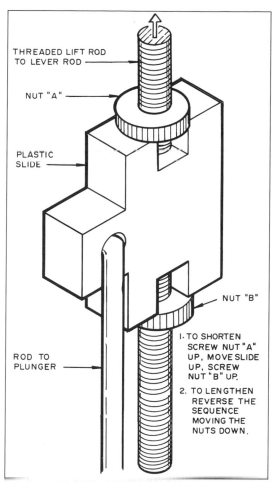

Labels in figure 1-118:
- THREADED LIFT ROD TO LEVER ROD
- NUT "A"
- PLASTIC SLIDE
- NUT "B"
- ROD TO PLUNGER
- 1. TO SHORTEN SCREW NUT "A" UP, MOVE SLIDE UP, SCREW NUT "B" UP.
- 2. TO LENGTHEN REVERSE THE SEQUENCE MOVING THE NUTS DOWN.

1–118. The length of the lift rod is changed by adjusting the nuts on each side of the plastic slide.

on it for making up-and-down adjustments. Loosen the nuts and move the plastic slide as shown in **1–118**. There are several other lift-rod designs, but the length adjustment is basically the

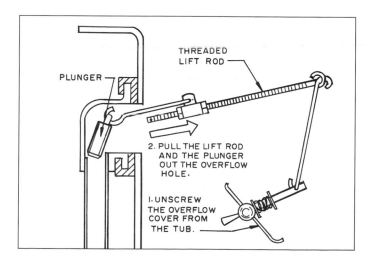

Labels in figure 1-117:
- PLUNGER
- THREADED LIFT ROD
- 2. PULL THE LIFT ROD AND THE PLUNGER OUT THE OVERFLOW HOLE.
- 1. UNSCREW THE OVERFLOW COVER FROM THE TUB.

same.

A pop-up drain using a **spring** is shown in **1–119**. The lower end of the lift rod is formed into a spring. The pop-up stopper is connected to a rocker linkage that can rock up or down like a seesaw. The spring end of the lift rod rests on one end of the linkage arm. When the operating lever is rotated in one direction,

the lift rod presses down on the spring; this causes the stopper to rise, allowing the water in the tub to drain. When the lever is rotated in the other direction, the pressure on the spring is removed and the stopper will lower, closing the drain.

The **pop-up stopper** can be pulled up out of the drain for cleaning (**1–120**). If the stopper has an O-ring, replace it if it is worn. The **lift-rod linkage** may be removed by loosening the screws holding the overflow cover to the tub. Pull the linkage out of the overflow tube in the same manner as described for plunger drains. The amount of pressure the spring has on the linkage can be adjusted. Simply change the length of the lift rod by turning the nut that holds it to the spring. This controls the position of the stopper and will let the stopper be seated so that it does not leak.

Soak the parts in vinegar to remove mineral deposits and brush them thoroughly. Make certain that the linkages on the rocker arm are clean and move freely.

The Step-On Bathtub Pop-Up Plug

The step-on bathtub pop-up plug uses a spring-loaded mechanism to control the opening and closing of the pop-up. It can be closed by stepping on the cover (**1–121**). To open it, step down on the cover and release it. This eliminates the need to have plungers and linkages as described earlier. These units are sold in a kit with the necessary plastic pipe and fittings

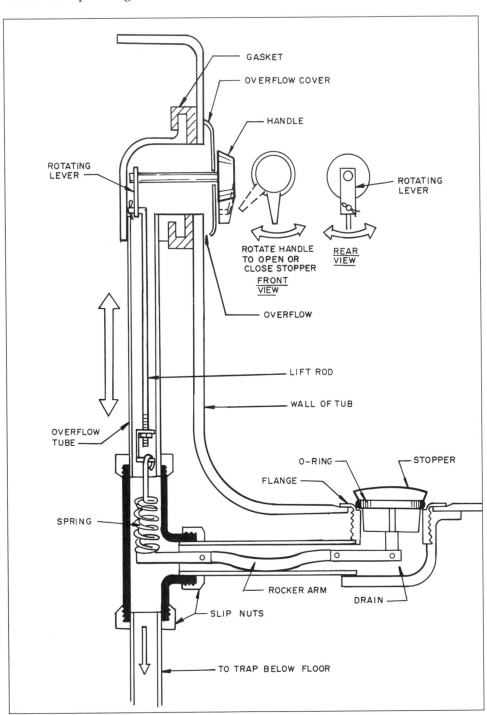

1–119. By rotating the handle, you can compress the spring opening or the stopper or release the spring, letting the stopper close. There are a number of different mechanisms available, but they all basically follow the design shown.

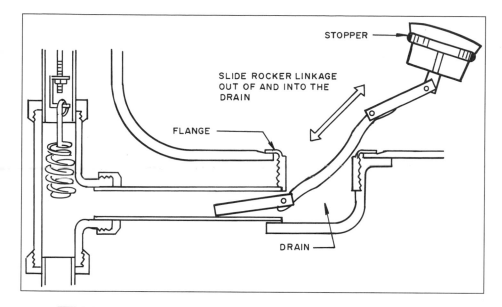

1–120. The rocker linkage can be removed by lifting the stopper and pulling it out. It is replaced by sliding it back into the drain.

needed to install the unit.

Repairing a Washer-Type Toilet Ball Cock

A common problem with a ball cock (refer to **1–60**) is that the inlet valve does not shut off. This condition is often caused by worn washers. To replace the washers, follow these steps:

1. Turn off the water. Flush the toilet to empty the tank.

2. Remove the screws holding

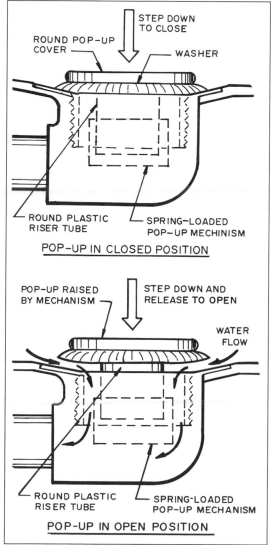

1–121. The step-on pop-up is a simple mechanism that eliminates the need for plungers and linkages used with other systems.

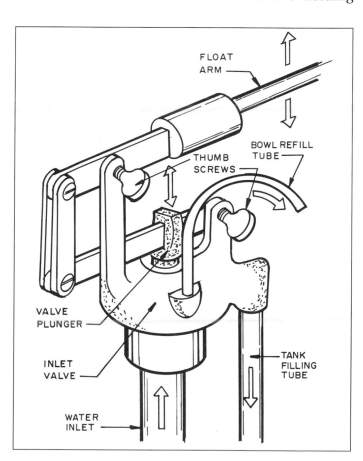

1–122. A typical inlet valve for a washer type toilet ball cock. As the float rises and lowers with the water level in the tank, the linkage moves the valve plunger up and down, controlling the flow of water into the tank and bowl.

the float-ball arm to the valve (**1–122**).

3. Lift the float ball and valve plunger from the tank.

4. Remove the split washer and bottom washer (**1–123**). Take the plunger with you to the plumb-

ing supply house to be sure of getting the correct-size washers.

5. Remove all corrosion on the parts before installing the new washers. Examine the surface of the washer seat in the valve. If it is worn, a new washer will not fit tightly and the leak will continue. Replace the entire unit with a newer type of flush mechanism (refer to **1–61**).

6. Install a new split washer and bottom washer.

7. Put the valve back together.

8. Turn on the water and check for leaks.

Frequently when the ball cock is old, it is simply replaced with the new type shown in **1–61**.

Repairing a Diaphragm-Type Toilet Ball Cock

Illus. 1–124 is a simplified drawing that shows a diaphragm-type ball cock. This unit fills the tank more quietly than the washer type and generally operates longer before needing repairs. It is installed in the tank in the same manner as other types of ball cocks.

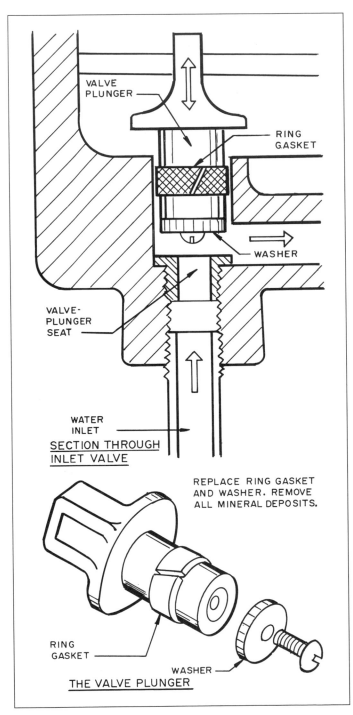

1–123. The ring gasket and washer can be replaced when worn. If the valve-plunger seat is worn, it is best to replace the entire ball cock.

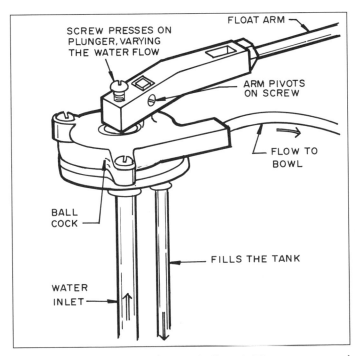

1–124. A typical diaphragm-type ball cock. There are several different designs manufactured, but the operation is much the same.

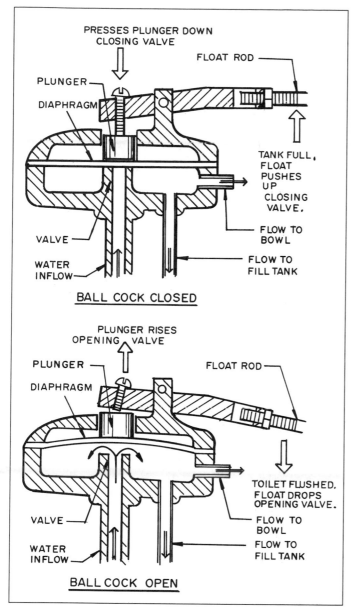

1–125. A generalized illustration showing how a diaphragm ball cock operates.

lever lowers as the toilet is flushed, the water pushes the diaphragm up, allowing water to flow into the tank and bowl. When the tank is filled, the float rises and the float lever pushes the plunger down; this seals the inflow at the valve by placing the diaphragm over the inlet (**1–125**).

When a diaphragm ball cock starts to leak, take it apart and replace the diaphragm. Clean mineral deposits from moving parts and inside the assembly.

Repairing Leaks Between the Toilet Tank and Bowl

A toilet tank is joined to the bowl with several bolts. Between the tank and bowl are a large washer at the flush valve, a **spud washer,** and a gasket called a **tank cushion** (1–126). If the tank leaks between it and the bowl, first try tightening the connecting bolts slightly. Do not overtighten them or the ceramic tank or bowl could crack. If tightening the bolts does not stop the leak, do the following:

1. Shut off the water to the tank.

2. Drain the tank by flushing the toilet. Remove any remaining water with a sponge.

3. Disconnect the slip nut from the inlet water line that connects with the ball cock.

4. Remove the bolts and their washers. With the bolts removed, the tank can be lifted off the bowl.

5. Unscrew the locknut holding the valve seat in place and remove it. If the valve seat is worn, now is a good time to replace it also. Replace the old washer and spud washer.

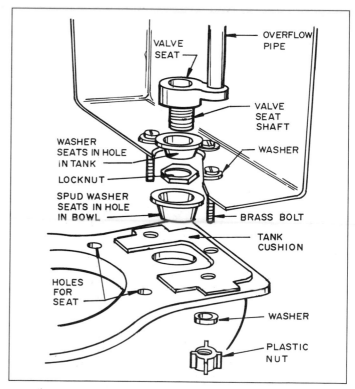

1–126. Leaks between the tank and bowl could be caused by defective bolt washers, spud washers or the large washer below the valve seat.

6. Set the washer in place inside the tank and install the valve-seat shaft through it. Install the locknut on the valve-seat shaft below the tank. Place the spud washer in the hole in the bowl.

7. Replace the tank cushion if it is worn.

8. Set the tank back on the bowl and install the bolts with new washers. Tighten the bolts until the unit is solid. Again, do not overtighten or the tank or bowl may crack.

9. Reconnect the water inlet, fill the tank, and check for leaks.

Unclogging Sink Drains

The surest way to handle sink-drain problems is to avoid them. Do not run anything but wastewater in the drain. Hair, food particles, and grease of any kind should not be allowed to enter the drain.

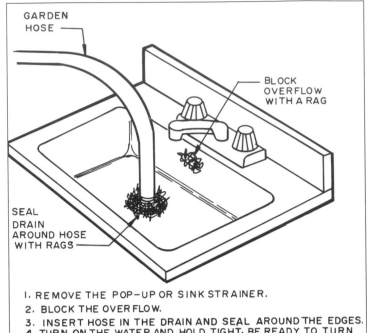

1. REMOVE THE POP-UP OR SINK STRAINER.
2. BLOCK THE OVERFLOW.
3. INSERT HOSE IN THE DRAIN AND SEAL AROUND THE EDGES.
4. TURN ON THE WATER AND HOLD TIGHT. BE READY TO TURN OFF THE IF THE DRAIN DOES NOT CLEAR.

1-128. Some clogged drains can be cleared using water pressure. Be certain to have someone ready to turn off the water if the clog does not clear.

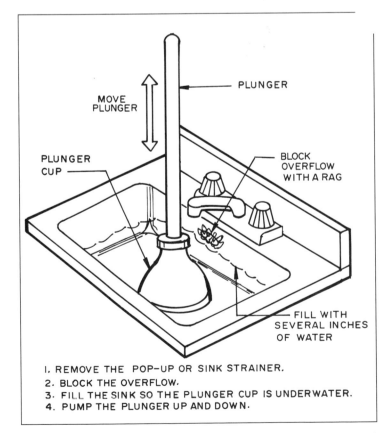

1. REMOVE THE POP-UP OR SINK STRAINER.
2. BLOCK THE OVERFLOW.
3. FILL THE SINK SO THE PLUNGER CUP IS UNDERWATER.
4. PUMP THE PLUNGER UP AND DOWN.

1-127. When a sink drain flows slowly or clogs, first try to clear it with a plunger.

A slowly emptying drain means there is something blocking the pipe that must be cleared. There are several choices of action. The easiest tool to reach for is a plunger. Before using the plunger, seal the overflow opening with a rag. It also helps to remove the sink or tub pop-up (1-127).

Commercial drain cleaners are made to dissolve grease and hair, both of which are a major cause of sink- and tub-drain clogs. Many of the commercial cleaners are caustic. Take great care when using them to avoid damage to your skin and eyes. Follow the manufacturer's directions. To avoid any chance of splashing the caustic cleaner back on you and in the room if the cleaner does not work, do not use a plunger after a caustic cleaner has been used.

Sometimes a drain can be opened with water pressure (1-128). Attach a garden hose to an exterior water faucet, run it into the room, and insert the other end in the drain. Wrap rags

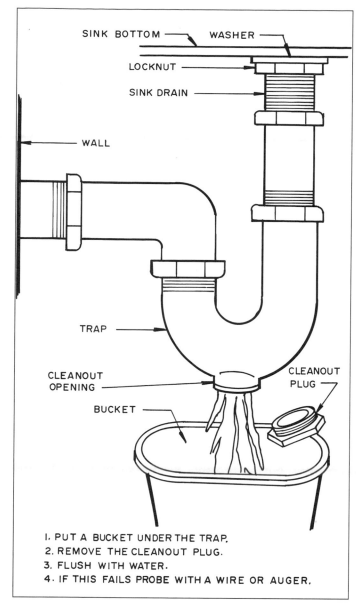

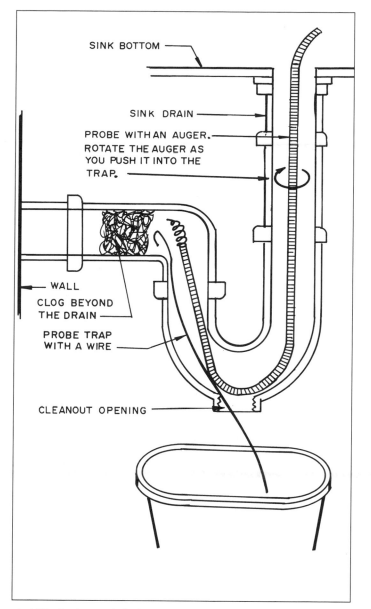

1–129. A trap with a cleanout plug can be drained and possibly cleared by removing the plug and running a little water through the trap.

1–130. A clogged drain can sometimes be cleared by running an auger or wire down the drain or through the cleanout opening in the trap.

around the end of the hose to seal it tightly in the drain. Also seal the overflow opening with a rag. Turn on the water, hold the hose and rags very tightly, and let the water pressure build against the clog. Have someone ready to turn off the water if the clog does not clear. If not, a backsplash of water may hit you in the face. If the drain clears, continue running water for a while to push the clog to the larger-diameter main sewer pipe.

There are commercially available short hoses made for this purpose. They clamp on the sink faucet and have a tapered end that fits tightly into the drain.

Another choice is to try to clean the trap. Some traps have a drain plug. Put a bucket beneath the trap to catch the water and remove the plug (**1–129**). If whatever is causing the clog does not flow out, try probing with a wire to pull it out. If the trap does not have a drain plug, the trap will have to be removed. Another option is to insert an auger (also called a **snake**) or a wire down the sink opening or through the cleanout plug on the trap (**1–130**). If the drain is

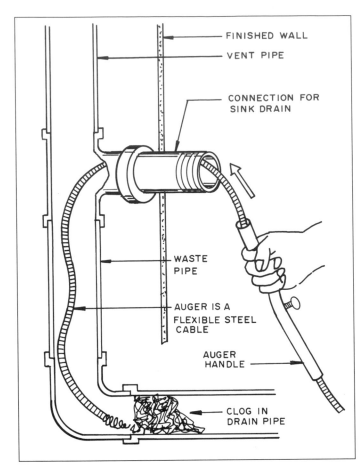

1-131. If the trap is clear, the clog will be somewhere in the waste pipe. Remove the trap and run an auger down the waste pipe.

clear to the wall but still is clogged, remove the trap and run the auger down the waste pipe that is sticking out of the wall (1–131).

Using an Auger

To use an auger, begin rotating it with the crank handle while pushing it into the pipe (1-132). The handle is clamped to the auger with a thumbscrew. As the handle gets near the drainpipe opening, loosen the setscrew, move the handle back along the auger around 24 to 30 inches (609 to 762 millimeters), and resume rotating. If forward progress is stopped before the clog is reached, move the auger in and out while continuing to rotate it. When the auger hits the clog, slide it back and forth so that the point breaks it up. Then flush the opening with water to clear the debris.

Unclogging Bathtub Drains

If the bathtub is clogged or running slow, try to clear the clog by running an auger down the overflow tube. Remove the popup from the drain and the flow-control linkage that is in the overflow tube (refer to 1–117 and 1–120). Carefully run the auger down the overflow, rotating it with the handle (1–132).

The trap for bathtubs is usually below the floor. If the area below the floor is unfinished, there is access to it (1–133).

If the trap is clear and the drain is still slow, the clog is in the waste-disposal lines beyond the trap. See Unclogging Soil and Waste Pipes, the House Drain, and the House Sewer on pages 70 to 73 for ways to unclog the waste pipe.

Unclogging a Toilet

The bowl of a toilet has a built-in trap. If it gets clogged, the easiest way to try to free the clog is with a plunger. Should the bowl be full to the rim with water, either wait until some of the water seeps past the blockage or remove some water with a pail. Place the plunger over the opening in the bottom of the bowl (1–134). Pump several quick, short strokes

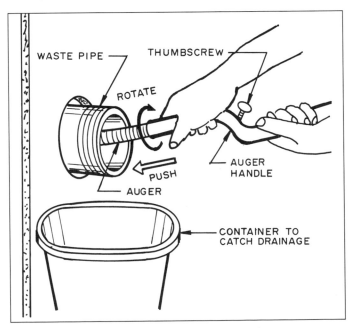

1–132. As you move the auger into the drain, rotate it with the crank handle. Move the handle back on the auger when it gets approximately within 12 inches of the end of the pipe.

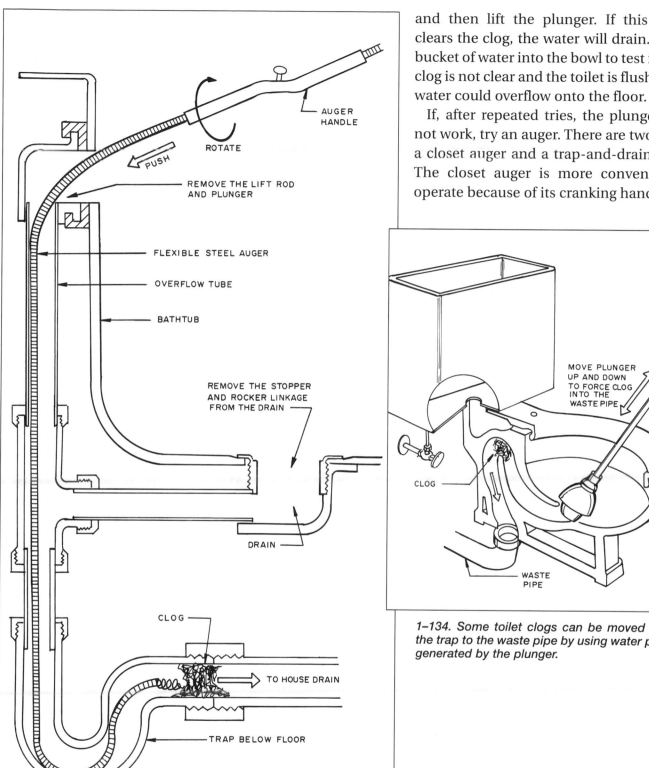

and then lift the plunger. If this action clears the clog, the water will drain. Pour a bucket of water into the bowl to test it. If the clog is not clear and the toilet is flushed, the water could overflow onto the floor.

If, after repeated tries, the plunger does not work, try an auger. There are two kinds: a closet auger and a trap-and-drain auger. The closet auger is more convenient to operate because of its cranking handle.

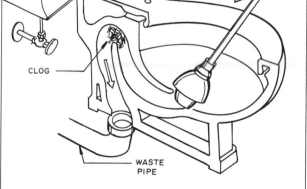

1–134. Some toilet clogs can be moved through the trap to the waste pipe by using water pressure generated by the plunger.

1–133. The bathtub drain can be cleared by running the auger down the overflow tube.

Guide the auger into the trap. Some toilets have the drain toward the front, while others are toward the back (**1–135**). Crank the auger clockwise and work the point through the trap. If it hooks onto something, pull it back into the bowl. If it cannot be hooked, try to break up the clog. Remember, the bowl is made of vitreous china and will chip or crack if hit too hard.

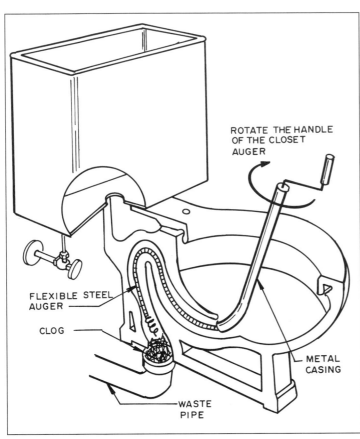

1–135. A closet auger can clear toilet clogs that the plunger will not move. Hold the casing in one hand and rotate the handle as you carefully push the auger through the trap.

Unclogging Soil and Waste Pipes, the House Drain, and the House Sewer

Once it has been determined that the traps to the fixtures are clear, but the water drains slowly or not at all, the clog is in the waste pipe, soil pipe, house drain, or house sewer. If only one fixture does not drain, the clog is probably in the waste pipe leading from that fixture. If all the fixtures do not drain, the clog is probably in the soil pipe, house drain, or house sewer. If the water takes a while to back up in

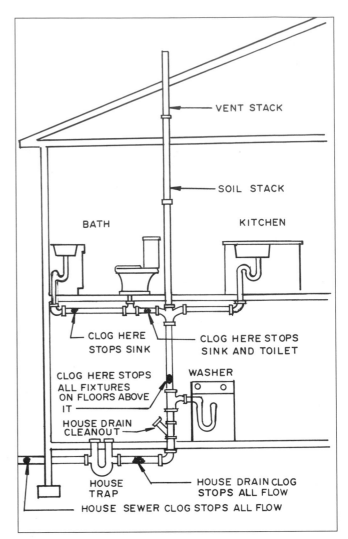

1–136. The location of the clog will determine whether the soil pipe, waste pipe, house drain, or house sewer is clogged.

the fixture, the clog is probably some distance away (**1–136**).

Sometimes **chemicals** can be used to clear a clog in a waste pipe. But if the clog has been building for a long time, chemicals will probably only ease the clog and not remove it completely. In a short time, the clog will rebuild.

Chemicals are caustic and must be used with great care. Protect your skin and eyes, and keep children away from the area.

A **garden hose** may clear a clog as described for sink drains (refer to **1–128**). This is especially effective for clearing small-diameter floor drains.

Seal the opening around the hose with rags and turn on the water. Try to force the hose down into

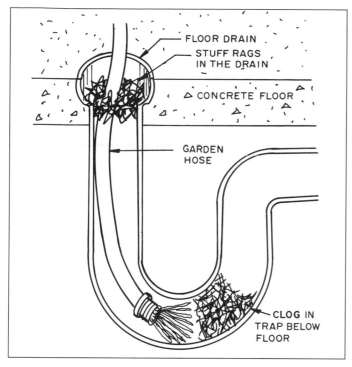

1–137. A hose can be used to build up water pressure against a clog in a drain below the floor. Do not do this if caustic chemicals have been placed in the drain. Use an auger instead.

the trap (**1–137**). Water pressure will sometimes clear the pipe. Do not use this method if you have tried and failed to clear the clog with chemicals. The water under pressure that does not clear the clog may flow back into the room, carrying chemicals with it. The chemicals, though diluted, could still cause injury.

The house drain or house sewer can be cleared with an auger. Hand-operated augers are usually 15 to 30 feet (4.5 to 10 meters) long. Electric-powered augers are also available. They can be rented.

If the clog appears to be in the house trap, remove a plug and probe it with an auger as shown in **1–138**. If the clog is in the house drain, it can be entered through the house trap. Work toward the nearest cleanout. If the line clears, replug the trap and run water through the cleanout opening through the house drain and house trap.

There are frequently one or more cleanouts; they occur usually in the basement, crawl

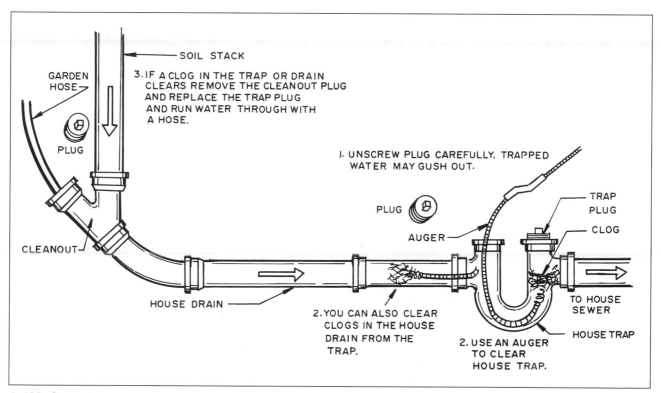

1–138. Open the trap cover and probe it with an auger to clear the trap. Poke until you get some flow. Then continue probing to break up the clog. Open both plugs and work from both sides. Close them and run water through the trap from the nearest cleanout. (A cleanout is a short section of pipe protruding above the sewer or waste line that has a removable plug that allows access into the pipe for cleaning purposes.) If the clog is not in the trap, work the auger toward the nearest cleanout. Close the trap and run water in the drain from the cleanout.

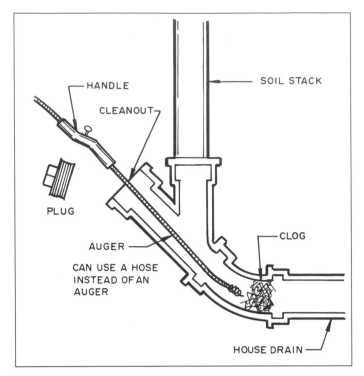

1–139. The cleanout at the base of the soil stack is the best place to try to clear a clog in the house sewer. Unscrew the plug and run an auger in the pipe. You can try a garden hose instead of an auger.

space, or utility room if there is a concrete floor (**1–139**). Frequently the house sewer will have access through cleanouts located on the sewer between the house and the city sewer or septic tank.

Within the house, the cleanout will be located at the bottom of the soil stack. When removing the cleanout plug, be ready to catch any water backed up above it. It may be advisable to wait and let the water slowly leak through the clog, lowering the level before removing the plug.

While working the auger, push it into the pipe. A clog may feel like a soft spot where the auger is difficult to turn. A turn in the pipe may stop the auger. It is hard, which makes it easy to distinguish from a soft spot. Continue to rotate the auger and push it to move it past the bend. If you think the auger has entered the clog, continue to turn it in the same direction, but pull rather than push it. If the clog is something solid, such as cloth, it will be pulled out with the auger. If the clog cannot be pulled out, try to break it up with the auger. Once you think the auger has cleared the pipe, replace the trap or cleanout plug and run lots of water down the drain.

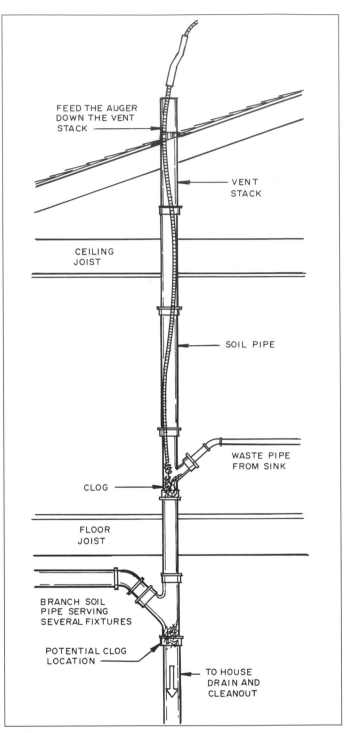

1–140. The soil stack and vent stack can have clogs cleared by running an auger down from the vent pipe on the roof.

Flushing all the toilets is a good way to produce this water rapidly.

Removing the cleanout or trap plug may be difficult. Soak the threads with penetrating oil and try turning the cleanout or trap plug with a large pipe wrench. A short length of pipe can be added to the wrench handle to gain some extra leverage. But be careful: If too much force is used, some of the joints along the drainpipe will loosen. Also try removing a difficult plug by cutting a nick in its edge with a cold chisel. Then, holding the chisel in the nick, hammer on the chisel to turn the plug.

Clogs in the vent stack and soil pipe can be cleared by running an auger down the pipe from the roof (**1–140**). After doing this, flush the line down the vent stack with water from a garden hose. Station someone by the fixture to let you know if the water begins to back up into it. If it does, that method to clear the clog did not work. Repeat the augering process.

It may be necessary to take apart some of the waste line to get to the clog. This means cutting out a section of pipe, clearing the clog, and then inserting a new piece into a union. Install a cleanout plug at this point.

If all these attempts fail, seek professional help to remove the clog. Sometimes the clog is caused by tree roots that have worked their way into the sewer line. All the efforts described in this chapter will not clear roots. The professional will run a power auger with cutting blades on the end to clear the line (**1–141**). Try not to plant trees near the sewer line.

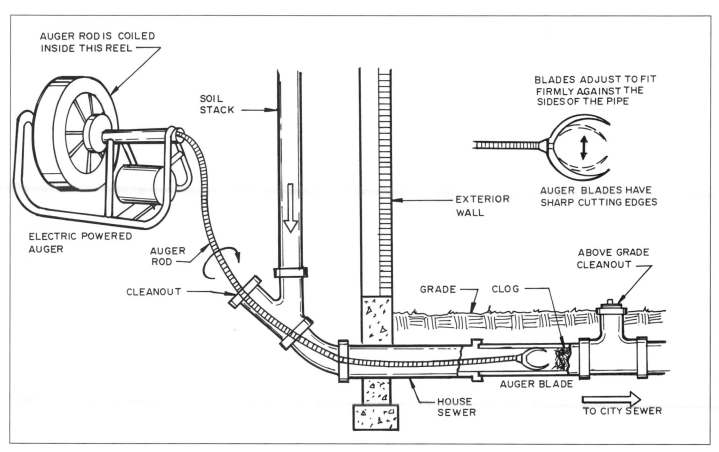

1–141. This power auger has knife-like blades on the end that will cut tree roots and other blockage. Start the motor and feed the auger into the pipe. When it starts cutting the blockage, run water into the pipe and move the auger rod back and forth to do a thorough cutting job.

CHAPTER TWO

Electrical Repairs and Replacement

Electricity is probably the most useful and widely used energy source used in homes. It lights the rooms, is used to power furnaces, air conditioners, and heat pumps, and runs the many appliances. Basic repair and replacement operations are relatively easy and safe *if the power to the unit being repaired has been shut off.* When repairs are being made, be certain the job is done so that it meets electrical codes. The repair parts commonly used in residential construction, such as light switches and duplex outlets, are standardized. Therefore, regardless of where they are bought they will serve as a replacement for the home.

Electrical repairs require only a few simple tools. A good knife, screwdrivers, pliers, electrician's tape, and wire caps are all that are needed for most jobs. Other special tools such as a wire stripper, continuity tester, voltage tester, and fish tape are important to have available (**2–1**).

WHAT IS ELECTRICITY?

Electricity is something that cannot be seen or smelled, but when contacted is felt as a strong, tingling shock. This shock can kill. Electricity is a component of matter. **Matter** is anything that has weight and occupies space. It may be a liquid (such as water), gas (such as oxygen), or a solid (such as steel).

Matter is made of **atoms**. Atoms, while very small, are made up of even smaller particles. Some particles carry a negative charge, while others carry a positive charge. Those with a negative charge are called **electrons**. The flow of electrons (negatively charged particles) along a wire produces what is called an **electric current**. The electric current is produced by these electrons' bumping into each other as they flow along the wire. They push each other along.

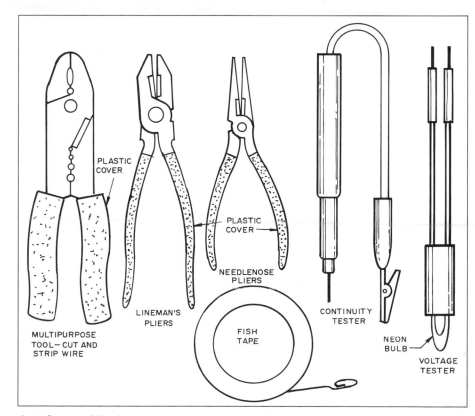

2–1. Some of the important tools used to make electrical repairs.

NATIONAL ELECTRICAL CODE

The National Electrical Code is sponsored by the National Fire Protection Association. It was developed to safeguard persons and property from the hazards arising from the use of electricity. The Code is standard throughout the United States and serves as the basis for most local codes. A copy can be secured from the National Fire Protection Association, P.O. Box 9146, One Battingerymarch Park, Quincy, MA 02269, or the local building inspector can be consulted. The Code is a large publication, having over 1,000 pages and very detailed specifications. Generally, it is not necessary to review it. For repairs, replace the worn unit with a high-quality unit of similar size and design. For more ambitious projects, check with your local building-inspection department.

UNDERWRITERS LABORATORY (UL)

All electrical parts such as switches, outlets, and sockets and other electrical devices such as motors, power tools, and appliances should have a label indicating that they have been tested and meet the standards of the Underwriters Laboratory. This means that these parts and devices are safe when used for the purpose intended. Products are submitted voluntarily from manufacturers in the United States and other countries. Inspectors make unannounced visits to the manufacturing plants to inspect the processes used to make the product. This ensures that the quality of the product will remain as approved.

ELECTRICAL THEORY

To be useful, electrical energy must flow in a **circuit,** or circular path. The current flows from a power source through conductors to a load, such as a lamp, a motor, or a toaster. A **load** is anything that uses electrical energy. After the current is used in the load, it flows back to the power source. **Illus. 2–2** clarifies why electricity needs a complete circuit to work.

To be useful, the electricity in your home also has to follow a circuit. In fact, the wiring in the home forms several circuits that "branch off" from one or more **main circuits**. If something in the wiring crosses across the circuit and interrupts the flow to the load, the result is a **short circuit** (refer to **2–2**).

The electric current supplied to the home from the power company is **alternating current (AC)**. Alternating current moves in one direction, stops, moves in the other direction, stops, and moves back in the first direction. It goes through this sequence many times per second. The alternating current used in the United States and Canada reverses itself 60 times per second. This current is called **60-hertz**, or **60-cycle**, **current** (2–3).

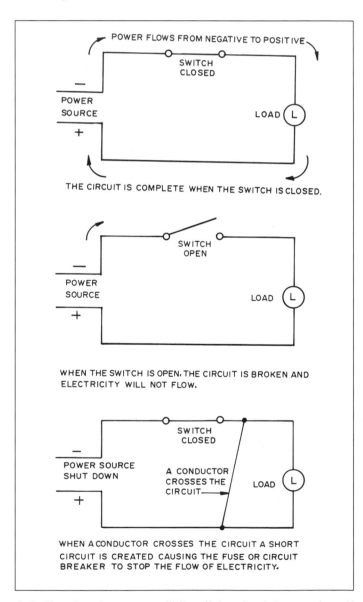

2–2. The electric current will flow if the circuit is complete. If there is a short circuit, the fuse will blow or the circuit breaker will trip, shutting off power to the circuit.

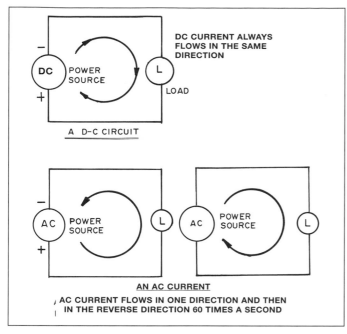

2–3. *Direct current (DC) always flows in one direction. Alternating current (AC) reverses direction 60 times per second.*

Direct current (DC) flows from the negative terminal of the source to the positive terminal and always flows in that direction (**2–3**). It does not reverse the direction of flow, as does alternating current. It is typically used for heavy-duty motors and other industrial equipment.

VOLTS, AMPERES, WATTS, AND OHMS

Electricity (the flow of electrons) flows under pressure to homes from the power company. **Electrical pressure** is measured in **volts (V)**. The circuits in the home are generally 120-volt circuits.

The rate of flow of electricity is measured in **amperes (A)**. The rate of flow is the amount of current passing any point on a circuit in one second. It is a useful measurement for determining the size of wire needed for a circuit or determining how much current is needed for an appliance.

To know how much power is flowing in a circuit, multiply the rate of flow by the pressure (that is, multiply the amps by the volts) to get **watts (A x V = W)**. Many electric devices have their wattage ratings noted on them.

Another useful electrical measurement is the **ohm**. Ohms are a measure of the resistance of the circuit to the flow of electricity. Almost all conductors offer some resistance to electrical flow, as does any load in a circuit. This resistance is what produces heat in wires such as the heating elements in an electric heater.

READING THE ELECTRIC METER

Just before the electricity from the power company enters the home, it passes through a **kilowatt-hour meter** to measure how much power is being used. As is undoubtedly well known, the amount of electricity used must be paid for. The meter records the watts of power used in terms of **kilowatt-hours**. A kilowatt is equal to 1,000 watts.

By reading the electric meter once each month, the electric company can determine how much electricity was used during that month. They subtract the beginning (lower) meter reading from the second (larger) reading to determine the number of kilowatt-hours used. Then they multiply this number by a rate to determine how much is owed for their service (**2–4**). The two types of electric meters in common use are the cyclometer and the clock electric meters. The clock meter is most frequently used.

To read the clock-hour meter, it is important to know that the dial on the left indicates kWh (kilowatt-hours) in 10,000's, the next in 1,000s, the center dial in 100s, the next in 10s, and the last one on the right 0 to 9. Refer again to **2–4** for an example of reading a watt-hour meter. It shows a reading taken May 1 as 12,220 and one on June 1 as 13,579. The difference is 1,359 kWh, which is the amount used in May. Notice that some dials rotate clockwise and others counterclockwise.

THE SERVICE ENTRANCE

Electric power is supplied to a building through the service entrance. The service entrance provides an entry for the wires that bring electricity into the home. The design of the service entrance depends on whether it is overhead or underground. It also depends on the location of the entrance, the height of the house, the distance from the utility pole to the

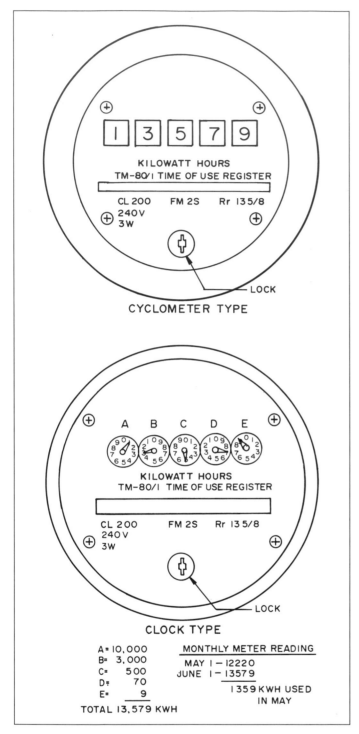

2–4. The amount of electricity consumed is found by taking the differences between two readings. The readings are in kilowatt-hours. One kilowatt-hour is equal to 1,000 watts.

increasingly popular because it eliminates unsightly wires leading to the house (**2–7**).

The service entrance receives power from a transformer on the power company's line. A typical residence will have a three-wire entrance. This consists of two 120-volt power sources. Since some electrical devices require 240 volts, this is available by putting the two 120-volt lines together to provide 240 volts (**2–8**).

The service entrance panel is grounded, providing protection to the entire electrical system. Many systems are grounded by connecting the bus bar

house, and local electrical codes. **Illus. 2–5** shows a two-wire service entrance that is often found on homes built before the mid 1940s. **Illus. 2–6** shows a three-wire service entrance typically used on homes built after the mid l940s. Underground service is

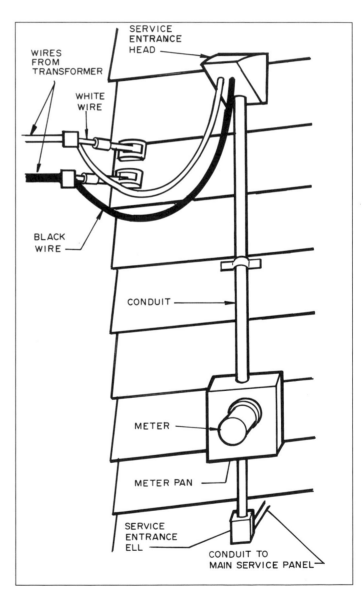

2–5. A typical two-wire service entrance found on older homes. This system does not provide the electrical service needed for operating the electrical appliances in the modern home.

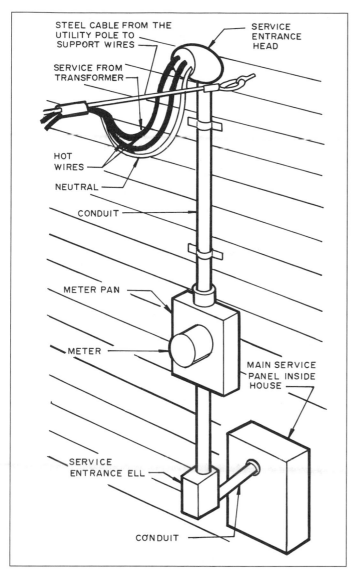

2–6. A typical three-wire service entrance that provides 120- and 240-volt electrical service at the main service panel.

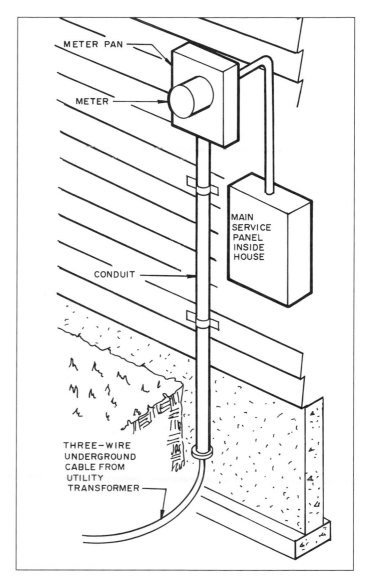

2–7. The underground service entrance eliminates the unsightly wires found on aboveground installations.

(which collects electric currents and distributes them to feeders) in the service panel to the metal water line of the city water service. While this provides an excellent ground, some claim it could pose risks for waterworks employees who may be working in the area. It is also claimed that the pipes tend to corrode faster.

The alternate ground that is widely used consists of installing an 8-foot (2½-meter) -long copper rod and connecting the service panel to it. Some codes require that the rod be installed up to eight feet from the house in moist soil. If it is in dry soil, it will not be effective. Some codes may recommend using two rods about six feet apart.

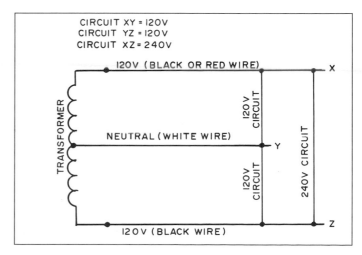

2–8. The three-wire service entrance provides both 120- and 240-volt service.

CIRCUITS WITHIN THE HOUSE

The electrical power enters the house through the meter and a service panel. From this panel, various circuits are run to the rooms for lighting and outlets. Other circuits go to the major appliances such as stoves, air conditioners, furnaces, and water heaters. Some of these are 120 volts and others are 240 volts, depending upon the needs of the device being used (**2–9**). A house will typically have 15 to 20 or more circuits.

There are several types of circuits used. An **appliance circuit** serves 120-volt appliances such as toasters, refrigerators, and coffeemakers, which require 20 amps of service. **General-purpose circuits** are also 120 volts and usually 20 amps. They are used for lighting, convenience outlets, and small low-power appliances. **Special-purpose circuits** may be 120 volts and 20 amps, but operate a single appliance such as a dishwasher. They may also be 240 volts for appliances such as a range, dryer, or water heater. These circuits typically range from 20 to 50 amps (**2–10**).

ANALYZING THE POWER SUPPLY

Most homes built before 1945 have an inadequate electrical supply for modern demands. They typically have only two wires at their service entrance. These two wires transmit 120 volts to the electric meter and **service panel** or **fuse box**.

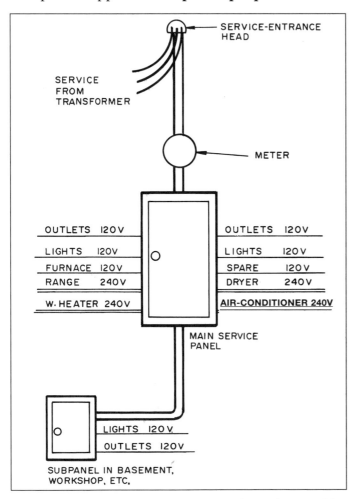

2–9. Various circuits are run from the main service panel for lights, outlets, and special-purpose applications. Power can also be taken to a subpanel, where additional circuits can be run.

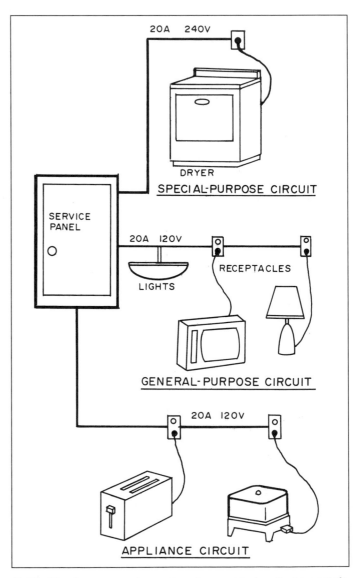

2–10. The house requires many types of circuit. Be certain these are clearly identified on the chart inside the service panel.

Service entrances are rated in amps. The typical service entrance in older houses is a 60-amp service. Sixty amps is not enough power to operate many appliances at the same time. Running an air conditioner along with an electric range or dryer would be difficult.

Newer houses have a three-wire service entrance rated at a minimum of 100 amps. This is also the minimum service entrance that should be provided when an older home is rewired. The three-wire system provides both 120- and 240-volt service. The 100 or more amps that the service provides is enough to power several major appliances at the same time.

If electric heat is used or the house is large, the service entrance needed will be from 150 to 200 amps. If a house is being wired or rewired, someone at the local electric utility office can figure the size of the service entrance that will be needed.

HOT AND NEUTRAL WIRES FOR 120-VOLT CIRCUITS

If the home was built after the mid 1940s, the 120-volt electrical lighting and convenience circuits should contain three wires. The three wires will be black, white, and bare or green.

The black wire is called the **hot wire** because it carries electricity under pressure (120 volts) from the service panel to the light fixtures and electrical outlets. Every hot wire must have a fuse or a circuit breaker to protect it from an overload of current. The hot (black) wire carries the electricity that will light a lamp, make a stereo play, or heat an iron.

After the electricity has done its work, it must return to the service panel to complete the circuit. The return wire is white and is called the **neutral wire**. The current flowing through this wire must go directly to the service panel. Therefore, the white wire must never be connected to a switch. This is because a switch can interrupt the flow of current.

The black wire is always "hot" as long as the power is on. Touching a bare part of the wire will lead to a shock. The current reaching the white, or neutral, wire has spent the 120 volts of energy. It cannot cause a current to flow through the body or anything it may touch. Even though it is "safe," most electricians do not touch it because if someone wired the circuit backward the white would be the hot wire and the black the neutral.

At the service panel, the neutral wire is connected to a copper bar called a neutral busbar. The neutral busbar is connected by wire to a grounding rod buried in the earth or, if permitted by the local wiring code, to a metal water pipe that enters the house. Because the current from the neutral wire flows directly into the ground, the current is said to be "grounded." Every circuit in the house must be connected to a ground in a safe way.

HOT AND NEUTRAL WIRES FOR 240-VOLT CIRCUITS

It should be noted that the cable for a 240-volt circuit may contain three wires color-coded in two different ways. It may have a bare wire (has no insulating cover) for grounding and black and white hot wires or a white wire for grounding and red and black hot wires. There is no neutral wire. One of the hot wires serves as the return wire. The bare or white wire serves to ground the circuit.

GROUNDING

Electrical circuits are grounded to reduce the danger of shocks or fire. Electrical appliances are designed so they are grounded through the grounded circuit. Older appliances may not have this feature and can be dangerous even though attached to a grounded circuit. If such an appliance develops a short, you will get a shock. Some items, such as portable electric power tools, are made with double insulation and a plastic case and do not require grounding.

The typical 120-volt electric wire will have a ground wire that is either bare or green. This, if properly connected, provides a continuous ground from the appliance through the circuit and to the grounding connection. This connection may be to a metal water pipe that runs into the ground or to a long metal rod driven into the ground. Usually the electrical code requires the ground rod even when the circuit is grounded to metal water pipes.

Before beginning to do repairs or renovation on the electrical system, examine it to see what type of grounding system is in place. Very old homes are wired with a metal-armored cable and have metal electric boxes. The electric fitting is connected to the metal box with metal screws. The metal-armored cable is also connected to the metal box. The armored cable is grounded at the service panel. Therefore, a continuous ground is provided (2–11). While this provides a ground, it could fail over time due to loose connections or corrosion forming between the cable and the box. Plastic-armored cable is available but will not provide this type of ground.

As plastic-sheathed cable became widely used, a third wire was added to serve as a ground (2–12). The wire was connected to the metal box and relied on the connections to the box. This system still does not ground the appliance.

The system in 2–13 connects a ground wire to a grounding screw on receptacles, switches, and light fixtures; this provides a direct ground. It does not rely on the screw connection with the box to complete the ground circuit. To make the system work when a duplex receptacle is involved, a three-prong plug is used. The receptacle has a round hole for the ground prong (2–14). This receptacle is for 120-volt circuits.

If there is a three-wire cord on an appliance, such as an electric drill, and the receptacles do not have the opening from the grounding prong, a grounding adapter plug can be used if the receptacle box is grounded. Check the receptacle cover screw to see if it is grounded. To check for grounding, insert the voltage tester into the "hot" side and against the screw (2–15). The bulb should light. If it does not light in either slot, the cover plate screw is not grounded. Replace the screw with a longer one and recheck. If the tester still does not light, the receptacle is not grounded.

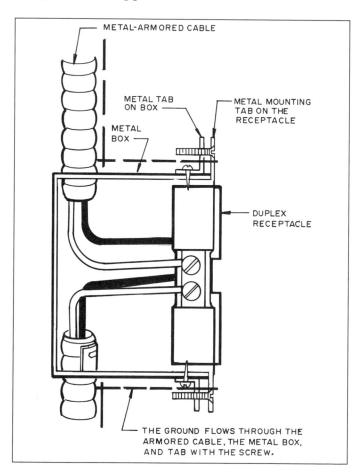

2–11. The older type of grounding relies on connections among the metal-armored cable, the metal box, and metal tabs on the receptacle. The armored cable must be grounded at the service panel.

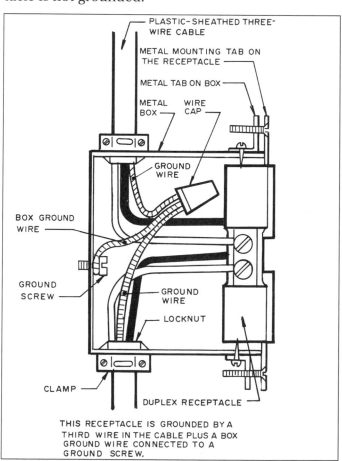

2–12. This older type of grounding system depends upon the tabs, screws, and the metal box to ground the receptacle. Loose or poor connections can jeopardize the ground.

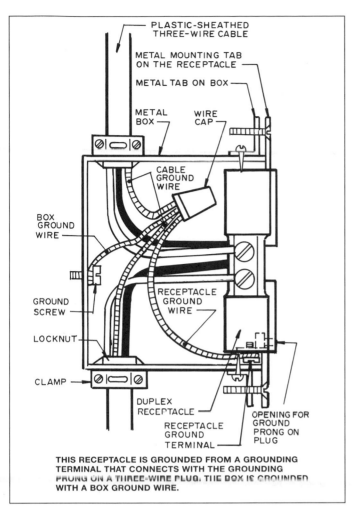

PLASTIC-SHEATHED
THREE-WIRE CABLE

METAL MOUNTING TAB
ON THE RECEPTACLE

METAL TAB ON BOX

METAL
BOX

WIRE
CAP

CABLE
GROUND
WIRE

BOX
GROUND
WIRE

GROUND
SCREW

RECEPTACLE
GROUND
WIRE

LOCKNUT

CLAMP

DUPLEX
RECEPTACLE

RECEPTACLE
GROUND
TERMINAL

OPENING FOR
GROUND
PRONG ON
PLUG

THIS RECEPTACLE IS GROUNDED FROM A GROUNDING
TERMINAL THAT CONNECTS WITH THE GROUNDING
PRONG ON A THREE-WIRE PLUG. THE BOX IS GROUNDED
WITH A BOX GROUND WIRE.

2–13 (left). The current-grounding system uses a direct wire connection between the receptacle and the cable ground wires that provides a reliable ground.

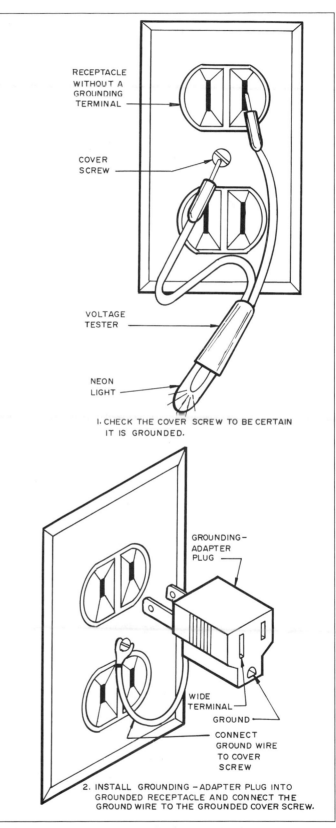

RECEPTACLE
WITHOUT A
GROUNDING
TERMINAL

COVER
SCREW

VOLTAGE
TESTER

NEON
LIGHT

1. CHECK THE COVER SCREW TO BE CERTAIN
IT IS GROUNDED.

GROUNDING-
ADAPTER
PLUG

WIDE
TERMINAL

GROUND

CONNECT
GROUND WIRE
TO COVER
SCREW

2. INSTALL GROUNDING –ADAPTER PLUG INTO
GROUNDED RECEPTACLE AND CONNECT THE
GROUND WIRE TO THE GROUNDED COVER SCREW.

2–15. A grounding-adapter plug can be used to connect a three-wire cable to a receptacle that has no grounding open-ing. Connect the plug ground wire to the cover screw. Be certain to check that the receptacle box is grounded.

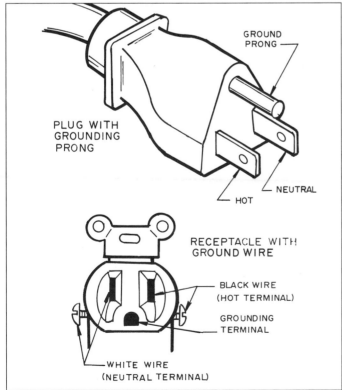

GROUND
PRONG

PLUG WITH
GROUNDING
PRONG

NEUTRAL

HOT

RECEPTACLE WITH
GROUND WIRE

BLACK WIRE
(HOT TERMINAL)

GROUNDING
TERMINAL

WHITE WIRE
(NEUTRAL TERMINAL)

2–14. A three-wire cable has a ground wire connected to a ground prong. It is inserted into the grounded opening on the receptacle.

WIRES FOR VARIOUS APPLICATIONS

Choose the right wire for the job. This is done by considering where it is to be used, the type of sheathing required, and the amount of current it will carry. The larger the current flow, the larger the diameter of the wire required (**2–16**).

Wire diameters are specified by gauge numbers. The larger the wire diameter, the smaller the gauge number. The standard system for specifying wire sizes is called the American Wire Gauge (AWG) system. As wires increase in diameter, they begin to be made in wrapped strands rather than as solid wire. This makes them easier to handle and bend.

Nonmetallic sheathed cable is most frequently used for house wiring. It contains two plastic-insulated wires and one ground wire all bound together in a plastic sheath (**2–17**). These are specified by gauge number and number of wires, for example, 14–2; if a bare ground wire is included, they are **14–2 with ground**. Wires used in house systems generally have diameters from 14- to 10-gauge and are normally solid single strand. The allowable current-carrying capacities of copper, aluminum, and copper-clad aluminum wires are shown in **Table 2–1**.

The types of nonmetallic sheathed cable are **NM cable,** used in house wiring in dry locations; **NMC cable,** used in damp aboveground locations; and **waterproof UF,** used in belowground installations.

Two of the frequently used flexible cables are **lamp cord** and **parallel cord**. Lamp cord is a very flexible, small-diameter, stranded, plastic-coated wire. The two wires are encased side by side with the plastic sheathing (refer to **2–17**). Lamp cord is designated as type C and is available in wire gauges 18 through 10. Polarized lamp cord has a ridge or grooves on the side of the wire to serve as the hot wire.

Other widely used **flexible parallel cords** used on lamps, clocks, radios, typewriters, refrigerators, and room air conditioners are specified as types SP, SPE, and SPT (refer to **2–17**). Each is designated by wire gauge and sheathing. SP has thermoset plastic sheathing, SPE has thermoplastic elastomer sheathing, and SPT has a thermoplastic sheath. They are specified by wire diameter. Those designated as 1 (such as SP-1) have 20- or 18-gauge wire, those with

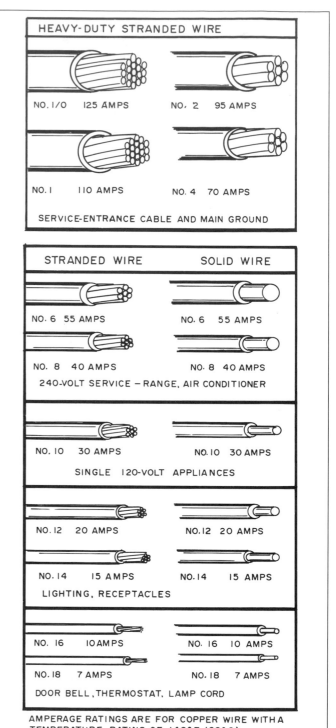

2–16. Commonly used stranded and solid copper wires and their maximum carrying capacities in amperes. Some typical uses are shown.

a 2 (such as SP-2) have 18- or 16-gauge wire, and those with a 3 designation have wire gauges from 18 to 10. The 3 designation has heavier gauges and is used on refrigerators and room air conditioners.

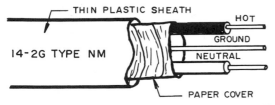

TWO−WIRE NONMETALIC PLASTIC-SHEATHED CABLE FOR DRY LOCATIONS.

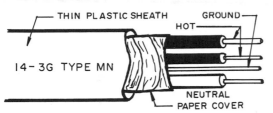

THREE−WIRE NONMETALLIC PLASTIC-SHEATHED CABLE FOR DRY LOCATIONS.

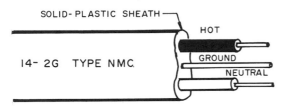

TWO−WIRE NONMETALLIC SOLID PLASTIC-SHEATHED CABLE FOR ABOVE GROUND DAMP LOCATIONS.

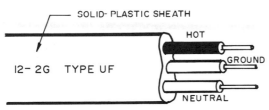

TWO−WIRE WATERPROOF PLASTIC-SHEATHED CABLE FOR UNDERGROUND INSTALLATION.

LAMP CORD AND FLEXIBLE PARALLEL CORD

TYPICAL FLEXIBLE CORD			LAMP CORD
SP−1 SPE−1 SPT−1	SP−2 SPE−2 SPT−2	SP−3 SPE−3 SPT−3	TYPE C
20,18 AWG	18,16 AWG	18 THRU 10 AWG	18 THRU 10 AWG

HARD-SERVICE AND JUNIOR-HARD-SERVICE CORD

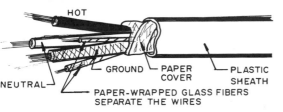

2–17 (left). Commonly used conductors for residential wiring. Be certain the wire size will carry the intended load. Check the building code to be certain it approves the type of wire to be used.

Heavy-duty cords used on power tools have two or three plastic insulated, stranded wires bound inside a very tough plastic sheathing. The green wire is the ground. The strands are separated by several strands of paper-wrapped glass fibers or paper cord (refer to **2–17**). Hard service cords are identified as SE, SEO, and SEOO. **Junior hard service cords** are identified by a series of SJ designations. For example, computer and copier cords are SJT.

Metal-armored cable contains two insulated wires wrapped in paper and a bare ground wire covered with a flexible metal sheath. This is typically referred to as BX cable. It was widely used in older homes and is currently used where the wire may be damaged and needs extra protection. It is more difficult to cut, splice, and make connections than nonmetallic sheathed cable (**2–18**). Plastic-armored cable is also available.

A **conduit** is a solid metal or plastic pipe through which wires are run. The conduit itself does not contain wires. It is installed and then individually insulated wires

TABLE 2–1. ALLOWABLE CURRENT-CARRYING CAPACITIES OF SELECTED WIRES

Wire Size	Amperes	
	Copper Size	Aluminum or Copper-Clad-Aluminum Size
18	7	--
16	10	--
14	15	--
12	20	15
10	30	25
8	40	30
6	55	40
4	70	55
3	80	65
2	95	75
1	110	85
0	125	100

are pulled through it (**2–18**). It is used where wires are exposed to possible damage and to provide protection against moisture. The service-entrance cable at the meter is one typical application (**2–19**). This cable may be joined with threaded couplings and elbows at corners. Thin-walled conduit is somewhat flexible and can be bent at large-radius bends. Bend radii are specified by the electrical code.

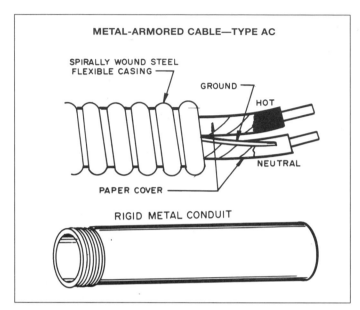

2–18. *Rigid metal conduit and metal-armored cable protect the wires from damage.*

ALUMINUM WIRE

Aluminum wire was used in some homes in the l940s. Since aluminum has a higher resistance to the flow of electricity than copper, aluminum wires must have a larger diameter than copper wires to conduct current of the same amperage. A rule of thumb is to use aluminum wire two sizes larger than the copper wire required. Always check local codes before using and selecting the gauges (sizes) of aluminum wire. Always use switches and receptacles that are approved for aluminum wire. These will have screw connectors, not push-in connectors. All wiring devices — switches, lamps, receptacles, etc. — cannot be connected to aluminum wire unless they are marked "CO/ALR."

If the home has aluminum wiring and you notice that the switch and receptacle faceplates are warm, lights are flickering, or there is the smell of burning plastic, there is a major problem. Sometimes alu-

2–19. *This rigid plastic conduit is protecting the high-amperage service-entrance cable from possible damage.*

minum wire connections fail without these warnings. If you have these trouble signs, call an electrician. *Do not try to make repairs yourself.*

A way to determine if there is aluminum wiring is to expose a section of the wire or find an exposed piece in the attic or basement. Every few feet it will be marked "AL" or "Aluminum." Whenever possible, abandon the aluminum circuit and rewire with copper. A system can be saved by an experienced electrician who knows the specific types of connections that must be used.

CIRCUIT-PROTECTION DEVICES

As has been discussed, an electrical circuit can cause shock or fire under certain conditions. The two main hazards are **overloaded circuits** and **short circuits**. The different items on a circuit that are powered by electricity are called **loads**. If the loads on a circuit require more current than the wire can carry, an **overload** occurs. The overloaded wire can become hot enough to melt its insulation and start a fire in the surrounding materials.

In a short circuit (or "short"), the current does not follow the proper path through the circuit. The current takes a shortcut to ground, which may be the nearest metal object. Someone touching that object will get a shock. Also, the current can be hot enough to start a fire.

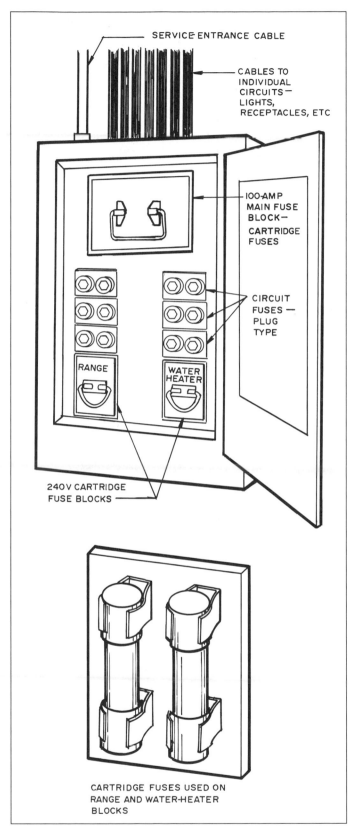

SERVICE ENTRANCE CABLE

CABLES TO INDIVIDUAL CIRCUITS — LIGHTS, RECEPTACLES, ETC

100-AMP MAIN FUSE BLOCK — CARTRIDGE FUSES

CIRCUIT FUSES — PLUG TYPE

RANGE

WATER HEATER

240V CARTRIDGE FUSE BLOCKS

CARTRIDGE FUSES USED ON RANGE AND WATER-HEATER BLOCKS

2–20. A typical service panel that uses plug and cartridge fuses. If the main fuse block is pulled, power to the entire house is cut off. The plug fuses control the branch circuits. They are typically 15 or 20 amps. The 240-volt appliances are controlled by the fuse blocks at the bottom of the panel.

To prevent either of the above hazards, the hot wires of circuits are protected by **fuses** or **circuit breakers**. When a short circuit or overload occurs, these devices open, or "break," the circuit. This prevents the current from flowing in the circuit.

THE FUSE PANEL

After the electrical power passes through the meter it enters the service panel, where it is distributed by circuits to various parts of the house. Each circuit may be protected by a **plug fuse**, and the main power-line entrance by a **cartridge fuse**. These panels will be found in older houses. Newer houses will use circuit breakers instead of fuses. A typical fused service-entrance panel is shown in **2–20**. Notice that cartridge fuses are also used on the circuits for a water heater and electric range, because these items draw high amperage and require 240-volt service.

FUSES

A fuse is a circuit-protection device that has a metal strip that melts when an overload or short circuit occurs, thus breaking the circuit. To restore power to the circuit, a new fuse must be put in. *Be sure to remove the overload or repair the short circuit before replacing the fuse.* If the cause of the trouble is not corrected, the new fuse will "blow" and break the circuit again.

Another device, the **ground-fault circuit interrupter,** is used to protect the circuit when current leakage is detected that is too small to be caught by a fuse or circuit breaker.

The types of low-amperage fuses used in circuits in houses include the plug, time-delay, and S-type fuses (**2–21**). The **plug fuse** is the most commonly used type. It screws into a socket in the service panel. The metal strip that protects the circuit can be seen through a window. If the fuse is blown by a short circuit, the window may be clouded or blackened by the flash as the metal strip melts. If the circuit is overloaded, the strip will melt but the window will remain clear (**2–22**).

The **time-delay fuse** is much like the plug fuse except it has a stretched spring anchored to the top

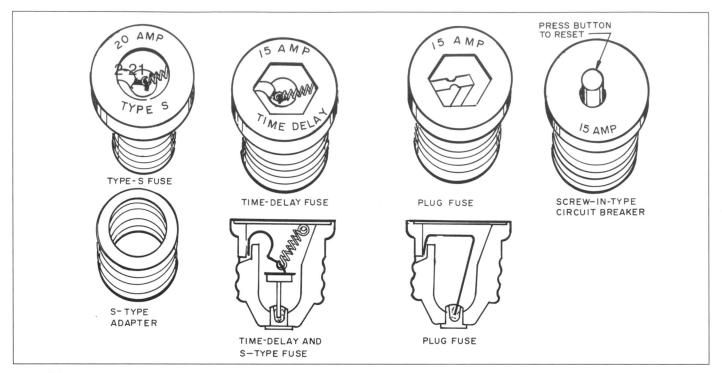

2–21. Three types of low-amperage fuses used in older service panels.

of the fuse and soldered at the base. A momentary overload is not enough to cause it to fail. A sustained overload or short circuit will melt the solder at the base of the spring, pulling it away from the base and breaking the circuit (**2-21**).

The **type-S fuse** is a time-delay fuse, but requires that an adapter base be screwed into the socket in the service panel. The adapters are sized for fuses of different amperage ratings, so a fuse with a higher amperage (such as 30 amperes) cannot be screwed into a base that was installed for a small-size fuse (such as 15 amperes).

Another fusing device that can be used is a **screw-in circuit breaker.** When something occurs to trip it, a reset button can be pressed rather than the device replaced. Be certain the amperage is the same as the fuse it replaces (**2–22**).

Another type of fuse is the **cartridge fuse**. Cartridge fuses are used for higher amperages. The **ferrule cartridge fuse** is used for currents up to 60 amperes, and the **knife-blade fuse** for amperages 60 and higher (**2–23**). These are used to protect heavy-current-drawing appliances such as a range and the link circuits connected to the main power

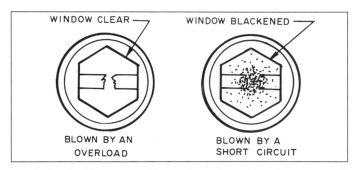

2–22. By looking at the blown fuse, it can be determined if there is an overload or a short circuit.

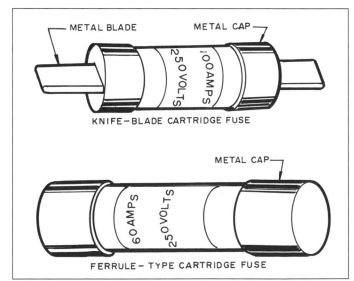

2–23. Knife-blade and ferrule cartridge fuses are used on lines having high amperage requirements.

line. *It is important to replace a cartridge fuse with another of the same size.*

A blown cartridge fuse shows no visible sign of damage. It must be checked with a continuity tester to see if the internal connection has been broken.

Replacing Fuses

When replacing a screw-in plug fuse, be certain you are not standing on a wet floor. Rubber-soled shoes are a good safety precaution. Wear heavy rubber gloves while removing and installing the fuses. If there is any doubt, pull the main fuse block; this shuts off power to the service panel.

Replace the plug fuse with one having the same amperage rating. If there are overload problems, do not put in a larger amperage fuse. It could cause a fire. Find and remove the overload.

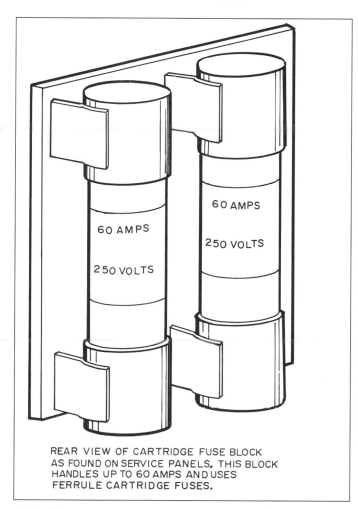

REAR VIEW OF CARTRIDGE FUSE BLOCK AS FOUND ON SERVICE PANELS. THIS BLOCK HANDLES UP TO 60 AMPS AND USES FERRULE CARTRIDGE FUSES.

2–24. *These ferrule cartridge fuses are used on a fuse block such as those used on a service panel for ranges, water heaters, and other appliances.*

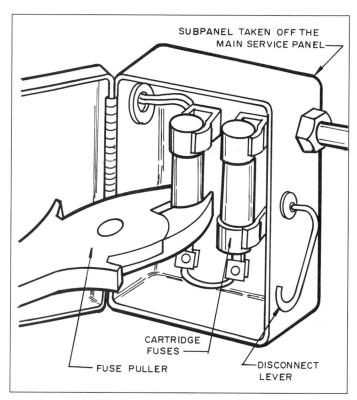

2–25. *Fuse pullers are used to remove cartridge fuses after the disconnect lever has cut off the power or the fuse block has been removed from the panel.*

Cartridge fuses are usually in a removable block. Pull the block and remove and replace the fuses (**2–24**). If the fuses are in a box, shut off the power with the lever on the side and use a fuse puller to grip and remove the fuses. The fuse puller also helps when removing cartridge fuses from a fuse block (**2–25**).

SERVICE PANEL WITH CIRCUIT BREAKERS

Circuit breakers are switch-like devices used instead of fuses to provide each circuit protection against overloads and short circuits. They are mounted in a service panel. A typical panel is shown in **2–26** on the next page. The breaker at the top is the main cutoff and is rated to carry the total service-entrance amperage. Typically this will be from 100 to 200 amperes. Individual circuit breakers are used on each 120-volt circuit, and double-breakers are used on 240-volt circuits.

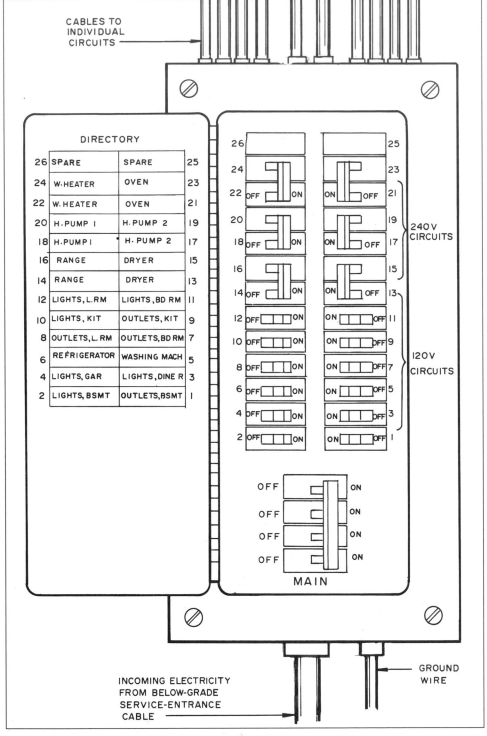

DIRECTORY		
26	SPARE	SPARE	25
24	W. HEATER	OVEN	23
22	W. HEATER	OVEN	21
20	H. PUMP 1	H. PUMP 2	19
18	H. PUMP 1	H. PUMP 2	17
16	RANGE	DRYER	15
14	RANGE	DRYER	13
12	LIGHTS, L. RM	LIGHTS, BD RM	11
10	LIGHTS, KIT	OUTLETS, KIT	9
8	OUTLETS, L. RM	OUTLETS, BD RM	7
6	REFRIGERATOR	WASHING MACH	5
4	LIGHTS, GAR	LIGHTS, DINE R	3
2	LIGHTS, BSMT	OUTLETS, BSMT	1

CABLES TO INDIVIDUAL CIRCUITS

240V CIRCUITS

120V CIRCUITS

MAIN

INCOMING ELECTRICITY FROM BELOW-GRADE SERVICE-ENTRANCE CABLE

GROUND WIRE

2–26. A modern service panel uses circuit breakers for both 240- and 120-volt service.

CIRCUIT BREAKERS

Circuit breakers are electrical devices that automatically open a circuit when an overload or short circuit occurs (**2–27**). When the overload or short circuit is corrected, the lever on the front of the circuit breaker is thrown just like those used on light switches. It is a reusable device and can be repeatedly reclosed and reused as an automatic overcurrent protection device without replacement. Circuit breakers are more convenient to use than fuses because they are reusable and reset by simply throwing a switch. Some types have a push button instead of a switch.

When a circuit fails, go to the service panel and look for a switch that is in the center of the "on" position.

A toggle-switch circuit breaker will have two or three positions. A two-position toggle-switch circuit breaker will be in the "off" position if it is toward the middle of the panel and in the "on" position if it is toward the outside. When the switch of a three-position toggle-switch circuit breaker is in the center, it indicates that it has been "tripped" and opened the circuit (**2-28**).

To restore power with a two-position circuit breaker, move the lever to the "on" position. The three-position type usually requires the lever to be moved to "off," then to a "reset" position, and then to "on." Before resetting the breaker, be certain the short circuit has been repaired or the overload removed.

The amperage rating of circuit breakers is clearly marked on the front. If you ever replace one, be certain to get one with the same rating.

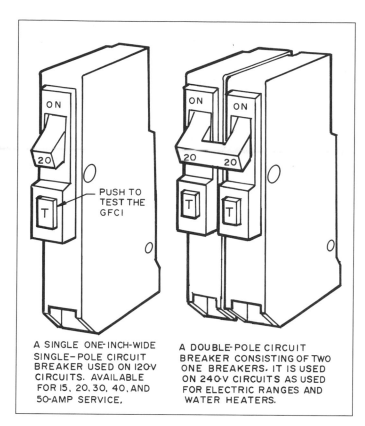

A SINGLE ONE-INCH-WIDE SINGLE-POLE CIRCUIT BREAKER USED ON 120-V CIRCUITS. AVAILABLE FOR 15, 20, 30, 40, AND 50-AMP SERVICE.

PUSH TO TEST THE GFCI

A DOUBLE-POLE CIRCUIT BREAKER CONSISTING OF TWO ONE BREAKERS. IT IS USED ON 240-V CIRCUITS AS USED FOR ELECTRIC RANGES AND WATER HEATERS.

2–27. Typical 120- and 240-volt circuit breakers. This type of breaker also provides ground-fault interruption capabilities for the circuit.

GROUND-FAULT CIRCUIT INTERRUPTERS

The ground-fault circuit interrupter (GFCI) is designed to protect against a common type of electrical shock called a ground fault. A **ground fault** is an electrical leakage too small to be detected by a fuse or circuit breaker but of sufficient size to cause great physical harm and possibly death. It is especially dangerous if you are working in wet conditions, such as when trimming the hedge with electric clippers in moist conditions. A minute electrical leakage (about 0.01 ampere) passing through the body to a wet ground is enough to kill. Think of all the conditions around the home where this could happen. Danger lurks in the kitchen, bath, deck, patio, beside the swimming pool or hot tub, and in a wet basement or crawl space — to mention a few areas. Building codes require GFCI installations in all dangerous locations (**2–29**).

The GFCI electronic circuit monitors the amperage coming into a circuit through the black wire and compares it with that leaving the circuit on the white

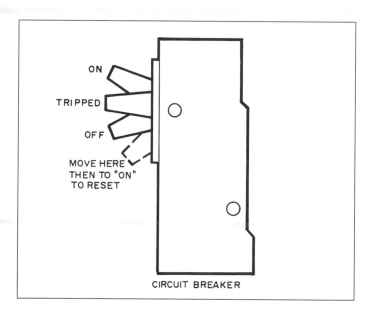

ON
TRIPPED
OFF
MOVE HERE THEN TO "ON" TO RESET
CIRCUIT BREAKER

2–28. When the lever is in the tripped position, the circuit has been opened due to a short or overload. When corrections have been made, move the switch to the "reset" position and then to the "on" position. To shut down the circuit for repairs, move the lever to the "off" position.

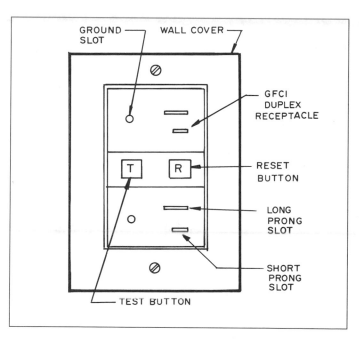

GROUND SLOT
WALL COVER
GFCI DUPLEX RECEPTACLE
RESET BUTTON
LONG PRONG SLOT
SHORT PRONG SLOT
TEST BUTTON

2–29. This GFCI duplex receptacle protects you from shock if any appliance plugged into it has minute current leakage. When leakage is detected, the "reset" button pops out and the circuit is broken. Remove the defective appliance and press the "reset" button to restore power. To check the receptacle to see if it is in working order, press the "test" button. It should cut the power to the outlet. Press "reset" to restore power.

wire. If it detects a difference of 0.005 ampere or more, a leak is occurring and within 1/40 of a second it shuts down the circuit. This is so fast that a serious shock will not occur.

If the service panel has fuses, GFCI protection can be ensured by replacing the first duplex receptacle. This will provide protection for this receptacle and all the other receptacles following this on the circuit (**2–30**). If the service panel has circuit breakers, install GFCI circuit breakers in place of the existing circuit breaker on each circuit. Another approach is to buy a portable GFCI that plugs into the regular grounded outlet. Then plug the tool into the GFCI (**2–31**).

TESTING A CIRCUIT OR ELECTRICAL DEVICE

There are many times when it is helpful to make a test on a circuit or on an electrical device. The following tests can be easily made if care is taken when performing them.

Making Continuity Tests

A **continuity tester** has a probe that contains a neon bulb and a penlight battery connected by a wire to an alligator clip. It can be used to determine if a current will flow in an electrical device (**2–32**). For example, to determine if a wire in a cord is broken, touch the

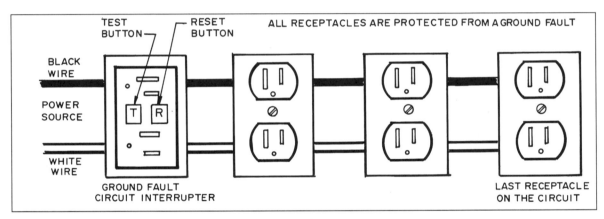

2–30. A ground-fault interrupter receptacle on the first box in a circuit will provide protection for all the receptacles on the circuit following it.

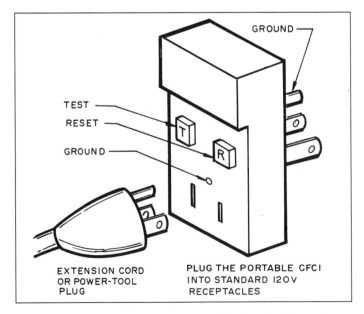

2–31. If the circuit does not have GFCI protection, plug a portable GFCI into it and plug the extension cord or power tool into the portable GFCI.

probe to one end and the clip to the other end. If the bulb lights, the current is getting through and the wire is not broken. Before making a continuity test, be sure the object being tested is not connected to an electrical source.

A continuity tester can also be used to determine if a current will flow in a circuit.

USING THE VOLTAGE TESTER

The voltage tester has two probes and a neon bulb. It is used to see if a circuit has power. For example, if work will be done on a circuit and there is a question as to whether the power to it has been turned off, this can be verified by using the voltage tester. This is a standard safety practice. A receptacle can be

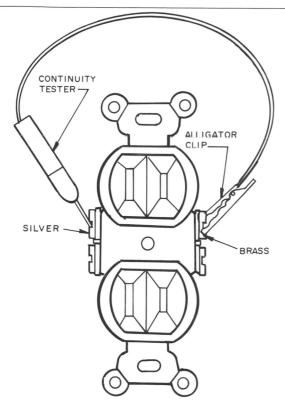

CONTINUITY TESTER

ALLIGATOR CLIP

SILVER

BRASS

REMOVE THE RECEPTACLE FROM THE CIRCUIT.
ATTACH THE ALLIGATOR CLIP TO ONE TERMINAL.
TOUCH THE PROBE TO A TERMINAL ON THE OTHER
SIDE. IF THE TEST GLOWS THERE IS CONTINUITY.
IF IT DOES NOT REPLACE THE RECEPTACLE.

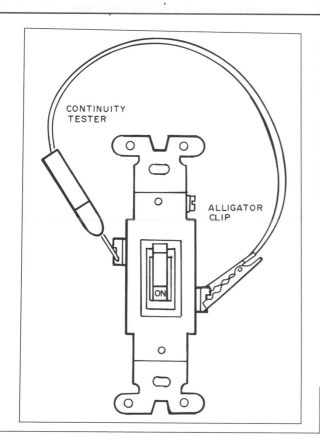

CONTINUITY TESTER

ALLIGATOR CLIP

ON

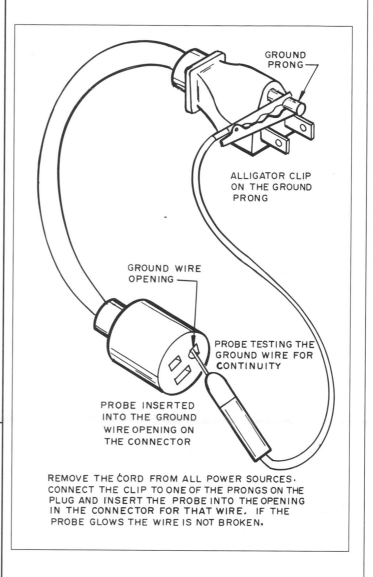

GROUND PRONG

ALLIGATOR CLIP ON THE GROUND PRONG

GROUND WIRE OPENING

PROBE TESTING THE GROUND WIRE FOR CONTINUITY

PROBE INSERTED INTO THE GROUND WIRE OPENING ON THE CONNECTOR

REMOVE THE CORD FROM ALL POWER SOURCES.
CONNECT THE CLIP TO ONE OF THE PRONGS ON THE
PLUG AND INSERT THE PROBE INTO THE OPENING
IN THE CONNECTOR FOR THAT WIRE. IF THE
PROBE GLOWS THE WIRE IS NOT BROKEN.

REMOVE THE SWITCH FROM THE CIRCUIT. CONNECT
THE ALLIGATOR CLIP TO ONE TERMINAL AND TOUCH
THE PROBE TO THE OTHER. THE TESTER SHOULD
GLOW WHEN THE SWITCH IS "ON", IF IT DOES NOT,
REPLACE THE SWITCH.

2–32. The continuity of various electrical devices is easily
checked with a continuity tester.

tested as shown in **2–33**. A light fixture can be tested by lowering it and touching the tester to the black and white wires (**2–34**). A switch can be tested by touching one probe to the ground and the other to the terminals (**2–35**). Before testing 240-volt circuits, be certain the tester is designed for this voltage.

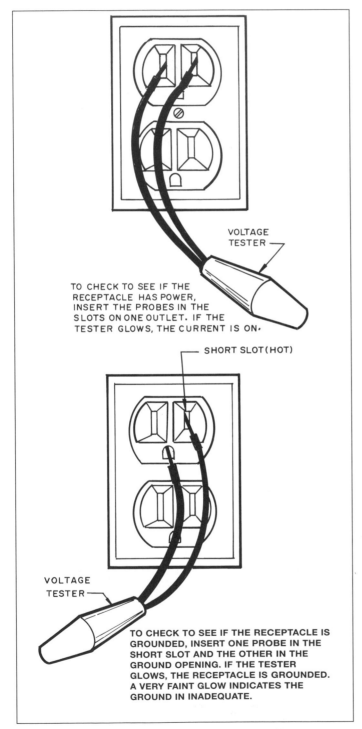

VOLTAGE TESTER

TO CHECK TO SEE IF THE RECEPTACLE HAS POWER, INSERT THE PROBES IN THE SLOTS ON ONE OUTLET. IF THE TESTER GLOWS, THE CURRENT IS ON.

SHORT SLOT (HOT)

VOLTAGE TESTER

TO CHECK TO SEE IF THE RECEPTACLE IS GROUNDED, INSERT ONE PROBE IN THE SHORT SLOT AND THE OTHER IN THE GROUND OPENING. IF THE TESTER GLOWS, THE RECEPTACLE IS GROUNDED. A VERY FAINT GLOW INDICATES THE GROUND IN INADEQUATE.

2–33. A voltage tester is used to see if receptacles are hot and properly grounded.

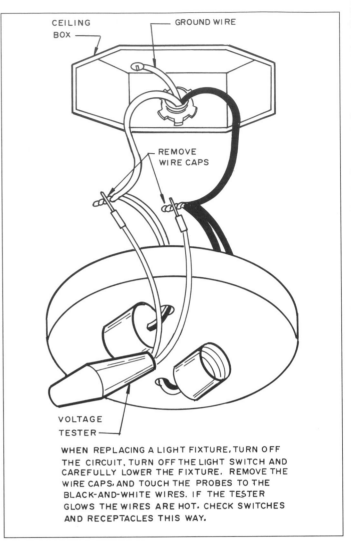

CEILING BOX — GROUND WIRE

REMOVE WIRE CAPS

VOLTAGE TESTER

WHEN REPLACING A LIGHT FIXTURE, TURN OFF THE CIRCUIT, TURN OFF THE LIGHT SWITCH AND CAREFULLY LOWER THE FIXTURE. REMOVE THE WIRE CAPS, AND TOUCH THE PROBES TO THE BLACK-AND-WHITE WIRES. IF THE TESTER GLOWS THE WIRES ARE HOT. CHECK SWITCHES AND RECEPTACLES THIS WAY.

2–34. Before touching the bare wires when removing a fixture or other electrical device, check it with a voltage tester to see if the current is really "off."

GENERAL SAFETY GUIDELINES

In order to avoid injury when working with the electrical system, follow these guidelines:

1. Always have respect for electrical power. Be alert, cautious, and consider the steps about to be performed when working with electricity.

2. Be certain to have adequate lighting in order to see clearly what is being done. It is often necessary to rely on battery-operated lighting devices when making repairs.

3. Never touch several bare wires with your bare hands—even if you think the power is off. There

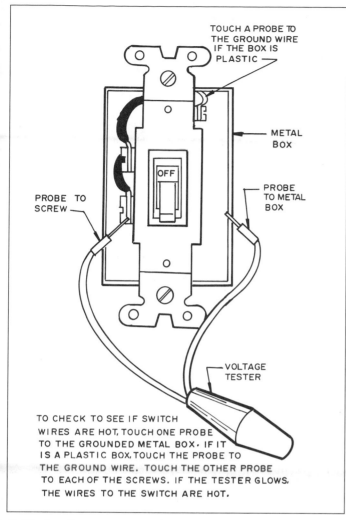

TOUCH A PROBE TO THE GROUND WIRE IF THE BOX IS PLASTIC

METAL BOX

PROBE TO SCREW

PROBE TO METAL BOX

OFF

VOLTAGE TESTER

TO CHECK TO SEE IF SWITCH WIRES ARE HOT, TOUCH ONE PROBE TO THE GROUNDED METAL BOX. IF IT IS A PLASTIC BOX, TOUCH THE PROBE TO THE GROUND WIRE. TOUCH THE OTHER PROBE TO EACH OF THE SCREWS. IF THE TESTER GLOWS, THE WIRES TO THE SWITCH ARE HOT.

2–35. A voltage tester can be used to check if the power to a switch is on or off.

may be a time when, through error, the power is actually on. Use a voltage tester to verify that the power is off.

4. Position bare wires so that more than one will not be accidentally touched at a time.

5. When making splices, join one pair of wires and tape them. Then join the other pair of wires.

6. Never enter the electrical system with the power on. Always turn off the power to the circuit before working on any device on the circuit.

7. Do not rely on insulated handles on tools or insulating gloves for protection against shock. They do protect, but only against accidentally hitting a wire.

8. Avoid working with electrical circuits when in damp places. If there is any dampness at all, put a dry board down and stand on it. Wear shoes with rubber soles as added protection.

9. Before leaving a repair, recheck every step to be certain nothing has been overlooked.

10. Always cover all connections with approved wiring connectors or electrical tape. Never use masking tape or any other substitute for the proper material.

TROUBLESHOOTING SUGGESTIONS

If all the lights and appliances on a circuit go off, the first thing to check is the fuse or circuit breaker. If the fuse is blown or the circuit breaker is in the "off" position, there is a problem with the circuit. It will usually be an overload, open circuit, short circuit, or a problem with the ground. Each is discussed below.

Overload

If the circuit works most of the time, but blows a fuse or trips a circuit breaker once in a while, the problem is probably an overload. A blown fuse caused by an overload will usually show the metal link broken, but the window will not be burned.

To fix the situation, note which units were operating on the circuit when it shut off. Add their total load in amperes and compare that number with the design load for the circuit.

Table 2–2 on the following page is a list of common wattages of appliances. Most appliances are identified with the number of watts they use. The voltage for most home circuits is 120, except for special circuits that are 240 volts, such as those for an electric range. Find the number of amperes in each appliance by dividing the number of watts by the volts ($A = W \div V$). Add these to get a typical load. The fuse or circuit breaker is clearly marked with the maximum load in amperes. In houses, 15- or 20-ampere circuits are common. If the problem is an overload, remove one appliance from the circuit.

TABLE 2–2. TYPICAL APPLIANCE WATTAGES

Major Appliances	
Appliance	***Watts**
Automatic Washer	700
Built-in Heating Elements	1,000 to 2,000
Central Air Conditioner	5,000
Clothes Dryer	4,500
Dishwasher	1,800
Garbage Disposal	900
Gas- or Oil-Fired Furnace	800
Range (All Elements and Oven on)	8,000 to 14,000
Room Air Conditioner	550 to 4,000
Water Heater	2,500

Small Appliances	
Appliance	***Watts**
Clock	2 to 3
Coffeemaker	500 to 1,000
Electric Blanket	150 to 200
Fluorescent Lamp	15 to 60
Electric Frying Pan	1,000 to 1,200
Incandescent Lamp	40 to 300
Iron	600 to 1,200
Mixer	120 to 150
Portable Fan	50 to 200
Portable Heater	1,000 to 1,750
Radio	40 to 150
Refrigerator	150 to 300
Roaster	1,200 to 1,600
Room Air Conditioner	800 to 1,500
Sewing Machine	60 to 90
Television	200 to 400
Toaster	500 to 1,200
Vacuum Cleaner	350 to 800
Waffle Iron	600 to 1,000

To convert watts to amperes, divide watts by the voltage.

Short or Grounded Circuit

A **short circuit** occurs when bare hot and neutral wires touch. A **ground problem** occurs when a bare hot wire touches something metal that serves as a ground. In either case, the fuse will blow or the circuit breaker will trip. Both are very dangerous situations. A blown fuse will usually show a burn on its clear cover if a short is the problem.

To check for a short or grounded circuit, follow these steps:

1. Unplug all appliances connected to the circuit.

2. Replace the fuse or throw the circuit breaker to the "on" position. If the fuse blows or the circuit breaker trips again, there is probably a short or ground problem in the wiring.

3. The location of the problem can probably be determined by smelling for burned material at receptacles, junction boxes, or box-mounted light fixtures.

4. If the problem cannot be located by smell, open each box or outlet on the circuit to check for bare wires and signs of burning. Be sure to first turn off the power. There is seldom a break in a wire. Breaks almost always occur in boxes where wires are joined.

5. Replace any wire that is found with broken or burned insulation.

6. If all boxes are safe and the short or ground was not found, begin to check each section of wire for continuity. There may be a wire that is broken somewhere along its length. To make this continuity check, use a continuity tester and follow these steps:

A. First turn off all power at the service-panel main switch.

B. Unfasten the wires for the circuit at the service panel. Unfasten the other end of the wires at the first junction box.

C. Make a continuity check between the hot and neutral wires by putting one probe on the hot (black) wire and the other probe on the neutral (white) wire. If there is continuity, it means the two wires are touching somewhere between the power panel and the first box. The wires will have to be replaced.

D. If a short is not found by a continuity test between the hot and neutral wires, check for continuity between the hot and ground wires. If they have continuity, it means they are touching and the circuit is grounded out. Replace those wires.

E. Continue checking each succeeding section of wire on the circuit if no continuity problems are found in the first section.

F. If a fuse is not blown or a circuit breaker tripped after all the appliances are removed from the circuit, there is probably a short circuit in one of the appliances. One at a time, carefully plug in each appliance until another fuse blows or the circuit breaker trips again. Remember, the appliance with the short is dangerous, so do not touch it during this procedure. Touch only its cord.

G. Sometimes the problem is in a receptacle or a circuit breaker. To test the receptacle, first turn off the power to the circuit at the service panel. Unfasten the receptacle from the box and remove its connecting wires. Check for continuity between the terminals at each side. The circuit breaker can be checked in the same way with its switch in the "on" position.

Other Possible Causes

Sometimes the base of a fuse becomes pitted, causing a loss of power to a circuit. Clean the base with steel wool or simply replace the fuse. Sometimes the screw in the bottom of the fuse socket becomes loose. Turn off the main power switch, tighten the screw, and replace the fuse.

If all the light fixtures on a circuit work except one, first check the bulb. If the bulb is working, check the switch. To do so, turn off the power to the circuit and remove the switch from its box. Check for continuity with the switch in the "on" position. If there is none, replace the switch.

cut through all three wires in a Romex cable. **Needle-nose pliers** are used for forming loops in wire and have a small wire cutter (**2–36**). **Diagonal cutting pliers** (**2–36**) will also cut single small-diameter wire. Their shape gives them the advantage of being able to get into tight places where other cutting tools cannot reach. A most useful tool is the combination **wire-stripper pliers** or **multipurpose tool**. It is used for gauging wire size, stripping insulation, crimping fittings, making small terminal loops, and cutting wire (**2–37**).

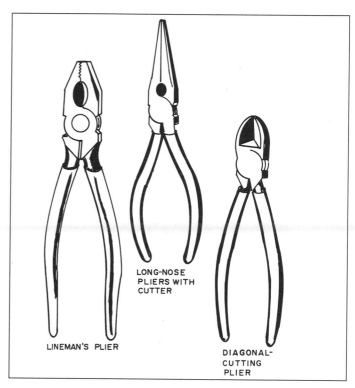

2–36. *These pliers are very helpful when doing electrical work.*

PREPARING THE WIRE AND MAKING CONNECTIONS

Before making connections, the wire has to be cut to length and the insulation stripped off the end. There are several tools designed for cutting wire. Be sure to buy tools with insulated handles. Heavy wire can be cut with **lineman's pliers** (**2–36**). They are large enough to

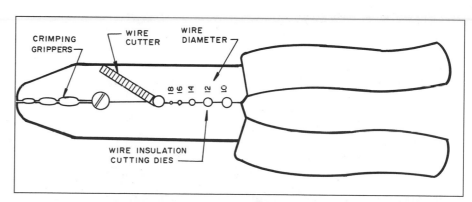

2–37. *Wire-stripper pliers are a multipurpose tool used to strip insulation, cut wire, measure wire diameters, make terminal loops, and secure crimped fittings.*

Stripping Wire

The plastic insulation must be stripped from the ends of the wire before it can be connected to a terminal or spliced to another wire. A variety of tools may be used for stripping wire. Take care to not cut into the wire when stripping it. Doing so would weaken the wire and possibly reduce its size. Reducing a wire's size reduces the amount of current it can carry. Stranded wire should not have any of the strands cut away.

The first step in stripping the wire of plastic-sheathed cable is to cut the heavy outside insulation to release the individual wires. To do this, place the cable against a solid surface. Then use a sharp knife to cut the cable in the center for the length you want the individual wires exposed. Be careful not to cut into the insulation on the individual wires. Strip back the outer insulation and cut it off as shown in **2–38**.

A pocketknife may be used to cut away the insulation from the individual wires. Make small, carefully controlled cuts to avoid cutting into the wire. Cut the insulation on a taper. Cut in a direction away from your body (**2–39**). Do not cut a circle around

the wire with a knife and try to slide the insulation off. You will most likely cut into the wire.

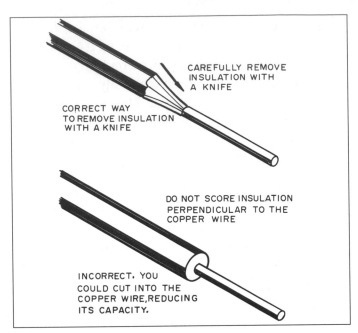

2–39. Insulation can be removed from wires by cutting it on a long angle with a knife. Be careful that the wire is not nicked. It is safer to use the multipurpose tool.

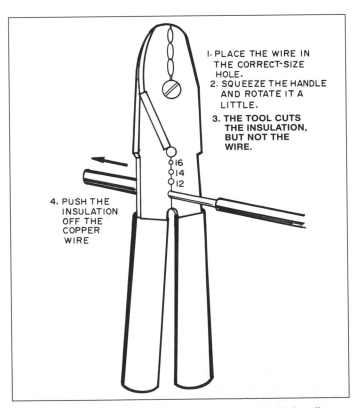

2–40. Place the wire in the hole marked for that wire diameter. Squeeze the handles to cut the insulation. It will not cut the wire. Rotate the tool around the wire a little to complete the cut. Then push insulation off the end of the wire.

2–38. When stripping the plastic sheath off the cable, be very careful that the insulation on the individual wires is not cut. If it is, cut back to the nick and start over.

The best way to strip wire is to use a stripping tool such as the multipurpose tool (**2–40**). To use this tool, select the stripping notch that is the same diameter as the wire. Slip the wire into the notch, squeeze the jaws closed, and turn the pliers in a complete circle around the wire. Doing so will cut the insulation all around the wire. Slide the loose piece of insulation off the wire.

Terminal Connections

Terminal connections may be either a screw terminal or a push-in terminal. To make a screw-terminal connection, do the following:

1. Strip the wire to be connected to a length equal to three-quarters the distance around the screw.

2. Form the wire into a loop with needle-nose pliers (**2–41**).

3. Place the loop around the screw so that it will wrap around the screw as it is tightened in a clockwise direction.

The push-in terminal has an opening into which the bare wire is pushed (**2–42**). Strip the wire the length indicated by the strip gauges on the device. The connection automatically grips the wire. Near the opening will be a release slot into which a screwdriver is fitted to release the wire. On the back of the switch is a groove that shows how much bare wire is needed for insertion into the terminal hole.

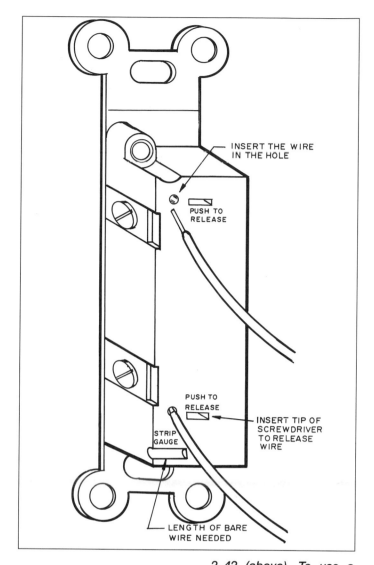

2–42 (above). To use a push-in terminal, strip ½ inch (13 millimeters) on the end of the wire and insert it into the hole. It will grip it and hold it in place. To remove the wire, insert the tip of a small screwdriver or rigid wire into the release slot and pull the wire out of the hole.

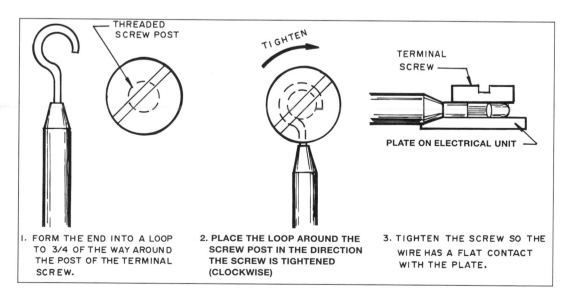

1. FORM THE END INTO A LOOP TO 3/4 OF THE WAY AROUND THE POST OF THE TERMINAL SCREW.

2. PLACE THE LOOP AROUND THE SCREW POST IN THE DIRECTION THE SCREW IS TIGHTENED (CLOCKWISE)

3. TIGHTEN THE SCREW SO THE WIRE HAS A FLAT CONTACT WITH THE PLATE.

2–41. The wire should wrap about three-quarters of the way around the screw post. The loop should face in a clockwise direction so that it will wrap around the screw as it is tightened.

Splicing Wire

Solid-wire splices are made by removing about ⅝ inch (16 millimeters) of the insulation on the end of the wire (**2–43**). Place the wires together. Slide the wire cap over them. Some home owners twist the wires together in a clockwise direction before sliding the wire cap over them. Rotate the wire cap clockwise. The cap should completely cover all bare wire. If it does not, remove the cap and shorten its bare ends. Some like to apply a couple layers of electrician's tape over the connector, securing it to the wire. Stranded wire can be connected to solid wire in this same manner.

Small-diameter **stranded wire** such as that used for lamps and small appliances must not be spliced. The cord should be a single, uninterrupted length. If such a cord is damaged, replace the entire cord.

ELECTRICAL BOXES

All receptacles, switches, and fixtures must be installed in electrical boxes. All connections must be made in electrical boxes. The electrical code regulates the number of conductors that can connect in a box,

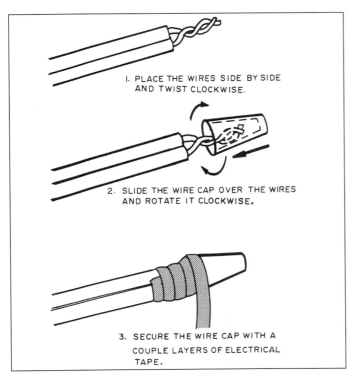

1. PLACE THE WIRES SIDE BY SIDE AND TWIST CLOCKWISE.

2. SLIDE THE WIRE CAP OVER THE WIRES AND ROTATE IT CLOCKWISE.

3. SECURE THE WIRE CAP WITH A COUPLE LAYERS OF ELECTRICAL TAPE.

2–43. Wires are joined in electrical boxes and spliced with a wire cap. Be certain to get the correct size cap. Use electrical tape to make certain the cap stays in place.

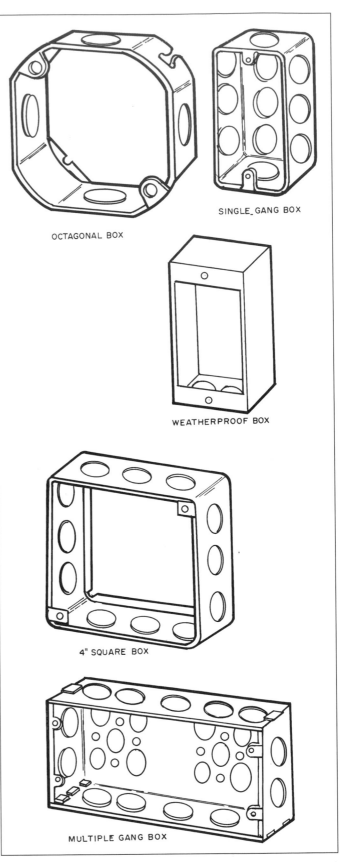

OCTAGONAL BOX

SINGLE-GANG BOX

WEATHERPROOF BOX

4" SQUARE BOX

MULTIPLE GANG BOX

2–44. These are the various types of most frequently used metal electrical boxes. Each shape has a number of different styles and features available.

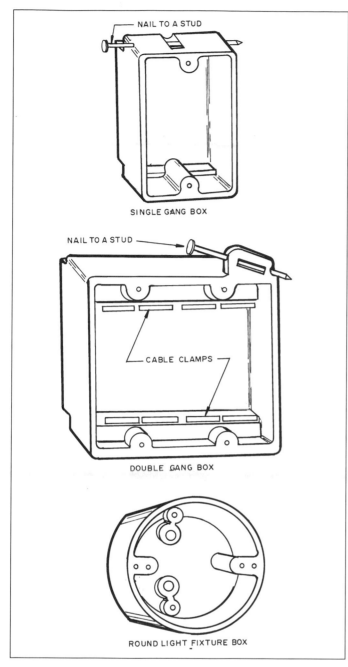

2–45. Typical plastic electrical boxes. They are available in the same basic sizes as metal boxes, but do not have the knockouts on all sides. The knockouts are on the top and bottom of the boxes. Knockouts are plugs that can be removed so cables can enter.

how it is installed, and how the connectors are brought into the box. Consult the local building-inspection department before starting an installation.

Electrical boxes are available in metal and plastic. Metal and plastic boxes are available in the same sizes and shapes. Both are approved for use with the nonmetallic plastic-sheathed cable used in residential wiring. One difference is that metal boxes must be grounded and plastic boxes do not require a ground. This feature makes plastic boxes easier and faster to install, and they find wide use in residential construction. A few of the commonly used metal and plastic boxes are shown in **2–44** and **2–45**.

Plastic boxes are referred to as nonmetallic boxes. They are made from polyvinyl chloride (PVC) or a thermosetting polyester. While they are approved for use with nonmetallic plastic-sheathed cable, they are not approved for use with metal conduits or armored cable. These require the use of metal boxes. Some PVC boxes can be used for outdoor installations with PVC conduit.

Connections to Electrical Boxes

Wires can be connected to wires and devices in electrical boxes. The electrical cable entering the box must be held firm with a mechanical connection. To help you make these connections, boxes have plugs, called knockouts, which can be removed so that cables can enter. A knockout in a metal box can be removed by inserting the tip of a screwdriver in its slot and bending it out. It will have to be worked back and forth several times until it breaks loose (**2–46**).

Round knockouts in metal boxes can be removed by using a nail set and hammer. Drive the knockout into the box and break it off by bending it back and forth with pliers (**2–47**).

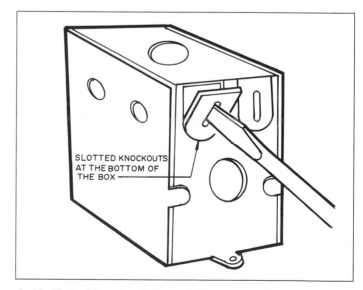

2–46. Slotted knockouts in metal boxes can be removed by bending them out with a screwdriver and working them back and forth until they break off.

Plastic boxes are made in the same sizes as metal boxes. However, they do not have the multiple knockouts commonly found on metal boxes. They have very thin plastic knockouts, which can be removed by pressing down on them with a screwdriver (**2–48**). Some codes permit cables to enter the plastic box and not be clamped if the cable is stapled to a stud within 8 inches (203 millimeters) of the box. The local building inspector can verify this requirement.

Some boxes have **internal clamps**. After the sheathing has been cut on the end of the cable and the length of wires needed to make the connection in the box are exposed, slip the cable through the knockout and tighten the clamp around the sheathed end of the cable (**2–49**).

A locknut connector is shown in **2–50**. To use this connector, first remove a knockout. Take the locknut off the connector, slide the threaded part of the con-

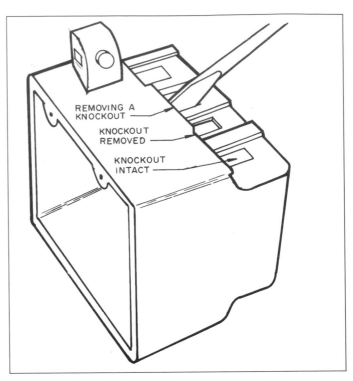

2–48. Knockouts in plastic boxes are removed by pressing down on them with a screwdriver.

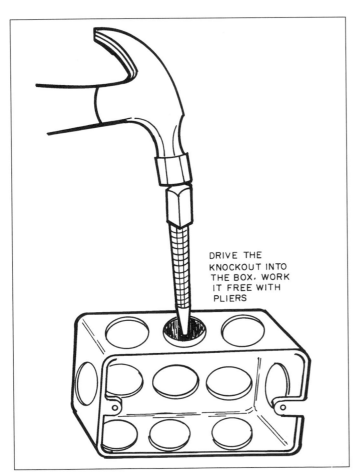

2–47. Round knockouts in metal boxes can be removed by driving them into the box and working them back and forth with pliers until they break off.

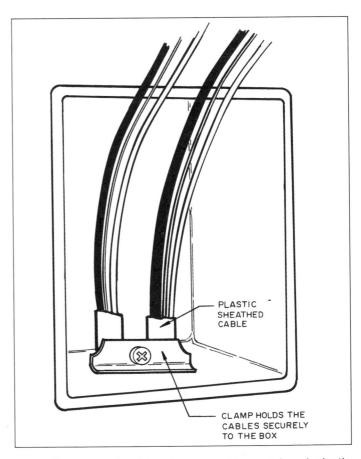

2–49. One type of cable clamp used in metal and plastic boxes.

nector through the knockout hole, and then reattach the locknut from the inside of the box. Slide the wire through the connector and lock it in place by tightening the clamping screws on both sides of the cable (**2–51**).

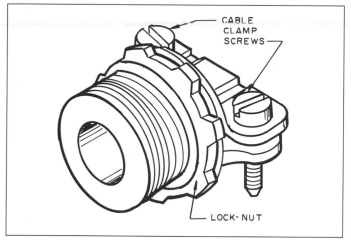

2–50. A typical locknut connector for nonmetallic cable in metal boxes that do not have connectors built in. There are a number of different designs for this connection.

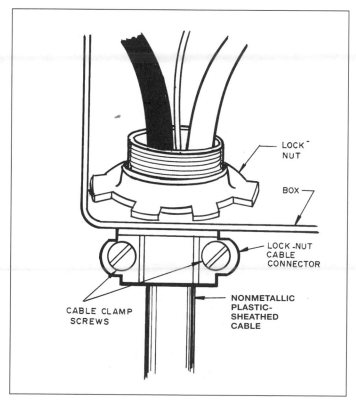

2–51. Remove the locknut, insert the threaded stem of the connector, and screw on the locknut.

PLUG-IN RECEPTACLES

Over the year, receptacles become worn and will not hold a plug securely. It is best to replace them. Begin by observing the openings in the receptacle. They tell a lot about its use, and the new one must have the same arrangement of slots. Those in common use are shown in **2–52**.

The receptacles for 120-volt service have one slot larger than the other. These are called **polarized receptacles**. The narrow slot is the one to which the hot (black) wire will be connected. A polarized plug on appliances has a wide and a narrow prong. The hot wire of the appliance is connected to the narrow prong on the plug.

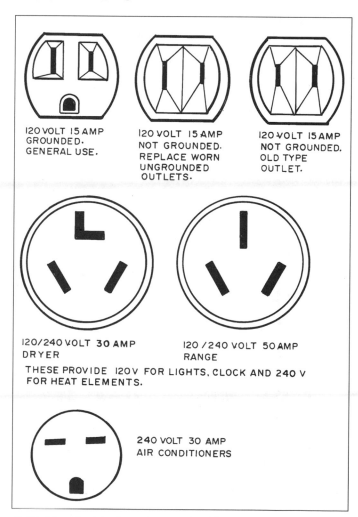

2–52. The electrical service can be identified by the arrangement of the slots on the receptacle. Always replace a receptacle with one having the identical slot configuration.

REPLACING A THREE-WIRE END-OF-THE-RUN GROUNDED RECEPTACLE

The last receptacle on a circuit (end of the run) has one cable entering the box. It is replaced as follows:

1. Turn off power to the circuit. Use a voltage tester to determine that no current is flowing.

2. Remove the cover plate.

3. Remove the receptacle from its box by loosening the screws at the top and bottom.

4. Pull the receptacle from its box and remove the wires attached to it.

5. On the new receptacle, attach the hot (black) wire to either of the brass screws. Next, attach the neutral (white) wire to either silver screw (2–53).

6. Finally, attach the ground (bare or green) wire to the green terminal. If it is in a metal box, connect the ground to the ground terminal on the box. If it is in a plastic box, it need not be grounded.

7. Attach the receptacle to the box and replace the cover.

8. Restore power to the circuit.

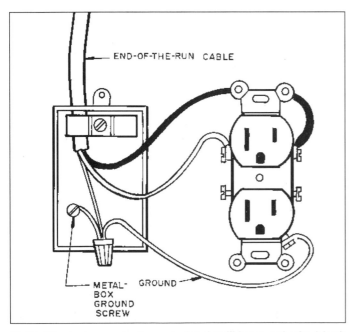

2–53. The last receptacle on a circuit will have only the black and white wires and the ground wire. Plastic boxes do not need to be grounded.

REPLACING A RECEPTACLE IN THE MIDDLE OF A RUN

Often there are several receptacles on one circuit. Each receptacle except the last will have four wires connected to it. The power flows from one receptacle to the next on the circuit.

One set of black and white wires are the **power-in wires**; the other set are the **power-out** wires (2–54). The power-out wires go to the next receptacle or other device on the circuit. When replacing a receptacle with four wires connected, place them on the new receptacle in the same order as they were removed from the old one. Look to see if the metal link between the screws for the top and bottom outlets has been broken. If it has, break the metal link on the new receptacle too. The broken link usually means half of the receptacle is always "hot," while the other half is controlled by a switch.

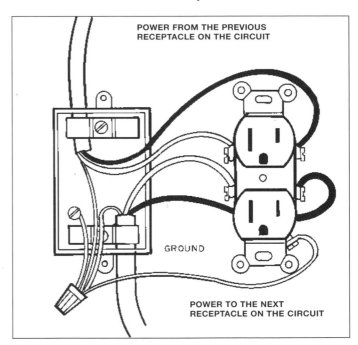

2–54. A middle-of-the run receptacle will have black, white, and ground wires coming into the box and also running out to the next receptacle.

INSTALLING A GROUND-FAULT CIRCUIT INTERRUPTER

Ground-fault circuit interrupters provide protection from shock due to minute current leakages. They may replace a standard receptacle in the middle of the run of a circuit or one that is on the end of the run.

If the electrical box into which the GFCI receptacle will be installed has only one black and one white wire entering it, connect the black to the brass-colored terminal and the white to the silver-colored terminal. Connect the ground wire to the green terminal. This provides protection for anything plugged into this receptacle (**2–55**).

If you are wiring for a middle-of-the-run GFCI receptacle, attach the black and white incoming wires to the brass and silver terminals marked "line." The outgoing wires to the next receptacle are connected to the brass and silver terminals marked "load" (**2–56**).

It should be noted that some GFCI units have wires instead of screw terminals. Connect these to the incoming and outgoing wires with wire caps.

To install a GFCI in the middle of a run, follow these steps:

1. Turn off the power to the circuit. Test it with a voltage tester to be certain it is off.

2. Remove the wall cover and unscrew the receptacle from the box.

3. Disconnect the wires. Note which are incoming and outgoing. If not certain, test them to find out. To do this, carefully separate the four wires. Turn on the power and touch one probe of a voltage

tester to the metal box or the grounding wire if it has a plastic box and the other to one of the black wires. If the tester lights, that is the incoming hot wire (**2–57**).

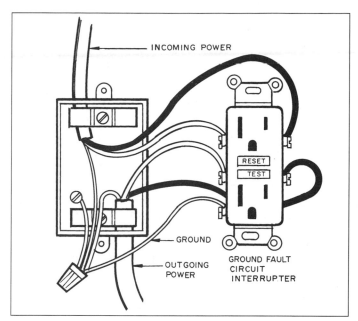

2–56. When installing a GFCI in the middle of a run, be certain the incoming and outgoing power are connected to the proper terminals.

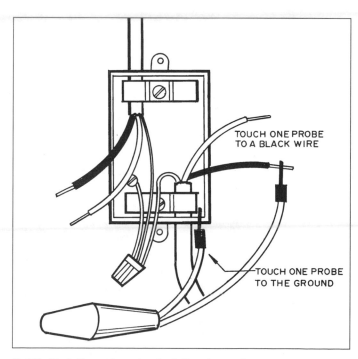

2–57. Test the wires to find the incoming power wires if unsure which set brings in the power. Touch one probe to a black wire and the other to the ground. If the tester glows, that black wire is the source of the incoming power. Be very careful doing this procedure, because a slight mistake could produce a shock.

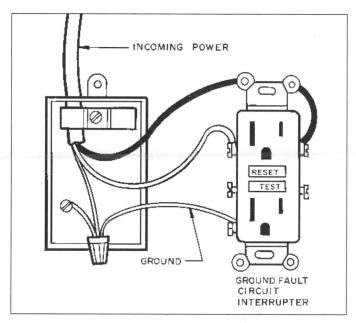

2–55. This ground-fault circuit interrupter (GFCI) is installed at the end of a run of a circuit. It has only the two wires from the incoming power to connect, plus a ground wire.

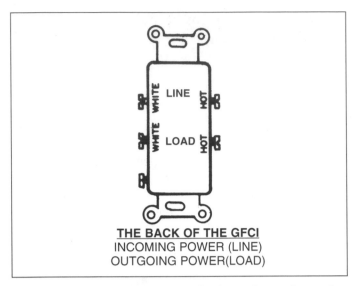

THE BACK OF THE GFCI
INCOMING POWER (LINE)
OUTGOING POWER (LOAD)

2–58. The line and load terminals (for incoming and outgoing power) and the hot (black) and white (negative) terminals are marked on the back of the GFCI.

4. Turn off the power. Mark the outgoing black wire with a piece of tape so it can be identified.

5. Connect the black incoming wire to the brass terminal and the white incoming wire to the silver terminal on the end marked "line" (**2–58**).

6. Connect the outgoing black and white wires to the brass and silver terminals on the end of the receptacle marked "load" (**2–58**).

7. Connect the ground wire to the metal box or, if it is plastic, to the other ground wires and the green terminal on the GFCI.

8. Install the GFCI in the box and replace the cover. Turn on the power.

9. Test the installation by plugging in a lamp. Press the test button. If the reset button pops out and the lamp stays lit, the receptacle is wired backward. Turn off the power and rewire the receptacle.

REPLACING A SINGLE-POLE WALL SWITCH

There are a number of ways this switch might be wired. It depends on where in the circuit the switch is located. Always connect the wires to the new switch exactly as they were connected to the old switch. The black wire is always the hot wire. If a red wire is used,

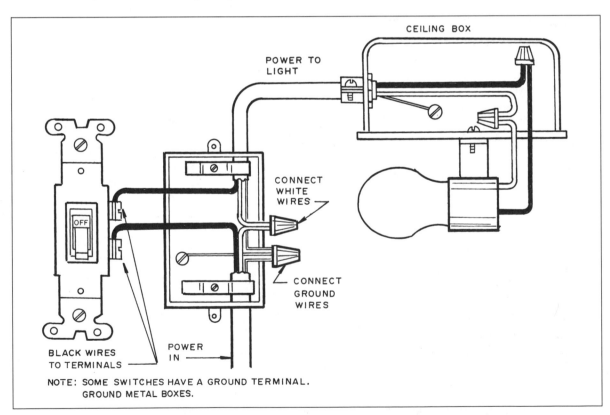

2–59. The technique for placing a switch on the line to a light located on the end of the run. Shut off the power, check with a voltage tester, remove the defective switch, and wire as shown. Notice that the switch is placed on the black wire ("hot"), which breaks the circuit when it is "off."

it is also hot. The white wire is sometimes neutral, but on some circuits it becomes a hot line. If this is the case, the electrician will paint the end black or wrap a layer of tape around it.

Before replacing any switch, turn off the power to the circuit. Remove the switch cover, unscrew the switch from the box, and carefully pull the switch out of the box. At this point, be very careful. *If the wrong circuit at the service panel is shut off, the wires will still be hot.* Check for a current with a voltage tester by touching one probe to each terminal on the switch and the other probe to a grounded metal box or the ground wire. If the switch has rear push-in terminals, insert the probe in each of the release slots. If the tester glows at any connection, the wires are hot. Recheck the service panel and get the correct circuit (refer to **2–35**).

The following discussion presents several frequently used wiring diagrams.

Connecting the Switch on the Power Source to a Light on the End of a Run

This is a very common installation. It involves putting the switch on the source of power ("hot" wire) located on the end of the run. The "hot" wire is cut and secured to the two switch terminals. The white wires from the power source and light are connected and the ground wires are connected (**2–59**).

Switch on a Loop

This installation has the power coming directly to the light fixture and the switch located in the circuit between the power source and the fixture. In this case, the white wire in the cable from the switch is connected to a black wire in the box and serves as a hot wire. The end is painted black. The two hot wires from the switch (one black, one white) form a loop that connects the switch to the light power source (**2–60**).

Additional light circuitry is shown later in this chapter.

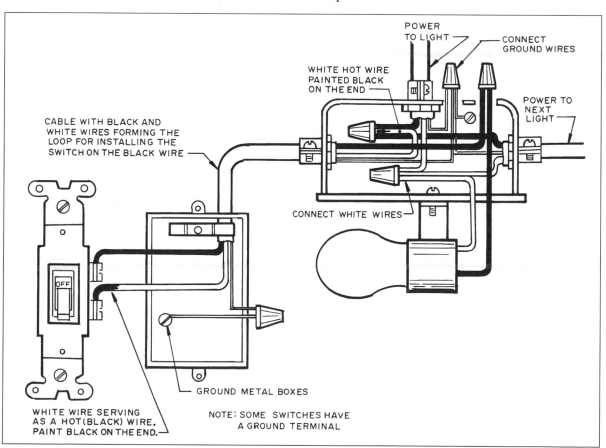

2–60. By installing the switch on a loop, a switch may be introduced into a light circuit when the power goes directly to the light. The switch is placed into the black wire, thus breaking the circuit when it is "off."

Replacing a Three-Way Switch

Three-way switches control a light from two positions, such as the top and bottom of a stairway. When they fail to turn on the light, the faulty switch has to be located. Do this by checking for continuity as discussed earlier.

Replacing a three-way switch is similar to replacing a single-pole switch. However, this switch has a common terminal on it. When this terminal is unscrewed from the faulty switch, put a piece of tape on its end so it can be identified for connection to the new switch. The common terminal on the three-way switch is darker in color than the others. It may be black or a dark-copper color. It is always darker than the brass- and silver-colored terminals. Notice that one cable has three wires and a ground. It will have black, red, and white wires.

Remember to turn off the power to the switch and test it using a voltage tester by touching one probe to the ground and the other to each of the three terminals.

Unscrew the switch from the box, mark the common wire, and disconnect the other two wires. Reconnect them to the new switch, attaching the common wire to the common (dark) terminal. The other two wires can be connected to either of the other terminals (**2–61**). These are referred to as **traveler terminals**. **Illus. 2–61** shows the diagram for a circuit when the light is on the end of the run. There are other circuits, such as one in which the light fixture is between two switches. However, when replacing a switch, connect the new switch exactly like the worn switch.

Replacing an Incandescent-Light Dimmer Switch

Incandescent-light dimmer switches allow the intensity of light to be controlled by rotating a knob. On some switches, the light is turned on and off by pushing in on the knob, while others operate by turning the knob to the left for "off" and the right for "on." Incandescent-light dimmer switches cannot be used on fluorescent lights. A special fluorescent-

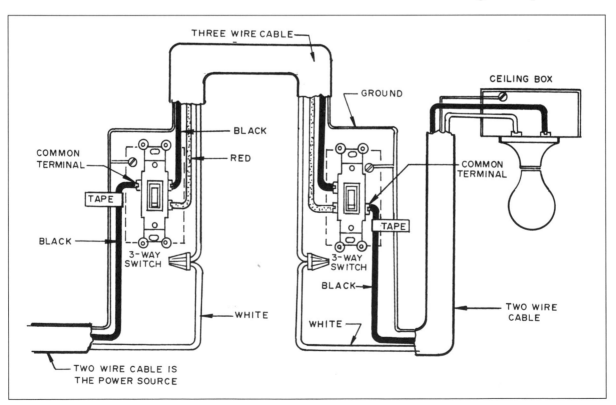

2–61. The wiring diagram for a light on the end of a run that is controlled by two 3-way switches. The common wire at each switch should be marked with a piece of tape so that when the switch is installed it can be easily identified and secured to the proper terminal on each switch.

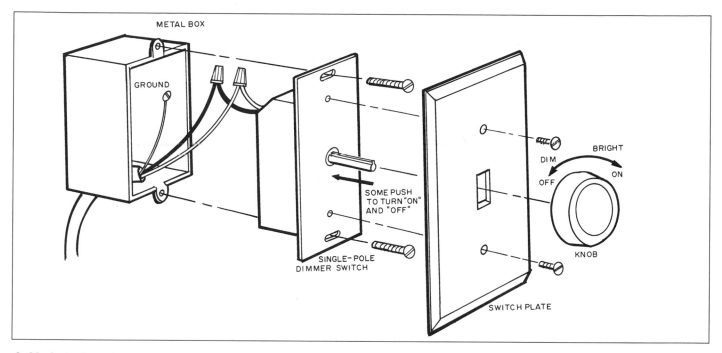

METAL BOX

GROUND

SOME PUSH
TO TURN "ON"
AND "OFF"

SINGLE-POLE
DIMMER SWITCH

DIM — BRIGHT

OFF — ON

KNOB

SWITCH PLATE

2–62. A single-pole dimmer switch can replace a standard single-pole switch. It is installed in the same manner as the single-pole switch.

light dimmer switch and dimmer ballast must be used. (A **dimmer ballast** stabilizes the current in a circuit.)

Single-pole dimmer switches are installed in the same manner as single-pole switches. Usually they come with wire leaders, which are connected to the electric cable with wire caps. Be certain to shut off the power to the circuit before replacing the switch (**2–62**).

Dimming can also be provided if there is a three-way-switch circuit. The three-way dimmer switch will have a common wire and two travelers. Only one dimmer switch can be installed on this circuit, so the light can be dimmed from only one of the two switches. Be certain to tape the common wire on the old switch before removing the wires. Connect the traveler wires on the switch to the black and red wires from the cable (**2–63**).

REPLACING A CEILING LIGHT FIXTURE

A ceiling light fixture has its electrical connections to the circuit enclosed in a box in the ceiling. There are many ways of hanging fixtures. Two common ways follow, but other systems exist. Study the instructions that come with the new light. To replace a ceiling fixture, follow these steps:

1. Turn off power to the circuit. If the old fixture was working, turn the wall switch to the "on" position to be sure there is no power in the circuit. Then turn the switch to the "off" position again. If the fixture was not working, check the circuit with a voltage tester.

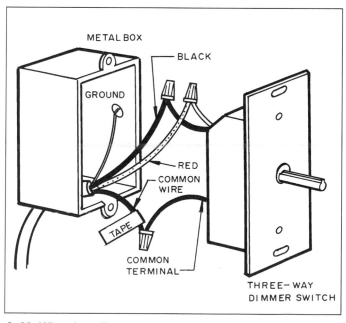

METAL BOX

BLACK

GROUND

RED

COMMON
WIRE

TAPE

COMMON
TERMINAL

THREE–WAY
DIMMER SWITCH

2–63. When installing a three-way dimmer switch, be certain to mark the common wire. Only one dimmer switch can be used on a three-way circuit.

2. Unscrew the screws or nuts holding the fixture to the electrical box to release the fixture from the ceiling. There is no standard hardware to hold fixtures in place, so examine the fixture to see what devices are holding it.

3. Disconnect the wires to the old fixture. This usually means unscrewing wire-cap connectors and pulling the wires free. The wires in the fixture are usually stranded, while the wires to the box are solid. Someone should help hold the fixture while it is being disconnected, so that the fixture does not fall.

4. Before connecting the new fixture, read the instructions packed with its hardware. Find out how it is meant to be held to the box. Some fixtures have screws that align with threaded holes in the box (**2–64**). Center-mounted fixtures are held to the box by a threaded metal tube called a nipple. The light fixture has a hole in the center through which the nipple runs, and is held with a decorative nut (**2–65**).

5. Connect the wires using wire-cap connectors. Have someone hold the fixture while doing so. Connect the black wires together, and the white

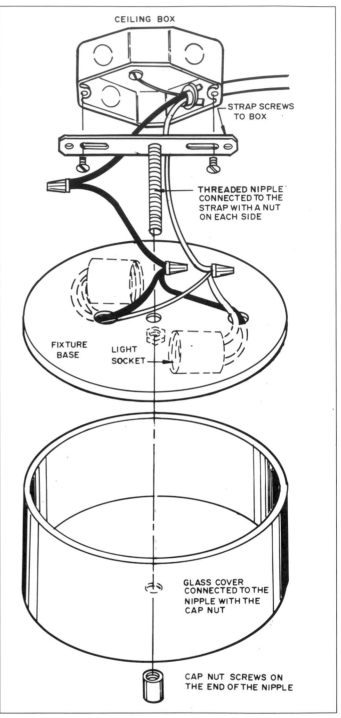

2–65. This light fixture is hung from a threaded nipple that is secured to the strap.

wires together. Connect the ground (green) wire, if there is one, to the bare ground wire or to the box.

6. Hang the fixture. Push the wires into the box and lift the base of the fixture against the ceiling. Align the screws in the base with the holes in the box. This may require much patience. Tighten the screws to pull the base to the ceiling.

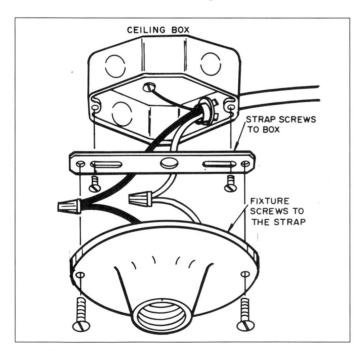

2–64. Some light fixtures are installed by screwing them to a strap. Connect black wires to black wires and white wires to white wires. Connect the ground to a metal box or to a bare ground wire if one is in the box.

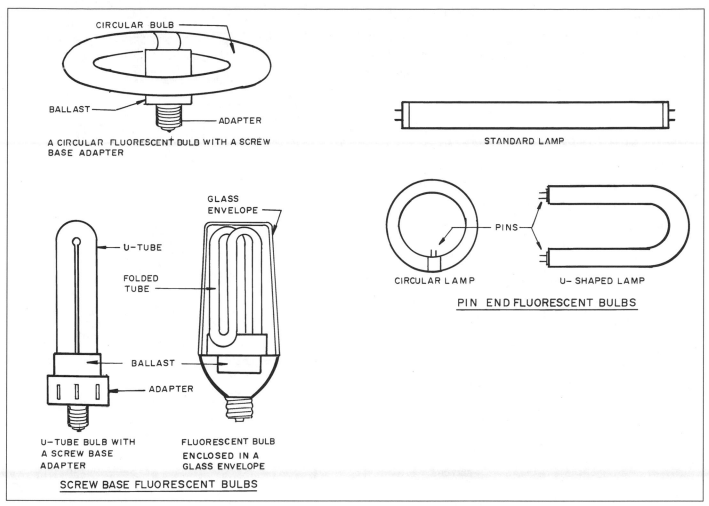

CIRCULAR BULB

BALLAST — — ADAPTER

A CIRCULAR FLUORESCENT BULB WITH A SCREW
BASE ADAPTER

STANDARD LAMP

GLASS
ENVELOPE

U–TUBE

FOLDED
TUBE

PINS

CIRCULAR LAMP   U– SHAPED LAMP

PIN END FLUORESCENT BULBS

BALLAST

ADAPTER

U–TUBE BULB WITH   FLUORESCENT BULB
A SCREW BASE   ENCLOSED IN A
ADAPTER   GLASS ENVELOPE

SCREW BASE FLUORESCENT BULBS

2–66. Commonly available fluorescent lamp bulbs.

FLUORESCENT LIGHTS

Fluorescent tubes use a lot less electricity than incandescent bulbs. They are available as straight, circular, and U-shaped tubes. A tube with a screw-type base that allows it to be screwed into incandescent sockets is also available (**2–66**).

The typical fluorescent fixture has a **ballast,** which is a transformer used to increase the standard 120-volt current to 300 volts to light the bulb and then reduce the voltage to that needed to keep it lighted.

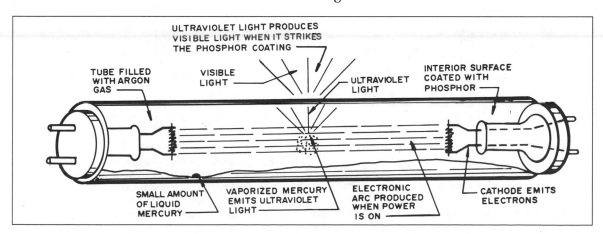

ULTRAVIOLET LIGHT PRODUCES
VISIBLE LIGHT WHEN IT STRIKES
THE PHOSPHOR COATING

TUBE FILLED
WITH ARGON
GAS

VISIBLE
LIGHT

ULTRAVIOLET
LIGHT

INTERIOR SURFACE
COATED WITH
PHOSPHOR

SMALL AMOUNT
OF LIQUID
MERCURY

VAPORIZED MERCURY
EMITS ULTRAVIOLET
LIGHT

ELECTRONIC
ARC PRODUCED
WHEN POWER
IS ON

CATHODE EMITS
ELECTRONS

2–67. A generalized illustration showing how a fluorescent bulb produces visible light.

The **tube** has cathodes at each end. The inside is coated with phosphor (a substance that emits light) and the space filled with argon gas and a low-pressure mercury vapor (**2–67**). Tubes are available in a range of whites and colors.

Mounting a Fluorescent Fixture

If the fluorescent fixture is old, it is best to replace it with a new fixture. The newer units are more efficient. New fixtures come ready to hang. Generally, the metal base is secured to the ceiling with screws or by hanging it from a stud if the ceiling box has one (**2–68**).

When selecting a new fluorescent fixture, you will find a wide array of designs. Some commonly available are shown in **2–69**. Basically the ballast is

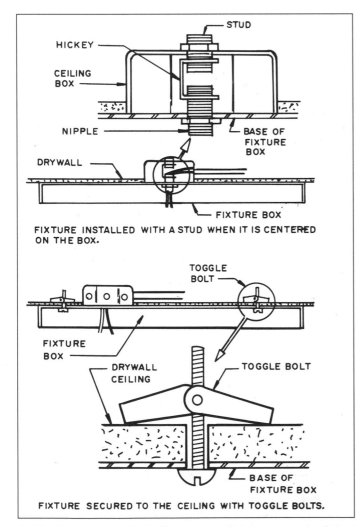

FIXTURE INSTALLED WITH A STUD WHEN IT IS CENTERED ON THE BOX.

FIXTURE SECURED TO THE CEILING WITH TOGGLE BOLTS.

2–68. Ceiling-mounted fluorescent fixtures are mounted using a stud from the ceiling box or by securing them to the ceiling. Sometimes they can be secured to a ceiling joist.

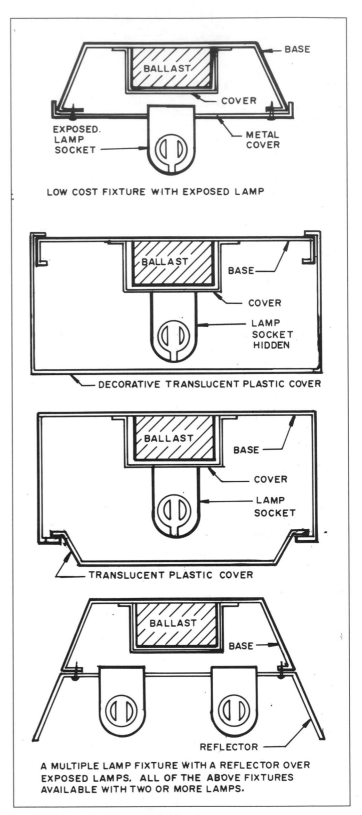

LOW COST FIXTURE WITH EXPOSED LAMP

DECORATIVE TRANSLUCENT PLASTIC COVER

TRANSLUCENT PLASTIC COVER

A MULTIPLE LAMP FIXTURE WITH A REFLECTOR OVER EXPOSED LAMPS. ALL OF THE ABOVE FIXTURES AVAILABLE WITH TWO OR MORE LAMPS.

2–69. Fluorescent fixtures are available in a range of designs and sizes. Some use an exposed lamp and are not suitable where appearance is important. The bare lamp also is objectionable because it bothers the eyes. Various translucent lamp-covered models are available.

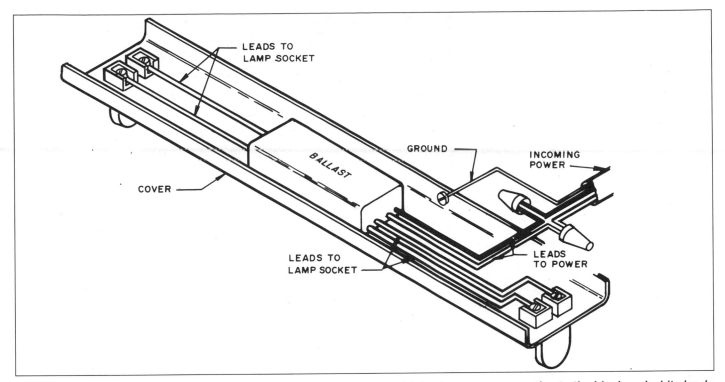

2–70. This shows the wiring layout for a rapid-start fluorescent fixture. Make the power connection to the black and white leads provided.

secured to the base and protected with a metal cover. The fixtures are sold fully wired so all that has to be done is to make the connection from the power source to the leads from the fixture. This is a black-to-black and white-to-white wire connection. **Illus. 2–70** is a typical wiring layout for a rapid-start fluorescent fixture.

The old fixture will be one of three types. A **starter-equipped preheat** unit will have a small, round starter on one end of the fixture (**2–71**). Some malfunctions require that the starter be twisted counterclockwise to remove it and replaced with an identical starter. This fixture uses tubes with two pins.

Instant-start fluorescent lights have a light tube that has only one pin on each end. The ballast provides the high voltage needed to ionize the gas in the tube. As the tube lights, this voltage is reduced. There is some danger of getting a shock when the tube is replaced, but most brands have a switch that cuts off power to the ballast if the tube is removed. The rapid-start system is replacing the instant-start system. Instant-start fixtures are generally used in industrial buildings.

Rapid-start fluorescent lights have a light tube with two pins at each end. The start ballast provides

a low voltage charge to quick-heating cathodes, enabling the tube to light rapidly. This is the most frequently used type for residential construction.

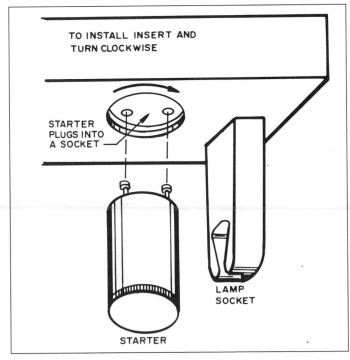

2–71. Starter-equipped preheat fluorescent fixtures have a circuit that heats the tube cathodes and fires an arc that lights the tube. The tube is installed by inserting it into the socket and twisting it counterclockwise.

TABLE 2-3. THINGS TO CHECK IF THE FLORESCENT LIGHTS DO NOT WORK PROPERLY

Problem	Possible Causes	Possible Solutions
Lamp will not light	1. Lamp burned out (ends appear black) 2. Poor connections in lamp socket 3. Defective starter (on starter-type fixtures) 4. Low air temperature 5. Improperly wired fixture 6. Low line voltage 7. Ballast failure	1. Replace lamp 2. Clean lamp pins and socket 3. Replace starter 4. Raise room air temperature to above 50° F (10° C) 5. Check wiring diagram often found on the ballast 6. Call electric company to correct 7. Replace ballast
Lamp flickers	1. Poor contact of tube pins 2. Low air temperature 3. Defective starter 4. Defective lamp 5. Defective ballast 6. Incorrect lamp	1. Clean pins 2. Raise air temperature 3. Replace starter 4. Replace lamp 5. Replace ballast 6. Install correct lamp
Ballast hums	1. Wrong ballast for the fixture 2. Defective ballast 3. Ballast not secured firmly	1. Replace ballast 2. Replace ballast 3. Tighten ballast screws

Table 2–1. Things to check if the fluorescent lights do not work properly.

While fluorescent lights are very reliable, sometimes there will be a malfunction. **Table 2–3** describes some common problems and possible solutions.

DOORBELL AND CHIME REPAIR

A doorbell or chime is controlled by a push-button switch. It receives its power from a transformer producing 12 to 20 volts. The transformer is operated by a 120-volt line and uses small-diameter cloth-covered wire typically 18 to 20 gauge. No ground is required, and the wires can be connected to any terminal on the bell or chime. The transformer can be installed in any convenient place such as the attic, basement, garage, or crawl space. The bell or chime is typically installed in the hall.

Two typical circuits are shown in **2–72**.

If the doorbell or chime fails to operate, follow these steps to find the trouble:

1. First test the 120-volt line at the transformer with a voltage tester.

2. If there is power to the transformer, next test the push-button switch. Remove the wires from the switch and touch them together. If the doorbell or chime rings, the switch is not functioning properly and needs to be replaced.

3. If the doorbell or chime does not ring when tested, power is not getting through to the switch, indicating that the transformer is not functioning properly. Replace the transformer. Be certain the new transformer has the same voltage as the one being replaced.

4. If the chime or bell is defective, be certain the old transformer provides the voltage needed by the new chime or bell. If not, replace the transformer.

A variety of wireless chimes are available. They enable a new system to be installed without a transformer or running wires. One type comes in a kit that contains front and rear door buttons and a chime as well as a sending unit in an attractive plastic case. It is battery-powered. The signal will pass through walls, floors, and ceilings. Install the chime unit in the house in a convenient place. Install the batteries and the job is finished.

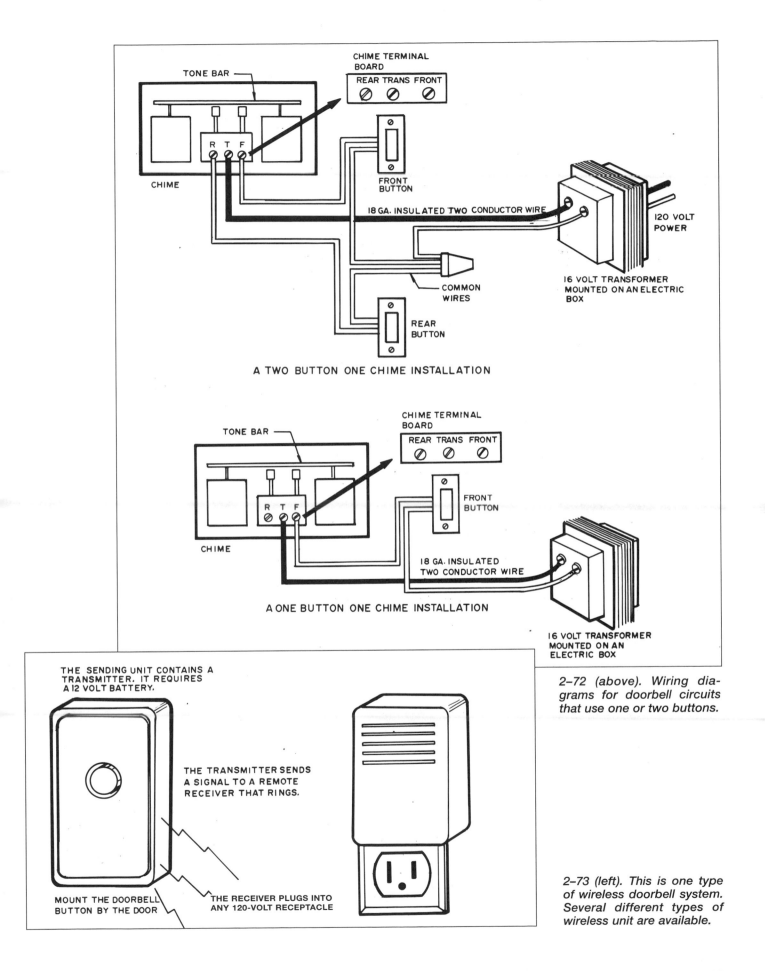

TONE BAR

CHIME TERMINAL BOARD

REAR TRANS FRONT

R T F

CHIME

FRONT BUTTON

18 GA. INSULATED TWO CONDUCTOR WIRE

120 VOLT POWER

COMMON WIRES

16 VOLT TRANSFORMER MOUNTED ON AN ELECTRIC BOX

REAR BUTTON

A TWO BUTTON ONE CHIME INSTALLATION

TONE BAR

CHIME TERMINAL BOARD

REAR TRANS FRONT

R T F

CHIME

FRONT BUTTON

18 GA. INSULATED TWO CONDUCTOR WIRE

A ONE BUTTON ONE CHIME INSTALLATION

16 VOLT TRANSFORMER MOUNTED ON AN ELECTRIC BOX

2–72 (above). Wiring diagrams for doorbell circuits that use one or two buttons.

THE SENDING UNIT CONTAINS A TRANSMITTER. IT REQUIRES A 12 VOLT BATTERY.

THE TRANSMITTER SENDS A SIGNAL TO A REMOTE RECEIVER THAT RINGS.

MOUNT THE DOORBELL BUTTON BY THE DOOR

THE RECEIVER PLUGS INTO ANY 120-VOLT RECEPTACLE

2–73 (left). This is one type of wireless doorbell system. Several different types of wireless unit are available.

Doorbell and Chime Repair ■ 115

Another type of wireless chime has the transmitter as part of the doorbell button unit, and the receiver is plugged into any convenient 120-volt receptacle (**2–73**).

DRIVEWAY MONITOR

One way to know every time someone comes into the driveway or some other part of the property is to install an infrared sensor directed across the path of travel. When it detects motion, it will sound a chime on an indoor receiving unit. The range and size of the detection area will vary depending upon the unit purchased. Both units require batteries (**2–74**).

REPLACING A CIRCUIT BREAKER

Illus. 2–75 shows a partial view of the circuit breakers in a service-entrance panel. The panel will have a hook strip into which a prong on the breaker is inserted. It will also have some type of metal protrusion, often called a **stab**, connected to the load bus-bar that fits into a slot on the bottom of the breaker. A bus bar for the neutral wires typically runs along the side of the hook strip (**2–76**). A typical circuit breaker is shown in **2–77**. There will be some design differences between the various brands of panel and breaker.

Following are steps to replace a circuit breaker:

1. Switch the main circuit breaker to the "off" position or pull the main fuses for the entire house. Check with a voltage tester to make certain the system is off. *Warning: If there is no main shutoff to the building, do not attempt to replace the circuit breaker.* Call an electrician to do the job.

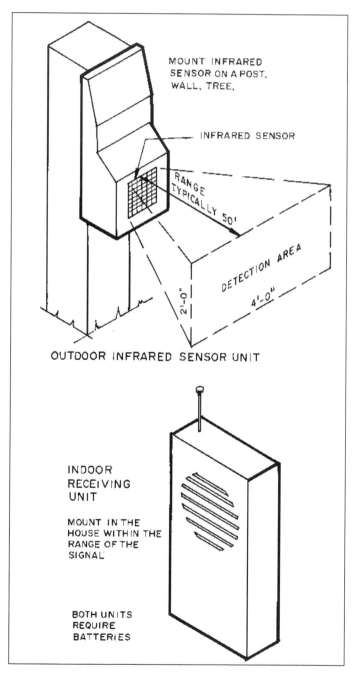

2–74. *An infrared driveway monitor can be used to send a signal to the house whenever something breaks the infrared ray.*

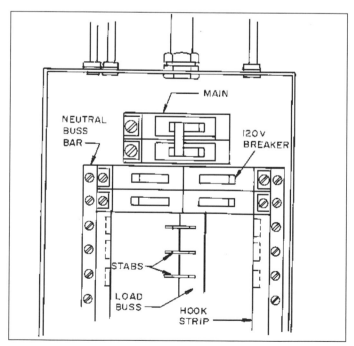

2–75. *The service-entrance panel contains the circuit breakers and the connections for their installation.*

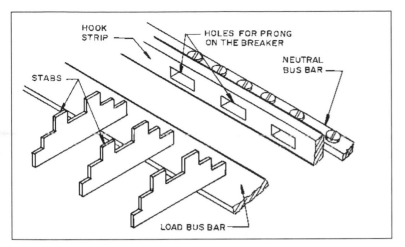

2–76. *A typical circuit-breaker connection on a service-entrance panel. The prongs on the circuit breaker fit into the hook-strip holes, and the circuit breaker is pressed down on the stab, which enters a connection slot in the bottom of the breaker. This design varies with different manufacturers.*

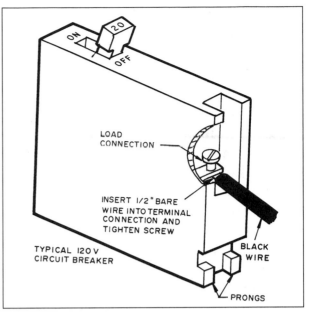

2–77. *A typical 120-volt two-pole circuit breaker.*

2. Put the circuit-breaker switch being replaced in the "off" position.

3. Disconnect the black load wire. *Warning: While working on the power panel, remember that the heavy cables bringing power to the panel are "hot." Do not go near them under any circumstances!*

4. Unplug the circuit breaker by pulling out on the end opposite the load connection (**2–78**). It should unplug from the panel.

5. Put the new circuit-breaker switch in the "off" position. Place one end on the hook strip. Then push the other side in place so it fits onto the stabs protruding from the bar in the panel.

6. Replace the load wire.

7. Replace the front of the power panel and turn on the main switch.

8. Turn the new circuit-breaker switch to the "on"

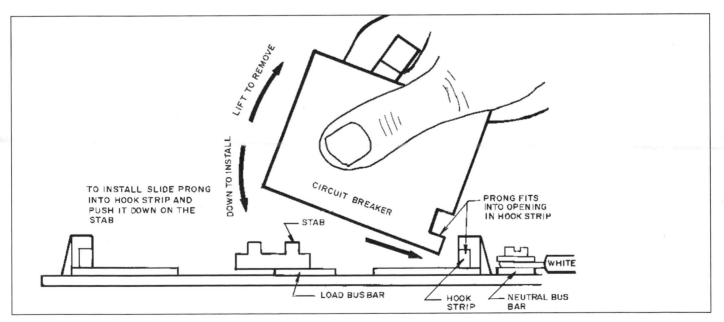

2–78. *The circuit breaker is removed by lifting the inside end. It is installed by sliding the prong into the opening in the hook strip and pushing it down on the stab. The circuit breaker has an opening in the bottom into which the stab enters and makes contact with the internal circuitry.*

position. Use a neon tester to see that the circuit is operating.

ADDING ON TO AN EXISTING CIRCUIT

Occasionally, there may be a need to add an additional duplex receptacle or a light in a dark area. This can sometimes be done by connecting the receptacle to an existing circuit. This requires some preliminary planning. First, it has to be determined if the circuit can carry additional loads. If it can, the next step is to figure out how many feet of plastic-covered wire will be needed and to purchase the boxes and fixtures. Finally, consider the structure of the wall or ceiling into which the receptacle or light switch will be installed. Most often, the wall will be made with 2 x 4-inch (50 x 102-millimeter) wood studs resting on a 2 x 4-inch bottom plate and having a 2 x 4-inch top plate. It is hollow, and the original wires were run through it. If the wall is masonry, it will be easiest to use a surface-mounted wiring system.

Planning Method

To determine if the circuit can handle an additional load, first trace the circuit on a sheet of paper to determine how many lights and receptacles are on it. Verify the number of lights and receptacles by checking the list made and posted at the power panel. Next, determine what load the circuit can carry. This can be done by examining the fuse or circuit breaker. The amperage is clearly indicated on each of them.

To determine the load on an existing circuit, follow these steps:

1. Add the total watts now in use on the circuit. Be sure to include the appliances plugged into receptacles.

2. Estimate in watts the load that will be added to the circuit.

3. Add the estimated watts to the total watts now in use.

4. Divide the total by 120 volts to find the total amps on the circuit. The number arrived at repre-

sents the load if every appliance and fixture is on at the same time.

5. Compare the number arrived at with the ampere capacity of the circuit. The ampere capacity for the circuit is found at the service-entrance panel. If the calculated number is smaller, the circuit may have excess capacity and the extra devices can be safely added. On typical 15- and 20-ampere branch circuits used in residential construction for lights and cord- and plug-connected equipment, the load rating should not exceed 80 percent of the branch circuit rating. Check your local code for specific requirements.

When estimating the new load, also consider the area in which the circuit is located. In a bedroom, the load on the receptacles would mainly be light. A bedroom load would consist of lamps, clocks, radios, an electric blanket, vacuum cleaner, etc. A good estimate might be 100 watts per receptacle. If the circuit is in the kitchen or workshop, the load on the receptacles would be heavier. Try to estimate which appliances or tools, such as coffeemakers, toasters, blenders, circular saws, etc., are in use at the same time. Find the number of watts each appliance uses to make the estimate.

ADDING A NEW RECEPTACLE

Several decisions have to be made when planning the addition of a new receptacle. These include determining where to locate it on the wall, where it will get its power, and how to install it. Typically, a new receptacle will get its power from a nearby existing receptacle if this will not overload the circuit. If this is the case, the next step is to decide how to run the cable.

Once the details have been worked out, locate and cut the opening. Place an electric box on the wall and mark around it. The opening can be cut by scoring gypsum drywall with a knife, cutting over and over until the knife breaks through (2–79). Tap the part to be removed with a hammer if it has to be popped loose. Another option is to drill a hole into each corner and cut the opening with a keyhole saw or a power saber saw (2–79). Openings in wood paneling

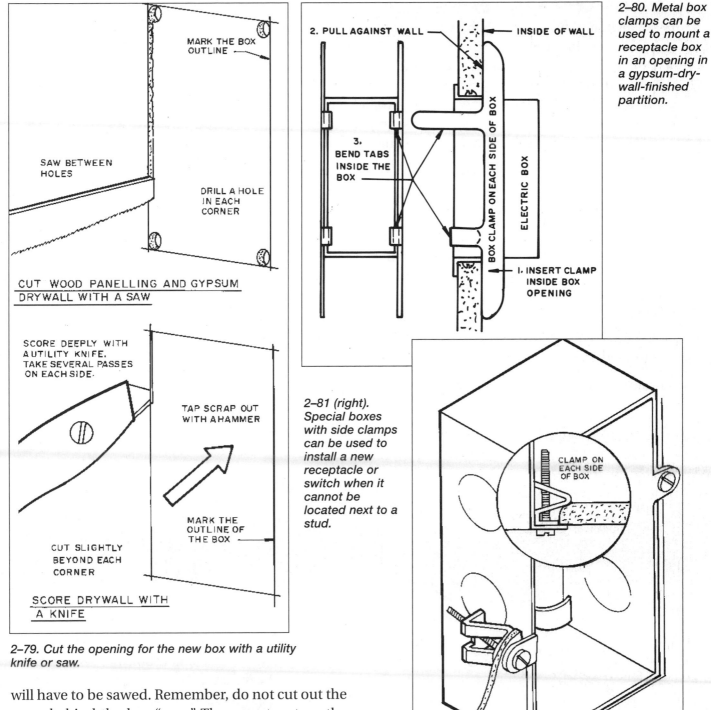

MARK THE BOX OUTLINE

SAW BETWEEN HOLES

DRILL A HOLE IN EACH CORNER

CUT WOOD PANELLING AND GYPSUM DRYWALL WITH A SAW

SCORE DEEPLY WITH A UTILITY KNIFE. TAKE SEVERAL PASSES ON EACH SIDE.

TAP SCRAP OUT WITH A HAMMER

CUT SLIGHTLY BEYOND EACH CORNER

MARK THE OUTLINE OF THE BOX

SCORE DRYWALL WITH A KNIFE

2–79. Cut the opening for the new box with a utility knife or saw.

2. PULL AGAINST WALL — INSIDE OF WALL

3. BEND TABS INSIDE THE BOX

BOX CLAMP ON EACH SIDE OF BOX

ELECTRIC BOX

1. INSERT CLAMP INSIDE BOX OPENING

2–80. Metal box clamps can be used to mount a receptacle box in an opening in a gypsum-dry-wall-finished partition.

2–81 (right). Special boxes with side clamps can be used to install a new receptacle or switch when it cannot be located next to a stud.

CLAMP ON EACH SIDE OF BOX

A SPECIAL SIDE CLAMP BOX

will have to be sawed. Remember, do not cut out the areas behind the box "ears." They must rest on the surface of the wall. If there are electric wires in the area, cut the opening carefully with the utility knife.

Securing Boxes to the Wall

If the new box is next to a stud, it can be secured to it with wood screws. If it is on a space between studs, box clamps can be used. These are used on plaster, gypsum drywall, and wood-paneled walls.

After cutting the opening for the box, pull the cable out of the opening and attach it to the box with the box clamps. Then slide the box partway into the opening and work the box clamps in on each side (2–80). This is not easy and it is possible to drop the box inside the wall. When both side clamps are in place, bend the tabs over the edge of the box. Pull them very tight and firm up the bend with pliers.

A box can be set into the wall using a special side-clamp box (**2–81**). It is not attached to a stud, but clamps on the drywall or paneling. The box has "ears" on the outside that rest against the finish wall material and, as the screw is tightened, the clamp on the back squeezes against the inside of the finish wall material.

Adding Boxes Back to Back

If possible, the new box should be placed next to the stud facing the existing box (**2–82**). If this is not possible, plan to mount the new box on the finished wall material as just described.

To install the next box so that it faces the existing box, use the following steps:

1. Cut the opening for the new box.

2. Cut off the power to the existing box. Check it with a voltage tester to be certain it is off.

3. Remove a knockout in the bottom of the existing box and run fish tape through it toward the new box opening. Move the boxes around until the hooks on the ends connect. It takes a little patience to hook these together (**2–83**).

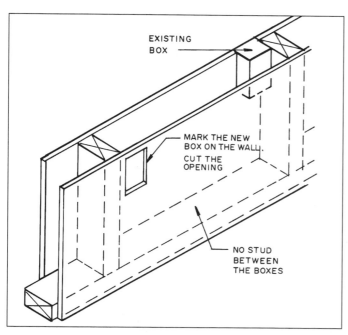

2–82. Locate the new box on the wall and cut the opening. Place the box next to a stud if possible.

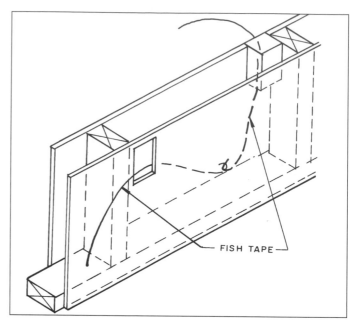

2–83. Run fish tape from each box location and hook the boxes together inside the wall.

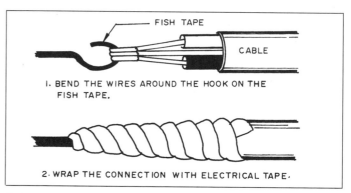

2–84. When pulling nonmetallic cable with fish tape, wrap the wires around the tape hook and cover the connection with electrical tape so it will slide through any openings and not get caught.

4. Connect a piece of nonmetallic cable to the fish tape (**2–84**) and pull it to the new box opening (**2–85**). Run it into the new box and secure it with a clamp. Leave enough wire to make the connections to the receptacle (**2–86**).

5. Install the new box in the opening and connect the wires to the receptacle. Install the receptacle.

6. Now connect the wires to the receptacle in the existing box. Connect black wires to black wires and white wires to white wires and join the ground wires.

7. Turn on the power and check to see that everything is working properly.

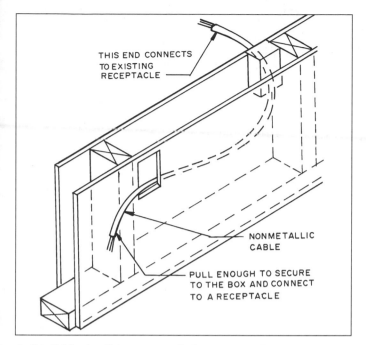

2–85. With the fish tape, pull the nonmetallic cable to the new receptacle opening. Allow enough wire to make the connections to the box and receptacle or switch.

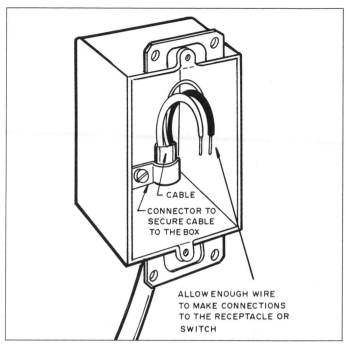

2–86. Run the cable into the box and secure it with the connector. Leave enough wire to make the connections to the receptacle or switch. Now install the box in the opening in the wall.

When running new cable, be certain to use a size that is large enough to carry the amperage in the circuit. The capacities of copper and aluminum wire are shown in **Table 2–1** (page 85). These sizes are printed on the side of the plastic cable. Refer also to **2–16**.

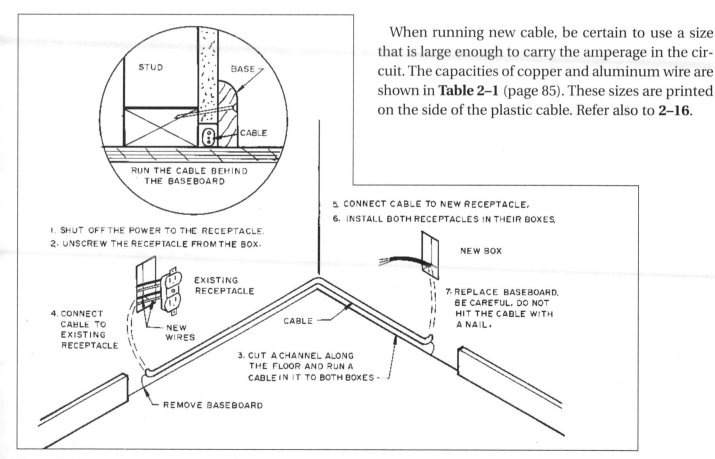

2–87. The power can be run to a new location by removing the baseboard, cutting a channel in the bottom of the finish wall material, and running the cable in the channel behind the baseboard.

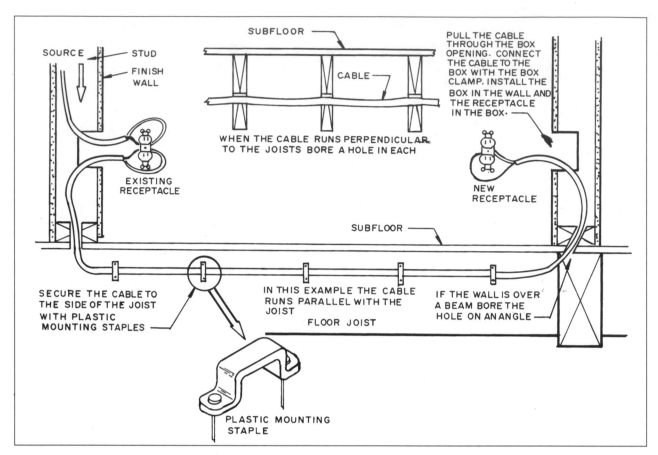

2–88. One way to add a new receptacle across the room is to run the new cable below the floor. It is important to locate each wall below the floor very accurately.

Adding Other Receptacles

If the new receptacle is farther down the wall, possibly the easiest thing to do is to remove the baseboard and cut a channel in the bottom of the gypsum wallboard or other finish wall material (**2–87**).

Once the channel is cut, turn off the power to the circuit, unscrew the receptacle, and pull it out of the box. Remove a knockout in the bottom of the existing box. Feed the wire or, if things are tight, drop a fish tape down through this knockout. Work the wire down until it reaches the new box.

Cut an opening for the new box in the wall. If possible, place it next to a stud, so the box can be secured to it. Pull the wire out of the opening and through a knockout in the new box. Tighten the clamp on the cable. Insert the box in the opening and fasten it to the stud. It is easiest to use wood screws for this connection. Then install the receptacle and put on the cover plate. When reinstalling the base, be very careful that a nail is not put through the cable.

It is more difficult to run a line across the room to put a receptacle on the other side. Possibly the easiest way is to go under the floor, if there is open access below the floor joists (**2–88**). The wall will have to be located from below and a hole drilled through the subfloor and bottom plate. It should be very near the existing receptacle. If it is off by much, it will be very difficult to get the wires in place. This requires great accuracy in measurement; if there is a mismeasurement, a hole can be drilled into the finished floor of the room. The wall plate is typically 3½ inches (89 millimeters) wide, so the margin of error is small.

If there is a carpet on the floor, a nail could be driven through it and the subfloor next to the wall. Measurements can then be made from this nail under the house to locate the hole (**2–89**). A small-diameter hole could be drilled through hardwood flooring. Once the hole location is established, drill the hole through the subfloor and bottom plate (**2–90**).

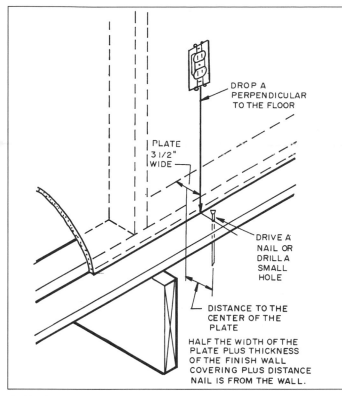

2–89. The center of the wall can be located by driving a nail through the carpet and subfloor or drilling a small hole through hardwood flooring.

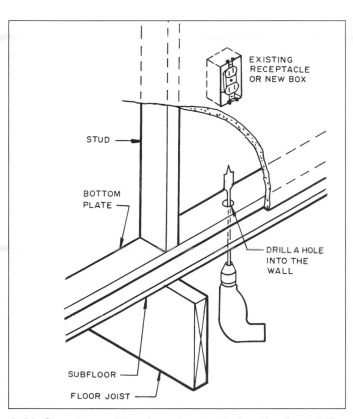

2–90. Once the wall has been located below the floor, drill a hole into the wall cavity. It should have a diameter large enough so that the cable moves through it easily.

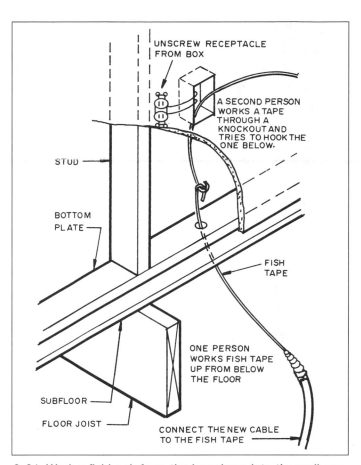

2–91. Work a fishhook from the box down into the wall cavity and one up from below the floor. Work the fishhooks around until they connect.

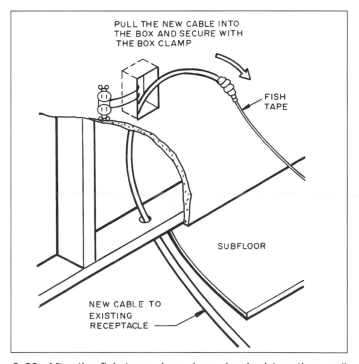

2–92. After the fish tapes have been hooked together, pull the cable up through the box and secure it with the box clamp.

Adding a New Receptacle ■ **123**

Now shut off the power to the receptacle and unscrew and pull it out of the box. Next, run fish tape up through the drilled hole and down through a knockout in the existing box and try to hook the looped ends (**2–91**). Then the cable can be connected to the fish tape and pulled into the box (**2–92**). Repeat this at the location of the new box. Connect the wires to the receptacles, install the receptacles in the box, turn on the power, and check the circuit. Refer to **2–88**.

Another way to run the cable is to remove the baseboard, bore a hole through the floor, and notch a piece out of the bottom plate as shown in **2–93**.

Power can be run in a wall by dropping the cable inside the wall from the attic as shown in **2–94**.

If you are planning to cover the old wall with new gypsum wallboard or paneling, a groove can be cut in the old finished wall and the studs notched as needed to prepare a channel for the new wire. Codes require that a metal plate be nailed over the wire at each stud (**2–95**).

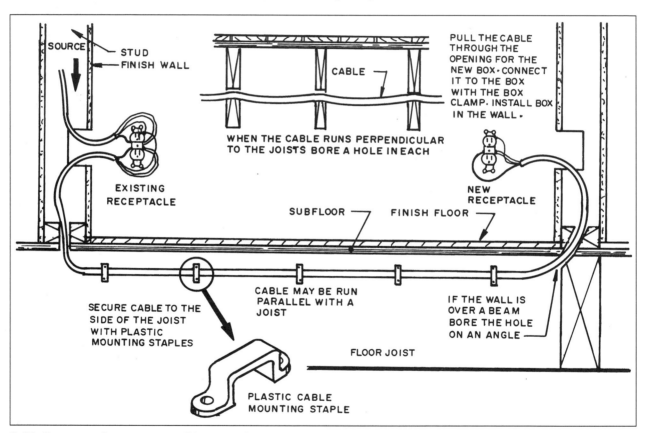

2–93. Power can be run up a wall by removing the base and boring a hole down into the basement or crawl space. Notch the bottom plate with a wood chisel to get enough room to run the cable.

2–95 (facing page, bottom). If a new wall finish material is being installed, a channel in the old wall covering can be cut and the studs notched as needed to provide access from an existing box to a new box. Notice that a ¹/₁₆-inch- (1.5-millimeter-) thick metal strip is nailed over the cable at each stud to prevent any nails from striking the cable.

2–94 (right). Power can be run from the attic to the wall below or to the basement by dropping a cable through the wall.

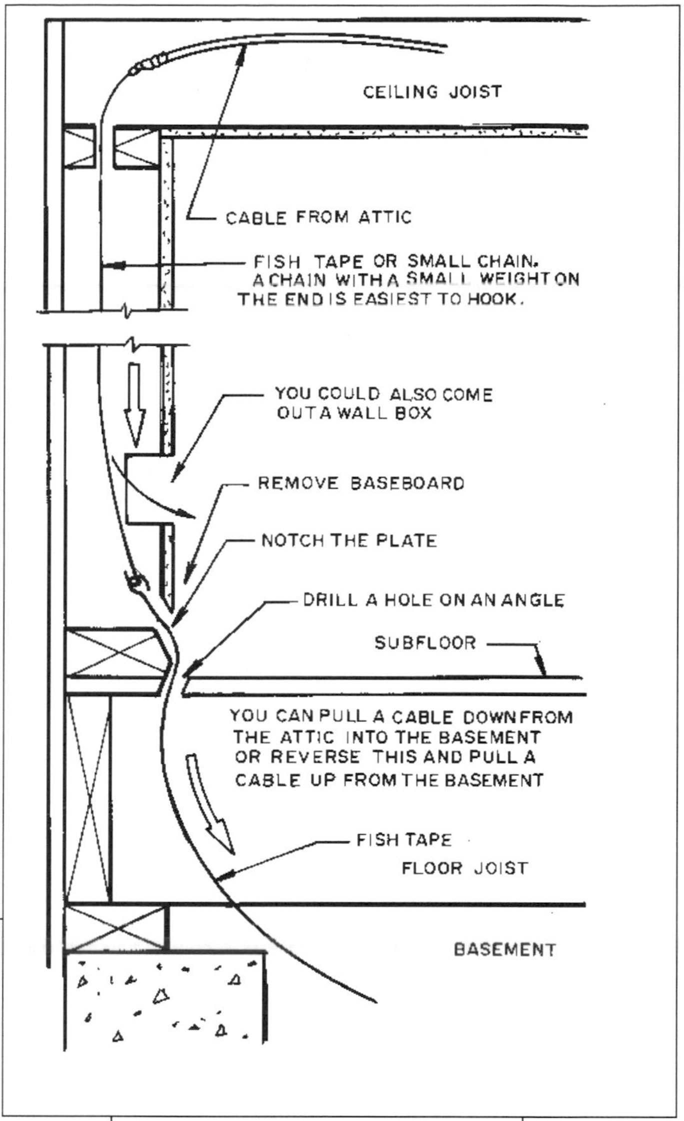

CEILING JOIST

CABLE FROM ATTIC

FISH TAPE OR SMALL CHAIN.
A CHAIN WITH A SMALL WEIGHT ON
THE END IS EASIEST TO HOOK.

YOU COULD ALSO COME
OUT A WALL BOX

REMOVE BASEBOARD

NOTCH THE PLATE

DRILL A HOLE ON AN ANGLE

SUBFLOOR

YOU CAN PULL A CABLE DOWN FROM
THE ATTIC INTO THE BASEMENT
OR REVERSE THIS AND PULL A
CABLE UP FROM THE BASEMENT

FISH TAPE

FLOOR JOIST

BASEMENT

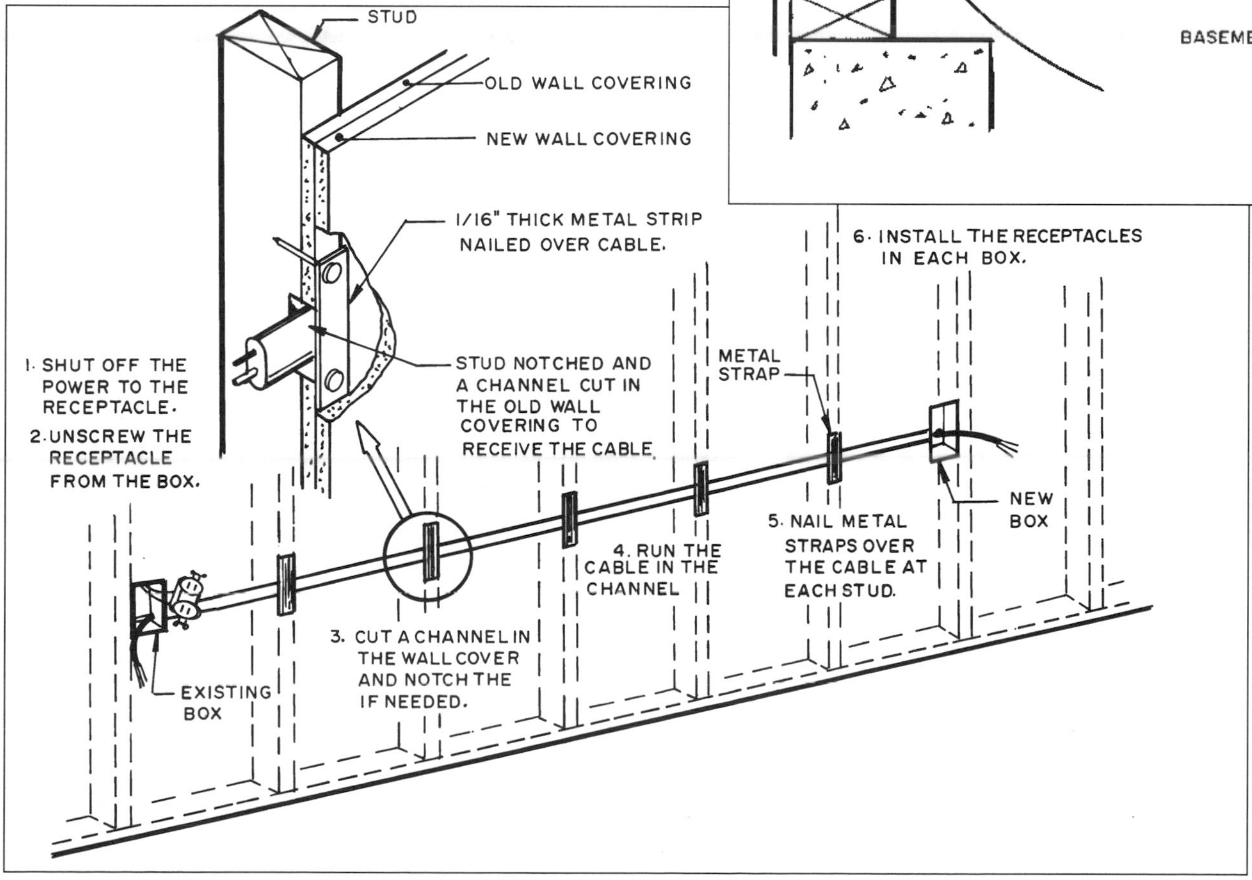

STUD

OLD WALL COVERING

NEW WALL COVERING

1/16" THICK METAL STRIP
NAILED OVER CABLE.

STUD NOTCHED AND
A CHANNEL CUT IN
THE OLD WALL
COVERING TO
RECEIVE THE CABLE.

1. SHUT OFF THE
POWER TO THE
RECEPTACLE.

2. UNSCREW THE
RECEPTACLE
FROM THE BOX.

3. CUT A CHANNEL IN
THE WALL COVER
AND NOTCH THE
IF NEEDED.

4. RUN THE
CABLE IN THE
CHANNEL

METAL
STRAP

6. INSTALL THE RECEPTACLES
IN EACH BOX.

5. NAIL METAL
STRAPS OVER
THE CABLE AT
EACH STUD.

NEW
BOX

EXISTING
BOX

ADDING A NEW LIGHT

A new light presents two major problems. One is the installation of a box to contain the wires and carry the weight of the light. The other is to get an uninterrupted source of power to the light and permit it to be controlled by a switch. If it is connected to another light, its switch will control the new light. A typical installation for a new light that requires a switch is shown in **2–96**. Notice that the power source is run to a junction box nailed to a joist. The wires to the light and switch are connected to power and each other in this box. When the connections are finished, a cover is placed over the box and secured with screws. **Illus. 2–97** is a wiring diagram for this installation.

Following is a possible way to install a new ceiling light and switch from an unfinished attic. Begin by locating the center of the light fixture on the ceiling. Drill a small hole through the ceiling. Check in the attic to see if the ceiling is at a far enough distance from the joists to enable the box with its hanging bracket to be installed. This usually takes about a 4-inch clearance. If the hole hits a joist or is close to one, the location of the light will need to be moved a little.

Now, place the box to be used against the ceiling with the hole in the center. Mark around the box. Drill holes at the corners and cut out the opening (**2–98**). Use a compass saw or a power saber saw. The holes can be cut from the attic or from below the box. If cutting from below the box, wear goggles and a mask because a lot of gypsum dust will fall.

Next, install the ceiling box as shown in **2–99** on page 128. Ceiling lights are hung between ceiling joists with a hanger strap that has a ceiling box secured to it. The box connection permits the box to slide along the strap, enabling the location of the light to be adjusted. When the ceiling box is installed from the attic, the flanges are screwed to the joists. When the ceiling box is installed from below, the flanges can be screwed to the joists.

Finally, run the light cables into the box and secure it with a clamp. Then the wires can be con-

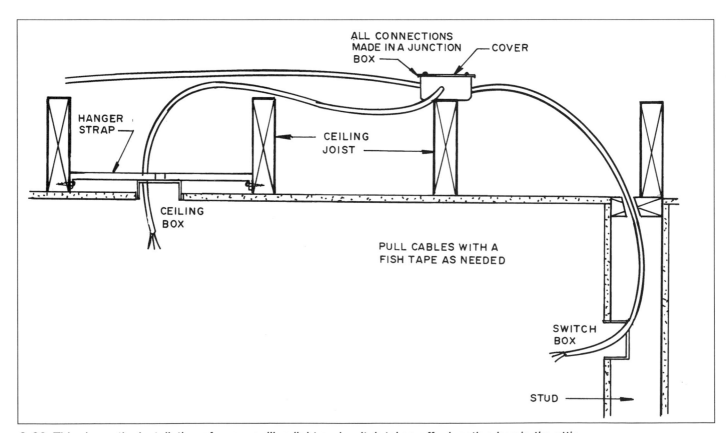

2–96. This shows the installation of a new ceiling light and switch taken off a junction box in the attic.

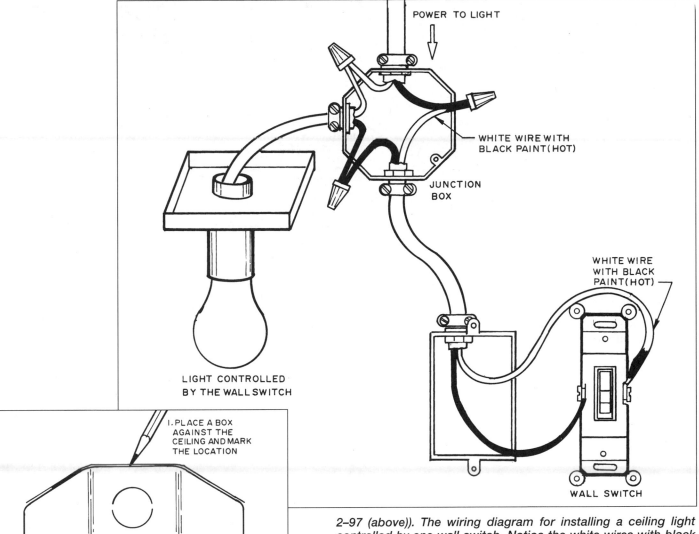

POWER TO LIGHT

WHITE WIRE WITH
BLACK PAINT(HOT)

JUNCTION
BOX

WHITE WIRE
WITH BLACK
PAINT(HOT)

LIGHT CONTROLLED
BY THE WALL SWITCH

WALL SWITCH

2–97 (above)). The wiring diagram for installing a ceiling light controlled by one wall switch. Notice the white wires with black print on the end indicating that they are "hot."

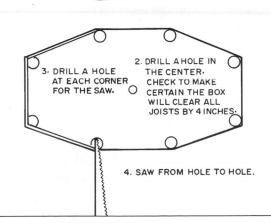

I. PLACE A BOX AGAINST THE CEILING AND MARK THE LOCATION

3. DRILL A HOLE AT EACH CORNER FOR THE SAW.

2. DRILL A HOLE IN THE CENTER. CHECK TO MAKE CERTAIN THE BOX WILL CLEAR ALL JOISTS BY 4 INCHES.

4. SAW FROM HOLE TO HOLE.

2–98 (left). Mark the location of the ceiling box, drill a hole in the center, and check in the attic to see that the box clears the joists. Then drill holes in each corner large enough for a compass saw to enter and cut the opening.

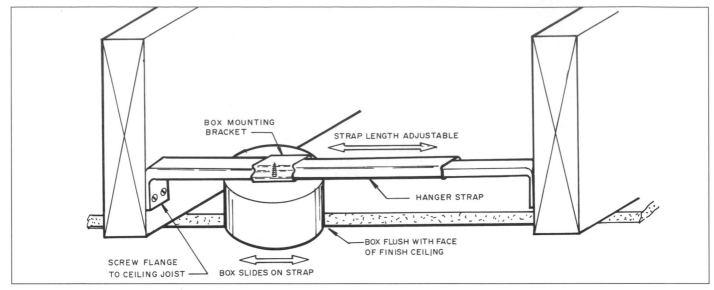

2–99. *The ceiling-light box is hung between ceiling joists with a hanger strap that comes from the store with the box attached. When installing from above, position the box in the hole so that it is flush with the face of the ceiling material. Mark the holes in the flange on the joists. Remove the strap and drill small holes at each mark. Replace the strap and drive screws through the flange into these holes.*

nected to the light fixture and mounted to the box (refer to **2–97**). If the box is mounted next to the joist, one of the boxes shown in **2–100** can be used. Metal boxes have a metal mounting flange, while plastic boxes have large-angled nailing flanges.

A word of caution: When working in the attic, be certain to lay wood boards or plywood sheets on top of the joists to provide a working platform. Do not try to work by standing on the edges of the joists. If the attic has a floor, you will have to remove a couple boards to get to the light location.

Installing a New Light from below the Ceiling

If access to the attic is not possible or the ceiling light is to be installed on the ceiling of a two-story house, a section of the ceiling material will have to be cut out, the hanger strap and box installed, and the ceiling repaired as shown in **2–101**. This illustration relates to a gypsum drywall ceiling.

2–100. *Typical ceiling-light boxes that can be secured directly to the side of a ceiling joist.*

2–101. *When it is not possible to get to the ceiling from above, a section of the drywall will have to be removed to install the ceiling box.*

WOOD SUBFLOOR

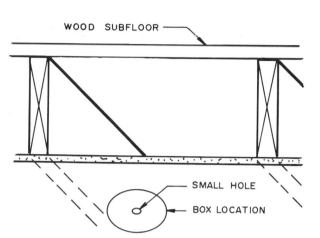

SMALL HOLE

BOX LOCATION

I. LOCATE BOX. DRILL A SMALL HOLE IN THE CENTER.

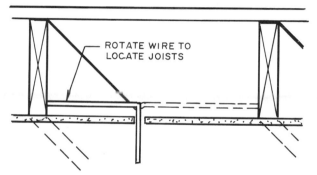

ROTATE WIRE TO LOCATE JOISTS

2. ROTATE A PIECE OF WIRE TO SEE IF THE BOX LOCATION CLEARS THE JOISTS 4 OR 5 INCHES.

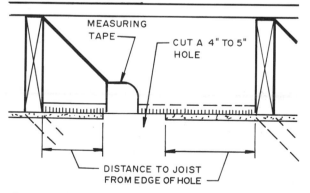

MEASURING TAPE

CUT A 4" TO 5" HOLE

DISTANCE TO JOIST FROM EDGE OF HOLE

3. CUT A HOLE, INSERT A MEASURING TAPE, AND FIND THE DISTANCE THE JOISTS ARE FROM THE EDGE OF THE HOLE.

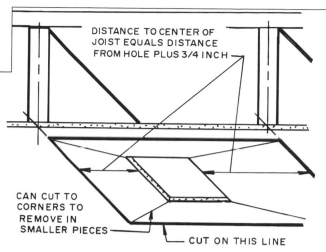

DISTANCE TO CENTER OF JOIST EQUALS DISTANCE FROM HOLE PLUS 3/4 INCH

CAN CUT TO CORNERS TO REMOVE IN SMALLER PIECES

CUT ON THIS LINE

4. MARK TO THE CENTER OF EACH JOIST AND THE WIDTH OF THE PIECE TO BE REMOVED. SCORE REPEATEDLY WITH A UTILITY KNIFE UNTIL YOU CUT THROUGH. CUTTING TO EACH CORNER MAKES IT EASIER TO REMOVE THE PIECES.

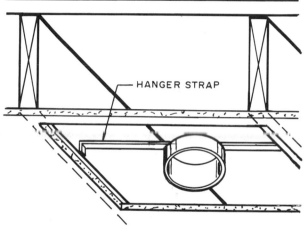

HANGER STRAP

5. REMOVE THE DRYWALL SECTION. INSTALL THE CEILING BOX WITH A HANGER STRAP.

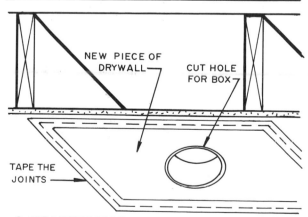

NEW PIECE OF DRYWALL

CUT HOLE FOR BOX

TAPE THE JOINTS

6. CUT A PIECE OF DRYWALL TO FIT THE OPENING. CUT A HOLE FOR THE BOX. NAIL TO THE JOISTS AND TAPE THE JOINT WITH DRYWALL TAPE AND FINISH WITH DRYWALL COMPOUND.

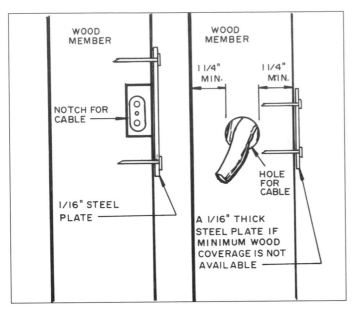

WOOD MEMBER

NOTCH FOR CABLE

1/16" STEEL PLATE

WOOD MEMBER

1 1/4" MIN.   1 1/4" MIN.

HOLE FOR CABLE

A 1/16" THICK STEEL PLATE IF MINIMUM WOOD COVERAGE IS NOT AVAILABLE

2–102. Cables installed in notches and holes in wood members must be protected from nails as specified by the local building code.

Notches and Holes in Wood Members

It may be that it will be helpful if a series of studs or joists are **notched,** forming a channel for running a cable. If this will be done, a metal strip 1/16 inch (1.5 millimeters) thick must be nailed over each notch. This protects the wire in case a nail happens to be driven directly over it (**2–102**).

When boring holes in studs or joists in which the cable will be run, the edge of the hole should be at least 1¼ inches (31.8 millimeters) from the nearest edge of the wood member (**2–102**). If this is not possible, a metal plate will have to be installed. If in doubt, check the local building code.

MAKING CONNECTIONS IN CIRCUITS

All cable connections must be made in an electrical box. Cable must never be spliced and taped.

2–103. Surface-mounted raceway wiring systems use surface-mounted boxes and channels to extend power from an existing source such as a receptacle. This illustration shows a system using plastic boxes and channels (products illustrated courtesy Carlon Electrical Products).

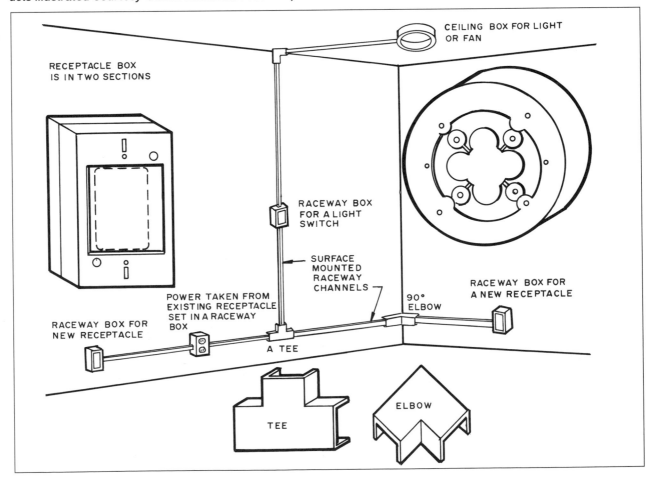

RECEPTACLE BOX IS IN TWO SECTIONS

CEILING BOX FOR LIGHT OR FAN

RACEWAY BOX FOR A LIGHT SWITCH

SURFACE MOUNTED RACEWAY CHANNELS

RACEWAY BOX FOR A NEW RECEPTACLE

90° ELBOW

POWER TAKEN FROM EXISTING RECEPTACLE SET IN A RACEWAY BOX

RACEWAY BOX FOR NEW RECEPTACLE

A TEE

TEE

ELBOW

SURFACE-MOUNTED WIRING

Surface-mounted wiring enables the installation of additional receptacles, lights, switches, and low-voltage wiring such as telephone, speaker, and computer cables without cutting into a wall or ceiling. The system consists of raceways to carry the wire and boxes for the receptacles and lights. It has preformed corners, enabling corners to be turned (**2–103**). Systems are available with plastic and metal components.

The system taps into an existing source of power, generally an existing outlet. Before using any outlet, be certain it is on a circuit that has the capacity to handle a little additional load.

Plastic systems use a two-piece raceway (**2–104**). The base is screwed to the wall or baseboard. Low-voltage raceways have an adhesive back that sticks the base to the surface. Plastic raceways are generally white or ivory. They can be cut with any fine-toothed saw used to cut wood or metal. After cutting, remove any burrs with a file. Remember, the plastic system components will not conduct electricity and therefore are not grounded.

The basic steps to install a plastic surface-mounted wiring system are shown in **2–105**, on the following page. Notice that the power has been taken from an existing receptacle. Following is a typical procedure:

1. Turn off the power to the existing receptacle.

2. Pull the existing receptacle out of its box, but leave the wires connected.

3. Install the back half of the surface-mounted box over the existing box.

4. Install the back half of new boxes at each location.

5. Run the plastic channel from the existing box to the new boxes. Be certain it is level.

6. Run the new wires to each box from the existing box and snap on the cover.

7. Install the outer half of the surface-mounted boxes on each.

8. Connect the wires to the existing receptacle and

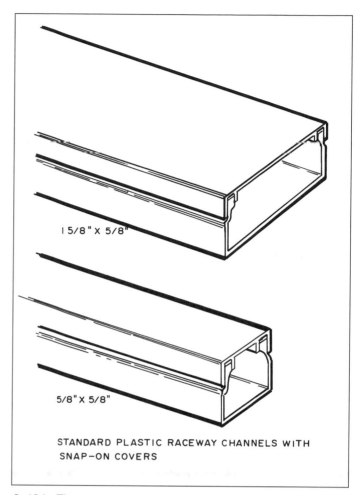

15/8" X 5/8"

5/8" X 5/8"

STANDARD PLASTIC RACEWAY CHANNELS WITH SNAP-ON COVERS

2–104. These are two commonly used standard plastic surface mounted channels (courtesy Carlon Electrical Products).

the new receptacles. Connect the black (hot) wire to the brass screw, the white (neutral) wire to the silver screw, and the ground wire to the green screw. The plastic system is a nonconductor and does not require grounding.

9. Secure the receptacles to the boxes and install the cover plate. Since there is some variance between the systems of different manufacturers, follow their instructions carefully.

The basic steps to installing a metal surface-mounted system are shown in **2–106** on page 133. It basically has the same components as the plastic system. One difference is that the channels are solid tubes and the wires must be pulled through them with fish tape. The system has boxes, ties, elbows, and round ceiling boxes as described for the plastic system.

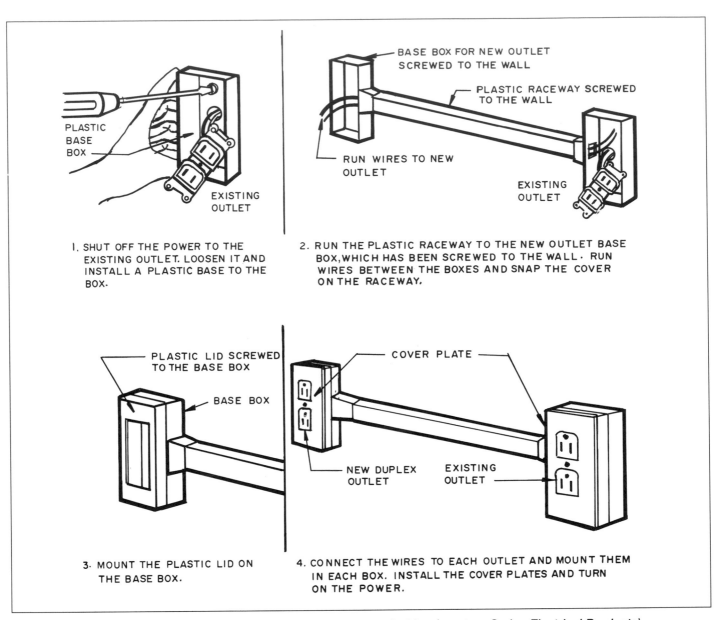

2–105. These steps are typical for installing plastic surface-mounted wiring (courtesy Carlon Electrical Products).

Before installing the system, turn off the power to the outlet that is to provide the current to the new outlets. To install this system, first install the starter box over the original receptacle. Connect the metal raceway to this box and run it to the new box. Cut it to length with a hacksaw and file the end to remove burrs and sharp edges. The metal raceway is mounted to the wall with metal clips that are screwed to the wall. Snap the raceway into the clips. Install elbows and brackets as needed.

Next, install the new box on the end of the raceway. Push the wires through the raceway. It is easiest if you start at an elbow (if there is one) and work the wires both ways. Connect the receptacle, switch, or light as discussed earlier in this chapter. Note that the metal system has the ground wires connected to a terminal at the switch, receptacle, or light fixture box.

Be certain to follow the manufacturer's instructions and ground the system.

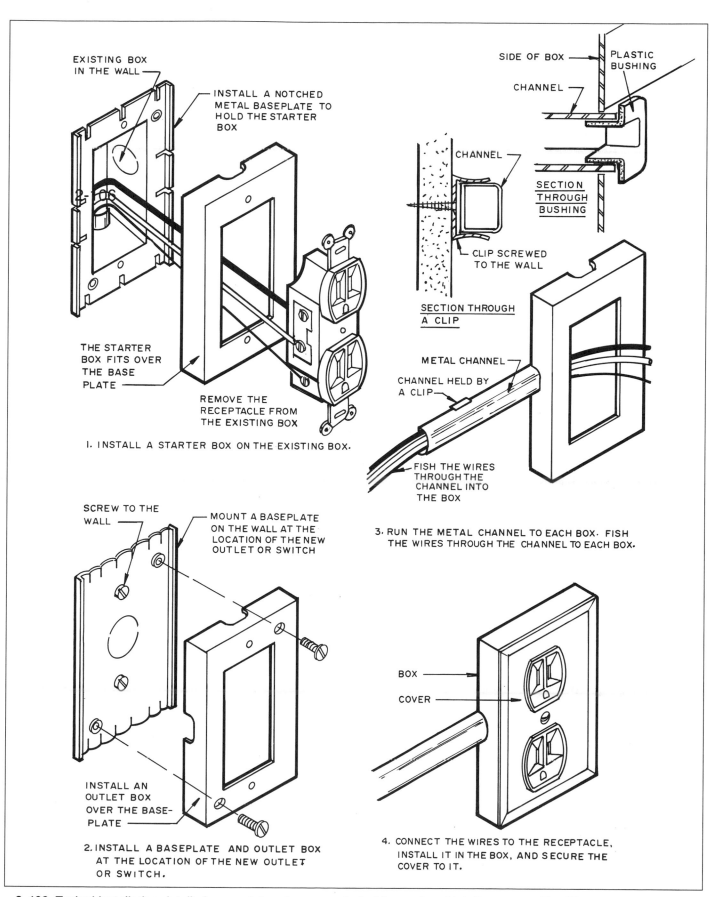

EXISTING BOX IN THE WALL

INSTALL A NOTCHED METAL BASEPLATE TO HOLD THE STARTER BOX

THE STARTER BOX FITS OVER THE BASE PLATE

REMOVE THE RECEPTACLE FROM THE EXISTING BOX

1. INSTALL A STARTER BOX ON THE EXISTING BOX.

SIDE OF BOX

PLASTIC BUSHING

CHANNEL

CHANNEL

SECTION THROUGH BUSHING

CLIP SCREWED TO THE WALL

SECTION THROUGH A CLIP

METAL CHANNEL

CHANNEL HELD BY A CLIP

FISH THE WIRES THROUGH THE CHANNEL INTO THE BOX

3. RUN THE METAL CHANNEL TO EACH BOX. FISH THE WIRES THROUGH THE CHANNEL TO EACH BOX.

SCREW TO THE WALL

MOUNT A BASEPLATE ON THE WALL AT THE LOCATION OF THE NEW OUTLET OR SWITCH

INSTALL AN OUTLET BOX OVER THE BASE-PLATE

2. INSTALL A BASEPLATE AND OUTLET BOX AT THE LOCATION OF THE NEW OUTLET OR SWITCH.

BOX

COVER

4. CONNECT THE WIRES TO THE RECEPTACLE, INSTALL IT IN THE BOX, AND SECURE THE COVER TO IT.

2–106. Typical installation details for a metal surface-mounted wiring system (details courtesy The Wiremold Company).

Surface-Mounted Wiring ■ **133**

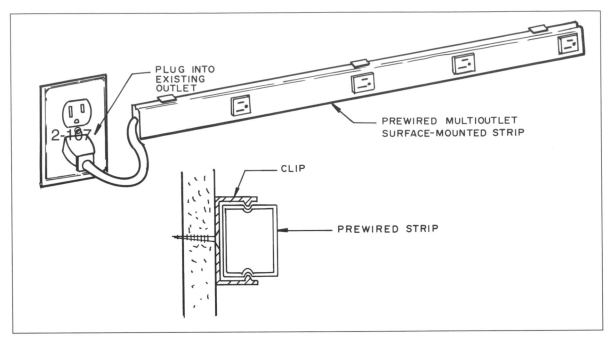

2–107. A prewired multioutlet electrical strip is powered by plugging it into an existing outlet (details courtesy The Wiremold Company).

Another simple surface-mounted device consists of a raceway with receptacles already installed and wired. It is mounted on the wall and plugged into a receptacle (**2–107**).

REPLACING WORN CABLE

When cable insulation has frayed, cracked, or worn, it must be replaced. The cable may not be easy to remove since it is generally inside wall and floor cavities. Before starting, be certain the power to the circuit has been shut off. Check the circuit with a voltage tester.

Disconnect the worn cable from the electrical fixtures. Loosen the cable from the box. Usually the receptacle, switch, or light has to be removed to allow room to work. Perhaps even the box will need to be removed. With luck, the old cable can be used to pull the new cable into place.

To pull new cable with the old one, strip the insulation from about 2 inches (51 millimeters) of each cable. Splice the new cable wires to the ends of the old wires. To make a splice, simply bend one wire into a loop and the other into a hook. Slide the hook through the loop and close the hook. Then wrap the splice with tape. The tape will help prevent the cable from getting caught as it is being pulled through the wall.

Pull the old cable out through a box opening. Have a second person help the process by pushing the new cable into the cavity at the other end. If the old wire is stapled to the studs or runs through holes in the joists, it may not pull through. The solution to such a problem is the same as running cable to a new location. There may be times when the only solution is to cut into the wall, replace the wire, and repair the wall or try to pull the new wire through with fish tape, leaving the old wire in the wall or floor cavity. First try working with small openings near studs, to keep the wall repairs to a minimum. Whenever replacing old circuits, upgrade them to the latest electrical code.

SPLIT-WIRED RECEPTACLES

Most outlets on duplex receptacles are connected to the same power source. However, each side of the receptacle can be connected independently. At the screw terminals of a receptacle is a tab that links the terminals together (**2–108**). Leaving the tab alone

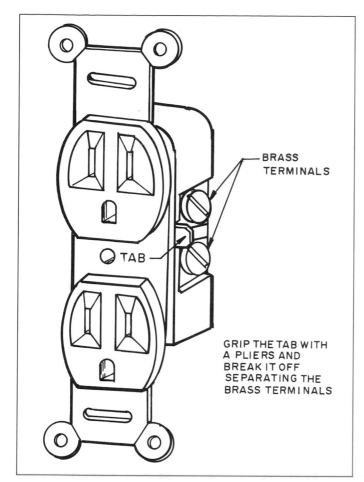

2–108. When the tab connecting the terminals on a duplex receptacle is broken away, each one of the receptacles can be individually controlled.

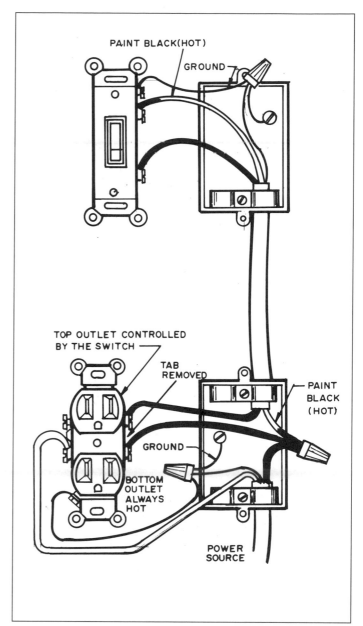

2–109. The top outlet is controlled by the switch in this diagram. The tab has been removed on the "hot" side.

allows one power source to serve both sides of the receptacle. Breaking the brass tab ("hot" side) means that the outlet on the receptacle can be wired separately to a power source. A receptacle wired this way is known as a **split-wired receptacle**. By breaking the tab, one side of the receptacle can be connected to a switch and the other to a different circuit (**2–109**).

OUTDOOR RECEPTACLES

Outdoor receptacles must be waterproof. They are installed in the same way as interior receptacles. The outdoor unit has a waterproof lid that closes over each side of the receptacle (**2–110**). It is very important that an outdoor receptacle be connected to a ground-fault circuit interrupter.

LIGHT CIRCUITS

Before replacing existing light fixtures or switches or installing new ones, it is important to understand the common light circuits in use. There are a variety of ways to control lights with switches. The most simple is when the light fixture contains the switch. The power is connected to the terminals on the fixture (**2–111**). The switch on the fixture controls the flow of electricity to the bulb.

2–110. Outdoor receptacles have waterproof covers and must be connected to a ground-fault circuit interrupter.

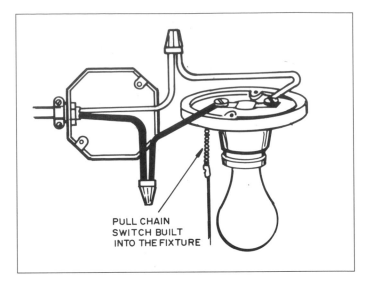

2–111. This light fixture has a pull-chain switch built into it, so no wall switch is required. It is located on the end of a run.

Using a Single-Pole Switch

The circuit that will most frequently be found has a **single-pole switch** controlling a single fixture. The incoming white wire is connected to the white wire on the light. The hot (black) wire is run through the switch and then to the light. The switch has two hot wires, and so both are considered black. Since cable does not come with two black wires inside, the ends of the white wire should be painted black to alert everyone that it is a hot wire.

If the light is at the end of a run on the circuit, wire the switch as shown in **2–112**. This light has the power coming to the ceiling box. If it comes into the switch box, it will be wired as shown in **2–113**. If the light is in the middle of the run, wire it as shown in **2–114**. Note that being in the middle of a run means anywhere along the circuit except the end. In a middle-of-the-run installation, the power source continues past the light to other locations on the circuit.

Using a Three-Way Switch

Use **three-way switches** to control a single light from two locations using two separate switches. Be certain to purchase three-way switches and three-way cable. Three-way cable has an additional black or red wire included. In addition to a neutral wire, two hot wires are needed for this installation. A three-way switch has three terminals. One is marked "common" and is a different color from the others. A push-in connection switch may only have an arrow pointing to the common terminal.

When wiring three-way switches, remember that the incoming hot (black) wire from the power source must connect directly to the common terminal of one of the switches. Then the black wire must be run from the common terminal of the second switch to the black wire or brass terminal screw of the light fixture.

Illus. **2–115** shows a circuit in which the power

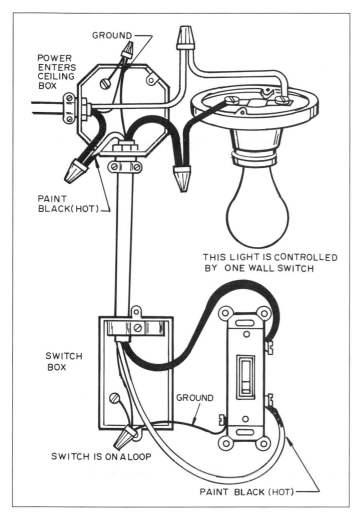

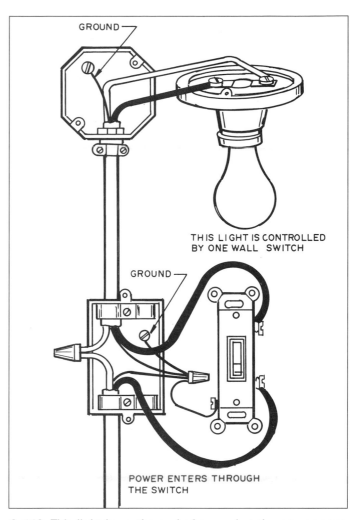

2–112. This light is on the end of a circuit in which the power enters the ceiling box before it goes through a switch. A switch is installed as a loop in the circuit.

2–113. This light is on the end of a run, but the power goes through the switch before it enters the ceiling box.

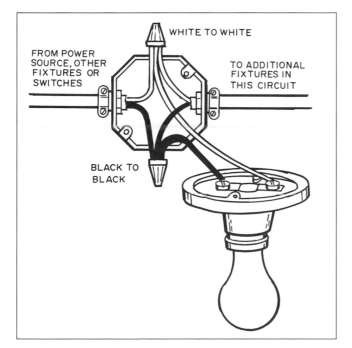

2–114. A light can be added in the middle of a circuit by installing a box and connecting the leads from the light fixture to the wires in the cable.

enters the circuit through a switch and the light is between the switches. Notice the black wire connections to the common terminal. Connect the white wires to each other as shown. The red wire connects a terminal on each switch. Be sure to also connect all ground wires to the proper terminal or to the boxes. If the light is located beyond both switches and the power enters one of the switches, it is wired as shown in **2–116**. The two switches are connected with a three-wire cable.

Another frequently occurring situation is when a light comes before the switches and the power enters the circuit at the light (**2–117**). Again, the incoming black wire is connected to the common terminal on each switch.

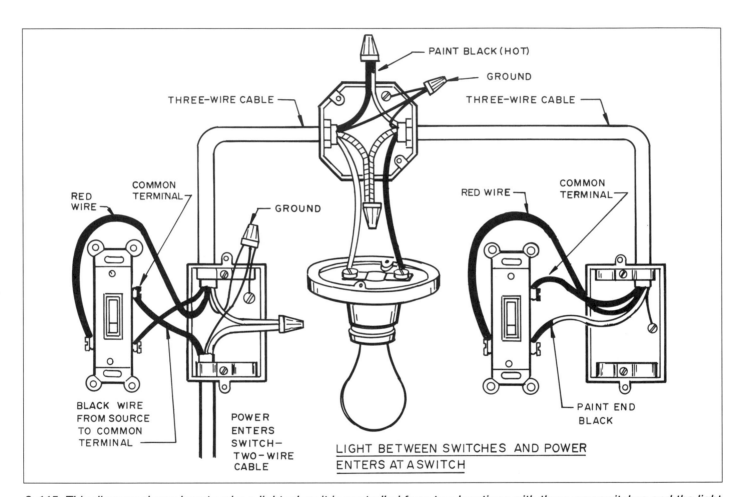

LIGHT BETWEEN SWITCHES AND POWER ENTERS AT A SWITCH

2–115. This diagram shows how to wire a light when it is controlled from two locations with three-way switches and the light is located between the switches. The incoming power-cable black wire is connected to the common terminal on the first switch, and the red and black wires from the outgoing cable are connected to the other two terminals. In the light ceiling box, connect the incoming white wire to the fixture, join the two red wires, and connect the outgoing white wires (painted black on their end) and the incoming black wire from the first switch. Connect the outgoing black wire (from the second switch) to the light fixture. At the second switch, connect the incoming black wire to the common terminal and the red wire and painted white wire to the other two terminals. Connect ground wires as required by code.

2–117 (facing page, at bottom). This diagram shows how to wire a light when it is controlled from two locations with three-way switches, the light is located before the switches, and the power enters at the light. The incoming black wire is connected to the common terminal on the first switch. The switches are connected with a three-wire cable. The black wire is connected to the common terminal on the second switch. The white wire serves as a "hot" wire and is painted black on each end. Connect the ground wires as required by code.

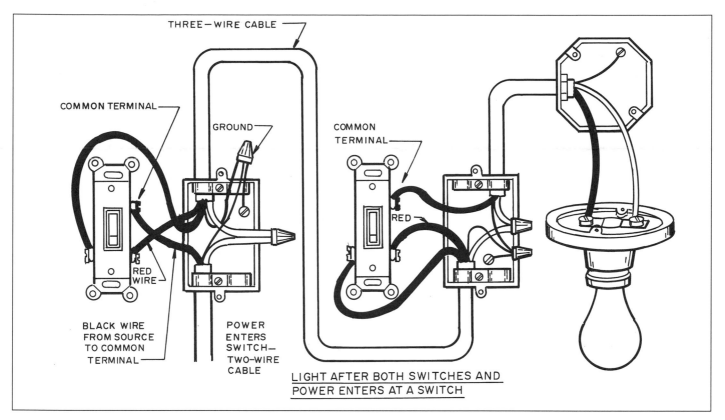

THREE—WIRE CABLE

COMMON TERMINAL

GROUND

COMMON TERMINAL

RED

RED WIRE

BLACK WIRE FROM SOURCE TO COMMON TERMINAL

POWER ENTERS SWITCH— TWO-WIRE CABLE

LIGHT AFTER BOTH SWITCHES AND POWER ENTERS AT A SWITCH

2–116. This diagram shows how to wire a light when it is controlled from two locations with three-way switches and the light is located beyond the switches. The incoming power cable black wire is connected to the common terminal on the first switch, and the red and black wires from the outgoing cable are connected to the other two terminals. These are then connected to the second switch, and the black wire from the outgoing cable is connected to the common terminal and to the light fixture. The white wires are connected in each box and to the light fixture.

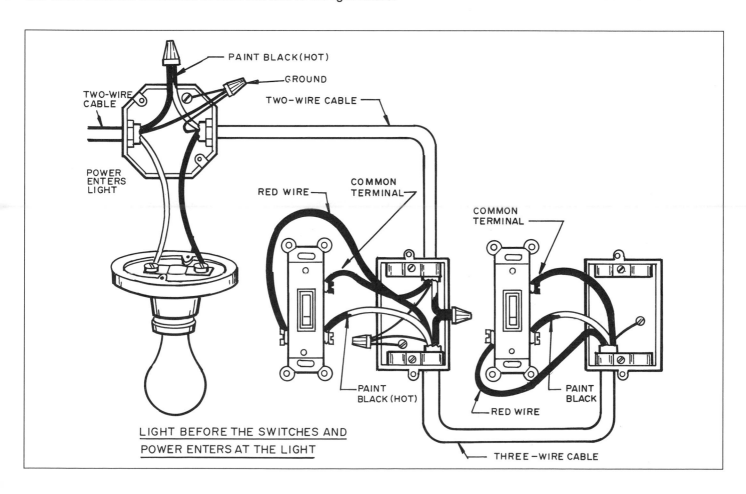

PAINT BLACK(HOT)

GROUND

TWO-WIRE CABLE

TWO-WIRE CABLE

POWER ENTERS LIGHT

RED WIRE

COMMON TERMINAL

COMMON TERMINAL

PAINT BLACK (HOT)

PAINT BLACK

RED WIRE

LIGHT BEFORE THE SWITCHES AND POWER ENTERS AT THE LIGHT

THREE—WIRE CABLE

POLARIZATION

The wiring in your home should have receptacles with a narrow slot for the hot (black) wire, a wider slot for the neutral (white) wire, and a round slot for the ground wire (usually bare or green). The plugs to fit into these outlets likewise must be polarized. This means the plug has prongs designed to fit into the openings in the receptacle in only one way (2–118).

A polarized cord is shown in 2–119. The large prong can only enter the neutral opening, so the hot (black) wire carries the current to the switch. When the switch is off, no current can reach the lamp socket. It can be touched when a bulb is being changed and there will be no shock.

If the receptacles and plugs are not polarized, an appliance can be plugged in with its "hot" side on the neutral side and the neutral side on the "hot" side. This means that the neutral wire leaving the appliance or tool is hot and can produce a shock even if it is off. A shock is even possible with a table lamp that is not polarized, when the metal socket is touched even if the lamp is turned off — because the current is not going through the switch but directly to the socket (2–120).

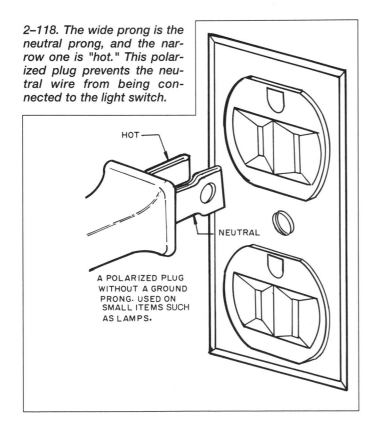

2–118. The wide prong is the neutral prong, and the narrow one is "hot." This polarized plug prevents the neutral wire from being connected to the light switch.

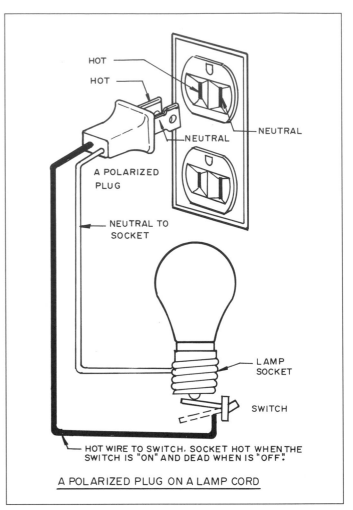

A POLARIZED PLUG ON A LAMP CORD

2–119. This polarized cord has a plug with a wide prong that fits only into the wide opening in the polarized receptacle. This prevents the "hot" wire (black) from running to the switch of the appliance. No current flows through the appliance when the switch is "off."

REPAIRING EXTENSION AND LIGHT-DUTY STRANDED CORDS

When choosing a cord, it should have a wire diameter large enough to carry the expected load over the length of the cord. Long cords provide additional resistance, which causes the voltage to be lower at the end; this affects the operation of the tool connected to the cord and is hard on the motor. **Table 2–4** gives some recommendations for selecting the cord. The longer the cord and the higher the amperage of the consuming tool, the larger the wire diameter required.

Extension cords are usually handled rather roughly and frequently abused. Therefore, they are

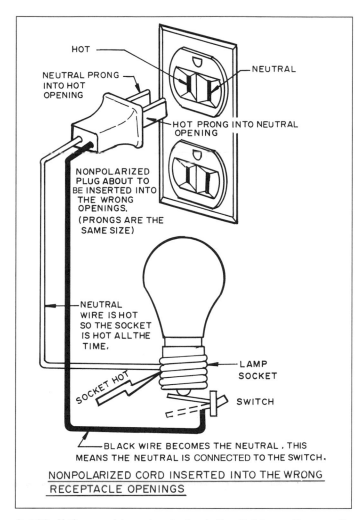

2–120. If the cord is not polarized, the light or other appliance can be turned off by the switch, but the current continues to flow through it in the "hot" wire.

TABLE 2-4 RECOMMENDED WIRE SIZES AND AMPERAGE REQUIREMENTS FOR EXTENSION CORDS OF VARIOUS LENGTHS

Amperage Consumption of Appliance	Length (Feet)	Length (Meters)	Wire Size (Gauge Number)
Up to 7	50	15.25	16
	100	30.5	12
	200	61	10
8 to 12	50	15.25	14
	100	30.5	10
	200	61	8
12 to 18	25	7.61	4
	50	15.25	12
	100	30.5	8
	200	61	6

subject to damage. Regularly examine extension and lamp cords for damage. These cords contain stranded, not solid, wire to make them flexible. When making most connections, the strands of bare wire have to be twisted to keep them all together. Remember, extension cords are for temporary use. They should not be used in place of a permanent installation.

If the insulation on a cord is cut or cracking from age or exposure, discard the cord. While temporary repairs may be made with electrical tape, it is a good investment to replace the cord. Heavy-duty extension cords used outside are exposed to the ground and moisture and must be fully sealed. Lamp cords and those on other small appliances could cause a shock or a fire. The cost is very small to replace the entire cord.

A **grounded extension cord** contains three wires. A continuity test can be made on this kind of cord. The third wire is the ground wire. It is green and should be connected to the grounding prong on a plug. The grounding prong is round, while the other prongs are flat (**2–121**). This is a polarized plug.

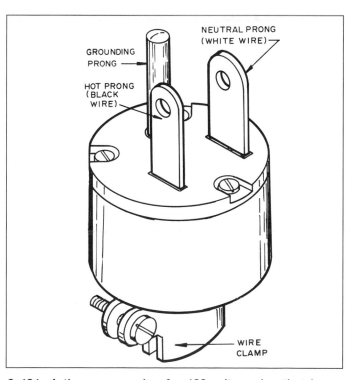

2–121. A three-prong plug for 120-volt service that has a grounding prong. It has a wider prong for the neutral (white) wire, which prevents the neutral wire from being connected through the light switch. This type of plug is referred to as a polarized plug.

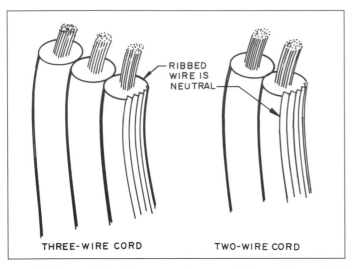

2–122. Some light-duty extension cords have the neutral wire ribbed so that they can be correctly installed using polarized plugs.

A two-wire cord is used for both lamps and light-duty extension cords. The insulation covering one wire on a two-wire cord may be ribbed (**2–122**). The ribbed conductor represents the neutral (white) wire. Fasten it to the silver screw of a plug or socket. The remaining wire is the hot (black) wire. Connect it to the brass screw of a plug or socket.

REPLACING PLUGS AND CONNECTORS

Examine the plug on a cord. It should cover the exposed ends of the wires and be free from damage. If the plug is damaged or the prongs are loose, replace it. To remove an old plug, cut the cord about 2 inches (51 millimeters) away from the plug. The section of cord close to the plug gets the most use

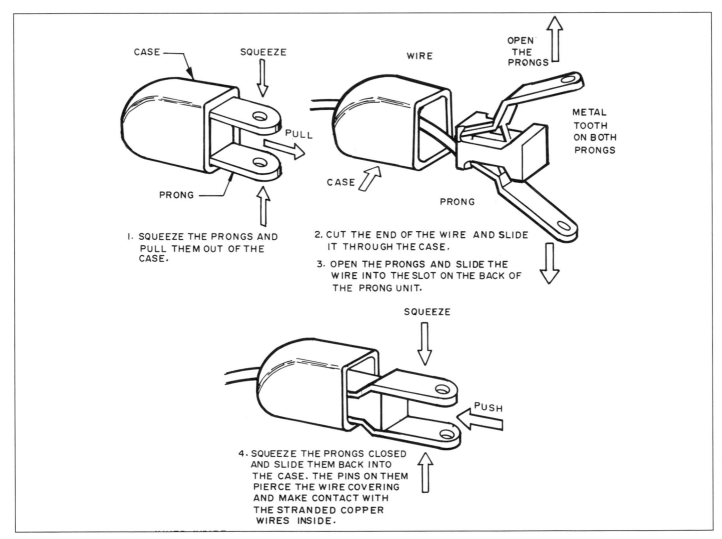

2–123. Installing one type of light-duty plug used on small electrical cords such as those found on lamps and radios. It has pins on the prongs that pierce the wire insulation and make contact with the stranded copper wire inside.

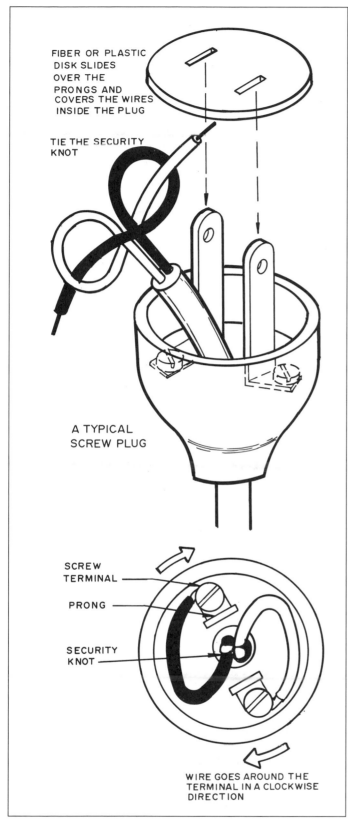

FIBER OR PLASTIC DISK SLIDES OVER THE PRONGS AND COVERS THE WIRES INSIDE THE PLUG

TIE THE SECURITY KNOT

A TYPICAL SCREW PLUG

SCREW TERMINAL

PRONG

SECURITY KNOT

WIRE GOES AROUND THE TERMINAL IN A CLOCKWISE DIRECTION

2–124. This type of screw-connection plug is used on light- and medium-duty appliances and extension cords.

because of bending, and is likely to be weaker than the rest of the cord — and so should be removed. When removing a plug from a receptacle, grip and pull the plug, never the cord. Pulling on the cord alone may either break the cord or pull the wires off the plug terminals.

A variety of replacement plugs are available. Plugs may be connected by piercing the cord insulation or with screw or clamp terminals. Some replacement plugs have features that attempt to reduce the strain on the electrical connections. Some plugs have a casing that grips the wires when it is screwed together. Some others have a clamp that grips the cord. Those used where grounding is intended have a third prong for the ground wire. It is round, while the others are flat (refer to **2–121**).

The installation of an **insulation-piercing plug** varies from brand to brand. The one shown in **2–123** is typical. This type of plug is used on light-duty appliances such as clocks, radios, lamps, and light-duty extension cords. Other designs of piercing plugs are available.

There are many types of screw terminal plugs. Some are for two-wire light- and medium-duty cable, while others are for three-wire cable used when grounding is required. Some have a wire clamp to provide strain relief if the cord is pulled from the outlet (refer to 2–121).

To install a new plug with screw terminals, slide the end of the wire through the shell (**2–124**). Separate the wires of the cord about an inch. Strip the insulation about ½ inch (12.5 millimeters) from the end of the wires. Tie a strain-relief knot (called an **underwriter's knot,** and shown in **2–124**) in the wire. This helps prevent the wires from being pulled loose from the screws. Twist the wire strands together and wrap the wire around the screws in a clockwise direction. Tighten each screw. Another type of plug with screw terminals for light-duty cords is shown in **2–125** on page 144.

Some two-prong plugs and receptacles are polarized. A polarized plug has one prong wider than the other. A polarized receptacle has one slot wider than the other. This arrangement permits a plug to be inserted into a receptacle in only one way. Doing so ensures that the hot wire of the plug is matched to

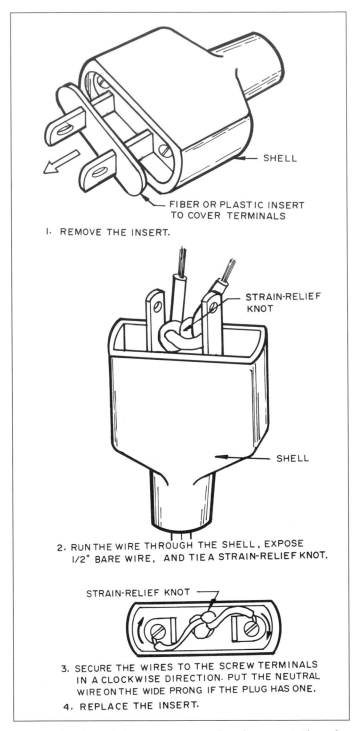

1. REMOVE THE INSERT.

2. RUN THE WIRE THROUGH THE SHELL, EXPOSE 1/2" BARE WIRE, AND TIE A STRAIN-RELIEF KNOT.

3. SECURE THE WIRES TO THE SCREW TERMINALS IN A CLOCKWISE DIRECTION. PUT THE NEUTRAL WIRE ON THE WIDE PRONG IF THE PLUG HAS ONE.

4. REPLACE THE INSERT.

2–125. Another of the many types of replacement plugs for light-duty cords such as those used on clocks and lamps. This type has screw terminals.

the hot wire of the receptacle. *Connect the hot (black) wire to the narrow prong of the plug and the narrow slot and the neutral (white) wire to the wide prong.*

There are a variety of screw terminal connectors. They are installed much like the plug. A typical example is shown in **2–126**. A connector is on the end of an extension cord and receives a plug.

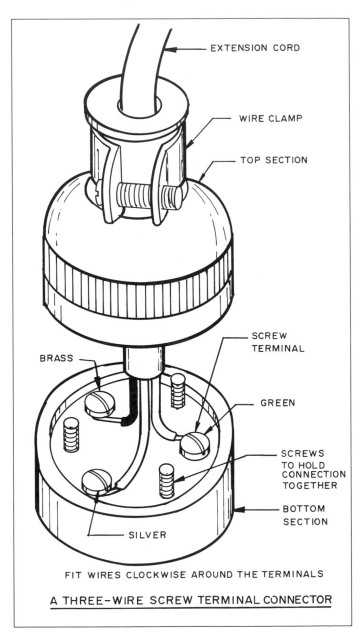

FIT WIRES CLOCKWISE AROUND THE TERMINALS

A THREE-WIRE SCREW TERMINAL CONNECTOR

2–126. A connector is placed on one end of an extension cord and a plug from a power tool is plugged into it. This connector has a ground terminal (green).

FEED-THROUGH SWITCHES

Feed-through switches are installed directly on the cord of an appliance. Light-duty switches, such as those for a lamp, have insulation-piercing connections. Heavy-duty switches usually connect with screw terminals. The procedure for installing either kind is about the same. Always follow the directions supplied by the manufacturer of the switch.

Following is a procedure for one brand of switch (**2–127**):

1. Make certain the cord is not connected to the power.

2. Cut the hot wire as directed.

3. Lay the wire into the back side of the switch case. Place the front side over it and tighten the screw that holds the switch together. Be certain to get the hot and neutral wires in the proper locations. When the screw closing the switch is tightened, this forces metal points into the hot wire, enabling the switch mechanism behind the wheel to open and close the circuit.

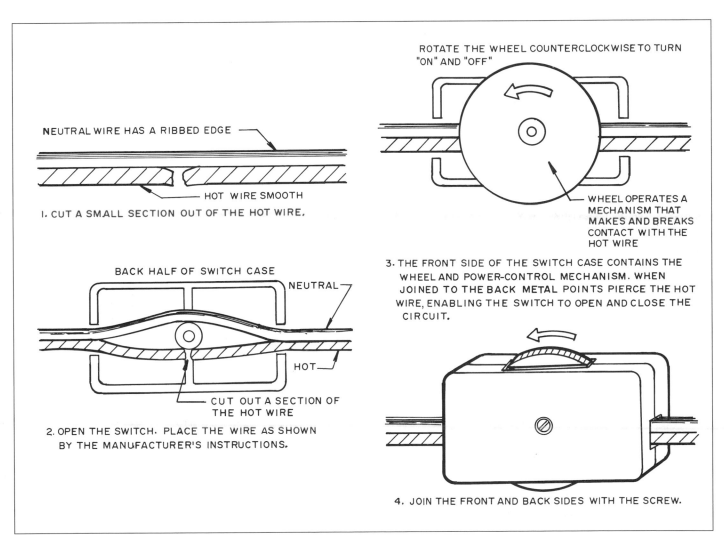

2–127. A feed-through switch mounts on the cord. The "hot" wire is cut and the circuit is controlled by a mechanism behind the control wheel that connects and disconnects the hot wire.

LAMP REPAIR

If a lamp flickers or will not light, it may be due to one or more possible problems. The first item to check is the bulb. Remove the old bulb and test it in a lamp that is working. If the bulb does not light, install a new one in the original lamp. If the new bulb does not light, plug the lamp into another circuit that is known to be operating. If it still does not light, the cord, plug, or socket may be defective.

Remove the plug from the receptacle. Open the socket, exposing the wires (**2–128**). Check the connections to the plug and socket terminals to be certain they are tight. Check the cord for continuity as explained earlier in this chapter. If each seems to be in working order, check the socket as follows:

1. To check the socket for an open circuit, remove it from the lamp. Connect the alligator clamp of a continuity tester to the metal-threaded socket and touch the probe to the silver (neutral) screw terminal. The tester will light if the neutral circuit is intact (**2–129**).

2. Next, check the socket switch. Connect the alligator clip to the brass (hot) screw terminal and touch the contact in the center of the socket. Turn the switch on and then off. The tester should light when the socket is on. If not, replace it (**2–130**). Do not attempt to repair a socket. Replace it with a new one.

To remove the socket from a lamp, begin by unplugging the lamp. Then squeeze the shell of the socket at the point marked "press" and lift off the shell. Unscrew the wire terminal screws and lift off the socket (**2–128**).

To install a new socket, screw the cap on the threaded pipe in the center of the lamp. Run the wire through the pipe, leaving enough to connect to the socket and tie a strain-relief knot. Connect the wires to the brass and silver screw terminals. Secure the neutral wire to the silver terminal. Place the insulated sleeve over the socket and the outer shell over this while pressing them down into the cap. The serrated edges will snap them together (**2–131**).

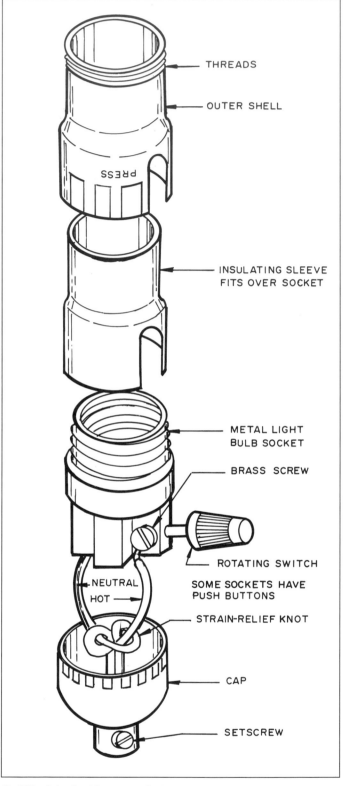

2–128. A typical lamp socket.

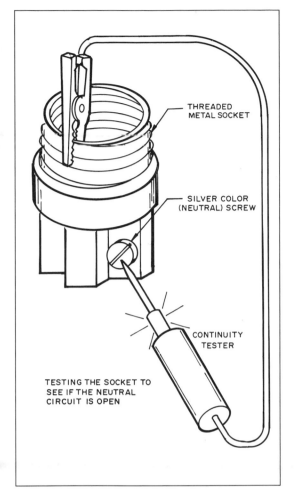

THREADED
METAL SOCKET

SILVER COLOR
(NEUTRAL) SCREW

CONTINUITY
TESTER

TESTING THE SOCKET TO
SEE IF THE NEUTRAL
CIRCUIT IS OPEN

2–129. If the continuity tester does not light, it means there is an open circuit in the neutral side of the socket.

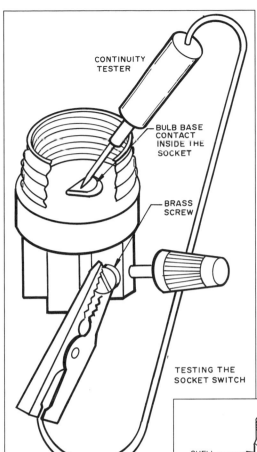

CONTINUITY
TESTER

BULB BASE
CONTACT
INSIDE THE
SOCKET

BRASS
SCREW

TESTING THE
SOCKET SWITCH

2–130 (left). Test the switch to see if it is working. Turn the switch on and off. If it is working, the continuity tester will light when "on" and go "off" when the switch is turned off.

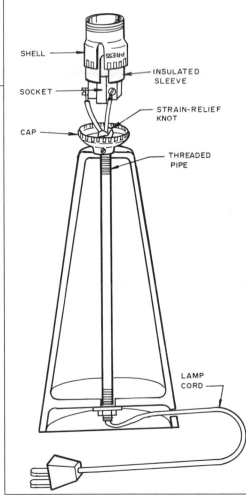

SHELL

SOCKET

CAP

INSULATED
SLEEVE

STRAIN-RELIEF
KNOT

THREADED
PIPE

LAMP
CORD

2-131 (right). Installing a new switch.

Lamp Repair ■ **147**

CHAPTER THREE

Heating and Air-Conditioning

Heating and air-conditioning systems need periodic care to keep them operating efficiently. This chapter presents ideas of how heating and air-conditioning systems operate and the routine maintenance that can be done to keep them running smoothly. Also discussed is the effect humidity has on comfort control and the steps that can be taken to control humidity.

Let's begin with heating systems.

HEAT FLOW

Heat moves from a hot material to a cold material. The flow will occur by convection, conduction, or radiation.

Thermal convection occurs when heat is transferred by the circulation of a heated liquid, gas, or air. Hot-air furnaces and hot-water systems use convection to heat the air in a room.

Thermal conduction occurs when heat is transferred through a material. Touch something cold and heat from your body will transfer to it. Touch something hot and your body will absorb heat from it.

Thermal radiation occurs when heat energy is projected by a source through space and is absorbed by the surface it strikes. The sun radiates heat to warm the earth. It is also used by solar collectors, which move the collected heat into a building.

EFFICIENCY-PERFORMANCE RATINGS

The National Appliance Energy Conservation Act established minimum efficiency-performance rat-

ings for heating and cooling equipment. Before buying a new system, be certain to check these ratings.

Annual Fuel Utilization Efficiency (AFUE) is a ratio of the annual fuel output energy to the annual input energy. Typical minimum ratings for gas- and oil-fired warm-air furnaces are 78 percent and for oil- and gas-fired hot-water boilers 80 percent. The higher the percent, the more efficient the heating unit.

Seasonal Energy Efficiency Ratio (SEER) is the total cooling output of an electric air conditioner in Btu/h (British thermal units/hour) divided by the total electric energy input in watt-hours. SEER minimum ratings vary with the different types of cooling units and range from 6 to 10 or even higher. The higher the SEER, the more efficient the cooling unit.

Heat-pump cooling efficiency is also indicated by its **seasonal energy-efficiency ratio**. A typical minimum rating is 6.6 to 10.0 SEER. The heating cycle is rated by it **heated seasonal performance factor** (HSPF). A typical minimum rating is 6.6 to 6.8 HSPF.

TYPES OF HEATING SYSTEMS

Heating systems are either fired by natural gas, propane, oil, or electricity. Cooling systems are electrically operated. While reading the discussion of these systems in the following pages, remember there are many brands and while they are similar some will have different requirements and design features. Those discussed in this chapter are typical of most systems. It is important to get the manuals on the system from the manufacturer so that there is access to the correct details about it.

The commonly used heating systems are forced warm air through ducts, hot water or steam moved to radiators through pipes, and individual electric heating units in each room. Each is discussed below.

FORCED WARM-AIR SYSTEMS

Forced warm-air heating systems heat air in a furnace that is fired by gas, oil, or electricity. Air may also be heated by a heat pump or solar panels. The heated air is forced through pipes, called **ducts**, by a blower. The air blows through outlets, called **registers,** in each room of the house. The system is simple and easy to maintain.

Duct systems and the location of the furnace in homes will vary, and it is important to examine yours to know where the pipes run. If the house has a basement, the furnace will usually be located there. Air heated by an upflow furnace will be blown up into an extended plenum running the length of the house. From the plenum, the heated air is directed to the registers by ducts (**3–1**). If the house is over a crawl space, the upflow furnace can move air up to ducts run in the attic, or a downflow furnace that will blow heated air down into ducts under the floor can be used (**3–2**).

Some furnaces are designed to be installed horizontally and are placed in the attic or in a crawl space under the floor (**3–3**). A house built on a concrete-slab foundation can use either a downflow furnace that forces air into ducts placed in the concrete floor or an upflow furnace that forces air into ducts placed in the attic. Ducts located in the attic or under the floor should be insulated to prevent heat loss or gain. Some prefer to insulate all ductwork so that temperature can be controlled more accurately.

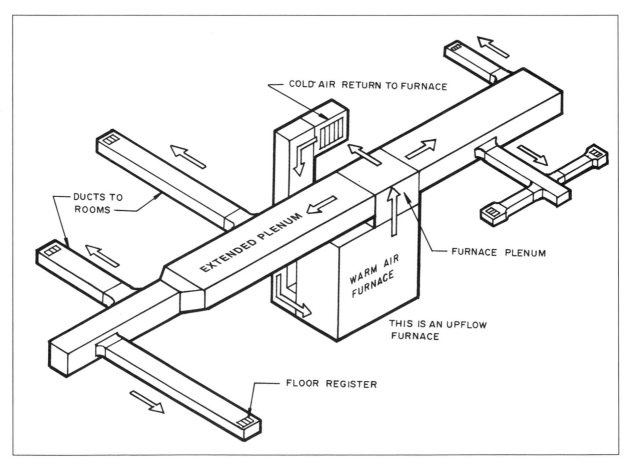

3–1. *This is a typical warm-air heating installation. The furnace plenum is extended the length of the house, and ducts to the various rooms are taken off it as needed. Notice the large cold-air return that carries the air in the house back to the furnace.*

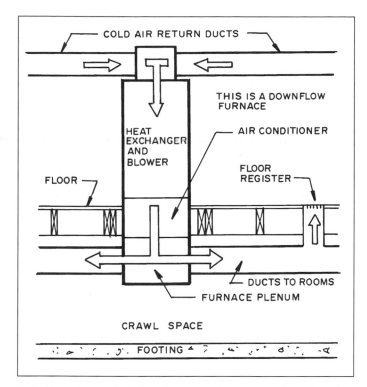

3–2. If the house is built with a crawl space, a downflow furnace can be used and the ducts run below the floor.

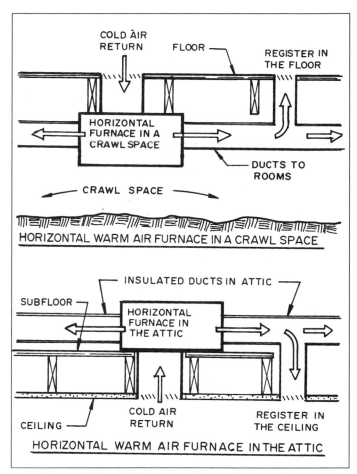

3–3. Horizontal warm-air furnaces can be installed in a crawl space or the attic.

When remodeling, locate the furnace near the center of the building. Doing so keeps the ducts to the various rooms as short in length as possible. Short ducts will, of course, deliver hotter air than long ducts. Locate registers in the floor along an exterior wall under a window when possible. The heated air should flow up the face of the exterior wall, forming a curtain of heated air that is needed to keep the occupants of the house comfortable. Do not locate registers on inside walls.

As the heated air cools, it settles to the floor and is returned to the furnace through another set of ducts, forming the **cool-air return system**. Return-air registers are located on inside walls.

Maintaining a Warm-Air System

The air filter of a warm-air system needs to be checked frequently — at least once a month during the heating season. A dirty filter needs to be cleaned or replaced. **Disposable filters** are easily and quickly replaced. Make sure there is a good supply of them at the beginning of the heating season. Some filters are permanent and may be cleaned by washing with mild soap and water. If the system includes an electronic air cleaner, remove and wash its filter often. How often depends upon the amount of dust and pollen in the air, but it could need washing every three or four weeks.

The inside of the blower chamber and the section with the filter should be vacuumed several times a year. Also, remove the heat registers and vacuum the dust from them at least once a year (see **3–4** on page 152).

The electric-blower motor and the blower bearings generally do not need lubrication. Both the motor and bearings are usually lubricated to last the life of the unit. However, if either does have oil fittings, lubricate the fittings with 20-weight nondetergent oil once or twice a year. Do not overlubricate the electric motor. It needs only two or three drops of oil. Using too much oil will allow it to get into the motor and cause coil damage.

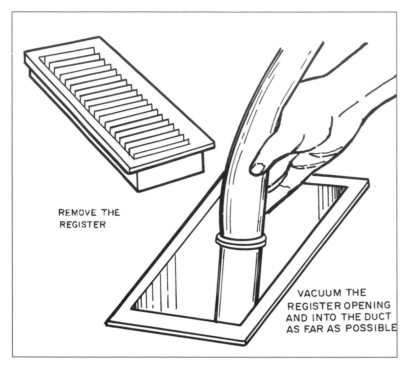

REMOVE THE REGISTER

VACUUM THE REGISTER OPENING AND INTO THE DUCT AS FAR AS POSSIBLE

3–4. At least once a year, remove the registers and vacuum the ducts.

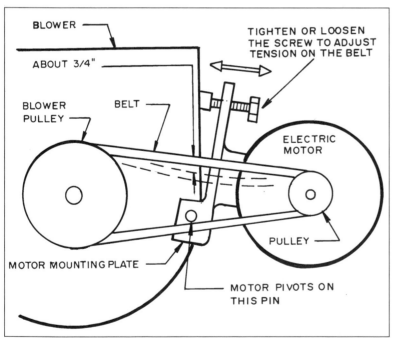

BLOWER

ABOUT 3/4"

TIGHTEN OR LOOSEN THE SCREW TO ADJUST TENSION ON THE BELT

BLOWER PULLEY

BELT

ELECTRIC MOTOR

MOTOR MOUNTING PLATE

PULLEY

MOTOR PIVOTS ON THIS PIN

3–5. A typical belt tension-adjustment mechanism. Other designs are used, but the principle is the same.

Check the tension on the belt between the motor and the blower fan. *Before adjusting the belt or pulleys, turn off the electric power to the blower motor.* The belt should be tight enough to turn the blower fan without slippage, yet not so tight that it places an unnecessary strain on the bearings. The belt should show about ¾-inch (19-millimeter) deflection. That means that when pressing down on the belt midway between the fan and motor, the belt should move only about three-quarters of an inch below its normal position. If the tension has to be changed, adjust a screw connected to the motor mount (**3–5**). If the belt is getting frayed or is cracking, replace it immediately. Take it with you to the heating-supply dealer or an auto-parts dealer for an exact replacement.

If the blower seems to be *running too slow or too fast*, the speed can be changed by adjusting the pulley on the motor. Generally the motor pulley is made in two parts. Each half is attached to the shaft with a setscrew. Loosen the setscrew on the outside half of the pulley and move that half closer to or farther away from the other half. If it is moved closer to the second half, the revolutions per minute will increase and the motor will turn the fan faster. If it is moved away from the second half, the revolutions per minute will decrease and the fan will run more slowly. What this adjustment does is change the diameter of the pulley on the motor (**3–6**). If you are making this adjustment, check the pulley's alignment.

Check to be certain the motor pulley and the blower pulley are in line. If they are not lined up, the belt will rub on one side and wear out quickly. It may also get hot and produce a burned-rubber smell. Check the pulleys for alignment with a framing square as shown in **3–7**. Move the pulley halves on the motor shaft until the alignment is correct. Be certain to maintain the desired pulley diameter while moving these parts.

Check the furnace for loose screws or

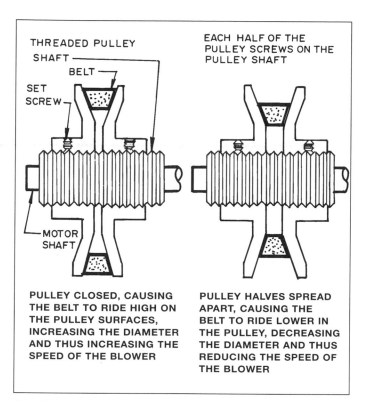

3–6. The speed of the blower can be adjusted by moving the sides of the adjustable pulley mounted on the shaft of the motor.

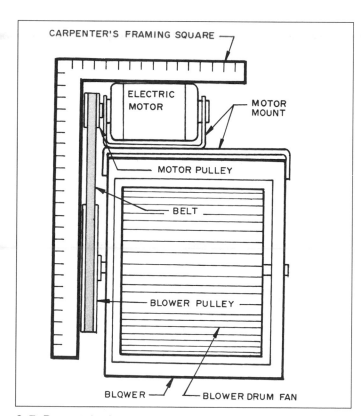

3–7. Be certain the motor and blower pulleys are in perfect alignment or the belt will wear out rapidly. Remember to recheck the alignment if you are adjusting the motor pulley to change the speed of the blower.

other parts. Tighten whatever is loose. Check the ducts wherever it possible to see if there are any leaks in the joints or if the joint tape is coming loose. Remove old loose tape and replace it with new duct tape. Repair or replace any duct insulation that is holding it in place.

If the furnace has a humidifier, check to see if minerals in the water have started to coat the intake valve and the mechanism used to put the moisture in the heated air. The chamber, valve, and float may have to be cleaned.

Balancing a Warm-Air System

Generally the intent is to have some rooms in the house receive more heat than others. Bedrooms are usually kept cooler than the living room. The kitchen generates heat from cooking and so requires less heat from the furnace. The warm-air system must be balanced to get the right amount of heat (or air conditioning) to each room. Follow these procedures to balance the heating system:

1. Set the thermostat on one setting, say 70° F (22° C), for several hours. Run the furnace with all the registers and dampers in the ducts open. Leave the doors open between rooms.

2. Put thermometers in each room and read the temperature three feet (one meter) off the floor.

3. If a room is hotter than it should be, partially close the registers. Remember, this forces more hot air (or cool air) into the other rooms.

4. Continue adjusting the registers until each room remains at a temperature close to the temperature desired. This may take a long time to get some type of balance, but it will improve the overall situation. Dampers in the ducts provide better control over airflow than registers.

Some systems have dampers in the pipes. To balance the system, adjust the dampers to change the amount of airflow. The damper is fully open when the handle on the damper is parallel with the duct. The damper is fully closed when the handle is perpendicular to the duct (3–8). Adjust the damper until the room maintains the temperature desired for several hours.

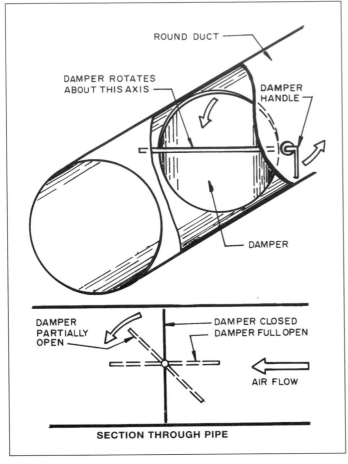

ROUND DUCT

DAMPER ROTATES
ABOUT THIS AXIS

DAMPER
HANDLE

DAMPER

DAMPER
PARTIALLY
OPEN

DAMPER CLOSED
DAMPER FULL OPEN

AIR FLOW

SECTION THROUGH PIPE

3–8. Dampers can be placed in round and rectangular ducts to help control airflow as the room temperature is maintained.

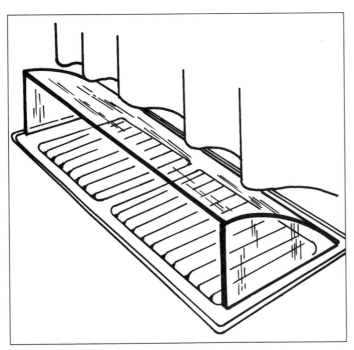

3–9. Transparent heat deflectors can be placed on warm-air registers to direct the flow of air.

If the ducts do not have dampers, it may be possible to buy and install them. Be sure to buy the right-size damper to fit the ducts.

Balancing the heating system of a two-story house is more difficult than a one-story house. This is so because heat rises and it is more difficult to control the temperature on the second floor. If the stairway to the second floor is enclosed and has a door, it will help to keep it closed during the process. In general, more heat should be released to the first-floor rooms because some will find its way to the second floor.

Adding plastic heat deflectors to each register may help by making it possible to direct the airflow in a needed direction (**3–9**).

STEAM HEATING SYSTEMS

Steam is a mixture of hot water vapor in hot air. Great pressure is created by steam within the heating system, and this pressure moves quickly to the radiators or convectors. A steam boiler is designed to withstand only so much pressure. The boiler has a relief valve that lets off steam if the pressure reaches a dangerous stage. Most valves release pres-

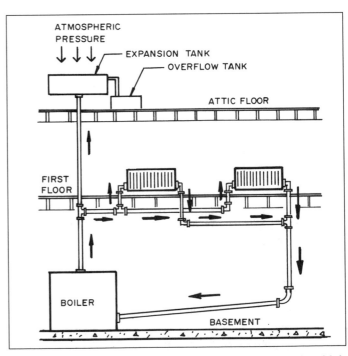

ATMOSPHERIC
PRESSURE

EXPANSION TANK

OVERFLOW TANK

ATTIC FLOOR

FIRST
FLOOR

BOILER

BASEMENT

3–10. A typical gravity-fed hot-water heating system in which the expansion tank is open to the atmosphere. These are found in older homes.

sure at about 15 pounds per square inch. A steam system looks and operates much like a force-fed hot-water system. It is not commonly used in the typical single-family residence.

HOT-WATER SYSTEMS (HYDRONIC SYSTEMS)

Hot-water heating systems may be either **gravity-fed** or **force-fed**. Gravity-fed systems are inefficient but can be found in older houses.

Gravity-Fed Hot-Water Systems

A gravity-fed hot-water system operates as follows. Water in a boiler is heated to about 180° F (82° C) by a gas- or oil-fired boiler. As the water is heated, it expands. The increase in water volume carries it to an expansion tank that is often located in the attic. The tank is open to the atmosphere, so the system is not under pressure. The heated water flows by gravity through pipes to radiators, where it gives off heat. As the water cools, it flows downward and returns to the boiler to be reheated and recirculated (3–10).

The gravity-fed system is slow to respond to sudden drops in temperature because the mass of water in the boiler must be heated before circulation can begin.

If the gravity-fed heating system heats poorly, there may be mineral deposits in the boiler or pipes. The size of the pipe is important for proper circula-

3–12. Currently used cast-iron radiators include freestanding units and baseboard sections (courtesy Burnham Corporation).

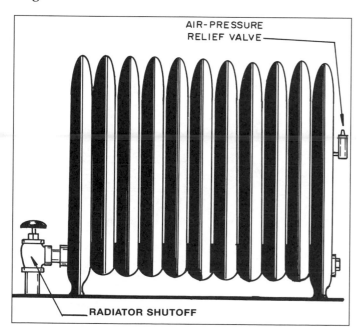
3–11. Cast-iron radiators have been used for years with hot-water heating systems.

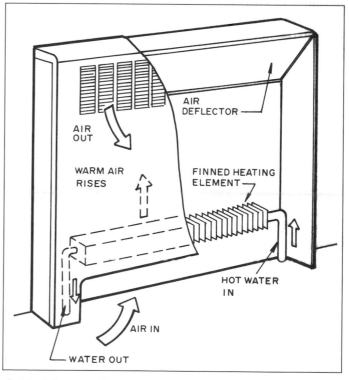
3–13. A freestanding hot-water convector provides efficient distribution of heat because it allows the air to flow over the heating coils.

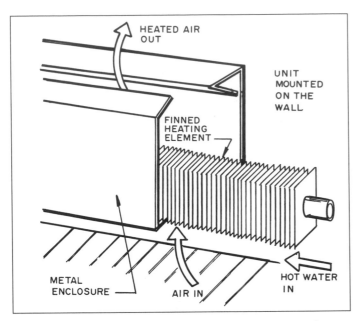

3–14. Finned baseboard hot-water convectors are inconspicuous and effective heating units.

tion. If the water has a heavy mineral content, use a water purifier before the water goes into the boiler.

Forced-Circulation Hot-Water Systems

A forced-circulation hot-water heating system is a closed system. In this system, heated water is moved through pipes and radiators by a pump that keeps it under pressure. The water flows through the circuit and returns to the boiler with some heat left in it. The boiler, then, does not have to raise the water temperature a great deal before recirculation.

Heat is transferred to the air in the room by some form of radiator or convector. Very old systems have **cast-iron radiators** through which the water circulates (**3–11**). Current types of cast-iron radiators are shown in **3–12**. Many systems use a **freestanding convector** that permits cool room air to enter at the bottom and exit, warmed, at the top after passing over heated coils (**3–13**).

Finned baseboard convectors are also available. They operate on a forced-feed hot-water supply. They are small and not noticeable because the piping is hidden, and they are effective heating units (**3–14**).

If there are old-style cast-iron radiators on a forced-feed system, consider replacing them with freestanding or baseboard convectors. These are

more efficient, attractive, and take up less space. Before doing this, check to be certain the boiler will provide the flow required by these replacement units.

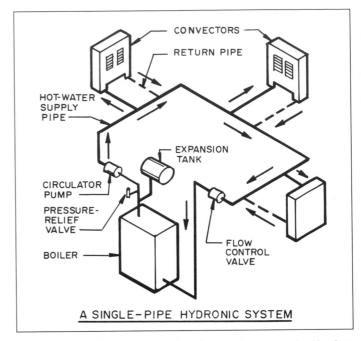

3–15. Single-pipe hot-water heating systems require the hot water to run through each convector and on back to the boiler. The convectors on the end of the run get the water at a greatly reduced temperature.

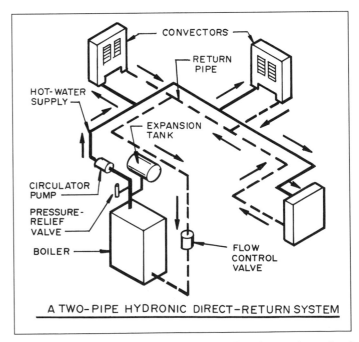

3–16. Two-pipe direct-return hot-water heating systems feed the hot water from the boiler to each convector with one pipe and carry the cooled water back to the boiler with a second pipe.

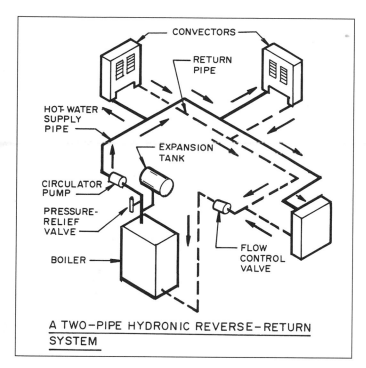

A TWO-PIPE HYDRONIC REVERSE-RETURN SYSTEM

3–17. Two-pipe reverse hot-water heating systems feed the hot water to the convectors from the boiler with one pipe system and return the cooled water in a second pipe system that flows in the same direction as the hot water. This provides about the same pipe resistance to the water flow at each convector, helping to balance the heat at each convector.

In some systems, a thermostat turns on the burner in the boiler and the motor in the pump when the temperature becomes lower than the set point. In other systems, the thermostat turns on the pump and the water-temperature control fires the burner in the boiler. If the water becomes overheated, a high-temperature limit switch shuts off the burner.

The heating system may have one of three different piping systems. The **single-pipe system** is inefficient and no longer used in new construction (**3–15**). The disadvantage with this system is that the heated water runs to the first radiator, then to the second, then the third, and so on through the whole house. Each radiator removes some of the heat from the water. When the water finally arrives at the last radiator, little heat is left and that room is cold.

The **two-pipe direct-return system** has water return to the boiler through a second set of pipes (**3–16**).

In the **two-pipe reversed system**, cooled water from the first radiator moves through a return pipe into which the cooled water from the other radiators

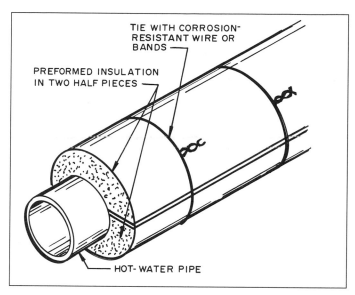

3–18. Hot-water pipes should be insulated to save energy.

also flows (**3–17**). The total flow of water that returns to the boiler has a constant temperature and all radiators are evenly heated.

Adjusting a Hot-Water System

There are a few adjustments that can be done to increase the efficiency of the hot-water heating system. Be certain to check the manual provided by the manufacturer and follow these instructions:

1. Have a service technician adjust the high-limit switch to give brief but more frequent on–off cycles. Doing so will allow better temperature regulation when outdoor temperatures make rapid changes.

2. In very cold weather, increase the pressure in the system. Doing so will increase the heat delivered to the radiators.

3. Too many short-turn elbows in the run of pipe also cut into the efficiency of the system. Replace the short-turn elbows with long-bend elbows in order to reduce resistance to the flow of water.

4. Insulate the pipes to reduce heat loss (**3–18**). This increases the amount of heat sent to the rooms while decreasing the heat to areas where heat is not needed, such as the basement. Insulation made for pipes can be purchased at most building-supply dealers.

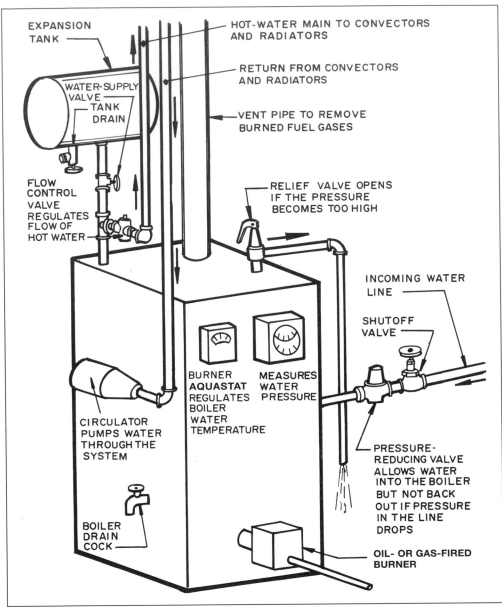

EXPANSION TANK

HOT-WATER MAIN TO CONVECTORS AND RADIATORS

WATER-SUPPLY VALVE

TANK DRAIN

RETURN FROM CONVECTORS AND RADIATORS

VENT PIPE TO REMOVE BURNED FUEL GASES

FLOW CONTROL VALVE REGULATES FLOW OF HOT WATER

RELIEF VALVE OPENS IF THE PRESSURE BECOMES TOO HIGH

INCOMING WATER LINE

SHUTOFF VALVE

BURNER AQUASTAT REGULATES BOILER WATER TEMPERATURE

MEASURES WATER PRESSURE

CIRCULATOR PUMPS WATER THROUGH THE SYSTEM

PRESSURE-REDUCING VALVE ALLOWS WATER INTO THE BOILER BUT NOT BACK OUT IF PRESSURE IN THE LINE DROPS

BOILER DRAIN COCK

OIL- OR GAS-FIRED BURNER

3–19. *A typical hot-water boiler used in residential construction. They sometimes differ slightly, so consult the owner's manual.*

MAINTENANCE FOR HOT-WATER HEATING SYSTEMS

Following are typical maintenance suggestions that can be done to improve the performance of the hot-water heating system. Be certain to review the recommendations in the manufacturer's manual. A simplified drawing of a typical boiler is shown in **3–19**. Consult it while reviewing these maintenance suggestions. The **temperature-pressure gauge** indicates the water temperature and pressure. The **aquastat** maintains the temperature of the boiler

water by starting the burner when the water temperature drops below the operating temperature, which is typically 180° F (83° C).

The **pressure-relief valve** relieves excess pressure within the system. Typically it is set for a maximum of 30 psi. The **air-cushion tank** accommodates expansion of water in the system as it is heated, providing a space for the extra volume of water without creating excessive pressure.

The **pressure-reducing valve** admits water into the system when the pressure drops below that set by the manufacturer, which is typically 12 psi. It has a check valve that prevents water in the boiler from reversing and flowing back into the water line. The **thermostat** fires up the boiler and circulating pump when the air temperature in the room drops below the setting on the thermostat.

Following are some things that can be done to maintain hot-water systems. Also consult the manufacturer's manual.

1. Lubricate the circulating pump motor if it has oil cups with a nondetergent 20-weight oil.

2. Check the entire system for leaks.

3. Vent the radiators in the fall when heating first takes place and occasionally during the winter. Air rises to the top of radiators and convectors and can be let out by opening the valve on each (**3–20**). When water begins to spurt out, close the valve.

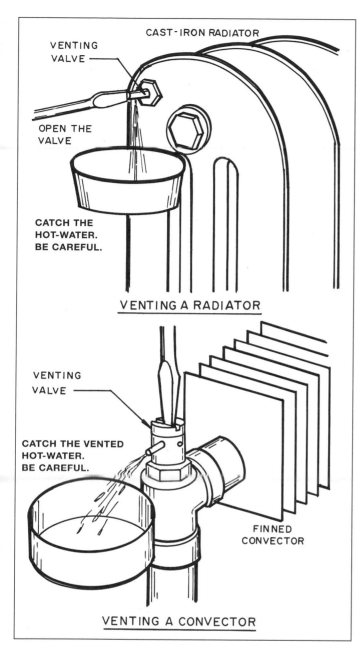

VENTING VALVE

CAST-IRON RADIATOR

OPEN THE VALVE

CATCH THE HOT-WATER. BE CAREFUL.

VENTING A RADIATOR

VENTING VALVE

CATCH THE VENTED HOT-WATER. BE CAREFUL.

FINNED CONVECTOR

VENTING A CONVECTOR

3–20. Typical radiator and convector vents used to bleed air out of the system. The vent on the system may be of a slightly different design than those shown.

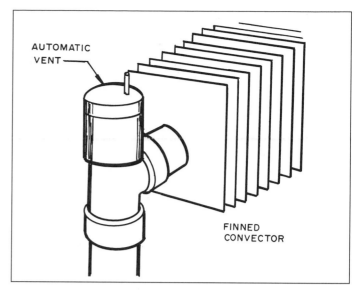

AUTOMATIC VENT

FINNED CONVECTOR

3–21. Automatic vents eliminate the need to regularly vent the hot-water system.

Have a pan to catch any water. Some units have automatic vents that release trapped air as the pressure increases. They close when water touches them. Consider replacing manual vents with automatic vents (**3–21**).

4. Remove rust, loose mineral deposits, and other sediment from the boiler by draining it. Be certain to review the manufacturer's instructions. To do this, shut off the power and water supply. Run a hose from the boiler drain cock and open it (refer

to **3–19**). Open the vent valves on the highest radiators in the house so air can flow into the system, permitting the water to drain. After it has finished draining, open the water-supply valve and flush fresh water through it. After it stops running, close the drain cock and vents and let the boiler fill with water. Some heating contractors recommend putting a rust inhibitor in at this time by removing the relief valve and pouring it into this opening. Keep filling the system as the boiler begins to heat.

If the boiler has a pressure-reducing valve, it will shut off the water flow when the boiler has filled. If there is not a pressure-reducing valve, let the boiler fill until the pressure gauge shows the reading as directed by the manufacturer. Then vent air from each convector until the gauge reads at the operating pressure specified for the boiler.

5. Occasionally the air-cushion tank becomes too full of water, leaving little air in the tank. This will usually force hot water out of the relief valve. To correct this, turn off the electricity to the boiler, close the water-supply valve, and let the water cool. Now drain the water from a valve on the bottom of the tank. When it is empty, close the drain and open the water-supply valve. The tank should be kept about half full.

New systems will have a combination valve on the tank that drains the water and lets air into the tank

(**3–22**). Since this lets air in, the water will drain. On systems without this valve, the water valve below the expansion tank will have to be closed and all the water drained out. Turn on the water to the tank.

Another type of air-cushion tank uses a **diaphragm** between the air and water (**3–23**). The tank connects to an air separator, which has an air vent to release excess air above the water. When the air pressure drops below the specified minimum, water will spray from the relief valve.

The valve on the bottom of the diaphragm tank is for adding air to the bladder side of the tank. When a system loses pressure, it is unlikely that it is the diaphragm tank that has lost air; it is more likely the system has lost water either through valve or shaft seals. So first consider adding water through the water make-up valve.

On many boiler pressure gauges, there is an altimeter scale. Determine the height of the highest baseboard or radiator above the location of the boiler gauge. From the altimeter scale, see what pressure that would be. Add about five pounds to that pressure — this is a safe operating pressure. If the bladder has in fact lost air, either the bicycle air valve has leaked or the bladder has a leak. If the

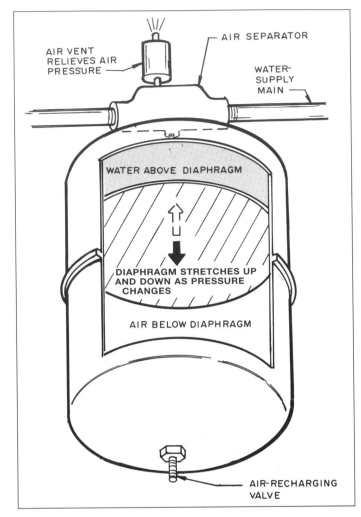

3–23. The diaphragm air-cushion tank uses a rubber diaphragm that flexes as the pressure varies, changing the amount of water and air space in the tank.

bicycle air valve has a slow leak, then a tight cap is needed. If the leak through the valve is fast, a new air-valve insert is needed. If the bladder has a leak, the tank needs to be replaced. The air pressure can be increased using an auto-tire pump connected to the air-recharging valve.

Unless the home owner knows that the system pressure loss is due to a loss of water or a loss of air from the diaphragm tank, it will be best to let a heating contractor determine the cause and allow the contractor to fix the problem.

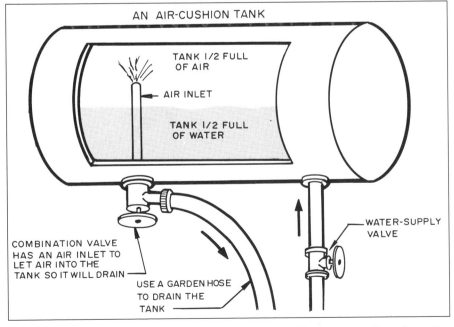

3–22. To drain the air-cushion tank, shut off the power to the boiler, close the water-supply valve, wait until the water cools, and then open the combination valve. On systems without a combination valve, close the valve below the tank on the line from the boiler.

TABLE 3–2. TROUBLESHOOTING A PORTABLE HUMIDIFIER

Problem	Cause	Solution
Humidifier will not run	Has no power	Check fuse or circuit breaker
	Power cord broken	Check power cord with a volt-ohm meter. Repair or replace it.
	Float switch defective	Replace float switch
	Humidistat defective	Replace humidistat
	Fan motor defective	Replace fan motor
Unit runs but provides inadequate humidity	Water level low	Fill water tank
	Belt worn or clogged	Wash belt in detergent or replace it
	Fan slipping on shaft	Tighten setscrew
	Belt or fan motor is defective or needs oiling	Test and replace the belt or fan motor or oil it as required

Another type of portable humidifier has a UV germicidal bulb, located inside the base of the humidifier, that shines on the water through a special glass tube as it passes from the cold-water reservoirs to the hot-water reservoir (**3–69**). The boiling action takes place in the hot-water reservoir just before the mist is distributed into the room. This eliminates potentially harmful micro-organisms from the water before they are spread by the mist into the air.

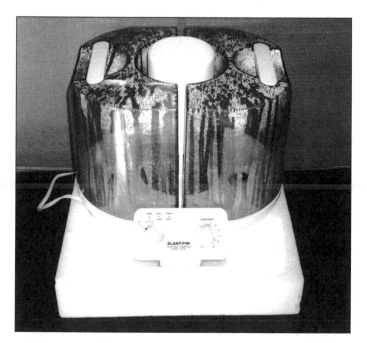

3–69. This humidifier heats the water to boiling and vents a very fine mist into the air. It uses an ultraviolet germicidal bulb to destroy harmful microorganisms in the mist, thus producing a germ-free warm mist.

Dehumidifiers

A dehumidifier removes moisture from the air. It has the same basic parts as a room air conditioner, including a compressor, fan, coils, and humidistat (see **3–70** on page 194). The dehumidifier works much like an air conditioner except that its main job is to remove moisture, not cool a room. Refrigerant passes through the coils, making them cold. A fan blows air past the coils. As the air is cooled, moisture that was in the air condenses on the coils. This action is similar to the outside of a glass of ice water "sweating" on a warm day. The condensed moisture drips off the coils and goes into a pan or down a hose that has been connected to the unit and which leads to a floor drain. When the pan is full, an overload prevention switch shuts off the unit. The pan must then be removed and emptied.

There is little maintenance to be done on a dehumidifier. Most of the routine maintenance operations discussed under Room Air Conditioners on pages 179 and 180 also apply to dehumidifiers. Periodically clean the dust from the coils, motor, and fan blade. Use a vacuum cleaner if the coils are dry. If it is necessary to probe between coils to loosen dust, use something soft such as a pipe cleaner. Be careful not to dent or break a coil. Be sure to unplug the unit before removing the cover to clean or do other work on it.

If the fan motor has oil cups, put No. 20 nondeter-

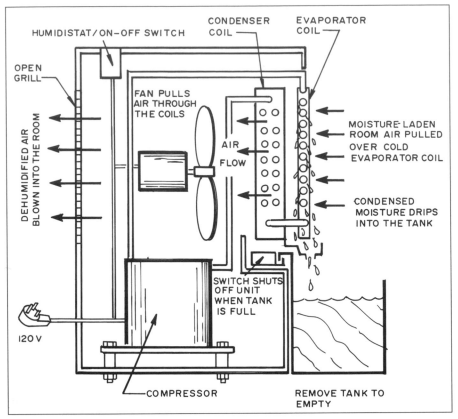

3–70. A dehumidifier removes moisture from the air by passing it over a cold coil, where it condenses and drips into a tank. This is the same principle used by air conditioners to remove moisture from the air.

gent oil in each one once a season. If the fan makes a squealing noise, it is probably slipping on the motor shaft. Tighten the setscrew. The fan blades should not be bent. If they become bent, they will cause vibrations that can damage the motor. A fan with bent blades should be replaced.

Check the motor-mounting nuts for tightness. They need to be firm, but not overtight.

Table 3–3 suggests some dehumidifier problems and their possible solutions.

THERMOSTATS

A thermostat is a switch that is heat-sensitive and controls the flow of electricity to a furnace or air-conditioning unit. When the thermostat senses a need for heat, it will activate the burner and let the heat exchanger warm up before it turns on the fan switch and starts the blower. This prevents a blast of cool air from coming through the ducts before the furnace is able to send warm air. When the thermostat is set for air conditioning, it senses a rise in room air temperature and activates the air conditioner. When the room air temperature set on the thermostat is reached, it shuts off the air conditioner.

Thermostats operate on 24 volts and are not generally covered by electrical codes used for 120-volt wiring.

The thermostat is placed in or near the living area

TABLE 3–3. TROUBLESHOOTING A DEHUMIDIFIER

Problem	Cause	Solution
Unit does not run	Circuit has no power	Check fuse or circuit breaker
	Power cord broken	Check power cord with volt-ohm meter. See the air-conditioner maintenance sections
	Overflow prevention switch faulty	Test and replace overflow prevention switch
	Humidistat faulty	Test and replace humidistat
Unit does not remove much moisture	Coils clogged with dust	Clean and vacuum coils
	Fan slips on shaft	Tighten setscrew
	Fan motor faulty – low rpm	Replace fan motor
	Compressor faulty	Call service technician
Coils become covered with frost	Air temperature too low to operate unit	Raise room temperature or discontinue use of unit
	Coils clogged with dust	Clean and vacuum coils

on a wall where the air temperature will be stable and not influenced by other factors such as direct sunlight or close proximity to a number of incandescent lights (which produce heat) or a heat register.

The furnace has a fan switch in the plenum that has a set temperature of 80 to 90° F (27 to 32° C). When the thermostat senses a need for heat, it activates the burner. When the furnace air reaches the **cut-in temperature**, the fan switch starts the blower. The blower and burner run until the room air reaches the temperature set on the thermostat. When this is reached, the burner is turned off and the blower continues to run until the air temperature in the furnace drops below the cut-in fan-switch temperature. This allows the furnace to move the heat generated into the room. If the fan-switch temperature is set too high, the fan will turn on and off frequently, and the short bursts of air will cause uncomfortable variations in air temperature.

The furnace also has a **high-limit switch**. If the temperature in the furnace reaches a dangerously high level, such as 200° F (94° C), the high-limit switch will shut off the burner. A typical situation is when the blower fails to run but the burner keeps firing the furnace. The furnace combustion chamber could become overheated.

Many thermostats have a **heat anticipator (3–71)**. It is a small heater built into the thermostat that turns on when the thermostat activates the furnace. It is located next to the bimetallic temperature-sensitive element of the thermostat. It heats this element, causing it to open the contact before the heated air in the room actually reaches the thermostat. The heat anticipator shuts off the heating system but lets the fan continue to run, moving the heated air in the system into the room. The idea is to keep from overheating the air in the room.

This anticipator can be adjusted until the desired balance in the system is reached. If the heat starts and stops frequently, move the anticipator lever toward the high setting. If it starts and stops infrequently, move the lever to a lower setting. After an adjustment, let the furnace operate for a day to determine if the furnace cycles on and off enough to keep the temperature stable.

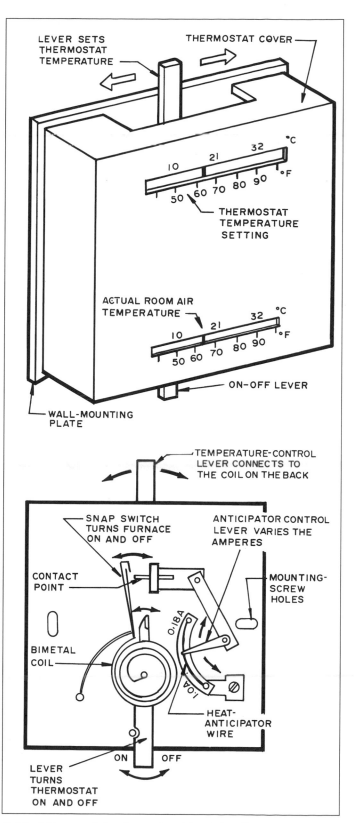

3–71. A thermostat using only a bimetal coil to control room temperature. It is used for controlling gas and oil warm-air furnaces, and operates on 24 volts. Notice that the heat anticipator can be adjusted from 1.0 to 0.18 amperes.

There is a wide range of thermostats available. One inexpensive type uses a bimetal coil that opens and closes a snap switch. The thermostat shown in **3–71** opens the snap switch when the bimetal coil receives enough heat from the air to cause it to expand. When the coil cools, it contracts, closing the snap switch and activating the furnace. This thermostat operates on 24 volts and is only used for gas and oil warm-air furnaces. Notice it has a heat anticipator to shut off the furnace burner slightly before the room air reaches the required temperature.

Another type of thermostat uses a bimetal coil and a mercury switch (**3–72**). The mercury is enclosed in a glass tube. As the coil uncoils or recoils, the glass tube changes positions, moving the mercury from one end to the other. When the mercury flows to one end of the glass tube, the circuit is completed and the furnace operates. When the mercury flows to the other end, the circuit is broken and the furnace ceases to operate. The mercury serves as a switch, making and breaking the circuit.

Another type of thermostat—a **clock-operated** one—can be set to keep the air at one temperature for a specific time and at a different temperature at another time (such as a lower temperature at night) so that heating and cooling costs can be reduced. The times are set on a timer switch (**3–73**). This type of thermostat uses a mercury-switch bulb that is moved by a bimetal coil and makes and breaks the circuit. This thermostat will save considerable energy. However, the same results can be achieved by remembering to turn down the manual thermostat at night.

Another thermostat used to control air temperature at different times is the **programmable thermostat** (**3–74**). It can be programmed to provide several different levels of heating and cooling during a 24-hour period. The programs are entered into the memory using the keypad on the face of the thermostat. The programming system is powered by batteries. This type of thermostat can save on energy bills by automatically lowering the temperature during the time when nobody is at home. If there is a heat pump, it is generally best to not lower the temperature during this time.

There is little that has to be done to maintain a

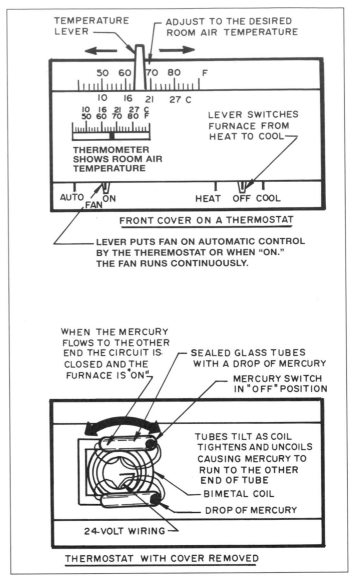

3–72. This thermostat uses a bimetal coil to operate a mercury switch. It is used to control both heating and air-conditioning systems.

thermostat. Basically keep it clean of lint and dust, and it will operate for years. Some types have the contacts enclosed in glass, dust-proof cylinders. If the contacts are open to the air, they will have to be cleaned occasionally. Run a piece of hard-surfaced paper between the points. Do not use sandpaper because it will damage the contacts.

If you are planning to replace the old thermostat, examine those available very carefully. Some types will not control both heating and air conditioning. Some will not work if a heat pump is being used. Be certain the voltage required is the same as that on the existing unit.

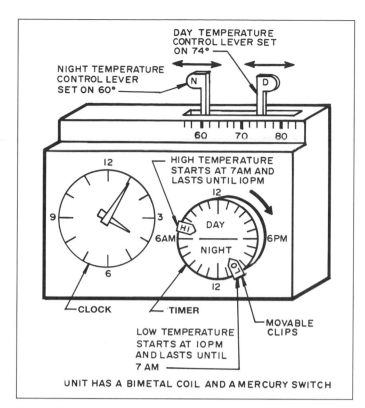

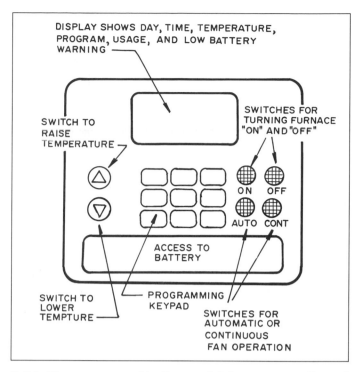

3–73 (above). A clock-operated thermostat can regulate the temperature of the air over a 24-hour period. When used with gas- and oil-fired furnaces, this thermostat can save money by lowering the temperature during the hours the house is not occupied.

3–74. The programmable thermostat is very versatile and can be programmed to change the air temperature several times a day and produce different temperatures on different days of the week.

Review the instruction sheet that accompanies the new thermostat. It will give a step-by-step procedure for removing the old unit and installing the new one. Following is a typical procedure:

1. Turn off the power to the furnace at the power panel.

2. Remove the cover and the thermostat, exposing the mounting plate and connecting wires (3–75).

3–75. To remove the old thermostat, turn off the power to the furnace, remove the cover, unscrew the thermostat control, and remove the old mounting plate from the wall. Be certain to mark the wires by the code letters before disconnecting them from the old thermostat.

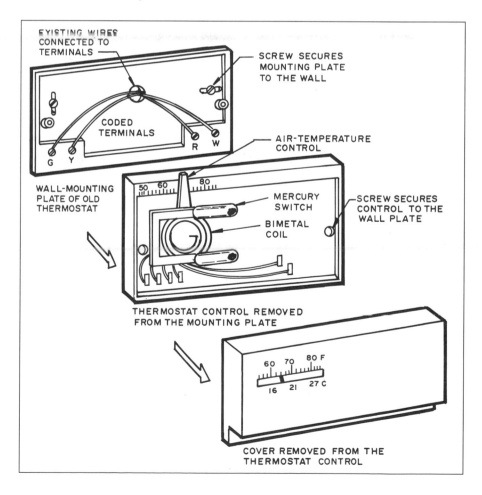

3. Each wire to the old thermostat is connected to a terminal point on the mounting plate. These are marked with a code letter (**3–76**). The new instruction booklet will indicate which to connect to the marked terminals on the new thermostat. On older thermostats, the terminals may not be labeled. The new booklet will instruct on how to make these connections. The color of the wires usually has no significance. Rely on the mounting-plate terminal code letter.

4. After labeling the wires, disconnect them from the old mounting plate.

5. Remove the old mounting plate from the wall.

6. Seal the hole in the wall through which the wires run with caulking to prevent cold air from hitting the back of the new thermostat, which can produce a false reading.

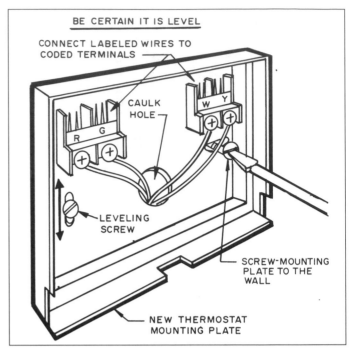

3–77. Pull the labeled wires through the hole in the new mounting plate and screw it to the wall. Be certain it is level. Then connect the wires to the coded terminals.

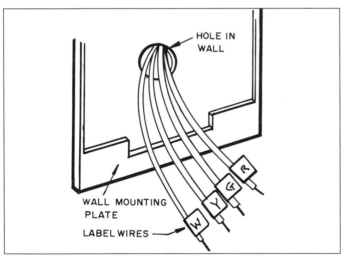

3–76. Label the wires from the old thermostat.

7. Mount the new mounting plate and pull the wires through the opening provided. Drill anchor holes in the wall and secure the new mounting plate with plastic anchors and screws. Be certain it is level (**3–77**).

8. Connect the wires to the terminals on the new mounting plate (**3–77**). Line up the thermostat with the mounting plate and secure it with screws. Install the cover by pressing on the plastic clips, which will snap it tight. The unit is ready to operate. Turn on the power and test it.

CHAPTER FOUR

Roof Repairs

The roof serves as the major barrier between the elements and the inside of the house. It is made of rafters, sheathing, and some form of exterior finished roofing material. The rafters or trusses and sheathing must be strong enough to carry the weight of the roofing material and also to withstand damage by wind.

Another essential part of the roof is flashing, which is usually made from sheet metal. The purpose of flashing is to prevent water from leaking through openings in the roof such as around a chimney, a skylight, or where the roof meets a wall.

A third part of the roof that may need attention is the gutters and downspouts. These carry away the water that drains from the roof and divert it away from the foundation.

USING A LADDER

A great number of roof and other exterior maintenance jobs require the use of a ladder. The two kinds of ladder in general use are extension ladders and stepladders. Follow these simple safety rules when using a ladder:

1. Do not use broken or bent ladders. A ladder must be sound and strong. Do not use a ladder on which an emergency repair has been made. If a ladder is repaired, the repair must make the ladder as strong as it was originally.

2. Always face the ladder when ascending or descending. Step on one step or rung at a time. Do not skip any steps or rungs.

3. When on the ladder, do not reach beyond a normal, comfortable distance. Move the ladder rather than stretch to reach something.

4. Do not climb a ladder with wet or muddy shoes.

5. Do not try to move a ladder that has tools or paint buckets hanging from it.

6. Set an extension ladder so the distance of its feet from the top support is about one-fourth the length of the ladder to that point (**4–1**).

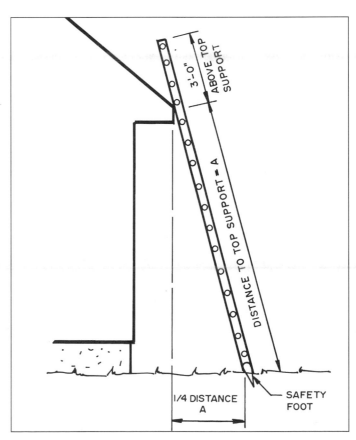

4–1. Position the feet of the extension ladder about one-fourth of its length from the top resting point. Use ladders with safety feet.

7. Set the feet of the ladder firmly on the ground. The ladder must have safety feet designed to reduce slipping.

8. If someone is going onto the roof, the ladder should extend at least three feet above the eave (**4–1**).

9. Use a ladder that is the correct length (**4–2**).

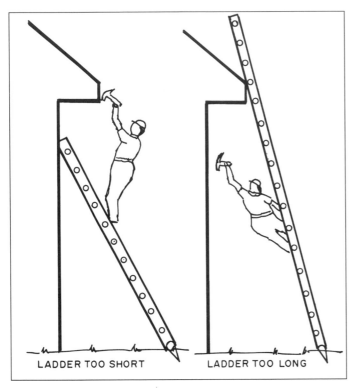

LADDER TOO SHORT   LADDER TOO LONG

4–2. Never work from a ladder that does not provide comfortable access to the work area.

10. Do not stand on the top three rungs of an extension ladder. If you must go higher, get down and increase the length of the ladder.

11. Extension ladders should have at least a three-foot overlap between sections.

12. To raise a ladder, place its feet against some fixed object and, using your hands on the rungs, "walk" it upright.

13. Be sure both top ends of the ladder rest on a firm surface.

14. When painting from an extension ladder, hang the paint bucket from a hook. Do not try to paint

from a full gallon can of paint. It is too heavy and easily spilled. Instead, use a plastic or metal paint bucket; pour from one-quarter to one-half gallon of paint into the bucket, and paint from it. Both buckets and hooks are sold in paint stores.

15. When working from a stepladder, be certain all four legs are on firm ground. Open the ladder fully and lock the leg braces in place.

16. Do not stand on the top step or on the shelf of a stepladder.

ROOF LEAKS

Roof leaks can cause serious damage to roof sheathing, rafters, trusses, ceiling joists, insulation, and interior ceilings and walls. A first sign of trouble may be minor damp spots that appear on an interior ceiling. Seeing these, assume that more serious damage has occurred in the attic. Rafters and sheathing that have been wet for years begin to rot and must be replaced. When a wet condition is noticed, first try to locate the leak.

The places to check for possible damage leading to leaks include:

1. Damaged or missing shingles, slates, or tiles.

2. Flashing around skylights, chimneys, vent pipes protruding through the roof, and dormers.

3. Valley flashing and flashing where a roof butts against a wall.

4. Clogged or damaged roof drains and gutters.

5. Ice dams.

6. Damaged hip and ridge shingles.

7. Chimney masonry that absorbs water or has damaged mortar joints.

8. Deteriorated sheet roofing on a flat roof or one with little slope.

Finding the Leak

First try to locate the leak from inside the attic. While it is unusual, sometimes the hole is found by looking for a pinhole of light showing through the attic. Generally the source is more elusive and takes more work to find it.

Look for water stains on the sheathing or, better still, go into the attic when it is raining and find the moist area on the sheathing or rafters. It will most likely be necessary to use a flashlight or a light on an extension cord to check the sheathing. The moist area will appear darker than the natural wood. Remember that the spot on the ceiling is probably not directly below the leak. Moisture will often run down the sheathing or rafter for some distance before it drops to the ceiling (4–3). Also check the insulation in the area of the suspected leak. Look for stains or damage to the insulation.

If the leak is spotted, measure the distance from it to the ridge or the edge of the roof and the distance from it to the gable end or nearest exterior wall (4–4). Lay out these distances on the shingles to find the damaged spot. Some home owners prefer to drive a large nail through the shingles that locates the leak on the outside.

Remember, there may be wet spots on the ceiling that could be caused by leaking water pipes, waste-

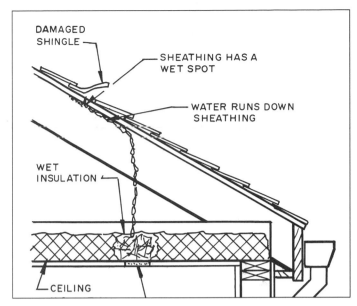

4–4. When a leak is found in the shingles, measurements can be made from the leak to the ridge or roof edge (if it is closer) and from the leak to the gable end in order to locate the hole on the outside. Some home owners simply drive a large nail through the leak so it protrudes above the shingles on the outside.

disposal pipes, or hot-water heating pipes if they are in the attic. If the house has a second floor, these pipes are more likely to be the cause than the roof.

Look for leaks from the outside, too. Look for cracked or broken shingles. Check the flashing to see if it has pulled away from the wall or chimney. Sometimes a leak can be found by spraying the roof with water from a garden hose while a helper watches in the attic for water to appear.

ASBESTOS-CEMENT SHINGLES

If the house is an older one that has asbestos-cement shingles, they cannot be removed or repaired. Asbestos fibers are a health hazard and the shingles must be removed by an approved asbestos abatement contractor. Contact the local building inspector for assistance.

REPAIRING FIBERGLASS AND ASPHALT SHINGLES

If a damaged shingle is spotted, an emergency repair can be made by sliding a waterproof material such as a plastic or metal sheet or a shingle between

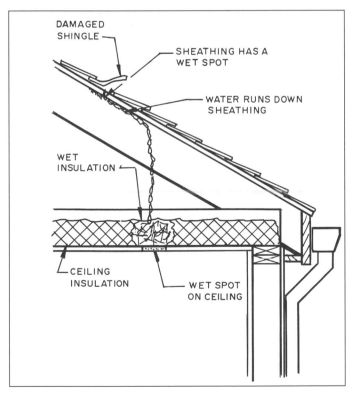

4–3. A roof leak often wets the insulation and ceiling down-hill from the actual leak.

the damaged shingles (**4–5**). If the weather is very cold, be careful when lifting the top shingles because they become stiff in cold weather and may develop a surface crack.

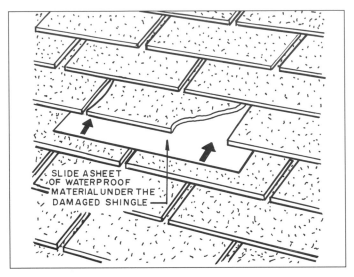

4–5. An emergency repair can be made by sliding a waterproof sheet under the damaged shingles.

Small cracks or splits in fiberglass and asphalt shingles can be repaired with roofing cement as follows:

1. Lift the shingle and spread a layer of roofing cement underneath it on both sides of the split (**4–6**).

2. Press the shingle into the cement.

3. Fill the split with more roofing cement. Be sure to spread the cement about 1 inch (25 millimeters) on each side of the split on the top of the shingle.

This procedure produces a good temporary patch. It will last longer if a piece of fiberglass cloth is pressed into the roofing cement.

Make a temporary repair on a badly torn shingle as follows:

1. Put a layer of roofing cement under the torn shingle as described above.

2. Press the shingle into the cement and nail the loose edges to the sheathing with 1½-inch (38-millimeter) galvanized roofing nails.

3. Apply a layer of fiberglass cloth and more roofing cement on top of the tear (**4–7**). If the wind raises the ends of the shingles but has not broken

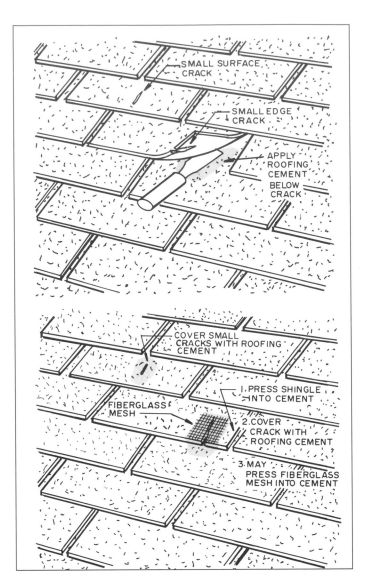

4–6. Minor cracks and small tears can be repaired by sealing them with roofing cement.

them, they can be recemented. Put 1-inch dabs of roofing cement under each tab and press it flat (**4–8**).

Shingles can be worked more easily when they are warm. Shingles may crack if they are worked on when cold. If the roof is very hot, the shingles can be damaged when they are walked on. In the summer, work early in the morning before the shingles get hot.

Replacing a Shingle

If a shingle has come loose and slides down but is in good condition, it can be replaced as described for installing a new shingle. Remember to put dabs of

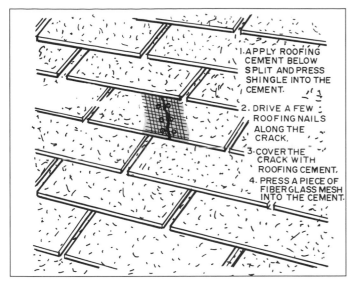

4–7. A badly torn shingle can be repaired temporarily using roofing cement, a few roofing nails, and a piece of fiberglass mesh.

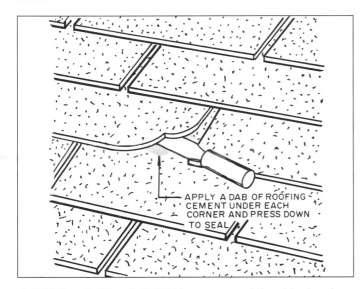

4–8. If the wind tends to lift the corners of the shingle, place a dab of roofing cement under each corner. A few dabs along the entire length of the shingle will increase resistance to wind, raising the entire shingle.

roofing cement along the bottom edge to prevent the wind from raising it and possibly breaking it off.

To replace a damaged shingle, use the following procedure:

1. Lift the shingles above it and remove the nails with a pry bar (**4–9**). Slide out all of the pieces of the damaged shingle.

2. Slide the new shingle in place. Make certain the edge lines up with the other shingles in its course (**4-10**).

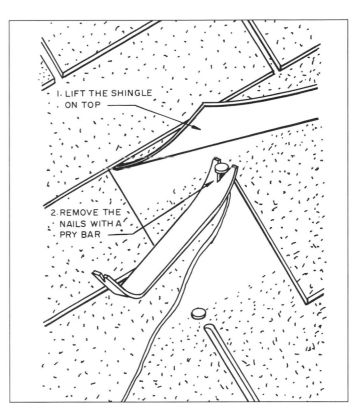

4–9. Remove a damaged asphalt or fiberglass shingle by lifting the shingle above it and pulling out the nails with a pry bar. Be careful not to crack the top shingles while lifting the damaged one out.

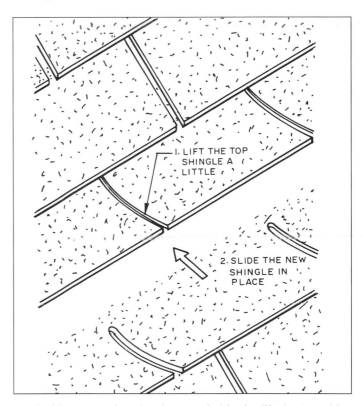

4–10. After removing the damaged shingle, lift the top shingle and slide the new one under it. Be certain the edge lines up with the other shingles in the course.

3. Nail the new shingle by placing nails in the recommended locations (**4–11**). Begin by raising the shingle on top and pressing the nail into the shingle with your thumb. If the shingles are warm and flexible, raise the top one carefully and drive the nail (**4–12**). If they are cold or old and brittle, they may crack if lifted, so the nail will have to be driven by placing a pry bar or large screwdriver on the nail and striking the pry bar or screwdriver as shown in **4–13**. Drive the nail so that the head rests firmly on the top of the new shingle. Do not drive the nail hard enough to break the surface.

4. Stick the replacement shingle to the top shingle and to the one below it with dabs of roofing cement.

If a **ridge** or **hip shingle** has developed a small surface crack, it can be repaired by applying a coating of roofing cement into the crack (**4–14**). If the damage is major, the damaged area will have to be

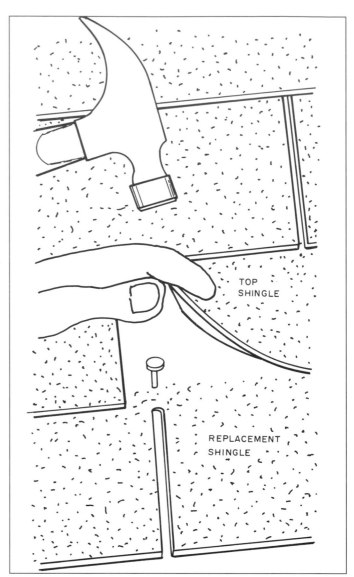

4–12. If the shingles are warm and flexible, it may be possible to lift the top shingle enough to allow the nail to be driven without cracking the lifted shingle.

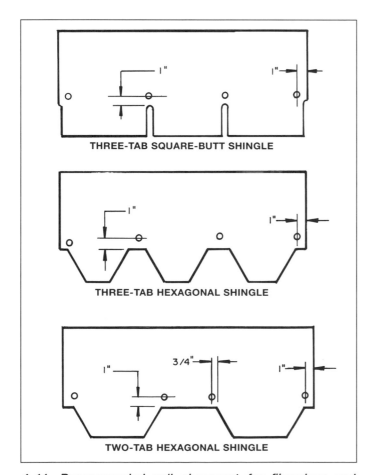

THREE-TAB SQUARE-BUTT SHINGLE

THREE-TAB HEXAGONAL SHINGLE

TWO-TAB HEXAGONAL SHINGLE

4–11. Recommended nail placement for fiberglass and asphalt shingles.

coated with roofing cement. Cut a piece of shingle to overlap the damaged shingle and nail it on all four corners with 2½-inch (63-millimeter) roofing nails. Before nailing, apply a spot of roofing cement where the nail will be installed and cover the head of the nail after it has been driven into place (**4–15**).

REPAIRING ROLL ROOFING

Roll roofing (asphalt roofing products manufactured in roof form) is often used on flat roofs or shed roofs that have a slight slope. This type of roofing is available in 36-inch (914-millimeter)-wide rolls that

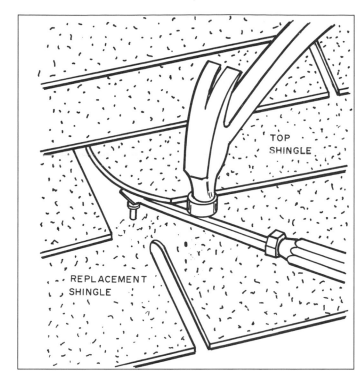

4–13. If the shingles are cold or brittle, carefully lift the top shingle enough to set the nail in place with your thumb. Then drive it in place by placing a bar on the nail and striking the bar with a hammer.

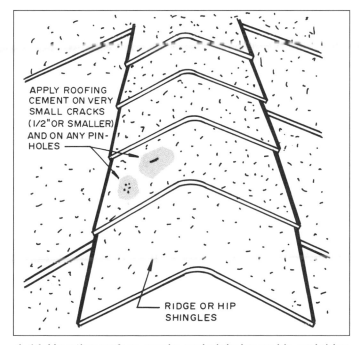

4–14. Very tiny surface cracks and pinholes on hip and ridge shingles should be sealed with a coat of roofing cement.

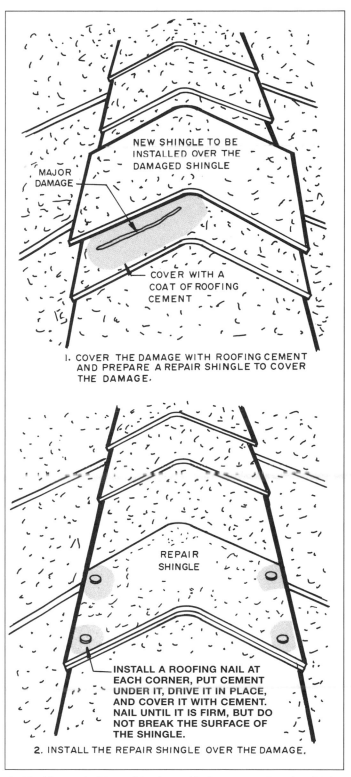

4–15. Hip and ridge shingles with large cracks should be repaired by bonding and nailing a new shingle over the damaged shingle.

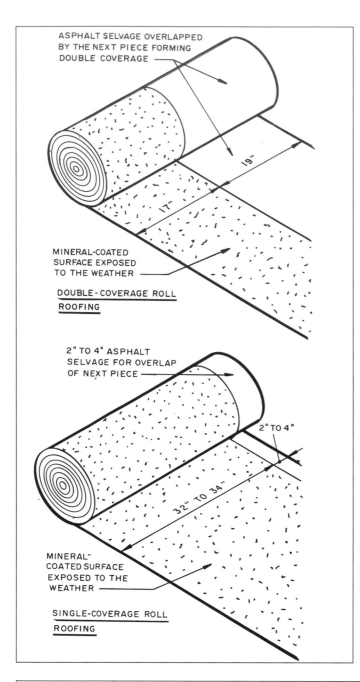

ASPHALT SELVAGE OVERLAPPED BY THE NEXT PIECE FORMING DOUBLE COVERAGE

19"

17"

MINERAL-COATED SURFACE EXPOSED TO THE WEATHER

DOUBLE-COVERAGE ROLL ROOFING

2" TO 4" ASPHALT SELVAGE FOR OVERLAP OF NEXT PIECE

2" TO 4"

32" TO 34"

MINERAL-COATED SURFACE EXPOSED TO THE WEATHER

SINGLE-COVERAGE ROLL ROOFING

4–16. Two commonly used types of roll roofing. One provides double coverage and the other single coverage.

have a part covered with a granular mineral and a part with an exposed asphalt surface (**4–16**).

Heat can cause a blister in this kind of built-up roof if water gets below it. The roll-roofing material will often crack at the blister, causing a major leak. If it is a **small** blister, slit the blister, lift the roofing, and dry the sheathing with a hair dryer or other blower. Force roofing cement under the roofing around the slit, press the roofing into the cement, and nail on both sides. Cover the slit with a coat of roofing cement about 2 inches (51 millimeters) around the slit. Cut a patch, nail it over this area, and cover the entire patch with cement (**4–17**).

If it is a large blister and the roofing around it is stretched and damaged, proceed as follows (**4–18**):

1. Cut away the blistered roll roofing and dry the exposed sheathing. The drying can be sped up by using a heated blower such as a hair dryer.

2. Be certain the roofing left around the cut-away area can be pressed flat. If it is irregular and buckled, cut this area away until what is left will lie flat on the sheathing. Be certain the sheathing below is dry.

3. Spread roofing cement below the edges of roll roofing, press it flat against the sheathing, and nail the edges. Spread roofing cement over the entire area of the exposed sheathing.

4. Cut a patch of roll roofing the same size as the exposed sheathing. The piece removed can be

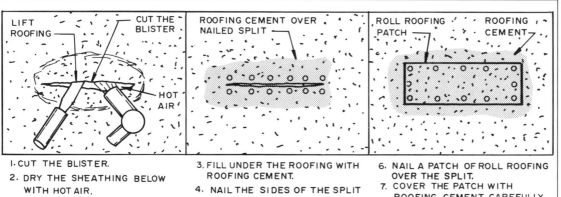

LIFT ROOFING   CUT THE BLISTER

HOT AIR

1. CUT THE BLISTER.
2. DRY THE SHEATHING BELOW WITH HOT AIR.

ROOFING CEMENT OVER NAILED SPLIT

3. FILL UNDER THE ROOFING WITH ROOFING CEMENT.
4. NAIL THE SIDES OF THE SPLIT TO THE SHEATHING.
5. COVER WITH ROOFING CEMENT.

ROLL ROOFING PATCH   ROOFING CEMENT

6. NAIL A PATCH OF ROLL ROOFING OVER THE SPLIT.
7. COVER THE PATCH WITH ROOFING CEMENT. CAREFULLY SEAL THE EDGES.

4–17. Small cracks and pinholes in roll roofing can be repaired by coating with roofing cement and nailing a patch cut from roll roofing over the break. Cover the patch with roofing cement.

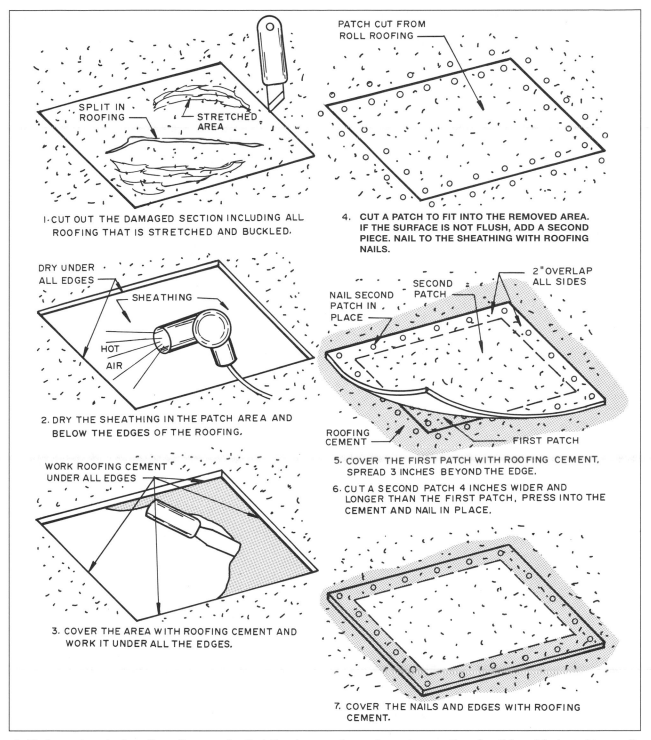

SPLIT IN ROOFING
STRETCHED AREA

1. CUT OUT THE DAMAGED SECTION INCLUDING ALL ROOFING THAT IS STRETCHED AND BUCKLED.

DRY UNDER ALL EDGES
SHEATHING
HOT AIR

2. DRY THE SHEATHING IN THE PATCH AREA AND BELOW THE EDGES OF THE ROOFING.

WORK ROOFING CEMENT UNDER ALL EDGES

3. COVER THE AREA WITH ROOFING CEMENT AND WORK IT UNDER ALL THE EDGES.

PATCH CUT FROM ROLL ROOFING

4. CUT A PATCH TO FIT INTO THE REMOVED AREA. IF THE SURFACE IS NOT FLUSH, ADD A SECOND PIECE. NAIL TO THE SHEATHING WITH ROOFING NAILS.

NAIL SECOND PATCH IN PLACE
SECOND PATCH
2" OVERLAP ALL SIDES
ROOFING CEMENT
FIRST PATCH

5. COVER THE FIRST PATCH WITH ROOFING CEMENT, SPREAD 3 INCHES BEYOND THE EDGE.

6. CUT A SECOND PATCH 4 INCHES WIDER AND LONGER THAN THE FIRST PATCH, PRESS INTO THE CEMENT AND NAIL IN PLACE.

7. COVER THE NAILS AND EDGES WITH ROOFING CEMENT.

4–18. Large breaks in roll roofing require that the damaged area be cut away, the sheathing dried, and two roll-roofing patches be applied.

used as a pattern. Nail this patch in the exposed area with galvanized or aluminum roofing nails.

5. Spread roofing cement over this patch and extend it at least 2 inches beyond the edge.

6. Cut a second patch of roll roofing 4 inches (102 millimeters) longer and wider than the first patch. Place it over the first patch, press it into the cement, and nail around the edges.

7. Apply a coat of roofing cement over the nails and carefully seal the edge of the patch.

REPLACING WOOD SHINGLES AND SHAKES

Wood shingles are sawn on both sides, so they are smooth. Wood shakes are hand-split from the log and are rough on both sides. Some types are split and then sawn; this forms two shakes, so one side is smooth.

Generally No. 1 grade (Blue Label) shingles and shakes are used for roofing. They are made from

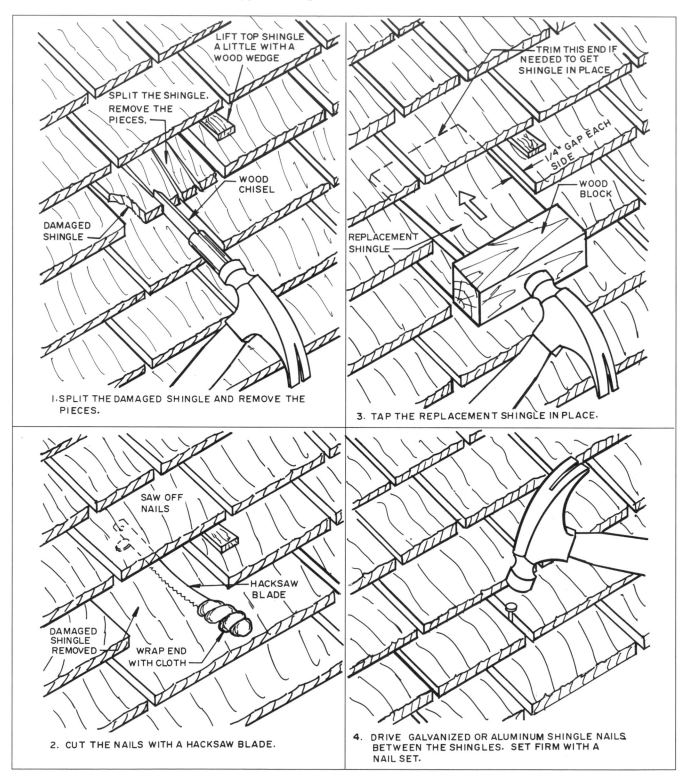

4–19. Work carefully when replacing damaged wood shingles or shakes. Since they do not bend, the old shingle has to be split and removed and the nails left sawn off before the new shingle or shake is installed.

cedar, spruce, and pine. It is recommended they be given a water-repellent coating every few years to help reduce the absorption of moisture.

Wood-shingle roofs can have mold and discoloration removed by power washing. Simply washing with bleach also cleans them up.

Over the years, wood shingles and shakes curl or cup due to being wet and then drying. A temporary repair can be made by slipping a piece of flashing under a defective shingle. Since the metal repair will be obvious, eventually the shingle or shake will have to be replaced. To replace the shingle or shake, do the following (**4–19**):

1. Remove the old shingle or shake. Drive a thin wood wedge under the shingle above, raising it just a little off the damaged shingle.

2. Split the damaged shingle with a chisel and remove the splintered parts.

3. Cut off the nails left by running a hacksaw blade or metal-cutting keyhole saw under the shingle.

4. If several courses must be replaced, start with the lowest course. Cut the replacement shingles to fit the space and match the pattern of the roof. The shingles should have a ¼-inch (6-millimeter) gap on the edges, so each replacement shingle will be ½ inch (13 millimeters) narrower than the space.

5. Slide the shingle in place. If it will not go all the way under, cut a little off the thin end. Tap it in place by putting a wood block on the edge and hammering on the block.

6. Nail the shingles to the sheathing with 4d galvanized or aluminum shingle nails. If several courses are to be installed, nail the lowest courses so the shingle above covers the nail about 1 inch (25 millimeters). The final shingle will have to be nailed between the shingles. Set it against the shingle with a nail set. Cover the exposed nails with roofing cement. Drive the nails so their heads rest firmly on top of the shingle but do not break the surface (**4–20**).

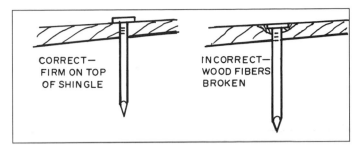

4–20. Set the shingle nails firmly on the surface of the wood shingle or shake, but do not break the wood fibers on the surface.

REPAIRING A METAL ROOF

The most commonly used metal roofing materials are copper, galvanized steel, and aluminum. Terne roofing is another type, but is not commonly found. It is steel-coated with an alloy composed of lead and tin and is generally painted. Copper is usually left unfinished and over the years develops a green patina (coating). Galvanized steel and aluminum roofing do not need painting, but often are coated to provide the color desired. This also protects steel from rusting. After years of exposure, the galvanizing tends to wear away. All metal roofs have a long life, however, and require little maintenance except for an occasional repainting.

In addition to sheets of roofing metal, shingles and shakes with embossed surfaces are available. The manufacturers of these products have designed methods for connecting the material and securing it to the sheathing.

It is important to remember that metal roofs can corrode if different metals are touching. For example, copper roofing installed with steel nails will corrode at each nail. Always use nails or screws of the same material as the roofing.

Steel, terne, and **copper roofs** can have minor damage repaired as follows (**4–21**):

1. Make certain the metal is flat against the sheathing. Clean around the damaged area; this includes the removal of any paint. Steel wool is good to use to clean and polish the surface. Also clean the bottom edge of the patch.

2. Cut a patch of the same material. Make it around 2 inches (51 millimeters) wider than the damaged area on each side.

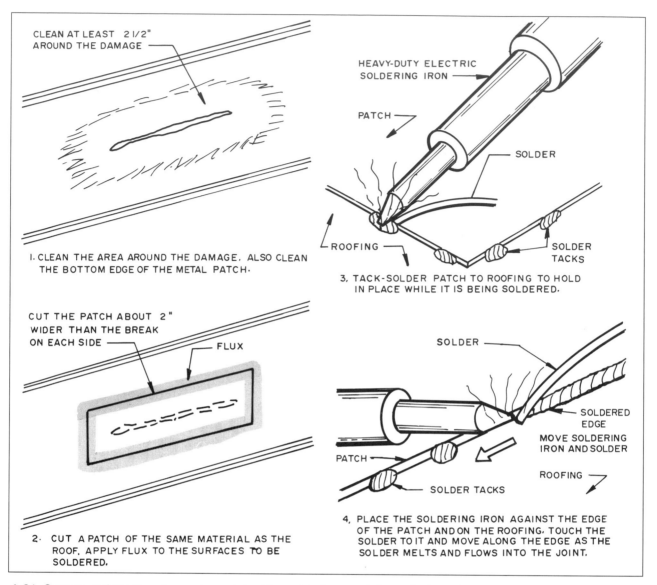

CLEAN AT LEAST 2 1/2"
AROUND THE DAMAGE

1. CLEAN THE AREA AROUND THE DAMAGE. ALSO CLEAN THE BOTTOM EDGE OF THE METAL PATCH.

CUT THE PATCH ABOUT 2" WIDER THAN THE BREAK ON EACH SIDE

FLUX

2. CUT A PATCH OF THE SAME MATERIAL AS THE ROOF. APPLY FLUX TO THE SURFACES TO BE SOLDERED.

HEAVY-DUTY ELECTRIC SOLDERING IRON

PATCH

SOLDER

ROOFING

SOLDER TACKS

3. TACK-SOLDER PATCH TO ROOFING TO HOLD IN PLACE WHILE IT IS BEING SOLDERED.

SOLDER

SOLDERED EDGE

MOVE SOLDERING IRON AND SOLDER

PATCH

ROOFING

SOLDER TACKS

4. PLACE THE SOLDERING IRON AGAINST THE EDGE OF THE PATCH AND ON THE ROOFING. TOUCH THE SOLDER TO IT AND MOVE ALONG THE EDGE AS THE SOLDER MELTS AND FLOWS INTO THE JOINT.

4–21. Copper and steel roofs can be patched by soldering a patch made from the same material over the damage. Be certain the surfaces to be soldered are clean and coated with the proper flux.

3. With a flux, coat the edges of the patch and the roof surface to be soldered. Use a flux recommended for the material being soldered. This removes any oxide that may be left on the surface.

4. Place the patch over the area. Tack solder in several places to hold it in position. (**Tack-soldering** consists of soldering the edges in several places with short strips of solder.)

5. Now, using a large soldering iron, place the face flat against the edge of the patch and down on the roofing. Touch the solder to the soldering iron. As the patch and roofing heat, the solder will melt and flow between them. Move the soldering iron

and solder along the edge, melting and flowing solder between the patch and the roof.

A small electric soldering iron may not produce enough heat to get the patch and roofing hot enough to melt the solder. A large soldering iron or a propane torch is needed. If using a propane torch, be aware that the metal could be overheated and a fire started on the roof.

Aluminum roofs cannot be soldered with equipment normally available. However, small breaks can be repaired by placing an aluminum patch over the area (**4–22**). The following steps show one way to make this repair:

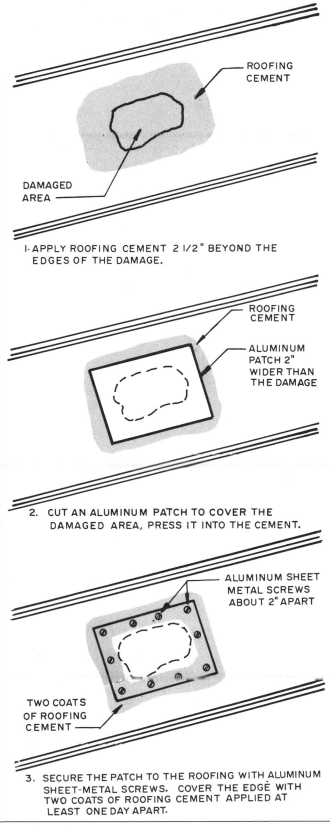

ROOFING CEMENT

DAMAGED AREA

1. APPLY ROOFING CEMENT 2 1/2" BEYOND THE EDGES OF THE DAMAGE.

ROOFING CEMENT

ALUMINUM PATCH 2" WIDER THAN THE DAMAGE

2. CUT AN ALUMINUM PATCH TO COVER THE DAMAGED AREA, PRESS IT INTO THE CEMENT.

ALUMINUM SHEET METAL SCREWS ABOUT 2" APART

TWO COATS OF ROOFING CEMENT

3. SECURE THE PATCH TO THE ROOFING WITH ALUMINUM SHEET-METAL SCREWS. COVER THE EDGE WITH TWO COATS OF ROOFING CEMENT APPLIED AT LEAST ONE DAY APART.

4–22. One way to patch damage on an aluminum metal roof is to combine layers of roofing cement below and over an aluminum patch secured with aluminum sheet-metal screws.

1. If the edges of the damaged area protrude above the surface of the aluminum roof, drive them flat with a hammer.

2. Spread a layer of roofing cement about 2½ inches (64 millimeters) beyond the edges of the damage. If the roof is over sheathing, coat the sheathing also.

3. Cut an aluminum patch about 2 inches wider than the damaged area on each side.

4. Press the patch into the cement. Secure the patch with aluminum sheet-metal screws. Drill the proper-diameter hole for the size screw being used. Tighten each screw until it is firm. Do not overtighten it or it will be stripped out of the metal roofing.

5. Apply a coat of roofing cement around the edge of the patch. Extend it about 2 inches beyond the sides of the damaged area. After it dries a day or so, apply a second coat.

REPAIRING A SLATE ROOF AND CONCRETE SHINGLES

Slate is a quarried stone that is split into thin sections that are cut to size. The colors vary depending upon the location of the quarry. It is an excellent, long-lasting roofing material, but is very heavy. The roof structure and supporting walls must be designed to carry the load.

A number of lighter-weight concrete shingles are available. They are long-lasting and attractive. Installation details vary, and it is important to follow those recommended by the manufacturer.

Slate and concrete shingles may crack if hit by falling debris, and after many years the nails may begin to fail. Loose pieces can slide off the roof and present a hazard. Roofing contractors have special tools for removing old slates and cutting them. *Slate- and concrete-shingled roofs are also very slippery and it is recommended that the average person not work on them or try to make repairs.*

CHIMNEYS

Sometimes a masonry chimney will absorb moisture and cause small amounts to work down into the house, so the area around the chimney at the ceiling will get damp. If the flashing is secure, the chimney will have to be coated with a water-repellent material. This is available in all building-supply and hardware stores. It is a clear liquid and will not discolor the masonry.

The mortar joints will also have to be checked. If a few minor cracks between the mortar and the masonry are found, they can be filled with caulking designed especially to seal cracks in masonry and concrete. It is highly weather-resistant and flexible.

If the mortar joints are badly deteriorated, the chimney will have to be tuck-pointed. **Tuck-pointing** consists of removing the defective mortar joints and filling the area in with fresh mortar.

If it is a small job and the roof is not too steep, you may want to try it yourself. Be certain to cover the shingles on the roof so they are not damaged.

Following are the basic tuck-pointing steps (**4–23**):

1. Chisel out the old mortar about ¾ to 1 inch (19 to 25 millimeters) deep. Use a tuck-pointing chisel. Be certain to wear eye protection.

2. After chiseling out the old mortar, clean all loose material out of the joint. Compressed air is best for this, but a good brush can be used.

3. When preparing to apply the new mortar, wet the joints with water.

4. The new mortar should be as similar to the old mortar as possible. If the chimney is very old, the exact mortar will most likely not be available or you will not be able to determine its composition. New mortars expand at different rates than older mortars and may produce enough pressure to cause the faces of the bricks to spall (break up) and fall off. When in doubt, some home owners use the currently available type-O mortar. Mix it as follows: one part type-O portland cement, two parts lime, and seven parts fine mortar sand. Add as little water as possible, so that the mix is rather stiff. If it is squeezed into a ball, it should retain that shape.

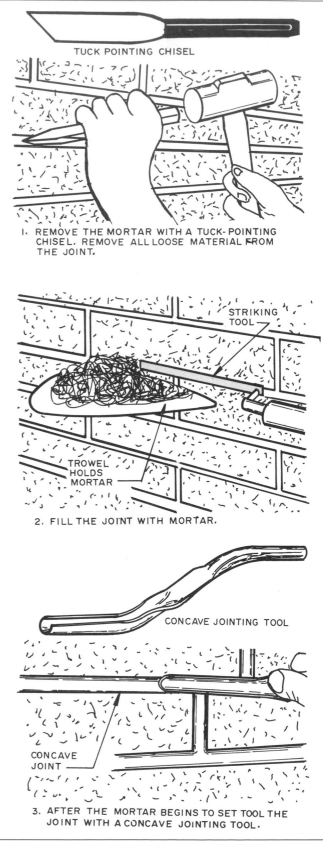

1. REMOVE THE MORTAR WITH A TUCK-POINTING CHISEL. REMOVE ALL LOOSE MATERIAL FROM THE JOINT.

2. FILL THE JOINT WITH MORTAR.

3. AFTER THE MORTAR BEGINS TO SET TOOL THE JOINT WITH A CONCAVE JOINTING TOOL.

4–23. *Badly deteriorated mortar joints should be tuck-pointed. This strengthens the chimney and reduces water leakage.*

5. Apply the mortar into the joints with a striking tool. After it has begun to set, go over the joints with a jointing tool, forming a slightly concave surface.

ROOF-FLASHING MAINTENANCE AND REPAIR

The most common places where roof flashing is required are where a pipe pierces a roof, a roof meets a wall, two roofs join forming a valley, or a roof butts up to a chimney.

Replacing Flashing on Pipes That Penetrate the Roof

Stack flashing is used to seal the roof around pipes. The metal and neoprene unit fits over the pipe and the shingles are laid over the base. When it deteriorates, the stack flashing should be replaced as shown in **4–24**.

Installing Flashing on a Frame Wall

When a roof butts a frame wall, the flashing is placed behind the wood siding (**4–25**). This is usually aluminum or copper and requires no maintenance. It is referred to as **step flashing**. Each piece of flashing is placed on top of a course of shingles and nailed to the wall sheathing. Then another course of shingles is laid on the wall and another piece of flashing placed on top of it. It is nailed to the sheathing with two nails in the top edge. The next flashing overlaps the first 2 inches (51 millimeters) of the original flashing and covers the nails.

After the flashing and shingles are in place, the siding is installed. It covers the flashing, but should be kept about 1 inch (25 millimeters) above the shingles. The siding serves as counterflashing.

If for some reason it is suspected that water may be leaking between the flashing pieces, the seams can be caulked with high-quality exterior caulking.

Installing Flashing on a Masonry Wall

When the roof butts a masonry wall, two layers of flashing are used. The first layer is step flashing. It is

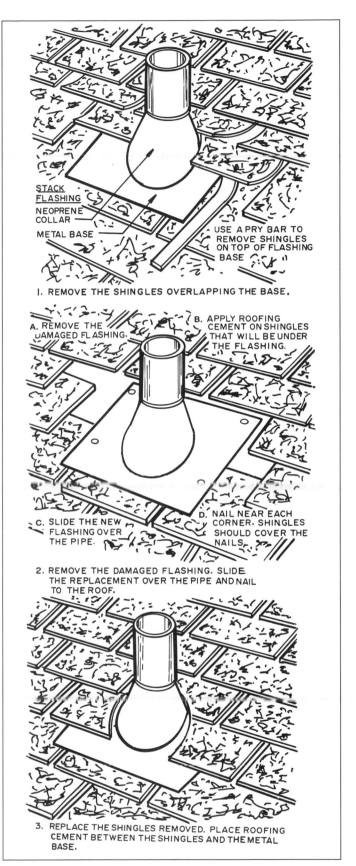

4–24. When stack flashing deteriorates, it is best to replace the flashing. Temporary repairs can be made with roofing cement.

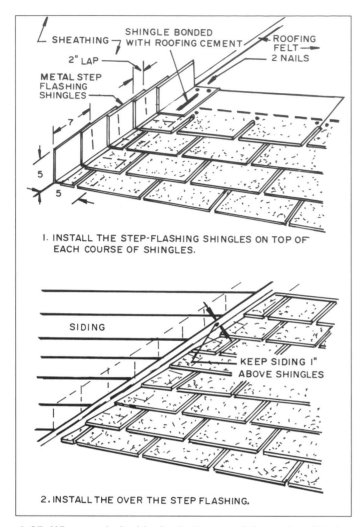

SHEATHING — SHINGLE BONDED WITH ROOFING CEMENT — ROOFING FELT — 2 NAILS

2" LAP

METAL STEP FLASHING SHINGLES

7

5

5

1. INSTALL THE STEP-FLASHING SHINGLES ON TOP OF EACH COURSE OF SHINGLES.

SIDING

KEEP SIDING 1" ABOVE SHINGLES

2. INSTALL THE OVER THE STEP FLASHING.

4–25. When asphalt shingles butt a wood-framed wall to be finished with wood, vinyl, or other siding, step flashing is installed and the siding is laid over the flashing. The siding serves as the counterflashing.

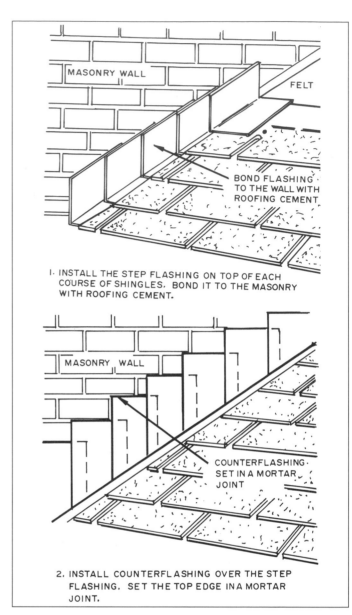

MASONRY WALL

FELT

BOND FLASHING TO THE WALL WITH ROOFING CEMENT.

1. INSTALL THE STEP FLASHING ON TOP OF EACH COURSE OF SHINGLES. BOND IT TO THE MASONRY WITH ROOFING CEMENT.

MASONRY WALL

COUNTERFLASHING SET IN A MORTAR JOINT

2. INSTALL COUNTERFLASHING OVER THE STEP FLASHING. SET THE TOP EDGE IN A MORTAR JOINT.

4–26. When a roof butts a masonry wall, the step flashing is bonded to the masonry with roofing cement and covered with counterflashing, which has the top edge set in a mortar joint.

nailed to the roof sheathing and bonded to the masonry with roofing cement (**4–26**). The second layer, often called **counterflashing**, is bent in an L-shape. One end is placed in a mortar joint, and the other overlaps the first layer. The mortar will have to be chiseled out at a depth of about 1½ inches (38 millimeters), the edge inserted into this opening, and the joint refilled with mortar (refer to **4–23**). When the mortar has set, recheck to be certain the counterflashing is pressed down snugly against the first layer (**4–27**).

Installing Flashing on Chimneys

Chimneys in common use are made of prefabricated metal or masonry. The prefabricated-metal chimney comes with a roof-flashing member similar to that for roof vent pipes. Install as directed by the chimney manufacturer. A generalized example is shown in **4–28**. If you wish to hide the pipe that sticks out of the roof, a frame can be constructed around the chimney with wood studs and an application of wood or some other siding added. Install the chimney flashing, but also install step flashing on the wood siding (**4–29**). Another option is buy thin bricks ½ inch (13 millimeters) thick, glue them to the chimney sheathing, and tuckpoint the joints with mortar.

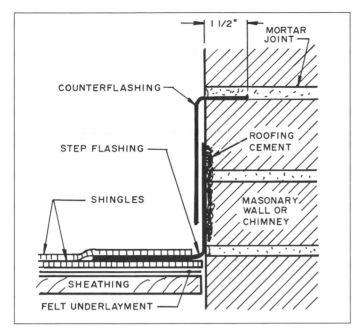

4–27. Counterflashing is set 1½ inches (38 millimeters) into the mortar joint.

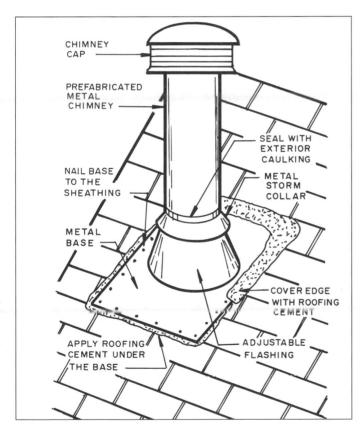

4–28. Typical installation for a prefabricated-metal chimney at the roof. The manufacturer will supply the required flashing and give installation instructions.

4–29 (right). A prefabricated-metal chimney can be hidden by building a wood-framed chimney around it. Install flashing to it as would be done to a roof meeting a wood-framed wall.

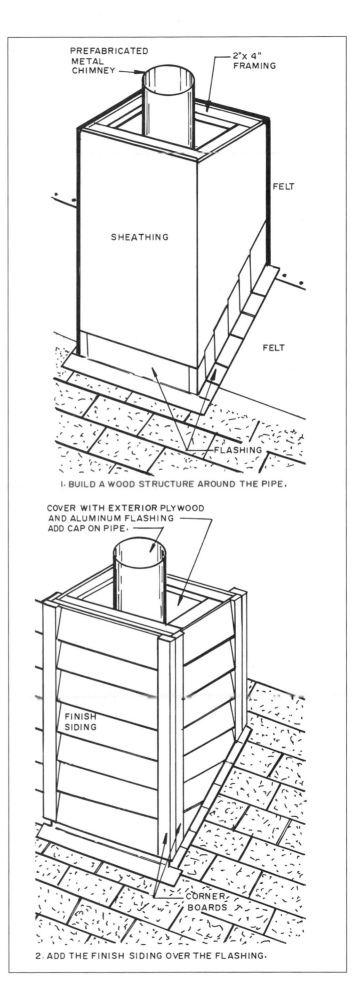

I. BUILD A WOOD STRUCTURE AROUND THE PIPE.

2. ADD THE FINISH SIDING OVER THE FLASHING.

Step flashing and counterflashing are used on masonry chimneys. They are installed as is that described for masonry walls. Needed are special-cut flashing for the front and back of the chimney.

Begin by building a wood cricket at the rear of the chimney (**4–30**). It should be covered with the asphalt underlayment that covers the entire roof. Then lay the shingles just past the front (down side) of the chimney. Cut and install the base flashing on the front (**4–31**). Cover the masonry with roofing cement and use it also to stick the base to the shingles. **Illus. 4–32** is a typical pattern for this base flashing.

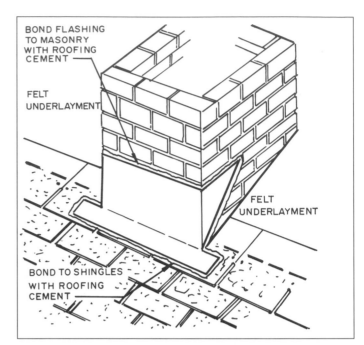

4–31. Begin flashing a chimney by installing the base flashing on the front (down side) of the chimney. Bond it to the chimney and shingles with roofing cement.

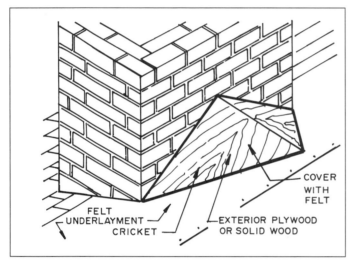

4–30. A cricket built behind a chimney helps turn the water and is especially helpful in areas with snow. Frame it with wood before applying the flashing.

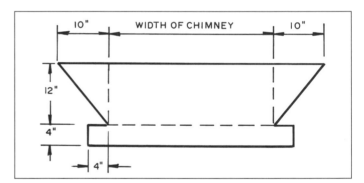

4–32. A typical pattern for the front base of the chimney flashing.

Next, install the step flashing by bonding it to the chimney with roofing cement. Bond one section to the chimney and nail it to the sheathing. Lay a course of shingles over it and bond the overlapping shingle to the flashing with roofing cement. Continue to the back of the chimney (**4–33**). This is the same as bonding flashing to a masonry wall (refer to **4–26** and **4–27**).

Now place the rear flashing over the cricket. It is bonded to the chimney with roofing cement and secured to the sheathing with cleats (**4–34**). Large crickets can be covered with shingles. A typical cricket flashing pattern is shown in **4–35**. Consider laying out the cricket on heavy paper, folding the paper, and placing the paper against the chimney

before using it as a pattern to mark and cut the aluminum.

Next, apply the counterflashing to the step flashing and then a single long counterflashing piece over the front flashing. Set these about 1½ inches (38 millimeters) into the mortar joint. On the back of the chimney, use counterflashing to cover the edge of the cricket flashing (**4–36**).

Chimney flashing may produce leaks after a number of years. Examine it to see where it has failed. Generally, the metal itself is in good condition and either the old mortar on the counterflashing has to be removed and replaced or, if it is not in bad condi-

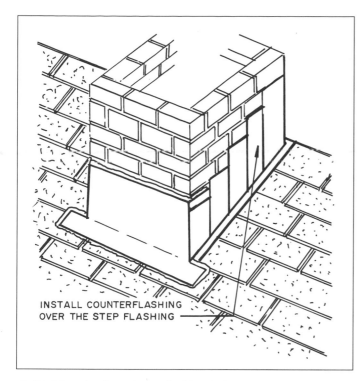

4–33. After the front-base flashing is in place, install the step flashing and counterflashing as detailed in 4-26 and 4-27.

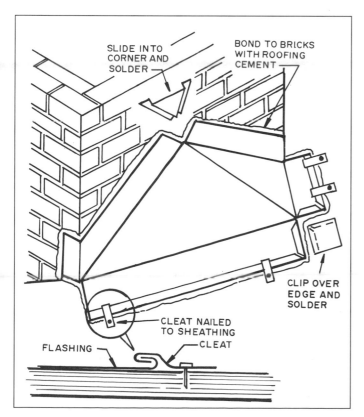

4–34. Cover the cricket with aluminum flashing cut to fit against the chimney, the cricket, and the roof sheathing.

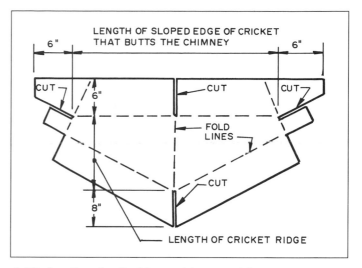

4–35. A pattern for flashing a chimney cricket.

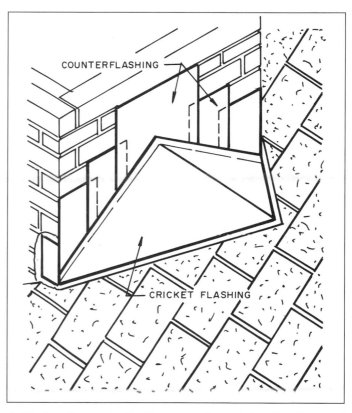

4–36. Install counterflashing over the cricket flashing and bond the shingles to the edges of the cricket flashing with roofing cement.

tion, sealed with a high-quality caulk. It may also be helpful to seal the edges of the counterflashing with caulking. Seldom is it necessary to tear off shingles and replace the actual metal flashing. If galvanized steel was used, it could be painted with a rust-retarding primer and a finish coat of a good exterior enamel.

Valley Flashing

Open-valley flashing may be made from mineral-surfaced roll roofing or galvanized steel, aluminum, or copper. Construction of mineral-surface open-valley flashing is shown in **4–37**. This is typical for use with asphalt or fiberglass shingles. While it will last a long time, when surface deterioration is noticed a decision has to be made as to replace it or coat it with an asphalt product such as cold tar. If you are replacing it, a sharp trowel or drywall trowel can be used to loosen shingles on each side. A better-looking finished job is likely if the old flashing is removed rather than a new one laid over the old. Consider replacing it with aluminum flashing.

A popular type of valley flashing is the closed woven valley (**4–38**). Here the valley has a layer of heavy roll roofing and the shingles are laid over each other, forming the watertight valley. Three-tab strip shingles must be used. Individual shingles do not work well with this technique.

Metal flashing is often used for open-valley construction. The valley is covered with a layer of asphalt felt. The metal valley has an inverted V which runs down its center. This stiffens the flashing and tends to prevent water from running across the flashing to the other side (**4–39**). The edges of the flashing are rolled and are used to secure the cleats, which hold the flashing to the sheathing and provide a drainage channel if water happens to get under the shingles. The shingles are bonded to the

4–37. This open-valley flashing is composed of two layers of mineral-faced asphalt roll roofing.

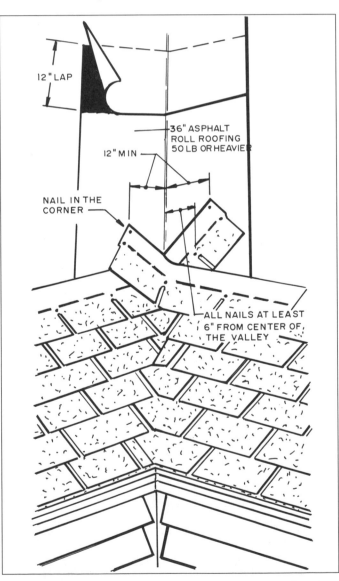

4-38. Woven valley flashing uses 50-pound roll roofing over the roofing felt underlayment. The three-tab asphalt or fiberglass shingles are laid over each other in the valley.

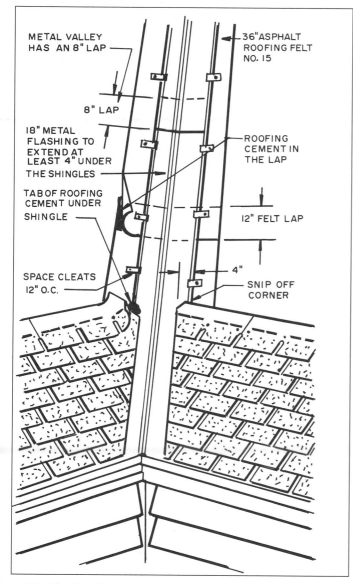

Labels in illustration:
- METAL VALLEY HAS AN 8" LAP
- 36" ASPHALT ROOFING FELT NO. 15
- 8" LAP
- 18" METAL FLASHING TO EXTEND AT LEAST 4" UNDER THE SHINGLES
- ROOFING CEMENT IN THE LAP
- TAB OF ROOFING CEMENT UNDER SHINGLE
- 12" FELT LAP
- SPACE CLEATS 12" O.C.
- 4"
- SNIP OFF CORNER

4–39. Metal valley flashing is held to the sheathing with cleats that fit into the curved edge of the flashing.

4–40. This detail shows how the metal valley flashing is held with cleats after it is installed over a roofing-felt valley.

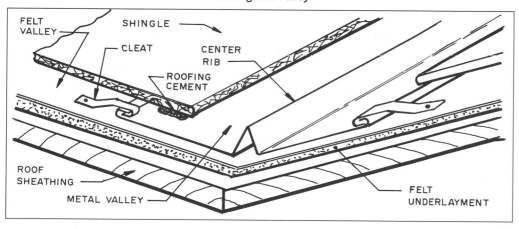

Labels in illustration:
- FELT VALLEY
- SHINGLE
- CLEAT
- CENTER RIB
- ROOFING CEMENT
- ROOF SHEATHING
- METAL VALLEY
- FELT UNDERLAYMENT

flashing with plastic asphalt cement (**4–40**). No nails should punch through the metal flashing.

If the valley flashing is galvanized steel, it would be wise to keep it painted. Aluminum and copper flashing require no special maintenance.

Protecting the Rake and Drip Edge with Flashing

The drip edge and rake edge of the roof should be protected with flashing designed especially for this purpose. This prevents water from running back under the shingles on the edges of the roof and wetting the fascia. If this happens, the fascia will eventually rot. **Illus. 4–41** contains installation details for this flashing.

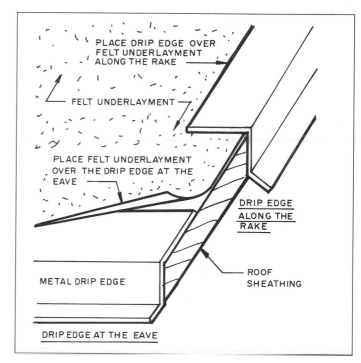

Labels in illustration:
- PLACE DRIP EDGE OVER FELT UNDERLAYMENT ALONG THE RAKE
- FELT UNDERLAYMENT
- PLACE FELT UNDERLAYMENT OVER THE DRIP EDGE AT THE EAVE
- DRIP EDGE ALONG THE RAKE
- METAL DRIP EDGE
- ROOF SHEATHING
- DRIP EDGE AT THE EAVE

4–41 (above). Metal drip edges are placed on the sheathing at the eave and along the rake. They prevent water from getting into the sheathing and starting to rot it.

Roof-Flashing Maintenance and Repair ■ **219**

GUTTER AND DOWNSPOUT REPAIR

Gutters and downspouts are essential to keeping the area beneath the house dry. **Gutters** collect the water that runs off the roof, and **downspouts** direct the water away from the house. By this redirection, water is prevented from seeping under the house or into the basement. Gutters and leaders are most frequently made from aluminum, plastic, or galvanized steel.

Gutter Maintenance

Gutters should frequently be checked to make certain they are free of leaves or other debris. In the autumn, they may need to be checked every few weeks. Clogged gutters will overflow, permitting water to run under the house. The water will also run over the fascia boards and possibly rot the roof sheathing and ends of the rafters.

Gutters can be covered with wire screen, or strainers may be put in the gutters at the downspouts to help prevent them from becoming clogged (**4–42**). While screens and strainers help keep gutters and downspouts free to drain water,

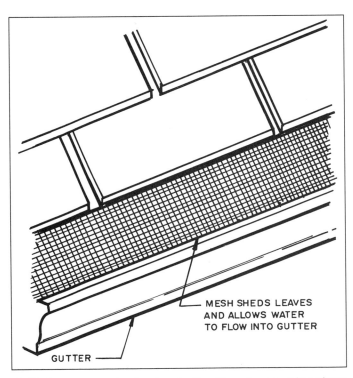

4–42. Leaves can be kept out of gutters by covering them with one of the several screening materials available at the local building-supply dealer.

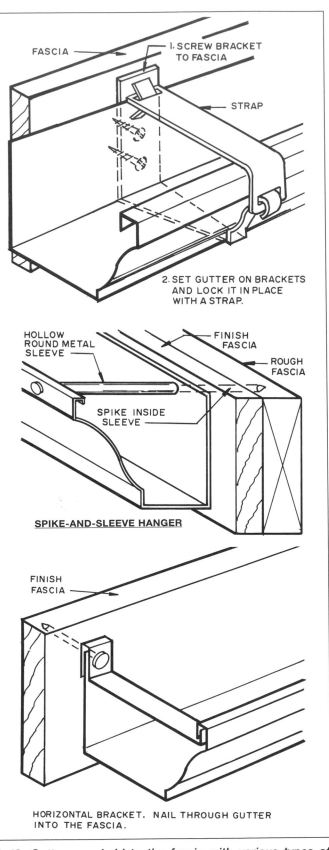

4–43. Gutters are held to the fascia with various types of hangers. These are provided by the company manufacturing the gutters that will be installed. These are a few of those available.

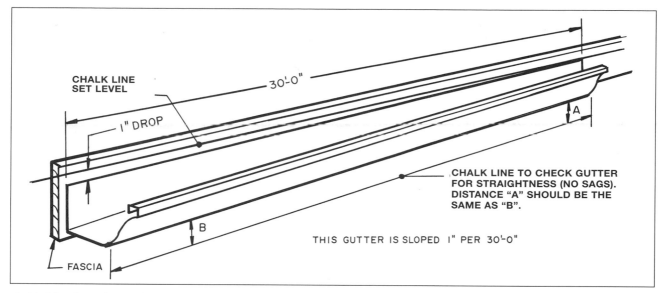

CHALK LINE SET LEVEL

30'-0"

1" DROP

A

CHALK LINE TO CHECK GUTTER FOR STRAIGHTNESS (NO SAGS). DISTANCE "A" SHOULD BE THE SAME AS "B".

B

THIS GUTTER IS SLOPED 1" PER 30'-0"

FASCIA

4–44. Check each section of the gutter for straightness and make certain there is a minimum slope toward a downspout.

they still must be cleaned periodically. After the leaves have been removed from the gutter, flush it with a garden hose.

Check the devices holding the gutter to the fascia. Sometimes these devices work loose and the weight of leaves, snow, and water causes the gutter to sag. This is a special problem in the snowbelt areas. Renail in a new spot and add additional hangers. Typical gutter hangers are shown in **4–43**.

Check to be certain the gutters are straight. If a gutter sags, it will not drain properly. A gutter's straightness can be checked by running a chalk line from one end to the other (**4–44**).

Remember, the gutter must slope toward a downspout. If water stands in the gutter, loosen the hangers and raise the gutter as needed to produce a slope of at least 1 inch (25 millimeters) per 30 feet (9 meters). Check for slope with a large level or run a chalk line with a line level (**4–44**).

Check for rot by sticking a knife blade into the fascia board and the sheathing. If they are soft, check to see if they need to be replaced. Their softness is an indication that the gutter is overflowing and wetting them.

Gutter Repair

The most frequent problem associated with repairing **galvanized-steel gutters** is that of rust on the inside of the gutter. Remove the rust with a wire brush and paint the inside of the gutter with a rust-inhibiting paint.

If small areas have rusted through, they can be patched. Clean the metal area of rust and wipe it down with paint thinner. When it is dry, apply a coating of epoxy over the area and press a piece of fiberglass cloth into it. This is the same cloth used in autobody repair. Put a second coat of epoxy over the patch (**4–45**, on page 222). Large holes may require several layers of fiberglass and epoxy. Some use roofing cement instead of epoxy as the binder.

A metal patch can also be used. After cleaning the area, coat it with epoxy and press the metal patch into it. The patch should be of the same metal as the gutter. Then blind-rivet the patch to the gutter. Seal the edges of the patch with epoxy. Generally, when steel gutters begin to rust and develop holes, the entire length is bad and should be replaced.

Another product used to seal small openings, rusted areas, and joints between gutter sections is referred to as **gutter seal** in most building-supply stores. It is sold in tubes like caulking. Gutter seals fit in a standard caulking gun and extrude a plastic-like sealer. Clean the surface and sand off all rust before applying the sealer. It is tough and not damaged by freezing.

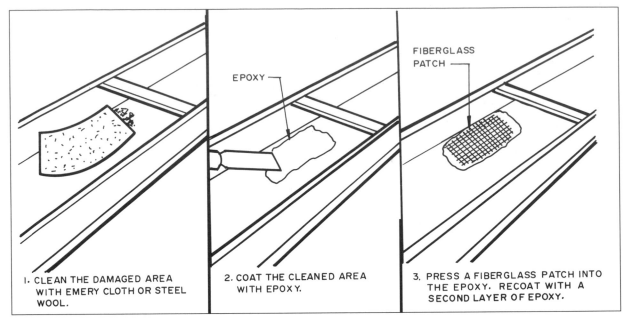

1. CLEAN THE DAMAGED AREA WITH EMERY CLOTH OR STEEL WOOL.

2. COAT THE CLEANED AREA WITH EPOXY.

3. PRESS A FIBERGLASS PATCH INTO THE EPOXY. RECOAT WITH A SECOND LAYER OF EPOXY.

4-45. A damaged area in a metal gutter can be patched with epoxy and a fiberglass patch.

REPLACING GUTTERS AND DOWNSPOUTS

The parts for a gutter system are shown in **4–46**. Galvanized steel gutters are available either unpainted or prefinished. If unpainted gutters are being used, before they can be painted they must be left exposed to the elements for a period of months or cleaned with mineral spirits to remove contaminants. Special galvanized-steel primer must be used before painting with regular house paint. Prevent

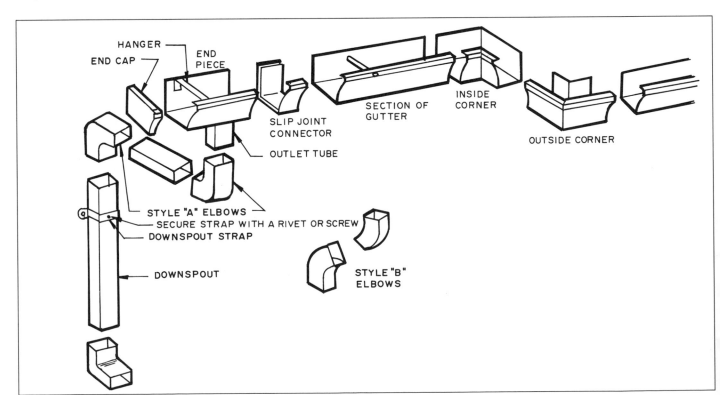

4-46. A gutter system is made up of these parts. Be certain all the parts that are used are from the same manufacturer.

rusting of prefinished steel gutters by painting all cut edges or scratches in a prefinished enamel.

Aluminum gutters, either prefinished or unfinished, will not rust. They are lightweight and easier to install than steel gutters. Aluminum gutters are not as strong as steel gutters, and may dent if a ladder and a heavy weight are placed against them. Try to place a ladder against a gutter near a hanger, because that is the strongest point.

Vinyl plastic gutters will not corrode or ever need painting. They are lightweight and easy to install. However, they will not withstand the weight of a ladder against them and, if not fully supported, may sag on hot days.

Replacing Gutters

To replace gutters, follow these steps:

1. Take down the old gutter, measure it for length, and determine the fittings needed. Leave the gutter on the ground by the wall from which it was removed as a reminder of how to assemble the new parts.

2. Mark, cut, and assemble the new gutter on the ground. Metal and vinyl gutters can be cut with a hacksaw; vinyl gutters can also be cut with a crosscut saw. It helps to put a piece of scrap 2 x 4 wood inside the gutter to reinforce it while cutting (**4–47**). Smooth rough edges with a file to help the pieces fit together (**4–48**).

3. If spikes are to be used for hanging, drill holes in the top of the gutter for the spikes to pass through

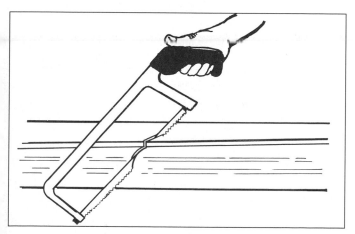

4–47. A hacksaw can be used to cut metal and vinyl gutters.

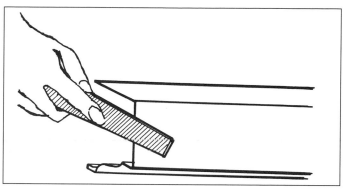

4–48. File or cut edges to remove any burrs. This makes it easier to slide them into slip-joint connectors.

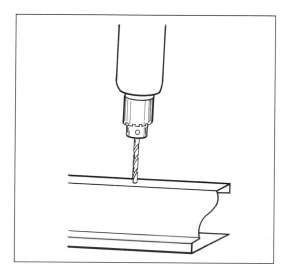

4–49. Drill ¼-inch (6-millimeter) -diameter holes 24 to 30 inches (600 to 750 millimeters) apart when the spike-and-sleeve hanger is used. Back up the gutter with a piece of 2 x 4 so that the gutter is not dented when it is being drilled.

(**4–49**). Back up the gutter with a 2 x 4 while drilling ¼-inch (6-millimeter) -holes in the gutter, spaced approximately every 30 inches (750 millimeters).

4. When assembling aluminum gutters, apply mastic to the inside of one end and to an end cap; then assemble the parts. Continue to join the other sections by applying mastic at each slip-joint connector (**4–50**). Installing sheet-metal screws or pop rivets can strengthen joints (**4–51**).

5. Some vinyl gutter systems are assembled by snap joints that fit tight without a sealant. If mechanical bonding is necessary, use cement that will bond vinyl materials.

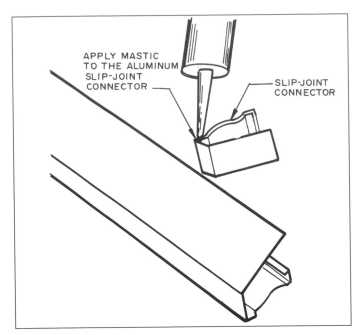

4–50. Apply mastic adhesive to the joints of all connections in aluminum gutters. The joints can be strengthened by installing sheet-metal screws or pop rivets.

6. Snap a chalk line on the fascia. Give it the correct slope toward the downspout end. A slope of 1 inch every 16 feet (5 meters) is commonly used, but more slope can be used if the situation calls for it. If the gutter has a downspout on each end, the chalk line will be set higher in the center than on the ends (**4–52**). Mark the line for the top edge on the fascia.

Check to be certain the gutter placement will allow water to drain off the roof into it, yet is high enough that a buildup of heavy snow will tend to flow over it (**4–53**).

7. With a helper holding the gutter in place, and the gutter aligned with the mark on the fascia, install the gutter hangers into the fascia. If metal straphangers are used, they can be nailed to the fascia first, and then the gutter set into them. Follow the manufacturer's instructions.

In mild climates, space the hangers every 32 inches (813 millimeters). In snow areas, space them 16 inches (406 millimeters). This spacing makes it possible to nail them into the end of the rafter. Good construction will have a 2-inch (51-millimeter) -thick rough fascia over which the ¾-inch (19-millimeter) finished fascia is nailed. In this case, there is

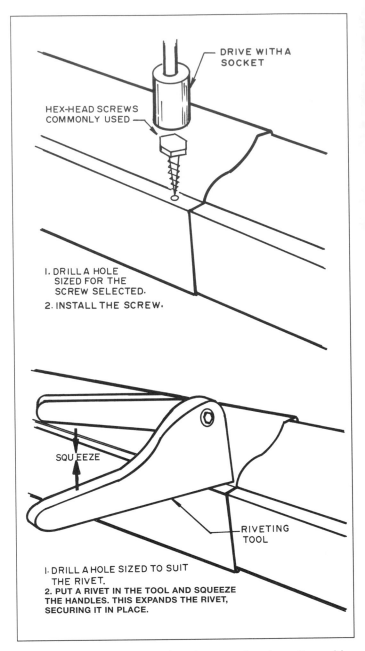

4–51. Connections in metal gutters can be strengthened by installing sheet-metal screws or pop rivets.

no need to try to nail the hangers into the end of a rafter. Nailing into just a single ¾-inch-thick fascia is not a good practice (**4–54**).

8. When possible, connect the ends of the pieces of gutters with the connectors provided while the parts are on the ground (**4–55**). If the run is long, it may be too difficult to handle and the connection can be made after each part is installed on the fascia. A number of different types of connectors are available.

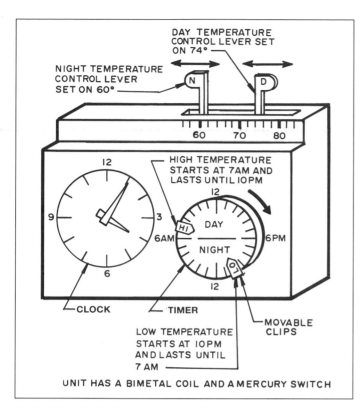

DAY TEMPERATURE CONTROL LEVER SET ON 74°

NIGHT TEMPERATURE CONTROL LEVER SET ON 60°

60 70 80

12

9 3

6

CLOCK

12

6AM HI DAY 6PM

NIGHT

12

TIMER

HIGH TEMPERATURE STARTS AT 7AM AND LASTS UNTIL 10PM

MOVABLE CLIPS

LOW TEMPERATURE STARTS AT 10PM AND LASTS UNTIL 7 AM

UNIT HAS A BIMETAL COIL AND A MERCURY SWITCH

3–73 (above). A clock-operated thermostat can regulate the temperature of the air over a 24-hour period. When used with gas- and oil-fired furnaces, this thermostat can save money by lowering the temperature during the hours the house is not occupied.

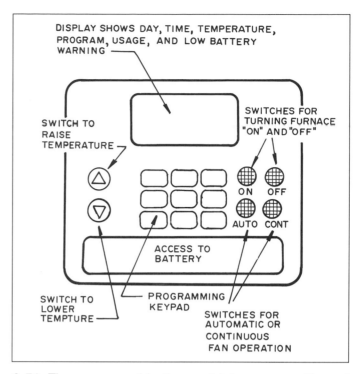

DISPLAY SHOWS DAY, TIME, TEMPERATURE, PROGRAM, USAGE, AND LOW BATTERY WARNING

SWITCH TO RAISE TEMPERATURE

SWITCHES FOR TURNING FURNACE "ON" AND "OFF"

ON OFF

AUTO CONT

ACCESS TO BATTERY

SWITCH TO LOWER TEMPTURE

PROGRAMMING KEYPAD

SWITCHES FOR AUTOMATIC OR CONTINUOUS FAN OPERATION

3–74. The programmable thermostat is very versatile and can be programmed to change the air temperature several times a day and produce different temperatures on different days of the week.

Review the instruction sheet that accompanies the new thermostat. It will give a step-by-step procedure for removing the old unit and installing the new one. Following is a typical procedure:

1. Turn off the power to the furnace at the power panel.

2. Remove the cover and the thermostat, exposing the mounting plate and connecting wires (**3–75**).

3–75. To remove the old thermostat, turn off the power to the furnace, remove the cover, unscrew the thermostat control, and remove the old mounting plate from the wall. Be certain to mark the wires by the code letters before disconnecting them from the old thermostat.

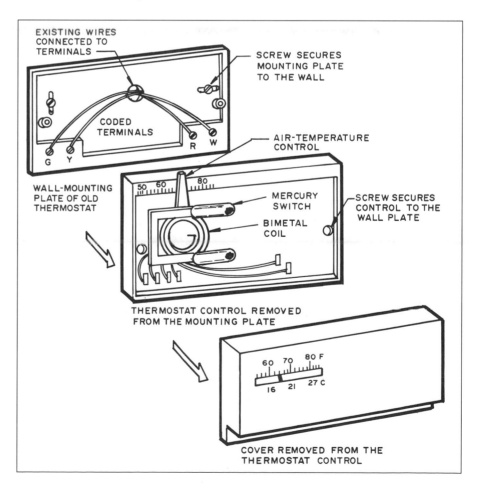

EXISTING WIRES CONNECTED TO TERMINALS

SCREW SECURES MOUNTING PLATE TO THE WALL

CODED TERMINALS

G Y R W

WALL-MOUNTING PLATE OF OLD THERMOSTAT

AIR-TEMPERATURE CONTROL

50 60 80

MERCURY SWITCH

BIMETAL COIL

SCREW SECURES CONTROL TO THE WALL PLATE

THERMOSTAT CONTROL REMOVED FROM THE MOUNTING PLATE

60 70 80 F

16 21 27 C

COVER REMOVED FROM THE THERMOSTAT CONTROL

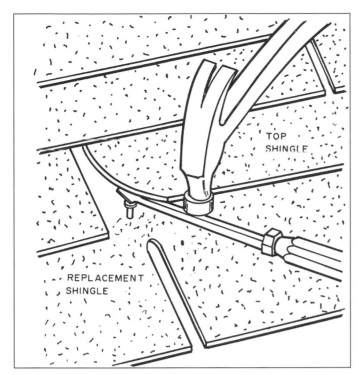

4–13. If the shingles are cold or brittle, carefully lift the top shingle enough to set the nail in place with your thumb. Then drive it in place by placing a bar on the nail and striking the bar with a hammer.

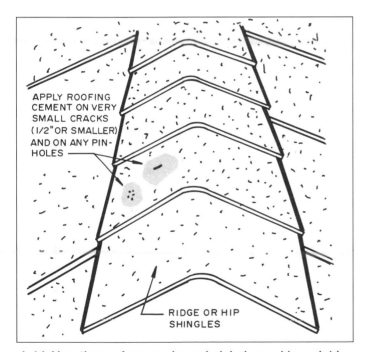

4–14. Very tiny surface cracks and pinholes on hip and ridge shingles should be sealed with a coat of roofing cement.

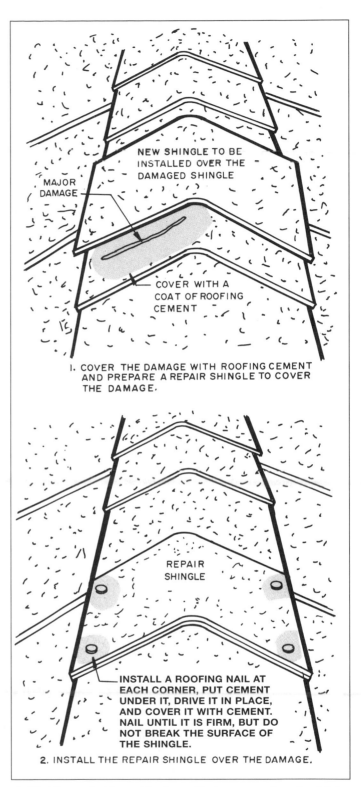

1. COVER THE DAMAGE WITH ROOFING CEMENT AND PREPARE A REPAIR SHINGLE TO COVER THE DAMAGE.

2. INSTALL THE REPAIR SHINGLE OVER THE DAMAGE.

4–15. Hip and ridge shingles with large cracks should be repaired by bonding and nailing a new shingle over the damaged shingle.

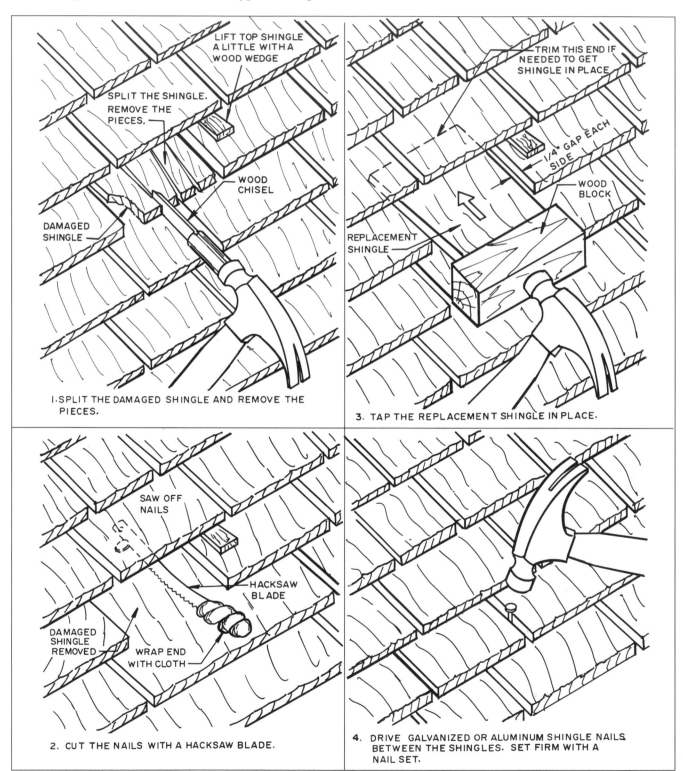

CHIMNEYS

Sometimes a masonry chimney will absorb moisture and cause small amounts to work down into the house, so the area around the chimney at the ceiling will get damp. If the flashing is secure, the chimney will have to be coated with a water-repellent material. This is available in all building-supply and hardware stores. It is a clear liquid and will not discolor the masonry.

The mortar joints will also have to be checked. If a few minor cracks between the mortar and the masonry are found, they can be filled with caulking designed especially to seal cracks in masonry and concrete. It is highly weather-resistant and flexible.

If the mortar joints are badly deteriorated, the chimney will have to be tuck-pointed. **Tuck-pointing** consists of removing the defective mortar joints and filling the area in with fresh mortar.

If it is a small job and the roof is not too steep, you may want to try it yourself. Be certain to cover the shingles on the roof so they are not damaged.

Following are the basic tuck-pointing steps (**4–23**):

1. Chisel out the old mortar about ¾ to 1 inch (19 to 25 millimeters) deep. Use a tuck-pointing chisel. Be certain to wear eye protection.

2. After chiseling out the old mortar, clean all loose material out of the joint. Compressed air is best for this, but a good brush can be used.

3. When preparing to apply the new mortar, wet the joints with water.

4. The new mortar should be as similar to the old mortar as possible. If the chimney is very old, the exact mortar will most likely not be available or you will not be able to determine its composition. New mortars expand at different rates than older mortars and may produce enough pressure to cause the faces of the bricks to spall (break up) and fall off. When in doubt, some home owners use the currently available type-O mortar. Mix it as follows: one part type-O portland cement, two parts lime, and seven parts fine mortar sand. Add as little water as possible, so that the mix is rather stiff. If it is squeezed into a ball, it should retain that shape.

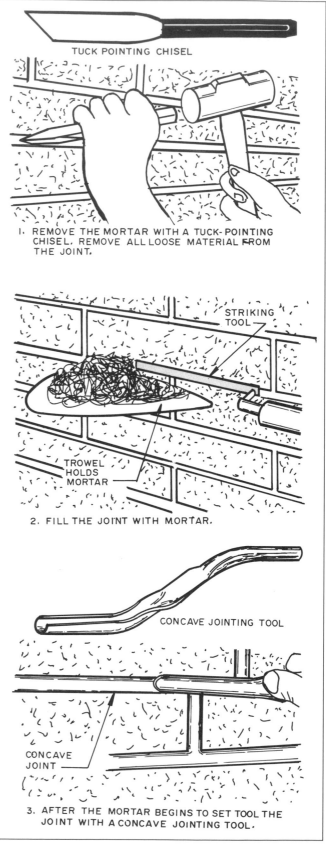

TUCK POINTING CHISEL

1. REMOVE THE MORTAR WITH A TUCK-POINTING CHISEL. REMOVE ALL LOOSE MATERIAL FROM THE JOINT.

STRIKING TOOL

TROWEL HOLDS MORTAR

2. FILL THE JOINT WITH MORTAR.

CONCAVE JOINTING TOOL

CONCAVE JOINT

3. AFTER THE MORTAR BEGINS TO SET TOOL THE JOINT WITH A CONCAVE JOINTING TOOL.

4–23. *Badly deteriorated mortar joints should be tuck-pointed. This strengthens the chimney and reduces water leakage.*

GUTTER AND DOWNSPOUT REPAIR

Gutters and downspouts are essential to keeping the area beneath the house dry. **Gutters** collect the water that runs off the roof, and **downspouts** direct the water away from the house. By this redirection, water is prevented from seeping under the house or into the basement. Gutters and leaders are most frequently made from aluminum, plastic, or galvanized steel.

Gutter Maintenance

Gutters should frequently be checked to make certain they are free of leaves or other debris. In the autumn, they may need to be checked every few weeks. Clogged gutters will overflow, permitting water to run under the house. The water will also run over the fascia boards and possibly rot the roof sheathing and ends of the rafters.

Gutters can be covered with wire screen, or strainers may be put in the gutters at the downspouts to help prevent them from becoming clogged (**4–42**). While screens and strainers help keep gutters and downspouts free to drain water,

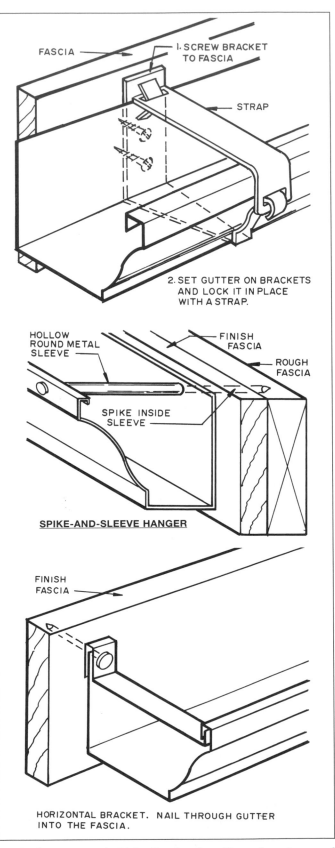

1. SCREW BRACKET TO FASCIA

FASCIA

STRAP

2. SET GUTTER ON BRACKETS AND LOCK IT IN PLACE WITH A STRAP.

HOLLOW ROUND METAL SLEEVE

FINISH FASCIA

ROUGH FASCIA

SPIKE INSIDE SLEEVE

SPIKE-AND-SLEEVE HANGER

FINISH FASCIA

HORIZONTAL BRACKET. NAIL THROUGH GUTTER INTO THE FASCIA.

4–43. Gutters are held to the fascia with various types of hangers. These are provided by the company manufacturing the gutters that will be installed. These are a few of those available.

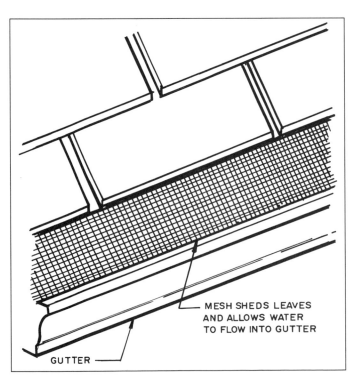

MESH SHEDS LEAVES AND ALLOWS WATER TO FLOW INTO GUTTER

GUTTER

4–42. Leaves can be kept out of gutters by covering them with one of the several screening materials available at the local building-supply dealer.

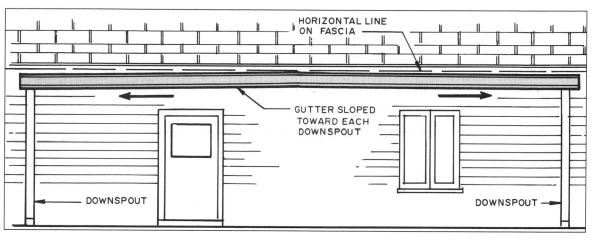

4–52. When a gutter has downspouts on each end, slope it from the center toward each downspout.

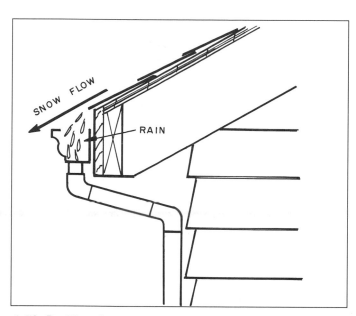

4–53. Position the gutter so that rain can flow into it and a massive snow buildup will tend to flow over it and fall to the ground.

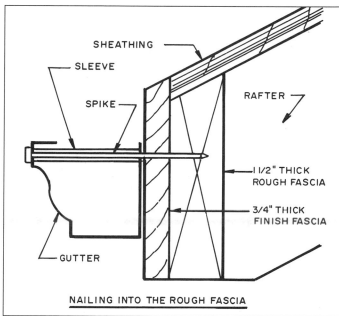

NAILING INTO THE ROUGH FASCIA

4–54. A rough fascia gives a strong nailing surface, and the gutter can be nailed into it anywhere desired along its length. If only a finish fascia is used, it is necessary to nail into the ends of each rafter.

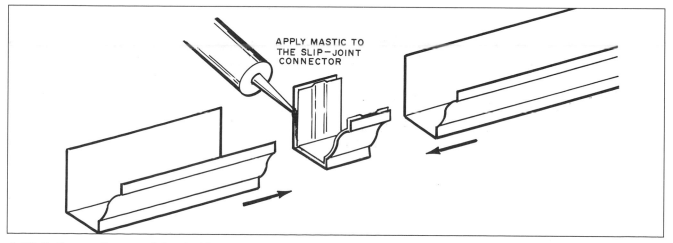

4–55. Gutter sections are joined with some type of a connector. This slip-joint connector is used with metal gutters.

9. After the gutter is up, cut and assemble the downspout sections (refer to **4–46**). Put an elbow at the bottom to turn water away from the house. A concrete splash block turns the water flow away from the foundation (**4–56**). If the lot is flat, it may be necessary to add a length of downspout pipe to the bottom elbow so the water is discharged some distance away from the foundation (**4–57**).

10. An elbow is also needed at the top so the downspout will run close to the wall of the house.

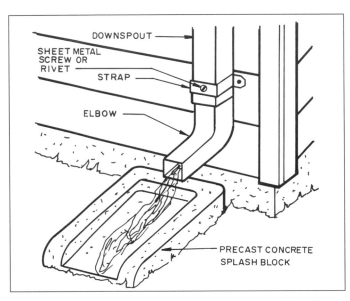

4–56. Put an elbow and splash block on the end of the downspout to direct the water away from the foundation.

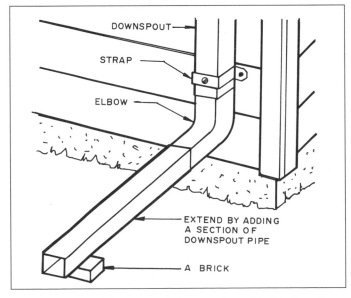

4–57. A length of downspout pipe can be added to the elbow at the bottom of the downspout to discharge the water some distance away from the house's foundation.

Hold the downspout close to the house with at least two straps. Fasten the straps to the downspout with a rivet or sheet-metal screw and to the exterior wall siding (refer to **4–46**).

ICE DAMS

Houses in areas of heavy snows can have damage to the ceiling along the exterior walls due to the backup of ice that forms under the snow. This backup is called an **ice dam**. Sometimes icicles will hang from the gutters. This signals an ice-dam problem.

Ice dams are caused by heat in the attic; this melts the snow, and the water trickles down the roof only to freeze on the overhang. As this continues, water builds up under the snow and eventually finds its way under the shingles and onto the interior ceiling (**4–58**).

Another contributing factor is inadequate ventilation. Ventilation should remove the heat escaping into the attic, permitting the air to be the same temperature as the outside air. Providing additional ventilation can reduce ice dams. Since snow may cover and seal off ridge vents and electric-vent fans, consider adding louvers in the gable ends. Fans can also be mounted on the louvers to increase the volume of airflow (**4–59**).

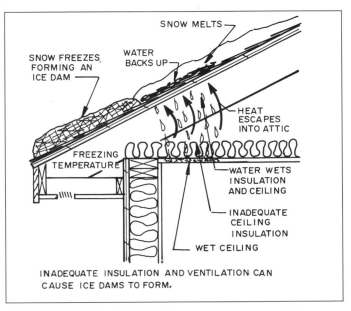

4-58. Inadequate ceiling insulation and attic ventilation can lead to the formation of ice dams.

4–59. In areas of heavy snowfall, ridge vents and power vents often are covered with snow, eliminating the means for ventilating the attic.

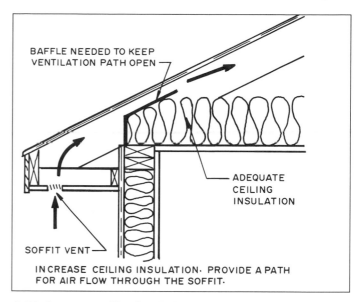

4–60. Increase celling insulation to reduce heat loss into the attic. Provide a baffle to ensure that the air flows openly from the soffit into the attic.

It is necessary to increase the amount of insulation in the ceiling to cut back on the heat loss to the attic (**4–60**).

The amount of insulation there should be in the attic will vary depending upon the climate and the type of insulation. Frequently the local electric-power representative can present some ideas about what is recommended locally. This also increases comfort in the summer by preventing attic heat from entering down through the ceiling.

Another technique is to place electric heat tape along the eave over the overhang. It prevents the water from freezing, so it drains off the roof. However, in some situations electric heat tape, instead of solving the problem, will move the ice dam a bit farther up the roof. The solution is more attic ventilation and insulation.

If a new roof is being added or a new home built, place a synthetic rubber shield or install cemented double layers of No. 15 asphalt roofing felt over the eave and extend it at least 24 inches (609 millimeters) over the interior ceiling. **Illus. 4–61** shows a typical installation.

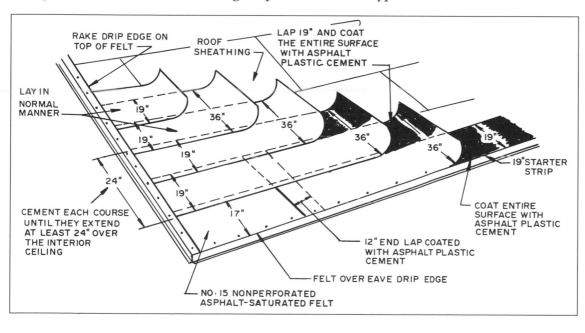

4–61. When reroofing or building a new house, install proper eave protection to prevent ceiling damage should an "ice dam" occur.

Ice dams can also form around skylights. Even if the attic is ventilated, snow tends to melt and freeze around skylights. It is difficult to insulate adequately around skylights to prevent the snow from melting there. Therefore, a membrane (a waterproof sheet material) must be installed on the roof deck before counterflashing is added around the skylight (**4–62**). The building-supply dealer can provide a self-adhering bituminous membrane for this purpose. This will help solve the problem when a skylight is added to new construction or during a remodeling job. If an existing skylight is causing ceiling damage, the shingles will have to be removed, the membrane installed, and the area reshingled.

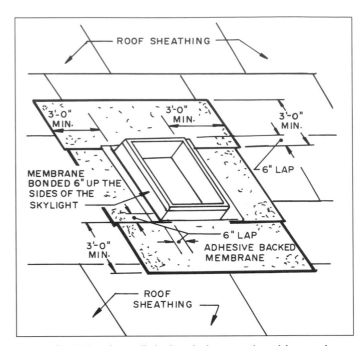

4–62. Skylights have little insulation on the sides and can melt snow and cause an "ice dam." The area around them must be prepared by bonding a membrane to the sheathing and the sides of the skylight before installing the counterflashing.

CHAPTER FIVE

Exterior-Wall Maintenance and Repair

Exterior walls are subject to the extremes of weather, which cause them to deteriorate. Regular examinations and maintenance are necessary so the materials in the wall are not damaged to the point where they must be replaced.

Start the inspection at the eaves. Make certain the soffit is securely fastened in place. Check all wood members on the fascia for loose, warped, or rotted parts. Rot could mean there is a roof or gutter problem. Repair any small cracks or checks with caulking. Renail any loose boards. Probe boards that appear spongy with a knife. If they are soft, they will have to be replaced.

CHECKING THE CAULKING AT JOINTS AND SEAMS

One of the most common maintenance activities is to check and replace the caulking at all joints and seams.

Check inside and outside corners where the siding meets a corner board or is covered by a metal corner unit. Caulk any openings as shown in **5–1**. Also check the seam between all doors and windows and the siding. This seam often opens because of the movement of the house. It is essential to caulk all cracks since they are the most common source of water leakage (**5–2**). This leakage will wet the sheathing and studs and, if not corrected promptly, the sheathing and studs will have to be replaced.

Silicone and polysulfide caulking have a long life and are elastomeric, but are not paintable. Polyethylene and polyurethane caulking also have a long life and can be painted. They all are satisfactory

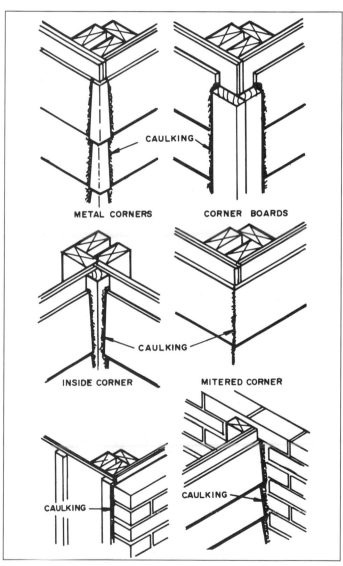

5–1. There are many joints in the exterior siding that must be kept watertight with caulking.

for exterior and interior use. Caulking is available in several colors as well as in clear form.

Caulking is most effective if done when the surface

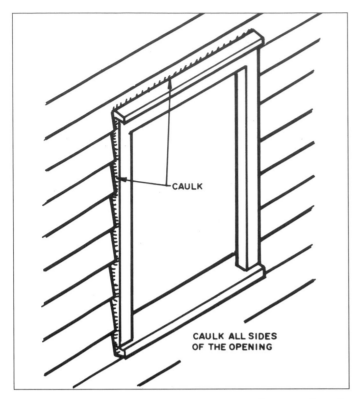

5–2. Caulk around doors, windows, and other openings in the exterior wall.

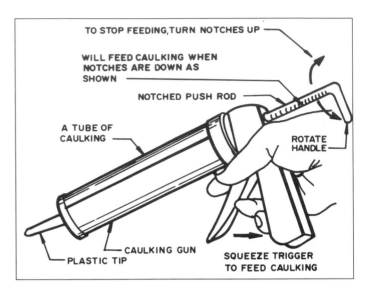

5–3. To operate the caulking gun, turn the push rod until the notched side is down and then squeeze the trigger.

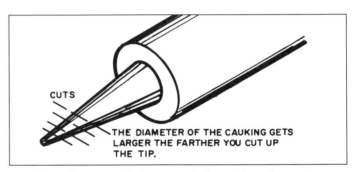

5–4. The diameter of the extruded caulking depends upon where the end of the tip is cut.

is dry and the temperature is above 50° F (10° C). Caulking should set several hours before becoming wet, so do not caulk on a rainy day. Most caulking can be painted 30 minutes after being placed. Be sure to check the manufacturer's instructions on the brand being used.

Before installing new caulking, remove the old material and any paint or dirt in the seam. Caulking is sold in tubes that are placed in a caulking gun (5–3). The end of the tube can be cut to allow the caulk to be forced out. The location of the cut determines the diameter of the extruded caulking (5–4). The tube tip can be pulled or pushed along the seam as it is filled. However, pushing seems to do a better job.

Caulking is also sold in small plastic tubes much like toothpaste. The end of the caulking is cut and the tube squeezed.

MOLD AND MILDEW

Another maintenance problem—very bad in many Southern states—is the formation of mold and mildew on the trim and siding. These can be removed by using a solution of three parts water and one part chlorine bleach. If the mold or mildew is difficult to remove, increase the amount of bleach and add about one-third cup of a strong detergent to each gallon of solution. This can be brushed on the surfaces (5–5) or sprayed on with a garden sprayer (5–6). It is wise to cover the shrubs with plastic drop cloths. After the solution has been on for a while, flush the surface with clean water; use the garden hose to get a hard, concentrated stream of water. Be certain to rinse all windows, doors, porches, light fixtures, and shrubs to remove any trace of the chlorine bleach. Protect your face from any spray and wear rubber gloves. It is suggested that a hat also be worn.

Vinyl siding can be cleaned with a mild soap, water, and a moderately stiff brush. A very stiff brush will scratch the surface.

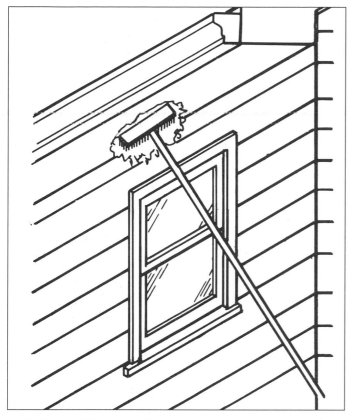

5–5. Mold, mildew, and dirt can be removed from parts of the exterior of a building by dipping a brush in a solution of one-part chlorine bleach and three-parts water and scrubbing the wall. Wear rubber gloves and eye protection.

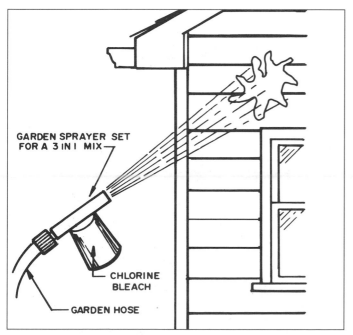

GARDEN SPRAYER SET FOR A 3 IN 1 MIX

CHLORINE BLEACH

GARDEN HOSE

5–6. One way to remove mildew from an exterior wall is to spray a solution of chlorine bleach mixed with water on the wall with a garden hose. This has little pressure, however, so will not dislodge dirt stuck to the surface. Wear rubber gloves and eye protection.

The best results are achieved if the high-pressure spray system used by companies that specialize in cleaning exterior walls is used. Some of these systems also remove mold from roofs. This spray system is used on all types of exterior siding, wood, plastic, and aluminum. It will also clean up concrete driveways and sidewalks, which can also get a green mold. In some localities, such a system can be rented.

EXTERIOR-TRIM MAINTENANCE AND REPAIR

Exterior trim is used to add to the architectural design of the exterior of a house and also serves the very important function of covering seams, thus preventing moisture from leaking into the exterior wall. It also helps stop air infiltration into the wall. Exterior trim includes door and window casing, corner boards, and cornice and rake boards. They should be primed on all sides before they are installed (**5–7**).

If the trim has begun to rot, the rot could be shallow and on the surface or it could be a large area possibly extending through the entire thickness of the piece. There are products on the market that enable these areas to be repaired without replacing the rotted piece. Two such products are manufactured by Abatron, Inc. One product, LiquidWood®, penetrates and cures the wood. It has great strength, strong adhesion properties, is clear, and has low viscosity. It regenerates and waterproofs as it hardens. Brush or pour it on the wood surface. It is good for shallow rot on door and window trim, frames, and on other wood products. Another product, WoodEpox®, is a structural wood substitute. It is a no-shrink putty used to fill large damaged areas and replace the rotted wood that was cut away (**5–8**). Follow the manufacturer's instructions.

If it is necessary to replace the deteriorated trim, follow these steps:

1. Carefully measure the piece of trim to be replaced. Be sure to write down the measurements because the piece will probably be destroyed when it is removed.

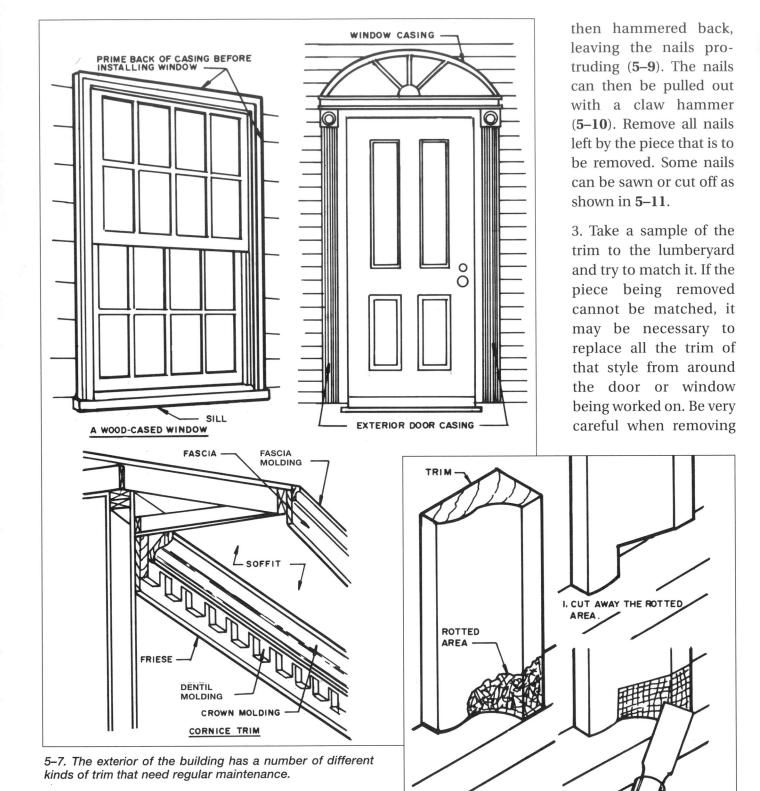

then hammered back, leaving the nails protruding (**5–9**). The nails can then be pulled out with a claw hammer (**5–10**). Remove all nails left by the piece that is to be removed. Some nails can be sawn or cut off as shown in **5–11**.

3. Take a sample of the trim to the lumberyard and try to match it. If the piece being removed cannot be matched, it may be necessary to replace all the trim of that style from around the door or window being worked on. Be very careful when removing

5–7. The exterior of the building has a number of different kinds of trim that need regular maintenance.

2. Attempt to carefully remove the piece with a pry bar. Be careful that the surrounding materials are not damaged. If necessary, use a chisel to split out the board to be replaced. Sometimes the board to be removed can be pried out a short distance and

5–8. Both surface rot and deep decay can be repaired with specially formulated wood-restoration liquids and putty.

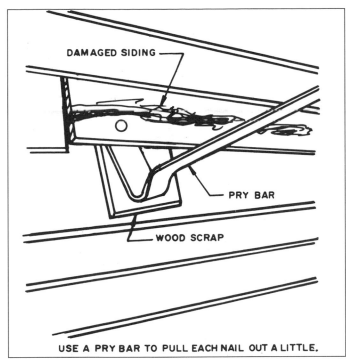

USE A PRY BAR TO PULL EACH NAIL OUT A LITTLE.

5–9. Use a pry bar to pull each nail out of the sheathing about ⅜ inch.

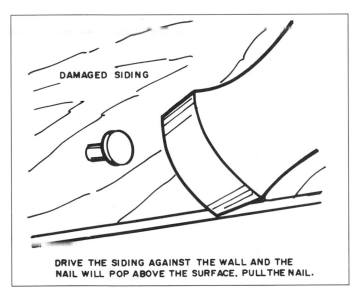

DRIVE THE SIDING AGAINST THE WALL AND THE NAIL WILL POP ABOVE THE SURFACE. PULL THE NAIL.

5–10. Drive the siding back against the sheathing. Use a pry bar or claw hammer to pull out the protruding nails.

the remaining trim that is sound. Those pieces should be saved for repairs to other windows or doors in the house.

4. Cut the new piece of trim to the proper size. Be sure to allow enough length to miter a corner when necessary.

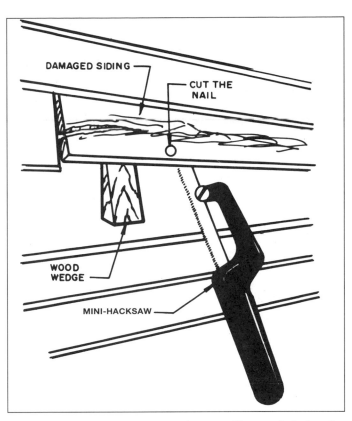

5–11. A mini-hacksaw can be used to cut off any nails below the siding that will not pop up.

5. Apply a primer to all four sides of the piece. After the primer dries, nail the trim in place. Be sure to use galvanized or aluminum nails. If the material below the new piece is wet, allow it to dry completely before covering it with the new trim. If it has deteriorated, replace it.

6. Set the nails, caulk the nail holes, and caulk around the edges of the new piece. After the caulking has set, apply the finish coats of paint.

REPLACING WOOD AND RECONSTITUTED-WOOD LAP SIDING

Small damaged or rotted areas on wood siding can be repaired by cleaning the area back to solid wood and filling the depression with a compound made especially for this purpose (refer to **5–8**). Larger damaged pieces of wood siding should be replaced. Follow these steps to replace wood siding:

1. Use a pry bar to raise the damaged piece. Put a thin scrap of wood under the pry bar so that the

siding below it is not damaged. Work carefully to raise any nails that are in the edge of the siding (**5–9**).

2. Tap the damaged siding back against the sheathing. The raised nail head will stick out. Pull the nail out with the pry bar or a claw hammer (**5–10**).

3. If the nail pulls through the siding when it is lifted or there are nails under the siding, use a mini-hacksaw or keyhole saw with a metal-cutting blade to cut them off (**5–11**). A small wedge can be driven under the siding to provide room for the blade. Pull the piece out when it is free.

4. If these steps do not work, use a wood chisel and hammer to split the siding and remove it in pieces (**5–12**).

5. Carefully measure the length of the replacement piece. Slide it under the top siding board and tap it in place until it is in alignment (**5–13**). Prime it on the back and edges before sliding it in place.

6. If the sheathing is wet, let it dry before installing the new siding. Replace the builder's felt if it has been damaged.

7. Nail as required for the type of siding. Use galvanized or aluminum nails (**5-14**).

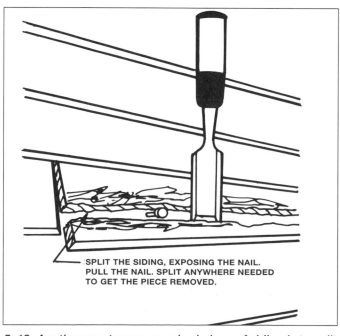

5–12. Another way to remove a bad piece of siding is to split it up and remove the pieces.

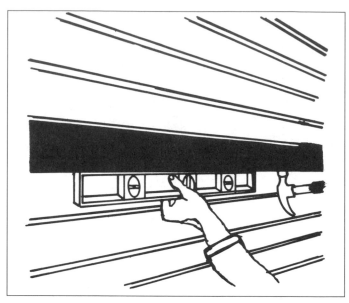

5–13. Slide the replacement piece into place. Line it up with the existing siding and check it with a level.

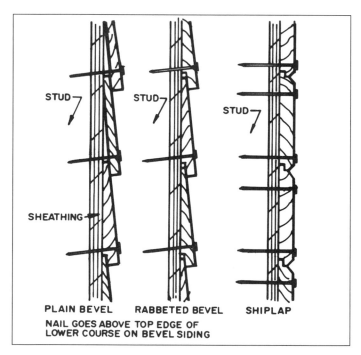

5–14. When the new siding is in place, nail it in the same manner as the original siding. Notice that on the bevel siding the nail is above the top edge of the lower course.

REPAIRING SPLITS IN WOOD SIDING

Occasionally, solid-wood siding will develop a split. This usually occurs where two pieces butt together, where a piece butts a corner board, or at a mitered corner. These splits must be repaired so moisture does not penetrate into the siding, causing it to eventually have to be replaced. To make a repair, do the following:

1. Open the split by inserting a screwdriver and spreading it a bit (**5–15**). Do not force it with so much pressure that the split is increased.

2. Inject a waterproof exterior glue into the split.

3. Push the split closed and nail it to the sheathing with aluminum finishing nails. Wipe off any glue that flows out of the split. Set the nails below the surface and cover them with caulking (**5–16**).

4. After the glue has thoroughly set, sand the area and cover it with two coats of the paint used on the wall.

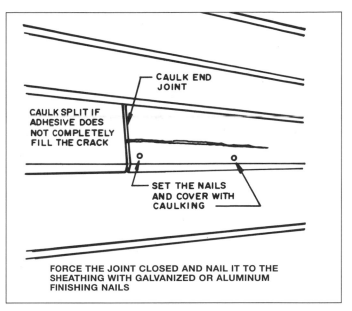

5–16. After inserting the adhesive, push the joint closed and nail it to the sheathing with galvanized or aluminum finishing nails. Set and caulk these nails.

1. Remove the damaged shingle by splitting it into small pieces. Split it with a wood chisel, but do not cut into the shingle below it.

2. Use a metal-cutting keyhole saw to cut off any nails below the overlapping shingle.

3. Cut a new shingle to fit into the space. Size it to allow a ¼-inch (6-millimeter) gap between it and the shingles on each side. Slide the new shingle into place and nail it to the sheathing with galvanized or aluminum nails.

REPAIRING ASBESTOS-CEMENT SIDING

For many years, asbestos-cement siding shingles were widely used. They are hard, brittle, and weather well. However, asbestos fibers have been found to be a major health hazard and asbestos is now banned from use in most construction materials. If an older house has asbestos shingles on the roof or as siding, they can only be removed or replaced by a qualified contractor. Consult the local building inspector, who can cite the regulations and provide contact with an approved asbestos abatement contractor. Additional information can be had by contacting the Consumer Product Safety Commission.

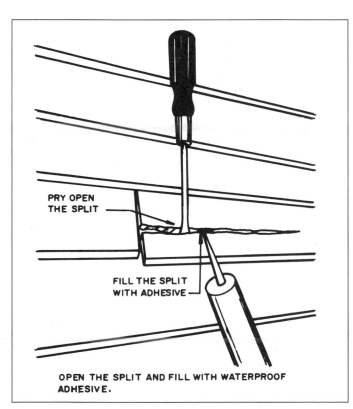

5–15. To repair a small split, pry it open enough so it can be filled with a waterproof adhesive.

REPAIRING WOOD-SHINGLE SIDING

When wood shingles become loose, warped, or split into narrow pieces, they should be replaced or renailed. The procedure to replace a shingle is shown in **5–17**. Follow these steps:

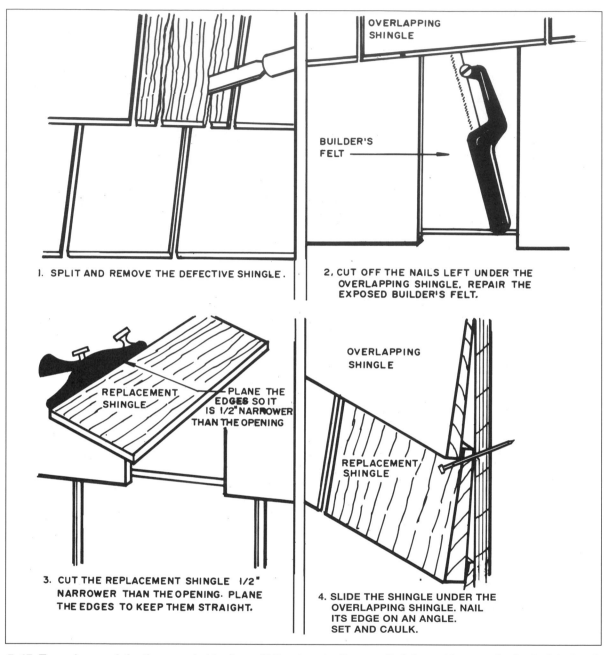

1. SPLIT AND REMOVE THE DEFECTIVE SHINGLE.

2. CUT OFF THE NAILS LEFT UNDER THE OVERLAPPING SHINGLE. REPAIR THE EXPOSED BUILDER'S FELT.

OVERLAPPING SHINGLE

BUILDER'S FELT

3. CUT THE REPLACEMENT SHINGLE 1/2" NARROWER THAN THE OPENING. PLANE THE EDGES TO KEEP THEM STRAIGHT.

REPLACEMENT SHINGLE

PLANE THE EDGES SO IT IS 1/2" NARROWER THAN THE OPENING

4. SLIDE THE SHINGLE UNDER THE OVERLAPPING SHINGLE. NAIL ITS EDGE ON AN ANGLE. SET AND CAULK.

OVERLAPPING SHINGLE

REPLACEMENT SHINGLE

5–17. To replace a defective wood shingle, split it out, cut off any nails left, and be certain the builder's felt is intact or replaced. Then cut and install a new shingle ¼ inch (6 millimeters) narrower than the opening.

REPAIRING A PORTLAND-CEMENT STUCCO EXTERIOR WALL

A portland-cement stucco wall is made of several layers (**5–18**). The sheathing is covered with two layers of waterproof, type-1 building paper. Over this is nailed expanded metal lath, woven-wire mesh, or welded-wire lath. Use galvanized steel-lath furring nails. Do not use aluminum nails; the cement will corrode them.

The cement plaster is applied in three coats. The **scratch coat** is troweled over the metal lath and pressed into it. The coat is about ⅜ inch (9.5 millimeters) thick. It is troweled smooth and, when it stiffens, the surface is covered with horizontal scratches about ⅛ inch (3 millimeters) deep. After it has dried for 10 or 12 hours, the brown coat is applied.

Before the brown coat is applied, the scratch coat

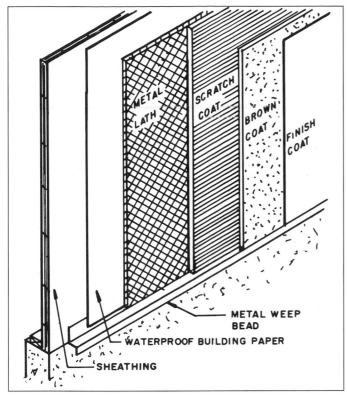

5-18. Typical construction of a portland-cement stucco exterior wall.

is moistened. Some contractors add a bonding agent to the surface. The **brown coat** should be applied about ⅜ inch thick with a steel trowel. Then it is roughed up a bit by troweling with a wood float. A wood float is a handheld tool much like a steel trowel but made of wood. Wait at least one day before applying the finish coat.

The **finish coat** is ⅛ inch thick and can be troweled over the brown coat. Usually, it can be applied with a steel trowel. However, a textured surface can be produced with a sponge or other technique after the steel-troweling. Keep the finished surface damp by spraying it lightly for three days. Color pigments can be added to this coat to match the existing wall.

Repairing Surface Cracks in Portland-Cement Plaster Walls

One common repair is to seal large cracks in the finish coat. These often appear around doors and windows, and are usually caused by settling. If water gets into the cracks and freezes, more extensive damage will occur. Before making a repair, deter-

mine what caused the damage and fix it. Cracks tend to indicate a settling foundation. If the material at the bottom of the wall is crumbling, it is usually caused by water standing in the bottom edge. Therefore, water is getting inside the wall.

To repair surface cracks in a cement-plaster stucco wall, follow these steps:

1. Remove all loose material in the crack. Use a cold chisel or other sharp tool to widen the crack. Undercut the opening so it is wider near the lath than at the surface. This helps form a key to hold the patch (**5–19**).

2. Purchase prepackaged stucco mix for covering the patch. It has the correct proportions of sand, cement, and plasticizers. In order to get the patch to stick to the old stucco around the edges of the patch, a bonding agent has to be added to the mix.

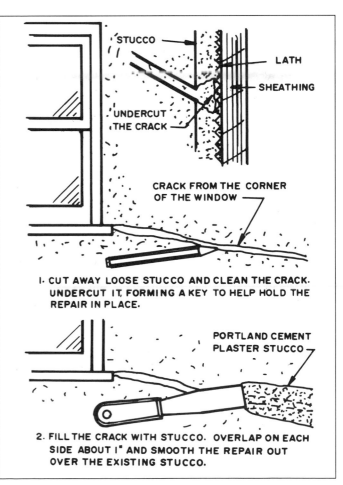

5–19. Large cracks should be cleaned out, undercut, and filled with stucco.

3. Wet the crack with a brush and allow it to dry until there is no surface moisture showing. Then fill the crack with mortar, working it into the crack. Overfill the crack a little and allow the mortar to overlap onto the stucco beside the crack. Then work the patch to match the existing surface texture.

4. If the stucco wall is colored, matching colored stucco can be purchased and applied to the surface of the patch. Dip a wet sponge into the material and dab it over the filled crack.

Fixing Hairline Cracks

Due to settling of the house, an occasional crack may be found in the stucco. Small cracks from a hairline break up to ⅛ or ³⁄₁₆ inch (3 or 5 millimeters) long can be sealed with a good high-quality exterior caulk. Cut the end of the caulking tube so it allows only a very thin amount to extrude. Work this into the crack. Try to keep the caulk off the face of the stucco (5–20).

Caulking is available in a wide range of colors, so choose one as close to the color of the stucco as possible. Remember, since the stucco wall may be painted sometime, choose a caulking that can be painted.

Repairing a Damaged Area on a Wall

Most damage to cement-plaster stucco walls is due to a physical blow or an opening caused by repairs on some part of the structure. The repair must be carefully made so it is watertight and blends in with the rest of the wall. Use these steps to make a repair:

1. Wearing a face mask and leather gloves, cut away all stucco that is not firmly attached to the metal lath. A cut can be made around the area with a mason's chisel or a bricklayer's brick-set chisel (5–21). The cut can also be made with a carborundum blade in a portable circular saw. Then use a chisel and small sledgehammer to break the concrete from the lath (5–22).

2. The exposed old metal lath will be rusty and clogged, so this part will have to be cut away with metal shears. Pry it loose from the sheathing with a pry bar, pulling out all the nails.

3. Cut the stucco back and leave 4 to 6 inches (102 to 152 millimeters) of the existing metal lath after cutting away the part that is rusted. If the sheathing has deteriorated, it will need to be replaced as shown in 5–22.

4. Cover the sheathing with waterproof builder's felt. Work it below the existing paper on the top

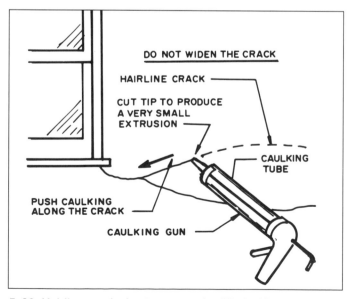

5–20. Hairline cracks in stucco can be filled with high-quality exterior caulking. Keep the caulking off the surface of the stucco.

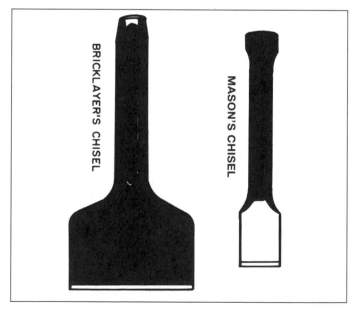

5–21. Bricklayer's and mason's chisels are designed for cutting concrete block, brick, and veined stone.

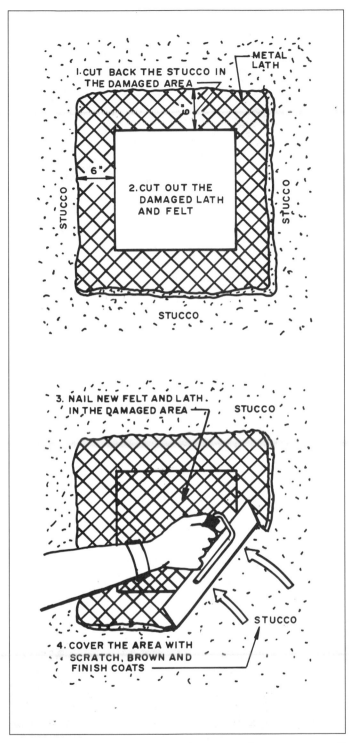

5–22. Severe blows to a portland-cement plaster stucco wall can cause sufficient damage that the entire section needs to be cut away and replaced.

and sides and over the bottom. Some home owners add two layers.

5. Cut a new piece of metal lath to fill the area. Nail it to the sheathing with galvanized furring nails. If the sheathing is one of the rigid, foam insulation types, nail the lathe into the studs.

6. Now apply three coats of portland-cement plaster stucco as described earlier.

Repairing Modified Stucco Walls

Modified stucco exterior-wall systems are referred to as exterior insulation and finish systems (EIFS). The system is a multilayer installation consisting of a water-resistant sheathing material that is covered with a waterproof weather barrier (5–23). Over this a sheet of expanded polystyrene insulation board with moisture-drainage panels is applied and held with mechanical fasteners. A base coat of synthetic plaster is troweled over the insulation board, and a fiberglass reinforcing mesh is embedded into it.

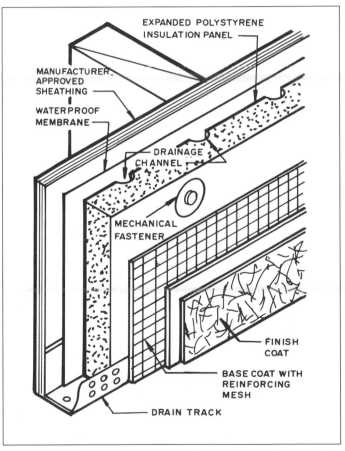

5–23. This exterior insulation and finish system (EIFS) is designed for use on residential buildings. It provides insulation plus a hard, tough exterior finish coating that is troweled over the reinforcing mesh (copyrighted by and used with the permission of Dryvit Systems, Inc.).

Repairing a Portland-Cement Stucco Exterior Wall ■ **239**

After this hardens, the plaster finish coat is troweled over the base coat.

The synthetic plaster is a special mixture available from the company supplying the various components of the system. It is available in a range of colors.

While the finish coat is very hard, a heavy blow may damage it. Following is an abbreviated discussion for making a repair following recommendations from Dryvit Systems, Inc. A detailed instruction booklet is available from the company.

1. Cut through the finished surface, exposing an area about 3 inches (76 millimeters) larger than the damaged area (**5–24**).

2. Cut out the insulation, exposing the sheathing. Clean off the old adhesive.

3. Sand through the finish coat around the edges of the opening, exposing the base coat.

4. Cut a piece of insulation board to fit in the opening and bond it to the sheathing.

5. Bond a piece of reinforcing mesh over the patch and the exposed base coat with the manufacturer-supplied adhesive.

6. After this has dried 24 hours, trowel on the finish coat. Work carefully and blend it into the surrounding finish.

MAINTAINING A BRICK WALL

There is very little to do to maintain a brick wall. An occasional check to see that all mortar joints are intact is helpful. A properly built brick wall will last for many years. Occasionally, a fine crack will appear in the mortar. If a brick wall leaks, it will usually be due to a separation between the mortar and the bricks. Fill any cracks with a special caulking made for this purpose. It is sold in tubes, and applied like regular caulking.

If the brick walls are very old and stained, they can be refreshed by cleaning them. Be careful when selecting the product to clean them; some products can damage the mortar joints. Various chemical

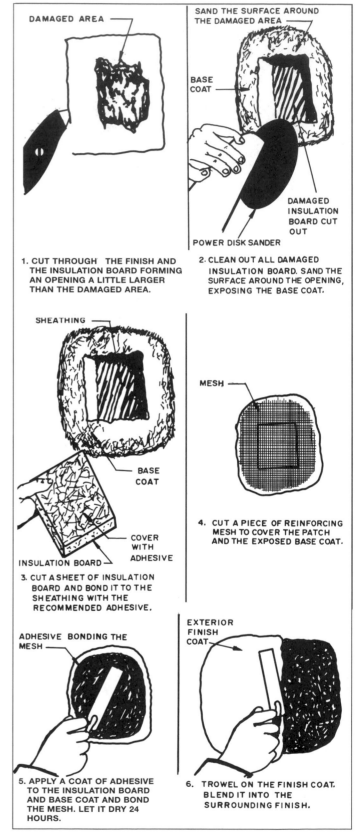

5–24. Physical damage to a modified stucco wall due to a heavy blow can easily be repaired. Follow the EIFS manufacturer's instructions.

cleaners are used, but typically contain acid and can cause trouble. Avoid these unless a professional cleaning company is employed.

The safest way to clean brick walls is to pressure-wash them using a very low pressure. A bristle brush can be used if it will help remove dirt and mold. High-pressure washing could penetrate the mortar joint and cause damage.

Do not wash brick walls during cold weather; any water within the masonry will freeze and cause spalling and cracking.

Brick can also be cleaned mechanically. This involves using a grinder or power sander to remove the surface material. The procedure will also remove some of the masonry surface and is not recommended.

Sandblasting is another mechanical cleaning method, but must be carefully done so as not to damage the masonry and the mortar joints. Again, professional help is recommended.

The National Park Service of the Department of the Interior recommends that water-repellent and waterproof coatings not be used on masonry walls. These tend to cause the wall to retain penetrating moisture and can cause more damage than they prevent.

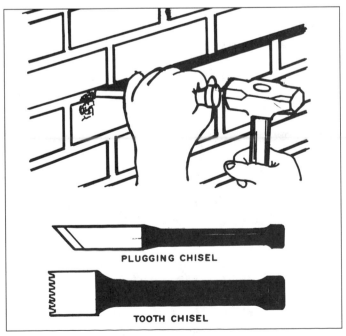

5–25. Use a tooth or plugging chisel to remove the deteriorated mortar from the joint.

Tuck-pointing a Brick Wall

If the house is old and the mortar between the bricks crumbling, the wall should be tuck-pointed. **Tuck-pointing** involves removing the old loose mortar and replacing it with new mortar. Follow these steps to tuck-point bricks:

1. Use a hammer and a toothing or plugging chisel (**5–25**) and a hooked mortar rake (**5–26**) to remove all loose mortar. Cut about 1 inch (25 millimeters) deep (**5–27**). Be certain to wear goggles or a full face shield. If cutting mortar with a carborundum

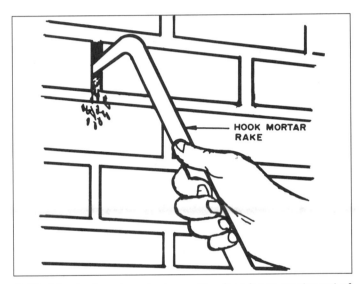

5–26. A hooked mortar rake is used to clean loose mortar out of the joint.

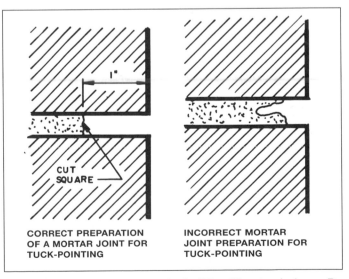

CORRECT PREPARATION OF A MORTAR JOINT FOR TUCK-POINTING

INCORRECT MORTAR JOINT PREPARATION FOR TUCK-POINTING

5–27. Cut the joint about 1 inch (25 millimeters) deep. Be certain to wear goggles or other face protection.

blade in a portable circular saw, also wear a respirator because considerable dust will be produced.

2. With a wire brush and garden hose, brush and wash the joint free of all loose mortar. The joints should be damp but have no standing water when they are filled with mortar.

3. Use prehydrated, type-N mortar for tuck-pointing. The proportions to use are by volume. Thoroughly mix one part of type-N, prehydrated portland cement with three parts of fine sand without water. Add enough water to produce a damp, unworkable mix that will retain its form when pressed into a ball. Wait five minutes and then add enough water to produce a workable mix. The mortar should be used within 30 minutes of final mixing.

4. Work mortar into the back ¼ inch (6 millimeters) of the joint. Pack it solidly into the joint. After doing several feet of the joint, return to the beginning and make another ¼-inch layer. Add additional layers until the joint is full (**5–28**).

5. When the final layer is hard enough to leave a print when a thumb is pressed into it, use a tool with a round blade to smooth and round the mortar joint to match the existing joints. See **Illus**. 4-**23** on page 212 for additional information.

MAINTAINING VINYL AND ALUMINUM SIDING

There is little that is needed to be done with vinyl and aluminum siding except be certain all joints are kept caulked. If the surface gets dirty, it can be washed with a brush and a household detergent. Heavy mold can be removed with pressure-washing.

Vinyl Siding

The color of **vinyl siding** tends to fade over the years. This is caused by ultraviolet radiation from the sun, aging, some minor water absorption, and surface contamination. Applying a nonabrasive, nonchemical paste wax to the vinyl siding will keep it in almost new condition. Commercial vinyl-restoring pastes are also available.

Painting an acrylic latex paint onto the vinyl surface is another means of keeping the vinyl siding in good condition, but this is a short-term solution. Lightly sand the surface with a fine abrasive paper to improve adhesion. Remember, sanding and painting is good for a few years, but the siding cannot be repainted. When this paint deteriorates, the siding will have to be replaced. Part of the problem is that the vinyl siding and the paint coating expand and contract at different rates, leading to failure in adhesion.

Some paint manufacturers have **specialty coatings** suitable for use on vinyl siding. Check with paint dealers to see if they have this product. They can give a predicted life for the finish and indicate if their coating can be reapplied as the old coating fades.

Aluminum Siding

Aluminum siding can be cleaned with a solution consisting of two tablespoons of trisodium phosphate (TSP) in one gallon of clean water. First wet the

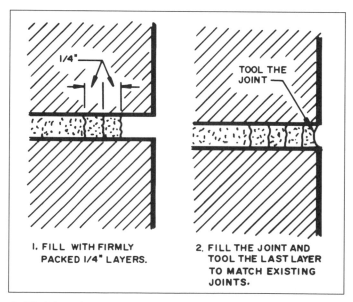

1. FILL WITH FIRMLY PACKED 1/4" LAYERS.

2. FILL THE JOINT AND TOOL THE LAST LAYER TO MATCH EXISTING JOINTS.

5–28. After cleaning and dampening the joint, work the mortar in by solidly packing 1/4-inch-thick layers.

siding and then rub it down with the solution using a soft brush or a sponge. Next, thoroughly rinse it with clean water. A poor rinse could cause the solution to damage the finish on the siding. It is a good idea to wear rubber gloves and face protection.

Coatings on aluminum siding are factory-applied and -baked. They are expected to last many years. The siding can be repainted. It is important to remove all dirt, mildew, and chalking from the original paint. Clean as mentioned above.

This clean surface can be repainted with acrylic latex or alkyd-based house paint. While this paint will not weather as well as the original one, it will refresh the surface. Be certain to paint the entire wall or the difference between the original and new paint will be obvious.

Acrylic latex touch-up paints are available in spray cans for repairs on a small damaged area.

Paint manufacturers provide products specifically designed for painting aluminum. For example, one company supplies a solution that cleans the aluminum surface and contains an acid that slightly etches the surface. It recommends the paint that should be the product's alkyd primer and enamel. Consult local paint dealers for products they have available. Follow the application directions carefully.

REPAIRING VINYL SIDING

Should a piece of vinyl siding crack, it is best to remove the damaged piece and replace it with a new one. Begin by unsnapping the piece above it and prying out the nails (**5–29**). The siding is rather flexible, so the top piece can be bent up some. Since vinyl is brittle in cold weather, make the repair when it is warm and more flexible.

Slide the new piece in place and nail through the prepunched nail slots. Drive the head of the nail to within ⅛ inch (3 millimeters) of the face of the panel. It must be left loose, so when the panel

5–29 (right). To remove a piece of vinyl siding, pop its bottom edge off the piece below, raise it up a bit, and slide a pry bar under it to pull out the nails.

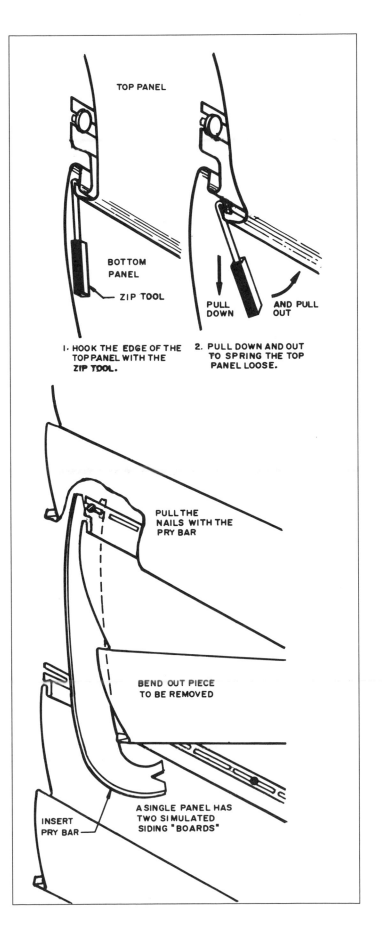

TOP PANEL

BOTTOM PANEL

ZIP TOOL

PULL DOWN   AND PULL OUT

1. HOOK THE EDGE OF THE TOP PANEL WITH THE ZIP TOOL.

2. PULL DOWN AND OUT TO SPRING THE TOP PANEL LOOSE.

PULL THE NAILS WITH THE PRY BAR

BEND OUT PIECE TO BE REMOVED

INSERT PRY BAR

A SINGLE PANEL HAS TWO SIMULATED SIDING "BOARDS"

expands and contracts it can slide on the nail. If the nail is driven hard against the panel, the panel will buckle as the temperature changes.

After the new piece is nailed in place, snap the top piece back over the lip on the new piece.

If the siding has been on for quite a few years, the new piece will stand out because the old siding has weathered. If the crack is small, it can be filled with a silicone caulking.

Some home owners repair cracked vinyl siding by removing the panel and gluing a vinyl patch on the back, as shown in **5–30**. Some vinyl siding manufacturers do not recommend this repair. Vinyl siding expands and contracts a great deal due to tempera-

ture changes. The patch will expand and contract at a different rate than the total panel, and this may cause the panel to bulge at certain temperatures. The one advantage to this patch is that the panel will be the same color (degree of fading) as the others on the wall.

Should several walls covered with vinyl siding be damaged (such as by a hailstorm or high winds), if only the damaged panels are replaced, their color will be different if the original wall has weathered over the years. This replacement would produce a wall that is varied in color. If this is the situation, consider replacing all the siding on one wall and using the good faded pieces that have been removed to repair damaged panels on an other wall. This will result in panels that are more uniform in color. Since the insurance company will most likely handle the repair, suggest this to the company.

REPAIRING ALUMINUM SIDING

Small dents in aluminum siding cause no problems other than aesthetic ones. Repairing aluminum siding is much like an autobody-shop repair. Clean and sand the area. Apply an autobody-repair filler over the depression and screed it level with a putty knife. When it hardens, sand the filler with a fine abrasive paper until it is flush with the surface. A light second coat can be added if necessary.

When the patch is hard and smooth, apply a metal primer and a finish consisting of two or three coats of aluminum-siding paint. Paint in a spray can is easiest to use and gives a smoother finished surface (**5–31**).

A repair like this may show up as a slightly different shade than the original paint. If the color cannot be matched and the dent is small, it may be less noticeable than the repair.

Should the siding be badly damaged from a heavy blow, repairs are more difficult. It is hard to remove a panel as described for vinyl siding because aluminum is not as flexible as vinyl. One thing that can be tried is to cut a piece to fit over the damage. Cut off the nailing flange so the piece

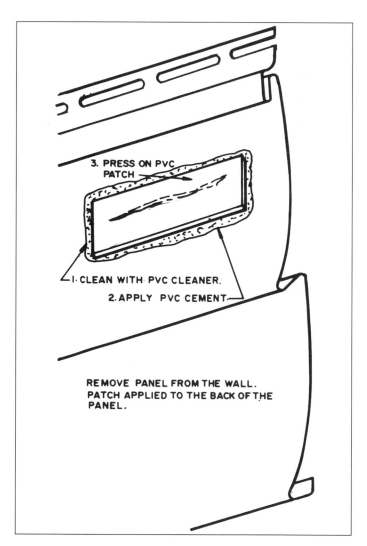

3. PRESS ON PVC PATCH

1. CLEAN WITH PVC CLEANER.

2. APPLY PVC CEMENT

REMOVE PANEL FROM THE WALL. PATCH APPLIED TO THE BACK OF THE PANEL.

5–30. *Some repair cracked vinyl siding by removing the panel and gluing a patch on the back. This is not recommended by some manufacturers because temperature changes may cause the panel to bulge or become wavy.*

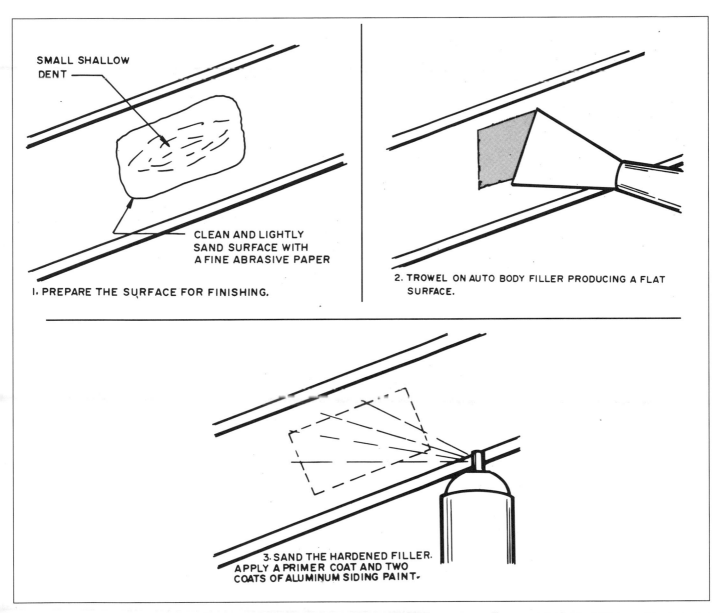

SMALL SHALLOW
DENT

CLEAN AND LIGHTLY
SAND SURFACE WITH
A FINE ABRASIVE PAPER

I. PREPARE THE SURFACE FOR FINISHING.

2. TROWEL ON AUTO BODY FILLER PRODUCING A FLAT
SURFACE.

3. SAND THE HARDENED FILLER.
APPLY A PRIMER COAT AND TWO
COATS OF ALUMINUM SIDING PAINT.

5–31. Small dents in aluminum siding can be repaired with auto-body filler.

fits up tight to the panel above and the lower edge butts tight against the bottom flange. Bond with an adhesive that will adhere metal to metal and withstand heat and cold and be waterproof (**5–32**), on the following page). These adhesives are available in tubes like those used for caulking. They are placed in a caulking gun and extrude a thick plastic-like ribbon of adhesive. If desired, lay a thin ribbon of silicone caulking alongside the adhesive to provide additional waterproofing protection.

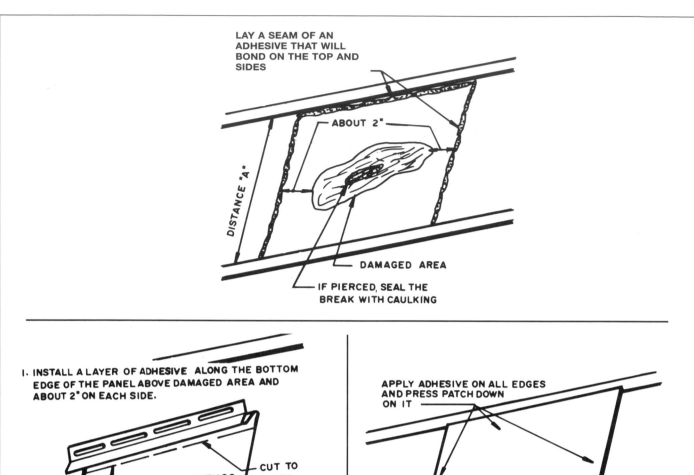

LAY A SEAM OF AN ADHESIVE THAT WILL BOND ON THE TOP AND SIDES

ABOUT 2"

DISTANCE "A"

DAMAGED AREA

IF PIERCED, SEAL THE BREAK WITH CAULKING

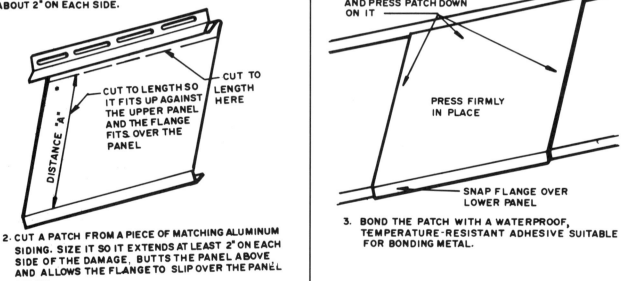

1. INSTALL A LAYER OF ADHESIVE ALONG THE BOTTOM EDGE OF THE PANEL ABOVE DAMAGED AREA AND ABOUT 2" ON EACH SIDE.

CUT TO LENGTH SO IT FITS UP AGAINST THE UPPER PANEL AND THE FLANGE FITS OVER THE PANEL

CUT TO LENGTH HERE

DISTANCE "A"

2. CUT A PATCH FROM A PIECE OF MATCHING ALUMINUM SIDING. SIZE IT SO IT EXTENDS AT LEAST 2" ON EACH SIDE OF THE DAMAGE, BUTTS THE PANEL ABOVE AND ALLOWS THE FLANGE TO SLIP OVER THE PANEL BELOW.

APPLY ADHESIVE ON ALL EDGES AND PRESS PATCH DOWN ON IT

PRESS FIRMLY IN PLACE

SNAP FLANGE OVER LOWER PANEL

3. BOND THE PATCH WITH A WATERPROOF, TEMPERATURE-RESISTANT ADHESIVE SUITABLE FOR BONDING METAL.

5–32. A large dent or pierced area on aluminum siding can be repaired by bonding an aluminum patch made from a piece of siding the same color as the original.

CHAPTER SIX

Painting the Exterior

Exterior finishing materials not only beautify the house but also form a weather-resistant seal over the exterior. Deciding which of the many paints, stains, or other finishing materials to use can be difficult. The quality of the finished job depends heavily upon using the correct finish on each of the exterior materials. Success also depends upon correct preparation of the surface to receive the finish and the use of proper application techniques. If the right finishing materials are applied correctly, the exterior finish will last many years.

PAINT FAILURES

Generally, the failure of an exterior finish is due to poor surface preparation or moisture damage caused by leaks into the wall that allow moisture to soak behind the finish coat. Before any repainting can be done, certain conditions must be corrected.

Some of the more frequently found failures include:

1. **Mildew**. Humid weather conditions will cause the growth of mildew on the surface, especially on walls that do not receive much sunlight (**6–1**). Mildew must be removed before the exterior of the house can be repainted. To do this, wash the surface with a solution containing one quart chlorine bleach to three quarts clean water. It helps if a cup of household detergent is added to the mix. After washing the surface, rinse it thoroughly and let it dry before painting. Wear rubber gloves and face protection. Cover any shrubs that may be damaged.

Warning: Do not mix ammonia in with the bleach. This mixture produces a lethal gas which, when breathed, leads to serious health problems. Likewise, never mix bleach with any detergent or cleansers containing ammonia.

2. **Bleeding**. This occurs when water-soluble extractives in the wood are wetted and penetrate through the paint coating. This produces a brown or pink stain. Wash the wall with a diluted solution of water and chlorine bleach as mentioned above. Rinse the wall thoroughly with clean water. When it is dry, add a coat of stain-blocking primer.

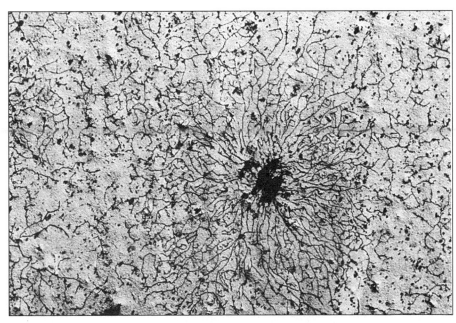

6–1. Mildew is a fungus that grows in warm, humid climates and is usually black. Many paints are vulnerable to attack from mildew and must be cleaned several times a year (courtesy USDA Forest Service, Forest Products Laboratory).

3. **Cracking**. This can be caused by moisture under the coating, using inferior coating products, improper mixing of the paint, and uneven application producing thick and thin areas. The paint cannot expand and contract, so it cracks. Generally, it is best to remove the old paint.

4. **Alligatoring**. This appears as cracks that run across the grain of the wood (**6–2**). It is caused when too many layers of paint have been applied over many years. The old paint has hardened and is unable to expand. The solution is to remove all the paint.

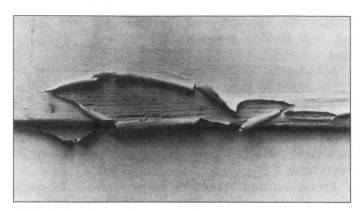

6–3. *Peeling is usually caused by poor preparation of the surface before applying the finish coats. Remove all the old paint before repainting (courtesy USDA Forest Service, Forest Products Laboratory).*

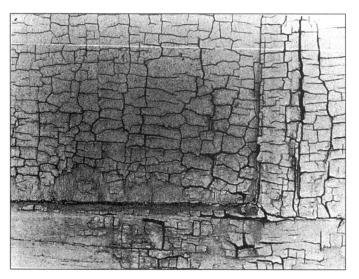

6–2. *"Alligatoring" identifies damage produced by the application of many layers of paint over many years. Before repainting, strip off all the old paint (courtesy USDA Forest Service, Forest Products Laboratory).*

5. **Peeling**. Large pieces of the coating lift off the surface and can easily be flaked off if they are touched (**6–3**). This is usually caused by water getting under the paint, so check the wall for leaks. Peeling also occurs when the new coating does not bond to the old coating. This can be avoided by cleaning and priming the old hard coat.

Peeling paint will have to be removed by scraping off the old paint down to the bare wood and an area 6 to 8 inches (152 to 203 millimeters) around it. Then sand the surface and feather any remaining paint out and away from the damaged area. Finally, prime and paint in the normal manner.

6. **Blistering**. Blisters are small bubbles formed on

the finish (**6–4**). They are produced when moisture gets below the paint and vaporizes due to heat from the sun. They also occur if the paint is applied in direct sunlight over hard or glossy surfaces. The surface must be scraped down to the bare wood and sanded, any remaining paint feathered out, and the surface primed and repainted properly.

Moisture gets behind the paint when water in the wall leaks behind the siding. Also, if the interior wall does not have a vapor barrier inside, moisture—such as that which results from cooking—will penetrate the wall and work through the siding.

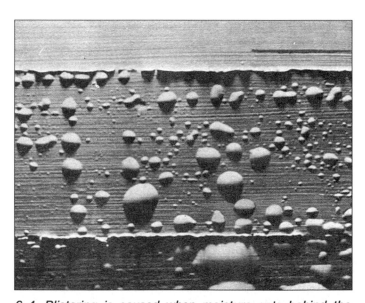

6–4. *Blistering is caused when moisture gets behind the paint and is then heated by the sun. Application of the paint in direct hot sunlight will also cause blisters (courtesy USDA Forest Service, Forest Products Laboratory).*

7. **Chalking**. Chalking is a stain caused by the paint pigment's washing down the wall. It is noticeable when wood is above a brick wall and the stain appears on the bricks. This is usually caused by using a poor-quality paint or because the paint has been on too long and needs recoating. Remove the chalk with a solution of water with ½-cup detergent per gallon. If the siding is above masonry, paint the siding with a nonchalking latex house paint.

8. **Peeling galvanized gutters**. This will occur due to the use of the wrong primer or failure to remove the oil that is on the surface of new galvanized gutters. Scrape off all loose paint down to the galvanizing. If paint is tight in places, lightly feather it by sanding. Be certain the gutter does not leak at the joints. Coat with a galvanized-steel primer and finish with the house paint.

9. **Nail-head stains**. If steel nails were used and the heads exposed, they will rust and produce stains down the wall. If possible, remove the nails and replace them with galvanized-steel or aluminum nails. If they cannot be removed, try to set them into the siding and cover them with caulking. Sand and prime over each nail head before applying the house paint.

PREPARING FOR PAINTING

No matter how good a paint is used, it will fail if the surface is not properly prepared. Following are surface-preparation guidelines:

1. The surface must be dry.

2. Paint will adhere only if the surface is clean, not glossy, sound, and properly sealed, sanded, and primed as recommended by the paint manufacturer.

3. All exterior wood, including wood siding, should be primed on the front, back, and all edges before being nailed in place. The first coat is thinned to permit penetration. After the board is nailed in place, set and caulk the nails, sand lightly, and prime with the recommended primer.

4. Fill all cracks with a quality caulk. Sand, spot-prime these cracks, and then apply the topcoats.

5. Caulk all seams on the exterior such as those around doors and windows.

6. Any paint defects such as peeling, blistering, and loose paint can be removed with a scraper. Sand to the bare wood. Feather out the remaining paint about a foot beyond the defective area. Prime this area before applying the topcoat.

Paint removal can be sped up using an electric hot-air gun as shown in **6–5**. It removes thick layers of paint and varnish. As the finish softens, scrape it away with a putty knife.

There are chemicals that soften the paint, allowing it to be scraped off. They are brushed on and allowed

6–5. Paint is easily and safely removed with an electric hot-air gun (courtesy HomeRight, Minneapolis, Minnesota).

to soak for a while before the surface is scraped. Clean away all the chemical before painting.

7. Wood knots contain a resinous material and will bleed through the paint. Wash the paint with mineral spirits or turpentine and seal it with a stain-block primer/sealer, which can be purchased at a paint store. If this fails to correct the problem, consider replacing these siding boards.

8. Rust and corrosion on iron and steel must be sanded or removed with a wire brush. Special primers that seal the surface are then applied.

9. If a masonry surface is very rough or porous, seal it with a masonry block filler. Fill all cracks with an epoxy crack filler.

10. Sand all glossy areas so the new paint will have maximum adhesion to the surface.

11. When possible, remove rusting nails and replace them with galvanized-steel or aluminum nails. If this is not possible, sand the rusty surface, set the nail, and cover it with caulking. Sand this smooth and cover it with a corrosion-resistant primer.

12. All dirt, mold, mildew, chalking, etc. should be removed with water. Add detergent and chlorine bleach as needed.

13. The edges of plywood panels readily absorb moisture. Therefore, all edges must be sealed even if they will not be exposed to the elements.

14. Vinyl siding and aluminum siding have special problems when repainted. See Chapter 5 for details.

15. The exterior hardboard siding used should always have a factory-applied prime coat. Usually latex and alkyd-oil house paints can be applied directly over this primer. Be certain all edges of the panels are sealed against water penetration.

APPLICATION TIPS

1. Do nothing until the instructions on the paint label have been read. The paint dealer will also have brochures that give helpful advice.

2. Paint new wood as soon as possible after installation.

3. Do not apply latex or alkyd-oil coatings when the temperature is below 50° F (10° C) or over 90° F (32° C).

4. Do not apply paint if the surface is damp from dew or rain. Latex paint will tolerate a slight amount of surface moisture.

5. The best condition for applying exterior paint is when the temperature is 70° to 80° F (21° to 26° C) and the humidity is below 75 percent.

6. Avoid painting when the surface is in direct sunlight. The heat generated could cause blistering. Work on the shady side as much as possible, and move as the sun moves.

7. Be certain the paint is thoroughly mixed. However, do not overmix. If it develops air bubbles, let the paint sit for several hours so the air can escape. The paint dealer will mix it with a shaking machine. Have this done each time more paint is purchased.

8. When a surface will require more than one gallon of a color, intermix the gallons to be used on that surface so that the color shading will be the same over the entire area.

9. When painting exterior siding, start at one corner at the top of the wall and paint across the building to the other side in 2- to 3-foot (.6- to .9-meter) -wide strips (6–6). At the end of the day, stop the paint at a natural boundary such as a corner, door, or window to avoid an overlap at the point where the painting was stopped. If working from a ladder, paint across the top and work down, but limit the length of painting to a safe distance that can be reached (6–7). Lower the ladder for each row. See Chapter 4 for information on ladder safety.

10. When painting lap siding, paint the bottom edge of several boards first and then cover the broad surface (6–8 and 6–9).

11. Paint from an unpainted surface into a freshly painted one.

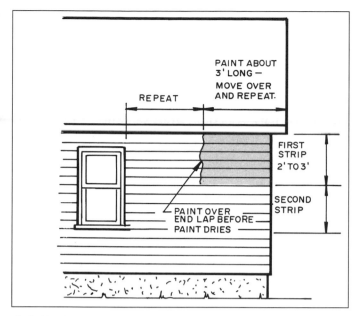

6–6. Begin painting exterior siding in an upper corner and paint a strip all the way across the wall.

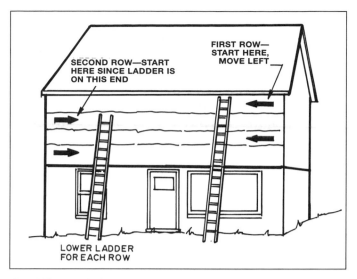

6–7. When painting on a long ladder, move it frequently and observe safety rules. Lower the ladder for each succeeding row.

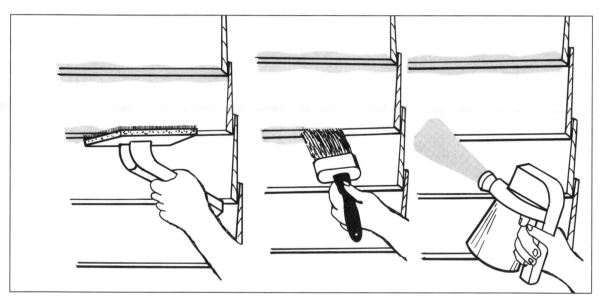

6–8 (above). When painting lap siding first, paint the bottom edge of several pieces about 3 or 4 feet (.9 or 1.2 meters) long. Smoothly brush any paint that may run down the face. Then paint the face, move down the wall, and repeat the process.

6–9 (right). After painting the edges of the siding in the area to be immediately painted, coat the broad surface and overlap the paint with the still-wet previous section.

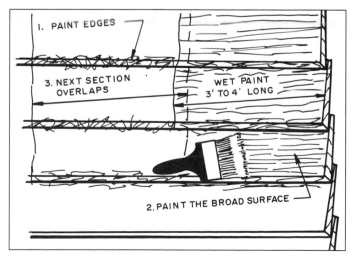

12. To get a uniform coating, apply paint generously and brush it out well.

13. Remove the shutters and clean and paint the wall surface behind them. Paint the shutters on both sides before replacing them. Clean, sand, and repair them in the same manner as any wood product.

14. After painting the siding, paint the wood trim, door, and window frames.

15. When painting double-hung windows, paint in the order shown in **6–10**. To paint areas covered by the sash, lower the upper sash and raise the bottom sash and paint the covered sides of the sash. Leave the sash open until the paint is dry or the windows will be stuck closed. Protect the glass by applying masking tape around the edges next to the wood sash and mullions.

16. When painting casement windows, crank them open and paint the various parts. Keep paint off the hinges and other hardware.

17. When painting a panel door, paint the molding and panels first, and then the frame. Finally, paint all the edges. It is helpful to seal the top and bottom edges against moisture penetration with a clear coating of thinned primer. Leave the door open until the paint is dry.

18. On new work, apply at least two topcoats over the manufacturer-recommended primer. The first coat should be applied with a quality brush so that an adequate coating is produced. The second coat can be applied with a brush, roller, or pad.

19. Review recommendations for the safe use of ladders in Chapter 4.

20. The proper way to load a brush is to dip the bristles about half their length into the paint (**6–11**) and remove the excess paint by tapping the bristles against the side of the paint container. Do not wipe the bristles on the container. Too much paint will be drawn from the brush.

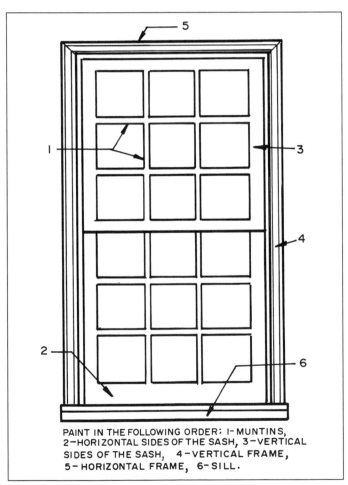

PAINT IN THE FOLLOWING ORDER: 1-MUNTINS, 2-HORIZONTAL SIDES OF THE SASH, 3-VERTICAL SIDES OF THE SASH, 4-VERTICAL FRAME, 5-HORIZONTAL FRAME, 6-SILL.

6–10. A suggested order for painting wood windows. Be certain to scrape, sand, and otherwise prepare the surface for priming and painting.

6–11. To load a brush, dip the bristles about halfway into the paint, lift the brush out, and tap the bristles against the side of the can.

THE CLEANUP

Follow these procedures for cleaning up during and after painting:

1. It is best to remove any spills or splashes as they occur. Wipe them off with a cloth and use the solvent recommended by the manufacturer.

2. Clean all paint brushes, rollers, and pads immediately after finishing with them. See the sections in this chapter describing the individual tools for details.

3. Be certain to use the solvents recommended by the manufacturer for cleaning the tools.

4. Keep your hands and arms clean. Clean them regularly during the day. Consider wearing disposable plastic gloves. Solvents may cause skin irritation, so wash with soap and water when using solvents other than water.

DETERMINING THE AMOUNT OF PAINT NEEDED

It is best if all the paint needed is bought at once. The color will more likely be uniform if the paint is from the same batch. The paint dealer identifies custom-mixed colors by recording identification codes on the paint can. Keep a record of these for possible future use.

How much paint is needed depends upon the kind of surface, the number of square feet to be painted, and the coverage produced per gallon on the paint selected. (Some paints get more square feet per gallon of coverage than others.) Rough surfaces such as masonry, rough-sawed wood siding, and abraded plywood will require 15 to 22 percent more paint than a smooth-surfaced product.

To find the number of square feet to be painted, first multiply the height of each wall by the width and then subtract any large unpainted areas such as doors and windows (**6–12**). The measurements can be rounded off to the nearest foot. For example, a wall that's 30 feet, six inches would be rounded off to 31 feet. Next, calculate the area of the soffit and fascia boards. Also determine the square feet in the gable end. To do this, assume that it is a rectangle,

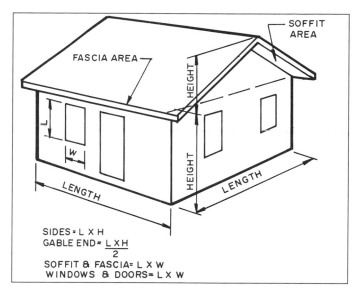

6–12. *Calculate the number of square feet of surface that must be painted and divide this number by the coverage per gallon specified for the paint that will be used. Add an additional 15 to 20 percent for rough surfaces.*

and multiple the length by the height and divide this calculation by 2. This will be an approximate measurement. Add these figures together.

The expected coverage for a gallon of the paint being used can be found on the paint can. Divide the total square feet to be painted by the square-foot-coverage per gallon in order to determine how many gallons of paint are needed.

VOLATILE ORGANIC COMPOUNDS (VOC)

The Federal Clean Air Act mandates National Air-Quality Standards that set health-based limits on ozone and carbon-monoxide releases into the atmosphere. They regulate many products, including finishing materials. Emissions from solvents in coatings are one source of air pollution. These products emit **volatile organic compounds** (**VOC**). Coatings have VOC limitations that manufacturers are trying to meet. Some products currently meet VOC standards. The VOC ratings are listed on the label of coating products. Architectural coatings are limited to not more than 2.09 lbs/gallon (250g/l[grams per liter]). Through the years many new paint products will be developed that have different or fewer solvents, which will change the way they are applied. Brush applications may become less viable and new application equipment will be developed.

PRIMERS

Primers are the first coat applied to the uncoated material or over repaired damaged areas. They protect the surface in a way that the finish topcoat cannot. Primers are formulated for a specific material and purpose. Some resist rust and corrosion on various metals. Some seal the wood surface, while others may stress penetration into the wood. In all cases, they provide the proper base upon which the topcoats are applied.

Since there are many primers, such as those for wood, metal, and masonry, the selection of primer must be coordinated with the topcoat to be used. The paint manufacturer's instructions must be carefully followed. The paint dealer can help with your selection.

CHOOSING THE TOPCOAT

Either latex or alkyd-oil paint will be used for an exterior house-paint topcoat. Each has advantages and disadvantages. The paint dealer may have some suggestions related to paint performance in your geographic area.

Latex House Paints

Latex paints use synthetic chemical polymers or resins (plastic-like substances) that are suspended in water. They are, therefore, thinned with water and brushes, and the hands should be cleaned with soap and water. Latex-paint spatters on windows, floors, and other places can be easily removed with a wet rag if it is cleaned up as soon as it occurs.

Latex paints have the following advantages:

1. They can be easily cleaned up.

2. They produce a paint film that breathes, therefore reducing blistering.

3. They can be applied over slightly damp surfaces, such as a slight dew on siding early in the morning.

4. They are fast-drying and, therefore, are usually dust- and bug-free in 30 minutes. They can be recoated in four hours.

5. They have excellent color retention.

6. Latex paints have little odor and no solvent smell.

7. They can be applied over a number of exterior materials including masonry, concrete block, wood, stucco, primed metal, and, in some cases, vinyl and aluminum siding.

8. Latex paints offer a range of finishes from flat to semigloss.

9. They can be applied with nylon or polyester bristle brushes, rollers, and pads. Do not use a pure (natural hog) bristle brush because the bristles absorb water and become soggy.

Alkyd-Oil House Paint

The most widely used oil-based house paint is the alkyd-oil type. It uses alkyd synthetic resins that are modified in oil. They are solvent-thinned, and solvents are used to clean brushes, rollers, and pads. The solvent used is turpentine or mineral spirits.

Alkyd-oil house paints have the following advantages:

1. They are very effective when coating wood that has been allowed to become excessively dry, such as bare wood that has weathered over the years. The paint penetrates the wood fibers and seals them against moisture.

2. They can be applied to wood, completely cured or previously painted concrete, brick, and primed metal.

3. They have good resistance to the accumulation of dirt on the surface.

4. They are good for hiding discoloration and colors from the previous coating.

5. They have good gloss- and color-retention properties and a range of gloss from flat to high.

6. They can bond to slightly chalked surfaces.

7. They are applied with a natural bristle or polyester bristle brush or a lamb's wool or polyester roller.

8. They are more tolerant to application and drying in colder temperatures than latex paint.

Possible disadvantages, though minor, are that they have a strong solvent odor, should dry overnight before recoating, and have a more difficult cleanup process.

NATURAL FINISHES

Natural finishes are used to protect wood surfaces. They have little or no pigment and so permit the natural color and grain of the wood to be seen. These finishes are generally used on redwood, western red cedar, and Philippine mahogany siding. They are easy to apply and maintain. Common natural finishes include water-repellent preservatives, penetrating or semitransparent stains, opaque stains, transparent coatings, and bleaches.

Water-Repellent Preservatives

Paintable water-repellent preservatives repel moisture, reduce swelling and shrinking, and protect against mildew and decay. They may be applied by brush, roller, or pad (**6–13**), or by dipping the wood in vats.

If water-repellent preservatives are to be the finish coat, at least two coats are necessary. The first coat should be applied to all faces, edges, and ends of the wood before it is nailed in place. If the wood purchased is already treated, be sure to coat every surface that is cut before installing it. The second coat can be applied after the wood is in place. Since this preservative is paintable, the first coat can also be covered with paint.

A water-repellent coating should be renewed every three to five years under normal weather con-

6–13. This applicator holds the strain, sealer, or water-repellent in the handle. It flows to the pad under pressure applied by the end of the stick (courtesy HomeRight, Minneapolis, Minnesota.)

ditions. Excessively wet climates will require more frequent application. When the wood begins to discolor, it is a sign that the preservative has broken down and needs recoating. Usually a single coating will renew the surface.

It is a good practice to treat doors, windows, and other exterior millwork with water-repellent preservatives before they are painted with any finish coating. The treatment will help resist moisture that eventually penetrates a painted topcoat. Work the preservative into all joints and end grain. Allow the coating to dry at least 72 hours before painting or staining.

Semi-Transparent Stains

Semi-transparent stains are also called **penetrating stains**. They contain a small amount of pigment, which slightly alters the color of the wood on which they are applied. However, much of the natural grain of the wood shows through this kind of stain. These stains are oil-based and available in natural and wood tones.

Semi-transparent stains are best applied with a brush or pad applicator. The stain may be applied with a roller or by spraying, if these techniques are followed by brushing. Two coats are usually required on new wood. One coat is usually enough when restaining a weathered, stained surface. When parts of the natural wood begin to show through the stain, it is time to apply a new coat.

Opaque Stains

Opaque stains, sometimes called **heavy-body stains,** have a high concentration of pigment. They have a high covering power and almost totally hide the natural color and grain of the wood. They appear more like paint than stain.

Opaque stains are available with a latex or oil base. Colors range from wood tones to pastels to deep tones. Water-thinned stains tend to last longer and retain their color better. However, they are more difficult to apply because it is a chore to avoid showing lap marks.

Usually a single coat of opaque stain will cover new wood, but two coats are recommended for long life. Opaque stain can be applied by brush, roller, pad, or spray. Brushing appears to be the preferred method.

Transparent Coatings

Varnishes, synthetic resins, and other transparent coatings are not recommended for exterior use on areas exposed to direct sunlight. The ultraviolet light penetrates the coating, degrading the wood below

and causing the coating to crack and peel. Before using any clear coating, consult a paint dealer.

Bleach

Bleach is applied to solid-wood siding and millwork to quickly produce a weathered appearance. Some bleaching oils contain a pigment to add to the grayish appearance of the wood treated.

New wood should have at least two coats of bleach. The wood does not have to be rebleached over the years, unless it develops dark spots or the gray color becomes spotty.

When bleaching, follow the manufacturer's directions carefully. Some kinds recommend a periodic spraying with water to help the bleaching action. Observe safety precautions when applying the bleach.

PAINTBRUSHES

Using the correct brush for the job at hand makes it easier and will produce more professional results. Generally, several sizes of brush are needed on an exterior painting job.

Use a trim brush to paint window sash, frames, molding, and narrow trim. Trim brushes are available in widths of ½, ¾, 1, and 1½ inches (13, 19, 25, and 38 millimeters). They have straight-, beveled-, and angled-cut bristles. Large straight-cut brushes (2½, 3, and 4 inches [63, 76, and 102 millimeters] wide) are used on larger surfaces such as siding, floors, and foundations (**6–14**).

Brushes with synthetic bristles, such as nylon and polyester brushes, can be used in latex and oil-based paints. They are most often used with latex because these bristles will not soak up water.

Natural-bristle brushes are used with oil-based paints and stains, varnishes, lacquers, and shellacs. They are not used on the water-based latex paints because the bristles will absorb water and swell.

To clean a synthetic-bristle brush used in latex paint, wash it in warm water containing a mild detergent. Work the bristles with your fingers until the paint is removed. Check all the way up to the ferrule (**6–15**). Shake the brush to remove excess

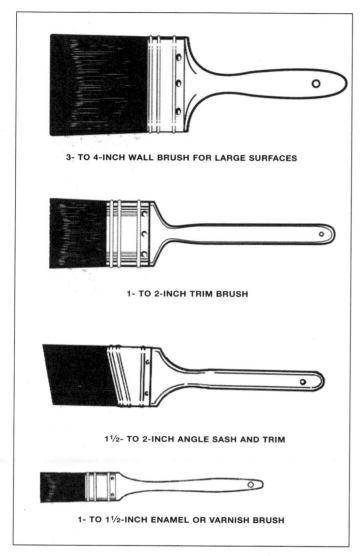

3- TO 4-INCH WALL BRUSH FOR LARGE SURFACES

1- TO 2-INCH TRIM BRUSH

1½- TO 2-INCH ANGLE SASH AND TRIM

1- TO 1½-INCH ENAMEL OR VARNISH BRUSH

6–14. Paintbrushes are available in a wide range of sizes and shapes. Use the proper brush for the job at hand (courtesy Purdy Corporation).

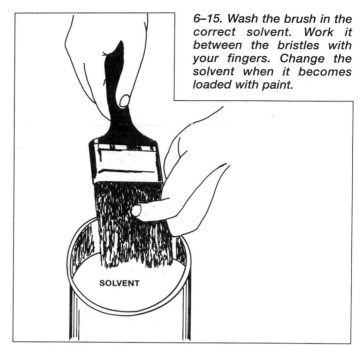

6–15. Wash the brush in the correct solvent. Work it between the bristles with your fingers. Change the solvent when it becomes loaded with paint.

SOLVENT

BRUSH COMB

6–16. A paintbrush comb can be used to loosen hardened pieces of paint and smooth and straighten the bristles.

moisture, smooth the bristles with your fingers, and hang it up to dry. A paintbrush comb can also be used to remove stubborn paint residue and straighten the fibers so they will dry straight (**6–16**). Store the dried brushes by wrapping them in wax paper or aluminum foil and hanging them from the hole in the handle or laying them flat (**6–17**).

Natural-bristle brushes are used only for oil-based paint and are cleaned as described above, with the exception that the solvent is paint thinner or mineral spirits. Synthetic-bristle brushes used for oil-based paints are also cleaned with these solvents. Wear plastic gloves when cleaning with them.

To load a brush in preparation for applying the paint to the surface, insert the brush into the paint about halfway to the ferrule, lift it from the paint, and tap the bristles gently against the inside of the paint container (refer to **6–6**).

PAINT ROLLERS

The most commonly used paint rollers are 7 and 9 inches (178 and 228 millimeters) long. For narrow spaces, 3- and 4-inch (76- and 102-millimeter) -long

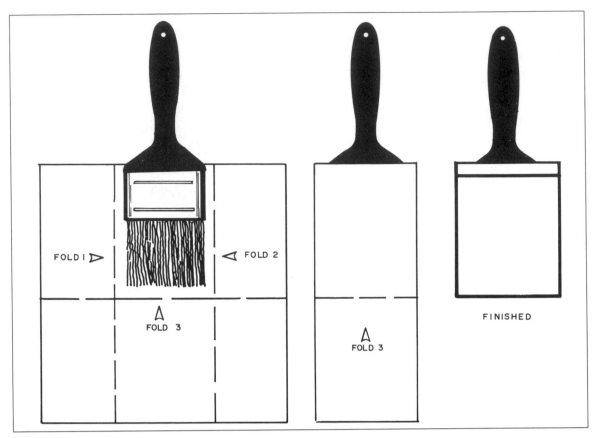

6–17. Wrap the clean, dry bristles in wax paper or aluminum foil.

paint rollers are available. For very large surfaces, 14- and 18-inch (355- and 457-millimeter) rollers are used. Roller handle lengths of 9 to 24 inches (228 to 609 millimeters) are commonly available (**6–18**).

Rollers do not give the penetration or thickness of coating required for a prime coat, so it should be applied with a brush.

Rollers have removable sleeves. Replace them when they no longer produce a uniform paint film (**6–19**). It is suggested that the best-quality covers available be used. They have a uniform texture, are lint-free, and have a water-resistant material on the interior. Covers with a short nap will produce a smoother finish and are required if enamel is being painted. A long-nap roller (about ½ inch [13 millimeters]) is good for porous masonry and rough surfaces such as stucco.

Select a cover made from Dynel fibers if water-based paints are being used. A lamb's-wool cover is good for oil-based paints. Polyester and acetate covers are used with both oil- and water-based paints. When applying enamels or varnish, use a mohair cover.

The most common way to load a paint roller is to pour some paint into a roller tray and move the roller back and forth in the paint in the shallow end. The roller should have a uniform coating but not enough paint to drip when it is lifted off the pan (**6–20**). Some painting-supply stores sell a plastic paint-tray liner that fits inside the tray and is thrown away after the job is finished.

To clean a roller, roll it on a sheet of paper to squeeze out the excess paint (**6–21**). Then remove the roller from the frame and wash it in the proper solvent (**6–22**). If latex paint was used, much of the paint can be removed by running the garden hose on the roller. When the roller is clean, squeeze it to remove the water from the nap. There is a tool available called a **spinner** that rapidly rotates the roller, causing water or solvent to spin off the surface.

Professional painters frequently discard the roller sleeve after one use. This avoids the cleaning process. It is difficult to get off all the caked paint, especially on the ends of the roller. A better job is produced with a new sleeve.

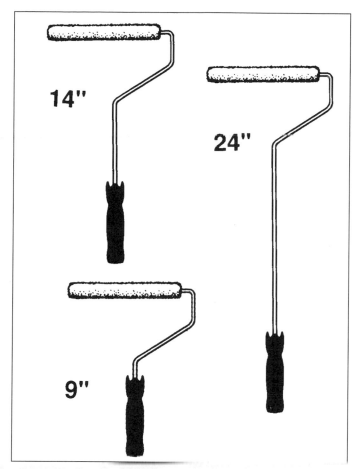

6–18. Rollers are available in several sizes and handle lengths.

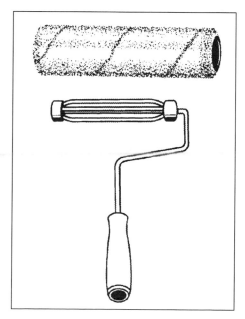

6–19. The roller handle and sleeves can be purchased separately to get a roller of the proper size and sleeve material (courtesy Purdy Corporation).

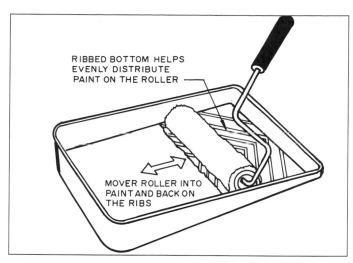

RIBBED BOTTOM HELPS EVENLY DISTRIBUTE PAINT ON THE ROLLER

MOVER ROLLER INTO PAINT AND BACK ON THE RIBS

6–20. Load the roller by running it into the paint poured into a roller tray and rolling it out on the ribbed pan bottom until it has a uniform coating.

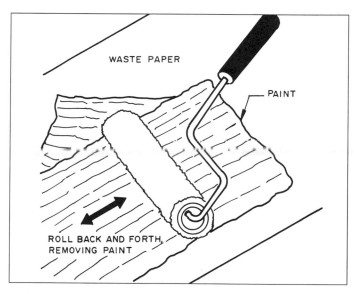

WASTE PAPER

PAINT

ROLL BACK AND FORTH, REMOVING PAINT

6–21. The first step when cleaning a roller is to run out as much of the paint as possible on a sheet of paper.

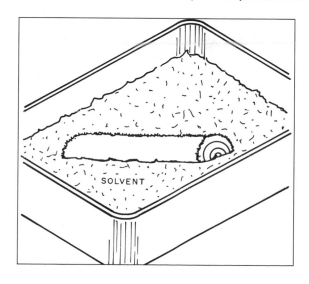

SOLVENT

6–22. Remove the roller from the frame and wash it in the proper solvent. Stand it on its end and let it dry.

To clean a roller used with latex paint, wash it in warm water with mild detergent. If the roller was used with oil-based paints, wash it in paint thinner or mineral spirits. Squeeze out the excess solvent, stand the roller on its end, and let it dry. When it is dry, wrap it in wax paper or aluminum foil and store it on its end.

PRESSURE-FED ROLLER SYSTEMS

Pressure-fed roller systems speed up the painting of large, flat surfaces. The paint feeder contains the one-gallon can of paint and moves the paint under pressure through a long hose to a paint roller (**6–23**). A button in the handle controls the flow of paint at the roller. The paint is fed from inside the core of the roller to the outside nap and requires the use of special roller covers. These cost more than the standard covers. The system shown in **6–24** operates on 120-volt electric current. It operates at 20 to 43 psi, uses oil-based paint, stain, and latex paint, and is suitable for both interior and exterior use.

To clean the system, remove the paint can and run solvent through the system. Some home owners clean the roller in a pan first and then run solvent through the system. Obviously, all the paint left in the system is wasted.

PAINT PADS

Pad applicators are available in a wide range of sizes and shapes (**6–25**). They are especially useful on flat, smooth surfaces, but unless they are used carefully it is possible to work the thickness of the coating down too thin. Some pads are triangular in shape for use in tight areas such as a corner, while narrow, rectangular pads can be used to paint windows and narrow strips.

There are two types of pads available. One is

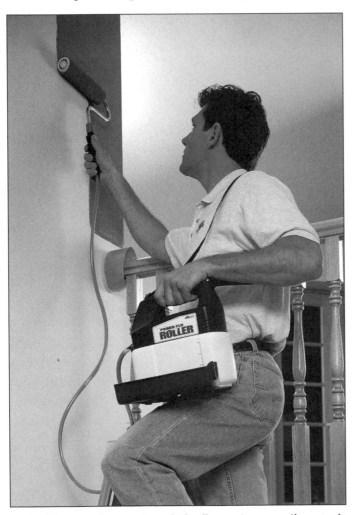

6–23. The use of a pressure-fed roller system greatly speeds up the painting of large surfaces. It can be used with oil and latex paints. This unit operates on four D-cell batteries (courtesy HomeRight, Minneapolis, Minnesota).

6–24. This large pressure-fed roller system has a long hose that enables the operator to move around while leaving the unit in a set position. The roller handle has an extension, so the ceiling can be easily reached (courtesy HomeRight, Minneapolis, Minnesota).

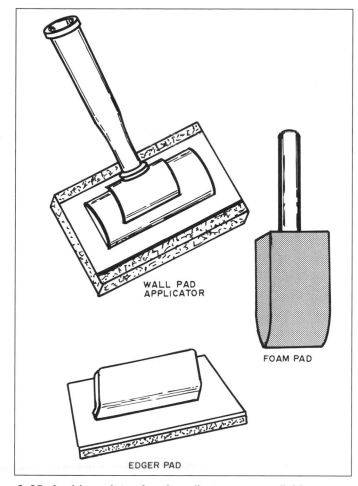

6–25. A wide variety of pad applicators are available.

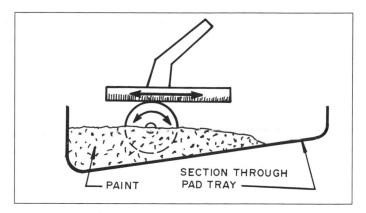

6–26. Load the pad with paint using a pad tray. Fill the tray about half full of paint. Running the pad over the roller coats the bottom surface of the pad with paint.

Place the pad on the roller and move it across the roller, allowing the surface of the pad to be coated. It is important that the sides and ends of the pad do not receive paint. This will cause problems when trying to get a smooth, uniform coating.

To clean a pad, squeeze out as much paint as possible by blotting it on newspaper. Then wash it in the proper solvent. Wash it in warm water containing a mild detergent for water-based paints and mineral spirits or in turpentine for oil-based paints. If the pad appears damaged, replace it. Replacements are inexpensive.

AIRLESS PAINT SPRAYERS

Airless paint sprayers allow large areas to be covered much more quickly than with a brush or roller. They also make it easier to coat irregularly shaped objects and rough surfaces. Some jobs will require the masking off of surfaces or edges that are not to be painted. Careful masking is very important and does take time.

The airless sprayer is a self-contained unit consisting of a paint container and the spraying mechanism (6–27). It is operated on 120-volt electric current. An explanation of how the unit works is given in 6–28.

Remember, the paint is forced out in a cone-shaped mist under great air pressure. This pressure can cause serious damage to the operator and those around him/her, so observe the following safety recommendations:

entirely made of foam, and the other, foam with fiber. Use the all-foam type only on smooth surfaces. The foam-with-fiber pads are used on brick, stucco, rough-sawn lumber, and other textured surfaces.

Use only high-quality pads having considerable fiber. Nylon is a commonly used fiber. Some of the pads are very inexpensive and can be discarded after they have been used a few times.

Pads should not be used to apply strong, solvent-based materials such as lacquer or shellac because they will dissolve. They are good for latex and oil-based paints and in some cases can be used to apply stains.

When applying paint with a pad, load the pad with a pad tray (6–26). It is difficult to evenly coat the pad without a tray.

A pad tray has a built-in roller. Fill the pan with paint so that half the roller is above the surface.

6–27. This airless paint spray operates on 120-volt current. It sprays latex, oil-, and alkyd-based paints and siding stains. The manufacturer provides detailed instructions for its proper use (courtesy Wagner Spray Tech Corporation).

eye- and breathing-protection devices. Eye-protection devices should fit tightly against the face. Respirators should be of high quality and have disposable filters, which should be changed frequently. Typical low-cost, inexpensive disposable dust masks are not recommended.

6. Always spray-paint in a well-ventilated area.

6–28 (below). The airless paint sprayer uses 120-volt electric current to operate an electromagnetic motor that drives the spraying mechanism (courtesy Wagner Spray Tech Corporation).

1. When the paint sprayer is not being used, keep it unplugged.

2. Do not use the sprayer if other people are in the room.

3. Do not point the sprayer at another person or yourself. The pressure is enough to puncture the skin, forcing paint into the system. It will destroy eyes and damage hearing should it hit the ear. In many cases, it is not possible to medically repair the damage.

4. Unplug the unit before attempting to unplug a clogged spray tip or make any other maintenance or repair effort.

5. Fumes and spray mist are damaging to the lungs and eyes, so always wear

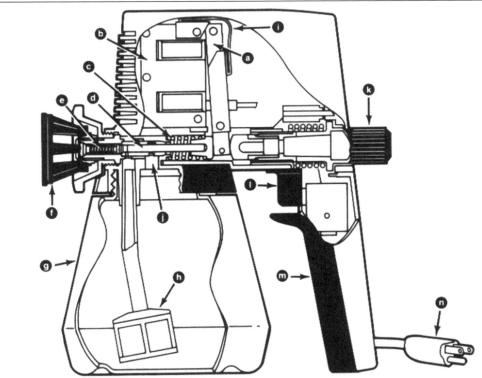

A ARMATURE
B ELECTROMAGNETIC MOTOR
C PISTON SPRING
D PISTON
E ATOMIZER VALVE
F SPRAY TIP WITH SAFETY GUARD
G CONTAINER
H FILTER
I LEAF SPRING
J OVERFLOW BYPASS
K CONTROL KNOB HANDLE
N 3-WIRE (GROUNDED PLUG)

HOW THE POWER PAINTER WORKS

THE ELECTROMAGNETIC MOTOR ACTIVATES AN ARMATURE THAT PUSHES A PISTON FORWARD. WHEN THE PISTON IS PUSHED BACK BY THE PISTON SPRING, PAINT FLOWS UP THE SUCTION TUBE INTO THE PAINT CHAMBER DUE TO THE PARTIAL VACUUM THERE. WHEN THE ARMATURE PUSHES THE PISTON FORWARD, IT FORCES THE PAINT THROUGH THE SPRAY TIP, CAUSING ATOMIZATION. BY TURNING THE CONTROL KNOB, THE PISTON STROKE IS CHANGED, RESULTING IN INCREASED OR DECREASED VOLUME.

Using an Airless Paint Sprayer

The surface preparation is the same as for any painting job. The airless sprayer requires the masking off of areas that will not be painted but may be hit by overspray when a nearby area is being painted. In addition, cover shrubs, floors, and other areas upon which the spray mist might fall. If working outdoors and it is a windy day, it is advisable to delay work to another day.

Preparing the System

Follow the manufacturer's instructions, which will describe how to assemble the unit. To be certain it is clean and operating, run some solvent through it. Then fill the paint can and select and install the spray tip required for the type of finish being used. Many spray tips are available, and it is necessary to follow the manufacturer's directions (**6–29**).

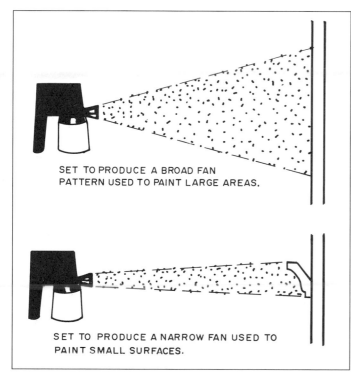

SET TO PRODUCE A BROAD FAN PATTERN USED TO PAINT LARGE AREAS.

SET TO PRODUCE A NARROW FAN USED TO PAINT SMALL SURFACES.

6–29. The size of the spray pattern is adjusted to suit the size and conditions existing on the surface to be painted.

If spraying a large surface or working on a ladder, you can replace the paint container with a hose that is run to a gallon can of paint or a special supply pack as shown in **6–30**.

6–30. When large areas are being painted, the paint container can be replaced with a hose running to a larger supply of paint (courtesy Wagner Spray Tech Corporation).

Spray-Painting a Surface

Before spraying on the surface to be painted, it is suggested that spraying be practiced on some scrap material, to check on the performance of the sprayer. The spray for a large surface should be a wide mist pattern that provides a uniform coating with a fine mist.

While working to get the proper spray pattern, you can adjust the pressure control on the unit to adjust the flow of paint. If, after this has been done, the paint is still not flowing properly, recheck the spray tip. If thin paint is being sprayed and the tip is too large, the spray will be coarse. If thick paint is being sprayed and the spray tip is too small, there will be light coverage at the edges and lumpy particles in the center of the spray. If the spray is still not flowing properly, check the viscosity of the paint.

Following are some things that can be done to ensure a good job with the sprayer:

1. Keep the spray tip about 12 inches (305 millimeters) from the surface. Check the manufacturer's instructions to verify if this is the normal, recommended distance. The farther away the sprayer is from the surface, the larger the pattern striking it (**6-31**). This also reduces the coverage, and the paint droplets may begin to set before hitting the surface, producing poor paint adhesion.

2. When painting a flat surface, move the sprayer horizontally and keep it parallel with the surface. This produces a coating with uniform thickness. Limit the strokes to about 3 feet (.9 meter) long

(**6–32**). If the sprayer is swung in an arc, the paint thickness will vary (**6–33**).

3. When spraying on a curved surface, keep the sprayer the recommended distance from the surface by moving the sprayer in an arc (**6–34**).

4. When an inside corner is encountered, it can be finished with a single downward stroke. Blend it into the ends of the horizontal strokes that approach the corner (**6–35**).

5. To finish grillwork, place a backing material behind it to catch the overspray (**6–36**).

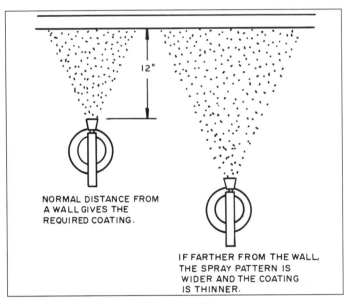

6–31. To get the recommended thickness of the finished coating, hold the sprayer the distance from the surface recommended by the manufacturer.

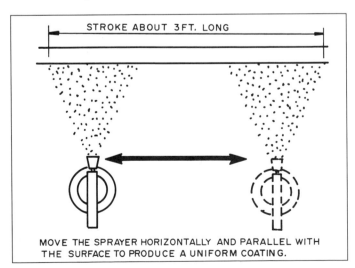

6–32. Move the sprayer horizontally and keep it parallel with the surface. This will produce a uniform coating.

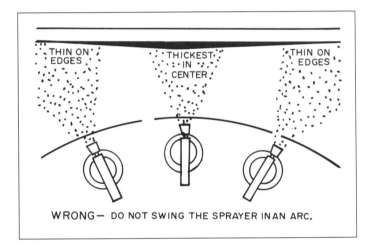

6–33. If the sprayer is swung in an arc, the coating will be thinner on the ends.

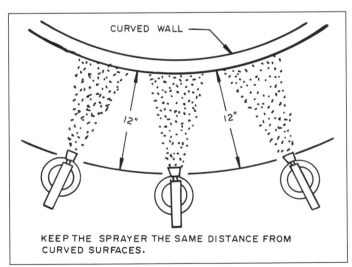

6–34. When spraying on a curved surface, swing the sprayer in an arc; keep it the same distance from the surface at all times.

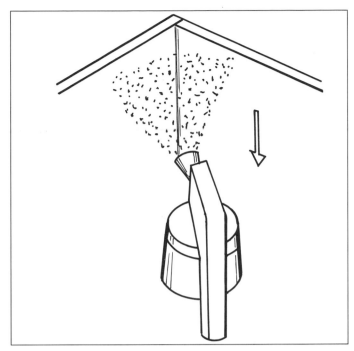

6–35. Finish inside corners by making a single downward stroke.

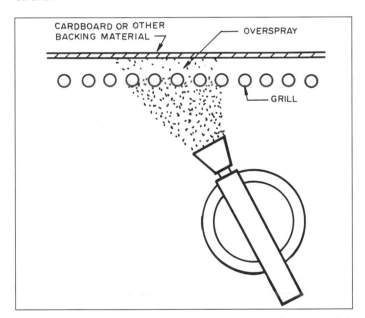

6–36. Grills and wrought iron require a backing material, such as cardboard, to catch the overspray.

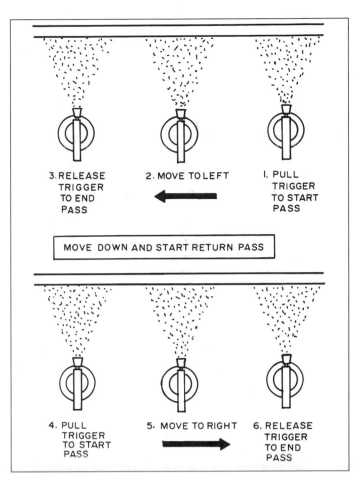

6–37. Start the pass by beginning the spray just as the tip reaches the beginning of the stroke. Release the trigger just as the tip passes the end of the stroke.

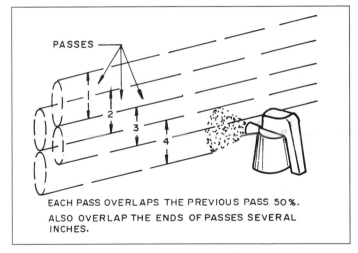

6–38. Start spray-painting on the top of the wall or other feature. Overlap the edges of each pass about 50 percent and the ends several inches.

6. Pull the trigger just before the spray tip reaches the beginning of the stroke. Release the trigger the moment the spray tip passes the end of the stroke (**6–37**).

7. Overlap the edge of the spray from the previous stroke about 50 percent. Also overlap the ends of each sprayed section (**6–38**). Start spraying at the top of the wall.

8. Some airless sprayers have spray tips that can be placed so that a ceiling or floor can be sprayed with the sprayer kept in a horizontal position (**6–39**).

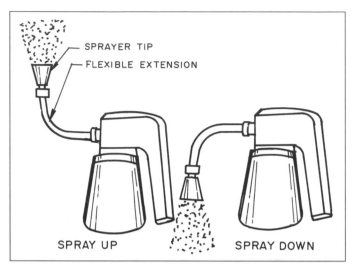

6–39. Some airless sprayers have a flexible extension enabling the tip to spray up or down.

Checking Paint Viscosity

One task when spray-painting is to get the paint the proper consistency so it will spray properly. A viscometer cup can be used to see if the paint has been thinned enough to spray properly (**6–40**). One type suitable for use on the job (versus in a test laboratory) is the **Zahn cup**. It has a hole in the rounded bottom of the cup. The diameter of this hole can be varied for use with various finishes. Dip the cup into the paint and record the time it takes for the paint flowing out of the hole to turn from a stream to a drip. Then match this time to a chart of established times. (Examples are shown in **Table 6–1**.) Use the directions supplied by the manufacturer of the device. When the paint is thinned until its viscosity matches that shown on the chart (in terms of the time it takes to turn from a stream to a drip), it is the correct viscosity to use in a paint sprayer.

TABLE 6–1. VISCOMETER TIME CHART

Materials test at 72°F (22°C)	Time (Seconds)
Latex paint	45
Floor and deck enamel	30
Semi- and high-gloss enamels	30
Oil-based paints	30

The typical times used when checking a finishing material with a viscometer to see if it is thin enough to apply with spray equipment.

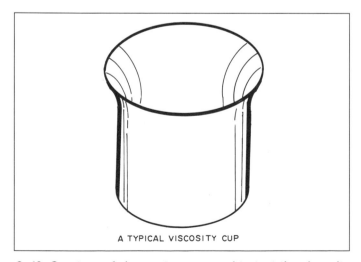

6–40. One type of viscometer cup used to test the viscosity of finishing materials.

Cleaning the Airless Sprayer

The manufacturer will give specific details for cleaning the sprayer. Since the parts will completely clog if not cleaned properly, this is an important step. Cleaning the spray tip, which has an opening measured in thousandths of an inch, is especially critical. Following is a typical procedure:

1. Empty the paint container and pump out as much paint as is possible from the hose.

2. Wash the paint container with solvent. Fill it with fresh solvent and run the solvent through the system.

3. Remove the individual parts as directed by the manufacturer and soak them in the solvent.

4. Dry and reassemble the parts. Some manufacturers recommend lightly coating the metal parts with a clear household oil to prevent rusting.

5. Should some part still have hardened paint on it, try to soften and remove it with a liquid paint remover. Never use sandpaper or scrape with a knife.

CHAPTER SEVEN

Exterior Maintenance and Repairs

A The exterior of the house is subject to constant deterioration due to exposure to the elements. Some routine maintenance activities will preserve the exterior materials, and these materials will serve for years. Some conditions, such as a house that has settled, will cause damage requiring a repair or replacement of some part. Following are some of the more frequent activities that are useful in maintaining the exterior of the house.

DEALING WITH MOISTURE UNDER THE HOUSE

A wet crawl space or basement not only causes deterioration of the wood-floor joists, but also moves moisture up into the house. Mold can develop almost anywhere, and an undesirable smell will develop. If the house was built on a lot that has some slope, there are several things that can be done to correct this situation. They are as follow:

1. As mentioned in Chapter 4, install gutters and direct the water away from the foundation with the downspouts.

2. Raise the level of the soil at the foundation and slope the soil away from it, as shown in **7–1**.

3. If the problem is severe, excavate around the foundation and apply a waterproof coating or a layer of rigid plastic drainage board to the foundation (see **7–2**, on the following page). Install perforated plastic drainage pipe around the edge of the

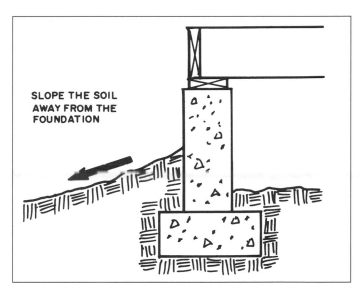

SLOPE THE SOIL AWAY FROM THE FOUNDATION

7–1. *Slope the soil away from the foundation to help surface water drain away from the building.*

footing and slope it toward a dry well (see **7–3** on the following page). Backfill the excavation with rock and earth as shown in **7–3**. A cement-plaster damp-proofing layer is recommended over concrete-block foundation walls.

Before waterproofing the foundation, carefully seal any cracks in it.

4. The earth floor of the crawl space should be covered with a 6-mil polyethylene vapor barrier. Overlap the sheets at least 6 inches (152 millimeters) and bond them to the foundation wall with roofing cement. Place bricks on the laps (the overhang) or cement to prevent them from blowing apart when the foundation vents are open.

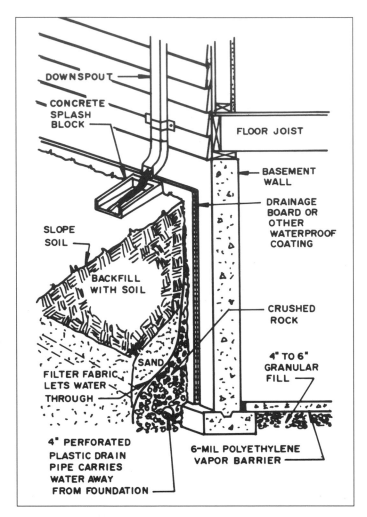

7–2. Wet basements can be dried up by excavating along the outside of the foundation, waterproofing the foundation, and providing for the removal of surface and subsurface water.

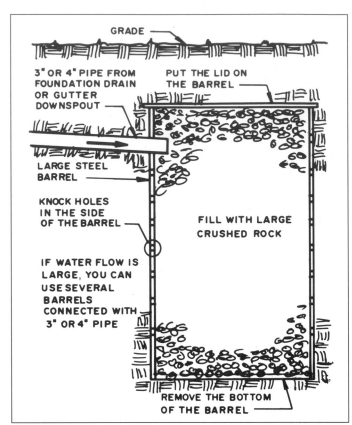

7–3. A simple dry well can be made using a large steel barrel. Put it deep enough in the soil so the water flows to it. The depth and distance from the house depend upon the slope of the lot.

5. If the outside air has low humidity, the foundation vents can be opened to allow fresh air to enter the crawl-space air and reduce the humidity there. However, most of the time the outside air will have more moisture than the air in the crawl space, so the vents should be closed.

CONCRETE-REPAIR PRODUCTS

Loose railings, anchor bolts, and other connections can be secured to a concrete surface by drilling the required hole, inserting the connection, and pouring a **liquid anchoring cement** around it. It sets quickly, so only mix enough for ten minutes' use.

Concrete **cure** and **sealer** products are sprayed on freshly poured concrete after it has taken on some set. They can be sprayed with a garden sprayer. They will seal the surface, thus holding the moisture in the concrete. This can be done instead of covering the concrete with plastic.

These products can also be applied to old concrete with a broom or roller. They seal the surface, keeping out moisture.

Concrete **bonding adhesives** are used to bond concrete to concrete or concrete block.

Concrete **liquid color** is added to the concrete mix as it is being made, to give it a permanent color. Be certain to mix it until the color is uniform throughout the mix. The manufacturer gives suggestions on how much to use per cubic yard (.76 cubic meter) of concrete.

Concrete **crack filler** and **patching** materials are commercially available in several types.

REPAIRING CRACKS IN THE FOUNDATION

Cracks are caused by the foundation settling. If they are small, they can usually be filled and waterproofed. If after filling they crack again, it means settling is still occurring and it is necessary to get a contractor to pump a special concrete under the footing or excavate under the footing a little at a time and pour larger sections of footing.

Cracks and patches in concrete are repaired with either a cementitious material or a polymer. Cementitious materials require the addition of water. Polymers require special setting agents other than water.

Using a Cementitious Material

Cementitious patching materials are prepackaged and require only the addition of water. They use a hydraulic-type cement that hardens rapidly, even when in a wet environment. The dry materials are mixed with water until it is in a soft, moldable, clay-like mixture. Since it hardens rapidly, work it into the crack rapidly. Do not mix more than can be installed in a few minutes.

Prepare the crack by cutting away loose particles with a cold chisel (**7–4**). If the crack is large, widen it at the bottom so that it forms a keyway that locks in

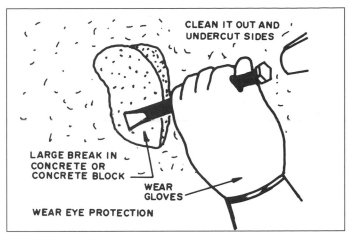

7–5. Large breaks in concrete and areas where pieces have broken off concrete blocks can be repaired by cleaning the surface and undercutting the edges before applying the patching material.

the concrete to be inserted. Work the mortar into the crack with a trowel and smooth it flush with the wall surface.

Cement patching material can also be used for larger repairs such as where a big piece of the concrete or concrete block wall has been damaged. Begin by cleaning and enlarging the area with a cold chisel (**7–5**). Wear gloves and eye protection. Wash the area with a garden hose to clean all loose debris, and moisten the area. Let the area sit until the moisture on the surface is gone.

Mix the patching mortar. It could be hydraulic cement or a mixture of one part portland cement, three parts sand, and about two-thirds part water. Fill the area slightly higher than the surrounding surface. After the patch begins to get stiff (in around 30 minutes), smooth it with a trowel and work it level with the surrounding concrete. Cover it with a heavy cloth and keep it wet for several days.

Using Epoxy

Epoxy is very effective for repairing small cracks (⅛ to 3/16 inch [3 to 5 millimeters]) in poured-concrete walls. The crack must be dry. If it is wet or water is leaking through, the flow must be stopped and the joint dried before proceeding. A hair dryer can be used to try to dry it out. After it appears dry, wait about 30 minutes to see if it gets wet again. If not, proceed with the patch.

Epoxy is sold at local building-supply stores in a

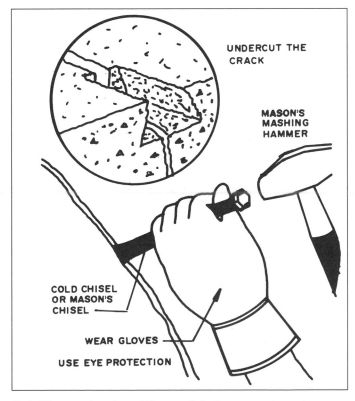

7–4. Clean and undercut the crack in the concrete and remove all loose particles before filling it.

kit containing a two-part epoxy paste, plastic ports, and a thin, injectable epoxy resin that is in a cartridge that fits the standard caulk gun. Be certain to wear eye protection and a mask.

Following is a brief explanation of the process (**7–6**). Observe the detailed instructions that come with the kit.

1. Clean the crack and the area around it with a wire brush. Be certain all loose particles are removed. Blow out the crack with compressed air to ensure cleanliness. Dry the crack and surface with a heat gun or hair dryer.

1. CLEAN THE CRACK AND THE SURFACE ON EACH SIDE.

2. DRY THE CRACK AND THE SURFACE ON EACH SIDE.

3. SECURE THE PORTS OVER THE CRACK EVERY 12 INCHES.

4. SPREAD THE SEALER PASTE OVER THE CRACK AND ALLOW IT TO HARDEN.

5. INJECT THE LIQUID EPOXY INTO THE LOWEST PORT UNTIL IT RUNS OUT THE PORT ABOVE. CAP THE FIRST PORT AND INJECT LIQUID EPOXY IN THE ONE DIRECTLY ABOVE. CONTINUE UP THE CRACK UNTIL IT IS FILLED.

7–6. Liquid epoxy provides a permanent seal of a crack in concrete and concrete masonry.

2. Glue the plastic injection ports into the crack, starting 12 inches (305 millimeters) above the floor and spaced 12 inches apart up the crack.

3. Mix the epoxy resin and hardener on a piece of cardboard with a putty knife. Put this mixture on the back of each port and secure the ports over the crack. Use rubber gloves when doing this. Let the epoxy cure.

4. Mix another batch of this two-part mixture and cover the surface of the crack. Press it into the crack, build a ⅛-inch (3-millimeter) -thick cover, and spread the glue over the sides of the crack onto the concrete. Let this cure overnight.

5. Now inject the thin epoxy liquid mix as directed by the manufacturer. Begin injecting the epoxy in the lowest port. When it runs out of the port above, cap the port and move up to the next one. Continue until the crack is full.

If this liquid epoxy is used on cracks wider than ⅛ inch, several cartridges will have to be used at each port.

6. Let the epoxy cure for five days and then break off the tops of the plastic ports if desired.

There are other products available for concrete-crack repair. One type is in a cartridge and is extruded into the cleaned crack. It can be troweled smooth and stays flexible. Any excess that may get on bricks or other surfaces can be wiped away with a damp cloth before it begins to set.

REPAIRING OPEN MORTAR JOINTS

Open mortar joints between bricks and concrete blocks are usually the result of careless masonry work. They may be caused because the mortar was too dry when used or because the brick or block was moved a little before the mortar had hardened.

To repair a defective mortar joint, do the following:

1. Wet the wall and mortar in the wall thoroughly.

2. Make a mix of one part mortar cement and two parts sand. Add water and mix the cement and sand until it is a plastic, workable substance. It should hold its shape as it is forced into the joint.

3. When the wall surface shows no moisture, force the mortar into the openings. Fill the opening with mortar until it is full and strike it off to match the original joint. The faces of the bricks can be kept clean by covering them with masking tape.

REPAIRING SIDEWALKS AND DRIVEWAYS

Concrete sidewalks and driveways can develop flaws due to poor mixing procedures, improper placement and finishing, and careless curing. Frequently occurring flaws are pop-outs, scaling, dusting, sandy or rough surfaces, and low spots.

Pop-outs occur when small pieces break out of the surface. These are typically caused by aggregates. To repair a pop-out, clean away all particles, wet the surface, let the moisture disappear, and trowel a patching cement over the hole.

Scaling is the breaking away of the surface of the slab in shallow layers of 1/16 to 3/16 inch (3 to 5 millimeters). This is often caused by the slab's freezing and thawing before the concrete has had a long cure. Applications of deicing salts also cause scaling.

To stop scaling, apply two coats of a mixture made of equal portions of boiled linseed oil and turpentine. Let the first coat cure before applying the second. These coats will have to be reapplied each fall for several years.

Dusting is the appearance of a chalky powder on the surface of the recently cured slab. It is typically caused by an excess of harmful fines, such as clay or silt particles, in the concrete mix. If the slab is floated or troweled before the excess water (called **bleed**) disappears from the surface, these fines are pulled up to the surface.

To stop dusting, brush the dust off the surface and coat it with a commercial concrete sealer. Follow the directions on the container.

Sandy surfaces occur when a slab surface is permitted to dry before it has set or if too much sand is used. To correct this situation, brush the slab clean and apply one or more coats of a commercial concrete sealer or a concrete paint.

Rough surfaces are smoothed by chipping away any loose particles, cleaning the surface thoroughly, flooding the surface with water, waiting until the water disappears from the surface, applying a bonding agent, and troweling on a ¼-inch (6-millimeter) -thick layer of mortar. Mix one part cement and three parts sand with enough water to make a throwable substance. Another option is to buy a ready-mixed patching mortar. Keep the patch moist for several days.

Another product useful for coating concrete is referred to as masonry coating. Clean and dampen the unpainted surface and apply the masonry coating with a stiff brush in a circular motion. Two coats are recommended, about 48 hours apart.

Low spots can be repaired by cleaning and roughening the surface and coating it with a bonding agent. Then flood the area and let the water disappear. Trowel on a mortar mix as used for rough surfaces. A wood screed can be used to level the patch (7–7). If the low spot is over 1½ inches (13 millimeters) deep, use two layers of mortar. Trowel one layer of mortar on the surface, but do not fill it completely. After the first layer has begun to harden, trowel a second layer over it. For a finer finish, run

the sand for the second layer through a sieve such as a window screen to remove the larger particles. Keep the patch moist for several days.

REPAIRING BROKEN CONCRETE

When a section of a driveway or sidewalk has a serious break, the damaged section can be broken away with a sledgehammer or hammer and cold chisel (7–8). It will take repeated blows to break away some parts. Be certain to wear eye protection and gloves.

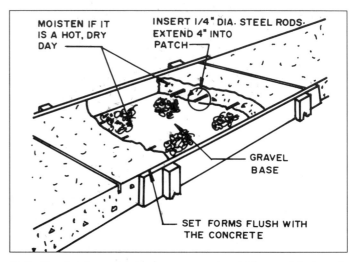

7–8. Break away the broken concrete until a solid area is reached. Form and prepare to pour the repair section.

Once the damaged concrete has been removed, put boards on each side and hold them in place with stakes. If the area below the damaged area is washed away, it may be necessary to put some crushed rock in and tamp it firmly. If the weather is hot and dry, wet the exposed edges of the slab and fill in the exposed area. Let all standing moisture disappear before pouring the patch. The bond between the patch and old slab can be improved by coating the edges of the slab with a commercial bonding agent. Consider drilling a few ¼-inch (6-millimeter) - diameter holes into each side of the slab about 1 inch (25 millimeters) deep and inserting large nails, bolts, or steel dowels that extend an inch or so into the patch. This helps hold the patch flush with the old concrete.

Fill the area with a mix of one part portland cement, three parts sand, and enough water to get a thick but workable mix. Typically two to three parts

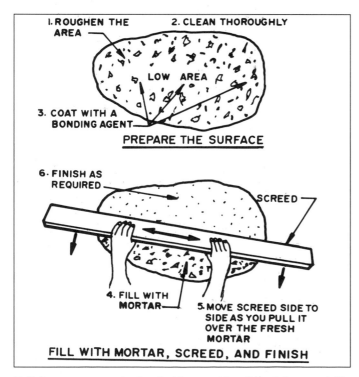

7–7. Low spots can be leveled by roughing the surface and filling it with mortar.

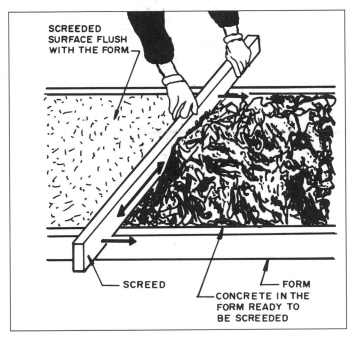

7–9. Pour the patch. Fill the area with concrete, level it with a screed, and add a finish as desired.

of water are required. After the area is filled, work the concrete against the forms (**7–9**). Then run a screed across the wood forms to level the concrete. This is the same as pouring a new sidewalk.

REPAIRING BROKEN CONCRETE ENDS AND EDGES

If a corner of a porch or step breaks off and the broken piece is available, cement it in place with epoxy cement. Be certain the concrete is dry. Coat and hold it in place as directed on the can of epoxy. Keep the joint warm until the cure time has been reached.

If the broken corner is in pieces, a new concrete corner can be cast. Drill a ¼-inch (6-millimeter) hole in the step about 1 inch (25 millimeters) deep using a concrete drill. Insert a steel dowel, large nail, or bolt in the hole and let it stick out as far as possible from the cavity (**7–10**). Build a wood form over the edge of the step, coat the concrete surface with a bonding agent, and fill the surface with a mixture consisting of one part portland cement, three parts sand, and enough water to make a thick but workable mix. Work it into the form and screed and trowel it smooth (**7–11**). It may be preferable to use ready-mixed patch cement available at the building-supply dealer.

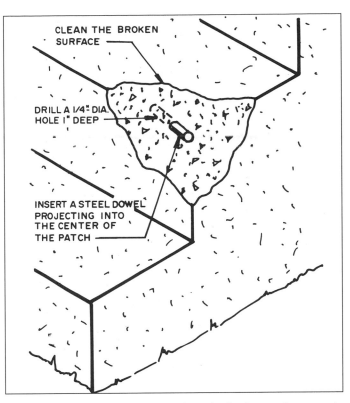

7–10. To repair a broken corner, clean the broken surface, apply a bonding agent, and install a steel dowel extending out into the area of the patch.

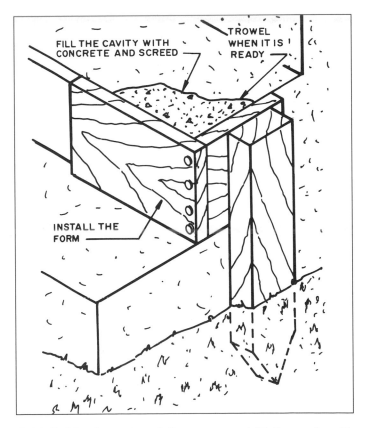

7–11. Build a form around the corner and fill the cavity with concrete.

After the patch has begun to set up (about one hour), carefully remove the form and trowel the edge of the patch (**7–12**). Be certain to place barriers around the patch for about two weeks, to let it firmly cure.

If the broken corner contains a post for a railing

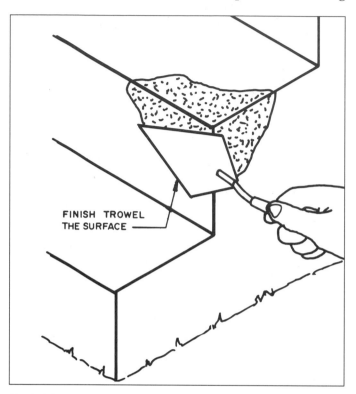

7–12. After the patch begins to set up, remove the forms and finish the surface with a metal trowel.

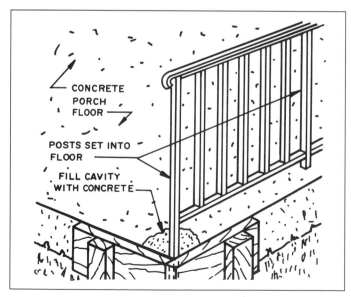

7–13. To repair a porch rail post that has broken loose in the concrete porch floor, clean the opening, enclose it with forms, set the post to the proper height, and pour concrete into the cavity.

repair as described above, position the post in the cavity. Rest it on a brick if necessary, to keep it level. Replace the corner as described earlier and shown in **7–13**.

REPLACING LOOSE MASONRY UNITS

Sometimes a brick or concrete block will become loose in a wall or will have crumbled. Generally, the blocks will not be carrying a load or they would not be loose. If the block is loose, stabilize it by forcing strips of lead solder into the cracks in the mortar. Tap the solder into the cracks with a blunt tool such as a screwdriver. This will seal off any water leak and stabilize the unit.

If the unit has deteriorated, it will have to be removed (**7–14**). Carefully chip away the unit and mortar with a cold chisel. Be careful that the other masonry units around it are not knocked loose. Clean away all particles and apply mortar to the bottom and sides of the opening and to the top face of the masonry unit. Slide the masonry unit into the opening, work the mortar joint to fill the gap, and finally tool it to match the other joints.

BUILDING A NEW SIDEWALK

The factors related to pouring on-grade slabs, such as those for a sidewalk or driveway, are many. The following discussion presents those factors that the home owner will commonly encounter.

Walk Size

The width of the walk varies, depending upon what the owner wants. Typically, residential walks are 3 to 4 feet (.9 to 1.2 meters) wide and 4 inches (102 millimeters) thick. If auto traffic crosses the walk, it should be at least 6 inches (152 millimeters) thick.

Laying Out the Walk

Drive stakes locating the corners of the walk. Dig 6 inches wider than this to make room for the forms. Run chalk lines locating the sides and ends of the

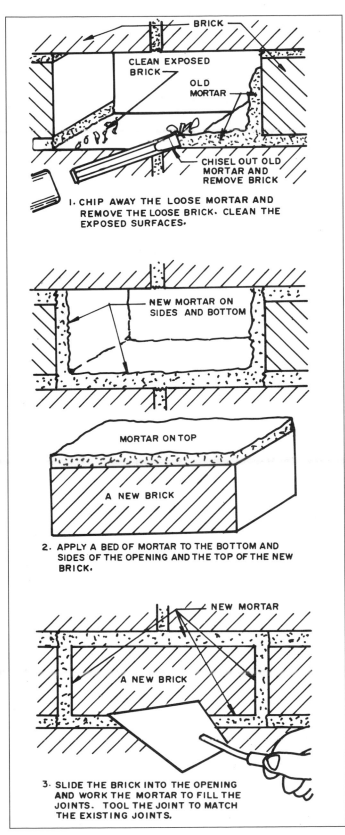

1. CHIP AWAY THE LOOSE MORTAR AND REMOVE THE LOOSE BRICK. CLEAN THE EXPOSED SURFACES.

2. APPLY A BED OF MORTAR TO THE BOTTOM AND SIDES OF THE OPENING AND THE TOP OF THE NEW BRICK.

3. SLIDE THE BRICK INTO THE OPENING AND WORK THE MORTAR TO FILL THE JOINTS. TOOL THE JOINT TO MATCH THE EXISTING JOINTS.

7–14. If you have to replace a loose or deteriorated masonry unit, carefully chip out the old mortar and remove the unit. Clean the exposed surfaces and coat the sides and bottom with a bed of mortar. Coat the new unit on top and slide it into place. Firm up the new mortar in the joint and tool as required.

excavation required, as shown in **7–15**. These are 12 inches (305 millimeters) wider than the sidewalk, to allow for the forms to be set.

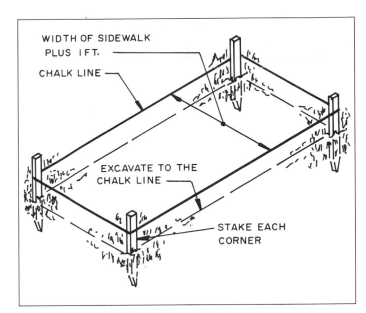

7–15. Details for laying out the length and width of the excavation.

The Excavation

Remove all sod and roots in the excavated area. The depth to dig can vary considerably. For example, if the soil is well drained and rather sandy, the concrete can be poured directly on it (**7–16**). This is especially true in warm climates. Compact the soil after the excavation is complete. If the walk is short, a hand tamper can be used.

If the soil tends to be wet and the area subject to freezing, it is best to lay down a 4- to 6-inch (101- to 152-millimeter) bed of gravel. This requires the excavation to be deeper (**7–16**). Compact the soil before placing the gravel.

Generally, the top of the slab should be 1 or 2 inches (25 or 51 millimeters) above the surface of the ground. Therefore, the amount of excavation can vary from 2 inches to as much as 6 inches. Remember that when the soil is compacted, it deepens the excavation, so a 3-inch (76-millimeter) excavation may only need to be dug 2 inches and compacted 1 inch.

Notice that in **7–16** the gravel fill extends below the form to the edges of the excavation.

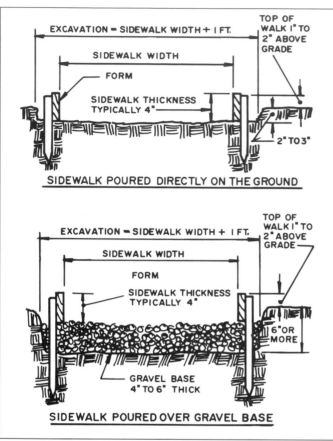

7–16. The base for the concrete sidewalk may be natural soil or gravel, depending upon local conditions.

Setting the Forms

The forms used are typically 1 x 4- or 2 x 4-inch lumber that are nailed to wood stakes to hold them in place (**7–17**). Lay out the edge forms and space them apart equal to the width of the sidewalk. A wood spacer may be used to make it easy to set the width. Once the side forms are in place, set the end forms. Be certain the forms are the required height above the ground. Generally, they are laid level or with a little slope from the horizontal. Slope them about G inch (6 millimeters) per foot (305 millimeters) toward the side or length to permit water to drain.

If the land slopes in the direction the walk runs, it may be advisable to pour a step. Form the step as shown in **7–18**. When doing this, set the gravel fill back about 8 to 10 inches (203 to 254 millimeters) from the end riser board, so the step is twice as thick as the slab. Steps can cause people to trip, so consider if you want to do this.

Now that the forms are in place, lay down the gravel base if one is required. Note that this step means the walk is not usable by someone in a wheelchair. The recommended slope for a ramp suitable for use by those in wheelchairs is 1:20 (1 foot for every 20 feet), but 1:12 is the absolute maximum permitted (**7–19**). Ramps should be at least 36 inches (914 millimeters) wide. Ramps are suggested instead of steps for use by everyone.

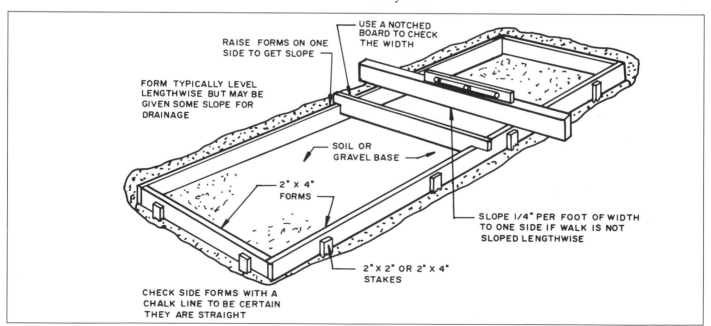

7–17. Typical forms for pouring a concrete sidewalk. Notice that they are either sloped to one side or lengthwise.

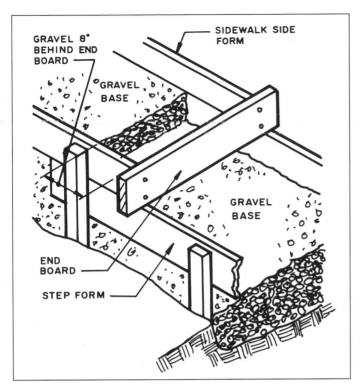

7–18. A step can be put in a walk that runs down a slope. If this can be avoided, do so because people often trip over steps. Steps also mean that the walk cannot be used by anyone in a wheelchair.

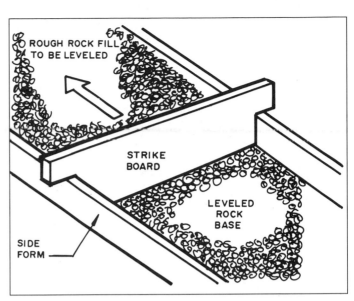

7–20. Move the strike board over the rough-filled gravel to level it; this forms the base for the concrete.

Setting Expansion Strips

Since concrete expands and contracts with changes in temperature, expansion strips should be installed every 25 feet (7.6 meters) or closer. They are resilient bituminous fiber strips placed in the form, separating two concrete pours. One way to do this is to use an end board to stop the first pour (**7-21**). After the concrete has stiffened, replace the end board with an expansion strip and make the next pour.

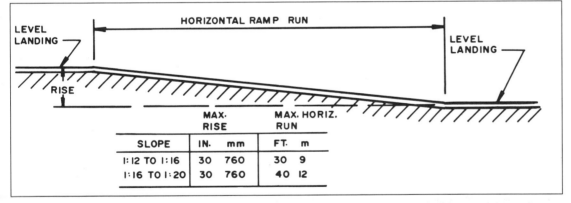

SLOPE	MAX. RISE		MAX. HORIZ. RUN	
	IN.	mm	FT.	m
1:12 TO 1:16	30	760	30	9
1:16 TO 1:20	30	760	40	12

7–19. A walk on a slope with a ramp rather than steps enables those in wheelchairs to use the walk.

Setting the Gravel Base

Use ¾- to 1-inch (19- to 25-millimeter) -size stone for the fill. Spread it evenly across the excavation and tamp it to firm up the base. Use a 4 x 4 wood member as a tamper. Be certain the base is level. An easy way to do this is to make a strike board and run it along the form as shown in **7–20**.

Isolation Joints

Where the slab meets a foundation, steps, or other fixed concrete surface, insert a strip of expansion material between the wall and the new slab. This allows each to expand and contract and not put pressure on each other. Seal this joint to prevent water from getting under the slab (**7–22**).

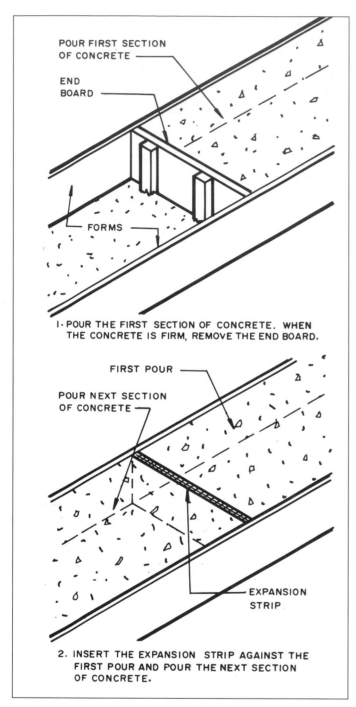

1. POUR THE FIRST SECTION OF CONCRETE. WHEN THE CONCRETE IS FIRM, REMOVE THE END BOARD.

2. INSERT THE EXPANSION STRIP AGAINST THE FIRST POUR AND POUR THE NEXT SECTION OF CONCRETE.

7–21. Pour a section of the walk, let the concrete firm up, remove the end board, insert an expansion strip, and pour the next section of concrete.

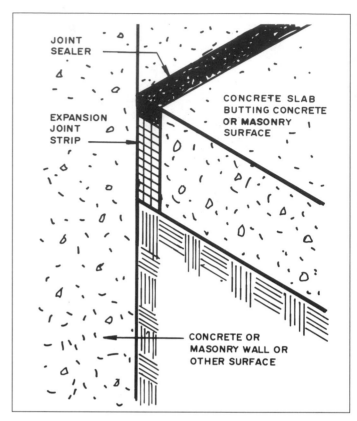

7–22. An isolation joint is used to separate a concrete pour from a wall, steps, or other concrete or masonry surface.

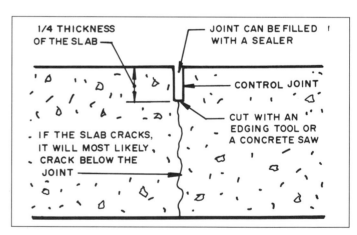

7–23. Control joints provide a place for the slab to crack without showing on the surface or running at an angle across the surface.

Control Joints

Control joints are recesses in the concrete slab that provide a thin section where the slab can crack and not show on the surface. The depth is typically one-quarter the thickness of the slab (7–23).

Control joints can be hand-cut with an edging tool or a concrete groover before the concrete has set up

(7–24). A concrete contractor will cut these with a concrete saw after the slab has firmed upa bit.

Reinforcing the Slab

If the soil is poor and the slabs in this area have a history of settling and cracking, a layer of welded wire fabric can be installed over the gravel base. Place it on pieces of brick or stone so it is about 1½

7–24. Control joints can be cut with an edging tool or a concrete groover.

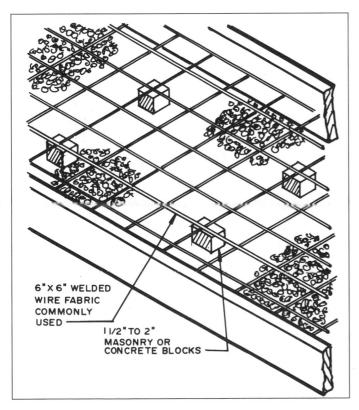

7–25. Welded wire fabric is used to reduce the size of any cracks that may occur in the concrete slab.

to 2 inches (38 to 51 millimeters) above the gravel. Usually a fabric with a 6 x 6-inch (152 x 152-millimeter) grid and a wire size of W2.0 x W2.0 is used. The main purpose of the fabric is not to strengthen the slab but to minimize the size of any cracks that may occur (**7–25**).

Rather than using welded wire fabric, a request can be made to the concrete-mix plant operator to add fiber reinforcement to the mixture. The types of fibers commonly used include glass, polymeric, and acrylic fibers.

The slab can be strengthened by adding metal reinforcing bars instead of the welded wire fabric, but this is unusual for sidewalk construction.

Pouring the Slab

Several people should be available to give assistance when the slab is being poured. It helps a great deal if it is poured in short sections of 10 to 15 feet (3 to 4.6 meters). Simply install an end board where the pour will be stopped (refer to **7–21**). A single pour of this size may be enough for one day's work unless experienced concrete workers are helping.

The first consideration is whether to mix the concrete yourself or have the local concrete plant do it. If you are mixing the concrete on a job this big, rent a concrete mixer and have the sand, aggregate, and portland cement on hand. Several sturdy wheelbarrows and shovels are necessary.

Generally, it is easier to have delivery from the local concrete plant. It will deliver a carefully controlled mix ready to place.

Before pouring the slab, wet the base and forms with water if it is a hot, dry day, but do not pour until there is no standing water. Begin pouring at one end of the form and fill 4 or 5 feet (1.2 or 1.5 meters) (**7–26**). Work the concrete into the form and rough-level it with a rake. Then screed it, beginning at the filled end and working toward the unfilled end. **Screeding** is done by placing a straight board across the forms and moving it back and forth, thus leveling the pour with the top of the form (**7–27**). If screeding over a low spot, fill it by moving some concrete from the loose end with a shovel.

Continue pouring sections, leveling and moving

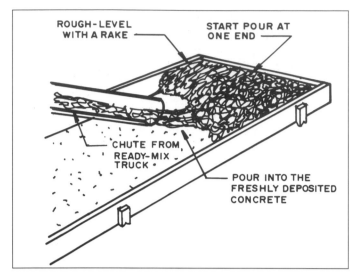

7–26. Start the pour at one end of the form and pour into the freshly placed concrete.

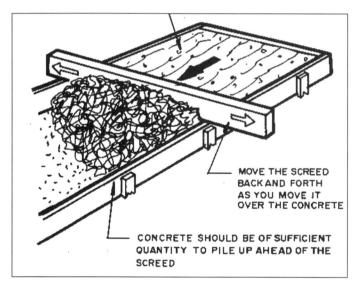

7–27. After some concrete has been deposited, rough-screed the surface.

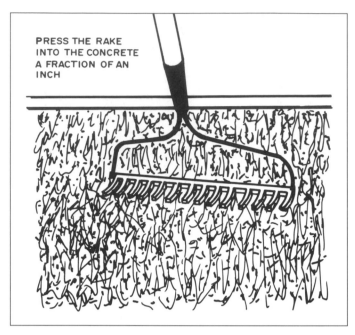

7–28. Lightly tamp the surface of the concrete to set any stones that have risen to the top below the surface.

on until the length of the form is full and screeded.

Now **tamp** the surface with a rake (**7–28**) to push any stones below the surface. Hold the rake perpendicular to the concrete and push it a fraction of an inch into the mix.

Finishing the Slab

Do not start the final finishing until the film of water (called **bleed**) on the top is gone, as well as any shine from moisture. How long this will take depends on the weather. On a hot, dry day, it may only be 30 minutes to an hour. On cool, cloudy, damp days, it will be much longer.

Now **float** the surface. On small surfaces, such as a sidewalk, a small hand float or darby is used to do this (**7–29**). Swing the tool in a circular motion, overlapping each swing. Do this over the entire walk.

When the surface is smooth and firm, the slab is ready to be edged. *Edging* rounds the sharp edges of the concrete slab so they are less likely to crack off if put under a load. The edges are rounded with an edging tool as shown in **7–24**. Work the tool back and forth along the edge inside the form (**7–30**).

Next, groove the concrete at the desired intervals with a grooving tool. Use a board as a guide to get the groove straight, as shown in **7–24**.

Now the **final finish** can be worked. Do not do this until all surface moisture (bleeding) is gone and the slab can be stepped on without leaving footprints more than ¼ inch (6 millimeters) deep. If the finish is started too soon, the surface will most likely develop craze (minute cracks) and dust.

When ready to do the final finish, begin by floating the surface. For small areas such as a sidewalk, use a darby as shown in **7–29**. This brings mortar to the surface and is needed if the final finish will be troweled.

At this point, one of two approaches can be taken. A steel trowel can be used on the surface to produce a

7–29. Smooth the surface and remove all high and low areas with a hand float or a darby.

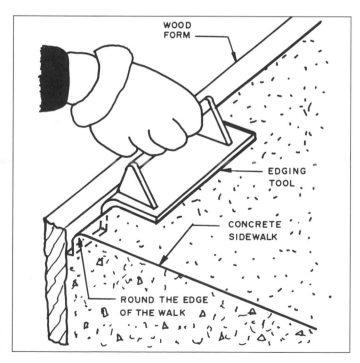

7–30. Edge the slab along the form so the sharp edges are rounded.

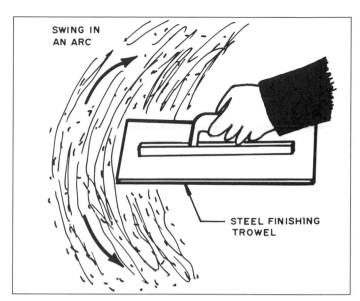

7–31. To get a hard, smooth finish, trowel the surface after it has been floated. Swing the trowel in overlapping circular arcs.

very smooth finish or the surface can be brushed, giving a striated finish. If a steel trowel is used, the smooth surface is produced by swinging the trowel across the surface in a circular motion (7–31). Keep the leading edge of the trowel raised a bit so it will not dig into the concrete. Continue troweling until enough cement has risen to conceal all the grains of sand.

If you are brushing the surface, pull a stiff brush across it perpendicular to the forms (7–32). Do this immediately after the slab has been floated. Do not overlap each stroke.

After the final finishing, go back over the edges with the edging tool and touch up the control-joint grooves.

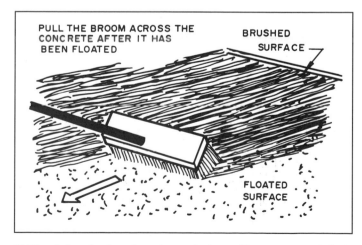

7–32. A brushed surface is made by pulling a coarse-bristle brush over the concrete surface after it has been floated.

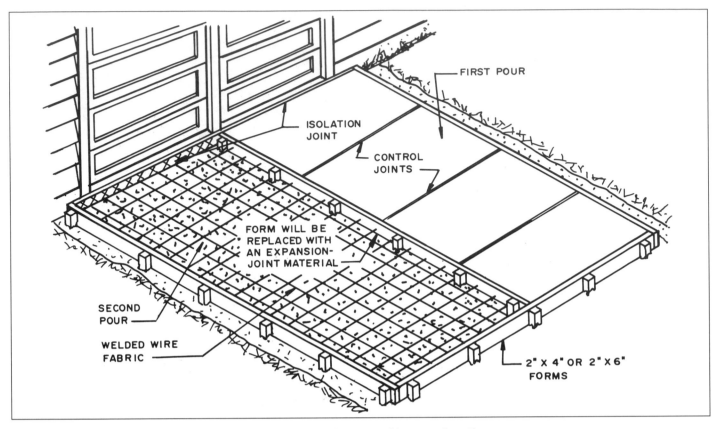

7–33. Since a driveway requires a large amount of concrete, it is poured in several sections.

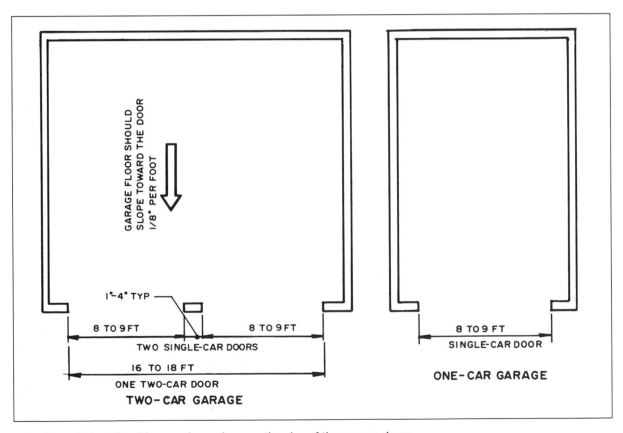

7–34. The width of the driveway depends upon the size of the garage doors.

BUILDING A CONCRETE DRIVEWAY

Building a New Sidewalk gives the basic information for laying out and pouring a driveway. The major difference between pouring a sidewalk and pouring a driveway is that much more concrete is to be poured for a driveway, so the job is laid out into several sections that are usually not poured all at the same time. A typical example is shown in **7–33**.

Residential driveways are poured 4 inches (102 millimeters) thick. They should be a little wider than the garage door. For example, a single-car garage with a 9-foot (2.7-meter) door usually has an 11- or 12-foot (3.4- or 3.7-meter) -wide driveway. A two-car garage could require a driveway 18 to 22 feet (5.5 to 6.7 meters) wide, depending upon the size and arrangement of garage doors. A garage with a single door that admits two cars will have a narrower drive than a garage with two single one-car doors (**7–34**).

The maximum driveway slope to the street specified by codes is usually 15 percent. A slope of 10 percent or less is much more desirable. A 10-percent slope is one that drops 1 foot in height for every 10 feet in length. If there is a sidewalk at the street, it is necessary to check the profile of the driveway to see if the bottom of the car or the bumper will hit it. Make a scale drawing like those shown in **7–35** and a scale drawing of the wheel base and rear bumper of the car and the amount they clear the driveway. If

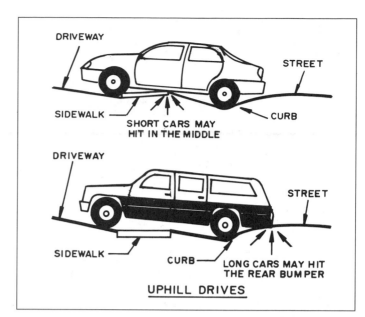

7–35. Check the profile of the proposed driveway to verify that the cars will not hit it when entering and leaving.

this shows that the car bottom or bumper could easily hit the driveway—especially if the car may bounce a little—then the angle of the drive must be changed.

Be certain to slope the driveway so water runs away from the garage. A slope of ¼ inch (6 millimeters) per foot away from the garage is adequate. The driveway can also be sloped to the sides as shown in **7–36**. Placing the driveway about 1 inch (25 millimeters) below the garage floor will help keep water out of the garage. If the street is sloped so water will

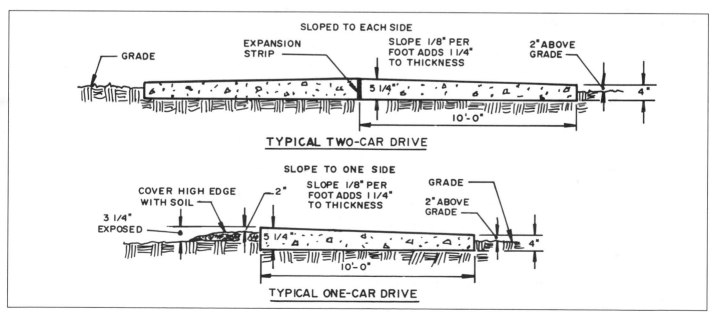

7–36. Slope the drive so rain will drain away from the garage and off to the sides.

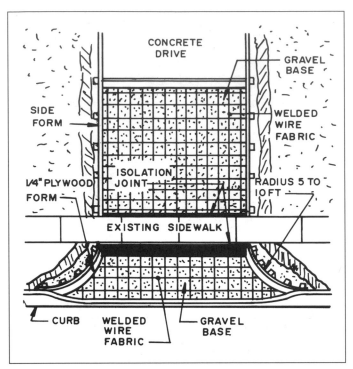

7–37. The concrete driveway is flared at the street to provide for turning onto the street. If there is no sidewalk, the drive runs uninterrupted to the street.

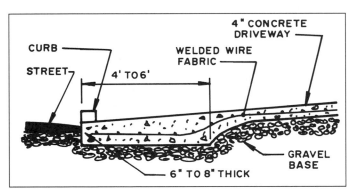

7–38. Thicken the driveway at the street so it resists heavier-than-expected loads from delivery trucks.

run down the driveway, pour the driveway about one inch higher than the street. The driveway should be 2 inches (51 millimeters) higher than the ground on each side.

A curved entrance slab has to be poured and formed at the street. The curved form can be made from ¼-inch (6-millimeter) -thick plywood. A radius of 10 to 15 feet (3 to 4.6 meters) is commonly used (7–37). It is usually poured thicker at the street to carry unexpected loads, as when a truck may use the drive to turn around (7–38).

ASPHALT DRIVEWAY MAINTENANCE AND REPAIR

Asphalt paving used on driveways is a cementitious mixture using a bituminous binder to hold together mineral aggregate, forming a flexible, plastic, waterproof paving. Over the years, freezing and thawing may cause cracks. The paving is also damaged by oil and gasoline.

Whenever a crack appears, it should be repaired so that water will not penetrate below the paving and cause more serious damage. There are a number of crack fillers available at the building-supply dealer. One type is referred to as **crack filler** and is used on cracks up to ¼ inch wide. It is in a cartridge just like those used for caulking (7–39).

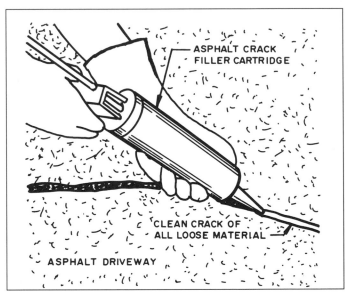

7–39. Fill cracks up to ¼ inch wide with a commercial asphalt crack filler. Deeper cracks may require a second layer. Clean the crack with a brush. Smooth the filler with a trowel.

Cracks wider than ¼ inch are filled with a **crack patch** (7–40). It is also used for larger areas such as where gasoline has damaged a section of the surface. To make a repair, cut back to an undamaged surface and clean away all debris (7–41). Fill the opening in 1-inch layers. Do not apply the patch if the temperature is below 50° F (10° C). Allow the patch to cure for at least 24 hours and then coat it with an asphalt sealer.

Every few years, cover the entire driveway with a **blacktop sealer**. First, fill all cracks and repair the damaged area. Remove any oil spots by scrubbing

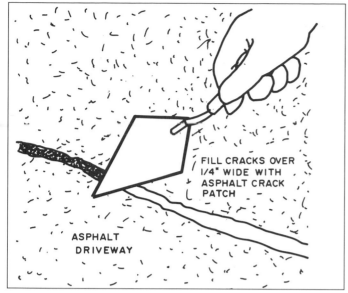

7–40. Wider cracks are filled by cleaning them thoroughly and filling them with crack patch. Lay it in with a trowel, using several layers if necessary. Trowel the final layer smooth and flush with the surrounding asphalt.

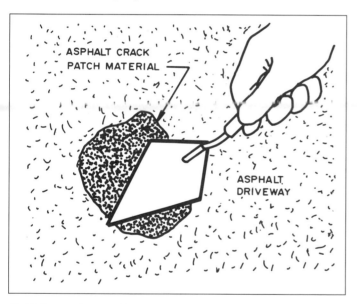

7–41. Large damaged areas require that all damaged material in the cavity and on the edges be removed. Lay in the crack-patch material in one-inch (25-millimeter) layers. Press it firmly in place. Add additional layers until it is flush with the surface. Trowel it smooth and protect it until it cures as recommended by the manufacturer.

not apply it too thick. Let it cure for 48 hours and apply a second thin coat. Let this cure for a day or so before driving on it.

Some asphalt patching and sealing products are

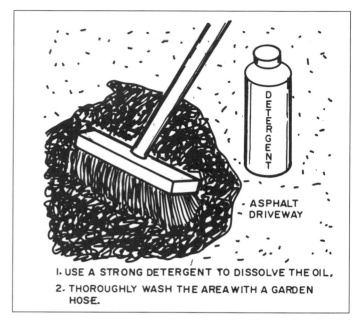

7–42. Before sealing the asphalt driveway, remove all oil spots with a strong detergent.

7–43. Seal the asphalt driveway by spreading the sealer coat on three- to four-foot-square areas. Brush in one direction and cross-brush perpendicular to the first brushing. Apply a second coat in 48 hours.

them with a strong detergent and then wash down the area with a garden hose (**7–42**). The sealer will usually fill tiny hairline cracks.

Apply the blacktop sealer with a brush or roller. Apply the sealer to a three- or four-square-foot (.28- or .37-square-meter) area, brushing in one direction. Then go back over it at right angles (**7–43**). Do

formulated so they are water-soluble. However, if any of these products get on the hands and tools, wash them before the product begins to harden; after it hardens, it is water-resistant.

REPAIRING ROTTED WOOD

Untreated wood tends to rot when exposed to the weather over a period of years. This can occur to painted wood if the moisture penetrates the paint or gets behind a painted surface such as wood siding.

Another type of rot is referred to as **dry rot**. It occurs when untreated wood is repeatedly wetted and dries over many years. A fungus carries the moisture into the wood. Wood not subject to the weather but in a damp area where fungi can flourish, such as floor joists, is vulnerable to dry rot.

The first thing to do is to remove the moisture problem. Wood exposed to weather can be replaced with wood treated with a wood preservative. All caulking should be checked and replaced as needed. Damp areas need to have the sources of moisture blocked and adequate ventilation provided.

Generally, it is best to replace the rotted wood members after moisture-control actions have been taken. However, for many smaller damaged areas, the rotted materials can be cut away and the area filled with an **epoxy wood filler**. Before doing this, be certain the wood is dry. It might be helpful to give it several coats of a wood preservative before filling it with the epoxy wood filler. Press the filler into the damaged area and smooth it with a trowel. Chapter Eight contains further information.

INSECTS

There are quite a variety of insects that like to inhabit houses. Some do major damage to the building materials, while others prefer to get inside the house and cohabit with the residents. Controlling these insects demands occasional use of chemical controls. It is essential to ascertain that these chemicals do not cause human injury. Many products are available at building-supply dealers,

plant nurseries, and garden shops. When buying such a product, pay close attention to the instructions and the safety requirements for using it. Typically, rubber gloves, eye protection, and a respirator are required. Also observe the recommended mixture of chemical to water. Do not try to increase the strength beyond that specified.

Spiders, Ants, and Crickets

These critters live in grass, the mulch around plants, and in the plants themselves. The area around the foundation outside the house can be treated with recommended chemicals. This greatly reduces the

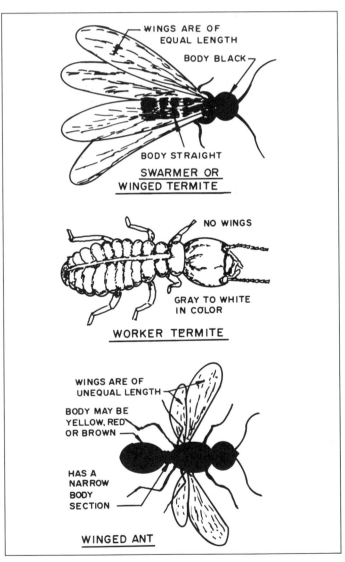

7–44. Soldier termites live and die in their colony. Winged termites leave and start new colonies. Winged ants are often mistaken for winged termites.

number trying to enter. Inside the house, use the various traps that are available. Be careful of sprays; they can damage eyes and lungs. Some people are allergic to the insect sprays available.

Subterranean Termites

Subterranean termites must have contact with damp soil. This is where they build their colonies. A colony is made up of winged, worker, and soldier termites (**7–44**).

Winged termites (also called **swarmers**) leave the colony and fly and are carried by the wind. They shed their wings, enter the earth, and form a new colony.

Worker termites make up most of the colony. They channel into and destroy wood, carry water, build the nest and mud shelter tubes in which they travel, and feed the young. When an infested board is broken open, white-gray worker termites will be found inside. Most of the termites in a colony are worker termites.

Soldier termites protect the colony from attack by other insects. They have pincer-like mouths to kill invaders. The workers repair any damage to the mud shelter tubes or the nest while the soldiers stand guard. A colony has only a small number of soldier termites.

Winged ants are often mistaken for termites (refer to **7–44**). Examine some of the insects before beginning treatment. Standard insecticides can kill ants.

As mentioned, **subterranean termites** require moist soil and dark, damp conditions in order to survive. It is here that they build their nests below the frost line. Because they must stay moist, they live in the earth and inside wood members and, when out of the earth, build mud tunnels for protection.

Subterranean termites are a major hazard to homes almost everywhere in the United States. They eat the cellulose in wood to survive. When they enter a wood member, they consume the inside; this leaves a thin wood shell to provide them protection, so when the wood member is examined, damage will not be spotted. However, the wood member has been structurally weakened and infestation can spread to nearby members.

Subterranean termites enter the house by building mud tunnels up foundation walls. They can enter around the edges of concrete slabs and go through wood porches, steps, and basement windows. They can also enter through the smallest cracks in any part of the house near the earth (**7–45**).

It is recommended that a professional exterminator be used to treat the soil around the house and inspect it once a year for signs of termite infestation. If termites are found, sometimes they can be killed. However, if the wood members are badly damaged they will have to be replaced.

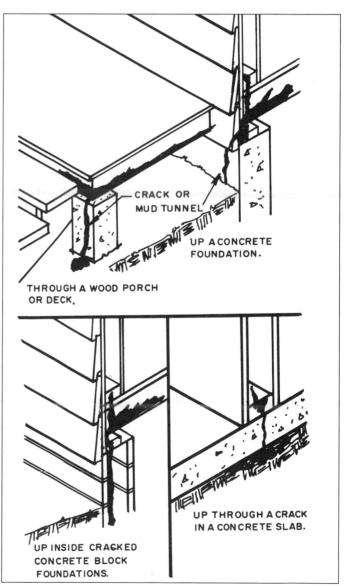

7–45. Termites enter the wood members of the house by moving from the damp ground up through cracks and mud tunnels to reach the wood.

If termites are under a concrete slab, such as in a garage floor, they will work their way up through cracks in the slab and attack the wall studs. The exterminator will drill holes through the slab in many places and inject under pressure the proper chemicals. If the house has a concrete-block foundation, termites can crawl up unseen inside the core holes. To control this when it is discovered, the exterminator will drill holes into each core hole and inject chemicals. Be certain to treat any piers and footings in the crawl space.

There are steps that can be taken that will help to minimize termite problems. Do not keep any wood products under the house or around the outside of the foundation. Dig up any wood that was buried when the house was built. Move firewood away from the house. Seal all joints between the siding and foundation and other openings. Fill all cracks in the foundation.

To check for termites, tap on wood members that appear to be infested. If they sound hollow, stick a knife into them. If they are infested, the knife will break through the thin wood exterior layer left by the termites.

Drywood Termites

Drywood termites are found in abundance in the Gulf states and up each coast to Virginia and California. Few are found in the band of states across the center of the United States, and they are almost never found in the upper half of the country up to the Canadian border. They live without contact with the soil and require little moisture. They are winged and make direct contact with dry wood members above the ground line. They build nests in the wood framing, siding, window frames, and other wood members. They can even move to the attic. A pair of winged reproductives enter the wood through cracks and tunnel inside to form a nest. They are hidden from view except when they make flights to other wood members. Their presence can be noted by the piles of tiny fecal pellets.

To prevent infestation by drywood termites, it is not necessary to treat the soil, because they do not live there. Use pressure-treated wood, steel, or con-crete structural members and masonry siding. Exterminators will dust any nests with a poisonous dust. If the house is extensively infested, the structure may have to be completely fumigated. This is a major action and must be done by qualified, insured exterminators, who will completely enclose the structure with plastic sheets. The chemicals are hazardous to pets, humans, and shrubs.

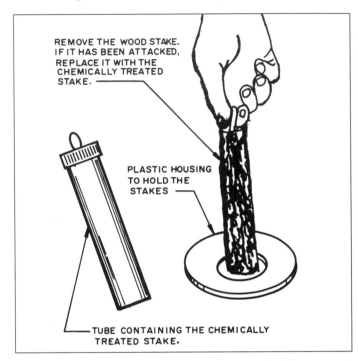

7–46. This termite-control system uses a wood stake to see if termites are available and then replaces it with poison bait if they are present. It is installed by a qualified pest-control operator.

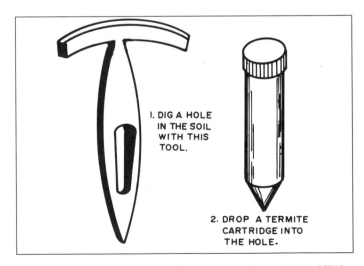

7–47. This termite-control system uses a poison bait to kill the worker termites. Since they do not bring food to the colony, the other termites starve. This is available at the building-supply dealer.

Since fumigation does not penetrate the wood, termites could return at some future time. Seal the exterior of the house to close all possible entry points for these flying insects.

Dampwood Termites

Dampwood termites do not require contact with the soil. They live in wet wood and areas having high humidity. They are found mainly in the Pacific Northwest and nationally cause little damage to residential construction. If they are present, call a professional exterminator. Try to reduce moisture accumulation in all members of the house and seal all exterior cracks that provide entry.

An Environmentally Friendly Way to Treat the Foundation for Termites

For years, the soil around houses has been treated for termites by pumping large quantities of chemicals into the soil. This provides a risk of contaminating the groundwater and possibly the basement. A new method uses solid bait in underground tubes that is eaten by the termites.

Several systems are available. Some are available only through the services of an authorized pest-control company. Others can be purchased at the local building-supply dealer. One system places wood stakes enclosed in hollow plastic stakes that are driven into the ground. If the wood is attacked by termites, the wood stick is replaced by a treated bait stick. The termites carry the bait back to the nest, where it poisons the entire colony (**7–46**).

Another type available to the home owner uses a solid bait in cartridges (**7–47**). The termites eat the bait and die. Since they cannot then bring food to the colony, all the termites starve.

WINDOW MAINTENANCE AND REPAIR

Routine maintenance should keep windows trouble-free and operating satisfactorily. Old windows that are loose, cracked, or have poorly fitting sashes should be replaced. Energy-efficient windows will reduce heating and cooling costs and make the occupants more comfortable.

One of the most common repairs on windows is replacing cracked and missing glazing compound. Scrape away all the old glazing compound. Use a chisel, putty knife, or other convenient tool. Avoid digging into the wood sash. If it is a metal sash, this is not a problem. Replace any loose glazier's points. Sand the frame lightly if it will help remove the final compound.

Now brush exposed wood frames with a wood preservative or linseed oil diluted slightly with turpentine. This prevents the wood from absorbing the oil out of the glazing compound. After this is dry, install new glazing compound as shown in **7–67**.

Double-Hung Windows

Double-hung windows have two sash that move up and down vertically. Some of the newer windows have the top sash fixed and only the lower sash moves (**7–48**).

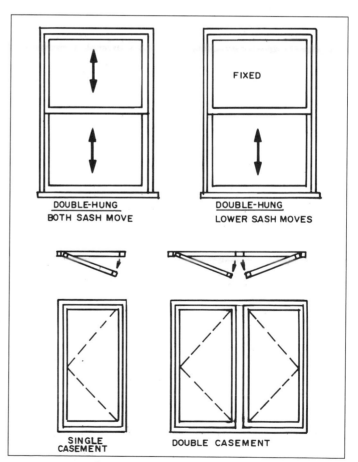

7–48. Typical double-hung and casement windows.

A common problem with double-hung windows is that when they are painted, the sash sticks to the frame. Run a putty knife between the sash and frame to separate the two (**7–49**). Clean away any lumps of paint that may cause the window to be difficult to move (**7–50**). If the sash slides on a wood frame, sand it lightly to remove paint. If the sash runs on a metal channel, remove paint with steel wool or dissolve it with paint remover. When it is clean, rub bar soap or paraffin on the slides.

7–50. Remove excess paint and any lumps with a wood chisel or a scraper.

Casement Windows

Casement windows are hinged on one side and swing out like a door (refer to **7–48**). They have a crank mechanism that enables them to be opened and closed by simply turning the handle of the crank.

7–49. Sash that has been painted and become stuck to the frame can be freed by cutting through the paint with a putty knife or some other thin, flat tool.

If moisture petrates the sash, causing it to swell, it may bind on the molding. Correct this situation by first preventing the moisture from entering the sash. Then carefully remove the molding and reinstall it, leaving a little more space between it and the window.

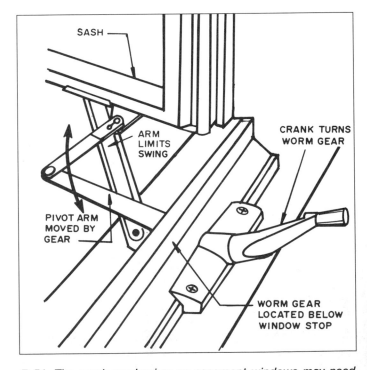

7–51. The crank mechanism on casement windows may need cleaning and lubricating after a few years.

Casement windows may have been been painted closed and, consequently, stick to the window frame. Cut the paint between the sash and the window frame with a putty knife. Sometimes a wood sash fits the frame too tightly because of swelling from moisture. To fix this problem, plane a small amount off the sash. Do not remove too much or the space between the frame and sash will become too big when the moisture content is lower. Treat the fresh wood surface with a wood preservative.

Another difficulty with casement windows may be a sticky cranking mechanism (7–51). The mechanism often does not work smoothly because of dirt or paint. Remedy this by cleaning the bar and the slot in which the end of the bar slides. Then spray both with silicone or light machine oil. Sometimes it is necessary to remove the cranking mechanism and clean the gears inside. Use any liquid cleaner that will dissolve dirt. Then lubricate the gears with silicone spray or light machine oil.

Sliding Windows

Sliding windows move horizontally in a metal track. One sash is fixed and the other slides horizontally (**7–52**).

Sliding windows are the simplest to maintain. If they stick, they are either painted closed or the track is clogged with dirt. Cut the paint that is causing the sash to stick to the frame. Wash or brush out any dirt and debris from the track. Lubricate the track with silicone spray. Some sliding windows may be lifted from the track for easy cleaning.

Hopper and Awning Windows

Hopper windows are hinged at the bottom and open into the room. They are manually pulled open and push closed (**7–52**). They provide ventilation but direct the draft up toward the ceiling and away from the occupants of the room.

Awning windows are hinged at the top and swing toward the exterior of the house. They may have a cranking mechanism similar to casement windows. Awning windows allow ventilation even when it is raining. They require the same maintenance described for other windows.

REPLACEMENT WINDOWS

There are a large variety of replacement windows available from window manufacturers. Before choosing one, review the types available and examine installation procedures. Some manufacturers will custom-make the window to fit the rough opening of the old window. Others have standard sizes and provide a means for filling in the rough opening to hold a slightly smaller unit as well as flashing and trim to waterproof the edges against the weather. Others enable the window to be replaced without

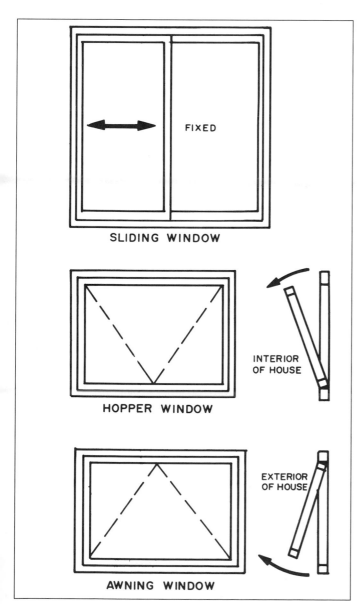

7–52. Typical sliding, hopper, and awning windows.

rebuilding the opening or removing and recutting the interior trim.

Windows are available in wood, wood clad with vinyl, composite, and vinyl. When choosing windows, inquire about the warranty. If a contractor is installing them, see what type of warranty is offered for the work.

After a brand of window has been chosen, measure the rough opening of the old window and the distance between the existing jambs. The dealer will need to know these measurements to supply the proper-sized unit. To measure the rough opening if this is needed, the interior window trim will most likely have to be removed. Measurements should be very accurate. Measure the width at the top, center, and bottom of the rough opening and on the right and left sides vertically from the bottom to the top of the rough opening. These measurements are necessary because the opening may vary and it is necessary to find the smallest size each way so the replacement window will fit into the opening.

If the old sill is to remain, repair or replace it if it is rotted. Small rot spots can be filled with epoxy wood filler. Complete replacement windows will have a new sill.

The window manufacturer will supply complete installation instructions and all the parts needed to make the installation. Following are some typical procedures for replacing different parts of a window:

Replacing Only the Sash

Old windows that use weights and cords can be replaced with a system using metal-pressure side channels. The channels have spring-loaded strips that are placed on both side jambs to hold each sash in the desired open position.

To replace the old windows, remove the inside trim and stop molding from the sides of the jamb and lift the old sash out of the frame (7–53). Cut off the old cord and remove the old pulleys.

To install the new sash, place it in the channels

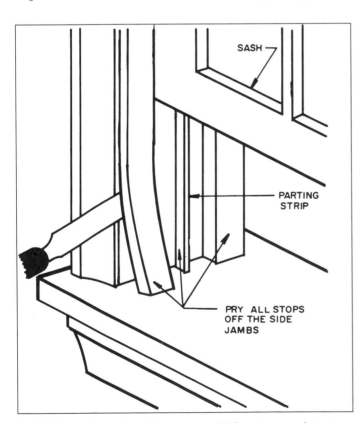

7–53. To replace old windows, pry off the stops and remove the sash. Cut the cords and remove the weights from the cavity in the wall. If the stops are in good condition, they can be nailed back after the metal channels are in place. Otherwise, get new ones.

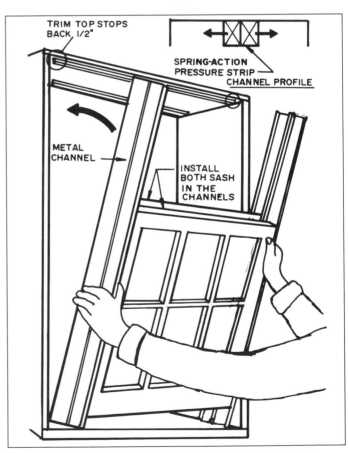

7–54. Put the sash into the metal channels, rest the channels on the sill, and swing them into the opening. Remember that the lower sash is to be on the outside.

and lift it into the frame (**7–54**). (If the old sash are sound, they can be used instead of buying new ones.) Now screw the channels to the frame (**7–55**). Next, fill the cavity that held the weights with fiberglass insulation and reinstall the interior trim. If it is difficult to get the insulation into the cavity, it can be filled with aerosol foam insulation, available in pressurized cans. If doing this, do not overfill the cavity or the pressure of the expanding foam may cause the window frame to bow.

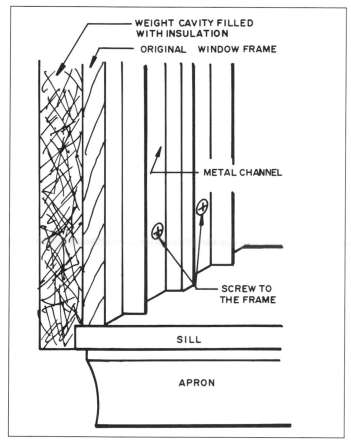

7–55. Screw the metal channels to the frame and fill the weight cavity with insulation

Replacing the Entire Window with One the Same Size or Smaller

Remove the sash and the entire frame of the existing window as well as the interior and exterior trim. This will leave the rough opening formed by the studs, header, and rough sill (**7–56**). If the new window is slightly smaller than the old one, blocking can be added on each side and at the sill as required.

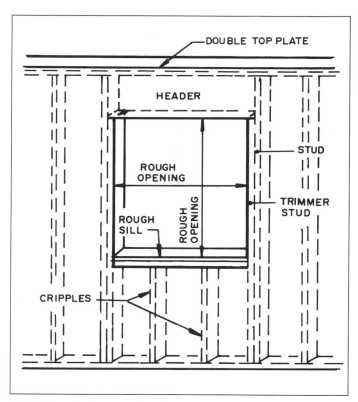

7–56. Completely removing the old window exposes the rough opening into which the replacement window will be installed.

Install the new window as directed by the manufacturer. One example is shown in **7–57**, on page 294. Wrap the sides of the rough opening with builder's felt if none is present. Then lift the window unit into the opening and nail through the nailing fin in one top corner with a 2-inch (51-millimeter) galvanized roofing nail. Level the unit and nail the opposite corner. Do not drive the nails in completely because one may have to be removed to readjust the window for levelness or plumb.

Now check the side jambs for plumb and shim at the sill to hold the unit vertical. Measure the diagonals to be certain the unit is square. It should measure exactly the same on each diagonal.

Next, nail the exterior head flashing if it is required. It is part of some units rather than a separate piece. Then nail around the nailing fin as specified by the manufacturer.

On the exterior, replace the trim that was removed. On the inside, fill any cavities around the unit with insulation and replace the interior trim.

Changing the Size of the Opening for Replacement Windows

If a window will be replaced with a larger or smaller one, some carpentry work is necessary because the opening has to be framed so it is the required size for the new window. Window manufacturers specify the required size of the framed opening. They call this the **rough opening**.

The framing for a typical window rough opening is shown in 7–56. The header spans the opening and is strong enough to carry the loads imposed upon it.

Preparing for a Smaller Window

Remove the old window completely. This will include the inside trim and may necessitate the removal of some of the exterior molding or siding

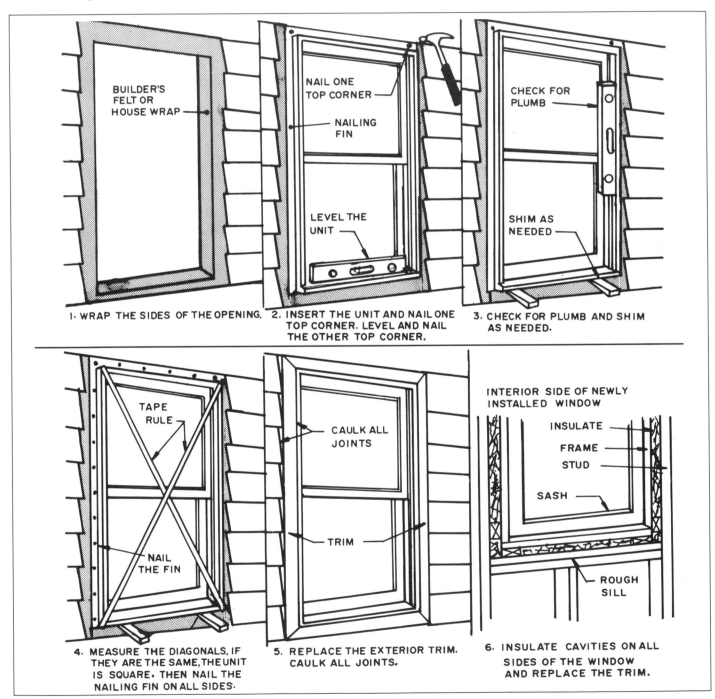

1. WRAP THE SIDES OF THE OPENING.

2. INSERT THE UNIT AND NAIL ONE TOP CORNER. LEVEL AND NAIL THE OTHER TOP CORNER.

3. CHECK FOR PLUMB AND SHIM AS NEEDED.

4. MEASURE THE DIAGONALS. IF THEY ARE THE SAME, THE UNIT IS SQUARE. THEN NAIL THE NAILING FIN ON ALL SIDES.

5. REPLACE THE EXTERIOR TRIM. CAULK ALL JOINTS.

6. INSULATE CAVITIES ON ALL SIDES OF THE WINDOW AND REPLACE THE TRIM.

7–57. A replacement window the same size as the old window is installed in the same manner as is done in new construction. This is one example. Follow the instructions provided by the manufacturer.

around the window. Then install the studs and rough sill; this provides the required rough opening (**7–58**). The tops of windows are usually kept 6 feet, 8 inches above the floor so that they align with the tops of doors.

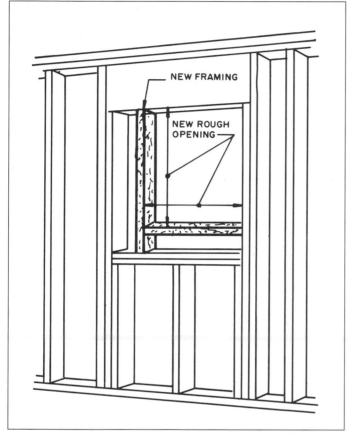

7–58. An existing rough opening can be made smaller by adding additional framing. Be certain the rough opening produced is the size specified for the window selected.

Preparing for a Larger Window

This is much more difficult because the header has to be replaced (**7–59**). Begin by removing the old window. Now replace the header. Some help will be needed because it is a difficult job. First, a stud wall must be constructed inside the room to hold up the ceiling, second floor, roof, and any other loads on the header. It is essential to be certain the floor is strong enough to carry this load. Remember, the load has been carried by the concrete foundation. It may also be helpful to install a beam under the floor and support it with concrete-block piers laid without mortar (**7–60**). It is also possible to damage the ceiling material.

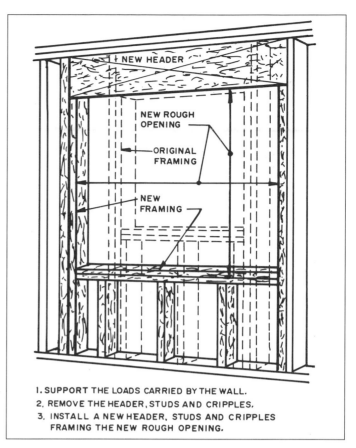

1. SUPPORT THE LOADS CARRIED BY THE WALL.
2. REMOVE THE HEADER, STUDS AND CRIPPLES.
3. INSTALL A NEW HEADER, STUDS AND CRIPPLES FRAMING THE NEW ROUGH OPENING.

7–59. An enlarged replacement-window opening requires considerable bracing of the overhead structure and the floor while the old window framing is removed and new framing is installed.

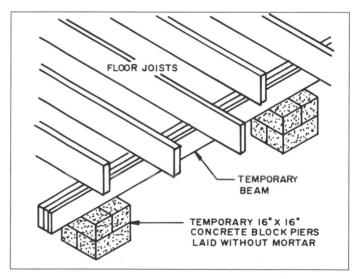

7–60. Temporary bracing below the floor could consist of concrete-block piers and a wood beam.

Once the floor is structurally sound, remove the header and studs and reframe the opening to fit the new window. This will also require cutting back on the exterior siding and repairs after the window is in place.

The manufacturer has instructions on how to install a new window. Many windows have a flange around the unit that is nailed to the studs in the rough opening (refer to **7–57**). Then the siding is butted to the side of the window frame and caulked.

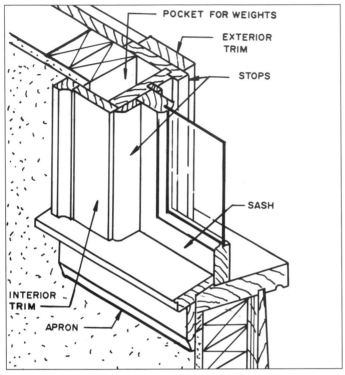

7–61. Windows with sash weights have a pocket prepared in the wall behind the window frame for the weights to move up and down.

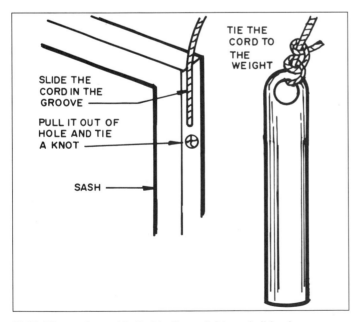

7–62. The sash cord is tied to the weight, and slides in a groove to a hole where a knot is tied.

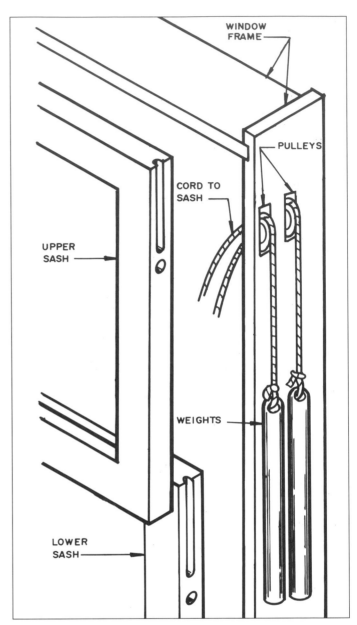

7–63. Run the new cord over the pulleys and connect it to the sash and the weights.

Replacing Sash Cord

Many older houses have double-hung windows. Each sash on a double-hung window is controlled by sash weights attached to the sash by a cord that runs in a pocket alongside the window frame (**7–61**). When the sash cord breaks, the weight falls to the bottom of the pocket and the sash will not stay at the height required.

To replace the sash cord, do the following:

1. Remove the interior trim around the window and the sash stops on the inside of the window.

(Try to avoid damaging the stops. However, they can be replaced.) This exposes the weights. Some older windows may have a board below the interior trim serving as a cover over the pocket.

2. Now pull the lower sash out of the frame. The cord is connected to the sash and the weight, as shown in **7–62**.

3. Remove the broken or damaged cord from the weight and the other end from the sash. It is recommended that all the cords on both sash be replaced while repairs are being made.

4. Run the new cord over the pulley and connect it to the sash. The correct length of cord can be determined by measuring the old cord. Tie it to the weight and slide it into the pocket (**7–63**).

5. If the upper sash has a broken cord, the lower sash and its stops will have to be removed before the upper sash is removed. Replace the upper sash as described for the lower sash.

6. Reinstall the stops and the interior trim.

It is recommended that broken sash cords be replaced with sash chain. The installation is the

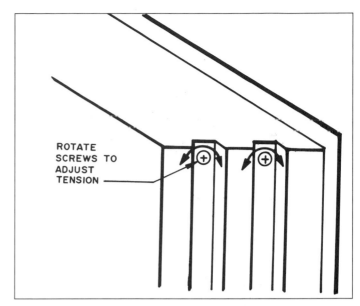

7–65. Some spring-balanced sash can have the tension adjusted by turning an adjustment screw.

same as for replacing cords, except that the chain has to be wired to the weight and secured to the sash with a screw as shown in **7–64**.

Repairing Spring-Balanced Sashes

Newer windows typically have spring-balanced sashes. These work satisfactorily for many years. However, if the window is not operating properly its spring tension may need adjusting.

There are several different types of spring mechanisms, and the one on the window will have to be carefully examined. One type has an adjustment screw in the window track. Turn the screw right or left until there is enough tension to permit the window to operate easily and stay open (**7–65**). Another type requires the loosening of the screw that holds the spring tube to the side jamb (see **7–66** on page 298). Be certain the screw stays through the tube because it holds the spring in place.

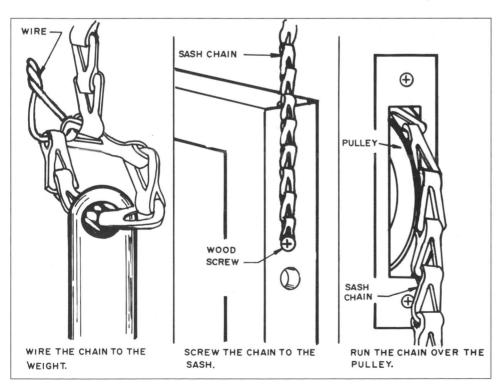

7–64. When you are replacing sash cord, consider using sash chain instead.

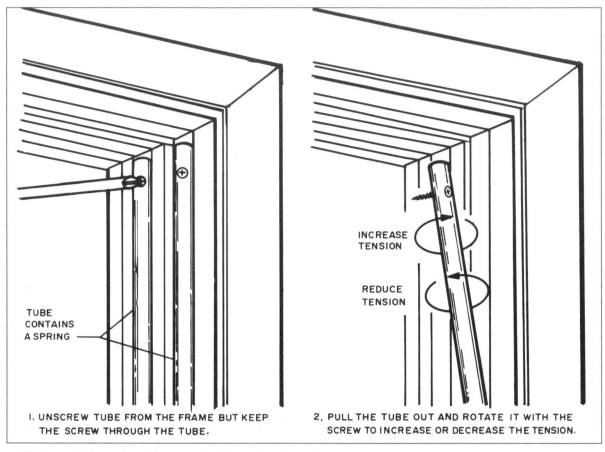

TUBE
CONTAINS
A SPRING

1. UNSCREW TUBE FROM THE FRAME BUT KEEP
THE SCREW THROUGH THE TUBE.

INCREASE
TENSION

REDUCE
TENSION

2, PULL THE TUBE OUT AND ROTATE IT WITH THE
SCREW TO INCREASE OR DECREASE THE TENSION.

7–66. *Spring-balanced sash is controlled by turning the spring tube. If the sash needs more tension, turn the tube clockwise. If it is too tight, turn it counterclockwise to loosen it.*

Rotate the screw and tube counterclockwise to reduce tension, making it easier to raise and lower the sash. Rotate the screw clockwise if more tension is needed to hold the sash in place. Then replace the tube and screw it to the window frame.

If the spring is broken, remove the inner stops and the screw at the top, pry out the tube, and remove the spiral rod from the sash. Install the new spring and adjust the tension.

Replacing Broken Window Glass

Older wood windows can have the glass replaced by cutting away the putty and removing the glazier's points (7–67). After clearing away the pieces of glass (make sure to wear gloves), remove all paint and lumps of putty so the frame for the glass is clean. A light coat of linseed oil, a wood preservative, or a primer can be added to this bare wood.

The replacement glass should be ⅛ inch (3 millimeters) smaller in width and length than the opening (7–68). Lay a thin layer of putty on the surface of the rabbet against which the glass is to be placed. Then lay the glass in the opening and press it into the putty until the putty is about ¹⁄₁₆ inch (1.5 millimeters) thick. Now secure it to the wood frame with glazier's points. Place the point flat on the glass and tap it into the wood with a screwdriver. **Illus. 7–69** shows the types of points available.

Now lay in the exterior layer of putty. Roll some into a long roll and place it on the edge of the glass. Smooth it out on an angle with a putty knife, forcing it firmly against the glass and the wood frame. Remove any excess putty on the inside and outside surfaces of the glass. Let the compound cure as directed on the can before painting it. This is typically two or three weeks.

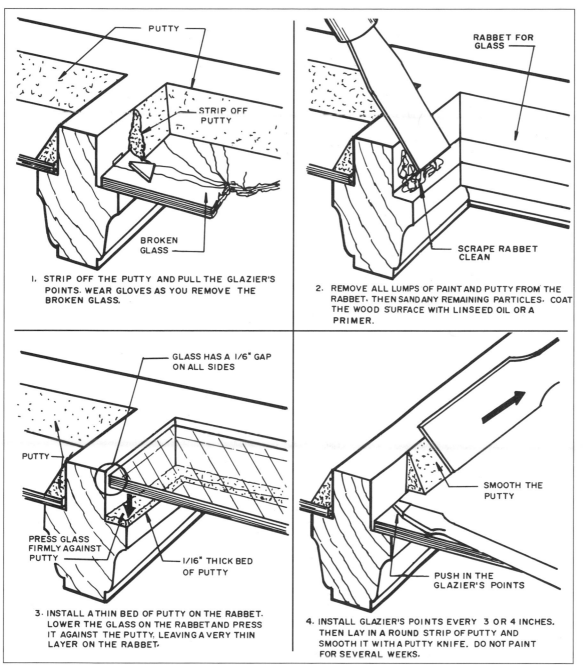

PUTTY

STRIP OFF
PUTTY

BROKEN
GLASS

1. STRIP OFF THE PUTTY AND PULL THE GLAZIER'S POINTS. WEAR GLOVES AS YOU REMOVE THE BROKEN GLASS.

RABBET FOR GLASS

SCRAPE RABBET CLEAN

2. REMOVE ALL LUMPS OF PAINT AND PUTTY FROM THE RABBET. THEN SAND ANY REMAINING PARTICLES. COAT THE WOOD SURFACE WITH LINSEED OIL OR A PRIMER.

GLASS HAS A 1/6" GAP ON ALL SIDES

PUTTY

PRESS GLASS FIRMLY AGAINST PUTTY

1/16" THICK BED OF PUTTY

3. INSTALL A THIN BED OF PUTTY ON THE RABBET. LOWER THE GLASS ON THE RABBET AND PRESS IT AGAINST THE PUTTY, LEAVING A VERY THIN LAYER ON THE RABBET.

SMOOTH THE PUTTY

PUSH IN THE GLAZIER'S POINTS

4. INSTALL GLAZIER'S POINTS EVERY 3 OR 4 INCHES. THEN LAY IN A ROUND STRIP OF PUTTY AND SMOOTH IT WITH A PUTTY KNIFE. DO NOT PAINT FOR SEVERAL WEEKS.

7–67. Carefully remove the pieces of broken glass. Strip the putty and remove the glazier's points. It is important to clean the rabbet before installing the new glass.

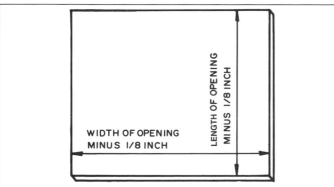

LENGTH OF OPENING
MINUS 1/8 INCH

WIDTH OF OPENING
MINUS 1/8 INCH

7–68. Cut the replacement glass 1/8 inch (3 millimeters) smaller than the glazed opening in both directions.

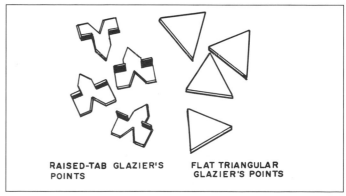

RAISED-TAB GLAZIER'S POINTS

FLAT TRIANGULAR GLAZIER'S POINTS

7–69. Raised-tab and flat, triangular glazier's points are commonly used to hold the glass to the wood sash.

If steel or aluminum window sash is being glazed, use a glazing compound formulated especially for them.

There are other ways of holding glass in the sash, including double- and triple-glazed panes with sealed airspaces between. These typically require professional help to get a proper, watertight replacement.

Cutting Glass

Generally, glass can be cut to size at the local hardware store. If not, buy a stock piece larger than needed. Wipe the surface of the glass clean. Place a straightedge on the glass with the edge where the cut is to be made.

Lubricate the cutting wheel of the glass cutter with a light machine oil or kerosene. Place it against the straightedge, press down on it, and draw it across the glass. The cutter wheel will score the surface

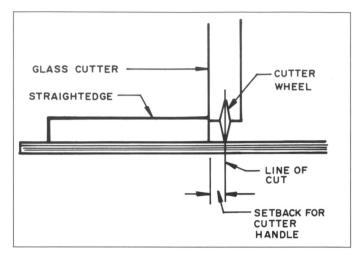

7–71. When starting the cut, remember to line up the cutter wheel with the line to be cut. Since the cutter handle has thickness, the straightedge is not placed on the line.

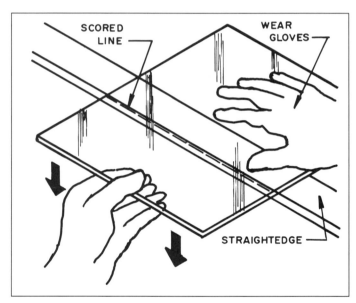

7–72. After scoring the glass, place the scored line over the edge of the straightedge and press down. It will break along the scored line. Wear gloves to protect the hands.

(7–70). Position the straightedge so the cutter wheel runs along the marked line (7–71). Run the cutter wheel across the glass only once. Do not go back over it several times. A double or triple score could cause the glass to break with an uneven edge.

If a large piece is to be removed, place the glass on the edge of a thin piece of wood or a steel rule with the part to be removed sticking over the edge. Press down on this part and it will snap on the scratch line (7–72). Wear gloves to protect hands.

If the piece to be removed is a narrow strip, position the glass so the part to be removed sticks over

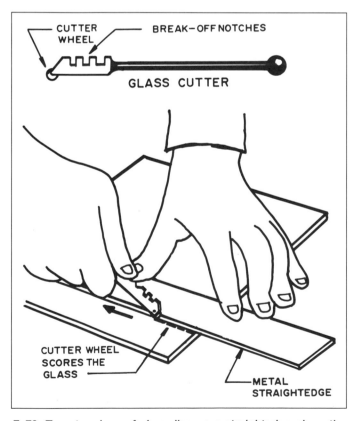

7–70. To cut a piece of glass, line up a straightedge along the line of the cut and pull the cutter wheel along it, pressing hard enough to score the surface of the glass. Run it across only once.

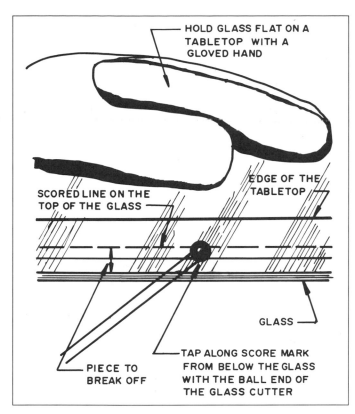

7–73. Narrow strips can be removed by scoring on the cut line, extending the glass over the edge of the tabletop, and tapping the score line from below with the ball end of the glass cutter.

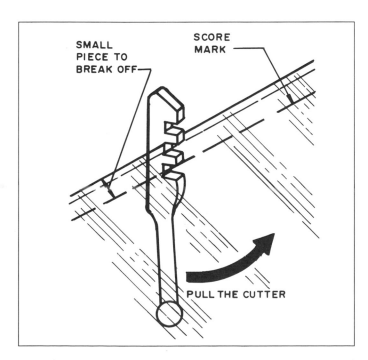

7–74. Narrow strips can be removed by scoring the glass and breaking them off using the break-off notches on the glass cutter. Place the notch that fits the glass thickness over the edge and rotate the ball end, providing leverage to break the glass on the scored line.

the edge of a table (**7–73**). Tap the underside of the glass along the crack with the ball end of the glass cutter. Tap along the line as the crack moves to the bottom side of the glass.

Another way to remove a narrow strip is to score it, place one of the break-off notches on the cutter over the edge of the glass, and pull the cutter down (**7–74**). This technique breaks away small pieces. Work along the scored line. Pliers can also be used to pull off the narrow strip.

Wear gloves when handling and cutting glass. The edges are always sharp and even small shards can pierce the skin.

Replacing Window Screen

Window-screen frames usually are made of either wood or metal. Either type of screen is easily replaced. Replace the screen in wood frames as follows:

1. Carefully remove the molding from around the edge and pull the old screen loose (**7–75**). Prime any exposed unpainted wood.

2. Cut a new piece of screen slightly larger than the opening. Place it over the wood frame with the mesh parallel to the edge of the frame.

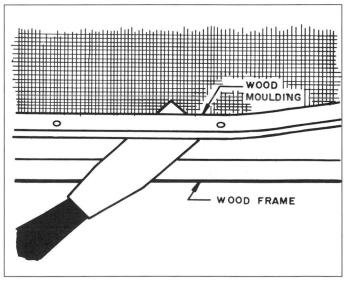

7–75. Use a chisel or putty knife to pry up the wood molding. After the nails lift a bit, they can be pulled out with a hammer. If the molding is not damaged, it can be used again.

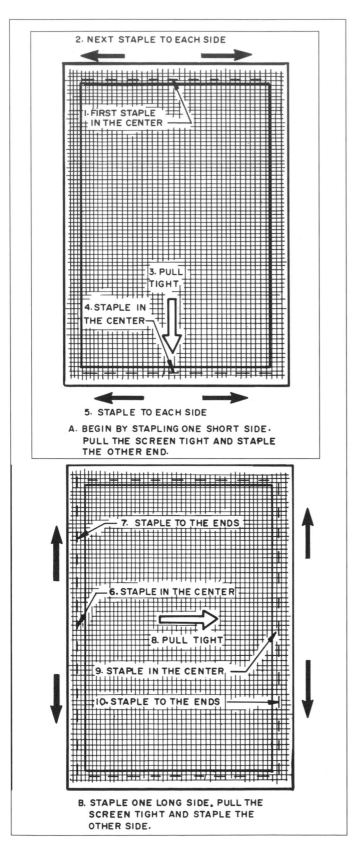

2. NEXT STAPLE TO EACH SIDE

1. FIRST STAPLE IN THE CENTER

3. PULL TIGHT

4. STAPLE IN THE CENTER

5. STAPLE TO EACH SIDE

A. BEGIN BY STAPLING ONE SHORT SIDE. PULL THE SCREEN TIGHT AND STAPLE THE OTHER END.

7. STAPLE TO THE ENDS

6. STAPLE IN THE CENTER

8. PULL TIGHT

9. STAPLE IN THE CENTER

10. STAPLE TO THE ENDS

B. STAPLE ONE LONG SIDE. PULL THE SCREEN TIGHT AND STAPLE THE OTHER SIDE.

7–76. Install new screen wire by stapling it at the center of a short side, pulling it to the other end, and stapling there. Repeat these steps on the long sides. It is helpful if there is someone to pull the screen tight and hold it as it is being stapled to the wood frame.

3. Staple the screen across one of the shorter ends (**7–76**). Place the staples so they will be hidden by the molding. Start stapling in the center of the short side and work to each side.

4. Pull the screen tightly to the opposite end and staple it.

5. Staple the long sides of the screen. Begin in the center and work toward each end. Pull the screen to keep it tight and flat.

6. Cut off any extra screen with a utility knife.

7. Replace the molding using ¾-inch (19-millimeter) wire brads (**7–77**).

Screens in aluminum frames are held in place with a neoprene spline that is forced into a groove in the frame. Follow these steps to replace the screen in a metal frame:

1. Pry the neoprene spline out of its channel on all four sides of the frame (**7–78**). The old screen will fall loose.

2. Cut a new piece of screen about 2 inches (51 millimeters) larger than each side of the opening.

3. Place the screen over the frame and align the mesh parallel with the edges of the frame.

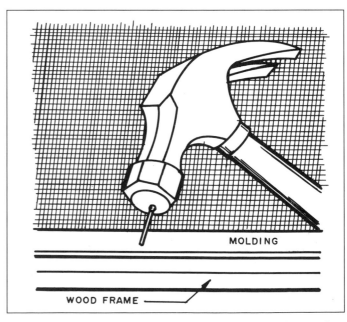

MOLDING

WOOD FRAME

7–77. Replace the wood molding by nailing over the staples. Rust-resistant wire brads are the best thing to use.

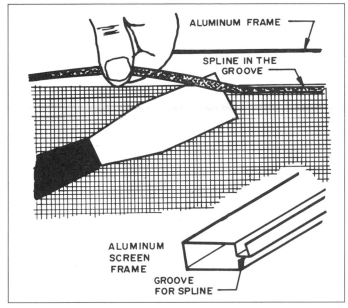

7–78. Screen wire is held to aluminum frames with a spline that presses the screen into a groove. To remove the screen, pull the spline out of the groove.

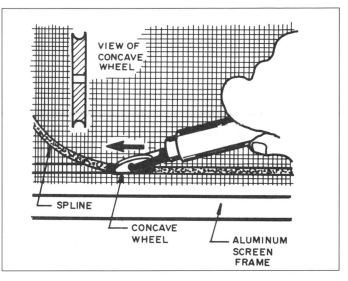

7–79. The spline is forced into the groove with a splining tool. A blunt-edge tool such as a large screwdriver can be used, but it is more difficult to force the screen and spline down into the groove.

4. Place the spline over the screen and on top of a groove. Starting at one corner, press the spline into the groove using a splining tool as shown in **7–79**. Continue pressing the spline into the groove until a corner is reached. Bend the spline around the corner and continue pressing the spline into the groove along the next side. Keep the screen stretched so there are no wrinkles. Be sure the new spline bought for the job is the proper diameter. Reuse old spline only if it is in very good condition.

5. Cut off excess screen with a utility knife.

Patching a Screen

A small hole in a **metal screen** can be patched using the following procedure (**7–80**):

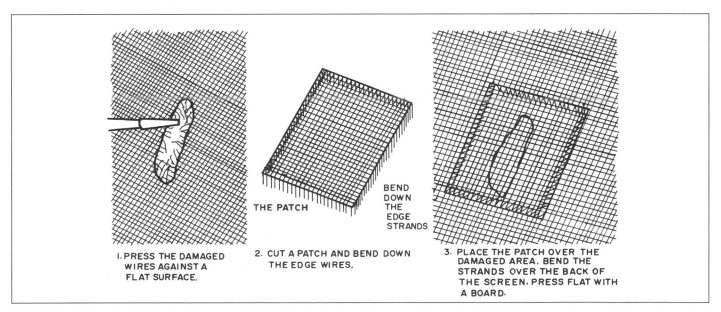

1. PRESS THE DAMAGED WIRES AGAINST A FLAT SURFACE.

THE PATCH

2. CUT A PATCH AND BEND DOWN THE EDGE WIRES.

BEND DOWN THE EDGE STRANDS

3. PLACE THE PATCH OVER THE DAMAGED AREA. BEND THE STRANDS OVER THE BACK OF THE SCREEN. PRESS FLAT WITH A BOARD.

7–80. Holes in metal-screen wire can be repaired by making a patch of the same material and joining it to the screen. A bit of glue can be added to help secure it.

1. Place the screen on a flat surface and press the damaged area flat. It may be necessary to snip off a few long, loose strands.

2. Cut a piece of screen that is 1 inch (25 millimeters) larger than the hole.

3. Remove two or more strands of wire on each side. Bend the ends of the these strands 90 degrees each in the same direction.

4. Push the bent strands through the mesh around the hole and bend the strands flat to the screen. To tighten the patch, put a block of wood on each side of the screen and push them together.

5. If needed, use a few spots of glue to keep the patch firmly in place.

Plastic and **fiberglass screen** are widely used and easily punctured. If the screen has a very small hole, realign the strands and seal them together with a waterproof glue (**7–81**). Be certain the glue that is chosen will not dissolve plastic. If the hole is larger, cut a patch an inch or so larger and glue it to the screen (**7–82**). Put glue on the patch and around the hole in the screen. Press on the patch and hold this pressure for a minute or so until it is set.

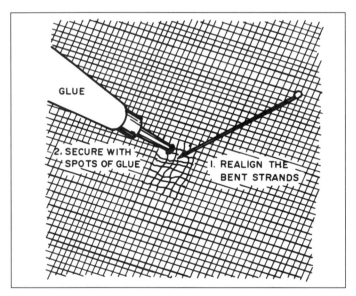

7–81. Realign the bent strands and secure them with a glue that will not dissolve the screen material.

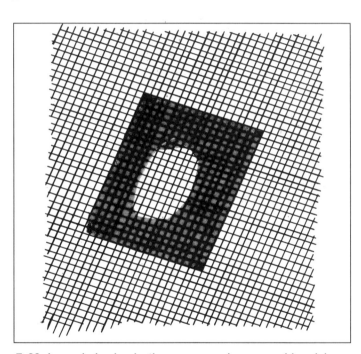

7–82. Large holes in plastic screen can be covered by gluing a patch of the same material over the hole. Put glue on the bottom of the patch and around the edge of the hole.

CHAPTER EIGHT

Renovating Interior Walls and Ceilings

The most frequently occurring maintenance tasks to be done on the interior of a house involve repairing and redecorating walls and ceilings, and repairing and recovering floors. There is a wide range of materials available for each of these tasks. Give careful consideration to the maintenance job about to be done and make a study of the choices of materials available to do it. Then choose the best material that can be afforded and follow the proper procedure for the job.

GYPSUM WALLBOARD

Gypsum wallboard is installed dry, which was why it is also called "drywall." It is easier to install than walls covered with plaster and less expensive. It consists of a gypsum core bonded between layers of a specially formulated paper. The side to be exposed is covered with a strong, smooth-faced paper. The back of the panel has a strong, natural-finish paper. The paper is folded along the long edges of the panel, and the ends are square-cut. The most commonly used panel is 4 feet x 8 feet (1.2 meters x 2.4 meters). However, larger panels are available by special order.

The commonly available kinds of drywall include regular, type-X, moisture-resistant, ceiling, and pre-decorated.

Regular drywall panels are used to finish interior walls. They have either a tapered, rounded edge or a standard taper with a beveled edge. The types of edges available on various panels are shown in **8–1**. Regular panels are available in thicknesses of ⅜, ½,

and ⅝ inch (9, 13, and 15 millimeters). The ½-inch thickness is most commonly used.

Type-X, fire-rated drywall has a specially formulated gypsum core that contains additives that increase its ability to resist fire.

Moisture-resistant drywall is used on walls and ceilings in areas where there will be higher-than-average moisture. It typically can be identified by

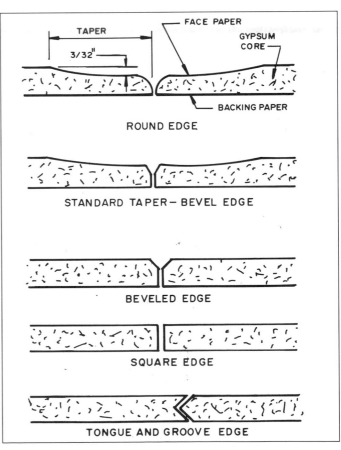

8–1. The common types of edge available on gypsum drywall panels.

the green-color paper. It is not used in areas having direct exposure to water, such as a shower. Use cementitious tile backer board in these areas.

Ceiling drywall is a high-strength ½- and ⅝-inch-thick gypsum panel used on ceilings. The special core is designed to resist sagging that can occur with regular panels on the ceiling over time.

Flexible drywall panels are ¼-inch thick and have heavy paper faces. They are used to bend around concave and convex walls. They bend best in the long direction, so are usually installed with the long edge perpendicular to the wall studs.

Predecorated drywall panels are covered with a decorative material such as fabric or vinyl. They do not require additional finishing. The joints are covered with moldings supplied by the manufacturer, and the nails are colored to blend in with the colors on the panel.

Gypsum sheathing panels are fire-resistant panels having a water-resistant core and a water-repellent paper on both sides. They are secured to the studs and covered with siding, masonry, and other exterior-finish materials.

DRYWALL FASTENERS

Annular ring nails provide the best holding power in wood studs. However **cement-coated nails** are also widely used. **Cooler nails** are used in some parts of the country.

Nails should be long enough to go through the

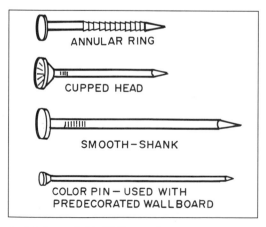

8–2 (above left). Nails used to secure gypsum drywall panels to wood framing.

8–3 (above right). A type-W drywall screw used to secure panels to wood framing.

panel and ⅞ inch (21 millimeters) into the wood stud. Fire-rated wall assemblies require nails that penetrate the stud 1½ inches (38 millimeters) (**8–2**).

Drywall screws are used to secure panels to wood and metal studs (**8–3**). They have greater holding power than nails, thus having fewer pop-outs. They are rapidly installed with a power screwdriver.

Adhesives are used to bond single layers of drywall to framing, masonry, or concrete. They are also used to bond panels together when multilayer assemblies are required. The adhesives are classified into two types. **Stud adhesives** are used to bond drywall panels to the studs. **Laminating adhesives** are used to bond one panel to another, forming a laminated panel.

INSTALLING DRYWALL PANELS

Drywall panels are easy to cut to size. While cutting them, be careful that the face paper is not damaged. Measure carefully. Since many measurements are long, use a tape measure.

Cutting Drywall Panels

To cut drywall panels, follow these steps (**8–4**):

1. Measure and locate the line of cut. A tape rule is generally used.

2. Score the drywall panel with a utility knife on the good paper side. Run the knife along the edge of a drywall T-square. A carpenter's framing square can also be used.

3. Bend the panel away from you and the core will snap along the scored line.

4. Cut the paper covering on the back side to complete the cut.

Cutting Openings in Panels

Openings in the panels for switches, electrical outlets, and other things that penetrate the wall have to be located and cut. One way to locate the openings is to measure their distance from the panel above and from the adjacent panel (**8–5**). Another way is to cover the edges of the outlet box with chalk and push the panel against it. Then drill holes at each

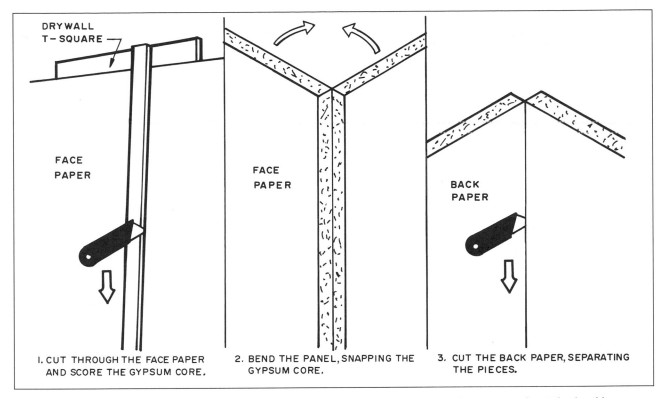

1. CUT THROUGH THE FACE PAPER AND SCORE THE GYPSUM CORE.	2. BEND THE PANEL, SNAPPING THE GYPSUM CORE.	3. CUT THE BACK PAPER, SEPARATING THE PIECES.

8–4. To cut a gypsum panel, score the core on the face side of the paper, snap the core, and cut the backing paper.

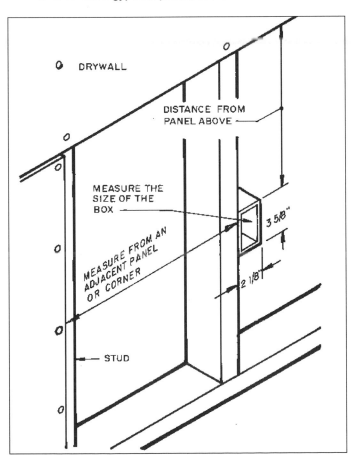

8–5. The openings in the gypsum panel can be located by measuring from adjoining panels or other surfaces.

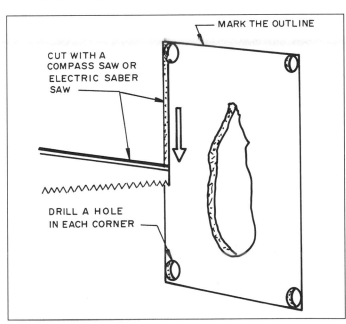

8–6. One way of cutting wall-panel openings is to drill a hole in each corner and saw between these corners.

corner, and cut the opening with a compass or electric saber saw (8–6). Another method is to cut the outline with a utility knife, cut diagonals across the opening, tap the pieces toward the back, and then cut the back paper (8–7).

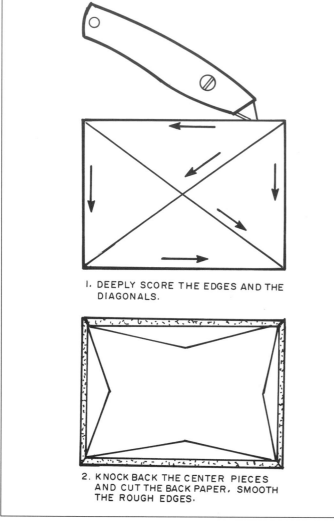

1. DEEPLY SCORE THE EDGES AND THE DIAGONALS.

2. KNOCK BACK THE CENTER PIECES AND CUT THE BACK PAPER, SMOOTH THE ROUGH EDGES.

8–7. Another way to cut an opening in the gypsum panel is to score the edges and diagonals and knock the pieces back with a hammer. Then cut the back paper.

Installing Wall Panels

A major room repair could require that a wall or ceiling be stripped to the frame and covered with new wallboard or that a new wall be added. Before installing any new wallboard, make certain the framing is strong and straight. To check for straightness, run a chalk line along the studs to see that they are all in line. If a stud is bowed, it can be straightened by cutting into the middle of the hollow side of the bow (**8–8**). Then drive a wooden wedge into the cut until the stud is straight. Nail scabs (short lengths of boards) made of ½-inch (13-millimeter) plywood on each side of the wedge to strengthen it. If a stud cannot be straightened, replace it.

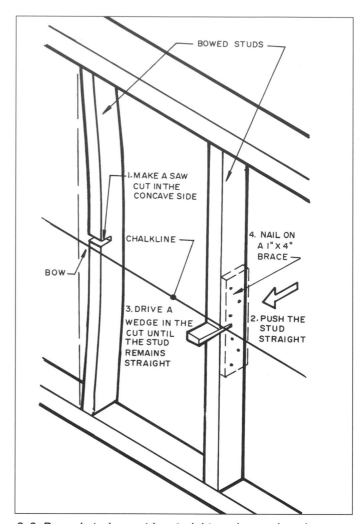

8–8. Bowed studs must be straightened or replaced.

Nailing the Panels

When driving the nails, set them in a small dimple so they can be covered with joint compound (**8–9**).

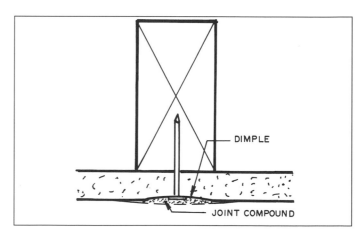

8–9. Set the nail head in a slight dimple in the panel, but do not break the paper or crush the gypsum core.

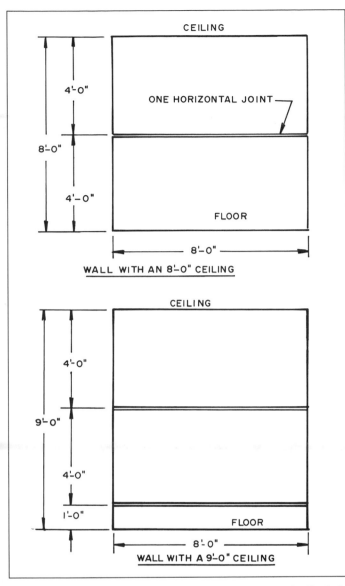

8–10. While gypsum panels can be installed vertically, it is recommended that horizontal construction be used.

Do not drive them so hard that they break the paper or crush the core. If this happens, put another nail about 2 inches (51 millimeters) away from the first. The panel should be held tightly against the stud and the nail must go straight into it. Use a hammer that has a rounded convex face that leaves a shallow dimple in the panel. A special drywall hammer is available.

Placing the Panels

If the ceiling is the standard 8-foot (2.4-meter) height, there will be fewer feet available for edge joints if the panels are installed with the long side perpendicular to the studs (**8–10**). This also places the strongest dimension across the framing members. If the ceilings are higher than this (9-foot [2.7-meter] ceilings are popular), place the narrow strip at the floor (**8–10**). Here it is less noticeable.

The recommended nailing pattern is shown in **8–11**. Double-nailing can be used to reduce nail pop-out. When driving the nail, remember to set it in a dimple.

If an entire wall has to be covered, follow the procedure shown in **8–12**. Start in an upper corner and lay the top row. Size the panels so that if there is a joint it occurs over a door or window. This reduces the length of the joint that will need to be covered. Never have a joint at the corner of an opening. It will tend to open up as the window jamb and framing expand and contract. Also, it is wise to use interior-angle construction at each interior corner (**8–13**). This allows for some wall movement without producing nail pop-out.

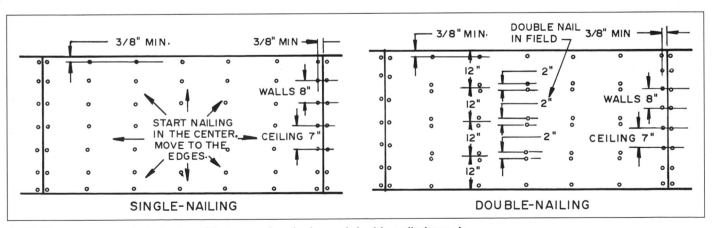

8–11. The recommended placing of fasteners for single- and double-nailed panels.

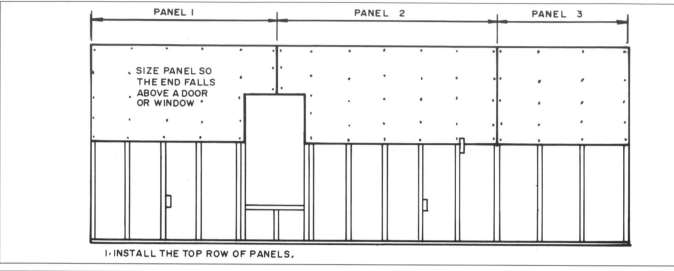

1. INSTALL THE TOP ROW OF PANELS.

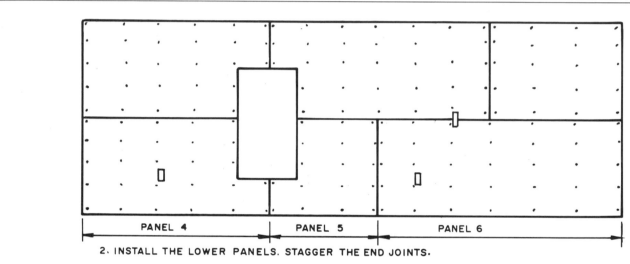

2. INSTALL THE LOWER PANELS. STAGGER THE END JOINTS.

8–12. When covering a wall, start in a corner and install the top row of panels first. Remember to stagger the joints and butt panels over doors and windows.

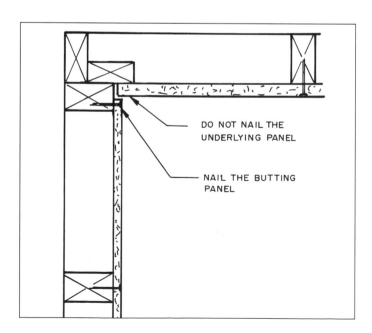

DO NOT NAIL THE UNDERLYING PANEL

NAIL THE BUTTING PANEL

8–13 (left). To allow for movement of the walls, omit the fasteners on one of the panels forming an interior corner.

In addition to nailing the panels, it provides a better job if a bead of stud adhesive is laid on each stud (**8–14**). Press the panel into the adhesive and nail it in the normal manner (**8–15**).

Covering Old Gypsum Wallboard

If the old wallboard is sound, although damaged, it need not be removed. Cover it with new ⅜-inch (9-millimeter) wallboard sheets. To install new wallboard over old, follow these steps:

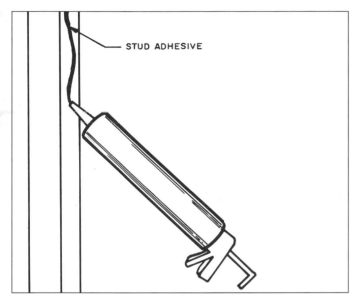

8–14. Stud adhesive, plus nails or screws, provides a superior bond between the panel and the stud.

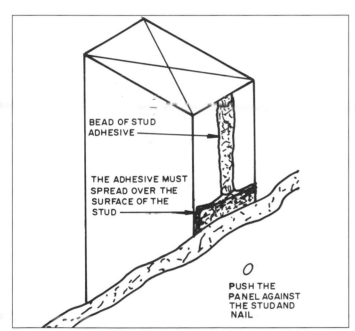

8–15. The panel must be pushed against the adhesive so it spreads over the face of the stud. Nail the panel so it is tight against the stud.

1. Go over the old wall, looking for loose spots. Renail as needed so the old sheets are firmly in place.

2. Apply an adhesive to the back of a new panel and spread it with a notched trowel (**8–16**).

3. Press the new sheet against the wall. Use a few nails to hold the sheet in place while the adhesive sets.

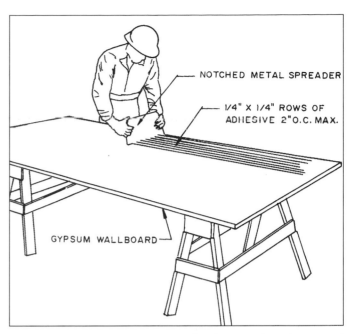

8–16. A double-layer panel application requires the use of a laminating adhesive that is applied to the back of the new panel.

4. If you are applying a new sheet to a ceiling, in addition to the adhesive use nails or screws long enough to reach the wood framing.

Installing Ceiling Panels

Ceiling panels should be installed before the wall panels. They are installed as shown in **8–17**. Start in a corner and work across the room. When installing the next row, cut a panel so the joints are staggered. Always place tapered edges together and square-cut ends together. The difference in thickness makes it difficult to tape over the joint. For best results, all edge and end joints should be backed by 2 x 4-inch blocking. Consider buying panels 12 feet (3.6 meters) long. While they are heavier, they reduce the number of end joints.

Ceiling panels are difficult to install because they are bulky and ½-inch (13-millimeter) panels weigh a bit over 50 pounds. It will take two or more people to lift a panel. Strong, stable scaffolding is needed (**8–18**). Make some T-braces out of 2 x 4-inch stock as shown in **8–19**. Pad the top of the brace with cloth or plastic so the paper on the panel is not damaged.

While installing the ceiling, consider using floating interior corner construction (**8–20**). This will allow for movement and reduce nail pop-out.

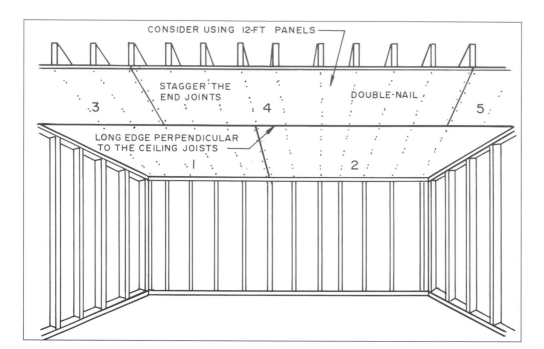

CONSIDER USING 12-FT PANELS

STAGGER THE END JOINTS

DOUBLE-NAIL

3   4   5

LONG EDGE PERPENDICULAR TO THE CEILING JOISTS

1   2

8–17. Begin installing ceiling panels in one corner and work across the room. Then start the next row. Stagger the end joints.

8–18. Ceiling installation is safer if good-quality scaffolding is used.

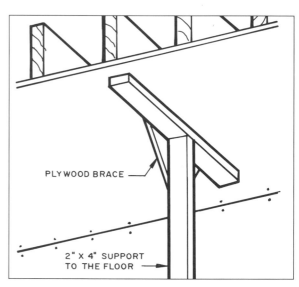

PLYWOOD BRACE

2" X 4" SUPPORT TO THE FLOOR

8–19. Make a couple of T-braces to help hold the panels as they are positioned and nailed.

INSTALLING CORNER BEADS AND TRIM

External corners should be protected with a metal or plastic corner bead. These protect the corner from damage and provide a base for finishing it with joint compound (**8–21**).

Various types of trim are also available. They are used to cover any exposed raw edges and provide a base for finishing them with joint compound (**8–22**).

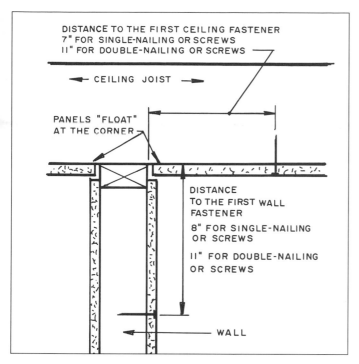

8–20. Typical floating corner construction where the ceiling meets a wall. This allows for movement and reduces cracking at the corner joint

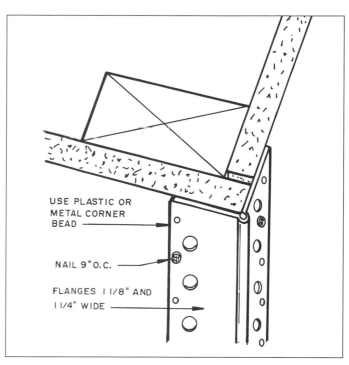

8–21. Metal and plastic corner beads are nailed over external corners. They provide protection from damage.

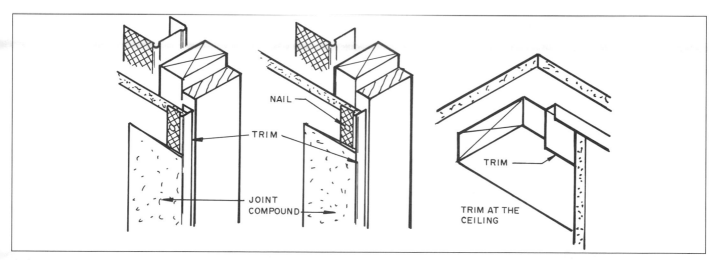

8–22. Metal and plastic trim are available for covering the exposed raw edges of the gypsum panel.

The bead and trim are nailed to the studs every 9 inches (228 millimeters) with standard annular ring nails or screws.

TAPING JOINTS, BEADS, TRIM, AND CORNERS

It takes a little patience and practice to get a good taped joint. Of importance are clean tools and joint compound that is workable and free of lumps.

There are several types of joint compound available; it is best to buy the **premixed all-purpose** type. The **quick-set** type is very good, but it has to be worked faster.

Paper-reinforcing tape is most commonly used to cover the joints between panels. It is bonded to the panel with joint compound. **Fiberglass tape** is available with a plain back and is stapled to the panel. It is also available with an adhesive back that sticks it directly onto the panel.

Taping Tools

The tools needed are 4- and 6-inch (102- and 152-millimeter) joint-taping knives and a 10-inch (254-millimeter) finishing knife (**8–23**). In addition, a pan is needed to contain the joint compound as the person taping the joint moves along the joint (**8–24**).

Very fine-grit **drywall sandpaper** is best to use for finishing. It is available in 80, 100, 120, and 150 grit. The larger the number, the finer the abrasive. Start with a coarser abrasive on the first coat and finish with a fine abrasive for the final coat.

Sanding sponges are used to wet-sand the compound. They are also used to lightly blend the compound's feathered edge to the surface of the drywall panel.

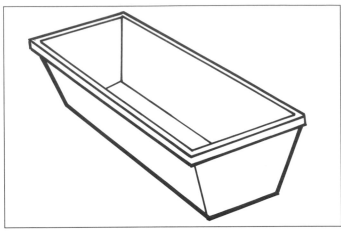

8–24. A typical mud pan used to hold the drywall joint compound needed by the person taping the joints.

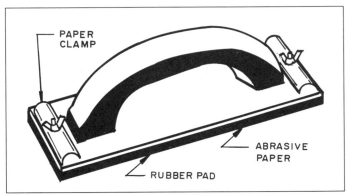

8–25. This is one type of handheld sanding pad. The abrasive paper is held by end clamps and is backed up by a rubber pad.

Handheld sanding pads are used to hold the abrasive. They make it easy to sand and prevent gouging (**8–25**). Pole sanders are available that enable the sander to reach the ceiling from the floor (**8–26**).

Sanding Safety Techniques

Sanding produces many fine gypsum particles. Wear eye protection, a good respirator, and a hat. The white particles will settle on cheeks, arms, and clothing, so stop and clean up frequently. A vacuum is a big help. It can also remove dust that has collected on the floor.

Taping the Joints

Tapered edge joints are covered by laying down a coat of joint compound in the tapered area and pressing the paper tape into it (**8–27**). Keep the knife at a slight angle. Be certain there are no air bubbles

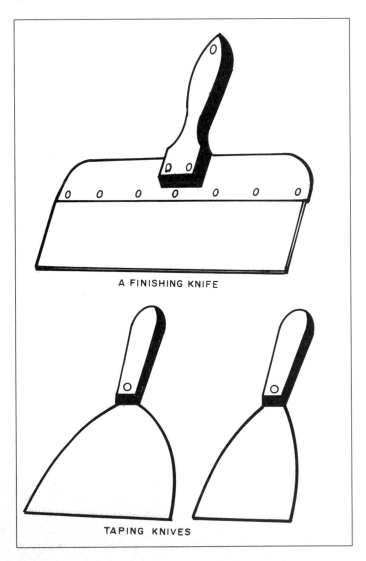

A FINISHING KNIFE

TAPING KNIVES

8–23. These are the most commonly used tools for installing and finishing the taping of the joints.

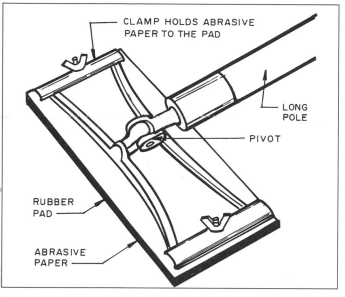

8–26. Pole sanders enable the sander to reach the ceiling while standing on the floor.

under the tape and that the excess compound has been wiped away.

After 24 hours, apply a second coating of compound. Feather it out 4 inches (76 millimeters) beyond the joint. Keep it smooth and uniform. Use a 6-inch (152-millimeter) finishing knife for this wider application.

After another 24-hour drying period, apply the third and final finish coat. Use a 10-inch finishing knife. Feather the coat out about six inches or more on each side of the joint.

Let the compound dry at least 24 hours and lightly sand it to get the smooth finish needed. Sponge-sand the feathered edge at this time if this is desired. Try not to dissolve the compound; if you do, another thin coating will have to be applied. A finished joint is shown in **8–28**.

Joints formed by square-cut ends of panels are more difficult to tape. While they are taped in the same manner as just described, they will produce a hump at the joint. This can be minimized by feathering out each coat of compound wider than that used on tapered edge joints. A typical application will be 18 to 24 inches (457 to 610 millimeters) wide.

Taping Corners

Outside corners are taped in the same manner as flat joints. The metal or plastic bead is nailed over

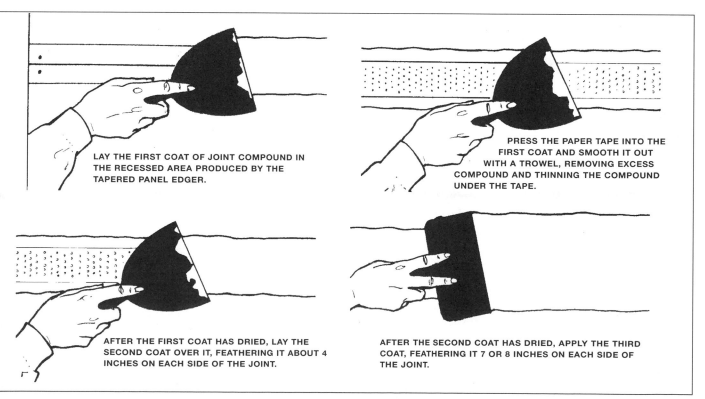

LAY THE FIRST COAT OF JOINT COMPOUND IN THE RECESSED AREA PRODUCED BY THE TAPERED PANEL EDGER.

PRESS THE PAPER TAPE INTO THE FIRST COAT AND SMOOTH IT OUT WITH A TROWEL, REMOVING EXCESS COMPOUND AND THINNING THE COMPOUND UNDER THE TAPE.

AFTER THE FIRST COAT HAS DRIED, LAY THE SECOND COAT OVER IT, FEATHERING IT ABOUT 4 INCHES ON EACH SIDE OF THE JOINT.

AFTER THE SECOND COAT HAS DRIED, APPLY THE THIRD COAT, FEATHERING IT 7 OR 8 INCHES ON EACH SIDE OF THE JOINT.

8–27. Four steps typically used to apply joint compound and tape to gypsum wallboard joints (courtesy National Gypsum Company).

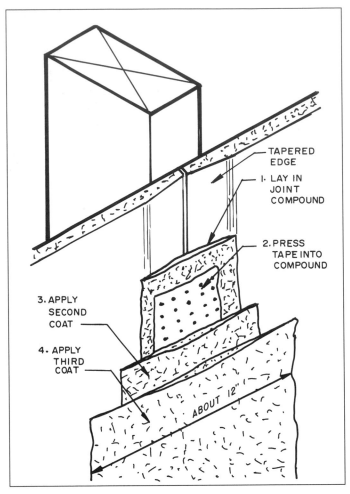

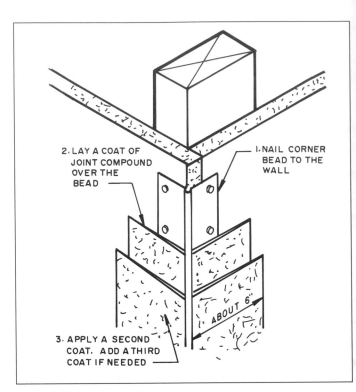

8–28. The parts of a typical finished edge joint.

8–29. A finished exterior corner.

the corner and a base coat of joint compound is feathered over it. After it hardens, additional coats are applied; each should extend more over the wall than the original coat — usually about 6 inches on each side (**8–29**).

Inside corners are taped by first laying a thin layer of joint compound down both sides of the corner with a taping knife. Bend a piece of paper joint tape, forming a right angle. Place it on the joint compound and press it into the compound by pulling the knife down the wall (**8–30**). After this hardens, apply additional thin coats and feather them out over the wall about 2 inches.

Covering Fasteners

The heads of fasteners are covered by troweling a thin layer of joint compound over them (**8–31**). Pick up a quantity of joint compound on the taping knife

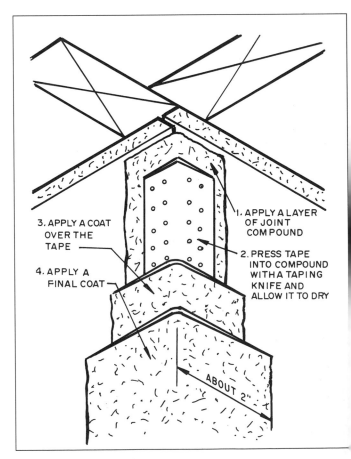

8–30. A finished interior corner.

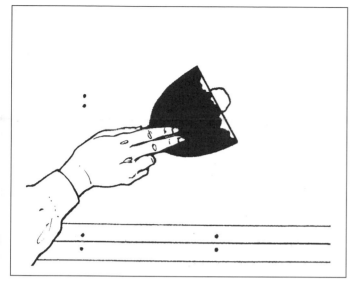

8–31. Lay the joint compound over the heads of fasteners with a 4-inch (102-millimeter) taping knife (courtesy National Gypsum Company).

and wipe it across the head of the fastener. Let this dry 24 hours before applying a second coat. If the surface is bumpy, sand it lightly between coats.

REPAIRING DRYWALL DAMAGE

The most common damages requiring attention are nail pops, dents that break the paper surface, holes broken through the panel, and cracks. They are discussed below.

REPAIRING PROTRUDING NAILS

Nails protrude because they get squeezed out of the stud as it dries and shrinks. This causes nail pops. To repair this problem, follow these steps (8–32):

1. Hammer the protruding nails back in place, but do not break the paper on the surface of the panel. The hammer blow should form a $\frac{1}{64}$-inch-deep dimple around the nail. Use a hammer with a crowned face to drive the nail.

2. About 2 inches (51 millimeters) from the first nail, drive a 1¼-inch (31-millimeter) annular-ring drywall nail or screw.

3. Fill each dimple with joint compound and sand after it hardens.

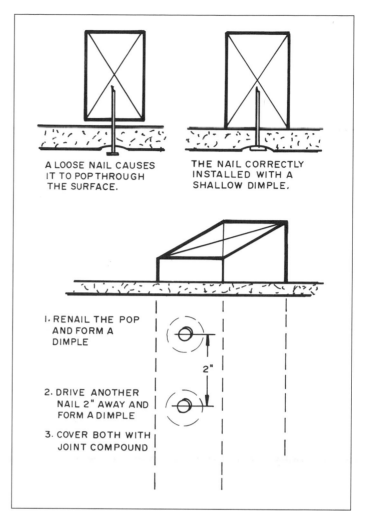

8–32. To correct a protruding nail, reset the loose nail and drive another about 2 inches (51 millimeters) away. Dimple and coat with joint compound.

Repairing Fastener Depressions

A fastener depression occurs when the area over a fastener is lower than the wall surface. It may occur when a fastener is driven too deeply or not enough compound is placed over the fastener. Sometimes not enough fasteners were used and the panel is pulling away from the wall. In this case, additional fasteners will have to be added.

To repair a depression, apply additional coats of joint compound over the area and sand as necessary.

Repairing Dents

Fill dents in wallboard with several layers of joint compound. Clean away all loose material from around the hole before filling it. The irregular edges of the hole will help hold the small patch in place. Larger holes are more difficult to repair and require more work.

Repairing Small Holes

There are several ways to repair small holes. Building-supply dealers have a number of kits that contain all that is needed to make the repair. One kit provides a fiberglass tape patch with an adhesive back. It is stuck over the hole and covered with tape and joint compound (**8–33**).

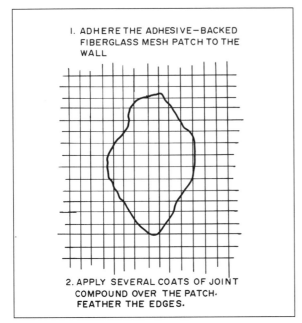

1. ADHERE THE ADHESIVE–BACKED FIBERGLASS MESH PATCH TO THE WALL

2. APPLY SEVERAL COATS OF JOINT COMPOUND OVER THE PATCH. FEATHER THE EDGES.

8–33. One repair kit supplies an adhesive-backed fiberglass patch that is pressed on the drywall over the hole. It is then covered with joint compound.

A repair can be made with a piece of scrap drywall by cutting the damaged area into a squared opening with beveled edges and then cutting a patch with beveled edges. Secure the patch in the opening with joint compound and finish with tape and compound in the normal manner (**8–34**).

A kit available at building-supply dealers uses metal clips that are screwed to the sides of the hole (**8–35**). Begin by cutting around the damaged area, forming a rectangular opening. Install the clips on the sides. Cut a piece of drywall and screw it to the

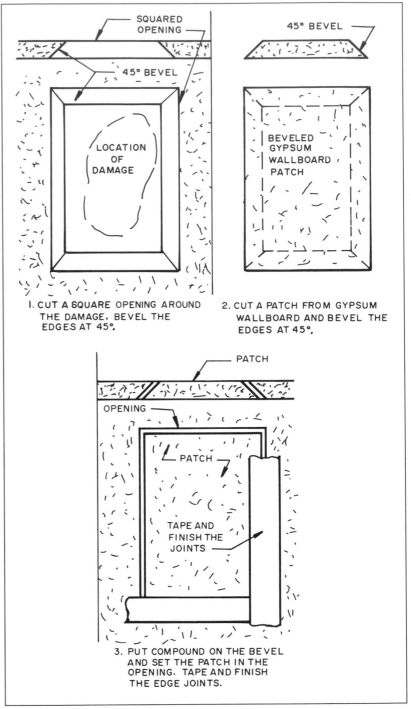

SQUARED OPENING

45° BEVEL

45° BEVEL

LOCATION OF DAMAGE

BEVELED GYPSUM WALLBOARD PATCH

1. CUT A SQUARE OPENING AROUND THE DAMAGE. BEVEL THE EDGES AT 45°.

2. CUT A PATCH FROM GYPSUM WALLBOARD AND BEVEL THE EDGES AT 45°.

PATCH

OPENING

PATCH

TAPE AND FINISH THE JOINTS

3. PUT COMPOUND ON THE BEVEL AND SET THE PATCH IN THE OPENING. TAPE AND FINISH THE EDGE JOINTS.

8–34. This patch requires that the edges of the squared opening and the edges of the patch be beveled.

clips. Then tape and finish the edges in the normal manner (**8–36**).

Repairing Larger Holes

Rather large holes can be repaired by installing wood strips behind the opening with wood screws, and cutting and fitting a drywall patch to them as

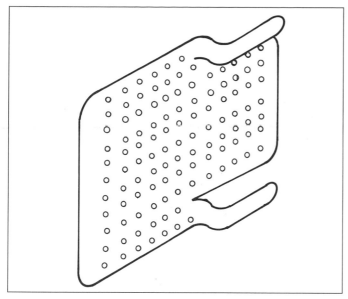

8–35. A metal drywall-repair clip that attaches to the edge of squared openings and supports a drywall patch, as shown in 8-36.

shown in **8–37**. Tape and finish the edges in the normal manner.

Holes that are very large are best repaired by cutting the drywall around them from one stud to the other (**8–38**). Then add wood blocking on all four sides and nail the patch to the blocking. Finish the joints in the normal manner.

REPAIRING PLASTER WALLS

Repairs are made using regular gypsum perlite plaster. Perlite is a siliceous rock that is ground and used as a lightweight aggregate in the plaster. It replaces the sand used in standard plaster. For the top finish coat, use a standard plaster finish-coat material.

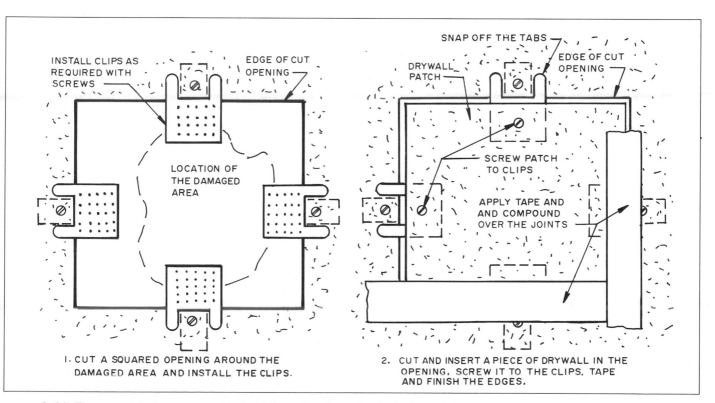

8–36. These metal clips are used to hold drywall patches in the hole, and the edges of the joints are taped in the normal manner.

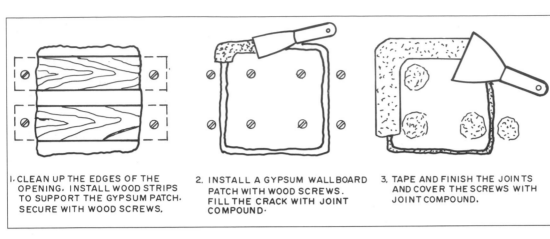

1. CLEAN UP THE EDGES OF THE OPENING. INSTALL WOOD STRIPS TO SUPPORT THE GYPSUM PATCH. SECURE WITH WOOD SCREWS.

2. INSTALL A GYPSUM WALLBOARD PATCH WITH WOOD SCREWS. FILL THE CRACK WITH JOINT COMPOUND.

3. TAPE AND FINISH THE JOINTS AND COVER THE SCREWS WITH JOINT COMPOUND.

8–37. Large holes can be repaired by installing wood strips across the opening and screwing the gypsum drywall patch to them. Then finish the edge joints in the normal manner.

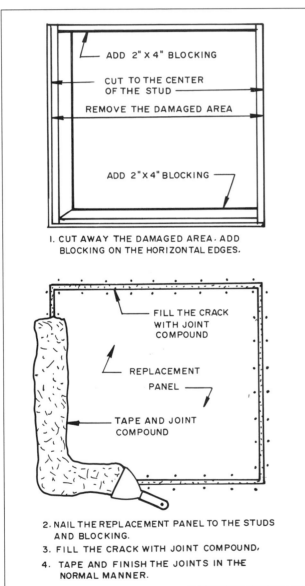

1. CUT AWAY THE DAMAGED AREA. ADD BLOCKING ON THE HORIZONTAL EDGES.

2. NAIL THE REPLACEMENT PANEL TO THE STUDS AND BLOCKING.
3. FILL THE CRACK WITH JOINT COMPOUND.
4. TAPE AND FINISH THE JOINTS IN THE NORMAL MANNER.

8–38. Large damaged areas are repaired by removing the damaged wallboard from one stud to the next, adding blocking on the horizontal edges, and nailing a replacement panel over the area. The horizontal edges could be supported with the metal clips shown in 8-36.

Houses built many years ago used wood lath. These strips are nailed to the studs with a small space between them. The base coat, called the **scratch coat**, is pressed through the spaces, forming a key that holds the finished plaster to the wall (**8–39**). A second coat, **the brown coat**, is applied over the scratch coat. The **plaster finish coat** is applied over the brown coat.

For many years now, gypsum lath has been used instead of wood lath. It is much like gypsum wallboard. It has a gypsum core covered with multilayer laminated paper that provides for the proper absorption of moisture from the plaster (**8–40**). The panels are ⅜ or ½ inch (10 or 13 millimeters) thick and 16 x 48 inches (406 x 1,219 millimeters). The plaster used may be for a one- or two-coat application. The two-coat system uses a special gypsum and wood-fiber plaster for the first coat and a standard plaster finish coat over it. The one-coat system uses a standard plaster finish material that has extra-high-strength gypsum gauging added.

Metal lath is used on the walls in commercial buildings.

PLASTER FAILURES

Several types of plaster failures require patching. Patches are required when the finish coat blisters and comes loose, when the scratch, brown, or finish coats deteriorate, when the lath and all coats come loose from the studs, and when holes are caused by heavy blows. The first three are usually caused by moisture, so the source of moisture must be detected and corrected before repairs are made.

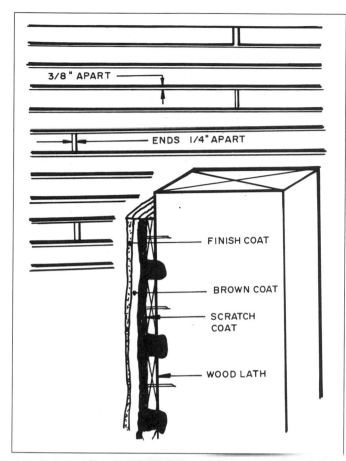

3/8" APART

ENDS 1/4" APART

FINISH COAT

BROWN COAT

SCRATCH COAT

WOOD LATH

8–39. Wood lath was used for years and is found in older homes. It is covered with a three-coat plaster wall system.

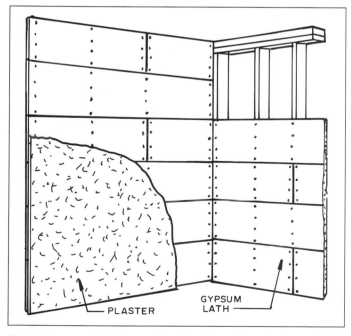

PLASTER

GYPSUM LATH

8–40. Gypsum lath is used as the base for plaster walls in residential construction.

Repairing Blisters

If the finish coat blisters and loosens because it is wet, the best solution is to remove the finish coat, dampen the exposed base coat, and apply a new finish coat. Paint the edges of the damaged area with a liquid bonding agent or moisten them with water before applying the new finish (**8–41**, on the following page).

Repairing Cracks

Sometimes plaster will develop surface cracks. These are generally caused by vibrations within the building, a weak base coat, or poor structural framing.

Small cracks can be repaired by cleaning them out with a sharp-pointed tool, cutting the crack so the inside is wider than the outside. This produces a wedge to help hold the plaster in place. Fill the crack with a quick-setting patching plaster. Be certain to wet the crack with a small paintbrush before applying the patching plaster. Any dust or particles on the surface can be removed by wiping the area down with a damp cloth. Work carefully, so the surface is not damaged.

Wider cracks should be cleaned out with a chisel, and any loose plaster on each side removed. This may widen a crack to 4 or 5 inches (102 or 127 millimeters). If the brown coat is sound, wet the area several times, let the moisture on the surface disappear, and apply a patching plaster over the area (**8–42**). If the lath is damaged, secure a piece of metal lath over it and then apply the scratch and finish coats as required.

Repairing a Damaged Area

Cut away all loose plaster down to the lath. If the lath has not been damaged, replaster over it. First, undercut the edges of the broken area to help hold the patch in place. Then wet the edges with a liquid bonding agent or moisten them with water. If gypsum lath is exposed, do not moisten it. This repair is made like the repair shown in **8–41**.

If the lath has been damaged, it will also have to be replaced. Wood and metal lath are less likely to need replacing than gypsum lath. Water on gypsum lath can cause the paper surfaces to separate from the core.

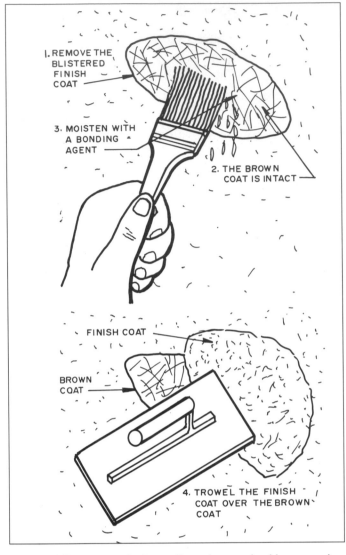

8–41. A blister on a plaster wall can be repaired by removing the damaged finish coat and applying a new finish coat to the brown coat. A repair on a small damaged area such as that caused by a blow is made in the same way, except that the plaster is cleared down to the lath.

Damaged lath in large damaged areas should have the repaired area cut back so the lath can be nailed to the studs (**8–43**). Then apply the base and finish coats. It will take two or three coats to build up the plaster layer to be flush with the plaster on the wall. Perlite plaster will harden in three or four hours, but should not be painted for 24 hours or longer.

Mix the perlite plaster with water until the mixture can be troweled. Do not apply this mixture if the temperature is below 50° F (10° C), and maintain this temperature or a higher one while the plaster is hardening.

If the hole is small and the lath is damaged, cut it away and replace it with a piece of metal lath as shown in **8–44**. Hold it in place with a wire and apply the first coat of plaster. Score this coat horizontally. When it is hard, cut the wire and apply the needed additional coats.

INSTALLING PLYWOOD AND HARDBOARD PANELING

Plywood paneling is available in a variety of wood species on the outer veneer. Typical thicknesses are $5/32$, $1/4$, $5/16$, and $7/16$ inch (4, 6, 8, and 11 millimeters). The most commonly used panel size is 4 x 8 feet (1.2 x 2.4 meters). Since most panelings are supplied prefinished, they should be handled with care.

Hardboard paneling has a wide range of surface finishes, including various simulated wood grains. The panels are typically $1/4$ inch thick and comes in sheets 4 x 8 feet.

The plywood and hardboard panels can be

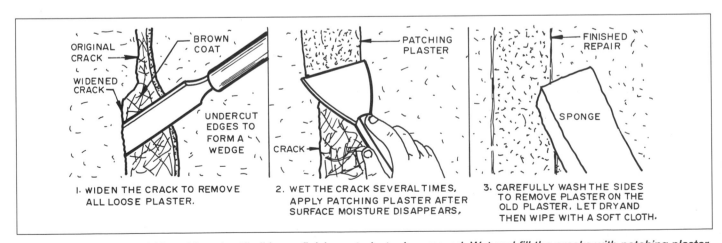

8–42. Wide cracks should be widened until all loose finish-coat plaster is removed. Wet and fill the cracks with patching plaster.

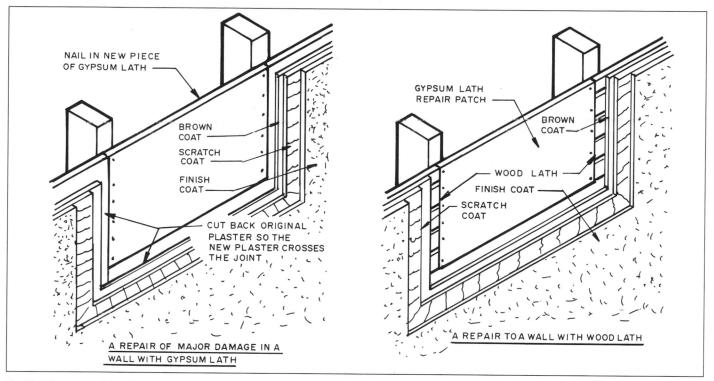

NAIL IN NEW PIECE
OF GYPSUM LATH

BROWN COAT

SCRATCH COAT

FINISH COAT

CUT BACK ORIGINAL PLASTER SO THE NEW PLASTER CROSSES THE JOINT

A REPAIR OF MAJOR DAMAGE IN A WALL WITH GYPSUM LATH

GYPSUM LATH REPAIR PATCH

BROWN COAT

WOOD LATH

FINISH COAT

SCRATCH COAT

A REPAIR TO A WALL WITH WOOD LATH

8–43. When repairing large, damaged areas in plaster walls, cut out the areas from stud to stud, install new lath, and replaster the areas.

installed with the long side vertical or horizontal. The direction used depends upon the appearance desired on the finished wall. When the panel is installed vertically, the edge of each sheet falls on a stud and is supported by it (**8–45**). When the panel is applied horizontally, the top edge of the panel must have 2 x 4 blocking installed at the joint (**8–46**). If the paneling has tongue-and-groove edges, the blocking may not be needed.

If possible, apply paneling over a backing material. The backing material may be ⅜-inch (9-millime-ter) gypsum wallboard, $^5{}_{16}$-inch (8-millimeter) plywood, or wood furring strips. (Furring strips are 1 x 2 or 1 x 3 strips that are nailed to the wall studs.) The backing prevents the paneling from bowing between the studs. If applied directly to the studs, the paneling should be at least ¼ inch thick.

Some building codes require paneling under ¼ inch thick to be installed over a fire-resistant material, such as gypsum wallboard. Check the local building code before starting the job.

Panels can be installed with nails or adhesive. If

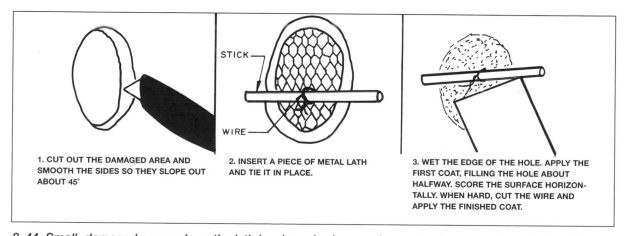

1. CUT OUT THE DAMAGED AREA AND SMOOTH THE SIDES SO THEY SLOPE OUT ABOUT 45°

STICK

WIRE

2. INSERT A PIECE OF METAL LATH AND TIE IT IN PLACE.

3. WET THE EDGE OF THE HOLE. APPLY THE FIRST COAT, FILLING THE HOLE ABOUT HALFWAY. SCORE THE SURFACE HORIZONTALLY. WHEN HARD, CUT THE WIRE AND APPLY THE FINISHED COAT.

8–44. Small, damaged areas where the lath has been broken can be repaired using a piece of wire lath.

Installing Plywood and Hardboard Paneling ■ 323

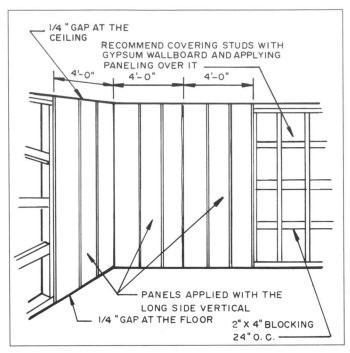

8–45. Plywood and hardboard wall panels are generally applied vertically using the 16-inch (407-millimeter) -long spaced studs for support.

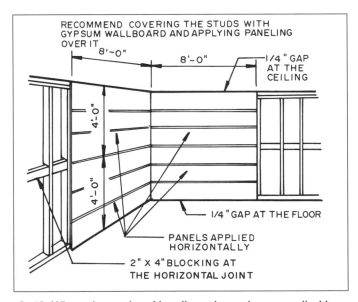

8–46. When plywood and hardboard panels are applied horizontally, the edge joint must be nailed to blocking.

covering an exterior wall, be sure it has a vapor barrier. (A **vapor barrier** is a plastic sheet secured to the studs to keep interior room moisture from getting into the wall cavity.) Staple sheet plastic to the studs or top and bottom plates if none are present. Install paneling as follows:

1. Begin by fitting a panel in a corner of the room (**8–47**). Scribe and plane the edge to fit the corner

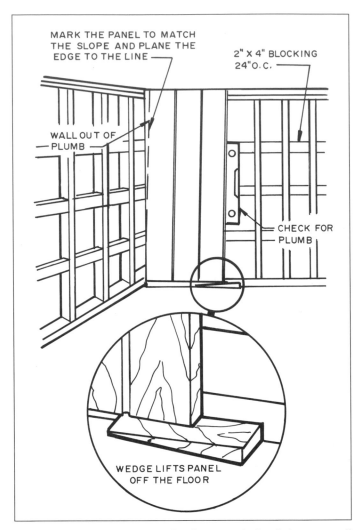

8–47. It is important to get the first panel plumb because all other panels come off it. Trim the edge in the corner as needed to get it plumb.

as needed. The panel edge must be plumb (vertical) and centered on a stud. Remember, the proper vertical look of all the other sheets depends upon the first sheet's being plumb. Drive wood wedges between the panel and floor until the panel is plumb and within ¼ inch of the ceiling. If a molding is used at the ceiling, this gap could get larger. While plumbing the panel, it may be necessary to plane parts of the edge in the corner to make it parallel with the intersecting wall. The panel should clear the floor by ¼ to ½ inch to allow for expansion.

2. Mark the openings needed for electrical outlets, doors, and windows. Use chalk around the electrical box, and then press the panel in place on the

wall. The outline of the box will show on the back of the panel.

3. Cut the openings marked. Drill a hole large enough to insert the saber-saw blade in the center of the marked area. The drill may cause the surface of the panel to splinter. Drilling in the center of the area will avoid marring the panel.

If you are cutting the openings from the finished side, use a fine-toothed blade and saw from the finished surface of the panel. If cutting the openings from the back side, putting masking tape on the finished side of the panel along the saw kerf will help avoid splintering. While installing the panel, it may be necessary to trim the edges of the opening to allow the panel to be plumb.

4. Nail or glue the panel to the studs. Some studs may not be accurately spaced to allow the edge of a panel to rest on them. To correct such a condition, nail a 2 x 2 to the inside of the stud (**8–48**).

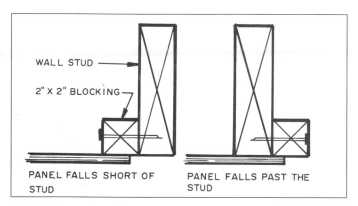

8–48. If the edge of the panel does not rest on the center of the stud, blocking will have to be added to get a proper nailing surface.

5. Nail panels with 1-inch (25-millimeter) paneling nails. Paneling nails have a ring shank and are painted to match the color of the grooves in panels. Use 3d 1¼-inch (31-millimeter) finishing nails if paneling nails are not available. When nailing over gypsum wallboard, use 1⅝-inch (41-millimeter) paneling nails or 6d 2-inch (51-millimeter) finishing nails. Space the nails 6 inches (152 millimeters) apart on the edges of the panel. Space nails 12 inches (300 millimeters) apart on the interior of the panel (**8–49**). Grooves in panels are spaced 16 inches (406 millimeters) apart, so they

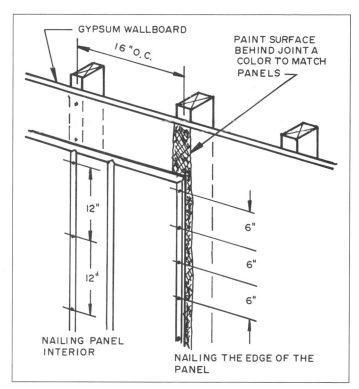

8–49. Specified nail spacing on the interior and edges of plywood and hardboard panels.

should hit a stud. Nail into the grooves to help hide the nails. Leave a hairline crack between plywood panels to allow for expansion.

Hardboard panels expand more than plywood. Leave ¹⁄₁₆ inch (0.5 millimeter) between hardboard panels. Paint the wall behind the panel at each joint a color similar to the panel color. This will help disguise the crack.

6. Use wood molding to cover the cracks at the ceiling (**8–50**) and in the corners (**8–51**). At the floor, install the baseboard. Some panel manufacturers provide aluminum corner moldings into which the panels fit (**8–52**). To install the panel, first nail the molding to the wall, properly spaced. Insert one edge of the panel into one molding, bend the panel a bit, and slip the other edge into the other molding. Before doing this, adhesive can be applied to the wall. If preferred, the panel can be installed without adhesive and the panel nailed in place.

7. To fasten a panel with adhesive, lay a continuous ⅛-inch (3-millimeter) -diameter bead around the perimeter of the panel. On the interior of the

Installing Plywood and Hardboard Paneling ■ 325

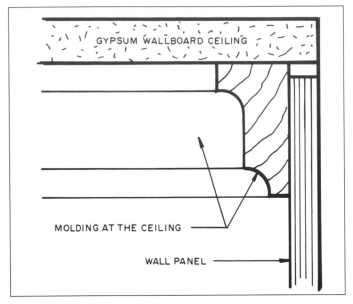

8–50. The space between the panel and the ceiling is covered with some form of molding.

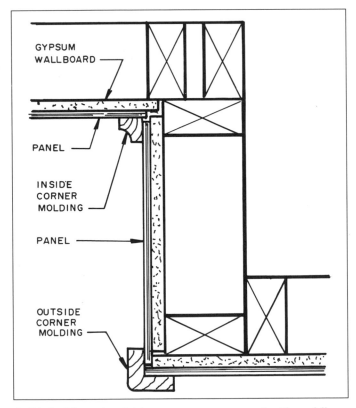

8–51. Inside and outside corners are covered with molding.

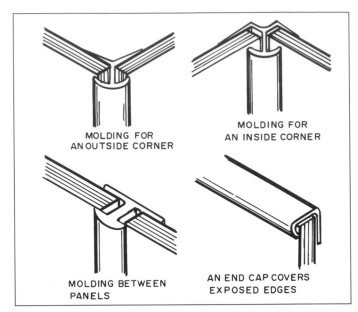

8–52. Vinyl-covered aluminum molding is available to conceal joints between panels.

gypsum wallboard, place these 3-inch-long adhesive beads on the back of the plywood or hardboard panel where the studs are located behind the drywall. Check it for plumb and add a wedge between the panel and floor to get the proper spacing (refer to **8–47**). Drive a few nails at the top

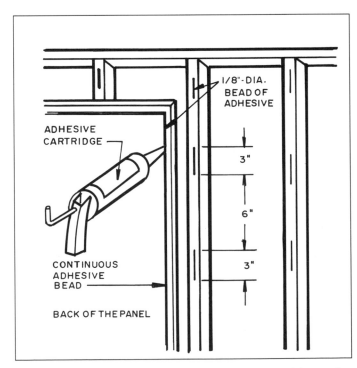

8–53. Adhesive is applied to the back of the panel in continuous beads and spaced applications on the studs or drywall on the interior of the panel.

panel, lay 3-inch (76-millimeter) -long beads spaced 6 inches (152 millimeters) apart on the studs that will hit the interior of the panel as shown in **8–53**. Place the panel against the studs and press it in place. If the wall is covered with

of the panel to hold it to the wall. Some companies recommend pressing the panel to the wall, pulling it out at the bottom for about 10 minutes to help the adhesive set, and then pressing it back against the studs.

When paneling over an existing wall, find each stud and mark its location on the wall. If the wall is somewhat out of plumb, is badly damaged, or is a masonry wall, nail furring strips to it and use wedges to make them plumb (8–54). Then install the paneling.

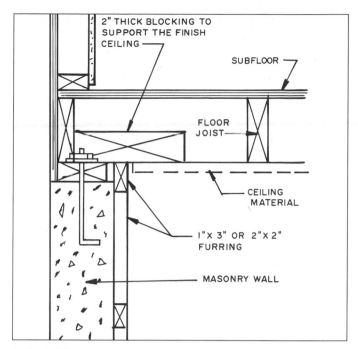

8–55. While preparing to panel the basement, remember to add blocking along the masonry wall to support the edge of the ceiling material.

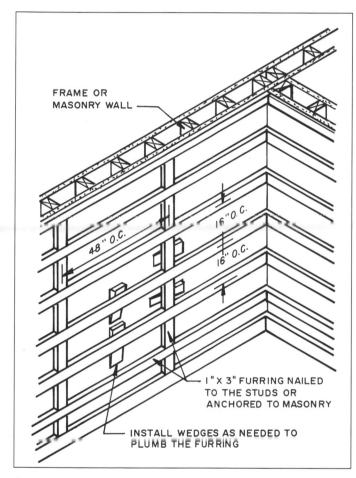

8–54. Damaged and out-of-plumb walls can be covered with paneling by nailing furring strips to them. Masonry walls can be paneled by anchoring furring strips to the masonry.

Special blocking is needed at the ceiling on basement walls where joists run parallel to the wall (8–55). Rigid plastic insulation can be glued to the masonry wall between the furring strips. Another way to panel a masonry wall, such as in a basement, is to frame a stud wall and place it next to the masonry wall (8–56). A stud wall will allow 3½ inches (88 millimeters) of

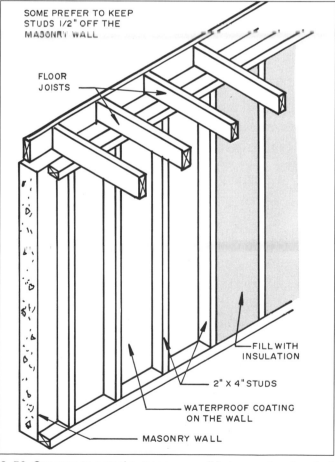

8–56. One way to panel a masonry wall is to construct a stud wall over it. This allows the wall to be insulated.

insulation to be installed. Place a waterproof membrane over the wall behind the studs.

INSTALLING SOLID-WOOD PANELING

Solid-wood paneling is available in a number of wood species and tongue-and-groove profiles. Square-edge boards can be used with a batten or molding at the edge joint.

The paneling to go over wall studs spaced 16 inches (406 millimeters) on center should be at least ⅜ inch (9.5 millimeters) thick. It should be kiln-dried to 8 percent moisture. If pieces over 8 inches (203 millimeters) wide are used, blocking is needed between the wall studs so they can be nailed in the center to reduce cupping.

Check the local building codes to see if a fire-retarding material such as gypsum drywall has to be used behind the paneling. Regardless of the code, this is a smart thing to do.

If the paneling is prefinished, be very careful not to scratch the surface. Store it flat in the room in which it will be installed so it can adjust to the moisture content in the air.

Preparing the Wall

Details for preparing the wall for new construction are shown in **8–57**. Notice that the horizontal blocking is spaced no wider than 24 inches (610 millimeters) on center. A plastic vapor barrier is placed over the framing; then the gypsum wallboard is applied and, finally, the vertical paneling.

If an existing room is being remodeled, apply horizontal and vertical furring strips on the wall and around doors and windows as shown in **8–54**. This will mean an extension has to be added to the window jambs so the window casing fits over the paneling (**8–58**).

Now make a plan detailing how to begin and the direction in which to work. Some prefer to start at an outside corner if one exists and work toward inside corners. Then they work from inside corners toward doors and windows or from one inside corner to the next inside corner. Often, the last board on a wall will be narrower than the rest, and this is less noticeable if it is on an inside corner.

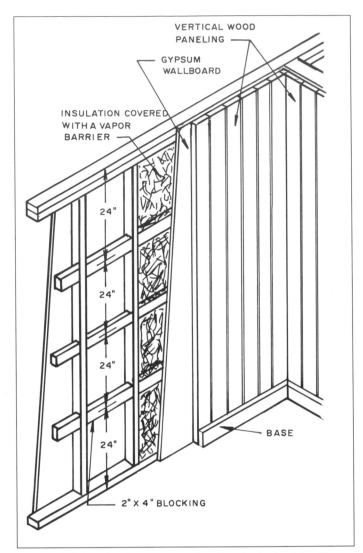

8–57. Wall framing for new construction includes blocking, a vapor barrier, insulation, and gypsum wallboard behind the wood paneling.

Set the first board in a corner and check for plumb. If the wall leans, the slope on the piece will need to be scribed and planed off so the exposed edge is plumb (**8–59**). Continue nailing across the wall, checking frequently for plumb. Leave a small gap at the floor and ceiling to allow for expansion. When arriving at the other wall, measure the space remaining and cut a board to fit this space.

Nailing patterns are shown in **8–60**. Use 6d finish nails. Notice that 6-inch (152-millimeter) -wide boards use one face nail and one blind nail, while 8-inch (203-millimeter) -wide boards have two face nails and one blind nail. Set the face nails and fill the holes. Be certain to leave a small gap between panels at each joint to allow for expansion.

The gap at the ceiling is covered with some type of molding, and a baseboard is installed at the floor (**8–61**). Interior and exterior corners do not need to be covered if they have a tight fit. However, if this is a problem, use molding to finish these as shown in **8–51**.

When a door or window is encountered, the window jamb will have to be extended by adding a piece equal to the thickness of the panel plus the furring (refer to **8–58**). If the window has a stool and apron, they will have to be removed. The stool will have to be notched to fit over the paneling and the apron nailed back below it (**8–62**).

INSTALLING WAINSCOTING

When solid wood paneling, plywood, or hardboard panels are used to cover the lower part of a wall,

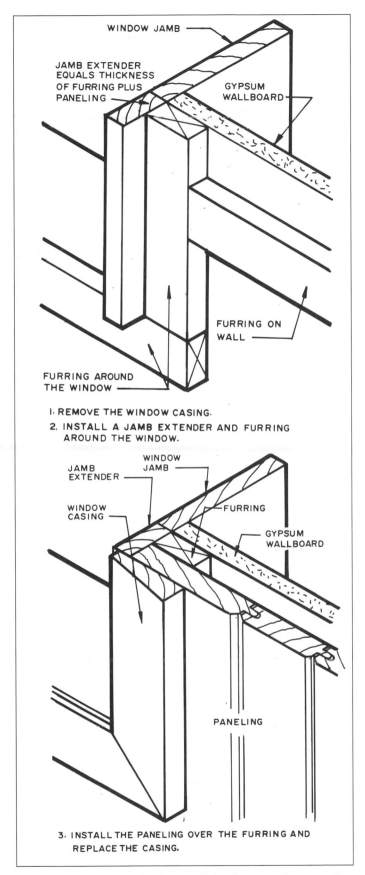

1. REMOVE THE WINDOW CASING.
2. INSTALL A JAMB EXTENDER AND FURRING AROUND THE WINDOW.

3. INSTALL THE PANELING OVER THE FURRING AND REPLACE THE CASING.

8–58. A jamb extender is needed wherever the paneling butts a window or door.

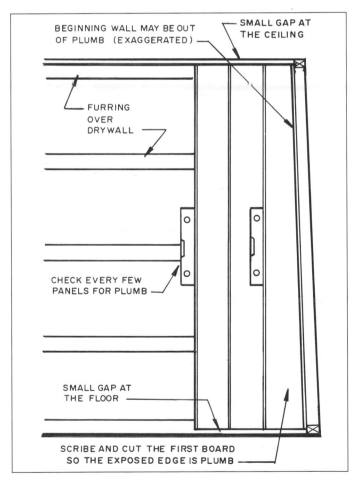

8–59. Check the wall where the first panel board is installed for plumb. Taper the first board so the exposed edge is plumb. When you get to the other wall, the same check and correction may be necessary.

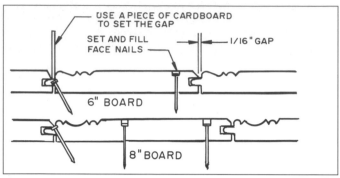

8–60. Recommended spacing and nailing patterns for vertical wood paneling.

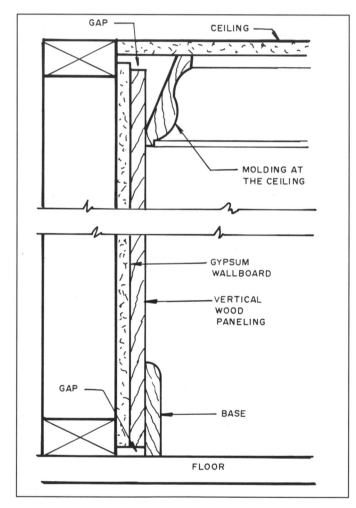

8–61. The gap between the paneling and the ceiling is covered with molding. The gap at the floor can be covered with a wood base, or carpet can butt the paneling, eliminating the need for the base.

this is referred to as **wainscoting**. It is typically installed in the same manner as described for full wall paneling.

To begin, decide on how high the wainscoting should be and run a chalk line along the wall (**8–63**).

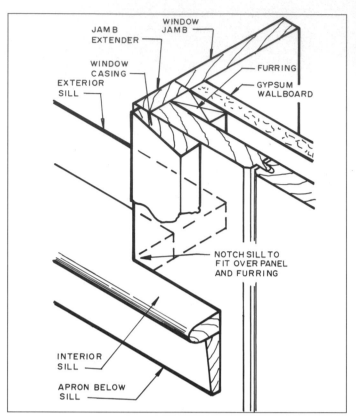

8–62. When the window has an interior sill, it will have to be removed and notched to fit over the jamb extender, which equals the thickness of the panel plus the furring.

This locates the top of the paneling. Start installation in one corner and proceed across the room. If this is over old gypsum wallboard, furring can be added to the wall and the panels nailed. If the wall is sound, paneling can be glued to it with paneling adhesive (**8–64**). Finally, install the wainscot cap. This can take several forms, and one can be made using stock molding (**8–65**).

INSTALLING A SUSPENDED CEILING

If the ceiling is cracked and patched, it is sometimes best to cover it with a suspended ceiling. A plaster or gypsum-board ceiling in bad shape is difficult to repair. Often, it must be entirely removed and a new one installed. Before starting to install a suspended ceiling, remove all portions of the old ceiling that may fall or nail them securely to the joists.

A suspended ceiling is a grid of metal runners that are hung from the ceiling joists on wire hangers. Panels are placed in the openings of the grid. These panels are typically ½ to ¾ inch (13 to 19 millime-

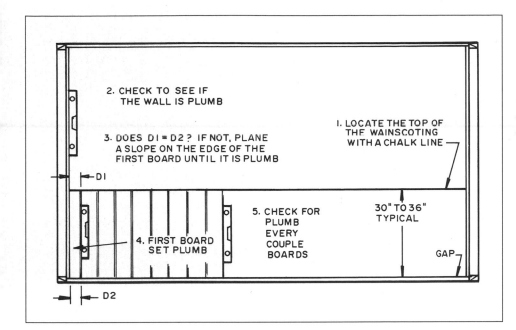

2. CHECK TO SEE IF THE WALL IS PLUMB

3. DOES D1 = D2 ? IF NOT, PLANE A SLOPE ON THE EDGE OF THE FIRST BOARD UNTIL IT IS PLUMB

D1

4. FIRST BOARD SET PLUMB

5. CHECK FOR PLUMB EVERY COUPLE BOARDS

D2

1. LOCATE THE TOP OF THF WAINSCOTING WITH A CHALK LINE

30" TO 36" TYPICAL

GAP

8–63. The steps for laying out and installing a wainscoting.

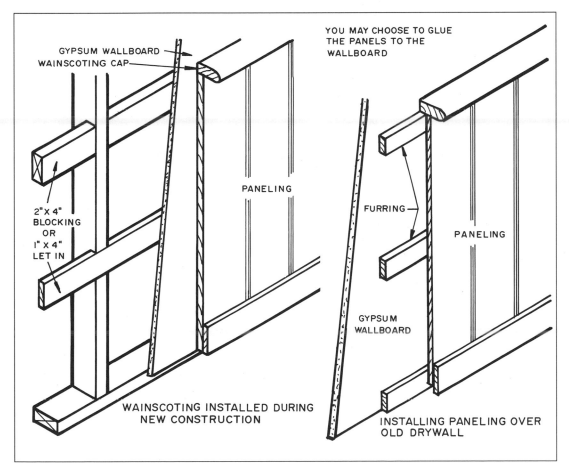

GYPSUM WALLBOARD

WAINSCOTING CAP

2" X 4" BLOCKING OR 1" X 4" LET IN

PANELING

YOU MAY CHOOSE TO GLUE THE PANELS TO THE WALLBOARD

FURRING

PANELING

GYPSUM WALLBOARD

WAINSCOTING INSTALLED DURING NEW CONSTRUCTION

INSTALLING PANELING OVER OLD DRYWALL

8–64. Two ways wainscoting is typically installed.

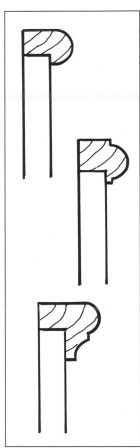

8–65. Various wainscoting caps are available. If desired, one can be designed and machined.

Installing a Suspended Ceiling ▧ **331**

The Grid

The grid is made of T-shaped metal runners available in 8- and 12-foot (2.4 and 3.7-meter) lengths (**8–67**). They run the length of the room. Short pieces called **cross-tees** run perpendicular to the runners, forming the openings into which the panels are placed. The grid is dropped 2 to 4 inches (51 to 102 millimeters) below the old ceiling or floor joists. The short pieces snap into slots in the runners (**8–68**).

Developing the Panel Layout

Make a plan that has the panels at each side wall the same width. Begin by making a drawing of the room. The long side of the panel is usually run parallel with the long side of the room. The main runners are placed perpendicular to the floor joists. Divide the long side of the room by 48 inches (1219 millimeters), which is the length of the panel. Add the inches left over to the length of one of the panels and divide by two. This gives the length of the end panels and the location of the first main runner from the outside wall (**8–68**).

8–66. A suspended ceiling provides an attractive acoustical finish with a space above to run utilities (courtesy Celotex Corporation).

ters) thick and available in 2 x 2- and 2 x 4-foot sizes. These panels are available in gypsum, fiberglass, wood fiber, and mineral fiber and have a wide variety of textures and finishes. Since they are laid in on the grid, they can be removed to give access to electrical, plumbing, and other systems hidden above the ceiling (**8–66**).

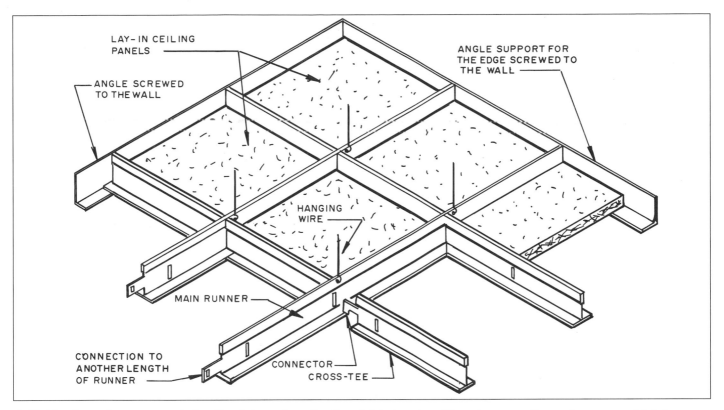

LAY-IN CEILING PANELS

ANGLE SCREWED TO THE WALL

ANGLE SUPPORT FOR THE EDGE SCREWED TO THE WALL

HANGING WIRE

MAIN RUNNER

CONNECTION TO ANOTHER LENGTH OF RUNNER

CONNECTOR

CROSS-TEE

8–67. The frame for a suspended ceiling is hung from the floor joists by wires. The wires carry the main runner, which is cross-connected by cross-tees. The panels are laid into the grid.

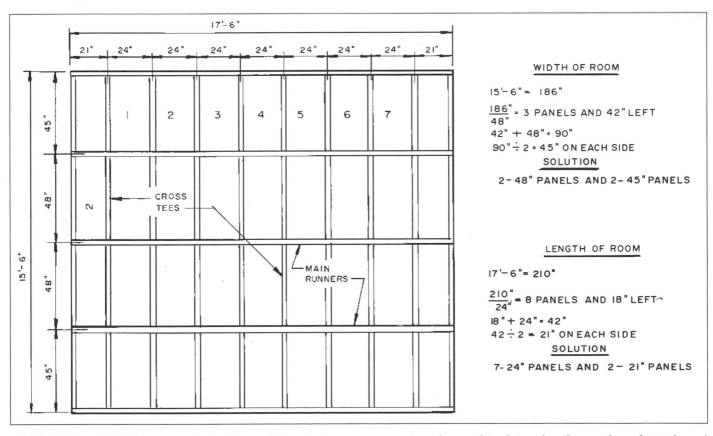

WIDTH OF ROOM

15'-6" = 186"

$\dfrac{186"}{48"}$ = 3 PANELS AND 42" LEFT

42" + 48" = 90"

90" ÷ 2 = 45" ON EACH SIDE

SOLUTION

2-48" PANELS AND 2-45" PANELS

LENGTH OF ROOM

17'-6" = 210"

$\dfrac{210"}{24"}$ = 8 PANELS AND 18" LEFT

18" + 24" = 42"

42 ÷ 2 = 21" ON EACH SIDE

SOLUTION

7-24" PANELS AND 2-21" PANELS

8–68. The layout for the suspended ceiling grid locates the runners and can be used to determine the number of panels and how much runner and cross-tee material is needed.

Repeat this to find the location of the cross-tees. The only difference is that the panel is 24 inches long instead of 48 inches.

Now it is possible to find the number of panels, the lineal feet of runner, and the number of cross-tees to buy.

An L-shaped runner in needed at the wall. It should be long enough to go around the perimeter of the room.

Installing the Wall Molding

The first step is to nail the wall molding to the wall. It supports the edge of the panel at the wall. Decide the height of the ceiling. Run a chalk line on each wall at this height plus the height of the main runner. Check the chalk line with a line level to see if it is level. Chalk the line and snap a chalk mark on each wall (**8–69**).

Place the top edge of the wall molding on the chalk line and nail it to the studs. Mark each stud on the wall so you can nail into it. Check it with a level while proceeding. Corners are formed as shown in **8–70**.

Installing the Main Runners

The main runners are made with a tongue on one

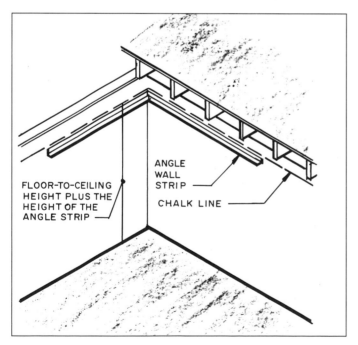

8–69. Locate the wall-mounted channel around the edge of the room with a chalk line.

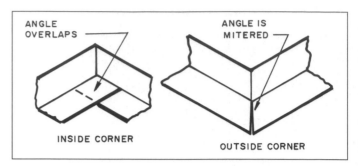

8–70. How to make the inside and outside corners on the wall-mounted channel.

end that fits into a slot on the end of the next piece. This splices runners together for long distances. The end of the runner that sits on the wall molding must be cut off. Measure from the first cross-tee-connection hole a distance equal to the width of the first panel and cut the main runner (**8–71**). In **8–68**, this was 21 inches (533 millimeters).

Run a chalk line the length of the room locating where the first runner will hang, and mark this. Mark where the runner crosses each joist. Install screw eyes at these points on every fourth joist. The screw eyes will be 48 inches (1219 millimeters) apart. Fasten a length of wire to each screw eye. It should be long enough to drop the ceiling the required amount and permit it to be wired to the main runner.

Slip each wire in the opening provided in the main runner (**8–72**). Bend the wire up temporarily until the entire runner is hanging. If a runner is not long enough, join another piece to it using the splice

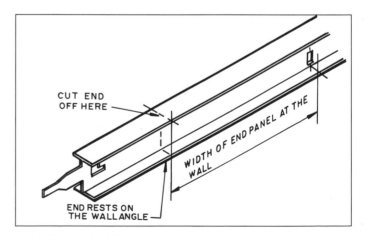

8–71. The end of the main runner is cut off and is supported by the wall-mounted channel.

8–72. Hang the main runner from screw eyes with wire. Be certain to check each for levelness before finally tightening the wire on the runner (courtesy Celotex Corporation).

8–73. The main runners have splice connections on the ends so they can be easily joined when they are being installed (courtesy Celotex Corporation).

connection provided (**8–73**). Run a chalk line at the desired ceiling height from one end of the runner to the other. Check to be certain it is level. Then raise or lower the main runner to match the chalk line and wrap the wire around itself to hold the runner in position. Repeat these steps for each main runner.

Installing the Cross-Tees

The cross-tees run perpendicular to the main runners. They have a special tab on each end that fits into holes on the main runner. Insert the cross-tees at 4-foot intervals and fasten them as specified by the manufacturer (**8–74**).

Installing the Ceiling Panels

The ceiling panels are sold cut to 24 x 48-inch sizes, so they fit into the runners. Slide them through the grid and drop them between the metal runners (**8–75**). If there are pipes, cut the panel in half at the pipe. Then cut the hole for the pipe and slide the two halves around the pipe as they are placed on the runners.

Installing Lights in Suspended Ceilings

The manufacturers of suspended systems offer various types of ceiling lights that will fit in place on a ceiling panel. These include fluorescent and incandescent fixtures (**8–76**). The manufacturer provides installation instructions for installing the lights in the ceiling. It will be necessary to develop an electrical plan to get

8–74. After the main runners are installed, the cross-tees are placed. They connect to openings provided in the main runner (courtesy Celotex Corporation).

8–75. After the grid is finished, the panels can be laid in (courtesy Celotex Corporation).

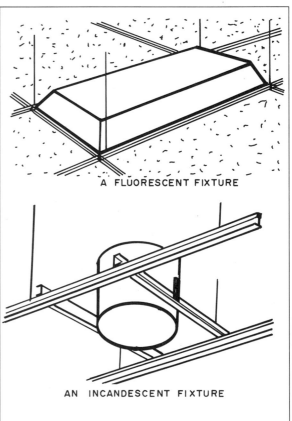

A FLUORESCENT FIXTURE

AN INCANDESCENT FIXTURE

8–76. Ceiling-systems manufacturers have a variety of light fixtures that fit into the grid, replacing a ceiling panel.

power to each fixture. Review Chapter 2 for electrical information.

INSTALLING CEILING TILES

Ceiling tiles are good to use to cover a damaged flat ceiling or over joists. The tiles are made of fiberboard or foam plastic. One side has a factory-applied finish, so they must be handled carefully. A wide variety of surface textures are available; they also have good acoustical qualities. Typical tiles are ½ inch (13 millimeters) thick and have tongue-and-groove edges. Typical tile sizes are 12 x 12, 12 x 24, 16 x 16, and 16 x 32 inches.

Developing a Flat-Ceiling Layout

To plan the layout, make a drawing showing the size of the room (**8–77**). The tiles next to the walls should be the same size on opposite walls of the room. Avoid using a small 2 x 4-inch strip along the wall.

To make the layout, divide the width and length of the ceiling (in inches or millimeters) by 12 inches (305 millimeters) or the tile size. This indicates that number of tiles needed. In **8–77**, 12 tiles were used for the short side, with 6 inches (152 millimeters) left over. Add 12 inches to the 6 inches and divide by 2. This gives the size of the outside tiles — which in

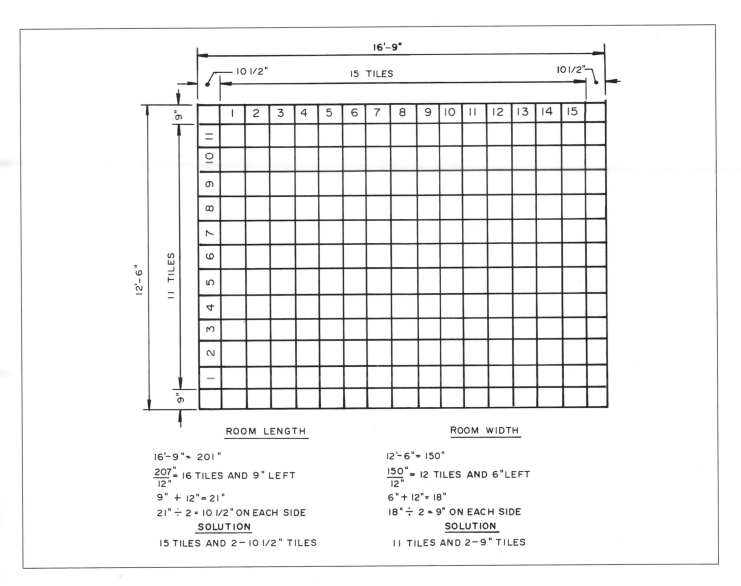

8–77. *A plan for installing ceiling tile. This locates the wood furring strips on the bottom of the floor joists and indicates how many tile are needed.*

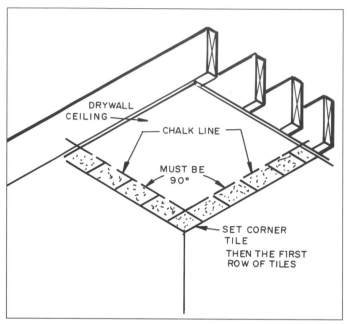

8–78. Use a chalk line to locate the edge of the first row of tile.

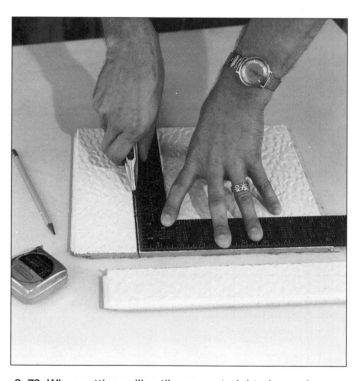

8–79. When cutting ceiling tile, use a straightedge and a very sharp utility knife. Cut with the finished surface on top (courtesy Celotex Corporation).

this example is 9 inches (228 millimeters). This avoids having a narrow strip along the wall.

The room length is figured in the same way. Remember, when using a different tile size, such as

16 x 16 inches (406 x 406 millimeters), divide the width and length by the actual tile size.

Installing Tiles over an Old Gypsum Drywall Ceiling

If the old ceiling is damaged but structurely sound, it can be covered by gluing the tiles to it. Go over the old ceiling and nail it to the joist wherever it seems to be weak. Repair any bulges or deteriorated areas. Once the ceiling appears sound, begin the installation. Use the adhesive recommended by the manufacturer.

Refer to the information from the tile layout (8–77). Use chalk lines to locate the edge of each outer row of tiles (8–78). Cut the tiles to the required width. Use a sharp utility knife and cut from the finished face. Use a straightedge to guide the knife (8–79). A sharp, fine-blade saber saw can also be used.

Place adhesive in spots on the back of the (8–80). Keep adhesive away from the edges of the tiles. Press the tiles against the ceiling and line them up with the mark. Put the cut edges next to the wall. If necessary, a staple can be driven through the tongue into the ceiling to hold the tiles while the adhesive sets. Continue along the wall. Check constantly to make certain this first row is straight. All other rows depend upon it.

When installing the outside row on the second wall, be certain the chalk lines cross at 90 degrees.

If the ceiling is in bad repair, install wood furring strips over it as described in the next section.

INSTALLING TILES USING FURRING STRIPS

Furring strips are 1 x 2 or 1 x 3 wood strips that are nailed to the ceiling joists. The ceiling tiles are stapled to the furring strips (8–81). If the joists are not level, place wood shims under the furring strips to bring them level. If the joist extends below the chalk line, plane some of it off (8–82). Check for levelness with a chalk line.

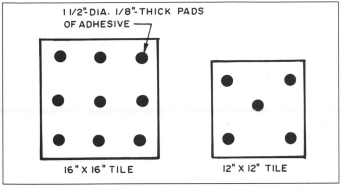

8–80. Place dabs of adhesive on the back of the tile in these patterns.

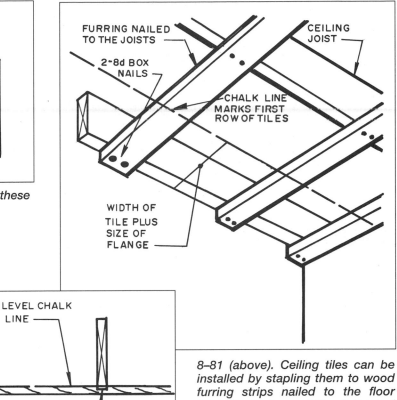

8–81 (above). Ceiling tiles can be installed by stapling them to wood furring strips nailed to the floor joist. The first row of tiles is located by a chalk line.

8–82. Adjust the furring so it is level the length and width of the room.

Developing the Furring-Ceiling Layout

This layout is made in the same manner as for the flat ceiling (refer to **8–77**). The chalk lines locate the center of each furring strip. The tiles must meet at the center of each strip (**8–83**).

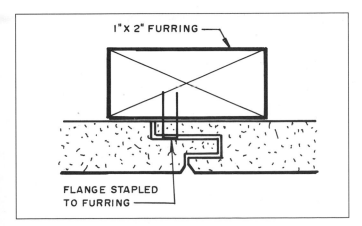

8–83. The tile is stapled to the furring through the flange. The edge of the finished face falls on the center of the furring.

Installing the Furring Strips

Nail the first furring strip next to the wall. Measure the width of the first row of tiles in from the wall. Nail the second row of furring strips with this line in the center. Locate each row in this manner. Nail the strips with two 8d box nails in each joist.

Framing Projections

Occasionally a heat duct or water pipe will extend below the ceiling joists. Projections can be boxed in using 2 x 2 or 2 x 4 framing (**8–84**). The tiles are then stapled to this framing.

Installing the Tiles

Run chalk lines locating the edges of the tiles on two meeting walls. Be certain they cross at right angles. Cut and install the corner tiles first (**8–85**). Cut off the side with the groove. The tongue is needed for

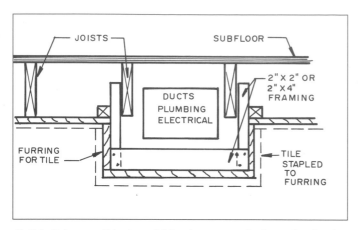

8–84. It is possible to add furring around obstacles in the ceiling and cover the area with the ceiling tile.

FIRST FURRING IS THE WIDTH OF THE TILE PLUS THE FLANGE

12" 12"

STAPLE

CHALK LINE

FACE NAIL

1. SET THE CORNER TILE.

FLANGE ON CENTER

CHALK LINE

2. STAPLE A ROW OF TILES ALONG EACH OF THE WALLS MEETING THE CORNER.

8–85. Start installing in a corner and complete a row along the two butting outside walls.

stapling it to the furring strips (**8–86**). Now cut and install the tiles on the outside row of two walls meeting in a corner. Staple through the tongue to the furring strip. Usually 9/16- or 5/8-inch (9- or 15-millimeter) staples are used. Use three staples on 12-inch tiles and four on 16-inch tiles. Twenty-four-inch panels need five staples. Then begin the second row and continue filling in the ceiling (**8–87**). The last row on the other side of the room will have to be face-nailed or stapled on the edge. Then install some type of molding around the entire ceiling (**8–88**).

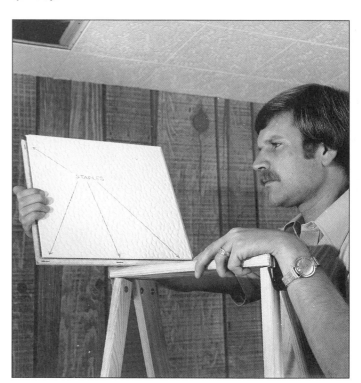

8–86. The tile is secured to the furring by stapling it through the tongue that is on two sides. The other two sides are grooves that fit over the tongue on the next tile. Put three staples in the tongue (courtesy Celotex Corporation).

Lights

Recessed and flush-mounted lights are available for installation with wood-furred ceilings (**8–89**). Follow the manufacturer's installation instructions. Protect the furniture part as you attempt to tap the joint apart.

8–87. After installing the row of tile along two walls, fill in the ceiling (courtesy Celotex Corporation).

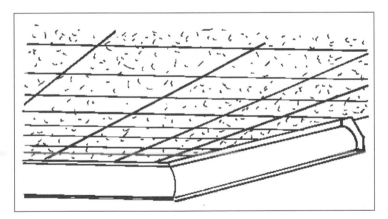

8–88. Cover the edge of the tile along the wall with some type of molding.

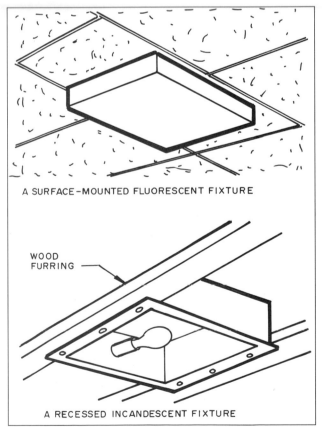

A SURFACE-MOUNTED FLUORESCENT FIXTURE

WOOD FURRING

A RECESSED INCANDESCENT FIXTURE

8–89. Several types of ceiling light are available.

CHAPTER NINE

Interior Painting

DECORATING WALLS

The first step in decorating a room is to select a color scheme. A color, surface texture, and pattern, if any, must be selected for the walls. The wall decoration must be coordinated with the color of the ceiling, trim, carpet, furnishings, and curtains or drapes. Color, as described below, is used to create a mood and to emphasize important architectural features. The local paint, wall-covering, or tile dealer will have examples and suggestions that will prove helpful when deciding which colors to use. The information below will also help.

COLOR

When considering color, remember that light colors make a room seem larger. A good example is to paint a long, narrow hall a white or very light color. White ceilings reflect light and brighten a room.

Dark colors are warm. A room painted with warm colors such as red, orange, and yellow seems to enclose a person and makes him or her feel comfortable. These colors can also hide or downplay a major defect or feature.

The cool colors are gray, green, blue, and violet. Some tints are more intense, while others are subdued, giving a soothing feeling.

The relationship of colors is shown on the color wheel in **9–1**. Red, yellow, and blue are the **primary colors**. Violet, orange, and green are **secondary colors**. These are made by blending two of the primary colors. When a primary and a secondary color are mixed, the result is referred to as a **tertiary color**.

For example, when yellow and green are mixed, they produce a yellow–green color.

Colors that are opposite each other on the color wheel, such as red and green, are **complementary colors** and are often used together in decorating. If a three-color scheme is desired, use colors equidistant from each other. This is referred to as a **color triad**. Red, green, and blue form a triad. One other possibility is to choose a primary color, such as yellow, and use it and the colors on each side, which are yellow–green and yellow–orange.

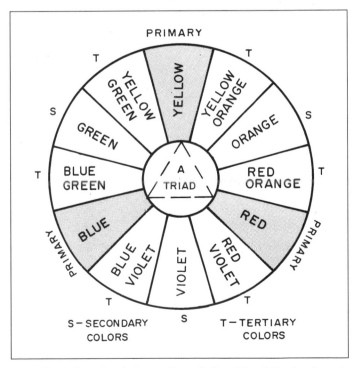

9–1. *The color wheel shows the relationship of the basic colors. Paint colors available are in these and lighter and darker values, but the color relationship within the room should be maintained.*

When working with color, also consider the intensity of the color. **Intensity** is the strength of the color. The intensity can be changed by varying the lightness or darkness of the color. This is referred to as the **value** of the color. Intense colors are generally used to emphasize a small, single feature and are reduced (lightened) when used on large areas.

LADDER SAFETY TECHNIQUES

The interior painting of walls and ceilings can usually be handled from stepladders. Information on major safety suggestions can be found in Chapter 6. A basic thing to remember is to move the ladder so there is no need to reach out beyond the safe reaching distance. Remember, stepladders come with a safety warning attached that instructs the user not to stand on the very top step or the one directly

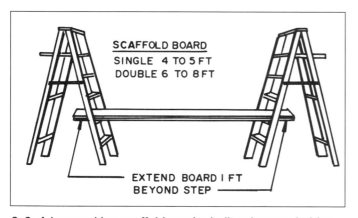

9–2. A low-working scaffold can be built using two ladders.

below it. Be certain to use strong, high-quality stepladders. Damaged, shaky ladders should be discarded.

Open the ladder fully and make certain the braces between the legs are in place and the paint-can shelf is down. Place it on a level, firm footing.

If the ceiling or top of the wall is high and difficult to reach, use a scaffold as shown in Chapter 8. Painting can be sped up somewhat if two stepladders are used with a plank between them (**9–2**). The plank should be of scaffold-board quality and at least 12 inches (305 millimeters) wide and 2 inches (51 millimeters) thick. Use one plank for spans of 4 to 5 feet (1.2 to 1.5 meters) and two planks for spans of 6 to 8 feet (1.8 to 2.4 meters). If the stepladders are more than 8 feet from each other, add a support in the center of the double plank.

If the second story of a building is being painted, the high walls and ceiling on the stairway present a special problem. Some solutions are shown in **9–3**. Since there is a greater safety hazard, clamp the plank to the ladders or nail a cleat below it so it locks onto the step of the ladder (**9–4**).

REDUCING THE HAZARDS OF LEAD-BASED PAINT

Many older homes were painted with lead-based paint. It was the major product for many years. Anyone living in a house painted with lead-based paint can be exposed to the lead by inhaling lead

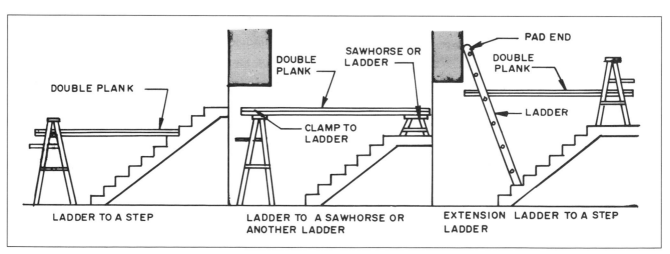

9–3. Various ladders and scaffold planks can be used to paint high walls and ceilings in difficult areas such as around a stair.

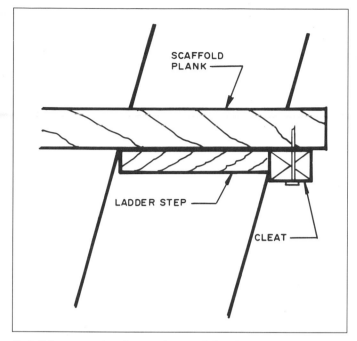

9–4. Whenever the danger from a fall exists, clamp the scaffold board to the ladder or sawhorse, or nail cleats on the bottom of the scaffold plank that fits up against the ladder tread.

dust created as the old paint chalks, peels, and is chipped from deteriorated surfaces. (Smaller children are especially susceptible by eating paint chips.) The dust settles on everything in the house and is ingested unknowingly. This causes brain damage and impairs mental functioning. It retards physical growth, and can sometimes even retard fetal development.

There are kits available that be used to check paint for lead. Some of these have not been approved by the U.S. Consumer Product Safety Commission. It is also possible to have paint chips tested for lead at a laboratory or by a certified testing technician. Your paint dealer can recommend a laboratory.

Following are several suggestions for reducing exposure to lead-based paint:

1. Replace the item. For example, replace all doors and cabinets and use an approved finish on the new doors and cabinets.

2. Cover the paint with gypsum drywall or an approved paint. This will reduce the hazard for a while. Eventually, the lead dust could penetrate the cover as it ages.

3. Employ professionals who are trained to remove the paint from all surfaces. They will protect themselves as they do this work. Do not try to remove the paint yourself.

4. As a temporary measure, wash all surfaces, floors, walls, and moldings to remove the dust. This is only a temporary measure and, while cutting down on the dust, does nothing to correct the situation.

SELECTING THE PAINT

The selection of the proper paint is critical when preparing to repaint the interior walls, molding, cabinets, and other features. Check with the experts at the local paint store for help. Following are some of the products available.

Latex paints (more accurately described as **emulsion paints**) are water-thinned and can be applied with a brush, roller, or pad. Cleanup is with soap and water. They are not flammable, have little odor, and dry to the touch in about an hour. When used on walls and ceilings, they provide satisfactory durability under normal conditions. Walls and ceilings can be easily cleaned by washing.

Latex paints are available in flat, eggshell (a satin finish), and semi- and high-gloss finishes. Textured latex products are available and produce an attractive wall finish. Since latex paints are water-thinned, they will cause steel to rust, so an adequate rust-inhibiting primer is necessary when painting over steel.

Latex primer is a water-thinned paint used as a first coat on all unpainted interior walls and ceilings made of wallboard or plaster. Regular latex paint can also be used as a primer.

Alkyd paints are oil-based and are thinned with a solvent such as turpentine. They can be applied with a brush or roller. Cleanup is done with turpentine, paint thinner, or mineral spirits. Alkyd paints have a strong odor that lasts longer (a day or two) than that produced by latex paints and are more resistant to damage from frequent cleaning. They are best used in rooms such as a bath or kitchen where frequent and vigorous cleaning is apt to take place.

Enamels are available in both alkyd and latex bases. They dry smooth and have a harder surface than most interior paints. Enamels may have high, medium, or low gloss. They produce a tough surface and are used where frequent use and severe cleaning conditions exist, such as on walls, ceilings, trim, and cabinets. Water is used to clean up latex enamel, while solvents are used to clean up alkyd enamel.

Enamel undercoats have an alkyd base and are solvent-thinned. They are used under all interior enamels and provide a good base for an enamel topcoat.

Clear finishes are used on wood trim, doors, and cabinets. These finishes include varnish, lacquer, shellac, polyurethane, and epoxy. See Chapter 15 for information on some of these.

DETERMINING THE AMOUNT OF PAINT NEEDED

The label on the paint can will indicate the number of square feet a gallon of that paint will cover when applied as directed. While the paint dealer can help in selecting the best paint for the job and insuring that the correct primer is used, those shown in **Table 9–1** are the ones that will most generally be used. Following are the steps to determine the amount of paint needed:

1. Find the area of the walls by multiplying the length by the height in feet. The ceiling area is the room width multiplied by the length (**9–5**). Round off any inches to the nearest foot.

2. Subtract the area of the doors and windows.

3. Divide the total square feet by the amount that one gallon of paint will cover. This is shown on the can.

4. If the trim is a different color and type of paint, allow 20 square feet for each side of a door and 16 square feet for the trim around a window. To determine how much paint is needed for the baseboard, determine the lineal feet of the baseboard and multiply it by the height in fractions of a foot. Divide this by the coverage per gallon.

Certain surfaces, such as unpainted plaster or porous wallboard, will absorb more paint than nor-

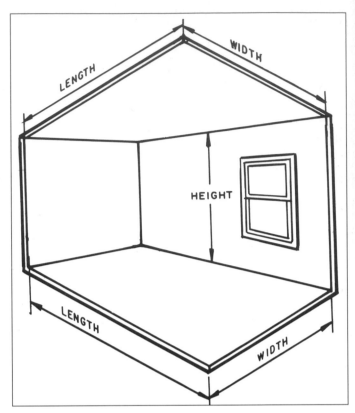

9–5. The area of walls and ceiling is found by multiplying the length by the width in feet, which gives square feet. Round off any inches to the nearest foot.

mal. These surfaces will require extra paint or primer.

If the color is custom-mixed, overestimate the amount of paint needed slightly so it does not run out before the job is completed. If another batch of a custom color is mixed, it may not exactly match the first batch. Fresh paint usually has a shelf life of several years if kept tightly closed, and an extra amount will often come in handy for touch-up repairs.

PREPARING THE SURFACE TO BE PAINTED

The time to prepare the surface for painting is frequently longer than that for the actual application of the various coats. If the walls, ceiling, and trim are new, they will be in good shape for priming and painting. Be certain they are free of dust, gypsum powder, and wood particles. A quick wipe with a cloth usually does this.

If the surfaces have been previously finished and are to be repainted, usually more extensive repairs

TABLE 9-1

Material Being Painted	Primers				Finishes				
	Alkyd	Latex	Aluminum Paint	Metal Primer	Latex Enamel	Alkyd Enamel	Latex Flat Paint	Alkyd Flat Paint	Textured Paint
New Gypsum Wallboard	*	*			*	*	*	*	*
Previously Painted Wallboard					*	*	*	*	*
New Plaster	*	*			*	*	*	*	*
Previously Painted Plaster					*	*	*	*	*
Uncoated Wall Covering	*	*			*	*			
Vinyl Wall Covering						*	*	*	
New Plywood	*	*			*	*	*	*	
Previously Painted Plywood					*	*	*		
New Wood Trim	*	*			*	*	*	*	
Previously Painted Wood Trim					*	*	*	*	
Steel (Window Frames, etc.)				*	*	*			
Aluminum (Window Frames, etc.)									
Galvanized Steel			*		*	*			
Cast Iron (Radiators, etc.)				*	*	*			
New Masonry	*						*		
Previously Painted Masonry	*						*		

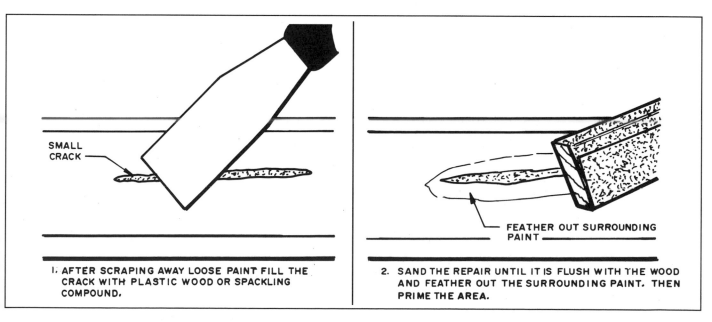

SMALL CRACK

1. AFTER SCRAPING AWAY LOOSE PAINT FILL THE CRACK WITH PLASTIC WOOD OR SPACKLING COMPOUND.

FEATHER OUT SURROUNDING PAINT

2. SAND THE REPAIR UNTIL IT IS FLUSH WITH THE WOOD AND FEATHER OUT THE SURROUNDING PAINT. THEN PRIME THE AREA.

9–6. Small cracks and dents can be repaired by scraping away the loose paint around them, filling them with plastic wood or a spackling compound, and sanding the area so the repair is flush with the surface and the edges of the paint around it are feathered out.

1. BRUSH ON THE PAINT REMOVER OVER A SMALL AREA. LET IT SIT UNTIL THE PAINT WRINKLES.

2. WHEN THE PAINT WRINKLES SCRAP IT OFF WITH A BROAD BLADE DRYWALL TAPING KNIFE.

9–7. A paste paint remover is easiest to use when the paint has to be removed down to the bare wood.

1. USE FOLDED SANDPAPER TO GET INTO SMALL SURFACES.

2. SAND FLAT SURFACES WITH A SANDPAPER HOLDER.

3. A SMALL ELECTRIC SANDER SPEEDS UP THE WORK.

9–8. After removing the old paint and washing off the paint remover, sand the surface so the wood is clean and ready for a primer.

are needed. Probably the biggest job will be checking the walls and ceiling for damage such as blistered paint, bulges, cracks, holes, and wet spots. Find out what caused the damage, such as a leaky roof, and repair it before refinishing the surface. Repairs to damaged gypsum drywall and plaster are explained in Chapter 8. After repairs have been made, prime the area with the recommended primer.

A wood surface can also have blistered and cracked paint. Some of these damages are shown in Chapter 6. If a piece is badly split or checked, replace it. Small cracks or chipped areas can be sanded so their edges are feathered out. Small cracks or dents can be filled with wood filler or a spackling compound and sanded (9–6). If there is greater damage such as blistering or heavy checking, it must be removed down to the bare wood surface. Paint remover can be used to soften the paint so it can be scraped off (9–7), or use an electric heat gun to soften the paint (see Chapter 6). Water-solvent paste paint removers are the best choice on solid wood. Benzine-solvent paint removers are used on veneers that may be damaged by water.

Brush the paint remover over a small area, for example an area 1- to 2-foot square, with an old paintbrush. As the paint starts to wrinkle, scrape it off with a broad-blade drywall taping knife. Have lots of newspaper with which to wipe off the knife. Apply remover to another part and scrape away the paint. It may be necessary to apply a light second coat over areas where some paint remains. Once all paint is removed, wash the surface with the solvent, whether it is water or benzine. Let it thoroughly dry before doing any sanding.

Before painting over a previously painted surface, sand it to dull it so the new coats will adhere. This can be done with a fine sandpaper or a liquid that when painted on dulls the surface. If hand-sanding the surface, fold the sandpaper to get into narrow places and buy a sandpaper holder with a rubber pad for large surfaces. A small electric sander is also very helpful (**9–8**).

Any dirt or grease is removed by washing the surface with a household cleaner. Let the surface dry before painting it. Sand off any black scuff marks that are on the baseboard. Paint will not completely cover them.

When using paint removers, wear rubber gloves and have eye and breathing protection. Remove cur-tain rods, shades, hooks, and switch and outlet covers, and lower light fixtures so they can be painted around easily. Remove as much furniture from the room as possible. Cover those items that cannot be moved with a drop cloth. Also cover the floor with drop cloths. If solvent-thinned paint is being used, turn off any appliance pilot lights. Do not use any open flame when painting. Provide adequate ventilation regardless of the kind of paint being used.

PRE-PAINTING PROCEDURES

Begin by reading the instructions on the paint-can label. It will give directions for priming, stirring, thinning, and applying the paint.

A wide variety of tools are used to paint. These include brushes, pads, rollers, and airless sprayers. Some of these are shown in Chapter 6. In addition to these, those shown in **9–9** and **9–10** are very helpful.

9–9. This roller application contains a paint supply in the long handle, and the paint is fed to the roller as needed by moving the end of the handle (courtesy HomeRight, Minneapolis, Minnesota).

Pre-Painting Procedures ■ **349**

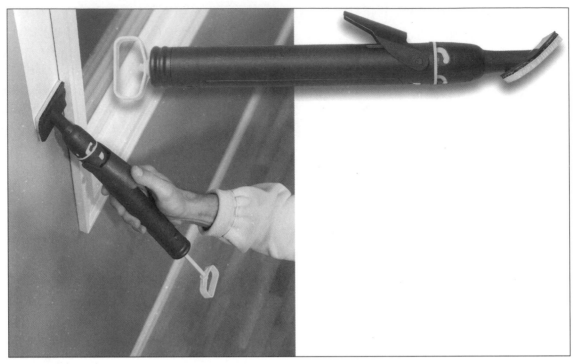

9–10. This pad-type painter is useful for painting around trim and the initial strip in corners, the ceiling, and along the baseboard. It contains a paint supply in the handle that is controlled by the handle on the end (courtesy HomeRight, Minneapolis, Minnesota).

MIXING THE PAINT

Since paint pigment settles and the solvent rises when the can sits, they must be thoroughly remixed. The paint dealer will place each can on a mixing machine, so the pigment and solvent for a recently bought can are pretty well mixed. If the paint can is used right away, it may require just a little manual mixing.

If the paint sits unopened for a while, it may need to be manually mixed. Begin by pouring one-third to one-half in a clean bucket. Stir the material remaining in the first can with a wood paddle. The paint dealer will provide several. Then pour a little from the bucket back into the paint can and stir it. Continue until all the paint is in the can. Be certain all pigment on the bottom of the can has been scraped loose and mixed. Paint stores sell a metal paddle that can be attached to an electric drill. This is the most effective way to get a good mix and is recommended. *Do not use it to mix solvent-based paints.* The sparks from the brushes in the drill motor may ignite the fumes.

HANDLING PAINT WHILE APPLYING IT

The one-gallon can of paint is very heavy and difficult to use, especially from a ladder. Pour some of the paint into a smaller paint bucket. Close up the paint can so evaporation does not occur.

If the brush is not being used, do not stand it up in the paint bucket. Lay it on a clean, flat surface or put a wire or two across the paint bucket and rest it on that (**9–11**).

9–11. It helps to put a couple of wires across the paint bucket to hold the brush.

CLEANING UP SPILLS

A few spills or splatters are always part of the painting process. Have available some rags or paper towels and a supply of the solvent for the paint being used. If there are some splatters on hard, washable surfaces, wash them off with a rag wetted with solvent as soon as they are noticed. Remember, water is used with latex paints and paint thinner with alkyd paints.

While painting, try to prevent the paint from running down the side of the bucket. It is smart to keep a piece of cardboard under the bucket to catch any runs.

If there is a major spill, pick up as much as possible with a dustpan or a flat piece of metal or plastic. Throw this paint away, because it is now contaminated. Then, with lots of rags or paper towels and solvent, wash the area and blot it dry. Do not rub the solvent in. This will force the paint into the surface.

Should the spill be on carpet and latex paint was being used, first blot up as much as possible with paper towels. Again, do not wipe or rub the solvent on. After repeated blottings, use a rag with a detergent and wash and rinse the area over and over until it is clean.

Should the spill be an alkyd paint, blot and then wash it with mineral spirits instead of water. Do not use paint thinner. This may damage the binders that hold the carpet fibers in place.

PAINTING A ROOM

When painting a room, begin at the ceiling and work down toward the floor. This means painting in the following order: the ceiling, then the walls, next the doors and windows, and finally any other woodwork and the baseboards.

The procedure will vary depending upon what is to be painted. If the ceiling is a different color than the walls, paint a strip 2 to 3 inches (51 to 76 millimeters) wide around the edge (9–12). Use a metal or plastic shield to keep the paint off the wall (9–13). Start painting in a corner and paint a 3-foot (915-millimeter) strip across the narrower width of the room. Paint in 3-foot-square sections while moving

across the room. Then move over and paint the next strip. Paint from the dry surface toward the wet area. This helps the paint blend and reduces excess thickness of paint at the overlapping area. Overlap the strips about 1 inch (25 millimeters) (9–14).

Paint walls by painting a 2- to 3-inch-wide strip

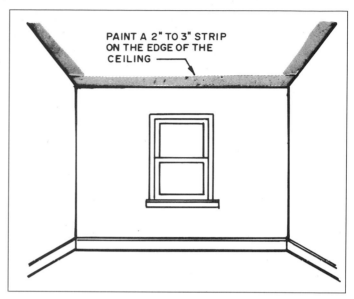

9–12. If the ceiling is a different color from the walls, paint a 2- to 3-inch-wide strip around the edge of the ceiling and then paint the entire surface. Keep the paint off the walls.

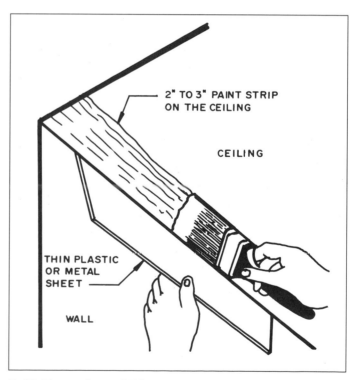

9–13. Use a piece of thin metal or plastic as an edging tool to keep the paint off an adjoining surface. Wipe it each time you move it to paint the next section of the strip.

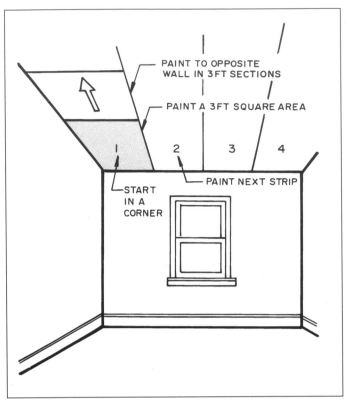

9–14. Start painting the ceiling in a corner and paint in 3-foot-wide sections to the other wall. Move over and paint the next area the same way.

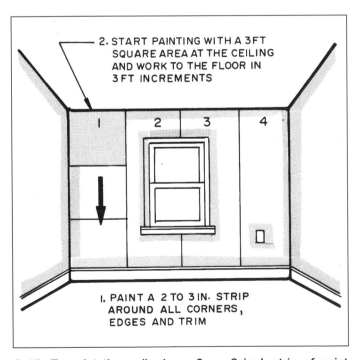

9–15. To paint the walls, lay a 2- or 3 inch-strip of paint around all corners, edges, and trim. Then, starting in a corner at the ceiling, paint toward the floor in 3-square-foot sections. Do not stop until the entire wall is covered.

around the edges, in the corners, and around doors and windows. Then paint a 3-foot-wide strip from the ceiling to the floor. Paint it in 3-foot squares while moving down the wall (**9–15**). Keep painting until the wall is finished. Do not stop partway and let the paint dry before finishing.

If the ceiling and wall are a different color, use a metal or plastic sheet to keep the paint off the ceiling. If they are the same color, this is not that big a problem. Still, try not to get additional paint on the ceiling when you paint the wall if the ceiling has dried.

When the walls and ceiling are the same color, all the corners can be trimmed out at the same time (**9–16**).

When arriving at a door or window, trim around it with a 2- to 3-inch strip (**9–16**). This paint can be applied with a trim brush, pad edger, or the edger shown in **9–10**. After painting the edges, do the ceiling and then the walls.

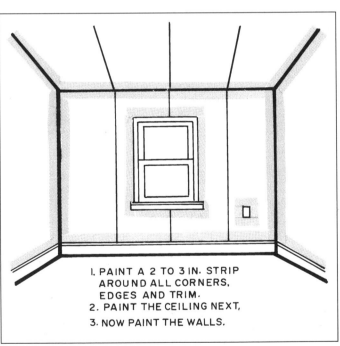

9–16. When the ceiling and the walls are the same color, the edges and corners on both can be trimmed out. Then paint the ceiling and finish up with the walls.

Painting Next to Wallpaper

When painting up to a wall covered with wallpaper, be very careful because the wallpaper tends to suck up the wet paint like a sponge. The edge of the wallpaper can be covered with masking tape, but this is

1. SWING SHORT CURVED STROKES OVERLAPPING EACH OTHER. SWING FROM SEVERAL DIRECTIONS.

2. SMOOTH THE PAINT WITH A SERIES OF HORIZONTAL STROKES FROM BOTH DIRECTIONS.

9–17. Lay on the paint in short, curved strokes. Lift the brush at the end of each stroke. Apply the paint from several directions. Use a 3- or 4-inch brush.

not a foolproof technique. Possibly the best approach is to paint to within ⅜ inch (9.5 millimeters) of the wallpaper and nail wood molding over this strip.

If you are planning to paint and wallpaper, first paint and then add the wallpaper. Feather the paint out on the wall for a few inches, so no gap shows along the edge of the paper. Allow the paint to dry completely before wallpapering.

Painting Techniques

One commonly used brushing technique for large brushes on large areas when using wall paint is to begin painting in a series of angled, overlapping strokes (**9–17**). Once the area (usually 3- or 4-foot square) is covered, use short strokes parallel with the floor. Feather out the edge next to the next strip. Begin painting on the dry surface and paint toward the wet edge (**9–18**, on the next page).

When using a roller on the ceiling or wall, lay out a coating with a series of angular, randomly spaced strokes using a freshly loaded roller. Do not lift the roller or there may be voids in the thickness of the coating. Now, without lifting the roller off the surface, run it across the surface perpendicular to the first layer until the coating is uniform (**9–19**, on the next page).

Painting Old Wallpaper

It is difficult to paint old wallpaper to your total satisfaction. The patterns are usually so dominant they show through several layers of paint. If vinyl wall covering is being painted, the problem is even worse. Before trying it, check with a paint dealer for suggestions.

If you decide to paint the wall, go over it and glue any loose sections and edges of the wallpaper. Next, test the paper for colorfastness. Wipe a place on the wall with a rag wetted with water, and another place with mineral spirits. If the color comes off with the water but not the mineral spirits, use an alkyd paint. If the mineral spirits remove the color but the water does not, use a latex paint. Remember, water is the solvent for latex paints and mineral spirits are the solvent for alkyd paints.

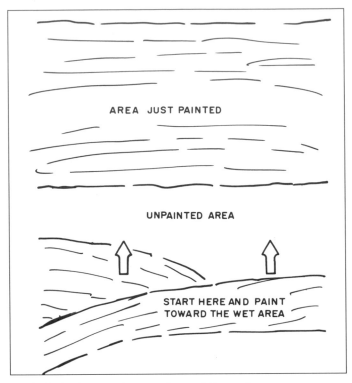

AREA JUST PAINTED

UNPAINTED AREA

START HERE AND PAINT
TOWARD THE WET AREA

9–18. Paint from a dry area toward the wet area.

Use a sealer such as shellac or one recommended by the paint dealer before applying the paint. Two coats are almost always required, and sometimes this is not enough. Consider working a trial area to see how things will look. If it is not satisfactory, cover the wall with paneling or strip the old wallpaper and repaper the wall.

DECORATING TECHNIQUE

Borders

A room can be made more interesting by painting a solid-color **contrasting border** or **stenciling** a border at the ceiling (**9–20**). To paint a solid border, follow these steps:

1. Measure the width desired and draw a light line that marks the bottom edge. The top edge will be the ceiling.

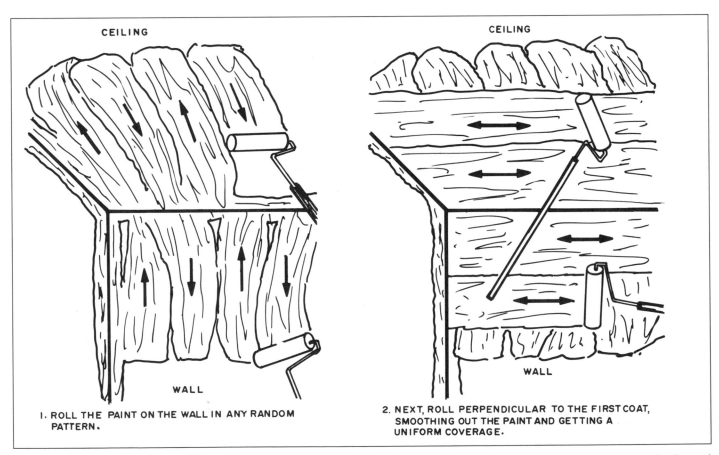

CEILING

WALL

1. ROLL THE PAINT ON THE WALL IN ANY RANDOM PATTERN.

CEILING

WALL

2. NEXT, ROLL PERPENDICULAR TO THE FIRST COAT, SMOOTHING OUT THE PAINT AND GETTING A UNIFORM COVERAGE.

9–19. Apply the paint to the ceiling and wall in 3-foot sections using a random pattern followed by a series of horizontal strokes. Do not add more paint to the roller for the horizontal stroke. Do not lift the roller from the surface during the entire application.

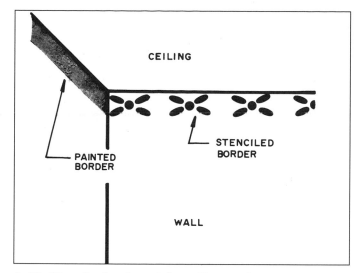

9–20. Attractive borders at the ceiling can be made by painting or stenciling.

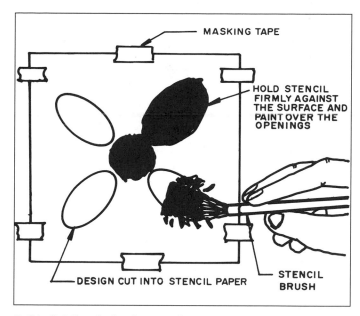

9–21. Cut the design in stencil paper. Tape it to the surface. Hold the stencil firmly to the surface and paint over the openings with a fine-bristle stencil brush. Work carefully so the paint does not run under the stencil. Do not overload the brush with paint. Practice on scrap material to get a feel for the process.

2. Stick plastic tape —the kind used to paint racing stripes on auto—along the line drawn and on the ceiling.

3. Paint the border and allow it to dry. Then remove the tape.

Stencils are used to paint a pattern on the wall. Stencil designs may be bought at paint stores. Stencil material can also be bought and individual patterns cut out. Stencil a border following these steps:

1. Buy or make a stencil pattern.

2. Plan the layout of the stencil so the pattern comes out with the design unbroken on the length of the wall.

3. When you are ready to paint, lightly tape the stencil in place on the wall.

4. Fill in the design using an artist's brush, a sponge, or a fine-bristle paintbrush. Work carefully and hold the stencil tightly to the wall (**9–21**).

5. After removing the stencil, wipe it clean before the next use.

Combing the Wall

Another interior wall treatment is to **comb the wall.** Combing produces the appearance of a satin-like fabric covering. The procedure is as follows:

1. Paint the wall with one or two coats of paint to get good coverage and let it dry.

2. Apply a coat of paint of a different color or a lighter or darker shade than the base paint.

3. Run a specially designed comb through the paint to form a pattern that allows the paint below to show through.

4. Form patterns with the comb such as a wavy motion from ceiling to floor, a diagonal pattern, or rectangular grids that alternate in different directions.

Sponging the Wall

Walls and ceilings can be given an interesting appearance using the **sponging technique**. Follow these steps to use this decorating touch:

1. Prepare and paint the wall in the color desired.

2. When the paint is dry, dab the wall with a sponge that has been dipped in paint. Applying small amounts of paint controls the design and prevents the buildup of paint. Use a slightly lighter or darker color to provide contrast.

Textured Paints

There are also **textured paints** available that give a wall a rough, plastered look. They are thicker than most paints and are good for hiding minor defects in a wall. Various patterns can be produced by using a brush, roller, sponge, or other applicator.

PAINTING DOORS AND WINDOWS

Doors and windows are usually painted after the walls are painted. If painting them before the walls, be certain no paint is splashed on them. Since they are subject to heavy use, they are usually painted with a semigloss or high-gloss enamel if a color is wanted. They can also be stained and finished with a transparent coating.

Painting Windows

The parts of a double-hung window are shown in **9–22**. When painting double-hung windows, follow these steps:

1. Mask the glass with masking tape. This step is not absolutely necessary, but it is possible to paint near the glass with more freedom if this is done. If the glass is not masked, wipe any excess paint off with a cloth before it dries on the window. Dried paint can be removed with a single-edge razor blade.

2. Lower the top sash an inch or so and paint the exposed surface (**9–23**).

3. Now raise the lower sash almost to the top of the frame (**9–24**). Lower the upper sash almost to the sill. Paint the entire upper sash, including the top edge of the top rail. Paint the rest of the lowered upper sash.

Paint the components of a window in the following order: 1, horizontal muntins; 2, vertical muntins; 3, top and bottom rails; and 4, stiles.

Move the sash occasionally to prevent it from sticking. Let the paint dry before painting the casing and sill.

4. Now that the paint on the sash is dry, paint the top casing, side casing, sill, and apron, in that order (**9–22**). If the window has wood parting

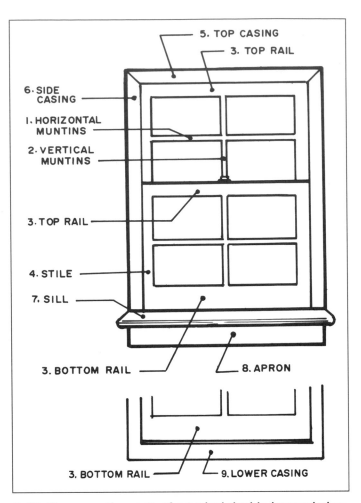

9–22. These are the parts of a typical double-hung window. Newer installations do not have the sill or apron, but run a piece of casing below the window frame.

strips, paint them. Again move the sash as the paint begins to dry, so it does not stick together (**9–25**). Never paint the aluminum channels. After all is dry, rub some paraffin on the channels to lubricate the slides.

Painting Doors

To paint a door, first remove as much hardware as is practical or cover it with masking tape. Do not forget to protect the hinges. It is uncraftsmanlike to slop paint on handles, locks, and hinges. Some prefer to remove the door from the wall and lay it across padded sawhorses for easy painting. Doors are usually painted with a semi- or high-gloss enamel.

Paint an interior panel door in the following order:

1. Paint the molding and then the panel (compo-

9–23. When painting windows, be careful you do not let them stick as the paint dries. Begin by pulling the upper sash down an inch or so and paint as much of the exposed surface as possible.

9–24. Next raise the lower sash and slide the upper sash down. Paint the entire upper sash and finish painting the lower sash. Slide the sash occasionally to prevent it from sticking.

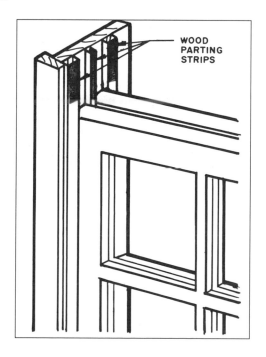

9–25. If the windows have wood parting strips, paint them after the sash has dried. Begin by lowering both sash and painting the strips on the upper sash. When the strips are dry, raise the sash and paint the strips on the lower sash. Keep paint off the sides and inside the track. Rub paraffin or wax on the slides.

Painting Doors and Windows ■ **357**

nents 1, 2, 3, and 4 as shown in **9–26**). Repeat this for each panel. Do not let the paint overlap on the face of the rails. If it does, wipe it off. Start at the top of the panel and paint vertically to the bottom.

2. Paint the top, lock, and bottom rails (components 5, 6, and 7 as shown in **9–26**).

3. Paint the stiles (components 8 and 9 as shown in **9–26**), beginning at the top of the door and painting to the bottom.

4. Paint the edge of the door that faces into the room when the door is open the same color as the door. This is designated by the number 10 in **9–26**.

If the door is new, prime the top and bottom edges to seal out moisture. If it is being repainted, do not paint them.

If a door has glass panes, paint them as follows (**9–27**):

1. Mask the glass to protect it from the paint.

2. Paint the horizontal muntins.

3. Paint the vertical muntins.

4. Paint the rest of the door as previously described.

When painting flush doors, work quickly. Paint from a dry surface into the just-painted wet surface. Following is a suggested plan (**9–28**):

1. Paint the edge of the door that faces into the room when the door is open.

2. Begin in an upper corner and lay on vertical strokes about one-third to halfway across the door and one-fourth the way down the length.

3. Then stroke this area horizontally without putting more paint on the brush.

4. Repeat this until you have painted across the top of the door.

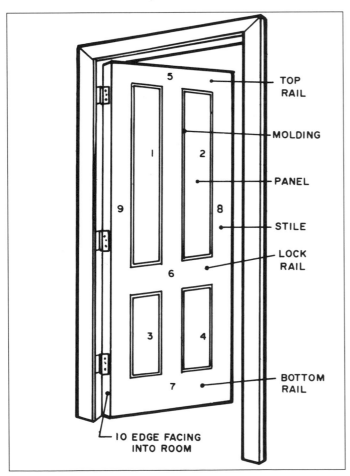

9–26. Paint panel doors in a logical order by completing the panels first and then finishing up on the rails and stiles. Start at the top and work toward the bottom of the door.

9–27. If the door has glass panes, paint the horizontal muntins first and then the vertical muntins.

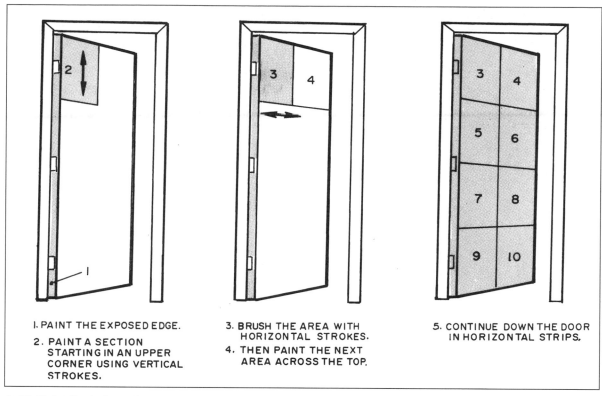

1. PAINT THE EXPOSED EDGE.

2. PAINT A SECTION STARTING IN AN UPPER CORNER USING VERTICAL STROKES.

3. BRUSH THE AREA WITH HORIZONTAL STROKES.

4. THEN PAINT THE NEXT AREA ACROSS THE TOP.

5. CONTINUE DOWN THE DOOR IN HORIZONTAL STRIPS.

9–28. Paint flush doors in horizontal strips. Paint in sections so the paint will be smooth and uniform in thickness before moving on across the door. Paint from a dry surface into the previously painted wet surface.

5. Drop down and paint another strip across the door. Repeat until the entire door has been painted.

FINISHING WOODWORK

If the woodwork is to be painted, follow these steps:

1. Apply a proper primer to new wood.

2. Set the nails and fill the holes. Sand any rough spots.

3. Remove any gloss on painted woodwork. Sand it with a medium-grit sandpaper to help the new topcoat adhere. An alternative is to rub the woodwork with liquid sandpaper. Liquid sandpaper is a clear liquid that cleans and prepares the old finish to receive the top coat of paint.

4. Repair any cracks or defects.

5. Protect the wall and floor from paint using masking tape or a metal or plastic paint shield.

6. Apply the paint to the trim with a 2-inch (51- millimeter) brush. Begin in one corner and work toward the next corner. Do not stop until the corner is reached, to avoid an overlap that will show when the job is finished (**9–29**, on the next page).

If the woodwork is to be stained or given a natural finish, begin by lightly sanding it. A sealer should be applied to softwoods such as pine before the stain is applied to prevent the stain from becoming too dark. The sealer can be omitted if a dark finish is preferred. Experiment on scrap wood to get the color desired. After the initial sealer is applied, stain the wood and then apply a second coat of sealer. Fill nail holes with a filler the color of the stain.

Open-grained woods such as oak are stained first and then filled with a paste wood filler. Then a primer is applied. On most clear finishes, a diluted coat of the topcoat material serves as a primer. Read the directions on the label for proportions. Fill nail holes with a filler to match the stain. The stain may be applied after the filler to minimize the appearance of the grain. Finally, apply a topcoat such as varnish.

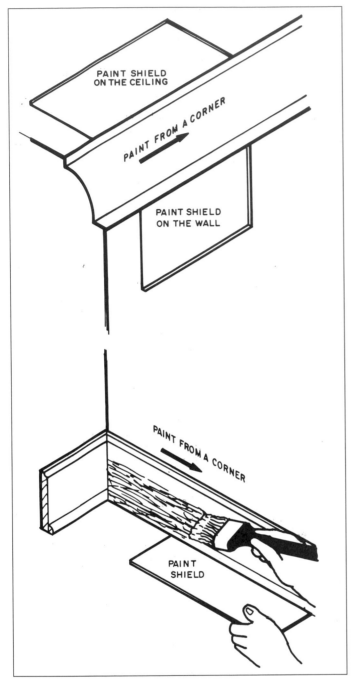

9–29. When painting baseboard or moldings, begin in a corner and paint to the next corner. Never leave a section only partially painted.

Close-grained woods such as birch can be stained and primed. Then the nail holes are filled and a topcoat is applied.

In all cases, be certain to allow each coat to dry thoroughly. The drying time will vary with the material, temperature, and humidity. Usually 24 hours is adequate.

CHAPTER TEN

Wall-Covering Materials and Techniques

The term **wall covering** is used to describe flexible wall decorations prepared and sold in roll form. The one most commonly used is **wallpaper**, which is a paper-based wall covering. There are many types of wall coverings available. Paint and wall-covering stores can show samples of many of these.

Fabric wall coverings include suede and other fabrics that are applied to a wall that has a covering of plastic applied to it to stick the fabric to the wall. Since fabrics stretch easily, they are difficult to apply.

Flocked wall coverings are made from very fine cotton, rayon, nylon, or silk fibers. They are applied to paper, cotton, linen, or vinyl backing that is coated with a slow-drying paint. This produces a soft, raised, velvety surface.

Liner paper is blank paper applied over walls that may be a bit too rough for the direct application of the wall covering. Liner paper is installed with the seams horizontal, while the wall covering is applied with the seams vertical.

Metallic and foil wall coverings are shiny and reflect light. They can also produce a bothersome glare if used in the wrong place. Foil wall covering consists of a thin sheet of aluminum foil laminated onto a paper or scrim (lightweight cloth) backing.

Natural materials are used to produce an array of textured, natural-colored wall materials. **Cork** is cut into a thin veneer that is laminated to a backing material. **Grass cloth** is made from the arrowroot vine. It is woven on looms with cotton threads, producing a product called **netting**. This is laminated to a paper backing and can be dyed, producing a range of colors. **Hemp** wall covering is made from the fibers of the hemp plant. It is woven much like grass cloth but has a finer weave. **Reed cloth** is made by inserting reeds into a cotton warp on a loom. Typically, the actual color and variance in the size of the reeds remain. **Rush cloth** is woven like grass cloth, but uses rush plant fibers that are woven in a cotton warp.

Photomural wall coverings have a paper backing onto which enlarged photos are laminated. They are usually supplied as quarter panels that are carefully aligned when mounted on the wall.

Standard paper (also called **wallpaper**) has a paper backing upon which the decorative design is printed. Some types have a very thin vinyl coating. Standard paper is not resistant to moisture. A light swipe with a damp cloth is all right, but it should not be scrubbed or heavily wetted. Standard paper is inexpensive and easy to hang, but will tear and wrinkle if not handled carefully.

Vinyl wall coverings include commercial vinyl, raised vinyl, and solid-sheet vinyl. **Commercial vinyl** is available in three weights: Type 1, Type 2, and Type 3. Type 1 is the lightest and probably the best for residential applications. **Raised vinyl** has a raised appearance created by heat-embossing a vinyl to a paper backing. **Solid-sheet vinyl** has a solid vinyl decorative surface laminated to a paper backing.

Vinyl wall coverings are good for use in areas where a durable, washable covering is needed, such as in a bath, kitchen, or hall.

Borders are narrow decorative strips used to provide accent around doors and windows, at the ceiling, and as chair rails. They are installed after the wall covering is in place.

TOOLS

The proper tools are needed to do a satisfactory job of hanging wall-covering material. Unless prepasted paper is being used, a pasting table is needed. Also needed are the following (**10–1**):

1. A piece of plywood

2. A 2 x 6-foot (610 x 1830-millimeter) stepladder

3. Sharp scissors

4. Long, metal straightedge

5. Seam roller

6. Razor-blade knife and extra blades

7. Paste bucket and either a water bucket or a water tray for prepasted paper

8. Chalk line and plumb bob

9. Paste brush

10. Pad applicator or paint roller

11. Smoothing brush for sweeping the paper to the wall

12. Drop cloth

13. Putty knife

WALL PREPARATION

Regardless of the type of wall covering being used, success is determined to a large degree by how well the walls are prepared to receive the material. Some wall coverings hide minor imperfections, while others, such as foil, clearly show them.

Following are suggestions for preparing the walls to receive the new wall covering:

1. Fill all cracks, repair any loose spots, and sand any rough spots smooth (review Chapter 8).

2. Prime any repairs with latex primer or a special primer supplied by the wall-covering dealer.

3. If the wall has been previously papered, it is best to remove the old paper. Papering over old paper presents many problems.

4. After removing the old wall covering, clean the wall as instructed by the manufacturer of the stripping material being used.

5. Coat the prepared wall with a wall-coating primer-sealer. An acrylic (latex) or alkyd primer-sealer is typically used.

6. If the wall is new plaster or gypsum wallboard, seal it with a coat of latex primer or a primer recommended by the wall-covering dealer.

7. If the wall is a bit rough, consider applying a layer of liner paper.

8. Some recommend that a coat of sizing be applied to the wall and allowed to dry. **Sizing** is a product that helps the wall covering adhere to the wall. It is applied with a paint roller. Check with the dealer to see if it is necessary that the recommended primer-sealer be used.

9. A wall painted with an oil-based paint or enamel must be lightly sanded with a medium-grit sandpaper or dulled with a deglosser available from the wall-covering dealer. Then cover the wall with a primer-sealer made especially for wall covering that is hung over glossy surfaces.

10. Paint all trim and the ceiling before hanging the wall covering.

REMOVING OLD WALL COVERINGS

First be certain you know the type of wall material behind the old wall covering. It will generally be gypsum drywall, but if the house is very old it could be plaster. Remember, drywall has a paper layer over a gypsum core and too much moisture can result in severe damage. Hopefully, the wall was sealed with a proper primer-sealer before the old covering was installed. This helps protect the wallboard as the old wall covering is being removed.

Some wall coverings are "strippable," which means they can be peeled off the wall without the use of chemical removers. Those that are not strippable require the use of a chemical remover or heat and moisture.

TOOLS YOU WILL NEED

IN ADDITION TO A PASTING TABLE, LADDER, AND DROP CLOTH, THE ESSENTIAL TOOLS MAY BE PURCHASED SEPARATELY OR ARE AVAILABLE IN KIT FORM. THE ACTUAL TOOLS ARE FEW AND QUITE SIMPLE. THE RAZOR KNIFE–AND LOTS OF NEW, SHARP BLADES THAT ARE CHANGED OFTEN–IS YOUR MOST IMPORTANT TOOL, FOLLOWED BY A WIDE PUTTY KNIFE USED IN CONJUNCTION WITH THE RAZOR KNIFE FOR TRIMMING.

ANOTHER TOOL IS A PASTING BRUSH (USUALLY 6") OR PAINT ROLLER. IF NOT USING PREPASTED WALLPAPER, ADD TWO BUCKETS — ONE FOR THE PASTE AND ONE FOR CLEAR WATER FOR WASHING DOWN THE WALL COVERING. IF PREPASTED WALLCOVERING IS USED, ONLY A WATER TRAY WILL BE NEEDED.

A YARDSTICK, PREFERABLY METAL, IS INVALUABLE FOR MEASURING AND CUTTING. TO INSURE STRAIGHT WALL-COVERING INSTALLATION, YOU'LL NEED A CHALK LINE AND PLUMB. A SMOOTHING BRUSH MEASURING AT LEAST 12" WIDE SHOULD HAVE FIRM BUT SOFT BRISTLES TO REMOVE AIR BUBBLES AND WRINKLES. THE SEAM ROLLER WILL MAKE IT FEASIBLE TO SET TIGHT JOINTS AT SEAMS AND AT THE EDGES OF THE WALL COVERING.

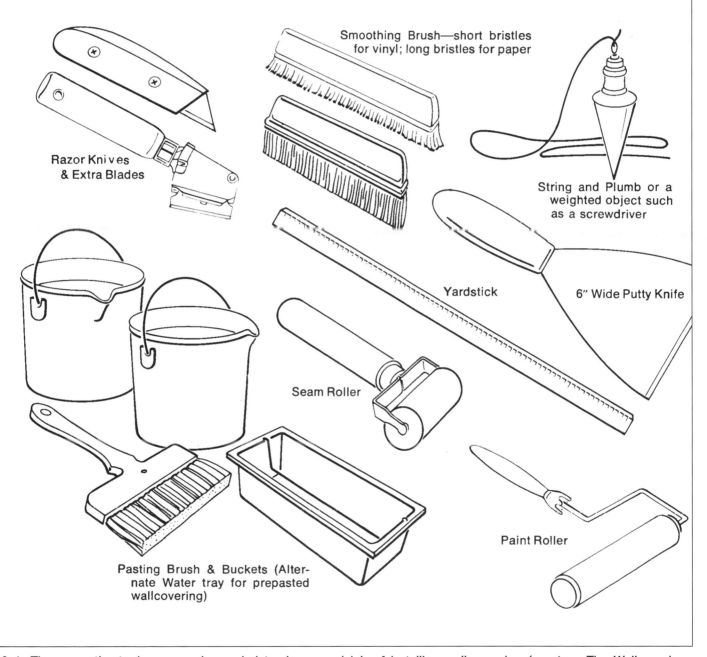

Razor Knives & Extra Blades

Smoothing Brush—short bristles for vinyl; long bristles for paper

String and Plumb or a weighted object such as a screwdriver

Yardstick

6" Wide Putty Knife

Seam Roller

Pasting Brush & Buckets (Alternate Water tray for prepasted wallcovering)

Paint Roller

10–1. These are the tools commonly needed to do a good job of installing wall covering (courtesy The Wallcoverings Association).

First try to **dry-strip** the covering. Fabric-backed and vinyl wall coverings will often strip off dry. Lift a corner of the covering and pull it on a slight angle from the wall. Often it will peel right off. It may leave a little paper behind, but if it is tight and smooth this can serve as a liner. Some wall coverings are more likely to strip off dry than others, so it is necessary to try dry-stripping first.

If dry-stripping does not work, buy wall-covering remover from a dealer. Mix the remover solution with warm water as directed on the container. Then wet one section with a brush, sponge, roller, or sprayer. Let it soak in as directed (usually 10 minutes) and then scrape off the wall covering with a wide-blade finishing knife or a stripping tool (**10–2**). Do not cut into the surface of the drywall or plaster. If the moisture does not penetrate the old wall covering, cut a series of scratches through it with a wall-covering perforating tool or a knife (**10–3**). The use of chemical removers will put water on the floor, so put down a drop cloth. Wear rubber gloves and, if necessary, eye protection.

Another type of wall-covering removal material is a gel compound that is brushed or rolled on the wall. It does not drip or run and will soften the paste

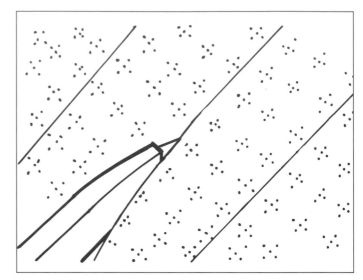

10–3. If the surface of the wall covering will not allow the chemical remover or steam to get to the adhesive, score the surface with a utility knife. Do not cut into the surface of the wall material. Just break the surface of the wall covering.

in about 20 minutes. Again, work in sections rather than doing the entire wall at one time.

Another method is to use an electric steamer (**10–4**). It heats water electrically and pumps steam to a pad that is held against the wall covering. Steamers can be rented at the local paint and wall-covering dealer.

It is also possible to use an electric heat gun. Wet the old covering with water and direct the heat from the gun on it. As it heats the water, the paste softens and the paper can be pulled or scraped from the wall (**10-5**).

Some home owners prefer to remove old wall coverings from plaster walls by dry-scraping them with a special scraper that can be bought at a wall-covering dealer. It will scrape away several layers of old paper. Wipe off any residue with an abrasive pad or nylon scrubber and warm water. When the wall is dry, apply the proper primer-sealer.

After the old covering has been removed, carefully scrape off any adhesive remaining. Do not gouge into the wall or a repair will have to be made. Then wipe down the wall with a mild household cleaner. Finally, rinse the wall several times with clear water to remove all of the cleaner (**10-6**).

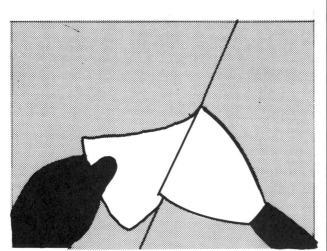

1. FIRST WET AN AREA SEVERAL FEET SQUARE WITH A LIQUID WALL-COVERING REMOVER.
2. LET IT SOAK. NOW PEEL THE COVERING OFF THE WALL. ADD MORE REMOVER TO SPOTS THAT ARE STILL STUCK.

10–2. Wet the wall covering with the remover and let the remover soak in for about 10 minutes. Then, starting at one edge, peel the covering off the wall. Be careful to not gouge the surface of the wall.

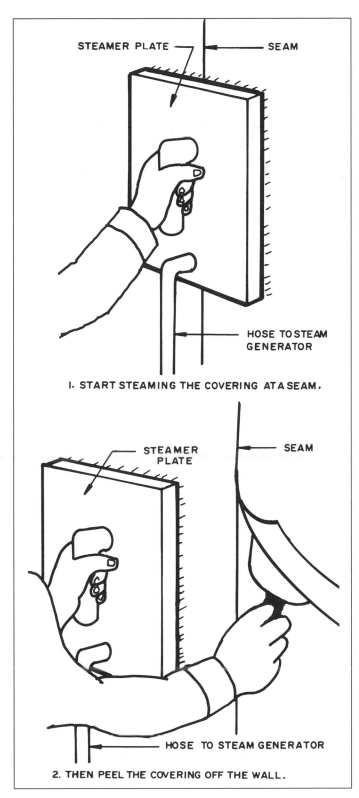

1. START STEAMING THE COVERING AT A SEAM.

2. THEN PEEL THE COVERING OFF THE WALL.

10–4. The electric steamer generates steam in a steam generator. The steam moves through the hose to the steamer plate that is held against the wall. The steam loosens the adhesive. Start at a seam and scrape off the covering. Move the steamer plate as needed and work small areas.

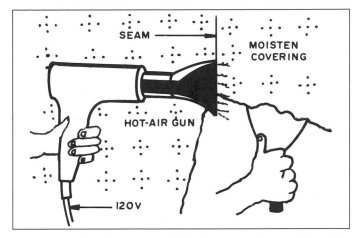

10–5. If an electric heat gun is being used, first moisten the covering with water. Then heat the area to loosen the covering. Scrape it off, starting at a seam.

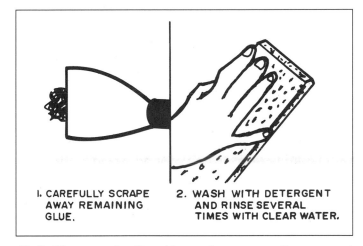

1. CAREFULLY SCRAPE AWAY REMAINING GLUE.

2. WASH WITH DETERGENT AND RINSE SEVERAL TIMES WITH CLEAR WATER.

10–6. After removing the old covering, go over the area and carefully scrape off any remaining adhesive. Then wash the wall with a mild detergent and rinse it thoroughly.

ADHESIVES

To hang some wall coverings, an adhesive is applied to the back of the material with a brush. It is important to use the correct adhesive. Other wall coverings are prepasted and need to be dipped in water to activate the paste.

Several types of adhesives can be used on wall coverings. **Starch-based adhesives** are made from natural products such as wheat and corn. They give good adhesion to paper- and cloth-backed wall coverings.

Cellulose adhesives are made from natural elements of plants such as cotton and wood pulp. They tend to stain less and make it easy to remove the old wall covering.

Paste is made from starches and dextrin. It has good bonding power.

Vinyl adhesives contain an acrylic resin that will bond almost any material. They are used to bond vinyl wall coverings over old vinyl wall coverings.

Clear premixed adhesives are a wheat paste that has been cooked with steam. They have good bonding qualities. They are not used if the wall covering is applied over oil-based paint or primer-sealer.

Using Prepasted Water-Remoistenable Adhesive

This adhesive is applied to the back of the wall covering as it is manufactured. The paste is activated by immersing the strip of wall covering in water for about 10 seconds. A special wall-covering water tray is available. Slowly pull the wall covering out of the water and fold it. Since it will expand after it is wet, wait about 5 to 10 minutes before installing it to insure that it has completely expanded.

ESTIMATING THE AMOUNT OF WALL COVERING NEEDED

It is important to buy enough wall-covering material to do the job so all the material will be from the same printing. Just in case there may not be enough material, record the dye lot number, pattern number, and name of the collection so you can try to get more wall covering from the same printing.

It might be best to figure the total area of the walls and ceiling and let the wall-covering dealer figure the number of rolls and amount of adhesive needed. To find the square feet of the ceiling, multiply the length by the width of the room in feet. Round out the measurements to the next highest foot; for example, if the ceiling is 12'-6", use 13'-0".

To find the square feet of the wall area, make a diagram of each wall showing the windows, doors, fireplace, built-in cabinets, and other things taking up wall space (**10–7**). Measure the wall height from the top of the baseboard to the ceiling or ceiling molding. Multiply the height by the length of each wall and subtract the area of windows, doors, fireplace, cabinets, and other items covering the wall. Take

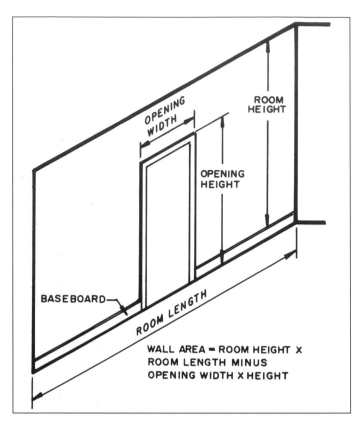

10–7. The wall area is found by multiplying the height by the length and subtracting the area of doors, windows, and other objects taking up wall space.

these drawings and figures to a wall-covering dealer, who will calculate the amount of materials needed.

Wall coverings are sold in single-, double-, and triple-roll bolts. Most rolls are 27 inches (686 millimeters) wide, although wider rolls are available. While the widths of the rolls vary, a single roll contains 36 square feet (3.3 meters²). Check with the wall-covering dealer to see if any rolls left over can be returned.

PLANS FOR HANGING WALL COVERING

Study the room and decide where to start the first strip and where the possible pattern mismatch will occur. It is inevitable that one seam at the end will not permit the pattern to match. This should occur at the most inconspicuous place possible, such as in a corner or behind a door. If the room has a fireplace or built-in cabinets, it is possible to begin on one side and end on the other side so no mismatch will occur.

A good place to start is often in a corner or along-side a window or door. Determine if it is possible to plan the seams to avoid large amounts of waste. In **10–8,** notice that on one example the seam falls at the center of the door, producing considerable waste. Planning to move the seam over reduces the amount of waste.

PATTERN-MATCHING

Unroll two rolls of wall covering to check the pattern-matching. The three common kinds of pattern are straight across, drop, and random (**10–9**). The matching to be done will determine how the rolls are cut and hung. Check the wrapping of random

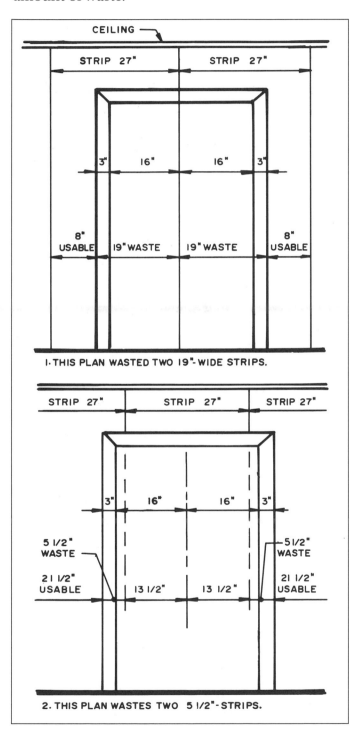

10–8. You can sometimes reduce the waste by carefully planning as to where your seams will fall.

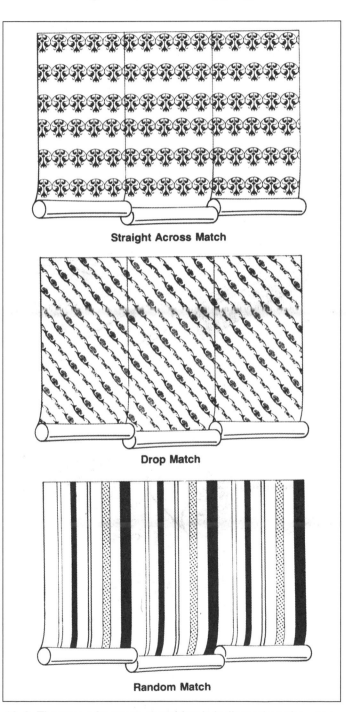

10–9. The type of pattern-matching is indicated on the wrapping of the roll of wall covering. Notice the three types that will probably be used (courtesy the Wallcoverings Association).

pattern and non-pattern wall covering to see if it is marked "reverse" or "nonreverse." If it is marked "reverse," the direction of each strip that is hung has to be alternated. When cutting strips from the roll, be certain to mark which end is the top on each strip.

ESTABLISHING PLUMB

The first strip is frequently hung along the casing of a door or window. From the casing measure ½ inch (13 millimeters) less than the width of the roll. Measure this width on the wall near the ceiling, and drive a tack to hold a plumb line. Drop the plumb line almost to the floor and chalk it. When the plumb

Plumb Line

10–10. Mark where the first strip of wall covering ends at the ceiling and drive a tack in the wall. Tie the plumb line to this and lower it to the floor. When it stops swinging, mark it above the baseboard. Rub the string with chalk and hold the string tight on the bottom mark. Pull the string out a little and let it snap against the wall. The chalk will mark the plumb line to be used to line up the first strip (courtesy the Wallcoverings Association).

Measuring

10–11. Once a decision has been made as to where the pattern will break at the ceiling, cut the strip to length, allowing 2 inches on each end. Place it against the wall to check it before applying the adhesive (courtesy the Wallcoverings Association).

bob becomes still, press the line against the wall at the base with one hand. With the other hand, snap the line to leave a straight, vertical chalk mark on the wall (**10–10**). This mark will be where the first strip of wall cover is aligned. If you chose to mark the line with a few marks down the chalk line, use a pencil instead of the chalk line. Mark lightly. Do not use ink because it may show through the wall covering.

MEASURING AND CUTTING THE WALL COVERING

Check the pattern and decide where it will break at the ceiling. Hold the roll of material against the wall and move it up and down until the best position for the pattern is found. Since some ceilings are uneven, the plumb line may have to be slanted to get an even pattern break.

When the position for the wall covering has been found, put a pencil mark where it breaks at the ceiling and the floor and add 2 inches (51 millimeters) to each end to allow room for adjustments. Mark the top with a "T" and cut it from the roll. Position the strip against the wall once again to check its length (**10–11**).

Cut and paste only one strip at a time. Doing so will avoid confusion and the possibility of wasting a strip. Keep good track of which end is the top on reversible coverings. After cutting each strip, immediately mark the roll next to the cut with a "T" or "B" to identify the top or bottom of the next strip. If the pattern is a drop match, each strip will have to be rechecked for match and length, including the 2 inches on each end.

Since the strips will be butted at the seam, it is very important that the wall covering be accurately trimmed. If the covering does not come from the manufacturer pretrimmed, ask the dealer to trim it.

PASTING WALL COVERING

Read and follow the directions on the package for mixing the paste or other adhesive. Place a strip facedown on a clean pasting table. Apply the paste with a roller or brush, working from the center out to the edges (**10–12**).

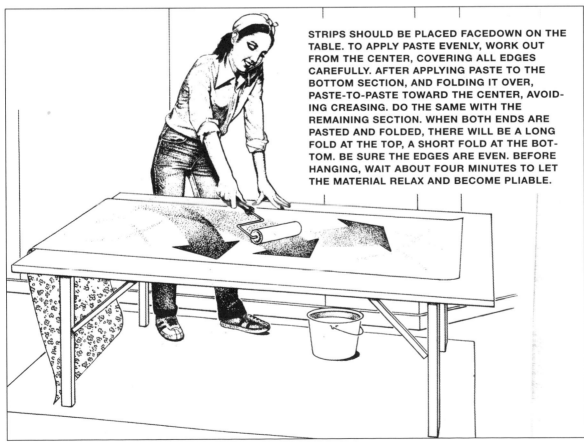

STRIPS SHOULD BE PLACED FACEDOWN ON THE TABLE. TO APPLY PASTE EVENLY, WORK OUT FROM THE CENTER, COVERING ALL EDGES CAREFULLY. AFTER APPLYING PASTE TO THE BOTTOM SECTION, AND FOLDING IT OVER, PASTE-TO-PASTE TOWARD THE CENTER, AVOIDING CREASING. DO THE SAME WITH THE REMAINING SECTION. WHEN BOTH ENDS ARE PASTED AND FOLDED, THERE WILL BE A LONG FOLD AT THE TOP, A SHORT FOLD AT THE BOTTOM. BE SURE THE EDGES ARE EVEN. BEFORE HANGING, WAIT ABOUT FOUR MINUTES TO LET THE MATERIAL RELAX AND BECOME PLIABLE.

10–12. Place the strip pattern side down on a clean flat surface and apply the adhesive, working from the center out over the edges (courtesy the Wallcovering Information Bureau).

Be certain the paste is evenly applied with no spots missed and is free from lumps and heavy streaks. Apply paste to about two-thirds of the strip and fold it over, paste to paste. Then apply paste to the rest of the strip and fold it over (**10-13**). This is called **booking**. Always apply the paste from the center of the strip off the edges. Never work in from the edge. After the strip is booked, let it sit around five minutes or so to allow the covering to expand and the paste to soak into the backing material.

USING PREPASTED COVERINGS

Cut the strips 4 inches (102 millimeters) longer than the height of the wall. Always review the manufacturer's instructions that come with the covering.

One way to handle prepasted covering is to place the water tray on some towels next to the wall. Reroll the strip loosely from the bottom end to the top with the pattern side in, pasted side out. Submerge the strip for the time indicated by the manufacturer. This is usually 15 to 30 seconds. If it is left in too long, some of the adhesive will be washed away. Now lift the strip from the water and raise the top edge to the ceiling (**10–14**). The manufacturer's directions may require you to hold it for a minute or so to allow the covering to expand. Then apply the strip to the wall as explained for wall covering using applied adhesive.

HANGING THE STRIPS

Lift the pasted (or wetted) strip to the wall with the top side to the ceiling. Allow about 2 inches (51 millimeters) to overlap on the ceiling. Align the vertical edge with the plumb line (**10–15**).

Use the smoothing brush to press the strip to the wall. Work from the center to the edges to get out all the air bubbles. Work the strip from top to bottom (**10–16,** on page 372). If there are bubbles that cannot be brushed out, lift the strip away from the wall, beginning at the bottom. Then repress the strip to the wall with the brush. The paste is slow-drying, so each strip can be moved and repositioned as needed.

After the strip is hung in position and all air bub-

Text continues on page 373

1. APPLY PASTE TO TWO-THIRDS OF THE STRIP AND FOLD OVER PASTE TO PASTE.

2. APPLY PASTE TO THE REMAINING STRIP.

3. FOLD THE END OF THE STRIP PASTE TO PASTE.

4. ROLL THE FOLDED BOOKED STRIP LOOSELY. ALLOW THREE TO FIVE MINUTES FOR THE ROLLED STRIP TO RELAX BEFORE HANGING.

10–13. After applying the adhesive, book the strip. This allows the adhesive time to soak into the wall covering. It lets you handle it from the pattern side while hanging it.

PREPASTED STRIP ROLLED FOR IMMERSING IN LUKEWARM WATER.

TOP EDGE TO THE CEILING

PATTERN ON THE INSIDE

PASTED SIDE

BOTTOM END

PLACE THE WATER TRAY ON THE FLOOR BY THE WALL. AFTER SUBMERGING THE ROLL THE REQUIRED TIME, SLOWLY LIFT THE TOP EDGE TO THE CEILING.

WATER TRAY

10–14. *Wet the prepasted wall covering in a water tray, raise it to the ceiling, and apply it to the wall.*

UNFOLD TOP SECTION AND PLACE IT ON THE WALL, WITH A 2" OVERLAP OVER THE CEILING JOINT. LINE UP THE EDGE WITH A PLUMB LINE. HOLDING UPPER SECTION OF STRIP TO THE WALL, GENTLY SMOOTH IT WITH A BRUSH. STROKE DOWNWARD WITH THE SMOOTHING BRUSH OUTWARD FROM THE CENTER OF THE STRIP. OPEN BOTTOM FOLDING SECTION, SLIDING IT INTO POSITION WITH PALMS OF HANDS. CHECK ALIGNMENT WITH PLUMB LINE. DON'T PANIC IF YOUR FIRST ATTEMPT DOESN'T ALIGN WITH THE PLUMB LINE. WALL-COVERING PASTE DRIES SLOWLY, AND YOU WILL HAVE PLENTY OF TIME TO REMOVE WALL COVERING AND REALIGN IT PROPERLY WITHOUT DAMAGE. IF YOU ARE WORKING WITH A FABRIC-BACKED WALL COVERING AND IT HASN'T ALIGNED PROPERLY, REMOVE THE ENTIRE STRIP AND REHANG. REPASTE IF NECESSARY.

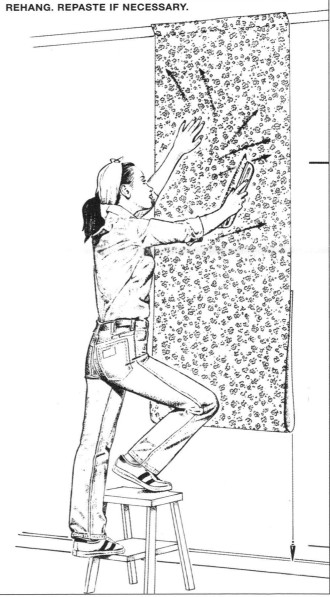

10–15. *Unfold the top, booked section and place it on the wall. Line up the top with the ceiling, allowing the two extra inches to flap over. Line up the edge with the plumb line. Gently smooth it with the brush, stroking outward from the center. Next, unbook the bottom section, sliding it against the plumb line and smoothing it (courtesy the Wallcoverings Association).*

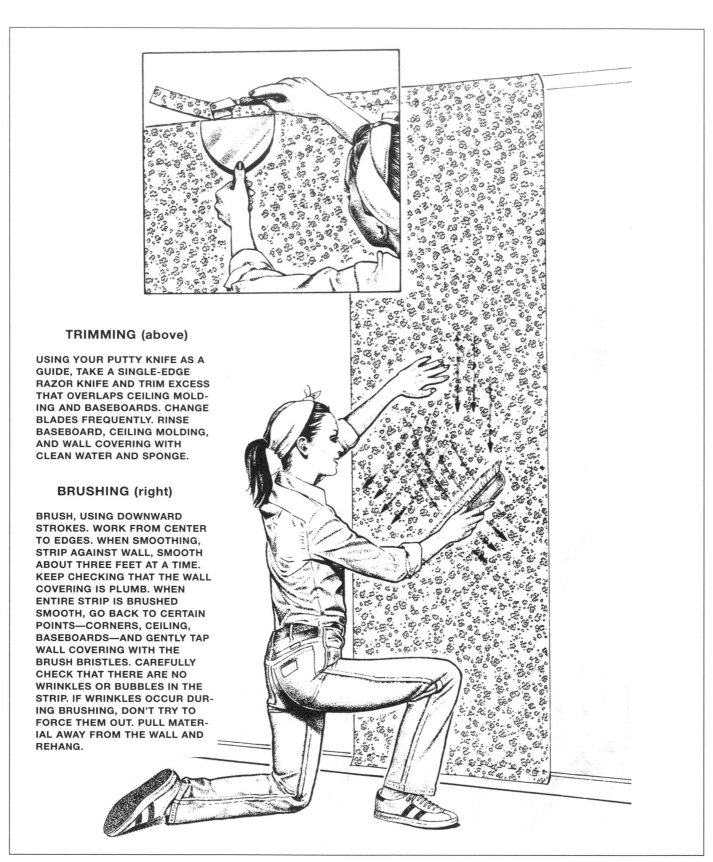

TRIMMING (above)

USING YOUR PUTTY KNIFE AS A GUIDE, TAKE A SINGLE-EDGE RAZOR KNIFE AND TRIM EXCESS THAT OVERLAPS CEILING MOLDING AND BASEBOARDS. CHANGE BLADES FREQUENTLY. RINSE BASEBOARD, CEILING MOLDING, AND WALL COVERING WITH CLEAN WATER AND SPONGE.

BRUSHING (right)

BRUSH, USING DOWNWARD STROKES. WORK FROM CENTER TO EDGES. WHEN SMOOTHING, STRIP AGAINST WALL, SMOOTH ABOUT THREE FEET AT A TIME. KEEP CHECKING THAT THE WALL COVERING IS PLUMB. WHEN ENTIRE STRIP IS BRUSHED SMOOTH, GO BACK TO CERTAIN POINTS—CORNERS, CEILING, BASEBOARDS—AND GENTLY TAP WALL COVERING WITH THE BRUSH BRISTLES. CAREFULLY CHECK THAT THERE ARE NO WRINKLES OR BUBBLES IN THE STRIP. IF WRINKLES OCCUR DURING BRUSHING, DON'T TRY TO FORCE THEM OUT. PULL MATERIAL AWAY FROM THE WALL AND REHANG.

10–16. Keep smoothing the strip, working from the top to the bottom and from the center toward the outer edge (courtesy the Wallcoverings Association).

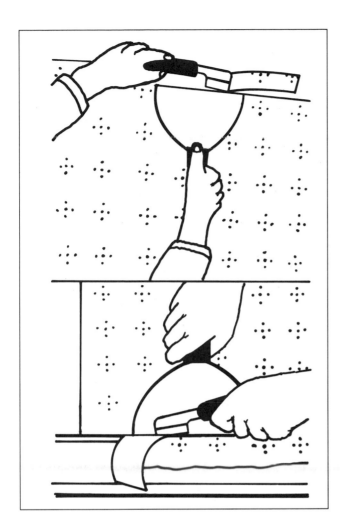

10–17 (left). After the strip is applied to the wall, trim the excess material at the ceiling and the floor.

bles are worked out, trim it at the ceiling and the casing (**10–17**). Use a wide drywall taping knife and a sharp razor knife. Change blades frequently because cutting the wall covering quickly dulls a blade. A dull blade will tear rather than cut wet wall covering. Trim each strip as it is hung.

When a strip meets a door or window casing, let it overhang the casing and cut the corners (**10–18**). Then fit it to the side of the casing and cut it with a wide-blade drywall knife or a razor knife (**10-19,** on the next page).

To cut the corner (**10–18**), cut the covering on a 45-degree miter on each corner. Then press the covering against the wall and cut off the excess.

Use a wet cloth or sponge to wipe off paste that has gotten on the ceiling, casing, or baseboard. Repeat this process with the other strips until the room is complete.

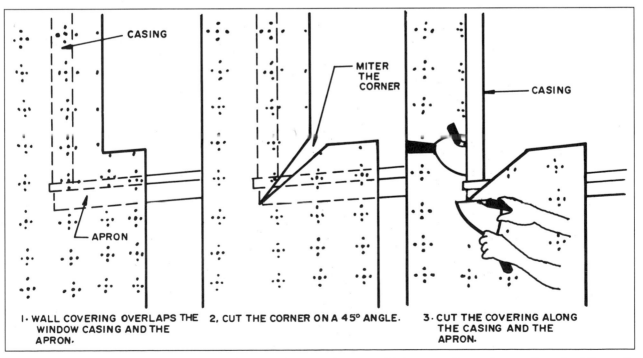

CASING

MITER THE CORNER

CASING

APRON

1· WALL COVERING OVERLAPS THE WINDOW CASING AND THE APRON· 2· CUT THE CORNER ON A 45° ANGLE. 3· CUT THE COVERING ALONG THE CASING AND THE APRON.

10–18. To fit around the corner of the casing, cut the covering on a 45-degree miter and press it against the wall.

Hanging the Strips ■ **373**

10–19 (left). *Press the covering into the corner of the wall and casing and cut it with a wide-blade drywall knife and a razor knife (courtesy the Wallcoverings Association).*

Since the corners of a room may not be plumb, extend the strip around the corner by ½ inch (13 millimeters) (**10–20**). Since the corner may not be plumb, measure the width for the corner strip in three places. Add ½ inch to this measurement to turn the corner. Mark and cut the corner piece.

Notice in **10–21** that the corner strip (A) has been applied and the first strip on the other wall (B) is in place. To position this piece, drop a plumb line to locate the edge and trim the edge in the corner to overlap the ½-inch corner from strip A.

A full strip can be wrapped around outside corners (**10–22**). Brush this strip away from the corner.

When arriving at a switch, outlet, or heat register, remove the cover before applying the paper. Then paper over the opening. After the strip is in place, use a razor knife to cut around the outside of the switch, outlet, or heat-register opening (**10-23**). Avoid electrical shock that can occur by cutting inside the electrical box. If in doubt, throw the circuit breaker or pull the fuse for that circuit for the time needed to cut the opening.

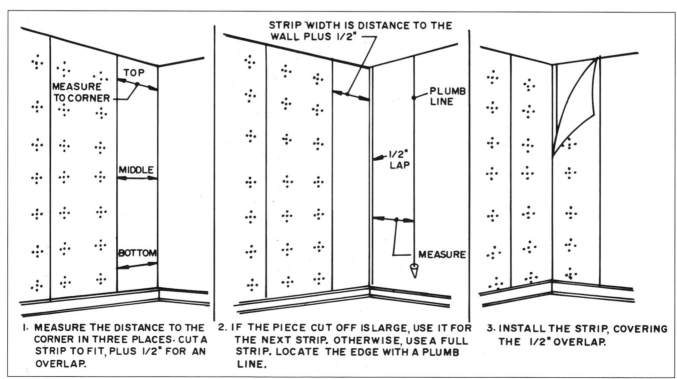

STRIP WIDTH IS DISTANCE TO THE WALL PLUS 1/2"

MEASURE TO CORNER

TOP

MIDDLE

BOTTOM

PLUMB LINE

1/2" LAP

MEASURE

1. MEASURE THE DISTANCE TO THE CORNER IN THREE PLACES. CUT A STRIP TO FIT, PLUS 1/2" FOR AN OVERLAP.

2. IF THE PIECE CUT OFF IS LARGE, USE IT FOR THE NEXT STRIP. OTHERWISE, USE A FULL STRIP. LOCATE THE EDGE WITH A PLUMB LINE.

3. INSTALL THE STRIP, COVERING THE 1/2" OVERLAP.

10–20. *Since the corner may not be plumb, measure and cut the last strip to fit. Add 1/2 inch so it can turn the corner.*

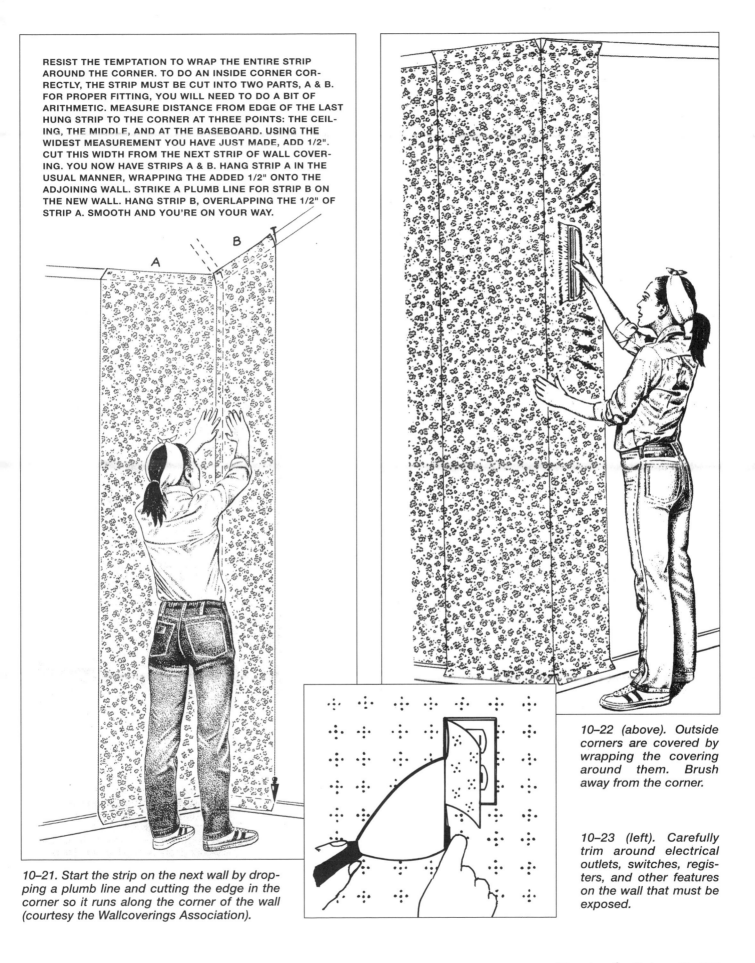

RESIST THE TEMPTATION TO WRAP THE ENTIRE STRIP AROUND THE CORNER. TO DO AN INSIDE CORNER CORRECTLY, THE STRIP MUST BE CUT INTO TWO PARTS, A & B. FOR PROPER FITTING, YOU WILL NEED TO DO A BIT OF ARITHMETIC. MEASURE DISTANCE FROM EDGE OF THE LAST HUNG STRIP TO THE CORNER AT THREE POINTS: THE CEILING, THE MIDDLE, AND AT THE BASEBOARD. USING THE WIDEST MEASUREMENT YOU HAVE JUST MADE, ADD 1/2". CUT THIS WIDTH FROM THE NEXT STRIP OF WALL COVERING. YOU NOW HAVE STRIPS A & B. HANG STRIP A IN THE USUAL MANNER, WRAPPING THE ADDED 1/2" ONTO THE ADJOINING WALL. STRIKE A PLUMB LINE FOR STRIP B ON THE NEW WALL. HANG STRIP B, OVERLAPPING THE 1/2" OF STRIP A. SMOOTH AND YOU'RE ON YOUR WAY.

10–21. Start the strip on the next wall by dropping a plumb line and cutting the edge in the corner so it runs along the corner of the wall (courtesy the Wallcoverings Association).

10–22 (above). Outside corners are covered by wrapping the covering around them. Brush away from the corner.

10–23 (left). Carefully trim around electrical outlets, switches, registers, and other features on the wall that must be exposed.

With a seam roller, roll each seam lightly after it has dried for 15 minutes (**10–24**). Rolling will often cause paste to come out of the seam. Wipe it off with a damp sponge or cloth (**10–25**). Also wipe the roller clean. Paste is easily removed with water before it dries.

COVERING A CEILING

Cover a ceiling before the walls. Use the same pattern as chosen for the walls or choose a white or contrasting solid color. This job requires two people: one to help hold and unfold the strips as they are installed, and one to position and smooth the covering (**10-26**). The job is made easier if a strong scaffold board can be suspended between two ladders. Since short strips are easier to handle, consider running them along the short dimension of the room.

To install the first strip, snap a chalk line in the direction the strips will run at a distance away from the wall that is 1 inch (25 millimeters) less than the width of a roll. The 1 inch will lap over at the corner and be trimmed, leaving a ½-inch overlap on the wall. Cut the pieces 4 inches (102 millimeters) longer so they can be trimmed back, leaving a ½-inch (13-millimeter) overlap on the wall. Apply the wall covering in the same manner as described for walls.

If the ceiling has the same pattern as the walls, use its pattern in the corner to align the wall pattern.

INSTALLING A BORDER

Cut a length of border about 2 inches (51 millimeters) longer than the distance from one wall to the other. Apply adhesive to the back, or, if it is prepasted, immerse the back in water as described for wall coverings. Fold the border paste-to-paste in loose folds. Start in one corner and allow a ½-inch (13-millimeter) overlap on the adjacent wall. Hang the strip, keeping the top edge against the ceiling. When you get to the next wall, let it overlap ½ inch.

Start the next wall by matching the pattern with the overlap at the corner. It can actually lie on top of the ½-inch overlap. Lay a border on the next corner

10–24. After a seam has dried for 15 minutes, roll it lightly with a seam roller. Wipe adhesive off the roller frequently (courtesy the Wallcoverings Association).

10–25. Install the border after the wall has been covered (courtesy the Wallcoverings Association).

UNWANTED BUBBLES
UNWANTED BUBBLES CAN ALSO BE HANDLED. JUST
CUT AN X IN BUBBLE WITH RAZOR AND CAREFULLY
LIFT CUT EDGE. APPLY PASTE TO SURFACE AND TO
WALLCOVERING. PRESS BACK AGAINST SURFACE,
USING SEAM ROLLER TO TIGHTEN INTO PLACE.
REMOVE EXCESS PASTE WITH DAMP SPONGE.

10–26. Install the ceiling strips in the same manner as wall strips. Allow them to overlap 1/2 inch (13 millimeters) on the wall (courtesy the Wallcoverings Association).

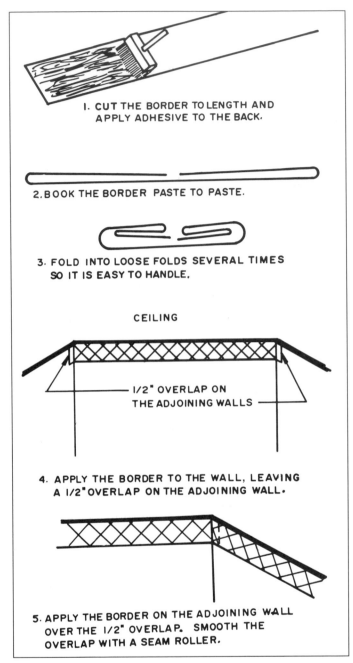

1. CUT THE BORDER TO LENGTH AND APPLY ADHESIVE TO THE BACK.

2. BOOK THE BORDER PASTE TO PASTE.

3. FOLD INTO LOOSE FOLDS SEVERAL TIMES SO IT IS EASY TO HANDLE.

CEILING

1/2" OVERLAP ON THE ADJOINING WALLS

4. APPLY THE BORDER TO THE WALL, LEAVING A 1/2" OVERLAP ON THE ADJOINING WALL.

5. APPLY THE BORDER ON THE ADJOINING WALL OVER THE 1/2" OVERLAP. SMOOTH THE OVERLAP WITH A SEAM ROLLER.

10–27. Install the border after the wall has been covered.

and proceed around the room. Press it against the wall with a wallpaper brush, and use a seam roller at each corner to firm up the overlap (**10–27**).

COVERING SWITCH AND OUTLET PLATES

Plates can be covered with wall covering so they blend into the wall. Fit and cut the piece so the pattern matches that on the wall. Notch as shown in **10–28**. Apply adhesive to the back and wrap the cov-

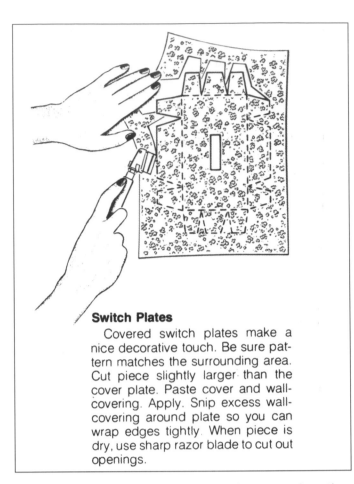

Switch Plates

Covered switch plates make a nice decorative touch. Be sure pattern matches the surrounding area. Cut piece slightly larger than the cover plate. Paste cover and wall-covering. Apply. Snip excess wall-covering around plate so you can wrap edges tightly. When piece is dry, use sharp razor blade to cut out openings.

10–28. Switch and outlet covers can be covered so they blend in with the wall covering (courtesy the Wallcoverings Association).

ering tightly around the cover. Fold the notches onto the back of the plate.

REPAIRING DAMAGED WALL COVERING

When paper or vinyl wall-covering materials become excessively soiled or torn, the damaged area can be replaced. A piece of the original wall covering is needed, so save the larger scraps and any leftover parts of rolls after covering a room. Follow these steps to make the repair (**10–29**):

1. Select a new piece of wall-covering material large enough to cover the damaged area. Match up the pattern.

2. Hold the piece firmly against the damaged area. Use a straightedge and a sharp razor knife to cut through both the patch and the damaged material at the same time. Do not cut into the

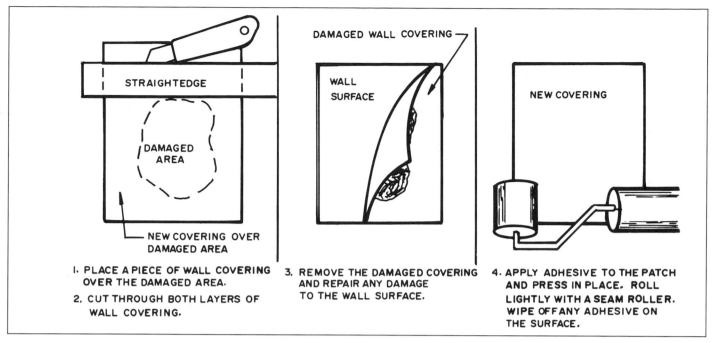

STRAIGHTEDGE

DAMAGED AREA

NEW COVERING OVER DAMAGED AREA

1. PLACE A PIECE OF WALL COVERING OVER THE DAMAGED AREA.

2. CUT THROUGH BOTH LAYERS OF WALL COVERING.

DAMAGED WALL COVERING

WALL SURFACE

3. REMOVE THE DAMAGED COVERING AND REPAIR ANY DAMAGE TO THE WALL SURFACE.

NEW COVERING

4. APPLY ADHESIVE TO THE PATCH AND PRESS IN PLACE. ROLL LIGHTLY WITH A SEAM ROLLER. WIPE OFF ANY ADHESIVE ON THE SURFACE.

10–29. A damaged area can be replaced by cutting through the new piece and the damaged piece at the same time. Remove the damaged covering and glue in the repair patch.

wallboard or plaster surface. Make the cut on all four sides. Be careful the patch does not slip in the process.

3. Remove the damaged material and paste in the patch.

Bubbles can be repaired by cutting an X across them with a sharp razor knife. Apply the adhesive to the back of each piece and press it in place. Carefully wipe off any adhesive that may squeeze out of the cuts (**10–30**).

Loose seams are repaired by carefully lifting the edge and inserting adhesive beneath it. Cover it with a thin layer. Do not use excess adhesive. Press the seam closed and roll it with a seam roller

Dirt can be removed from washable or vinyl wall coverings. Use a mild soap and warm water. A soft rag or sponge is necessary.

Cleaning nonwashable wallpaper is more difficult. Wall-covering dealers will have cleaning dough, or try a soft gum eraser. These will most likely lighten the stain, but seldom completely remove it. If it is bad, cut it out and patch it. If you have some extra pieces of the wall covering, try the cleaning process on them to see if it will damage the surface.

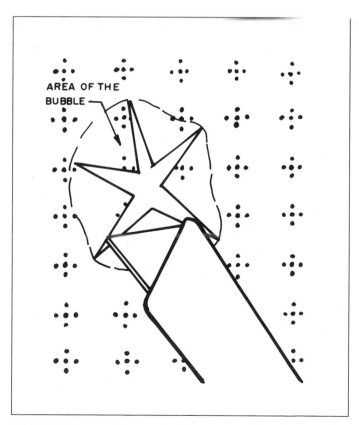

AREA OF THE BUBBLE

10–30. Blisters can be repaired by crosscutting them, applying adhesive to the back of the covering, and carefully pressing the covering in place. Be certain to wash off any adhesive that may have gotten on the surface.

CHAPTER ELEVEN

Ceramic Wall-Tile Repair

Over the years, some maintenance jobs will be necessary to preserve the attractiveness and integrity of a wall covered with ceramic wall tiles.

WALL-TILE ADHESIVES

There are a number of wall-tile adhesives available. Each has certain advantages and disadvantages. Consult your tile dealer for the type it recommends for the specific repair.

There are three groups of wall-tile adhesives: mastics, thinset adhesives, and epoxy thinsets.

Mastics are premixed and easy to use. They do not have the holding power of the other types. They require that the wall surface be very flat.

Thinset adhesives have good bonding and compressive strengths. They are cement-based, so they bond well to cement backer board and mortar beds and can be used in wet and dry areas. There are a variety of types, and your tile dealer should provide advice on which is best. Since they set fast, you have to work more rapidly than if using mastics.

Epoxy thinsets are possibly the strongest adhesives available. They can be used on any wall surface in wet and dry conditions. You have to mix the dry ingredients—the sand and cement—with the liquid epoxy resin and the hardener. The epoxy resin and hardener must be in exact proportions. They also set fast. Setting time is shown on the container.

GROUT

Grout is the material that seals the space between tiles. It must seal out all moisture and bond to the tiles. Grout contains cement or sand, and some types have a coloring material. **Dry grout** is mixed with water and allowed to stand (**slake**) for a short time before it can be used.

Another type of grout is a **premixed latex material**. This grout is very resistant to water and sets up quickly.

SUBSTRATES

A **substrate** is the material applied to the studs to which the tiles are bonded. There is nothing that can be done about the substrate presently used in your house, but it is helpful to know about the various kinds so if replacement is necessary the correct choice is made.

The type of substrate selected will depend basically on whether the tiles are used on a wall that will be exposed to water. If the tiles are on a wall where they will not ever be wet, it's possible regular gypsum wallboard was used. If they are in a wet area, such as a shower, water-resistant gypsum wallboard may have been used. The water-resistant coating is green, and the product is referred to as **green board**. This works well on walls where occasional moisture may occur, but if the wall is exposed regularly to water, such as in a shower, it would be best to use cement board. **Cement board** is a panel product with an aggregated portland cement core reinforced with polymer-coated glass-fiber mesh embedded on both sides. It is also used where fire-resistant walls are required.

REPLACING GROUT

A common problem with ceramic tiles is the loss of grout between tiles. Replace the grout as soon as you notice some damage. Cracked or lost grout allows water to get behind the tiles and loosen them. Regrout tiles by following these steps:

1. Remove all old loose grout from between tiles using a putty knife, an old screwdriver, or a grout saw. Be careful not to chip any of the tiles (**11–1**).

2. Mix enough grout for the job by following the instructions on the package. Grout is sold in small quantities, and there is a difference between wall and floor grout. Be sure to buy the correct kind.

3. Work the mixed grout between the tiles with a putty knife; pack it solid with your fingers (**11–2**).

4. Immediately wipe any excess grout from the wall. Use a damp sponge or cloth.

5. When you are finished, the grout should lie slightly below the surface of the tiles. When the grout has become slightly firm, run the handle

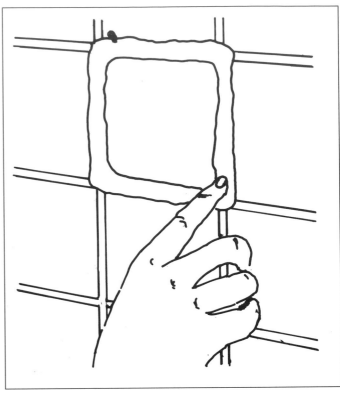

11–2. Fill the opening around the tiles with grout. You can lay it in with a putty knife and then pack it solid with your finger.

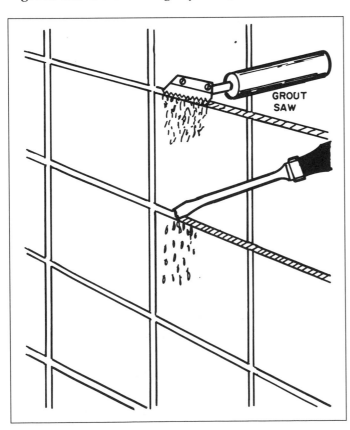

11–1. Carefully remove the damaged grout without dislodging or chipping the tiles.

end of an old toothbrush, a pencil eraser, or plastic spoon over the joints (**11–3**).

6. When the grout has been in place for 15 or 20 minutes, wipe the light haze off the tiles. Use a dry, folded cloth that you keep turning and folding (**11–4**).

7. After the grout has thoroughly hardened (several days), keep it clean by applying a coating of grout sealer. The sealer repels water and dark stains caused by mildew.

Another frequently occurring problem is the loss of grout between a tub or sink and the wall tiles. The best choice here is to remove all the old grout and fill the space with a silicone sealant. Silicone sealants are flexible, waterproof, mildew-resistant, and will stay white. They bond to most materials and are unaffected by heat, cold, moisture, and household chemicals.

Follow these steps to install silicone sealant:

1. Remove all the old grout with a putty knife or screwdriver. Be careful not to damage the wall tiles or the tub or sink.

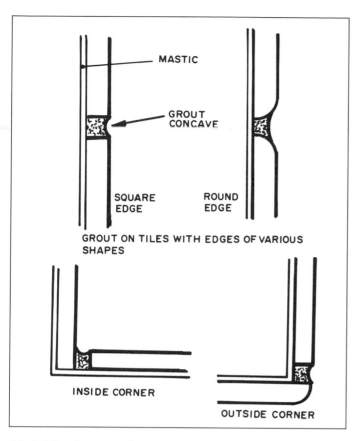

GROUT ON TILES WITH EDGES OF VARIOUS SHAPES

11–3. After the grout firms up a bit, shape it into a slight concave depression.

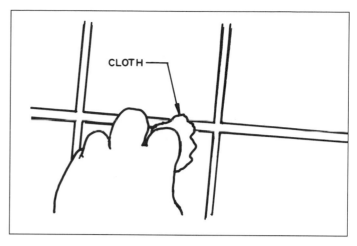

11–4. Wipe off any excess grout from the face of the tile immediately after smoothing the grout joint.

2. Wash away all traces of soap, dirt, or grease. Dry the area thoroughly.

3. Cut the tube nozzle on a slant to give a ³⁄₁₆-inch (5-millimeter) bead.

4. Squeeze the sealant from the tube into the joint. Keep the tube at a 45-degree angle (**11–5**). Push the sealant ahead of the tube, rather than pulling it.

5. If needed, smooth the bead with the tip of a plastic spoon. Do so within five minutes after applying the sealant. Wipe off any excess immediately with a damp cloth.

6. Allow the sealant to cure for 24 hours before using the tub or sink.

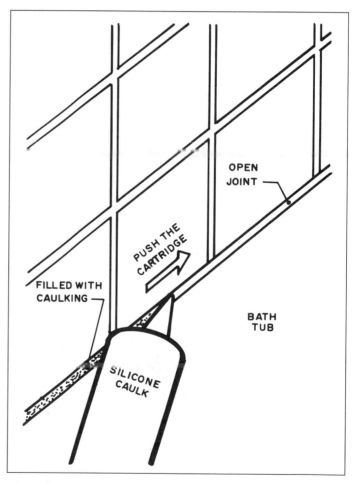

11–5. Seal the opening between the wall tiles and fixtures, such as a bathtub, with a silicone caulk.

REPLACING A SINGLE TILE

If a single tile is damaged or is loose, it must be removed. Clean all old adhesive off the back. Repair any damage to the wall surface. It should be flat and smooth. Old adhesive will have to be removed from it, also.

Use the following procedure to replace a tile:

1. Remove the grout from the joints and, if the tile is loose, pry it off the wall. If the tile has been broken, it may have to be broken up so it can be removed (**11–6**).

2. Repair any damage to the wall substrate. Let the repair material thoroughly dry.

3. Clean the substrate and the edges of the surrounding tile.

4. Apply a thin layer of adhesive to the back of the tile and a coating about ⅛ inch (3 millimeters) thick on the wall. Score it with a corner of the trowel. Keep the adhesive on the tile about ¼ inch (6 millimeters) from the edges.

5. Place the tile against the wall and carefully center it so the grout lines up with the adjacent tiles (**11–7**). Hold it in place with masking tape. Tap it lightly with a rubber mallet.

6. After the adhesive has hardened, dampen the joints with water and apply the grout.

REPAIRING A LARGE DAMAGED AREA

Frequently, moisture will cause many tiles to become loose. Begin by removing the loose tiles. Examine the substrate on the wall. Is it a water-resistant type? If it is regular gypsum wallboard or green board that has failed, you will have to cut it away from the studs and replace it with a cement backer board. Proceed as discussed in Chapter 8 (refer to **8–38**) for making large repairs on gypsum-covered walls. This involves installing a waterproof substrate from stud to stud (**11–8**). It should be screwed to the studs. Leave a ⅛-inch (3-millimeter) space between it and the surrounding substrate to allow for expansion. Then cover the joint with fiberglass tape as recommended by the manufacturer.

If you use cement board, cut it with a carbide blade in a portable circular saw. Wear eye protection.

Following are some suggested steps for repairing a large damaged area:

1. After repairing or replacing the substrate, spread the adhesive on the wall with a notched trowel (**11–9**). Do not place more than you can cover in 15 minutes.

2. Press the new tiles in the top row against the adhesive-covered wall. Line up these tiles with those already on the row so the grout line is straight (**11–10**, on page 386). Tap each tile with a rubber mallet and a rubber block.

11–6. Chip out the damaged tile with a cold chisel. Be careful you do not damage the substrate. Clean off adhesive on the substrate and repair it if it is damaged.

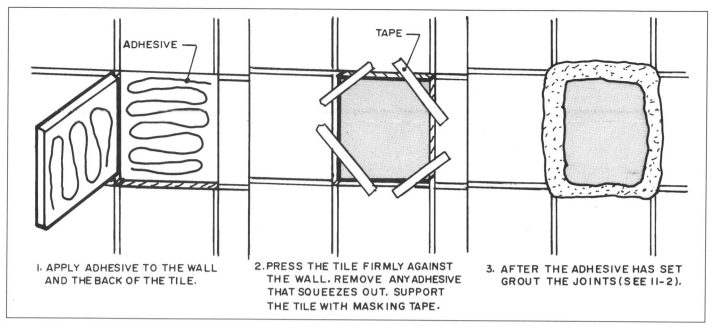

1. APPLY ADHESIVE TO THE WALL AND THE BACK OF THE TILE.

2. PRESS THE TILE FIRMLY AGAINST THE WALL. REMOVE ANY ADHESIVE THAT SQUEEZES OUT. SUPPORT THE TILE WITH MASKING TAPE.

3. AFTER THE ADHESIVE HAS SET GROUT THE JOINTS (SEE 11-2).

11–7. Single loose tiles can be replaced by cleaning the substrate and applying new adhesive to it and the tile. After it hardens, grout as usual.

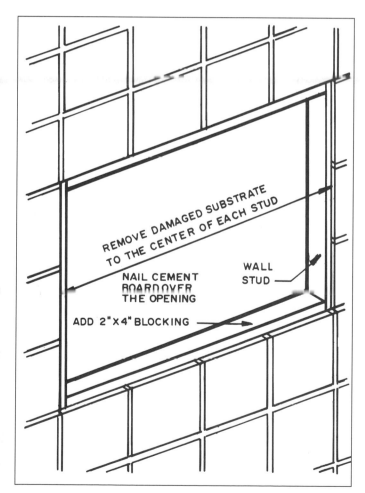

11–8. If the substrate on a large area is badly damaged, remove the tiles, cut away the damaged area from stud to stud, and install new cement board.

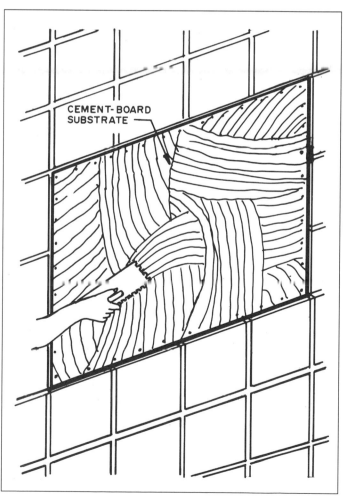

11–9. Spread adhesive on the new cement-board substrate. Keep it uniform in thickness by using a notched trowel.

3. Install the next row of tiles and proceed down the wall. Some tiles have spacer lugs on the sides to help you keep the grout line uniform. If these are not there, small strips of wood can be used (**11–10**). Continue until the damaged area is completely retiled.

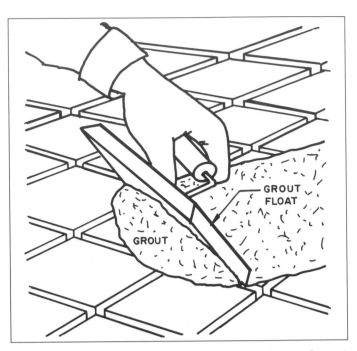

11–11. After the adhesive has set, spread a layer of grout over the tiles with a grout trowel. Move the trowel at an angle to the openings between the tiles.

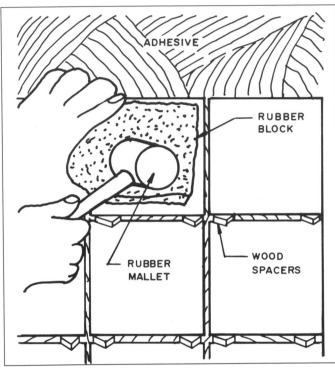

11–10. Position the tiles and press them firmly against the substrate. Use spacers to help keep them aligned. Tap them with a rubber mallet against a firm rubber pad to set the tiles firmly into the adhesive.

4. Apply the grout after the adhesive has set for 24 hours or longer. To grout large areas, use a rubber-faced trowel. Spread the grout in two passes (**11–11**). First, spread a layer of grout across the face of the tile. Hold the trowel on an angle of 30 to 70 degrees to the face and press the grout firmly into the openings. Make the passes on an angle to the openings. As you pack the grout, let the trowel scrape off the excess grout. Wipe the trowel frequently so the excess grout is removed. Finish the grouting as described earlier in this chapter.

CUTTING TILES

Frequently, tiles have to be cut to fit in an area where partial tiles are needed (**11–12**) or to fit around a pipe (**11–13**).

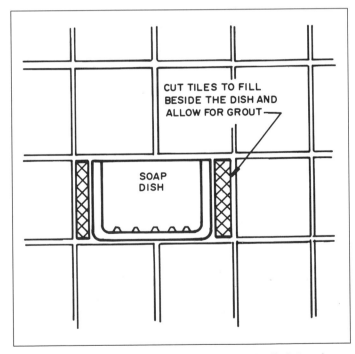

11–12. It is often necessary to cut tiles to fit into places smaller than the full tiles.

To make a straight cut, score the face of the tile with a **glass cutter**. With the glazed face up, place a finishing nail under the tile below the scored line and press on each half (**11–14**). If the edges are a bit rough, they can be smooth on an electric grinding wheel or a Carborundum stone.

A better way is to rent a **tile cutter** (11-15). Position the tile against the fence and score the face

11–13 (above). Holes in tiles must frequently be cut.

11–14 (right). To cut a tile, score the line of cut on the face side, place this score mark over a finishing nail, and press on each side. You can smooth the edges with a Carborundum stone or an electric grinder. Wear goggles.

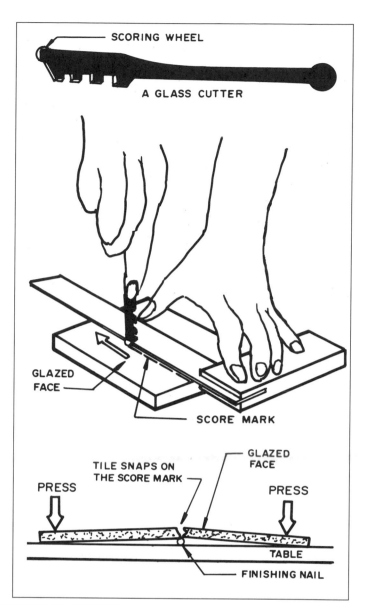

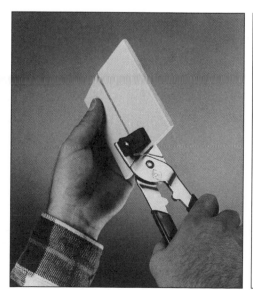

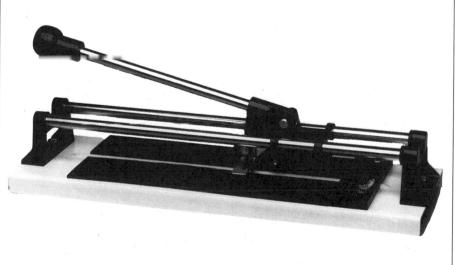

11–15. A commercial tile cutter speeds up the work and produces accurate cuts (courtesy Red Devil, Inc).

with the cutting wheel. Then press down on the sides to snap the tile.

Holes can be cut with a **carbide-tipped hole saw** (**11–16**). It is placed in a portable electric drill. It gets very hot as it drills, so you should let it cool frequently.

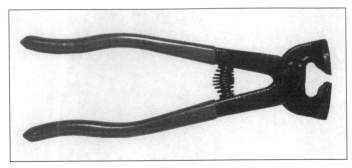

11–17. Irregular openings can be cut with tile nippers. Take very small bites or you may crack the tile (courtesy Red Devil, Inc).

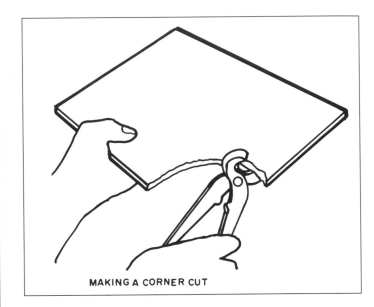

MAKING A CORNER CUT

11–18. When using the nippers, work from the center of the desired opening toward each side. You can smooth the rough edges with a Carborundum stone or your electric grinder. Wear goggles.

You can use the nippers to cut an opening around a pipe by drawing the outline of the opening on the glazed face. A grease-type marker works best. Then score the centerline of the opening and begin nipping away. Work from the centerline toward each edge (**11–18**). The rough edges can be smoothed with an electric grinding wheel or a Carborundum stone.

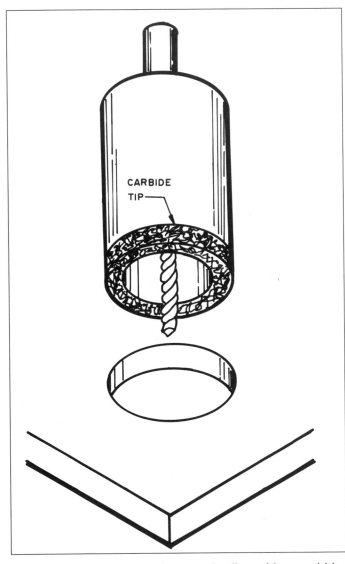

CARBIDE TIP

11–16. Holes can be cut in ceramic tiles with a carbide-tipped hole saw that is placed in your electric drill. Since it gets very hot while you are drilling, stop and let it cool frequently or you may crack the tile.

If a large arc or an unusually shaped area has to be removed, use **tile nippers** (**11–17**). Take very small bites with the nippers. Use only part of the nipper cutter to crack away small pieces. It is slow work, but the shape can gradually be developed with many small bites.

CHAPTER TWELVE

Floors and Floor Coverings

The floor in a house receives more wear and tear than any other part. In addition to regular cleaning, floor coverings need to be replaced occasionally. Squeaky floors ought to be silenced and weak or sagging floors need to be strengthened before a new finished floor is installed.

SOLID-WOOD FLOORS

Solid-wood flooring is manufactured in a variety of widths and is available as strips, wide planks, and parquet squares. The softwood species available include southern pine, western larch, bald cypress, and Douglas fir. Some of the hardwoods available are oak, beech, birch, pecan, and maple. They are specified by grade and are kiln-dried. Many are available prefinished, so require only installation.

Renovating a Solid-Wood Floor

If your floor appears dull, it may be loaded with old wax and dirt and not need refinishing. Try cleaning a small area by rubbing it with a steel-wool pad dipped in alcohol or kerosene. Commercial floor cleaners are also available. Wipe the trial area clean with a damp cloth and let it dry. Then apply a coat of paste wax and buff it. If the spot is clean and satisfactory to you, clean and wax the entire floor. You can speed up the cleaning by renting a power-buffing machine and some steel-wool pads. Put small amounts of alcohol or kerosene on the floor while buffing it. After waxing, use the power buffer with a buffing pad to bring up the shine.

Black scuff marks, such as from shoes, can sometimes be removed or reduced by rubbing them with a soft eraser or wiping them with a cloth dampened with turpentine.

Sometimes it is possible to touch up a faded spot on solid-wood floors by mixing brown shoe polish with some floor wax, applying this mixture to the spot, and buffing the spot. This is not a permanent fix, but gives some improvement.

If there are a few very fine scratches, they can sometimes be made less noticeable by rubbing them with a fine steel wool loaded with paste wax.

If you know the floor was finished with a **surface sealer**, you can clean it with a steel-wool pad. Remove all dust and recoat with the same brand of surface sealer originally used. Do not use wax to try to restore the luster.

Floors finished with **penetrating sealers** usually do not require sanding to be refinished. Clean the floor, remove all dust, and apply another coat of penetrating sealer. Do not use ammonia, oil soap, or any household cleaner if the floor was finished with a penetrating sealer.

If you do not know which type of sealer was used, scratch the surface in an inconspicuous location, such as in a closet. If the finish flakes, most likely a surface sealer was used.

Squeaky Floors

Squeaky floors have several causes, and each will have to be checked to discover how to correct a particular problem. Generally, squeaks are caused by the subfloor's working loose and sliding up and down on the nails. If subfloors were joined to the joists with adhesive and then nailed or secured with screws, most squeaks would never develop. Another cause is a gradual drying out of the subfloor and the solid-wood floor nailed to it. This permits the solid-wood floor to move a little, causing squeaks. Squeaks from these causes can be stopped by driving wood screws through the subfloor into the solid-wood floor to pull them together (12–1). Drill a pilot hole in the subfloor in the area of the squeak so the screw does not bind. Have someone stand on the spot to push the subfloor and finished floor together while you tighten the screw.

Select a screw that is long enough to go through the subfloor into the solid-wood floor. Do not use a screw that is too long or it will show through the finished floor.

Sometimes the squeak is caused by the bridging between the joists (12–2). If the floor has wood bridging, make certain it is nailed tightly. If metal bridging is used, check to see that each end is firmly in the joist.

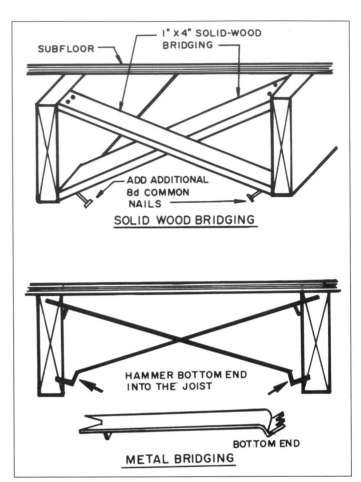

12–2. Sometimes tightening the bridging will reduce floor squeaks.

Warped and Curled Solid-Wood Flooring

Age and humidity can cause the wider solid-wood flooring boards to warp or curl. One way to handle this is to pull the deflection out by screwing the boards to the subfloor. Drill counterbored pilot holes through the flooring, but do not drill into the subfloor. Drill the counterbore about one-third of the way through the flooring (12–3). Drive the screw into the subfloor, pulling the warp out as much as possible. Very badly warped boards will have to be replaced. Then glue wood plugs of the same material over each screw and stain and finish them to the color of the flooring.

If you cannot make the repair from below, install pairs of 8d ring-shank flooring nails from above. These are angled toward each other at 45 degrees. Drill holes slightly smaller in diameter than the nail on a slant through the solid-wood floor, but not into the subfloor. Drive the nails through them. To be

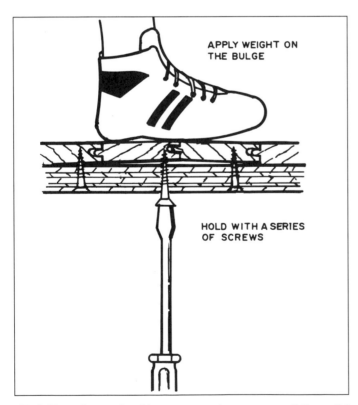

12–1. If you have a buckle or a squeak, you can pull the solid wood flooring tight against the subfloor with a series of screws.

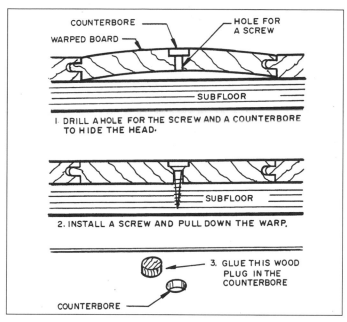

12-3. Strip flooring with a slight warp can be pulled flat by driving screws into the floor joist or subfloor.

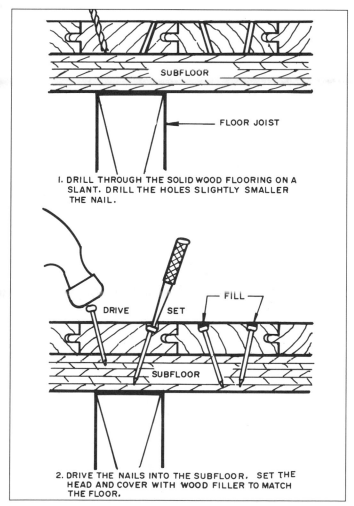

12-4. Squeaky solid-wood floors can be silenced by nailing through the flooring into the joist and subfloor.

most effective, they should go into a floor joist, but nailing into the subfloor does provide an alternate solution (**12-4**).

Some minor squeaks in solid-wood floors are the result of slight movement that causes the edges of the wood strips to rub together. You can reduce this by working talcum powder in between the boards.

If there is carpeting on the floor and the floor squeaks, most likely the squeaks are caused by the nails holding the subfloor in place. The best solution is to repair from below. One easy way is to cut wood strips and glue and screw them to the joist with the top of the strips just below the subfloor (**12-5**). Screw the strip to the joist and then to the subfloor. The strip can be predrilled before you go under the house, and can be any convenient length. Often two or three feet is enough.

If you cannot get to the subfloor from below, an effective repair can be made from above by nailing into a joist through the carpet (**12-6**). The nail should go through the pad and firmly into the joist. It is difficult to find the joist, so it may be necessary to try a few spots until the nail hits the joist. It will feel solid when this happens. There are commercially available screw-type fasteners that use this technique.

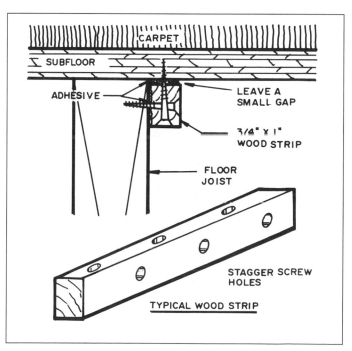

12-5. You can make wood strips and glue and screw them to the floor joist and subfloor in areas where the floor squeaks.

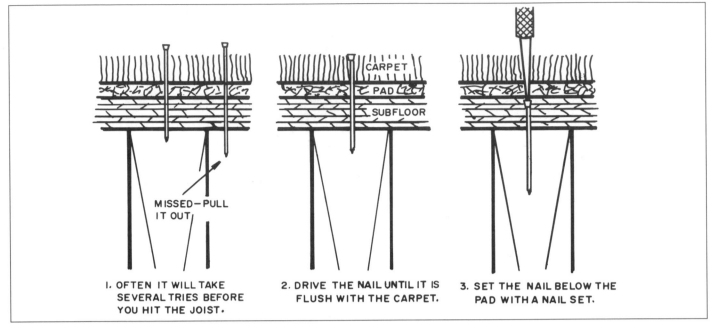

1. OFTEN IT WILL TAKE SEVERAL TRIES BEFORE YOU HIT THE JOIST.

MISSED—PULL IT OUT

2. DRIVE THE NAIL UNTIL IT IS FLUSH WITH THE CARPET.

CARPET
PAD
SUBFLOOR

3. SET THE NAIL BELOW THE PAD WITH A NAIL SET.

12–6. When you cannot get to the subfloor from below, you can sometimes muffle a squeak by nailing into the joist through the carpet.

Another approach if you can get under the floor is to drive and glue wood wedges between the subfloor and joist (12–7). This will stop the squeak, but be careful you do not produce a bulge in the floor. The wedge should be very thin. Sometimes minor squeaks can be fixed by running adhesive between the joist and subfloor.

If you are getting ready to install a new finish floor covering, you can drive screws or annular ring nails through the exposed subfloor into the joists. This is a good time to firm up the subfloor with the floor joists. Be certain the heads are flush or set and cov-

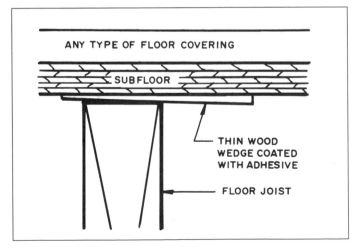

ANY TYPE OF FLOOR COVERING

SUBFLOOR

THIN WOOD WEDGE COATED WITH ADHESIVE

FLOOR JOIST

12–7. Squeaks can be silenced by driving very thin wood wedges covered with an adhesive between the joist and subfloor.

ered with a wood filler. Fastener heads can show through vinyl sheet and tile flooring.

Bouncy Floors

If a floor has a bouncy spot, additional support of the subfloor will firm up the area. To do this, cut some 2 x 6-inch pieces to fit between the floor joists. These are called **solid bridging** (12–8). Put an adhesive on the top edge, push it firmly against the subfloor, and nail the bridging to the joists. Run several pieces so you cross the bouncy area. Stagger the bridging and end-nail with three 10d common nails. Then drive nails down from above into the bridging or secure the bridging from below with wood strips.

Sagging Floors

Sagging floors indicate a serious structural problem. Examine the joists to see if they are sound. If they have been damaged by water or have rot or termites, they will need to be replaced. If they are sound, you can straighten and structurally strengthen the floor by adding a beam below it.

If you have a crawl space, concrete block piers can be constructed to support a new beam (12–9). Some of the various types of screw jacks can also be used. It is important to have a good concrete footing.

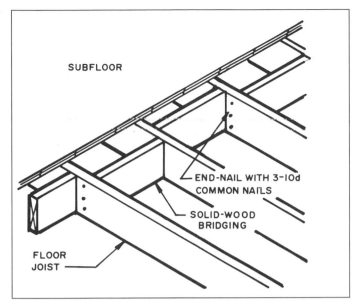

SUBFLOOR

END-NAIL WITH 3-10d COMMON NAILS

SOLID-WOOD BRIDGING

FLOOR JOIST

12–8. Add solid-wood bridging below bouncy floors. Glue the top edge to the subfloor. If possible, nail through the subfloor into the top of the bridging.

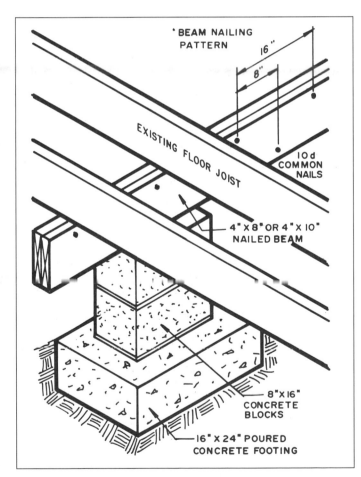

BEAM NAILING PATTERN

16"

8"

EXISTING FLOOR JOIST

10d COMMON NAILS

4" X 8" OR 4" X 10" NAILED BEAM

8" X 16" CONCRETE BLOCKS

16" X 24" POURED CONCRETE FOOTING

12–9. If the floor needs additional support, you can construct concrete block piers that support a new beam running under the sagging floor joists.

If you have a basement, jack posts can be used (**12–10**). A **jack post** is a metal post that enables you to adjust its length and make a final adjustment with a screw shaft on top. If the load is fairly light—for example, the beam supports a few floor joists—the steel base of the jack post can rest on a 2-foot (610-millimeter)-square, ¾-inch (19-millimeter)-thick piece of plywood on top of the concrete floor.

Sometimes the problem is a sagging beam. If the beam is sound, it can be shored up with jack posts as shown in **12–11**. If this is in a crawl space, a concrete footing will be needed. In a basement, you should spread the load by resting the post on a wood grid of 2-inch (51-millimeter)-thick members or two thicknesses of ¾-inch (19-millimeter) plywood.

When using jack posts or other types of jacks, do not try to correct the full sag with one adjustment. Set them tight and give the screw a one-quarter turn every 24 hours or so. Continue until the sag disappears and the floor is level. Adjusting the sag slowly allows the rest of the house to adjust to the new sup-

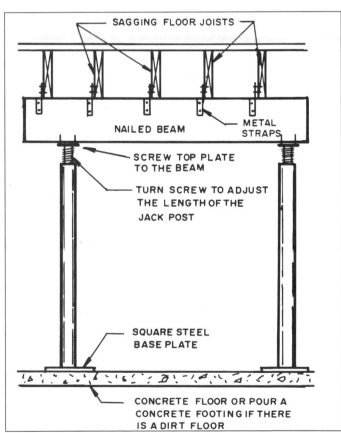

SAGGING FLOOR JOISTS

NAILED BEAM

METAL STRAPS

SCREW TOP PLATE TO THE BEAM

TURN SCREW TO ADJUST THE LENGTH OF THE JACK POST

SQUARE STEEL BASE PLATE

CONCRETE FLOOR OR POUR A CONCRETE FOOTING IF THERE IS A DIRT FLOOR

12–10. Jack posts and beams can be used to shore up sagging floor joists. The manufacturer will specify load carrying capacities of the posts.

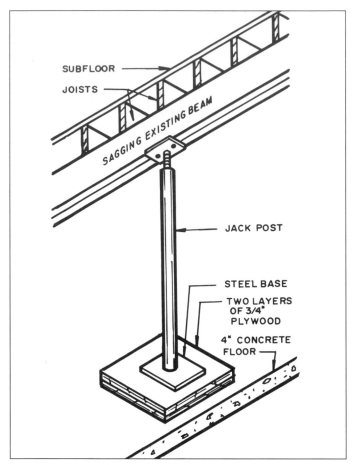

12–11. Jack posts can be used to shore up sagging beams. If the load is great consider installing a permanent steel column mounted on a concrete footing cut through the basement floor.

ports. If you raised the floor to level it all at one time, the sudden shift and strain would probably crack plaster or pop out wallboard nails.

While this column is strong and will hold the load, consider installing a permanent support. Following are some more permanent solutions.

Install steel columns set on a concrete footing. You will have to cut through the basement floor for the footing. This will meet building codes, so if you sell the house it will be approved.

If the floor sags because of just a few floor joists, you can construct a load-bearing partition below it. Raise the joists with jack posts until the floor is level and build the partition below them. The basement floor should be able to carry this load.

Sagging joists can also be corrected by adding new joists on each side. These are called **sister joists**. Raise the sagging joists, install the new straight

joists, and remove the posts. This leaves the area in the basement free of posts.

Damaged Subfloors

If a tiled or carpeted subfloor has rotted, remove and replace all of it. If one section is bad, the rest is likely to become bad also. Check floor joists for rot and replace any that are not sound. If the original subfloor has rotted because of moisture, the source of the moisture must be eliminated or the replacement will also rot. Drain any water collecting in a crawl space and fix the foundation so water does not get under the house. See Chapter 7 for ways of preventing water from getting under a house.

A good subfloor material is ¾-inch (19-millimeter) tongue-and-groove plywood or oriented strandboard. Both of these are strong and smooth, and some finish flooring is laid directly upon them. Other floor coverings require an underlayment. Bond the new subfloor to the joists with an approved adhesive and use annular ring nails or screws.

Now is a good time to insulate the floor (**12–12**). Chicken wire stapled to the bottom of the floor joists will hold insulation in a crawl space. Use insulation that has a moisture barrier attached or lay a plastic vapor barrier on top of the joists before replacing the subfloor. The vapor barrier belongs on the floor side of the joists.

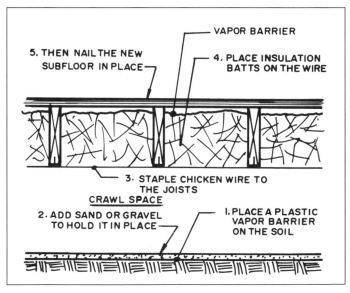

12–12. If you have to replace the subfloor, it is a good time to cover the ground with a vapor barrier and insulate the floor.

Repairing Damaged Solid-Wood Flooring

If a board in a solid-wood floor has been damaged, follow these steps to replace it:

1. Drill a series of holes across the damaged board at each end of the damage (step 1 in **12–13**). Do not bore into the subfloor.

2. Cut across the outside ends of the drilled holes with a chisel until the section of board is free (steps 2 to 6 in **12–13**). You will have to split off part of the side of the board with the chisel in order to free it from the tongue and groove.

3. Cut and fit the patch to size. Cut off the bottom side of the groove so the board will fit over the tongue of the next floor board (step 7 in **12–13**).

4. Put glue under the patch and set it in place (step 8 in **12–13**).

5. Drill a hole close to each corner of the patch that is slightly smaller than the finishing nails to be used. Do not drill into the subfloor.

6. Nail the patch. Set the nails and fill the holes with wood putty (step 9 in **12–13**).

7. Finish the patch to match the old floor and finish (step 10 in **12–13**).

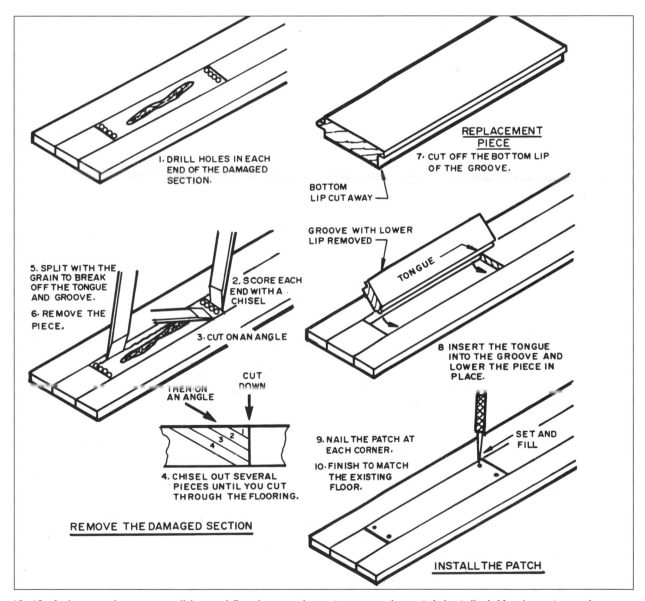

12–13. *A damaged area on solid-wood flooring can be cut away and a patch installed. You have to work carefully to get sharp cuts on the end to get the patch to fit.*

Refinishing Solid-Wood Floors

If you decide the floor needs refinishing, you face a big task. Many people choose to hire a floor-refinishing company. Should you try it first, make certain the flooring is thick enough to be sanded. If it is old and has possibly been refinished many times, check the thickness. Maybe you can remove a floor register and check the remaining thickness. It should be about ⅜ inch (9.5 millimeters). Be certain it is not a laminated floor made by bonding thin veneers as is done when making plywood. Usually these cannot be sanded even once.

Sanding the Floor

The goal is to sand away the old finish and any stains and irregular bumps or ridges. Set any nails or screws that are showing (**12–14**). While you do not have to remove the shoe molding, it makes it easier to get next to the wall. If you remove it, label each piece so they can be put back (**12–15**). If the floor has cracks or gaps between boards, fill them with a floor putty that matches the color of the sanded wood. When it is hard, it can be sanded. Rent a drum sander designed especially for this purpose and an edge sander to sand along the walls where the drum sander will not reach.

For floors that are not in too bad shape, use 30- or 40-grit sandpaper for the first pass and 120-grit for the second pass on hardwood floors. On softwood floors, begin with a 60- to 80-grit sandpaper and finish with 120-grit. If the floors are in bad shape and have a heavy varnish finish, a second sanding with 100-grit sandpaper may be needed before the final 120-grit sanding. The drum sander uses sheet material, and the edge sander uses discs.

Sanding Strip Flooring

Start sanding along the right side of the room and stay a few inches away from the baseboard. Remember, when you turn on the sander the drum is rotating and it will sand a gouge in the floor if it sits still as it runs. Lower the drum onto the floor and move from the center of the room to one wall (**12–16**). Sand in the direction the flooring was laid.

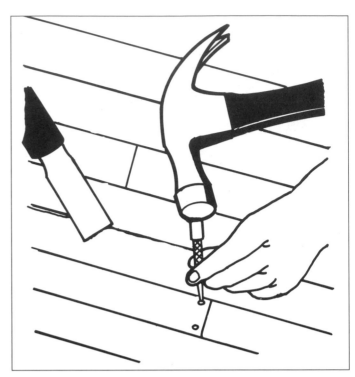

12–14. Before refinishing the solid-wood floor, repair all defects. This includes setting and filling over all visible nails and filling all cracks with a wood filler the color of the floor.

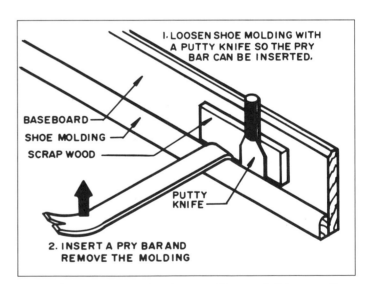

12–15. If you remove the shoe molding, pull it loose with a pry bar. Put the bar behind each nail and pull it loose. If you pull between nails, molding will break.

As you approach the end wall, raise the drum gradually, producing a feathered end to the sanded surface. Move the sander over and lower it as you cut back to the center of the room. Let it overlap the first cut about half the width of the drum. After you reach the other wall, turn around and sand the other half of the room.

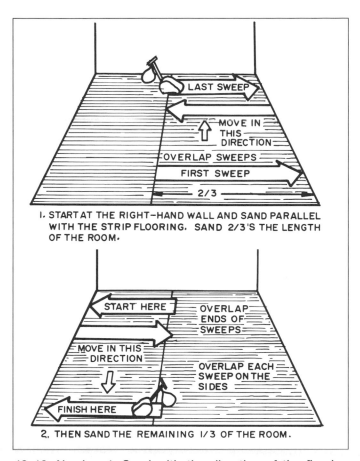

1. START AT THE RIGHT–HAND WALL AND SAND PARALLEL WITH THE STRIP FLOORING. SAND 2/3'S THE LENGTH OF THE ROOM.

2. THEN SAND THE REMAINING 1/3 OF THE ROOM.

12–16. Number 1: Sand with the direction of the flooring strips. Start at the right wall and sand one-half to two-thirds of the way across. Keep the sander moving forward and backward. Do not let it sit still. Let each pass overlap the previous one about half the width of the drum.
Number 2: After reaching the other wall, reposition the sander and sand the other side of the room.

Be certain to wear a dust mask while sanding. While disposable masks are inexpensive, it is recommended you get a high-quality mask with replaceable filters. Close off adjoining rooms. Vacuum the floor frequently as you work.

Once the room is sanded, use the edge sander along the wall (**12–17**). Place the sander on the floor and tilt it back so the disc is clear of the floor. Turn it on and, when it reaches full speed, lower the disc to the floor and immediately move it along the wall. Move it back and forth in a sweeping movement as shown in **12–18**. Always keep the sander moving when the disc is on the floor.

The edge sander will not get into the corners. These are cleaned with a scraper (**12–19**). If the edge sander leaves a few marks where it overlapped the drum-sanded area, smooth these out with a portable electric sander.

Sanding Parquet Solid-Wood Flooring

If you are certain the parquet flooring is solid wood, it can be sanded in much the same way as described for strip flooring. But you do not have a straight grain to follow and must start the first grit (coarse) on a 45-degree angle, then sand with the medium grit on the opposite 45-degree angle, and finish with the fine grit running parallel with the long wall

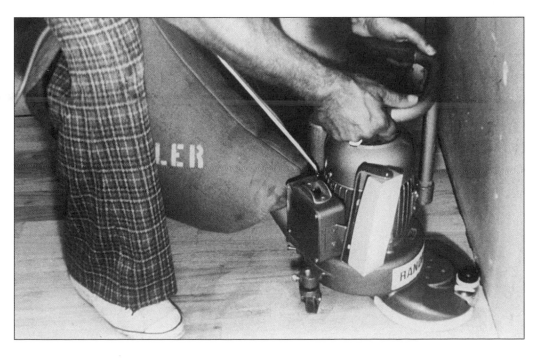

12–17. Sand the area around the baseboard with an edge-sander. (courtesy National Oak Flooring Manufacturers' Association).

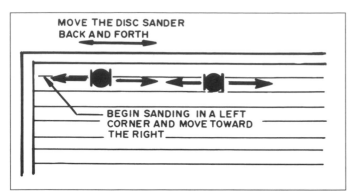

12–18. Start sanding the edge along the wall starting in the left corner with an edge sander. Move it back and forth in a slow sweeping motion about 18 inches (457 millimeters) long.

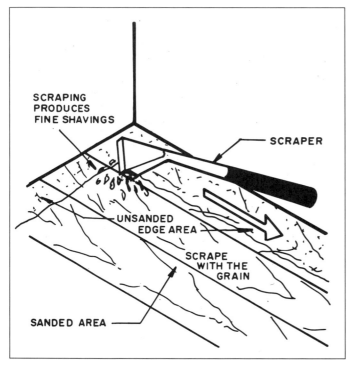

12–19. A scraper is used to finish the areas in the corners that cannot be reached with the edge sander. Scrape with the grain.

(12–20). On each pass, move the sander toward the wall and then pull it directly back before you move it over for the next pass. Overlap each pass about half the drum's width.

STAINS AND SEALERS

Stains are applied to the freshly sanded wood floor to produce the color desired. They are available in a range of shades.

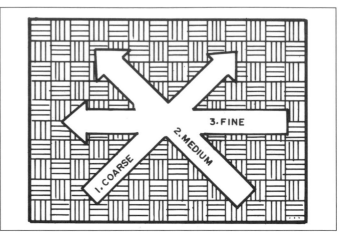

12–20. Sand solid-wood parquet flooring with coarse and then medium-grit abrasive paper on opposite 45 degrees angles and finish with a fine grit running parallel with the long wall.

Stain-sealers add color to the wood and provide a degree of sealing. Some will produce a matte finish, while others require covering with a surface finish coating. Check on the can of stain-sealer to see what kind of finish must be applied.

Penetrating sealers are a floor wax that prevents the penetration of liquids into the flooring. Some types of liquid buffing wax can be applied over them to provide additional protection.

Surface sealers do not penetrate the wood, but form a surface layer that bonds to the wood. The common types include polyurethanes and urethanes.

Polyurethanes have good moisture resistance and durability. They are available in water- and oil-based types and in satin, matte, semigloss, and high-gloss finishes.

Urethanes are available as moisture-cure and acid-cure types. Both types provide a harder surface than polyurethanes but are more difficult to apply. Consult a floor-finishing company if you want to use these.

APPLYING THE FINISH COATING

Stains and other floor finishes are applied in strips starting along one wall and running the length of the room. To apply a **penetrating sealer** (wax type), begin by making certain the surface is absolutely free of dust. Then apply a 12-inch (305-millimeter) strip along the wall with a wide brush (**12–21**). Then start the next strip, overlapping the first strip several inches. Paint to the end wall. Repeat strip after strip until the floor is covered (**12–22**). Make certain you

12–21. When applying the finish coating, start with a strip along a wall and apply the finish parallel with the strip flooring. Be certain to feather the edge of each coated section as you move down the wall. Coat the next section, painting into the wet feathered edge.

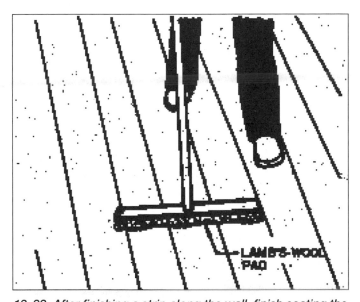

12–22. After finishing a strip along the wall, finish coating the floor. Apply with a lamb's wool pad in the direction of the strip flooring. Overlap each of the strips about 3 inches (76 millimeters).

have planned the work so you can leave the room as you finish the last strip.

Let the sealer cure for 24 hours or longer. Then power-buff with a steel-wool pad. Remove all the dust and apply a second coating.

Polyurethane finishes are applied in much the same way as penetrating sealers. However, you should not overlap the brush strokes but apply the finish toward the wet edge. Feather the edge strokes so any overlap will have a uniform thickness. Allow the finish to completely dry and buff it with a fine steel-wool pad. Apply a second coat, let it dry, and buff it. A third coat adds considerably to the protection of the floor and the durability of the finish coating. Do not wax the final coating.

LAMINATED WOOD-FLOOR COVERING

High-pressure laminate flooring is a prefinished assembly of a top surface of a high-pressure laminate material bonded to a core of medium-density fiberboard and backed with a balancing layer of high-pressure laminate (**12–23**). Should you decide to replace the floor covering, this system is relatively easy to install and produces a wood-grain top surface. It can be installed over most existing flooring.

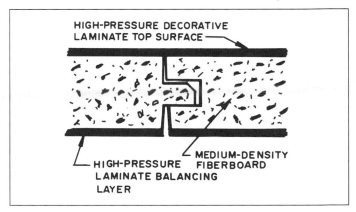

12–23. A typical construction and edge joint for laminated wood-floor covering. (courtesy Wilsonart International).

The manufacturer can verify if it will go over your old floor covering.

High-pressure laminate flooring is a floating floor that is installed over a special foam padding. The strips are laid on the surface and end- and edge-glued (**12–24**). The manufacturer provides detailed installation instructions. It is available in planks 7¼ inches wide and 4 feet long and in 15½-inch squares.

RESILIENT FLOOR COVERINGS

Resilient floor coverings are available in vinyl, cork, and rubber. Vinyl-composition tiles and sheet materials are the most widely used. These are called "resilient" because they are flexible and give when pressure is applied, and then return to their original condition. You can do a good job of laying resilient tiles, but the installation of sheet material is more difficult.

Some types are bonded to the floor with an adhesive, while others have an adhesive backing and you only have to peel off the paper and stick them in place. Installation procedures are the same for both, except adhesive-backed tiles do not have a messy adhesive application.

Before beginning installation, get the subfloor in first-class condition. All holes and dents must be filled, nail heads set, and ridges or bumps sanded down. If the subfloor is in poor condition, install a ⅜- to ½-inch (9.5- to 13-millimeter) underlayment grade plywood.

The flooring can be cut with sheet-metal shears or a utility knife. Use the adhesive recommended by the manufacturer. Your floor-covering dealer will have it available.

Cleaning Scuff Marks

If the vinyl has marks, such as crayon, buff them with silver polish, being careful to not cut through the finish. Sometimes kerosene or turpentine can be used to dissolve black marks such as from your shoes.

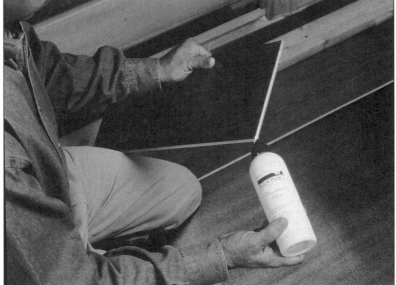

12–24. The steps for installing laminated wood-floor covering. Top: Cover the subfloor with the special form padding. Middle: Apply adhesive to the end and side joint of each piece as it is laid. Bottom: After putting the piece in place and lightly tapping the joint closed, wipe off the excess adhesive (courtesy Wilsonart International).

Repairing Damaged Resilient Tiles

A badly damaged tile can be replaced by heating it with a hair dryer and prying it out with a putty knife. Then scrape away all old adhesive on the subfloor, repair any damage to it, apply new adhesive, and carefully place the new tile into the opening (**12–25**).

If a tile comes partially loose, it will usually curl, and you can trip over it and possibly break off the corner. To repair this, heat the tile with a hair dryer on a medium setting until the tile is flexible. Curl up the tile a little and scrape away the adhesive on the tile and subfloor. Apply new adhesive, press the tile in place, wipe off excess adhesive with the specified solvent, and place a weight on it for a day or so (**12–26**).

If a tile develops a blister, you will most likely want to replace it. Any repair does not produce a quality

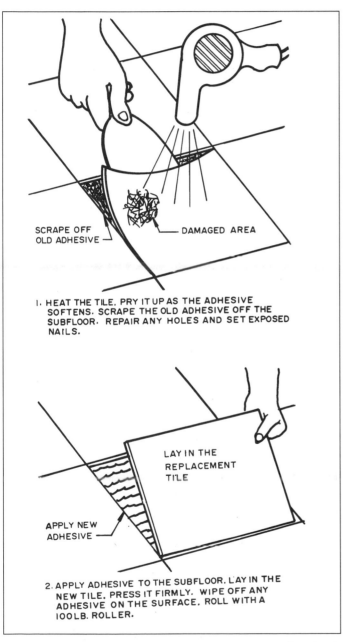

SCRAPE OFF OLD ADHESIVE — — DAMAGED AREA

1. HEAT THE TILE. PRY IT UP AS THE ADHESIVE SOFTENS. SCRAPE THE OLD ADHESIVE OFF THE SUBFLOOR. REPAIR ANY HOLES AND SET EXPOSED NAILS.

LAY IN THE REPLACEMENT TILE

APPLY NEW ADHESIVE —

2. APPLY ADHESIVE TO THE SUBFLOOR. LAY IN THE NEW TILE. PRESS IT FIRMLY. WIPE OFF ANY ADHESIVE ON THE SURFACE. ROLL WITH A 100 LB. ROLLER.

12–25. A damaged resilient tile can be removed by heating it until the adhesive becomes soft. Carefully install the new tile and be certain to remove any of the adhesive that may get on the surface.

1. HEAT THE TILE WITH A HAIR DRYER ON LOW HEAT UNTIL IT BECOMES FLEXIBLE AND THE ADHESIVE SOFTENS.

2. APPLY A THIN COAT OF ADHESIVE ON THE BACK OF THE TILE AND PRESS IN PLACE. CLEAN OFF ANY ADHESIVE ON THE SURFACE. PLACE A WEIGHT ON IT UNTIL IT SETS.

12–26. A tile will sometimes come loose at a corner and curl up from the subfloor. Clean away the adhesive below it, apply new adhesive, and rebond it to the subfloor.

appearance. If you decide to make a repair, cut across the blister, heat the tile with a hair dryer until it is flexible, carefully place a thin layer of adhesive under the blister, and press the blister against the subfloor (**12–27**). Wipe off any adhesive that squeezes out with the recommended solvent and place a weight on it until it dries.

Installing Resilient Floor Tiles

Sweep and vacuum the floor so it is perfectly clean. Divide the room along its centerlines. Mark these with a chalk line (**12–28**). Lay a row of uncemented tiles on the wall in one quadrant of the room (**12–29**). Arrange the layout so there is approximately one-half a tile or more at each wall. If necessary, move the centerline a little until you work this out. Allow for a ¼-inch (6-millimeter) gap at the baseboard. This is needed to allow for expansion.

Begin applying adhesive with a notched trowel to one quarter of the room. Place one tile at the center and lay a row along the chalk line to one wall (**12–30**). Then fill in the quarter. Do not slide a tile after it has been placed because adhesive will build up along the edge. After placing tiles on some of the area, roll them. One-hundred-pound rollers are available from tile dealers (**12–31**). As a substitute, use an ordinary rolling pin and press firmly on the tiles.

2. HEAT UNTIL THE TILE IS FLEXIBLE.

1. CUT THE BLISTER BEYOND THE EDGE.

3. INSERT A THIN LAYER OF ADHESIVE UNDER THE BLISTER AND PRESS IT IN PLACE. CLEAN OFF ANY ADHESIVE ON THE FACE. PUT A WEIGHT ON IT.

12–27. If your resilient tile has a blister, slit it, put a thin layer of adhesive below it, and press it firmly against the subfloor.

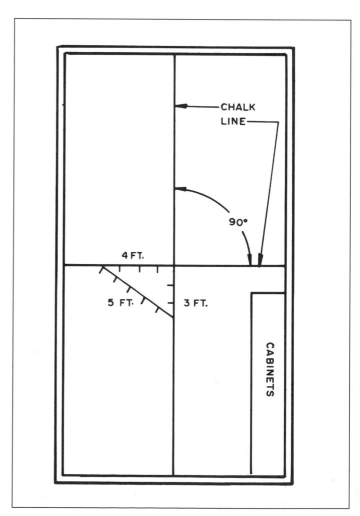

12–28. As you plan the tile layout, run a chalk line through the center of the length and width of the room.

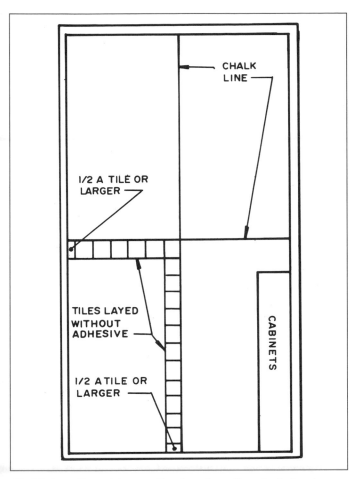

12–29. Lay tiles without adhesive along the chalk line to see how they will come out along each wall.

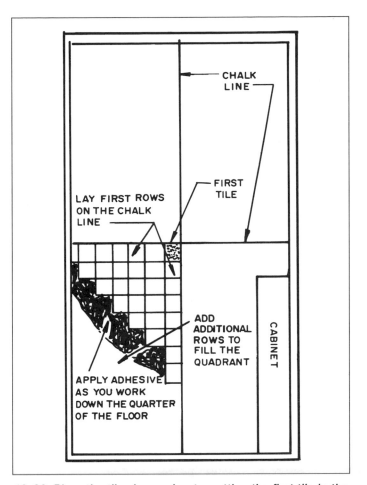

12–30. Place the tiles in quadrants, setting the first tile in the center of the room and working toward the walls. Drop the tiles in place. If you push them, adhesive will squeeze onto the surface.

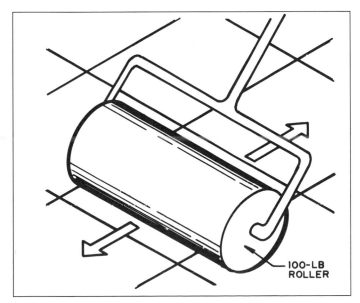

12–31. After pressing the tiles in place, clean off any adhesive on the surface and roll the tiles with a 100-pound floor-tile roller. A rolling pin can be used as a substitute if you bear down on it.

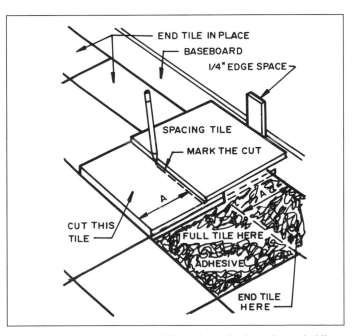

12–32. Mark and cut the end tiles along the baseboard. Allow 1/4 inch for expansion.

Now measure and cut the partial tiles along the wall. To get the correct size, place two uncemented tiles on the end tile and mark the line of cut as shown in **12–32**.

To fit tile around pipes or other protrusions, make

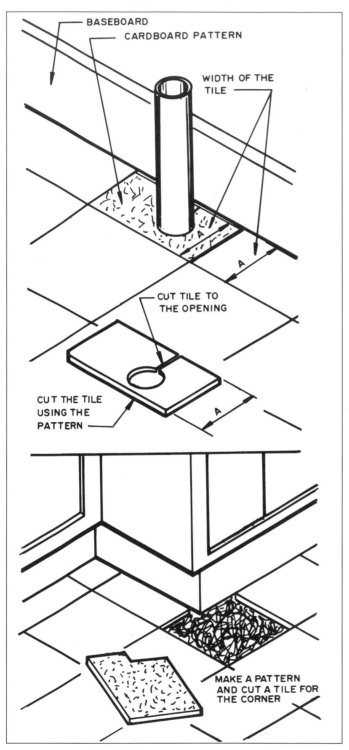

12–33. It is possible to fit tiles around difficult corners or projections by making a pattern and cutting the tiles from the pattern.

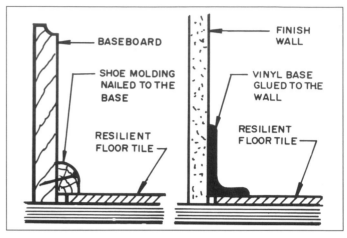

12–34. The space between the resilient floor tiles and the wall can be covered with wood shoe molding or a vinyl base.

a cardboard template. Cut the tile and trim as necessary. To get around a pipe, cut from one edge to the hole (**12–33**).

Finish the job by installing shoe molding or a vinyl base around the wall (**12–34**).

CERAMIC FLOOR TILES

There is a wide range of ceramic tiles available. Some are unglazed and are the color of the clay. Others are glazed. The **glaze** is a coating applied to the natural tiles and bonded by firing. It can be clear or colored.

When selecting tiles for your floor, be certain they were made for that purpose. **Vitreous tiles** have a glaze that makes them impervious to penetration by water. They are used where water is present and are recommended for use on floors. **Floor tiles** are thicker than wall tiles, so they can withstand the pressures exerted upon the floor.

Subfloor Preparation

The subfloor must be strong and stiff enough so there is no deflection. Any deflection will cause the tiles to crack or come loose. A ½- to ¾-inch (13- to 19-millimeter) underlayment-grade plywood nailed over the existing subfloor gives solid construction. Some prefer to nail a cement backer-board underlayment over the old subfloor (**12–35**). Stagger the joints so they do not line up with those in the sub-

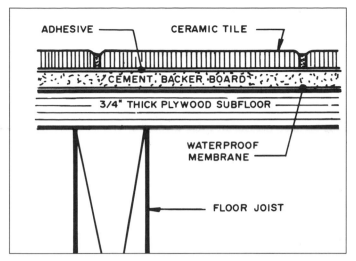

12–35. A good subfloor assembly for ceramic-tile floor covering. If the floor is bouncy, nail it securely and install a second layer of 3/4-inch plywood.

floor. Secure them with 1⅝-inch (40-millimeter) wood screws or 1½-inch (38-millimeter) hot-dipped galvanized roofing nails spaced 8 inches (203 millimeters) on center. Before laying the tiles, fill the joints between the cement backer board with tile-setting mortar or adhesive and press a fiberglass tape into the mortar or adhesive (**12–36**).

Ceramic floor tiles can be applied over concrete floors and, with careful preparation and proper adhesives, can be applied over existing resilient or ceramic tiles.

Ceramic floor tiles are cut in the same manner as ceramic wall tiles. Refer to Chapter 11.

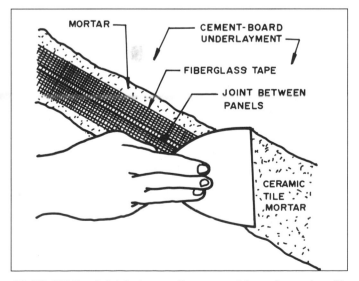

12–36. Fill the joint between the cement-board panels with tile-setting mortar, cover this with fiberglass tape, and cover this with a thin coat of mortar.

Adhesives and Mortars

Various types of adhesives and grouts are available. Your tile dealer can provide advice on the type to use. Those available are discussed in Chapter 11. Epoxy adhesive seems to be the choice for bonding ceramic tiles to plywood or cement board in damp areas. Epoxy mortars are also widely used in damp areas.

Installing Ceramic Floor Tiles

If you are tiling a floor in a room where the baseboard is in place, you can tile to within the width of the grout line that was selected. You may decide to remove the wood baseboard and install a tile base border (**12–37**).

Decide on the width of the grout line. Your tile dealer can supply plastic spacers of various widths

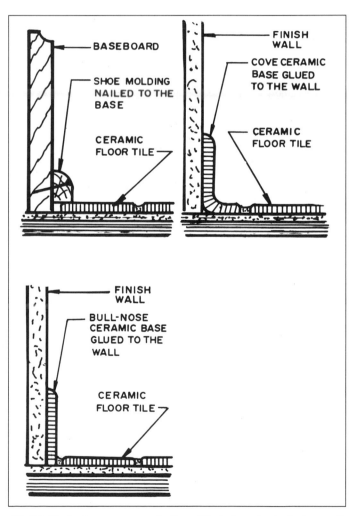

12–37. Typical ways ceramic floor tile is terminated at a wall.

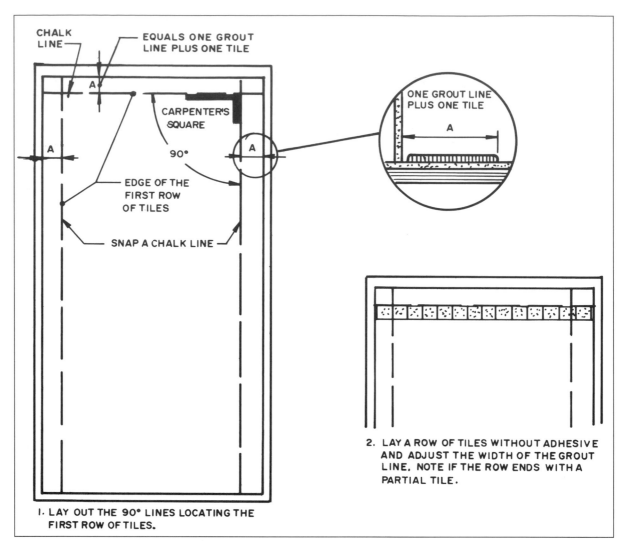

12–38. Locate the edges of the starting row of tiles, lay the tiles dry, and adjust the width of the grout line as you space the tiles over to the other wall. The tiles on the other wall may have to be cut.

that you place between the tiles while setting them.

Remember, the walls of the room may not be straight or square and you may have to make some adjustment for them.

It is usually best to remove the doors to the room so they are not in the way as you lay the tiles. Remember to check to see if you will have to cut some off the bottom of the door.

Now measure out from the end wall or the baseboard—if there is one—a distance equal to one grout line and one tile, and snap a chalk line (**12–38**). This establishes the line for laying the first row of tiles. Repeat this for the sidewalls. Check to be certain the chalk lines are at 90 degrees. This can be done with a carpenter's square.

Now lay a row of tiles without adhesive along each wall line to see if a tiny piece may occur at one wall. If so, you can adjust the width of the grout line. Typically, you will have to plan for cut tiles on one wall. Decide where these will be placed. It is a matter of appearance. Place full tiles in the most conspicuous places.

Setting the Tiles

Apply adhesive over the subfloor for the first row of tiles. Spread it with the smooth side of the trowel and then go over it with the grooved side. The adhesive container will provide instructions for the width of groove to use (**12–39**). Spread the adhesive up to

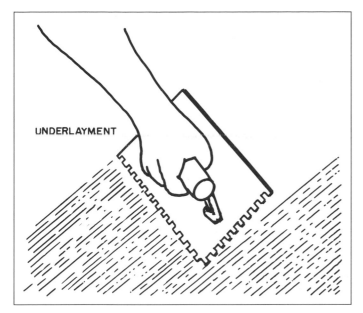

12–39. Spread the adhesive over the underlayment with a notched trowel. See the adhesive container for the recommended size of notch in the trowel.

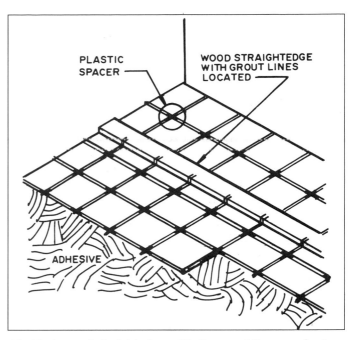

12–41. A wood straightedge with the grout lines marked on it can be used to help check the alignment of the tiles.

but not covering the chalk line. Start placing the tiles in one corner and move across the wall. Press each tile down firmly. Place plastic grout-line spacers between the tiles (**12–40**). Remove with the proper solvent any adhesive that gets on the face of the tiles. If the grout line has excess adhesive in it, scrape it away with a wood stick.

After the base course has been set, some tile layers prefer to set the rest of the floor in sections several feet square. You can measure and snap additional chalk-line marks across the floor to help keep the rows aligned. A straightedge marked with the tiles and grout-line spacers can be used as an additional check (**12–41**). After tiling an area, tap the tiles with

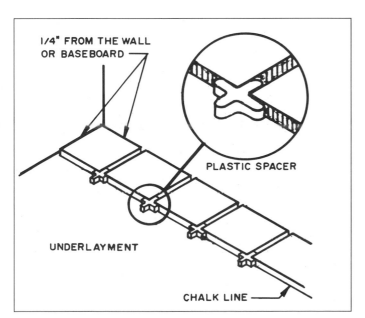

12–40. Place each tile on the chalk line and space it with the plastic spacer that establishes the width of the grout line.

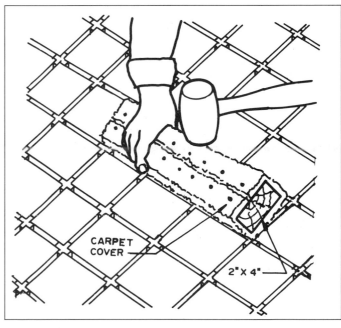

12–42. After tiling an area level and tapping and setting the tiles with a carpet-covered 2 x 4, you can remove the spacers.

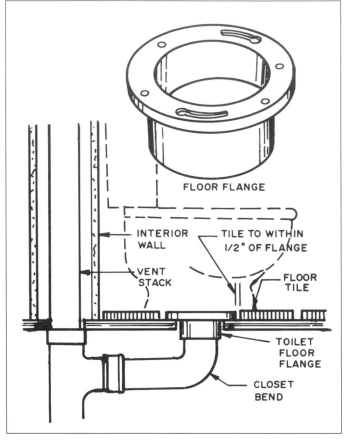

FLOOR FLANGE

INTERIOR WALL

TILE TO WITHIN 1/2" OF FLANGE

VENT STACK

FLOOR TILE

TOILET FLOOR FLANGE

CLOSET BEND

12–43. Remove the toilet and set the tiles within 1/2 inch (13 millimeters) of the flange.

12–44. After you install and grout the tiles and everything has hardened, set the toilet on top of the tiles. Be certain to install a new wax gasket.

a mallet and a piece of 2 x 4 covered with carpet. This levels and sets the tiles (**12–42**). You may remove the plastic spacers as you move down the floor or wait until the tiles have set.

When installing tiles in a bathroom, remove the toilet. Set the tiles to within ½ inch (13 millimeters) of the flange (**12–43**). After the grout has hardened, reset the toilet. It is smart to have a plumber install a new wax gasket and set the toilet. It is set on top of the tiles (**12–44**). Refer to Chapter 1.

Do not walk on the tiles after they have been laid. The adhesive container label will specify this time. Certainly several days would be reasonable. If you walk on the tiles too soon, they may slip out of line and the edges may break.

Grouting the Tiles

Select a grout that's the color you want. Your tile dealer has samples of actual hardened grout. He can figure how much is needed if you know the number of square feet to be covered. Refer to **12–44** to see a dark grout with a light-colored tile.

Pour a quantity of grout on the tiles and spread it diagonally over an area with a rubber-blade float. Work it into the openings so they are completely full (**12–45**). You can pack it with a small rod if necessary. Then sweep diagonally across the joints with a squeegee, scraping off any excess grout (**12–46**).

Wait about 15 minutes for the grout to begin to harden and start wiping the surface of the tiles with a sponge. Rinse the sponge frequently. Avoid damaging the grout in the joint. You can now smooth any grout that is a bit rough. This can be done with a special tool your tile dealer may be able to provide or with a plastic spoon.

To avoid damage to the soft grout, kneel on a large padded board or thick rubber pad.

Wait about 10 to 15 minutes and carefully wipe the surface of the tiles with a damp sponge. Use one with rounded edges so it does not dig into the grout

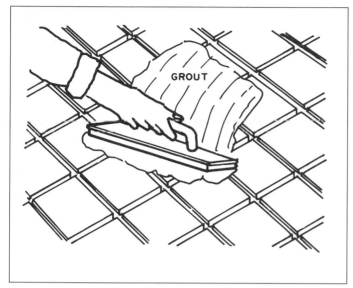

12–45. Work the grout between the tiles with a rubber-blade float. Sweep it on an angle to the grout lines. Force it firmly into the grout lines.

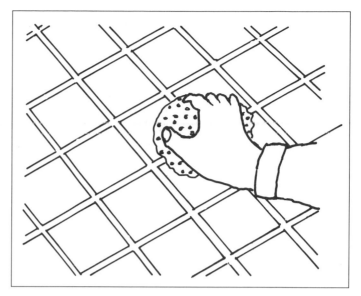

12–47. After the grout has hardened for 10 to 15 minutes, wipe the surface of each tile with a dampened, rounded sponge.

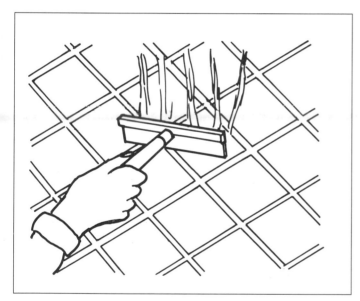

12–46. Use a rubber squeegee to sweep off the excess grout. Move at an angle to the grout lines.

(12–47). Now let the grout dry for 30 to 60 minutes and carefully wipe off any grout film still left on the tiles with a soft cloth. The tiles should be perfectly clean after this step. Allow the grout to cure as long as the manufacturer recommends.

Sealing Tiles and Grout

Some types of tiles and grout can be sealed to protect from dirt, mildew, and water. Consult your tile dealer about whether this is possible.

CARPET

As you consider which carpet to use, it becomes evident that there are many materials and types of construction to consider. A major consideration is where it will be used. Typical factors are areas of heavy traffic, the possibility of its getting wet, and the possibility of its developing mildew. Some carpets wear better, while others resist moisture. Other factors such as spilled food, muddy shoes, and animals living in the house create cleaning problems.

Types of Carpets

Following is a list of carpets available:

Wool carpets. These are made from natural fibers. They have good resistance to abrasion and aging and resist damage from sunlight and mildew.

Acrylic-fiber carpets. Acrylic fiber is a synthetic material that has a texture similar to wool. Acrylic-fiber carpets have good resistance to abrasion, mildew, sunlight, aging, and many chemicals.

Modacrylic-fiber carpets. Modacrylic fiber is a type of acrylic material. These carpets are soft, resilient, abrasive, and flame-resistant. They also resist sunlight, mildew, alkalies, and some acids.

Nylon-fiber carpets. Nylon fiber is a petrochemical product that is strong and resists staining. It also resists aging, mildew, abrasion, and has a low moisture-absorption rate.

Polyester-fiber carpets. Polyester fiber is a synthetic fiber that has high tensile strength and resists mineral acids, mildew, abrasion, and aging. Exposure to sunlight over a long time will cause loss of strength. These carpets are not as durable as nylon carpets.

Polypropylene-fiber carpets. Polypropylene fibers are synthetic fibers that have the lowest moisture-absorption rate of all these fibers. These carpets resist abrasion, aging, mildew, sunlight, and common solvents.

Carpet Construction

Carpet construction includes woven, tufted, knitted, flocked, and fusion construction.

The types of **woven construction** are shown in **12–48**. These carpets are woven on a loom and have different types of backing. **Tufted construction** (**12–49**) involves stitching the face pile into a backing material. **Knitted construction** (**12–49**) is made by looping the stitching, backing, and pile yarn together. **Flocked construction** (**12–49**) produces a carpet by electrostatically spraying short strands of

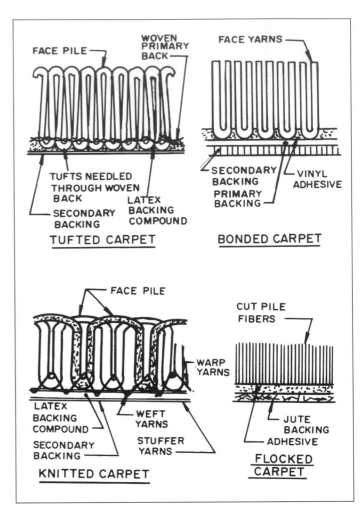

12–49. Tufted, knitted, flocked, and fusion-bonded carpet construction.

pile yarn onto an adhesive-coated backing. **Fusion-bonded construction** (**12–49**) bonds the pile yarn to sheets of backing material coated with a vinyl adhesive.

Carpet Cushions

Cushion is usually installed below the carpet to extend its life and provide a soft, resilient covering. Carpet cushions are available made from rubber, fiber, and urethane. They are made in Class 1 (light-traffic) and Class 2 (heavy-traffic) types.

Caring for Carpets

Carpets should be vacuumed frequently to prevent permanent damage from dirt and soil. Stains and dirt must be removed as soon as possible. A hot-water rug cleaner is a good way to keep your carpet

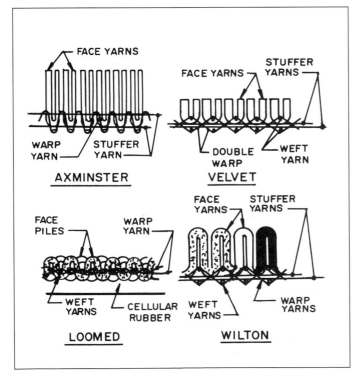

12–48. Woven carpets are woven on a loom and have different types of backing.

12–50. This hot-water rug cleaner uses a special cleaning solution that is spread on the carpet with a series of rotating brushes.

fresh (**12–50**). Most carpets are now treated with a stain-resistant chemical when they are manufactured. If yours is not, it can be applied by a professional carpet service after the carpet is thoroughly cleaned.

Before cleaning spots or even the entire carpet, try to find out the fibers used. A carpet dealer can tell you what cleaners and solvents are safe for that particular fiber. You can also test a cleaner on a small area where damage is not visible, such as in a closet.

Urine stains are removed using a solution of ammonia and water or vinegar and water.

Blood is best removed with cold water.

Sand and **soil** should be allowed to dry. Then scrape as much loose as possible and vacuum the area. A commercial carpet product, whether liquid or powder, will finish the job.

Food stains should first be blotted to soak up as much of the stain as possible. A mixture of dishwashing detergent and water will often remove the rest of the stain. It may take several applications.

Wax and **gum** are first hardened with ice and then scraped off. Any remaining particles are removed with a dry-cleaning fluid.

Burned or **torn** carpet can be repaired by cutting out the damaged area with a very sharp utility knife. Using the cut piece as a pattern, cut an exact fit from a new piece of carpeting. Keep the pattern and "grain" of the patch in the same direction as the original carpet. Do not cut into the carpet pad.

Now place double-sided carpet tape under the

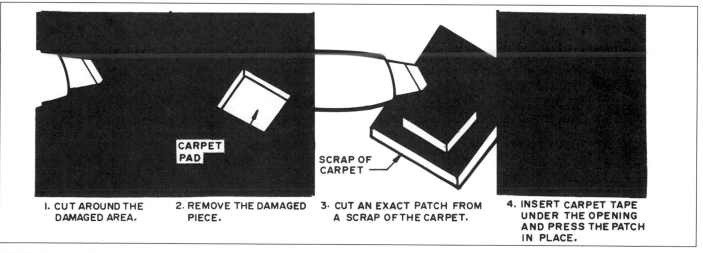

1. CUT AROUND THE DAMAGED AREA. 2. REMOVE THE DAMAGED PIECE. 3. CUT AN EXACT PATCH FROM A SCRAP OF THE CARPET. 4. INSERT CARPET TAPE UNDER THE OPENING AND PRESS THE PATCH IN PLACE.

12–51. Damaged areas of carpet can be repaired by cutting out the damaged section and taping or gluing in a patch of new carpet.

opening and press the patch in place. If you cannot get the tape below the carpet, glue the patch on the edges and the back (**12–51**). It is a good idea to keep some of the leftover pieces of carpet so you can make this repair.

If you use a steam cleaner, remove as much furniture as possible from the room. For large pieces that are remaining, put pieces of aluminum foil below each leg so the metal glide on the leg will not leave a rust spot.

Water and ammonia will remove many stains, such as grass stains. Club soda will remove some spots. Vinegar and water will remove stains such as ink and some glues.

Any wet spotting material should be blotted. Never wipe because this spreads the stain.

Any glob of sticky material should first be scraped off with a knife. Try not to spread it. Work from the edges to the center.

Clean any spill or soil as soon as it occurs.

After you clean a spot—and especially if water was used—cover it with several layers of paper towels and a few magazines so the moisture is rapidly soaked up. Replace the towels as necessary.

ADDITIONAL INFORMATION ON INSTALLING FLOOR COVERINGS

• Spence, William P., *Finish Carpentry: A Complete Interior & Exterior Guide;* New York: Sterling Publishing Co., 1995.

• ————*Carpentry and Building Construction;* New York: Sterling Publishing Co., 1999.

CHAPTER THIRTEEN

Home Security

Home security has become increasingly important and difficult to maintain. The home owner can improve the situation by installing proper locks and other security devices. Locks are operated repeatedly every day and usually are given little attention. They do wear out and need occasional maintenance. Sometimes they can be repaired, while other times it is easier and less expensive to replace the entire lock.

Below is information concerning security measures for doors and windows.

DOOR SECURITY

Doors should be able to withstand forced entry by having secure locksets and a construction that can withstand heavy blows. Exterior wood doors such as those made with wood and hardboard should be of solid-core construction. They should be 1¾ inches (44 millimeters) thick. While flush doors provide better protection than panel doors, if panel doors are used the panels should be at least ½ inch (13 millimeters) thick.

Steel-clad flush doors made with 24-gauge sheet metal bonded to a nonresinous wood core provide good security.

Doors with panes of glass or louvers are vulnerable. Replace the glass with an impact-resistant plastic sheet material. Louvers could have a metal grill bolted over them.

Door Frames

Wood door frames should be at least 2 inches (51 millimeters) thick. Metal-covered wood frames are even better. Door frames should have the doorstop cut into the solid wood (**13–1**). This is referred to as a **rabbeted jamb**. If the doorstop is nailed to the jamb, the intruder can pop it off in just a minute. If you have this type of doorstop, run a series of screws through it—especially in the area where the lock is located. Better still, mount an 18-inch (457-millimeter) piece of angle iron in the area where the door

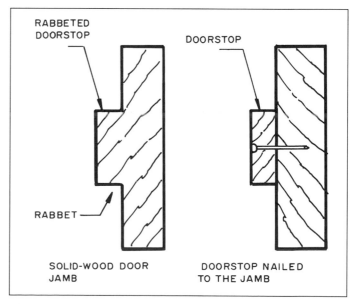

13–1. A door jamb with the rabbet cut into the jamb so it is one solid piece is more secure than the typical nailed door stop.

strike (lock) is located (**13–2**). This protects doors that open in. If the door opens out, bolt a metal escutcheon plate in the area of the lock and let it extend over the doorstop. Use screws that cannot be removed or fasten bolts through the door with round heads so they cannot be unscrewed (**13–3**).

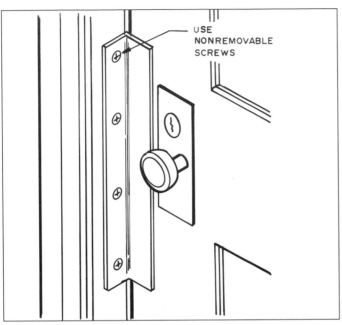

13–2. An angle iron installed by the lock makes it difficult to get to the latch and force it open. This is used on doors opening into the house.

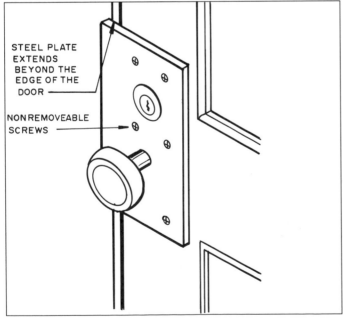

13–3. Security measures for doors that open out. A metal escutcheon plate is bolted in the area of the lock. It extends over the doorstop. Use screws that cannot be removed or fasten bolts through the door with round heads so they cannot be unscrewed.

Hinges

Hinges on exterior doors should be mounted with the barrel on the inside of the house. If they are on the outside, they must have nonremovable pins. If they do not, you must drill a hole into the hinge pin in the center of the barrel facing inside the house and insert a steel pin into the hinge pin (**13–4**). This prevents it from being removed.

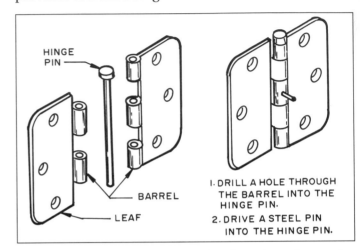

13–4. If the hinges on your exterior doors have loose pins that could be removed from outside the house, secure the hinge pin with a small steel pin.

Another technique is to partially set a screw into the edge of the door at each hinge. Drill a hole into the frame to receive the screw when the door is closed (**13–5**). This prevents the door from being lifted off the hinge even if the hinge pin has been removed.

Sliding Exterior Doors

Sliding glass exterior doors are especially vulnerable. If you are adding new doors, be certain they meet the standards set forth in the standard *Physical Security of Sliding Glass Door Units.* This specifies reinforced stiles at the locks, and the design should prevent the door from simply being lifted out of the tracks. If you have older doors, drive self-tapping metal screws through a couple of holes drilled in the channel above the door. This prevents them from being lifted out (**13–6**).

The locks on most sliding doors use a small hook to secure the door. This is easily broken with pressure from a wrecking bar. Two easy means for secur-

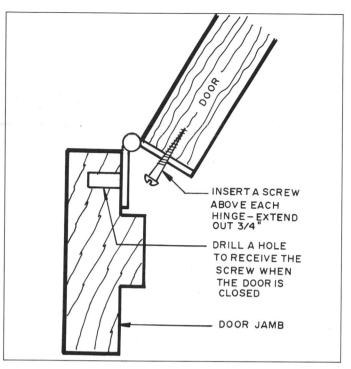

13–5. This is an easy way to prevent your door from being lifted out when the hinge pin has been removed.

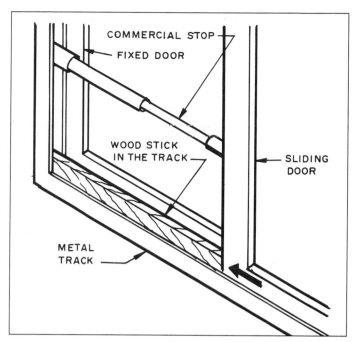

13–7. A wood stick or a commercial doorstop can be used to prevent the sliding door from being forced open.

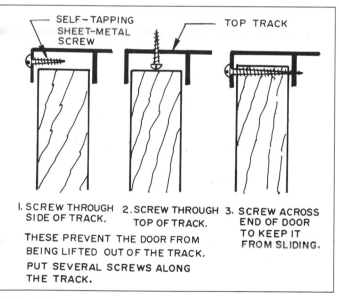

I. SCREW THROUGH SIDE OF TRACK.   2. SCREW THROUGH TOP OF TRACK.   3. SCREW ACROSS END OF DOOR TO KEEP IT FROM SLIDING.

THESE PREVENT THE DOOR FROM BEING LIFTED OUT OF THE TRACK. PUT SEVERAL SCREWS ALONG THE TRACK.

13–6. Sliding glass doors can be made more secure by installing sheet-metal screws to prevent them from being slid or lifted out of the frame.

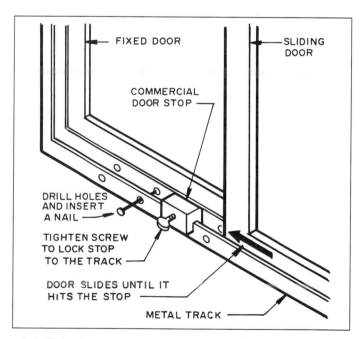

13–8. This clamp-on doorstop or a series of holes for a nail will let you open the door for ventilation, but prevents the door from being forced open for entry.

ing a door are to prop a wood stick in the track or buy a commercial stop that is adjustable to fit various door sizes (**13–7**). You can also purchase a stop that clamps on the track or drill a series of holes through the edge of the tracks and runner and insert a nail wherever you want a stop (**13–8**). These meth-

ods discourage or slow down the intruder. The glass can be broken to provide entry, but this is noisy and takes a considerable blow. You can protect your home from entry by breaking glass by using glass-protection sensors described in the section on security alarms later in this chapter.

Other Door-Protection Items

One weak part of any door is the strike plate that is screwed to the frame. A typical example is in **13–9**. This can be easily torn loose with a pry bar. To provide additional protection, use a reinforced strike plate as shown in **13–10**.

There are a number of locking devices that can be mounted on the door that connect to a unit mounted on the door casing (**13–11**). These do not provide much security because they can be torn

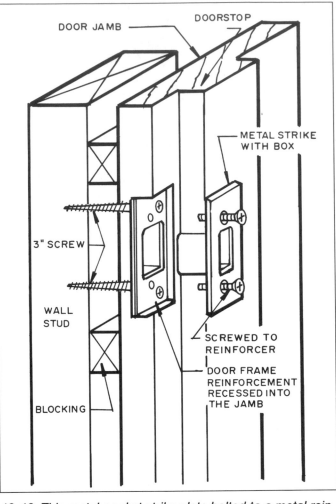

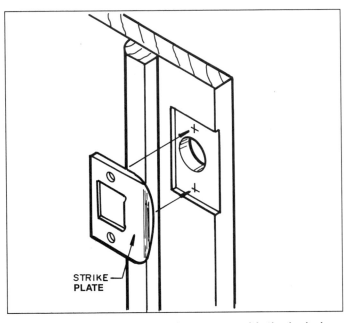

13–9. The typical strike plate that comes with the lock does not provide maximum protection.

13–10. This metal-pocket strike plate bolted to a metal reinforcement plate that is screwed to the wall stud provides good protection from "kick-in" attacks. It is especially recommended for dead bolts.

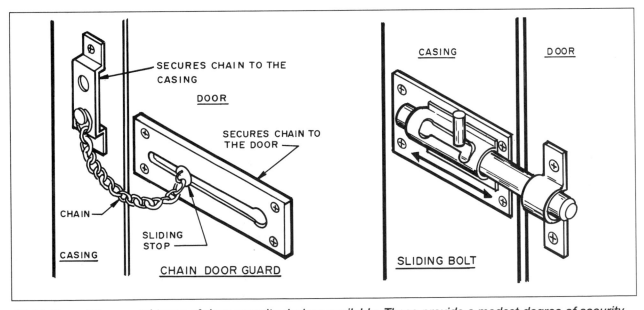

13–11. Two of the several types of door-security devices available. These provide a modest degree of security.

loose rather easily. They do provide a measure of safety if you open the door in response to someone at the door. Even better is to have an optical peephole in the door so you can view the person on the other side without unlocking the door (**13–12**). There are many types of peepholes available, so study each to find the one that suits your needs the best. Locate the peephole around 4 feet, 10 inches from the floor.

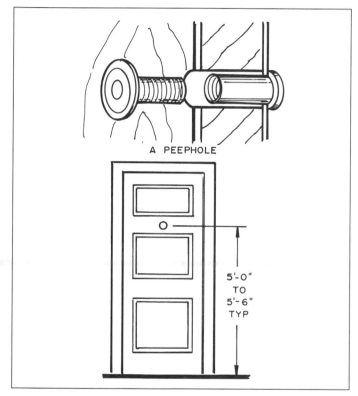

13–12. A peephole lets you see who is at the door before you unlock and open it.

Types of Locks

The **mortise locks** found in very old houses provide little security. They are set in a rectangular opening (called a **mortise**) cut into the edge of the door. When they no longer operate properly, they should be replaced with a cylindrical lock (**13–13**). It is usually best to glue wood pieces into the mortise. This will strengthen a very weak part of the door. You can install the cylindrical lock through this repair piece or move up or down on the door and install it in undisturbed solid wood. If you do not want to replace the old mortise lock but want to repair it,

TO REMOVE LOCK:
1. REMOVE THE KNOBS AND THEIR SPINDLE.
2. UNSCREW FROM THE DOOR.
3. PULL OUT THE LOCK.

TO INSTALL A NEWER LOCK, GLUE A SOLID-WOOD BLOCK INTO THE MORTISE.

13–13. Old mortise locks are not secure and should be replaced with a new type of lock.

consider installing a key-operated dead bolt above it. Heavy-duty mortise locks are available for use on commercial buildings.

A **cylindrical lockset** (**13–14**) has a heavy-duty mechanism and is a strong lock. It has a large cylindrical case surrounding the locking mechanism. It requires that a large-diameter hole be bored through the door.

13–14. A cylindrical lockset has a large cylindrical case surrounding the locking mechanism.

A **tubular lockset** (13–15) has a long, narrow mechanism and is not as secure as the cylindrical lock. A small-diameter hole has to be bored through the door. It is used on interior doors to provide privacy. Tubular locksets are not key-operated. They are locked by pressing a button in the center of the handle. They unlock when this handle is turned. They are installed in the same way as exterior locksets.

A **dead bolt** has a large, solid latch that enters a metal strike plate on the door jamb. The plunger is not spring-operated and can only be moved with a key or indoor handle; therefore, it cannot be slipped open with a plastic card. The two types of dead bolts are **tubular** (13–16) and **surface-mounted**, referred to as **rim locks** (13–17).

Servicing Locks

About once a year, squirt some graphite powder into the key opening. If the key still has difficulty entering the lock, it probably has dirt in it. Try to blow out the dirt with compressed air.

If the lock freezes in cold weather, heat the key with a match and work it into the lock. Repeat as necessary to thaw it out. Then plan some means for protecting the lock from direct exposure to the weather.

13–16. Dead bolts provide excellent security and are used in addition to the usual cylindrical and tubular locksets.

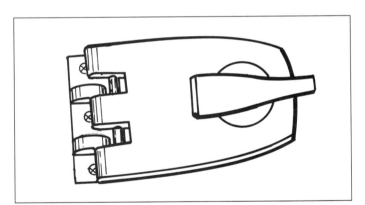

13–17. Surface-mounted dead bolts provide additional protection.

Sometimes you will break off a key in a lock that turns hard and needs maintenance. You might be able to grasp the piece with needle-nose pliers. If not, try to insert a wire in the key opening and work it out.

If the key turns the lock easily when the door is open but is difficult to turn when it is closed, the latch is probably rubbing against the side of the opening in the strike plate. You can move the strike plate over a little by filing a bit off that side of the opening in the strike plate.

If the lock tends to stick and it is difficult to move the mechanism, the lock is probably dirty or has a gummy substance or mold in it. Remove the lock from the door and clean it. Spray in graphite powder.

13–15. Tubular locksets are used on interior and exterior doors.

Replacing a Cylinder Lock

To replace a cylinder lock:

1. Remove the knob on the inner side of the door. Usually there is a small spring catch that can be pressed with a screwdriver, and the handle can be pulled off (**13–18**).

2. Slide off the rose that fits over the spindle. (The **rose** is the round part that fits around the shaft that enters the door.) It is usually held by friction to tabs on the plate below it or by a spring catch. It can be popped loose with a screwdriver.

3. Remove the two screws on the retainer plate. Pull the plate loose; then pull the mechanism and outside handle off the other side of the door. The latch can now be removed by removing the two screws in the edge of the door and pulling it forward.

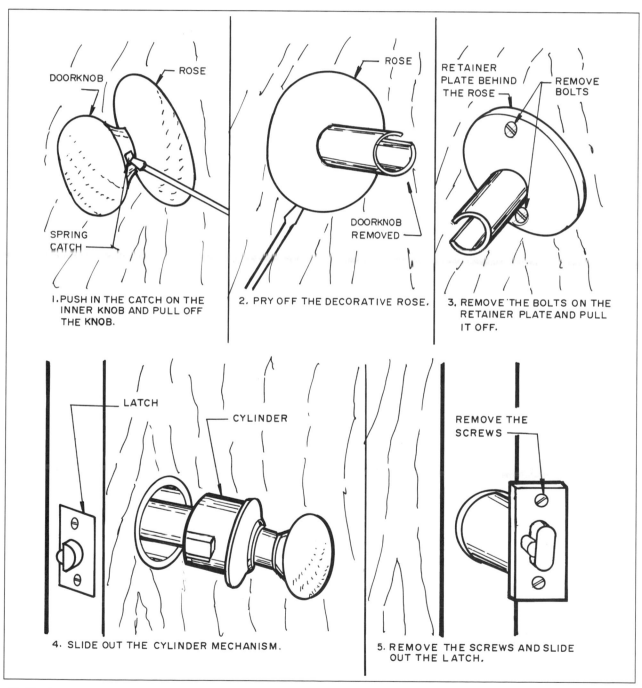

13–18. Steps to replace a cylinder lock.

Replacing a Tubular Lock

A tubular lock is replaced in the same manner as described for the cylinder lock. On some styles, the two screws are not hidden by the rose but extend through it. In this case, remove these screws and the knobs and spindle can be removed from the door (**13–19**).

Installing a New Tubular or Cylindrical Lockset or Dead Bolt

New locks come with complete instructions for installation and templates to locate needed holes.

Follow these instructions carefully. These steps are typical for locksets on the market:

1. Remove the old lock. If it was a cylindrical or tubular type, there will be a hole in the door. Measure its diameter and try to buy a lock using the same-size hole. Also check the size of the hole for the latch mechanism in the edge of the door.

2. If it is a new door or you are going to relocate the new lock, it will be necessary to bore new holes. Locate the centers of the holes using the template provided (**13–20**).

3. To bore a large hole, use an expansion bit, lockset bit, or a hole saw in your electric drill (**13–21**).

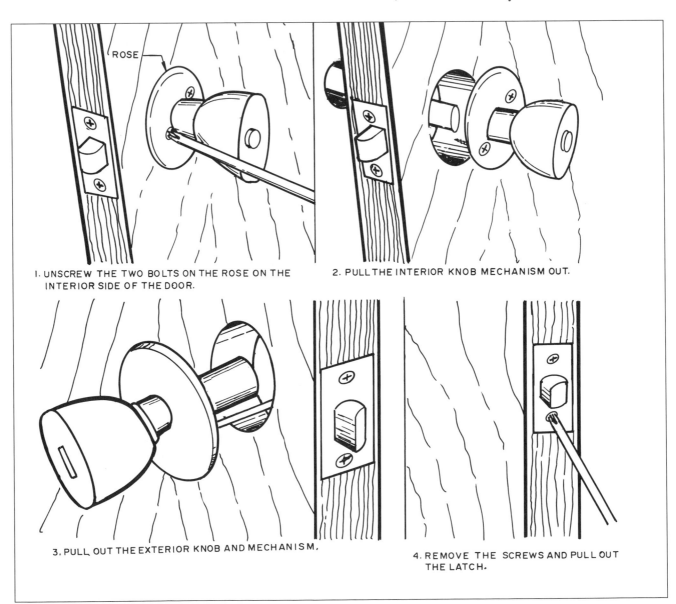

1. UNSCREW THE TWO BOLTS ON THE ROSE ON THE INTERIOR SIDE OF THE DOOR.

2. PULL THE INTERIOR KNOB MECHANISM OUT.

3. PULL OUT THE EXTERIOR KNOB AND MECHANISM.

4. REMOVE THE SCREWS AND PULL OUT THE LATCH.

13–19. Steps to replace a tubular lock.

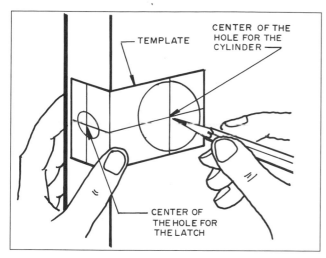

13–20. Use the template supplied with the lock to locate the centers of the holes.

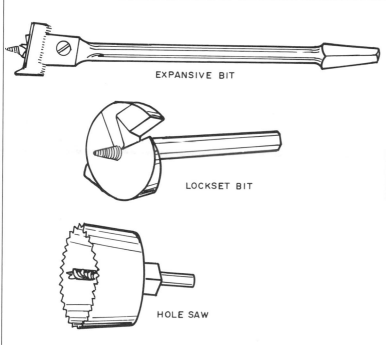

13–21. These tools are used to bore the large-diameter holes needed.

Do not bore all the way through or you will split the door on the other side. Bore until the tip of the bit shows on the other side. Then finish the hole by boring from the other side (**13–22**).

4. Mark the center of the small hole on the edge of the door using the template provided (refer to **13–20**). Bore a hole of the proper diameter until it breaks through into the large-diameter hole (**13–23**).

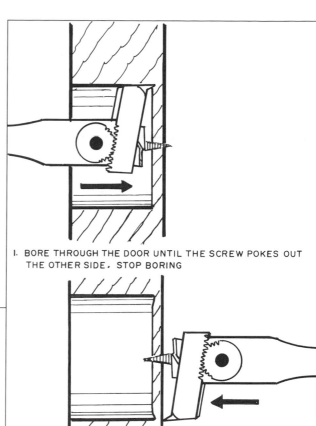

I. BORE THROUGH THE DOOR UNTIL THE SCREW POKES OUT THE OTHER SIDE. STOP BORING

2. THEN FINISH THE HOLE BY BORING FROM THE OTHER SIDE.

13–22. When you bore through the door, stop when the screw tip comes out the other side and finish the hole from the other side.

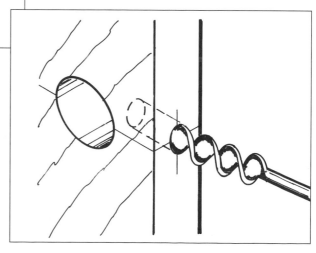

13–23. Bore the latch hole into the edge of the door through to the cylinder hole.

13–24 (right). Mark the edge of the latch and chisel out the gain so the latch will fit flush with the edge of the door.

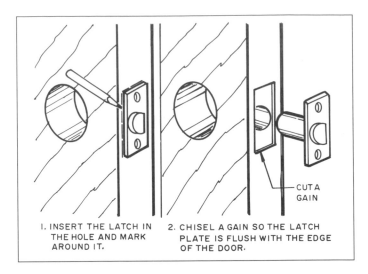

I. INSERT THE LATCH IN THE HOLE AND MARK AROUND IT.

2. CHISEL A GAIN SO THE LATCH PLATE IS FLUSH WITH THE EDGE OF THE DOOR.

5. Slide the spring latch into the small hole. Mark around the outside of its plate. Remove it and chisel out the area behind it so the plate is flush with the edge of the door (**13–24**).

6. Slide the spring latch back into the hole and secure it with the two wood screws provided.

7. Now install the knobs and spindle following the manufacturer's directions (**13–25**).

---

❶ MARK HOLES

MARK HEIGHT LINE ON EDGE OF DOOR 38" FROM FLOOR. POSITION CENTER LINE OF TEMPLATE ON HEIGHT LINE AND MARK CENTER POINT OF DOOR THICKNESS AND CENTER POINT FOR 2⅛" HOLE.

NOTE: CYLINDER LOCKS OF THIS TYPE ARE FACTORY-ASSEMBLED HALF RIGHT-HANDED AND HALF LEFT-HANDED UNLESS HANDEDNESS IS SPECIFIED ON ORDER. WHEN THIS LOCK IS MOUNTED ON A DOOR, THE KEY SHOULD BE IN THIS POSITION ⟡ AS IT ENTERS THE CYLINDER.

TO CHANGE HAND OF LOCK, REVERSE CYLINDER AS FOLLOWS:

TO REMOVE KNOB:
1. WITH OUTSIDE KNOB IN OPEN POSITION, TURN KNOB CLOCKWISE AS FAR AS IT WILL GO.
2. INSERT AWL OR SMALL PIN THROUGH SLEEVE HOLE, DEPRESS KNOB CATCH, AND PULL KNOB FROM TUBE.

TO REPLACE KNOB:
1. ROTATE KNOB 180 DEGREES AND PUSH KNOB BACK ON TUBE UNTIL IT HITS KNOB CATCH (FOR EASIER INSTALLATION, INSERT KEY HALFWAY AND WIGGLE CYLINDER).
2. TURN KNOB CLOCKWISE AS FAR AS IT WILL GO, INSERT AWL OR SMALL PIN THROUGH SLEEVE HOLE, AND DEPRESS KNOB CATCH. AS YOU DEPRESS KNOB CATCH, PUSH KNOB UNTIL KNOB CATCH CLICKS INTO UP POSITION.

FOR HOTEL LOCKS, FLOCK, DC LOCKS:

TO REMOVE KNOB:
1. INSERT KEY INTO CYLINDER.
2. INSET AWL OR SMALL PIN THROUGH SLEEVE HOLE AND WHILE EXERTING PRESSURE SLOWLY TURN KEY IN CLOCKWISE DIRECTION UNTIL KNOB DEPRESSES; THEN PULL OFF KNOB.

TO REPLACE KNOB:
1. PARTIALLY REMOVE KEY FROM CYLINDER, ROTATE KNOB 180 DEGREES, AND PUSH KNOB BACK ON TUBE UNTIL IT HITS KNOB CATCH. (FOR EASIER INSTALLATION, WIGGLE CYLINDER WITH KEY.)
2. INSERT KEY FULLY INTO CYLINDER. INSERT AWL OR SMALL PIN THROUGH SLEEVE HOLE AND WHILE EXERTING PRESSURE TURN KEY CLOCKWISE UNTIL KNOB CATCH DEPRESSES. THEN PUSH KNOB UNTIL KNOB CATCH CLICKS INTO UP POSITION. FOR PROPER INSTALLATION, ALL HOLLOW METAL AND STEEL DOORS MUST HAVE LATCH AND LOCK CASE SUPPORT BY THE DOOR MANUFACTURER.

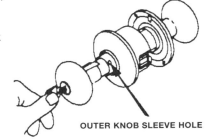

OUTER KNOB SLEEVE HOLE

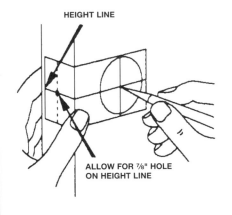

HEIGHT LINE

ALLOW FOR ⅞" HOLE ON HEIGHT LINE

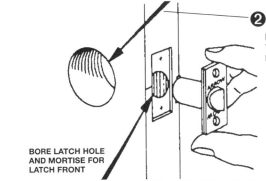

BORE LATCH HOLE AND MORTISE FOR LATCH FRONT

❷ BORING HOLES

BORE THE 2⅛" HOLE AT POINT MARKED FROM BOTH SIDES OF DOOR. BORE ⅞"LATCH UNIT HOLE STRAIGHT INTO EDGE OF DOOR AT CENTER POINT ON HEIONT AND INSTALL LATCH UNIT.

13–25. Complete installation instructions are supplied with each lock (courtesy Arrow Lock Manufacturing Co.).

❸ REMOVE INSIDE KNOB AND ROSE

DEPRESS KNOB CATCH WITH SCREWDRIVER. PULL KNOB OFF TUBE. REMOVE ROSE AND RETAINER PLATE.

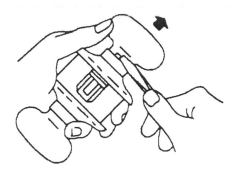

REMOVE ROSE AND RETAINER PLATE

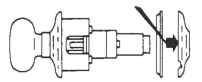

❹ ADJUST FOR DOOR THICKNESS

ROTATE OUTSIDE ROSE TO ADJUST LOCK FOR DOOR THICKNESS. LOCK WILL FIT ANY DOOR FROM 1⅜" TO 1¾" THICK

ROTATE AS FAR AS POSSIBLE FOR 1⅜" DOOR

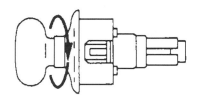

ROTATE OUT TO ³⁄₁₆" FOR 1¾"

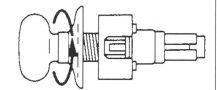

❺ INSTALL MAIN UNIT

MAIN HOUSING MUST ENGAGE WITH LATCH PRONGS AND RETRACTOR WITH LATCH TAILPIECE AS SHOWN.

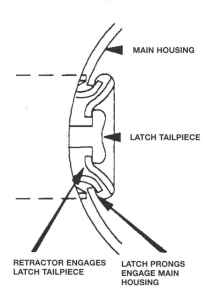

MAIN HOUSING

LATCH TAILPIECE

RETRACTOR ENGAGES LATCH TAILPIECE

LATCH PRONGS ENGAGE MAIN HOUSING

❻ ATTACH INSIDE ROSE

SLIDE ON RETAINER PLATE; INSERT AND TIGHTEN MACHINE SCREWS. SNAP ROSE OVER RETAINER PLATE.

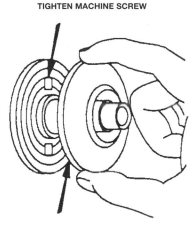

TIGHTEN MACHINE SCREW

SLOT FOR REMOVING ROSE

❼ REPLACE INSIDE KNOB

LINE UP DEPRESSION IN KNOB SLEEVE WITH SLOT IN TUBE. SLIDE KNOB ON TUBE. DEPRESS KNOB CATCH AND PUSH KNOB INTO POSITION.

DEPRESS KNOB LATCH

❽ INSTALL STRIKE

MAKE SHALLOW MORTISE IN DOOR JAMB TO ALIGN WITH LATCH FACE AND INSTALL STRIKE.

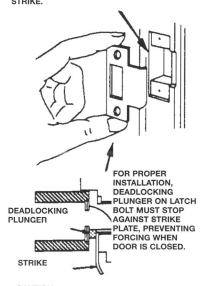

FOR PROPER INSTALLATION, DEADLOCKING PLUNGER ON LATCH BOLT MUST STOP AGAINST STRIKE PLATE, PREVENTING FORCING WHEN DOOR IS CLOSED.

DEADLOCKING PLUNGER

STRIKE

CAUTION:
DO NOT ATTEMPT TO MOUNT LOCK UNIT WITH DOOR CLOSED.

13–25 continued.

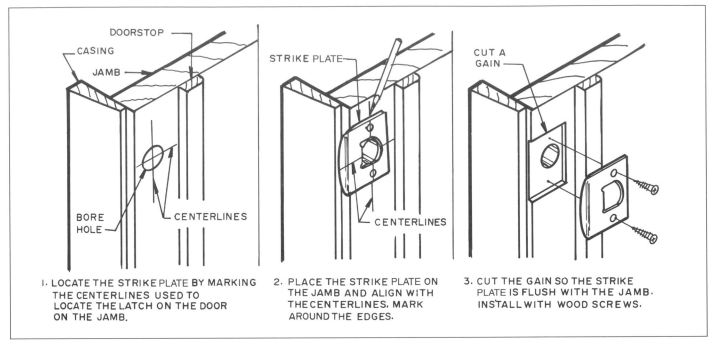

1. LOCATE THE STRIKE PLATE BY MARKING THE CENTERLINES USED TO LOCATE THE LATCH ON THE DOOR ON THE JAMB.

2. PLACE THE STRIKE PLATE ON THE JAMB AND ALIGN WITH THE CENTERLINES. MARK AROUND THE EDGES.

3. CUT THE GAIN SO THE STRIKE PLATE IS FLUSH WITH THE JAMB. INSTALL WITH WOOD SCREWS.

13–26. Install the strike in a gain. Check it to be certain the latch plunger enters it easily.

8. Finally, install the strike plate on the doorjamb. Mark a horizontal line on the jamb that lines up with the center of the hole in the edge of the door (**13–26**). Bore a ⅞-inch (22-millimeter) hole on this centerline about ¾ inch (19 millimeters) deep. Place the strike plate so the centerline runs through the screw holes. Mark around it and chisel out the area so the strike plate is flush with the surface. Install the strike plate with the two screws provided.

9. Now close the door and check the operation of the lock. Make adjustments as needed. If the latch gets stuck up in the mechanism, it means the screws holding the lock mechanism are too tight. If it does not enter the opening in the strike plate, the plate will have to be moved or the opening filed larger to permit the latch to enter without binding.

Installing Dead Bolts

Dead bolts are installed in the same manner as tubular locks. The sliding bolt enters a strike plate mounted on the door frame (**13–27**). Some dead bolts require a key to open from both sides. These are used on doors with glass lights that, if broken,

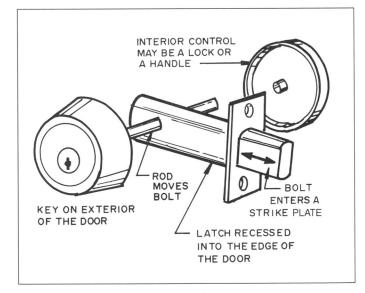

13–27. An internal-mounted dead bolt.

prevent the intruder from reaching inside and unlocking the door. However, they are banned by some codes because if there is a fire you cannot get out the door unless you find the key. Typical installation procedures are shown in **13–28**.

Surface-mounted dead bolts, also called **rim locks**, are excellent locks to prevent entry when mounted on a solid-wood door. On the exterior a

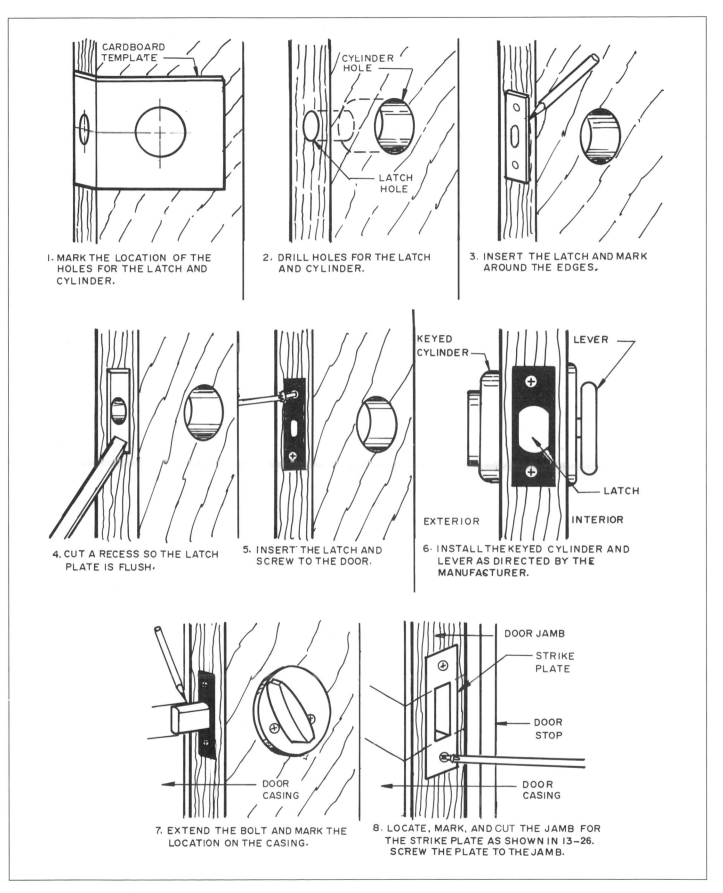

1. MARK THE LOCATION OF THE HOLES FOR THE LATCH AND CYLINDER.

2. DRILL HOLES FOR THE LATCH AND CYLINDER.

3. INSERT THE LATCH AND MARK AROUND THE EDGES.

4. CUT A RECESS SO THE LATCH PLATE IS FLUSH.

5. INSERT THE LATCH AND SCREW TO THE DOOR.

6. INSTALL THE KEYED CYLINDER AND LEVER AS DIRECTED BY THE MANUFACTURER.

7. EXTEND THE BOLT AND MARK THE LOCATION ON THE CASING.

8. LOCATE, MARK, AND CUT THE JAMB FOR THE STRIKE PLATE AS SHOWN IN 13-26. SCREW THE PLATE TO THE JAMB.

13–28. Steps to install an internal-mounted dead bolt.

rim lock requires a key, and on the interior it has a lever to open it (**13–29**).

Before you buy a lock, measure the door thickness and find out if the door is right-handed or left-handed. When the door is viewed from the "outside," as from a hall facing toward a room, if the hinge is on the right side it is a right-hand door—regardless whether it swings into the room or out into the hall.

The dead bolt will have a template that is positioned on the door. Drill the anchor holes for the screws and a large hole for the cylinder (**13–30**). Do not drill all the way through. Drill until the drill screw pokes through the other side. Then finish the hole from the other side. Insert the cylinder ring around the cylinder and insert on the exterior side of the door. Screw the back plate on the inside of the door as directed by the manufacturer's instructions. Screw the lock mechanism to the back plate.

Now install the lock strike plate. Hold it against the door casing with the lock closed. Mark around the strike. Remove the strike plate and cut a recess for it in the casing. Then secure it to the casing with screws. Check to see that the locking mechanism slides into the strike plate easily. Use screws long enough to penetrate into the door frame or a stud. In all cases, follow the manufacturer's instructions.

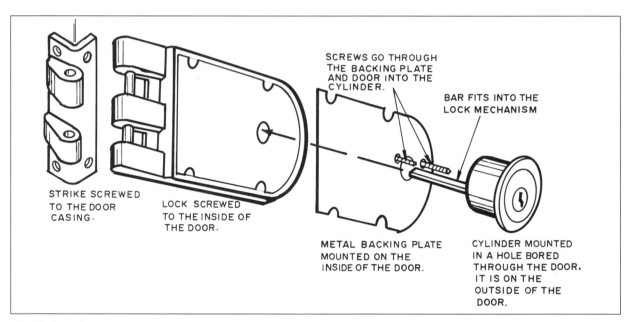

13–29. A typical surface-mounted dead bolt.

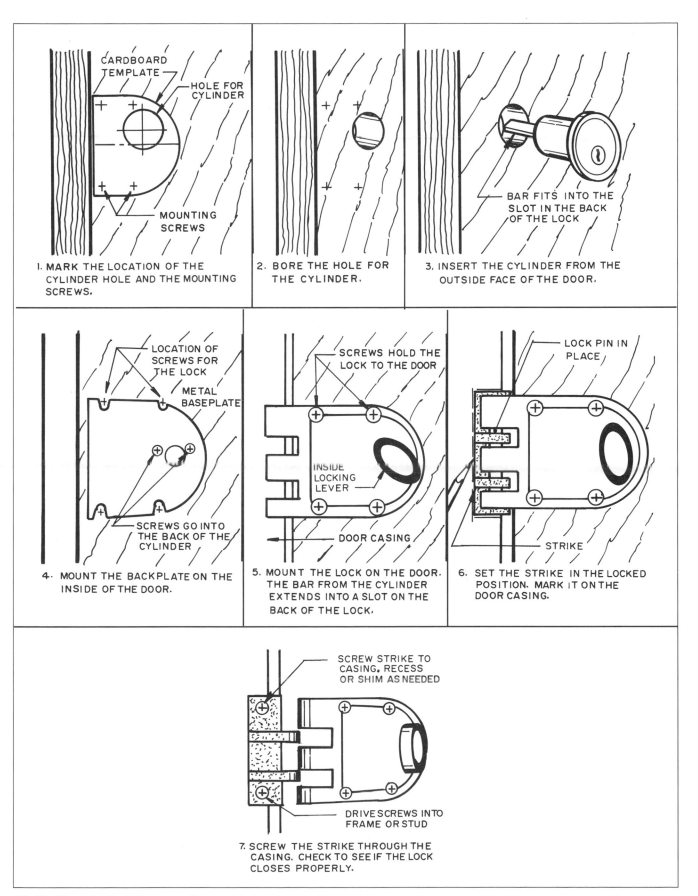

13–30. *Steps for installing a surface-mounted dead bolt.*

WINDOW SECURITY

Windows are difficult to secure and yet keep operational. The standard window sash locks found on most double-hung windows prevent minor entry attempts, but are too weak to stop a serious attempt. Their main value is to pull together the top and bottom sash to seal them to reduce air leakage (**13–31**). A more satisfactory lock for double-hung windows is installed by drilling small-diameter holes through the inside sash and ¾ inch (19 millimeters) deep into the outside sash and then run a nail or strong wire into the hole. Two of these per window provide excellent security (**13–31**). A stick placed between the sash also provides security (**13–31**).

There are a number of commercially available window locks available at your local building-supply dealer. Some require a key or special wrench to

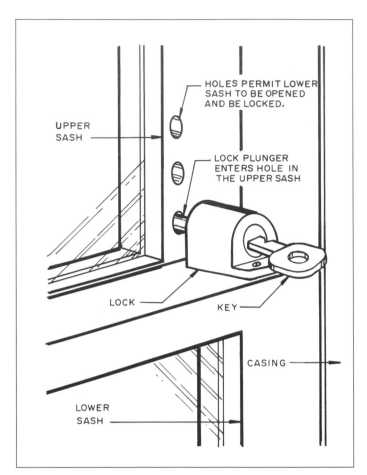

13–32. There are a number of commercially manufactured locks that are used to secure double-hung windows.

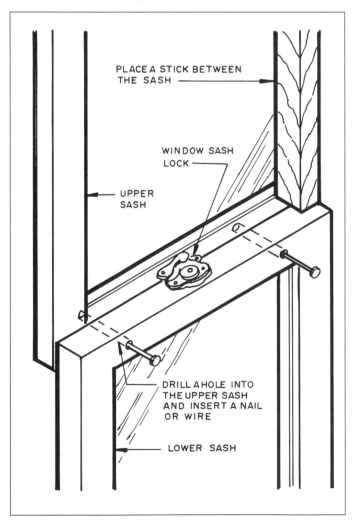

13–31. Several ways to easily and inexpensively secure double-hung windows.

unlock. These can be a problem in an emergency because the key or tool will eventually get misplaced and a means of escape is not available. One type that uses a key is shown in **13–32**.

Another technique is to install good-quality metal storm windows. While these are not burglar-proof, they do add another layer of protection as well as prevent the loss of energy that occurs with inefficient windows.

Sliding windows use the same protection devices mentioned earlier for sliding doors. A small rod placed in the channel is about as good as anything.

Glazing can be replaced with clear polycarbonate materials that look like glass but are virtually unbreakable. These are more expensive than glass and will scratch if they are cleaned with normal abrasive materials. You could install sheets over door glazing using nonremovable wood screws (**13–33**). Fire codes will probably prohibit the use of

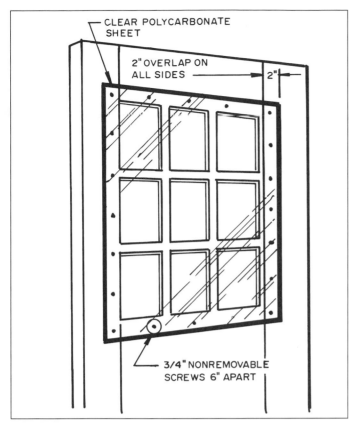

CLEAR POLYCARBONATE SHEET

2" OVERLAP ON ALL SIDES

2"

3/4" NONREMOVABLE SCREWS 6" APART

13–33. You can reduce the danger of someone breaking the glass in your doors by screwing a sheet of polycarbonate material over them.

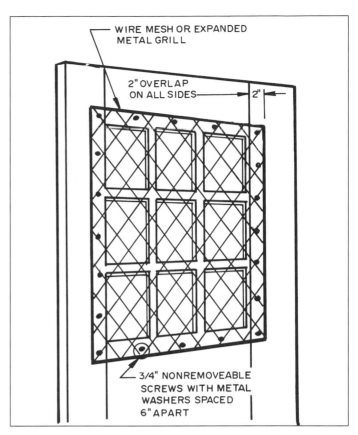

WIRE MESH OR EXPANDED METAL GRILL

2" OVERLAP ON ALL SIDES

2"

3/4" NONREMOVEABLE SCREWS WITH METAL WASHERS SPACED 6" APART

13–34. Metal grills will protect the glass in your doors and restrict entry.

these sheets over windows, because then escape is blocked.

In areas where there is a danger of thieves' breaking a glass window or door pane to gain entry, the window can be covered with expandable wire mesh. The mesh must be securely screwed or bolted to the wall surrounding the window. On doors, it can be fastened to the door itself. If it is used on windows, provide some means for removing it from the inside so a person could escape during a fire (**13–34**). Building codes will most likely prohibit mesh from being used on windows.

ALARM SYSTEMS

Security systems may be hard-wired or wireless. A **hard–wired system** has a control panel that has a transformer operating on 120 volts, but converts this to a low voltage. It is installed in a secure, out-of-the-way location. When turned on, the system has a complete closed circuit to switches placed at

doors and windows. When this is broken, for example if a door is opened, the alarm sounds. You may have it connected to a central security office or police station where the signal is received. Likewise, you may prefer to have it simply start a loud alarm inside the house and a siren outside the house (**13–35**).

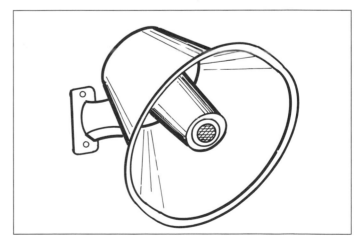

13–35. Alarm systems usually have a siren installed outside the house that alerts the neighbors that the house has been entered.

Hard-wired systems are usually installed as the house is built. The wires to the doors and windows are run in the wall cavities and under the floor or over the ceiling before the drywall is installed. To install such a system after the house is finished requires a great deal of work that includes cutting holes in walls.

Hard-wired systems have a foil alarm tape used to sound an alarm if the glass is broken. The thin, adhesive-backed metallic tape is bonded to the glass. It conducts the low-voltage electric current to a sensor mounted on the door or window. When the tape is broken, the alarm is sounded.

A general example of a hard-wired system installed after the house has been finished is shown in **13–36**. The baseboard is removed, lifted up about ⅜ inch (9.5 millimeters), and reinstalled; the ⅜-inch lift provides a space to run the low-voltage wire around the perimeter of the house to the doors and windows. This wire connects to the magnetic switch on each door and window.

After you remove the baseboard, cut a small hole in the drywall and feed the wires to a hole bored in the jamb. Review Chapter 2, Electrical Repairs, for information on how to do this. Cover the wire at the base with shoe molding.

A plunger switch is used at the doors (**13–37**). This is much like the switch on a refrigerator door. The unit is controlled at a keypad similar to that shown in **13–38**. Be certain to study the installation and operation manual.

The **wireless system** has a control panel operated on 120-volt electricity (**13–39**). It receives a signal from an electronic sensor and transmitter mounted on each door and window (**13–40**). When the control panel is activated and a door or window is opened, the sensor transmits a signal to the panel, which sounds the alarm, and, if you subscribe to the service, to a central monitoring office. The system also provides bedside alarms, medical alarms, and smoke monitors. Glass-breakage sensors can be put on glazing and signal an alarm if the glass is broken.

To install such a system, put sensors at each door and window. Each requires only the installation of a couple of screws (**13–41**). The transmitter is pow-

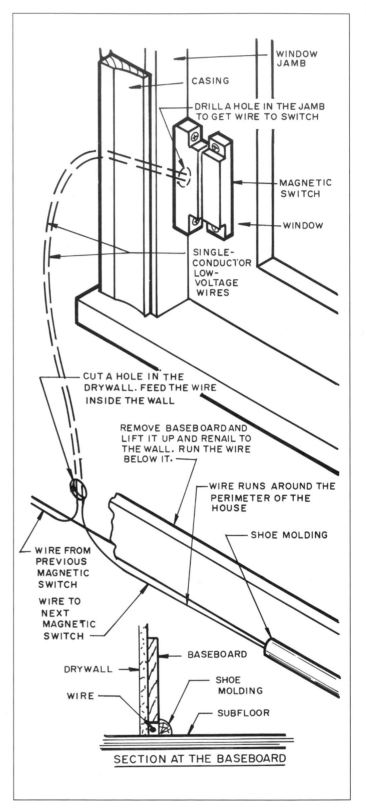

13–36. When you install a hard-wired alarm system after the house has been built, you will have to do some carpentry work and electrical wiring.

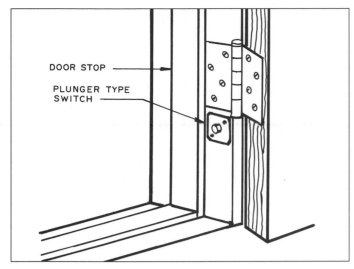

13–37. Doors on hard-wired alarm systems use a plunger switch to activate the alarm when the door is opened.

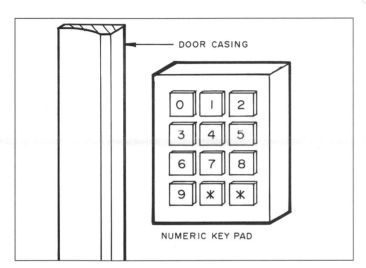

13–38. The home owner controls the hard-wired alarm system from keypads installed near the exterior doors frequently used to enter the house.

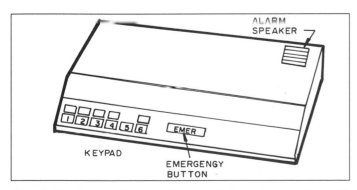

13–39. This is a control panel for a wireless alarm system. All functions are controlled from it, and it contains the receiver of the signals sent from the transmitters mounted on the doors and windows.

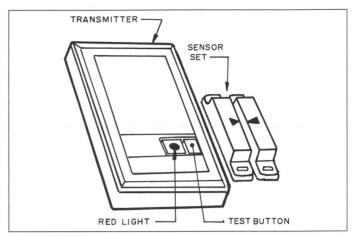

13–40. The transmitter and sensor set are mounted by each door or window. When the sensors are separated, the transmitter sends a signal to the control panel, which sounds an alarm.

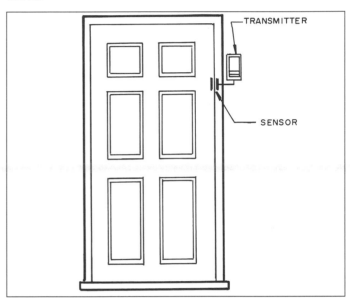

13–41. The transmitter is mounted on the wall near a door or window and is connected to one side of the sensor set with a wire.

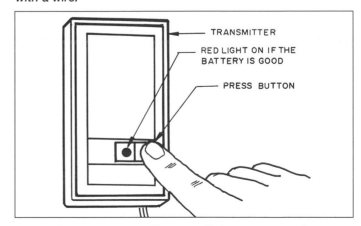

13–42. Check occasionally to see if the transmitter batteries are still good by pressing the button on each transmitter. If the red light glows, the battery is still good.

ered with a nine-volt battery, so you need to check each sensor occasionally to verify that the battery is still functioning. To do this, press the test button on the transmitter. If the red light fails to light, replace the battery (**13–42**).

One transmitter can operate several doors or windows if they are close together (**13–43**). Sliding glass doors can be secured as shown in **13–44**.

You can add a second sensor magnet a few inches above the original magnet on double-hung windows to permit you to provide some ventilation but maintain the security of the alarm system (**13–45**). Be certain the transmitter and sensor are high enough above the opening so a thief cannot reach in and disconnect the contacts.

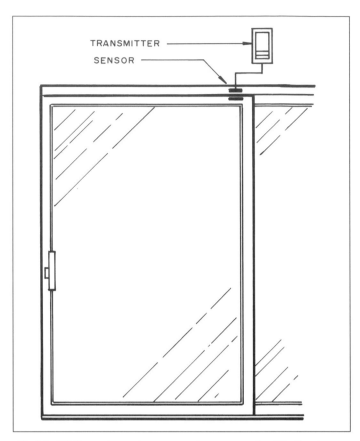

13–44. Sliding glass doors can be secured with the transmitter and sensor set.

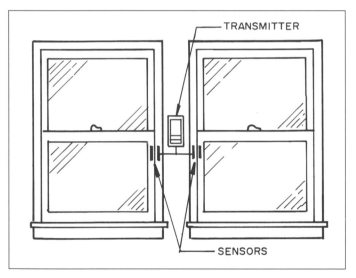

13–43. One transmitter can control several doors and windows. Each must have its own sensor set.

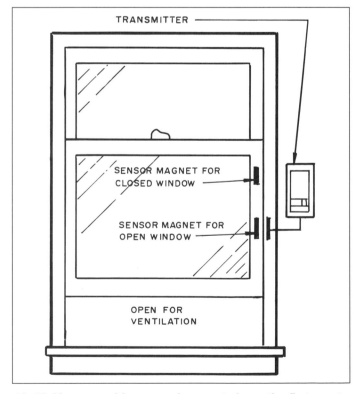

13–45. You can add a second magnet above the first one to provide a bit of ventilation yet keep the alarm system intact.

OTHER PROTECTION DEVICES

You can install an electric eye that sends an invisible beam from a sending device to a receiving device. If someone walks through the beam, an alarm is sounded (**13–46**). Remember, your dog or cat can set off the alarm if left free to walk around the house.

There are electric-eye systems that can be put on the driveway near the street. When a car enters the driveway, it sounds a brief alarm in the house, letting you know a car has entered.

Another device is a motion detector (**13–47**). These may be wired in or battery-operated. They scan an area of a room and sound an alarm if they detect motion in the room. Again, pets will set off some of these alarms.

Another protective device is a motion sensor that can be installed in an existing exterior light. This motion sensor will sense anything approaching your house and turn on an outside floodlight.

An effective deterrent is to install floodlights on the exteriors of the house. Those with two bulbs can illuminate a large area, and a series of floodlights can illuminate the entire area around your house (**13–48**).

MOTION DETECTOR MOUNTED ABOUT 7 FT ABOVE THE FLOOR

13–47. A motion detector is set high on the wall and scans a wide area. Anything moving into its beam will trigger an alarm.

13–48. If you put floodlights on each corner of the house, you can light the area around it. This discourages prowling thieves.

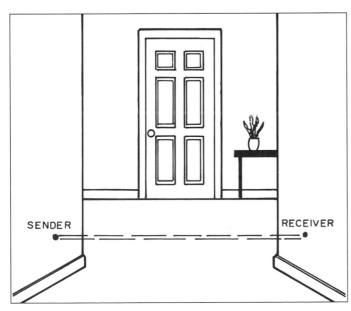

SENDER   RECEIVER

13–46. An electric eye will detect motion if something passes through the invisible beam.

If you are to be away for awhile, a low-cost electric timer can be used to make the house appear occupied. Connect a light, radio, or television to it. Set the timer to turn them on and off at the hours they are normally operating (**13–49**). The passersby will think you are home as usual.

You can also buy window screens that have low-voltage wires running through the mesh. Connect them to your alarm system. They will sound the alarm if the wires are cut.

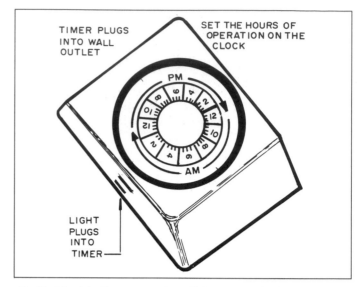

13–49. Electric timers can turn lights on and off during your absence, giving the appearance that the house is occupied. They can also turn on the television and radio, providing sound to reinforce this appearance.

CHAPTER FOURTEEN

Improving Interior Temperature Control

Thermal insulation is needed in a home in all seasons. In the winter, it helps keep heat inside the house. In the summer, it keeps the sun's heat outside the house. Thermal insulation reduces the passage of heat through walls, floors, and ceilings. It adds to the comfort of the living spaces and reduces heating and air-conditioning costs.

HOW HEAT ENERGY IS TRANSFERRED

Heat energy is transferred by convection, conduction, and radiation (**14–1**). **Convection heat transfer** occurs by transferring heat by the circulation or movement of heated liquids or gases (air). When air passes over a warm surface, it is heated. When it passes over a cool surface, it is cooled. **Conduction heat transfer** occurs when the heat is passed through a solid or liquid; for example, when the sun heats a masonry wall, the heat is conducted through the wall and is emitted on the other side.

In your home, a hot-air furnace transfers heat by convection (heated air). Heat built up in the attic is transferred down into the house by conduction through the building materials.

Radiated heat energy passes through the air between the source and the object being heated without heating the intervening air. It heats the objects it eventually strikes.

DETERMINING THE AMOUNT OF INSULATION NEEDED

Building codes now specify the minimum amount of insulation required. The actual code adopted varies from state to state, so consult your local building inspector.

An example of general recommendations of the Energy Policy Act (which is enforced by the

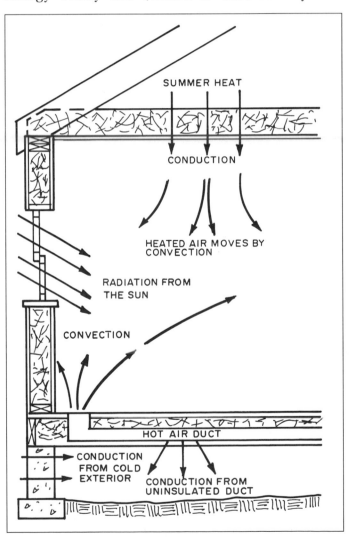

14–1. Heat energy is transferred by convection, conduction, and radiation. These must be controlled and properly directed if you want to have comfortable interior conditions.

Department of Energy) is shown in **14–2**. This does not indicate how many inches of insulation are needed, but gives the R-value of the insulation. (**R-value** is a measure of the ability of a material to resist the flow of heat through it. The larger the R-value, the greater the resistance.) The thickness will vary depending upon the insulation product used to get the required R-value.

Another insulation rating that you should become familiar with is the sound transmission class. **Sound transmission class (STC)** is a number rating indicating the effectiveness of a material or an assembly of materials to reduce the transmission of airborne sound through the material or assembly. The larger the number, the more effective the material is in reducing sound transmission.

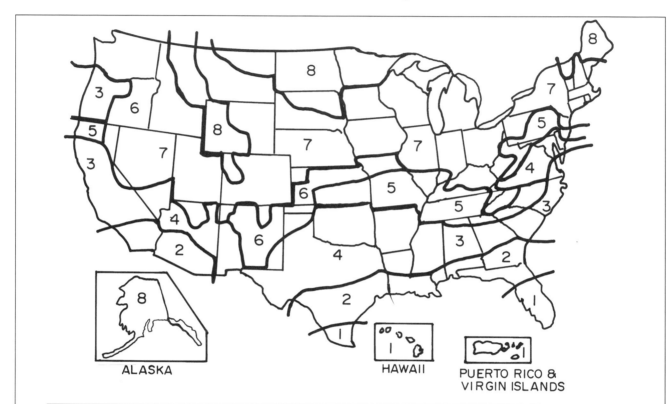

RECOMMENDED R-VALUES FOR EXISTING HOMES*				
ZONE	CEILING BELOW VENTILATED ATTICS		FLOORS OVER UNHEATED BASEMENTS, CRAWLSPACES	EXTERIOR WALLS (WOOD FRAME)	DRY CRAWL-SPACES, WALLS
	Electric Heat	Gas, Oil, Heat Pump		All Fuels	
1	30	19	0	0	11
2	30	30	0	11	19
3	38	30	19	11	19
4	38	30	19	11	19
5	38	38	19	11	19
6	38	38	19	11	19
7	49	38	19	11	19
8	49	49	19	11	19

* Try to upgrade your house to these levels. Chart courtesy of U.S. Department of Energy.

14–2. If possible, you should bring your insulation up to these levels (courtesy U.S. Department of Energy).

FIXING LEAKS

One major source of heat loss and heat gain is air leaks through various parts of the house. The following are suggestions for correcting these leaks.

Old, loose, ill-fitting doors and windows are a major problem. Correct them by installing storm windows and doors (refer to Installing Storm Windows on page 449), replacing them with new, energy-efficient windows and doors, or sealing around them with some form of weather stripping (refer to Weather-Stripping Doors and Windows on pages 449 to 451). You can also replace the threshold on the door and install a plastic strip on the bottom of the door (also discussed in Weather-Stripping Doors and Windows).

Electrical outlets, switches, pipes, and other things penetrating through the drywall let a lot of air filter into the house. You can remove the cover and seal around each switch or around the pipe with caulking (**14–3**) or get a foam-rubber gasket and place it behind the switch or outlet cover.

Leaks between the top of the foundation and the floor framing let air into the basement or crawl space. Fill the gaps around the foundation with foam insulation sold in pressurized cans. It comes out soft like shaving cream, expands a great deal (filling the crack), and hardens. It is good for filling any cracks or openings in the walls of the house. Caulking can also be used (**14–4**).

Be certain the cracks around doors and windows and the exterior siding are filled with latex caulking. It is sold in tubes and placed with a caulking gun (**14–5**).

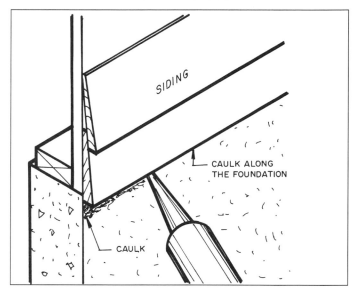

14–4. Caulk around the foundation. Be certain the caulking fills all cracks between the siding and foundation.

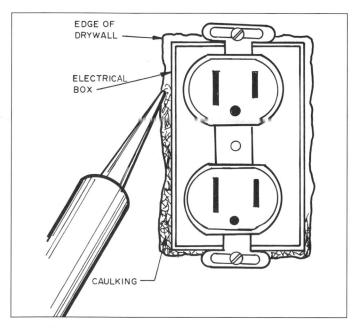

14–3. Seal the crack around electrical boxes, pipes and other items that penetrate the drywall.

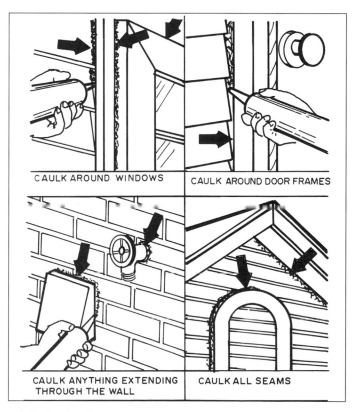

14–5. Caulk all exterior openings and joints where air and water could enter.

If your house has pull-down stairs or an access door to the attic, seal the edges with adhesive-backed foam-rubber tape.

Keep your fireplace damper closed when you do not have a fire going. Add glass doors to the opening to increase the seal. Having an open damper is much like leaving a window wide open.

KINDS OF INSULATION

Insulating materials are used to control the inflow and outflow of heat energy from the interior of the house. Insulation is available in batts 48 inches (1219 millimeters) long, blankets up to 8 feet (2.4 meters) and longer, sheet material, and loose materials sold in bags. There are many types available. Those most commonly used are shown in **Table 14–1**. Their effectiveness is rated by their R-value. The higher the R-value, the better they resist passage of heat energy.

Insulating foams commonly used include extruded polystyrene, expanded polystyrene, and polyurethane. These are produced in rigid sheets 16 and 24 inches (406 and 610 millimeters) wide and 48 to 96 inches (1219 to 2438 millimeters) long in thickness of 1, 1½, 2, 2½, 3, and 4 inches (25, 38, 51, 63, 76, and 102 millimeters). They are used as sheathing and foundation insulation.

Granular insulation includes perlite (expanded volcanic rock), vermiculite (expanded mica), and

TABLE 14–1. COMMON TYPES OF INSULATION AND THEIR R-VALUES

		Most Common Forms	R-Values per Inch Thickness
Mineral Wools	Rock Wool	Loose fill	2.7 to 3.0
		Blanket or batting	3.1 to 3.7
	Fiberglass	Loose fill	2.3 to 2.7
		Blanket or batting	2.9 to 3.8
		Semi-rigid boards	
		High-performance blankets	3.7 to 4.3
Wood Products	Cellulose	Loose fill	3.4 to 3.7
		Semi-rigid board used as exterior sheathing	1.6
Insulating Foams	Extruded polystyrene	Smooth-surface rigid boards	4.5 to 5.0
	Expanded polystyrene (molded beads)	Rigid boards	3.6 to 4.0
	Polyurethane	Rigid boards	6.2
		Foamed in place	5.6 to 6.3
	Polyisocyanurate	Foil-faced boards	7.0
		Unfaced boards	5.6 to 6.3
Mineral Fills	Perlite	Loose fill	2.4 to 3.7
	Vermiculite	Loose fill	2.4 to 3.7

Metal-foil reflective insulation with 3.5-inch air space	In ceiling and floor	2.0 heat upflow 8.17 heat downflow
	In wall	2.5

expanded polystyrene. These are used to fill cavities such as the cores in a concrete block wall.

Mineral-wool insulation commonly used includes fiberglass and rock wool. Fiberglass is made of very fine fibers spun out of glass. Rock wool is made of fine fibers formed from molten rock. These are available in batts and blankets 15 and 23 inches (381 and 584 millimeters) wide. Batts are 48 inches long and blankets are typically 7 feet (2.1 meters) and longer.

Loose-fill insulation may be rock wool, fiberglass, or cellulose. These materials are available in bags and can be blown into cavities and attics. Granular insulation is another type of loose fill. It is used mainly on ceilings.

Radiant insulation is composed of one or more layers of aluminum foil. It is stapled to the rafters inside the attic and reflects the heat coming through the roof back to the exterior.

Foamed insulation is a plastic mix that is pumped into wall cavities and other voids.

WHERE SHOULD YOU INSULATE?

Insulation should be placed in any wall, ceiling, floor, or foundation that is exposed to possible temperature variations. The common locations are shown in **14–6**.

VAPOR RETARDERS

Walls, ceilings, and floors should have a vapor retarder facing the inside (warm side) of the house. Unfaced blankets used with new construction are held in the wall cavity by pressure against the studs and are covered with a polyethylene sheet as shown in **14–7** on the following page. It is advisable to get sheets 8 feet (2.4 meters) wide and cover the wall with a single piece. If it is necessary to end-join pieces or turn a corner, lap it one stud over the previous piece.

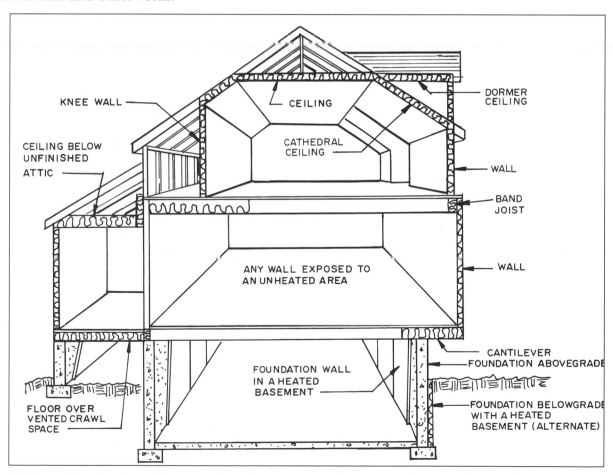

14–6. Insulate all walls, ceilings, and floors that are exposed to unheated areas or the weather.

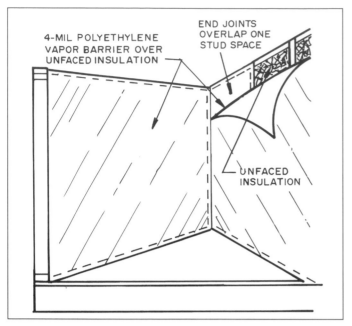

14–7. Unfaced insulation must be covered with a vapor barrier on the warm side of the wall.

14–8. The paper facing on faced insulation blankets serves as the vapor barrier.

If blankets faced with kraft paper are being used, push them into the cavity until they touch the sheathing and staple them to the studs. The top and bottom ends must fit tightly against the top and bottom plates. The paper covering is the vapor barrier. It must face the warm side (inside) of the wall (14–8).

If moisture penetrates the interior wall, wets the insulation, and gets on the siding, the exterior paint will fail. This is a special problem in kitchens and baths. It can also cause structural problems in the studs and damage some types of sheathing.

If you want to protect the insulation in an existing house from moisture and do not want to tear off the drywall to install a plastic vapor barrier, you can paint the wall with a special vapor-retarding primer that has a permeability rating of 0.6. Polyethylene sheeting 4 to 6 mil thick has a permeability rating of 0.10. The **permeability rating** is a measure used to express the resistance of a material to the penetration of water vapor. The higher the rating, the greater the resistance to penetration by water vapor.

One way to help control moisture is to install exhaust fans in areas where moisture is generated. Many bath ceiling lights have exhaust fans built as part of the fixture. Through-the-wall exhaust fans in the kitchen are common. Do not exhaust moisture into the attic. Get it out of the house (14–9).

INSULATION SAFETY TECHNIQUES

There are a few personal safety precautions you should follow when working with most kinds of insulation:

1. Wear proper clothing to protect your skin. For glass-fiber insulation especially, proper clothing means a long-sleeved shirt, a cap, and gloves.

2. Wear a filtering mask over your nose.

3. Wear safety goggles.

INSULATING WALLS

If your house was built without insulation in the exterior wall, you could consider having an insulation company blow it into the wall cavity. While this is not as effective as blanket installation, it will be a great help. One problem is that it may settle over time and leave the top of the wall without insulation. If doing it yourself, you will have to rent a special blower. It contains a hopper into which the loose fill insulation is put and a blower that moves the insulation through the hose.

Begin by removing siding at each level at which you will blow in insulation (**14–10**). Begin at the lower part of the wall. Drill a hole through the sheathing as required by the blower being rented.

Shut off the electricity to that wall before drilling the hole. Drill holes every 4 feet (1.2 meters) up the wall. A row is drilled between each set of studs. Begin filling at the bottom and, as the cavity fills, move up to

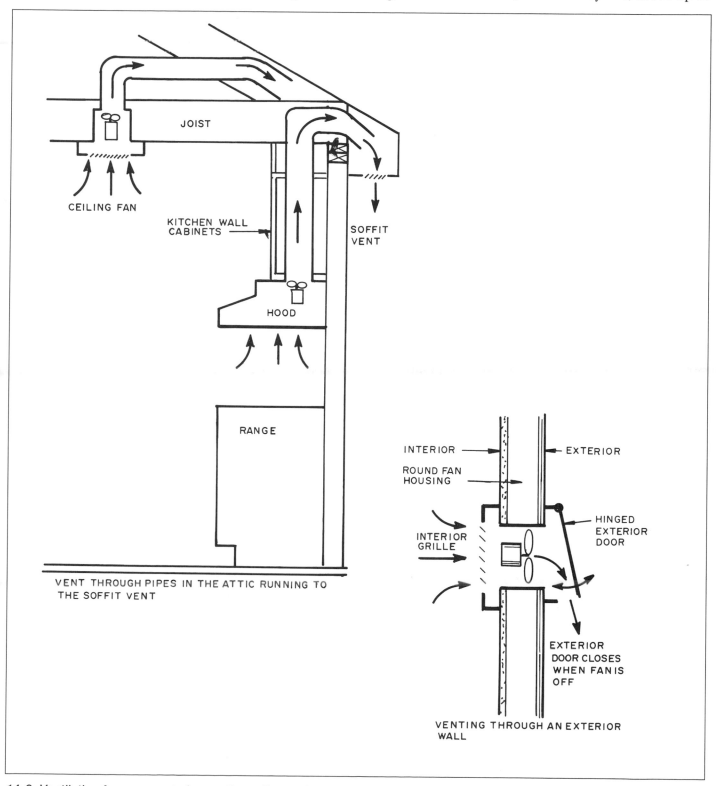

14–9. Ventilation fans can vent air over the ceiling and exhaust it at the soffit vent or through the wall.

the next hole. After one cavity is filled, glue cork into the hole. After the entire wall is finished, reinstall the siding and caulk the seams.

When there is a pipe, electrical box, or other item in the wall, carefully work the insulation behind it (**14–11**). Use scraps to fit into the spaces around the door and window frames (**14–12**).

INSULATING THE CEILING

When you insulate the attic ceiling, lay the blankets between the joists with the kraft-paper side down, facing the room. Make certain they fit snugly against the joists, and that any end-butt joints also fit tightly (**14–13**). If you still do not have enough insulation in the attic, lay a second blanket on top of the first

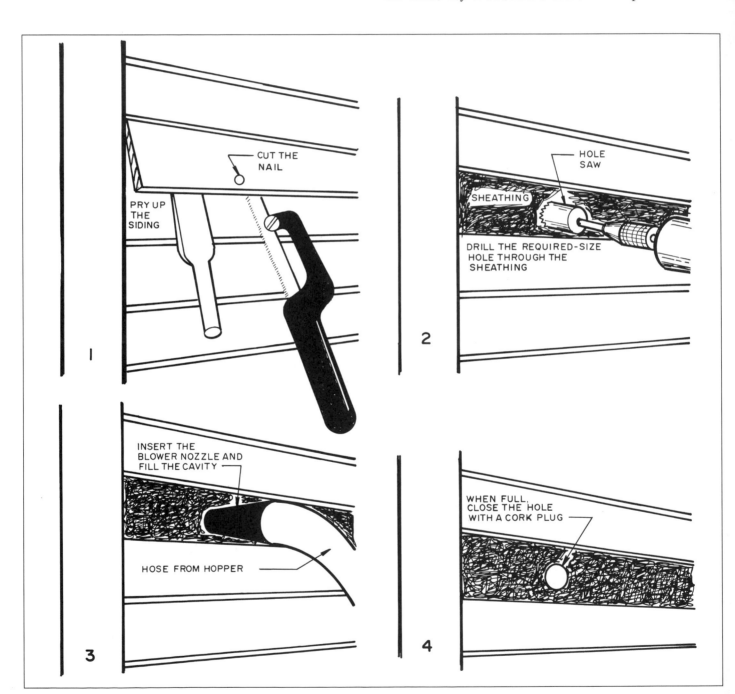

14–10. A typical procedure for installing blown-in insulation. (1) Pry up the siding to be removed and cut off the nails. Do not damage the siding. (2) Shut off electricity to that wall. Drill the required-diameter hole through the sheathing. Insert a wire to find each side stud. (3) Place the blower-hose nozzle into the hole and fill each cavity. (4) Plug the holes, replace the siding, and caulk any seams.

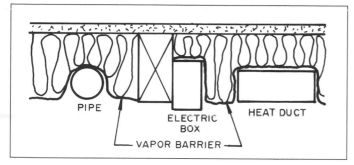

14–11. Carefully work the insulation around pipes and other items in the wall.

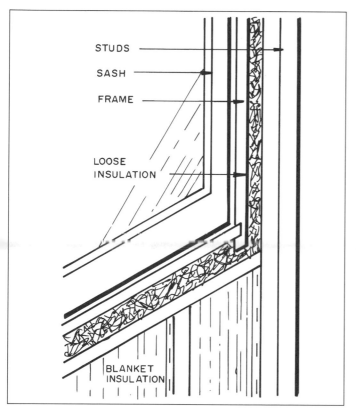

14–12. Work loose insulation into the spaces around door and window frames. Do not pack the insulation tightly, but leave it at its normal density.

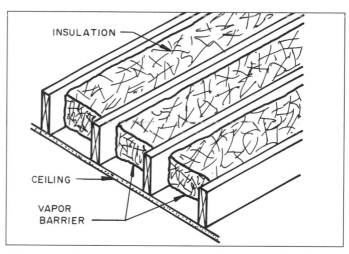

14–13. Ceilings are insulated by placing the blankets between the ceiling joists with the kraft-paper down against the drywall.

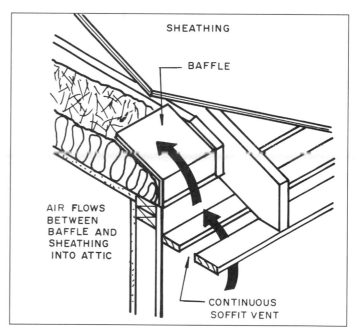

14–14. Do not let the insulation block the flow of air from the soffit vent into the attic.

layer. It does not have a kraft-paper vapor barrier on either side. Some prefer to lay the second layer at right angles to the first layer, which is between the joists. You could also blow in loose insulation over the existing insulation.

The insulation should go over the top plate of the exterior wall. Be careful you do not block the flow of air from the soffit into the attic. If this is a possibility, install baffles along the plate to keep the airflow open (**14–14**).

Should a light fixture extend up into the attic, the insulation must be kept at least 3 inches (76 millimeters) away on all sides. The use of metal dividers is a good way to do this. Place noncombustible insulation in the space between the chimney and the wood framing (**14–15**).

INSULATING FLOORS

Install insulation between floor joists. If there is no finish material below the insulation, install the insulation between the joists and hold it in place with

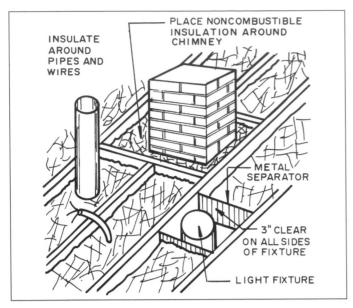

14–15. Keep insulation clear of any light fixtures recessed into the ceiling. Be certain the insulation fits tightly against any pipes, wires, or other items penetrating the ceiling.

metal wires as shown in **14–16**. Be sure the kraft-paper vapor barrier faces up toward the heated space.

Insulating the foundation and floor-joist header on unvented, unheated crawl spaces is shown in **14–17**. When a two-story house is under construction, insulate the header between floors (**14–18**). Cantilevered floors are exposed to the elements and must be heavily insulated (**14–19**).

If you are building a new building with a concrete floor slab, one way to insulate it is shown in **14–20**.

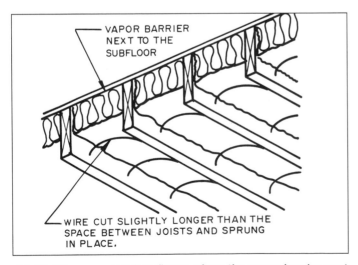

14–16. When you insulate floors, place the vapor barrier next to the subfloor and hold the blankets in place with wires bowed between the floor joists.

After you place and compact the gravel fill, place a plastic vapor barrier over it. Then place the rigid insulation around the perimeter. There are other designs that are also used.

If your house has already been built, the edge of the slab can still be insulated by installing insulation against the exterior as shown in **14–21**. Be certain to extend the insulation below the frost line.

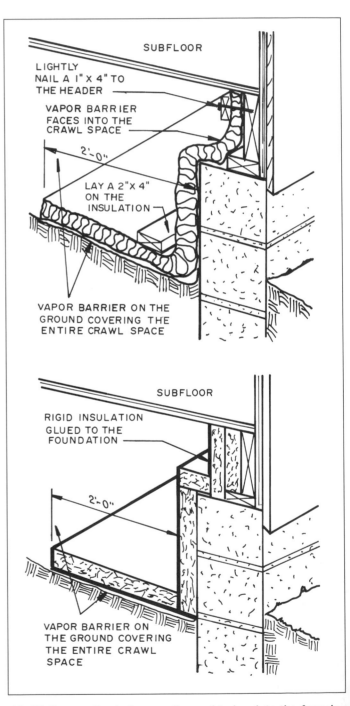

14–17. Two methods frequently used to insulate the foundation on unvented, unheated crawl spaces.

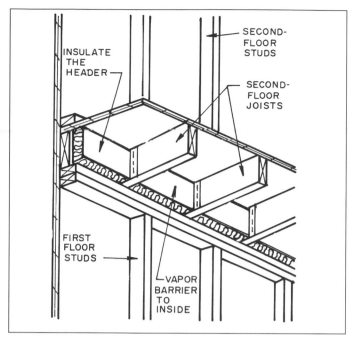

14–18. Insulate the header around the edges of the second-floor joists.

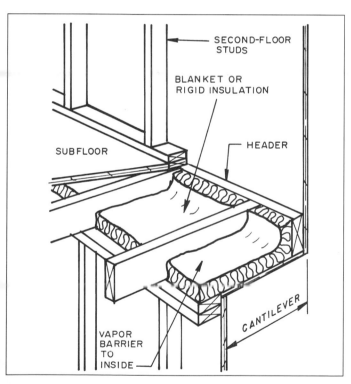

14–19. Cantilevered areas, including the header, must be fully insulated.

INSULATING ROOFS

Flat and shed roofs require that an air space be left between the roof sheathing and the insulation. The air can then flow through the soffit vents and this air

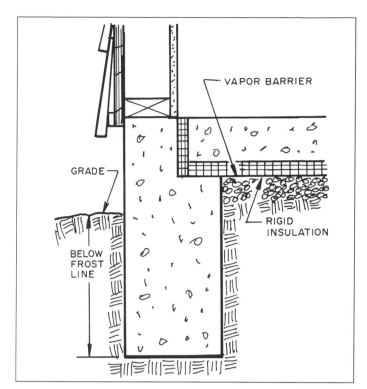

14–20. This is one way frequently used to insulate the perimeter of a concrete floor slab.

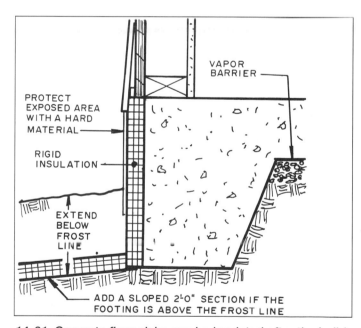

14–21. Concrete floor slabs can be insulated after the building has been built by installing insulation on the outside of the foundation running from the siding or up to the brick into the ground to the frost line.

space (14–22).

If you would like to add additional insulation to an existing gable or shed roof, add it to the exterior of the roof as shown in 14–23.

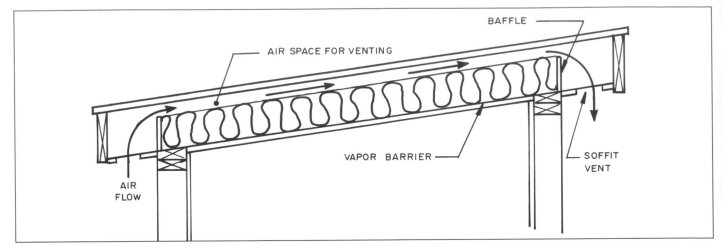

14–22. When you insulate a flat or shed roof, leave an air space so the heat and moisture that may collect can be vented out through soffit vents.

Flat and shed roofs can be insulated best at the time of construction using the technique shown in **14–22**. If you plan to install new shingles and want to increase the insulation, you must strip the old

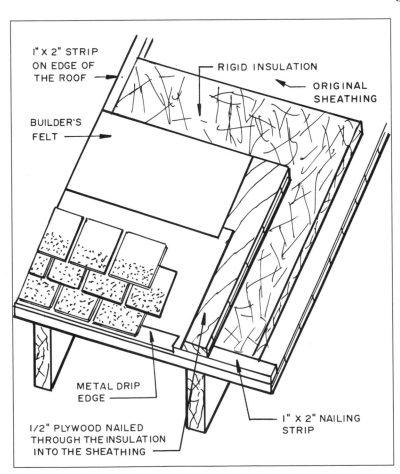

14–23. You can add insulation to the roof by removing the old shingles, installing rigid insulation over the sheathing, and nailing plywood over this as the base for the new shingles.

shingles from the roof. With no shingles on the sheathing, the procedure is as follows:

1. Lay a 1 x 2-inch (25 x 51-millimeter) wood nailing strip around the edge of the roof.

2. Apply rigid insulation over the sheathing within the boundaries of the nailing strip (**14–23**).

3. Place ½-inch (13-millimeter) -thick plywood sheets over the insulation.

4. Shingle the roof.

INSTALLING STORM DOORS

Storm doors are made of wood, polystyrene, or aluminum, and are available in many different types and styles. A good-quality storm door will come with all the hardware needed for installation. It will also have interchangeable screen and window panels (**14–24**).

Storm doors come hinged to their frames and may swing either left or right. Be sure to buy a door hinged on the correct side for your house. Generally, a storm door is hinged on the same side as the entrance door and swings out.

Carefully measure the size of the opening on the exterior-door frame. The storm door should fit tightly into the frame. Measure the width between the insides of the rabbets

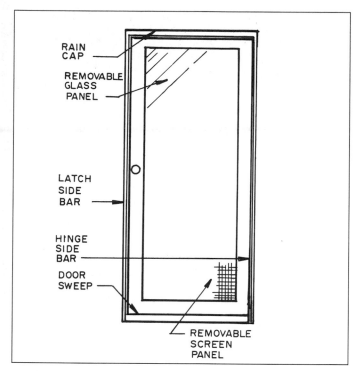

14–24. A typical storm door is supplied with all the mounting hardware and removable glass and screen panels.

(grooves) in the jamb at both the top and bottom (14–25). If there is a difference, use the smaller dimension for your size. The storm door usually fits into the outermost rabbet if the jamb has more than one. Measure the height of the door opening from

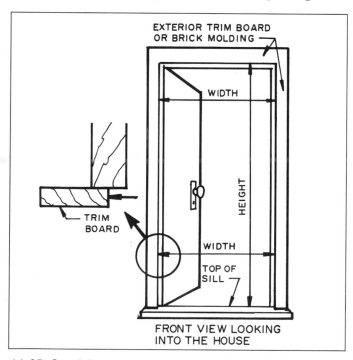

14–25. Carefully measure the opening into which the storm door will fit.

the rabbet at the top of the frame to the threshold.

The storm-door unit has two parts: the door and a metal frame. Usually the door comes with the hinge side bar attached to the door. The latch side bar may be separate.

The procedure for installing the door will vary, depending upon its design and manufacturer. Following are typical suggestions:

1. Open the carton and remove the door and all hardware.

2. Remove the glass panel and the sweep from the door. Keep the glass in a vertical position. Never lay it flat or it might break. The sweep is a flexible strip added to the bottom of the door to seal off air infiltration.

3. Install the rain cap (14–26). Center it on the door opening. Locate it so it provides the height of opening specified by the manufacturer.

4. Check the length of the hinge side bar. Some doors allow extra length and you may have to cut a little off with a hacksaw (14–27).

5. Insert the door in the rabbet in the jamb. Make certain the hinge side bar is perpendicular by checking it with a level. Check clearance at the top and bottom. Then install the screws provided, connecting the hinge side bar to the jamb (14–28).

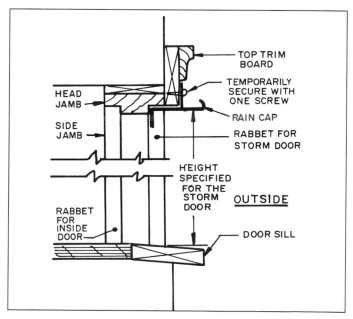

14–26. Start the storm-door installation by installing the rain cap the specified distance above the sill.

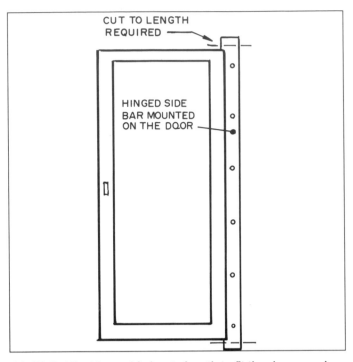

14–27. Cut the hinge-side bar to length to fit the door opening.

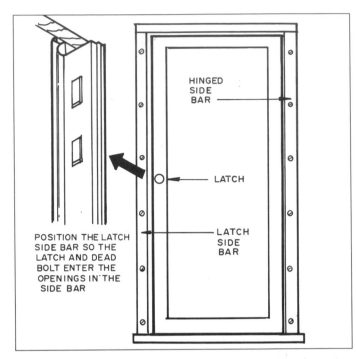

14–29. When you install the latch side bar, position it so the latch and dead bolt will enter the openings without rubbing on the edges.

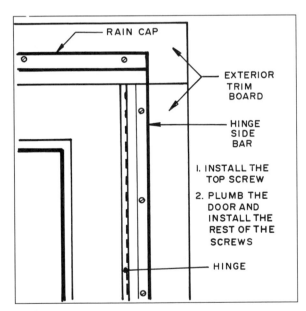

14–28. Set the storm door in place and position it with the rain cap. Install the top screw in the hinge side bar, plumb the door with a level, and install the rest of the screws.

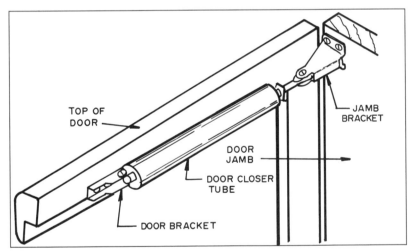

14–30. Your storm-door kit will have some type of door closer and sometimes a safety chain.

6. If the latch was not installed at the factory, do so now.

7. Cut the latch side bar to length if necessary. Place it on the jamb in the rabbet. Be certain the latch and dead bolt will move into the openings without binding. Then secure the latch side bar to the door frame (14–29).

8. Install the door closer (14–30). Some doors come with a safety chain in addition to the door closer.

9. Finally, reinstall the sweep. Adjust it so it seals the crack at the bottom of the door. You can caulk around the frame of the door if you feel it will be exposed to considerable moisture.

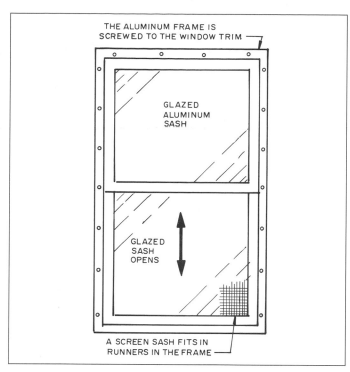

14–31. A typical aluminum storm window.

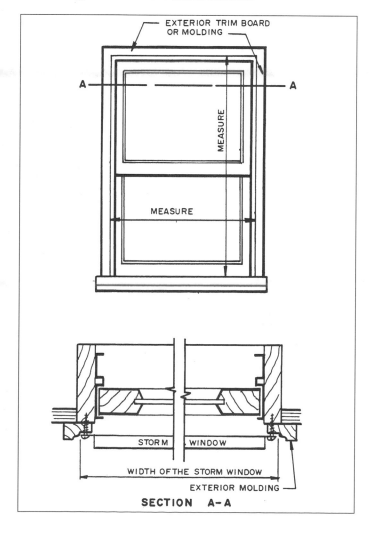

14–32. Measure the window to get the size of the storm window. You need to include the flat surface of the molding into which the window will be screwed.

INSTALLING STORM WINDOWS

One of the commonly used storm windows has an aluminum frame and glazed and screen inserts that run in channels in the frame (**14–31**). The glazed panel can be raised to allow ventilation, and a screen panel covers the open area. They are installed on the exterior side of the window, providing a dead air space which increases energy efficiency and protects the original window from damage by the weather. Aluminum storm windows are cut to size to fit your window opening, so measure the window opening carefully.

Where you measure the size of the window opening to receive the storm window can vary, depending upon the design of the window frame and molding. You need to measure so the storm-window flange will screw onto a flat surface around the window. This is typically a trim board or a molding, as shown in **14–32**.

Fit the window against the molding and install one screw in the top corner. Adjust it so it fits properly and put a screw in the other top corner. Then drill small holes in the molding or trim board for each screw. If you drive the screws without these small holes, they are difficult to get started and may split the molding because they are very near its edge.

Install one or two screws on each side and slide the glazed sashes up and down to be certain they operate freely. If all is working, install the rest of the screws. You can lay a line of caulking along the edge if extra protection is desired.

WEATHER-STRIPPING DOORS AND WINDOWS

If your house is very old, the doors and windows will most likely not have weather stripping around the perimeter of the opening. There are a number of products that can be used. Visit your building-supply dealer to see what is available. Some applications are shown in **14–33** and **14–34**, on the following page. You will find a number of other variations of these at your local building-supply dealer. It should be noted that new doors and windows are fully weather-stripped and energy-efficient.

Possibly the easiest weather stripping to apply is **adhesive-backed foam strips** or **felt strips**. You pull off the backing and press the adhesive side against the door or the window frame. These are effective if you do not open the window often, because if you do they will wear and have to be replaced. If the adhesive does not hold, you can nail it with short tacks. It lasts only a few years, so is a short-term solution.

Vinyl tube gaskets are applied from the outside. Press them against the door or sash so there are no gaps. **Metal spring strips** are made from bronze and aluminum. They fit into the door and window channels, so are not seen. They are nailed with special nails supplied with the strips. The nailing flange faces the exterior, so the door or window presses tightly against the strips. A similar product is a **vinyl spring strip** that has an adhesive backing but can be nailed in place.

The bottom of the sash at the sill can be sealed by a rubber strip that is nailed or screwed onto the bottom edge. Position it so the rubber flange seals tightly against the sill (**14–35**). Tubular gaskets are also used.

If your exterior doors have air leaks at the sills, there are a variety of sills and sweeps to close the

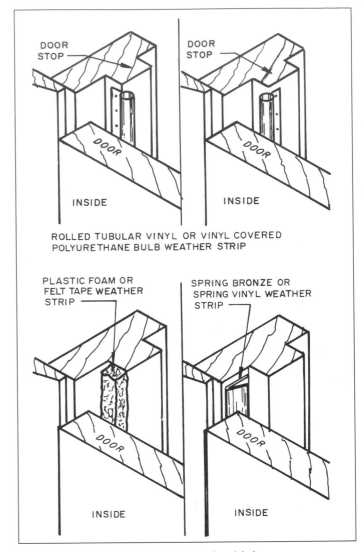

14–34. Several ways to weather-strip old doors.

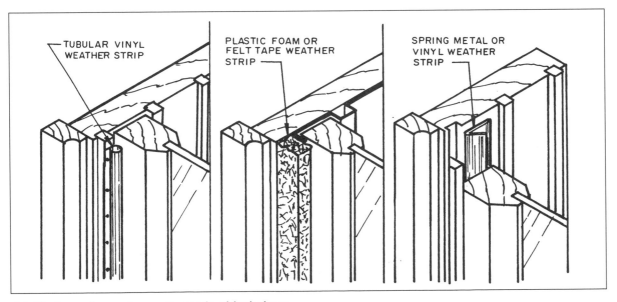

14–33. Several ways to weather-strip old windows.

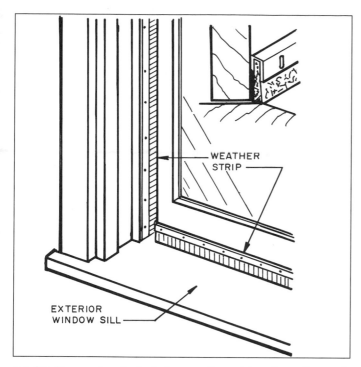

14–35. Remember to install a weather strip where the sash meets the window sill.

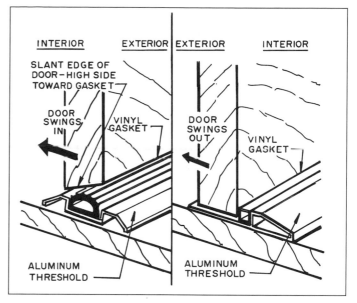

14–37. Two of the several exterior door thresholds available.

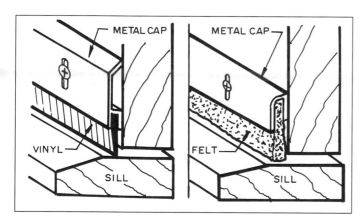

14–36. There are a number of different sweeps available to seal leaks between the door and sill.

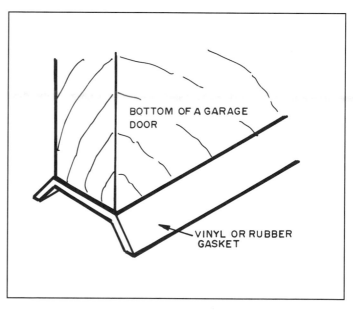

14–38. Special gaskets are available to seal the crack between your garage door and the concrete floor.

gap. The easiest to install is a sweep that fits on the bottom edge of the door, as shown in **14–36**. These are also available for storm doors. A typical threshold with a vinyl gasket is widely used (**14–37**). It is screwed to the sill. Slant the bottom edge of the door a little so it does not bind on the gasket but still closes the crack. You can also seal the bottom of your garage door with a rubber gasket secured to the bottom of the door (**14–38**). Plastic gaskets for sealing around the sides of the door are also available.

CHAPTER FIFTEEN

Furniture Repair

The furniture in our homes represents a substantial investment. Many pieces get heavy use and need occasional renovation. The life of furniture can be extended if routine maintenance and repairs are made as needed rather than letting pieces fall into a state of complete disrepair. Most repairs are easily made by the home owner and require only a few simple tools. The key to success is the use of the proper materials, such as the correct adhesive, for each job. This chapter gives the details you need to know to repair and refinish your furniture.

The most common types of furniture repair involve broken parts, loose joints, worn or torn upholstery, and a need for refinishing. Each situation needs to be studied, and some common-sense decisions must be made. Sometimes a part can be repaired, while other times it should be replaced. The following suggestions are general in nature and can be applied to a variety of situations.

GLUES AND ADHESIVES

There are a wide variety of glues and adhesives available. As you make a choice, consider the material to be bonded, its condition, the difficulty of holding the bonded parts together, and the specifications of the various bonding agents. If the bonded material is to be exposed to moisture, a moisture-resistant agent should be used. **Table 15–1** on the following page is a summary of the more frequently used bonding agents. When you visit your hardware store, read the specifications on the label to be certain it will do the job you expect.

REPAIRING DOWEL JOINTS

Through normal use, table and chair legs and rails begin to come unglued. They are often joined with dowel joints. To repair these, first separate the loose joints.

Generally, one part of a joint will be loose and another part will be a bit too tight to tap loose without possibly breaking something. If this part does not come loose easily, try to soften the glue by working in a solvent with a small brush or hypodermic syringe (**15–1**). Try various solvents such as acetone, lacquer thinner, and paint thinner. Allow the joint to

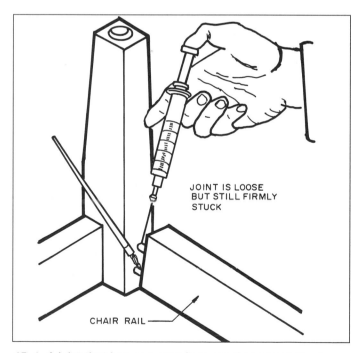

15–1. A joint that has one-part loose and one part stuck can sometimes be loosened by injecting various solvents to soften the adhesive. This helps separate the parts without damage to them.

TABLE 15–1. CHARACTERISTICS OF BONDING AGENTS

Type	Form	Solvent	Mixing Procedure	Applications	Service Durability	Clamping Time
Acrylic	Liquid and powder	Acetone	Mix liquid with powder	Wood, glass, metal	Water-resistant	Sets in 5 minutes, cures in 12 hours
Aliphatic resin (yellow glue)	Liquid	Warm water	None	Edge- and face-gluing, laminating	Interior use	1 hour
Casein glue	Powder	Soap and warm water before it hardens	Mix with water	Furniture, laminated timbers, doors, edge-gluing	Water-resistant	2 hours
Cellulose cement	Clear liquid	Acetone	None	Wood, glass, metal	Water-resistant	2 hours
Contact cement	Liquid	Acetone	None	Bonding plastic to countertops	Water-resistant	No clamping time
Cyanoacrylate (superglue)	Liquid or gel	None	None	Liquid-metal, plastic, rubber, ceramics	Water-resistant	Sets in 30 seconds, cures in 30 to 60 minutes
Epoxy	Liquid and a catalyst	Acetone	Mix liquid and catalyst	Wood, glass, metal, ceramics	Interior use	Sets in 5 minutes, cures in 2 hours
Hot-melts	Solid	Acetone	Melt with electric glue gun	Molding, overlays	Interior use	None

TABLE 15–1. CHARACTERISTICS OF BONDING AGENTS (*CONTINUED*)

Type	Form	Solvent	Mixing	Applications Procedure	Service Durability	Clamping Time
Liquid hide glue	Liquid	Warm water	None	Furniture, edge-gluing, laminating	Interior use	2 hours
Polyvinyl acetate (white glue)	Liquid	Soap and warm water	None	Edge- and face-gluing, laminating, paper	Interior use	Sets in 8 hours, cures in 24 hours
Polyvinyl chloride	Liquid	Acetone	None	Wood, ceramics, glass, metal, plastic	Water-resistant	Sets in 5 minutes, cures in 12 hours
Resorcinol resin	Liquid and powder	Water before it hardens	Mix liquid with catalyst	Laminated timbers, sandwich panels, general bonding, boats	Waterproof	16 hours
Urea-formaldehyde	Powder	Soap and warm water before it hardens	Mix with water	Lumber and hardwood plywood, assembly gluing	Water-resistant	16 hours
Urethane	Liquid	Alcohol before hardening	None	Gel-wood, porous materials, wood to wood, glass, and metal	Interior use	1 hour

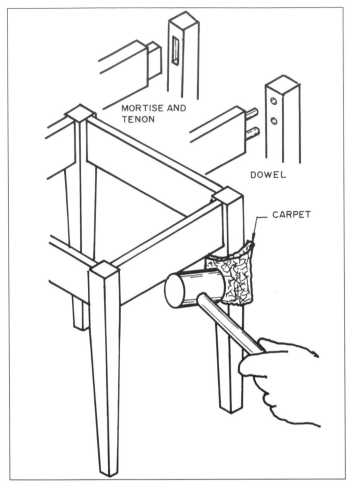

15–2. Protect the furniture part as you attempt to tap the joint apart.

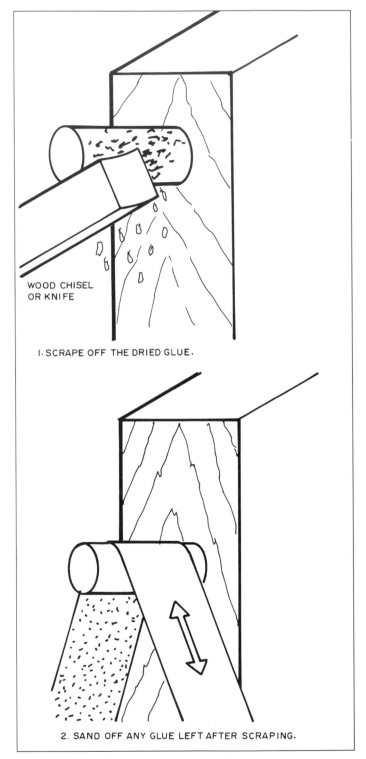

15–3. Scrape the glue off the dowel with a knife or chisel and clean up any left with fine sandpaper.

soak for several hours. Several applications may be necessary. You can help separate the joint by tapping it carefully with a rubber mallet. If you need to protect the finish, place a piece of wood with carpet wrapped around it against the part and tap on it (**15–2**). Once the joint comes apart, dry off the solvent and let the wood dry.

Now scrap and sand the old glue off the dowel (**15–3**). Be careful that you do not reduce the diameter of the dowel. The glue must be removed from inside the dowel socket. This can be done with a rolled-up piece of sandpaper. The sandpaper can be wrapped around a pencil or small dowel rod (**15–4**). Do not enlarge the diameter of the hole. Now put the parts together dry and see how they fit. They must fit tightly. Most glues and adhesives do not fill voids in the joint. If the fit is a little loose, mix some sawdust with the glue or use a gap-filling glue such as an acrylic or epoxy type. If the fit is very loose, the

dowel will have to be replaced with a larger one or repaired as shown in **15–9** and **15–10**.

Now apply adhesive to the dowel. For most jobs, the white polyvinyl resin is successful. Coat the entire surface of the dowel generously (**15–5**). Then

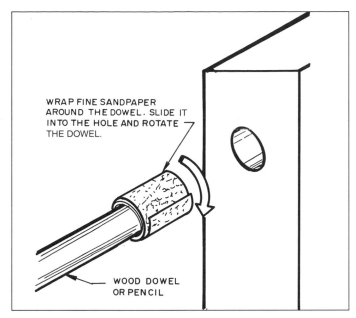

15–4. You can remove dried glue from the dowel hole by sanding it with fine sandpaper.

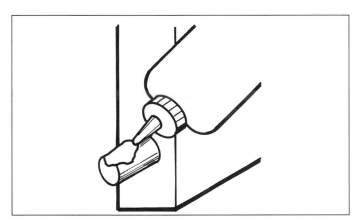

15–5. Coat the entire dowel with adhesive before you slide it into the dowel hole.

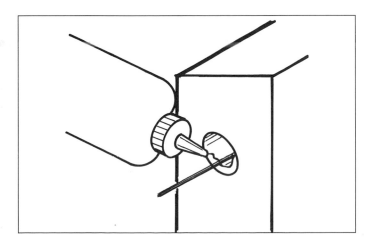

15–6. Apply adhesive to the walls of the dowel hole. Smooth it out. Do not fill the hole because this could prevent the dowel from fully entering.

apply the adhesive to the walls of the socket (15–6). Do not fill the socket with glue or you will not be able to get the dowel to go all the way in. Slide the dowels into their sockets. The excess glue will run out and can be wiped away with a wet cloth.

Next, clamp the joints so they remain firmly together until dry. Drying time varies, but it is wise to keep the unit clamped overnight (15–7). Rope can be used as a clamp as shown in 15–8.

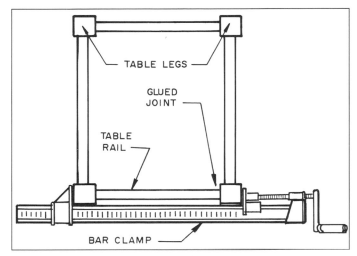

15–7. The best way to clamp a glued joint is with a bar clamp.

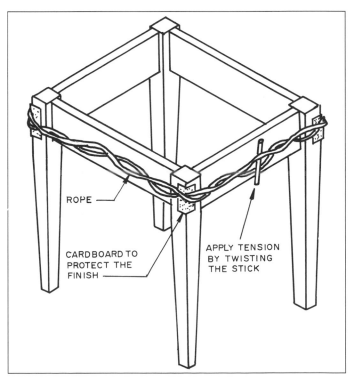

15–8. You can use a rope or length of rubber as an emergency clamp to hold a glued joint as it dries.

If a dowel or chair rung is too small to fit tightly into the socket, it can be enlarged by coating the end with glue and wrapping silk thread around it. Then apply more glue over the thread and insert it into the socket (**15–9**). If the thread will not enlarge it enough, saw a slot across the end of the dowel. Put a small wedge partway into the slot. Apply glue to the dowel and hammer it into the socket. The wedge will force apart the ends of the dowel, providing a tight fit.

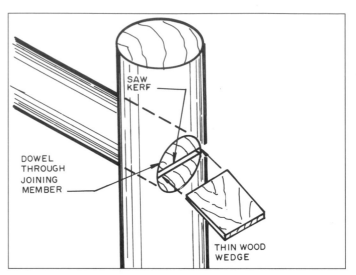

15–11. If a dowel runs through the joining member and is loose, a wedge can be glued and driven in from the outside.

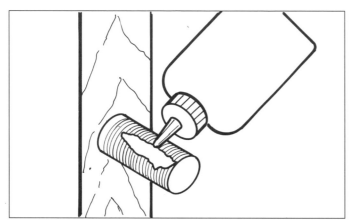

15–9. Sometimes you can enlarge a dowel by wrapping thread around it and coating it with adhesive before sliding it into the dowel hole.

It is important that the wedge be short enough to completely enter the socket (**15–10**). If the dowel goes completely through the part, the wedge could be driven in from behind and cut off flush with the surface (**15–11**). Be certain to wipe off any glue that is forced out of the joint.

If the dowel on the end of a leg breaks off, a smaller-diameter dowel can be installed (**15–12**). If the broken part in the dowel socket is firmly glued in place, drill a hole into it for the new dowel. If it is

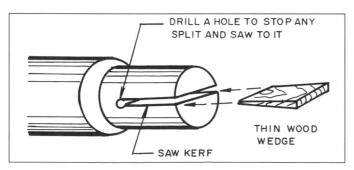

15–10. Put glue on the wedge and place the wedge in the kerf. Drive the dowel, into the dowel hole. The wedge expands the dowel, making a tight fit.

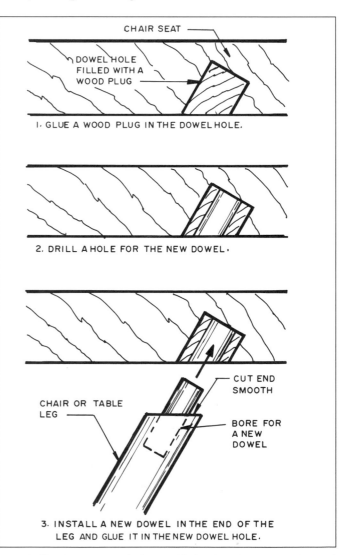

1. GLUE A WOOD PLUG IN THE DOWEL HOLE.

2. DRILL A HOLE FOR THE NEW DOWEL.

3. INSTALL A NEW DOWEL IN THE END OF THE LEG AND GLUE IT IN THE NEW DOWEL HOLE.

15–12. If a dowel on a chair or table leg breaks off, cut the end smooth and install a smaller dowel in it. Fill the dowel hole in the seat or tabletop and bore a hole for the new dowel.

loose or broken, remove it and glue a new piece into the hole. After it is dry, drill the dowel hole. In the leg, drill a hole for the new dowel. It may be necessary to smooth the broken end a little before you can get the drill started. Cut the dowel about ¼ inch (6 millimeters) shorter than the combined depths of the dowel holes.

A loose dowel joint can be strengthened by clamping the joint closed and installing a new dowel through one part, such as a leg, into the part containing the dowels, as shown in **15–13**. Locate the new dowel so it clears the original dowels. Cut the dowel about ¼ inch (6 millimeters) shorter than the total length of the hole.

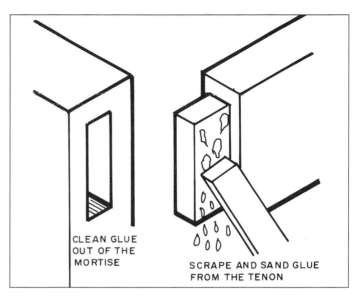

15–14. *Before regluing a mortise-and-tenon joint, scrape and sand off all the old glue on the tenon and in the mortise. Try to maintain their original sizes.*

clamp as shown in **15–8**.

If you prefer not to disassemble the joint, a good repair can be made by clamping the joint closed and installing a dowel through the leg, tenon, and back side of the leg (**15–16**). Put adhesive on the dowel and tap it in place. Some like to let a little of the dowel stick out and sand it flush after the adhesive dries. This is all right if you plan to refinish the leg. You might consider making a dowel of the same wood used for the leg. It will be easier to get it to blend in with the existing finish.

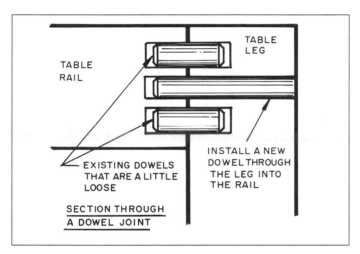

15–13. *If a dowel joint is a little loose, you can tighten it by installing a new dowel through the leg into the rail.*

REPAIRING MORTISE-AND-TENON JOINTS

If a mortise-and-tenon joint becomes loose, it has to be taken apart, cleaned, and reglued. This procedure is much like that for dowel joints shown in **15–1** and **15–2**.

Once the joint is separated, scrape the old glue off the tenon and inside the mortise and sand off any glue remaining on the surface (**15–14**). Insert the tenon into the mortise. It should have a tight fit. If it is loose, you might glue a very thin shim of veneer to the tenon. After it dries, scrape it until the tenon tightly enters the mortise (**15–15**). Apply adhesive to the tenon and mortise, insert the tenon, and clamp the joint closed. It can be held with bar clamps as shown in **15–7** or with a rope as an emergency

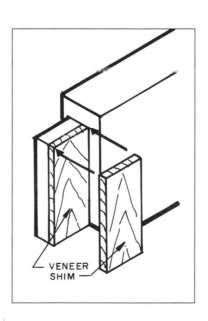

15–15. *If the tenon has become too small, you can glue a piece of veneer to one side and trim it to fit snugly into the mortise.*

LEG-RAIL BRACES

Loose leg-rail connections can be strengthened with wood corner blocks (**15–17**). Other types of connectors may be available at hardware stores.

REPAIRING SPLIT-WOOD PARTS

First, carefully open up the split with a chisel or screwdriver. If it is in **fresh wood** rather than an old glue joint, place glue into the split, work it in with a small stick, remove the tool, and clamp the split until it is dry. Remove the adhesive that squeezed out before it hardens (**15–18**).

If it is a **separated glue joint,** the old glue must be scraped away before new glue is applied. In extreme cases, the part may need to be sawed apart along the split and a new joint made.

If a round member, such as a round chair dowel, is split, open the split, insert glue, and clamp it (**15–19**).

When an edge splits, apply glue to the split piece and place it back on the edge. To hold it while it is drying, clamp it with masking tape (**15–20**).

REPAIRING LOOSE VENEER

When veneer loosens on an edge, work glue under it with a wire or thin piece of wood. Then pull the veneer down with masking tape. This holds it in place while the clamps are being installed (**15–21**). Wipe off all glue that squeezes out as you press down on the veneer.

REPAIRING HINGES

The screws in hinges sometimes loosen in their holes. This causes the door to sag. If they are not very loose, fill the hole with contact cement and replace the screws. Tighten them until they are in place, but do not overtighten. If this does not work, drill a hole where each screw was located. Glue a piece of round dowel rod the exact size of the hole in each place. When these are dry, drill the proper anchor holes for the screws in the dowel and install the hinges (**15–22**).

If the surface below the hinge is badly damaged, cut the hinge mortise deeper and glue a wood block in the recess. Install the hinge on this in the normal manner (**15–23**).

Sometimes a hinge bed on the edge of a door splits. Remove the hinge, pry open the split, force glue into the split, and clamp the split until it is dry (**15–24**).

REPAIRING WARPED TABLETOPS

Tabletops warp because they are exposed to changes in humidity. The wood fibers expand, putting stress on the board. When one side is protected from moisture by a finish and the other side (the bottom) is unfinished, the unfinished side absorbs moisture and begins to swell. The

1. CLAMP THE JOINT CLOSED. DRILL A DOWEL HOLE THROUGH THE LEG AND TENON·

2. GLUE A DOWEL IN THE HOLE·

15–16. *A loose mortise-and-tenon joint can be secured by clamping it tightly and installing a dowel through it and the leg.*

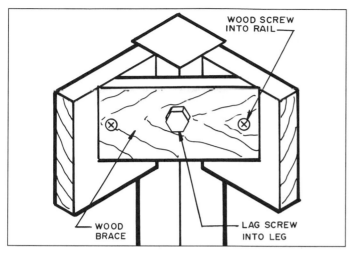

15–17. *If the leg-to-rail connection seems a bit loose, you can stiffen and strengthen it by installing a wood corner brace.*

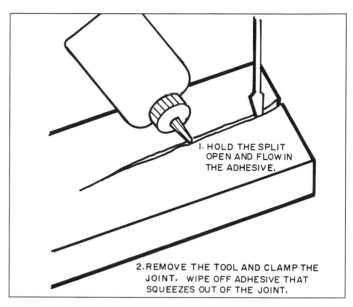

1. HOLD THE SPLIT OPEN AND FLOW IN THE ADHESIVE.

2. REMOVE THE TOOL AND CLAMP THE JOINT. WIPE OFF ADHESIVE THAT SQUEEZES OUT OF THE JOINT.

15–18. *A split in the wood can often be repaired by opening it up a little, filling it with adhesive, and clamping it until it is dry.*

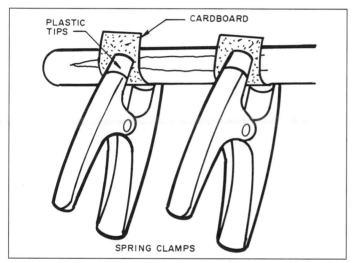

15–19. *Splits on round members can be glued and clamped. Spring clamps or C-clamps are generally used.*

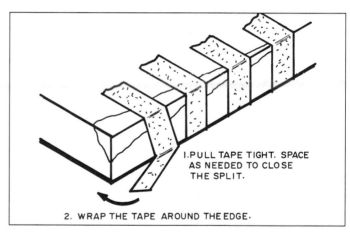

1. PULL TAPE TIGHT. SPACE AS NEEDED TO CLOSE THE SPLIT.

2. WRAP THE TAPE AROUND THE EDGE.

15–20. *Split edges can be repaired by regluing the split-off piece. Clean off as much glue as possible before taping it. Some surface-finish repair will usually be necessary.*

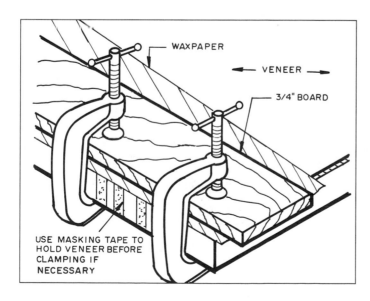

15–21. *Loose edges of veneers can be reglued and clamped until the adhesive dries.*

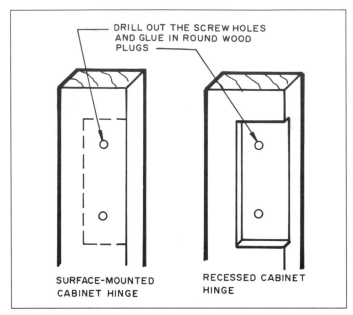

DRILL OUT THE SCREW HOLES AND GLUE IN ROUND WOOD PLUGS

SURFACE-MOUNTED CABINET HINGE

RECESSED CABINET HINGE

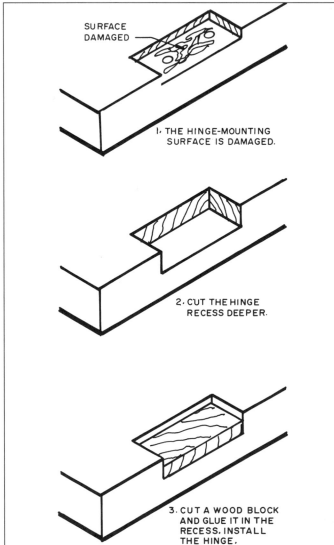

SURFACE DAMAGED

1. THE HINGE-MOUNTING SURFACE IS DAMAGED.

2. CUT THE HINGE RECESS DEEPER.

3. CUT A WOOD BLOCK AND GLUE IT IN THE RECESS. INSTALL THE HINGE.

15–23. If the hinge recess is badly damaged, cut it deeper and glue in a solid-wood block to reinstall the hinge.

15–22 (left). When hinge screws become loose and will not tighten, drill out the screw holes, glue in round wood plugs, and reinstall the screws.

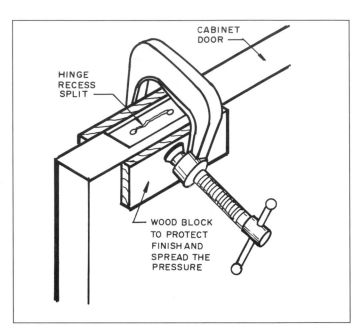

CABINET DOOR

HINGE RECESS SPLIT

WOOD BLOCK TO PROTECT FINISH AND SPREAD THE PRESSURE

15–24. A large screw can split the hinge recess in cabinet doors. When this happens, insert glue in the split and clamp it until it is dry.

other side does not absorb moisture, so the board warps. One thing that can be done is to watch the top during the seasons. If it flattens out on its own, the moisture in it must be stabilized. At this point, apply a finish to seal the unprotected bottom. Plywood and particleboard tend to warp less than solid wood because of the alternating grain in the veneers.

Cleats can be used to correct warp in particleboard, plywood, and solid-wood tops. The cleats on solid-wood tops are screwed to the bottom perpendicular to the wood grain. On other materials, the cleats are screwed perpendicular to the warp. This is most effective if done after the top has naturally returned to a nearly flat condition. After this occurs, apply a finish coat, such as a varnish, lacquer, or polyurethane, to the bottom to keep out moisture in the future.

Now clamp the top flat for 24 hours and then install the cleats (**15–25**). While 1 x 2-inch (25 x 51-millimeter) cleats are useful, 2 x 2-inch (51 x 51-millimeter) cleats are better. Be certain the screws do not break through the top.

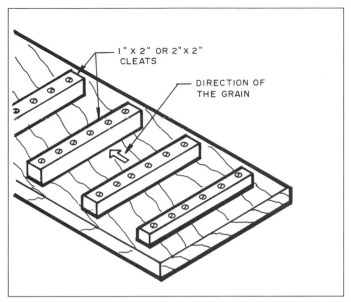

15–25. Wood cleats will help hold a warped tabletop flat. Let the moisture leave the top and then apply a finish coat to the unfinished bottom to seal out moisture before installing the cleats.

BANDING PLYWOOD EDGES

You can improve the appearance of the edges of plywood and particleboard that are exposed by bonding on them a layer of veneer tape. This is a wood product that is sold in rolls of various widths. Some types are bonded to the edge with a polyvinyl adhesive and clamped in place. Others have an adhesive back. To install them, remove the backing paper, press the veneer tape against the edge, and press it on with a hot iron (**15–26**). Rolling after heating firms up the bonding.

REPAIRING SCRATCHES

Scratches in the finish can be hidden somewhat by using one of the various touch-up sticks available (**15–27**, on the following page). These crayon-like sticks are available in a range of colors. Select the one that best matches your furniture and carefully mark it along the scratch. Note any special instructions that come with the product.

You can also touch up the scratch by applying wood stain to it with a fine-tipped watercolor brush or some type of ink (**15–28**). After the repair dries, carefully wax the surface.

15–26. The edges of plywood and particleboard can be banded with wood veneers made especially for this purpose.

RESTORING A FURNITURE FINISH

Sometimes a piece of furniture can have its finish restored without stripping and refinishing. The decision to try to revive an old finish will depend upon the desires of the person involved. Some prefer that the stains and distress marks be visible, while others want to remove them. If the old finish is to be restored, the stains and distress marks will remain. If the old finish is not cracked or blistered, it can be improved by thoroughly wiping the surface

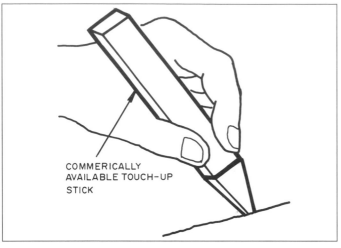

15–27. There are a variety of commercially available touch-up sticks They are made in many colors to match various woods and stains.

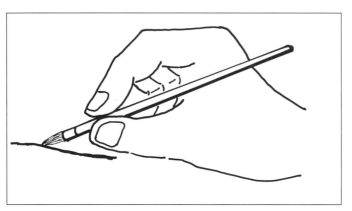

15–28. You can touch up fine scratches with oil stain or ink using a fine watercolor brush.

with a rag soaked in benzine. Rewipe it several times, using clean rags each time until the surface is clean. Then wipe it with a dry cloth and let the surface dry. Be certain to wear rubber gloves and work in a well-ventilated location.

At this point, you may decide the surface remaining is satisfactory, so you only need to apply a good furniture polish. Some prefer to use a furniture cleaner-conditioner before polishing because it helps restore the natural color of the wood and may blend into minor surface scratches.

If it appears after cleaning that the topcoat finish is not satisfactory but is not checked or cracked, you can apply a new topcoat over it. First find out if the topcoat is lacquer, varnish, polyurethane, or shellac. To do this, place a drop of denatured alcohol on an

inconspicuous spot. If the finish is shellac, it will dissolve it. If it is varnish, the alcohol will cause it to blister. If it is lacquer or polyurethane, it will not affect it. Apply a drop of lacquer thinner. If the finish is lacquer, it will slightly dissolve.

To restore the topcoat, gently rub the surface with 4/0 steel wool. Always rub with the grain and be certain to get into the grooves and crevices on turnings and carvings. The goal is to smooth the surface and remove any gloss. This helps the new finish to adhere. Do not cut through the old finish. Now, remove all dust and apply one or more coats of new finish of the same type that is on the furniture.

Restoring a Varnished Surface

If you want to try to restore a varnished surface, dissolve 4 ounces (0.11 kilogram) of trisodium phosphate in 1 gallon (3.8 liters) of hot water. Apply this to a small area and let it soak for about 15 minutes. Then scrub this area with a fine steel-wool pad dipped into the solution. Rinse the surface with cold water and allow it to dry. After it is dry, wipe it down in small sections with a cloth wetted with denatured alcohol. Wipe it dry and let it completely air dry before applying a new coat of varnish.

Another technique is to polish the surface with a steel-wool pad wetted with mineral spirits. Then wipe the surface clean and wipe it down with a cloth wetted with mineral spirits. Allow the surface to become completely dry before you apply a new coat of varnish.

Refinishing Furniture

If it is decided to remove the old finish and completely refinish it, the topcoat of varnish, lacquer, or shellac will have to be removed. There are a variety of commercial stripping compounds on the market. They dissolve the finish, allowing you to scrape it away.

There are two kinds of stripping compounds generally available. One contains methylene chloride and is available as a paste or cream. It dissolves the finish in 15 to 20 minutes. It is a hazardous material, so you must observe the safety directions of the manufacturer. The other type is a water-based material. It works well, but is slower in softening the finish. It has the advantage that it keeps the finish soft for an hour or longer, giving you more time to work. It also is nontoxic and nonflammable. Since it is water-based, it will raise the grain of the wood and you will need to lightly fine-sand the surface.

Read the directions carefully before using any stripper. *Be certain to wear rubber gloves and goggles, and work in a place with excellent ventilation.* Run an electric fan to help clear the air. Some strippers are volatile and should not be used near a flame, such as a pilot light on a stove.

To begin, place the furniture on lots of newspaper. Remove drawers, doors, and hardware. Lay on the stripping material in a heavy coat with a brush. It does not have to be spread uniformly or brushed on like a paint. When possible, place the section being stripped in a horizontal position. Confine your work to a small area such as an end panel or several drawer fronts. Complete them before proceeding to other parts.

Let the material remain for the recommended time or until the finish begins to wrinkle. Then scrape it off with a putty knife (**15–29**). If the knife has sharp corners, file them off so they do not gouge the surface of the wood. Use coarse steel wool or a toothbrush or other fine, soft-bristle brush to get into grooves and carvings (**15–30**). Usually several coats of stripper are needed to completely clean a surface. Very small round grooves can be cleaned with a piece of string.

Preparing the Surface for Refinishing

After stripping the furniture, wipe it with turpentine or a solvent recommended by the manufacturer. This removes all traces of the stripping material. Be certain to clean all crevices. Then let the furniture dry overnight.

Generally, the wood at this stage still retains some of the color from the stain originally used. This does not cause any problem and may even be attractive. Next, lightly sand the surface with the grain using a very fine abrasive such as No. 280 finishing paper.

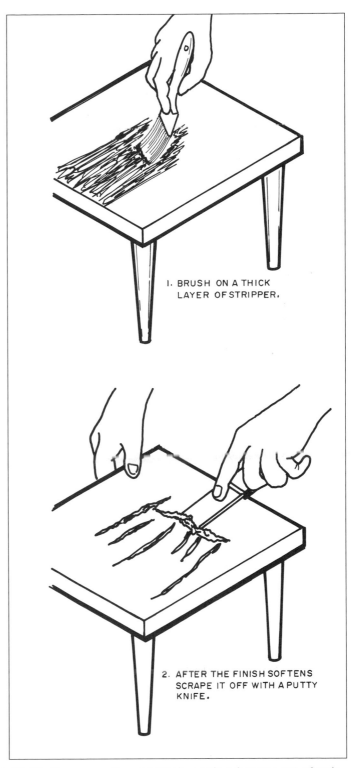

1. BRUSH ON A THICK LAYER OF STRIPPER.

2. AFTER THE FINISH SOFTENS SCRAPE IT OFF WITH A PUTTY KNIFE.

15–29. To remove the old finish, apply a heavy coat of stripper. After it soaks awhile, remove the finish with a putty knife.

Crevices can be smoothed with steel wool. If you wish to completely remove all color, the surfaces must be sanded until the color is gone. The early

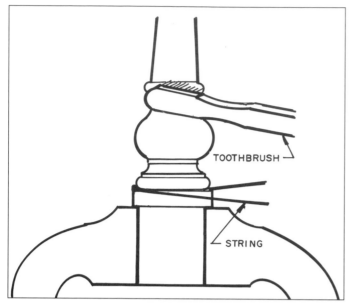

15–30. Remove the old finish on curved parts, narrow openings and carvings with a toothbrush and string.

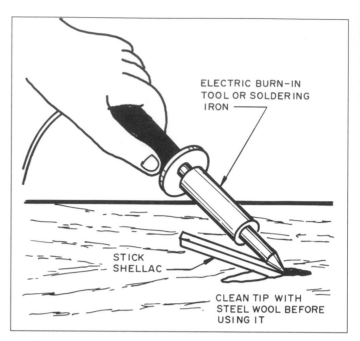

15–31. Melt the stick shellac into the defect. Press it into the defect with a wet finger while it is still warm. Let it harden and then carefully sand it smooth with very fine sandpaper or scrape it with the edge of a sharp chisel.

sanding can be done with an electric vibrating sander and the finishing touches by hand-sanding. Always sand with the grain. If the furniture is made from plywood or has a veneer, be careful you do not sand through to the layer below.

Bleaching

If there are stains such as water marks that were not sanded out, they can be reduced by bleaching. Household bleach or ammonia used full strength will often remove the blemish. Commercial bleaches are also available. After bleaching, clean the area with a 50/50 solution of white vinegar and water. Let it dry and hand-sand it with a fine finishing paper. Protect your hands and eyes and provide ventilation during this process.

Removing Dents and Defects

Dents and cuts in the surface can be filled using **stick shellac**. This is made in many colors. Choose a color as near to the desired finished color as possible. The stick shellac is melted into the crack with a special burn-in knife, but a soldering iron or other hot tool such as a heated knife can also be used (**15–31**). The stick shellac hardens immediately and can be sanded smooth. It does not take stain, so the color should be as near the finished stain as possible.

Small depressions where the surface of the wood has not been broken can be raised by applying **warm water** to them (**15–32**). If you punch a small hole or two in the dent with a pin, the wood will absorb water faster (**15–32**). In difficult cases, place a folded, damp cloth over the dent and steam it out by placing

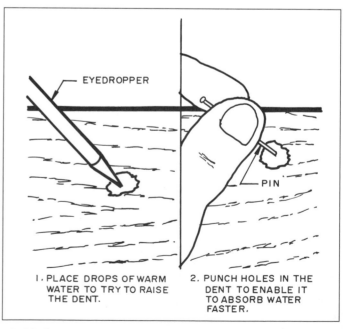

15–32. Small shallow dents can be raised some by wetting them with warm water.

an electric clothes iron or soldering iron on the cloth (**15–33**). After the surface is raised and has dried, dry-sand it smooth with a fine finishing paper.

There are other products available at hardware stores. Very small dents and nail holes can be hidden somewhat by filling them with a **wax-based stick product**. It is rubbed over the hole and leveled with a cloth. **Wood putty** and **plastic wood** can be used to fill holes and dents. They are usually used on surfaces to be painted, since they do not absorb stain.

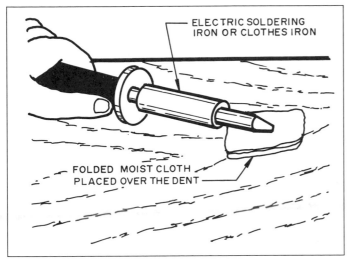

ELECTRIC SOLDERING IRON OR CLOTHES IRON

FOLDED MOIST CLOTH PLACED OVER THE DENT

15–33. You can apply mild heat to a moist cloth over a shallow dent to try to raise the wood.

Staining the Surface

Stains are applied to the raw wood to enhance the color and darken light areas so they blend with darker areas. **Oil stain** is the easiest to use. It can be applied with a cloth or brush. After it is on the surface a few minutes, it is wiped off with a clean cloth. The length of time it is left on the surface depends upon the darkness desired. The longer it is on, the darker the surface. Some can be wiped off in two or three minutes, while darker tones may require 15 minutes. Oil stain can be thinned with turpentine to cut it so it will produce lighter shades. It should dry 24 hours before additional finishing materials are applied.

Another effective coloring agent is **non-grain-raising stains**. They dry rapidly and produce a transparent color. They are most effective if applied with a spray gun because it gives a more uniform coating. However, they can also be applied with a brush. Since these stains dry rapidly, you must work quickly and avoid overlapping the strokes. Lacquer sealer can be mixed with the stain and the surface stained and sealed in one operation. It should dry in six hours.

All types of stains soak into the porous end grain faster than into the face grain; therefore, the end grain gets darker faster. This can be prevented by wiping the end grain immediately after staining or applying a coat of turpentine or boiled linseed oil to it before staining.

A **gel stain** is in a creamy condition. Wipe it on with a cloth and let set for three or four minutes. Then wipe it off across the grain. You can restain the wood until the desired color is produced. Gel stain will not run when applied to slanted or vertical surfaces. After it dries for 24 hours, it can be coated with clear polyurethane.

After the stain has dried, it should be sealed so following operations do not pick up the stain. A sealer is a diluted coat of shellac, varnish, or lacquer. **Shellac sealer** is a mix of one part shellac and eight parts denatured alcohol. **Varnish sealer** is an equal mix of varnish and turpentine, while **lacquer sealer** is an equal mix of lacquer and lacquer thinner. Consult the directions with the product finish coat to see if a sealer is necessary and, if so, what is recommended. **Table 15–2**, shown on the following page, provides general guidelines.

Be certain the surface is free of dust before the sealer is applied. Brush the sealer with the grain and let it dry. Then sand it gently with 4/0 steel wool. You are now ready to apply the finish coats.

Review the section on one-step finishes to find additional ways to stain your work.

Filling the Grain

The grain can be filled after the furniture has been stained and sealed.

Some wood species, such as oak and walnut, have an **open grain**. They have small, pore-like openings that can be filled with a wood filler. On some refinishing jobs, the pores remain filled even after sanding, unless the surface has had

TABLE 15–2. SEALERS FOR CLEAN FINISH MATERIALS*

Finish Material	Sealers
Nonsynthetic oil-type varnish	Varnish thinned 50 percent with specified solvent
Polyurethane	Lacquer-based sealer or polyurethane thinned 50 percent with mineral spirits
Lacquer	Lacquer-based sealer or one pound cut shellac mixed with eight parts denatured alcohol**
Shellac	One pound cut shellac**

* Always check the manufacturer's recommendation on the can.
** One pound of shellac dissolved in one-gallon denatured alcohol

Table 15–2. Sealers commonly used with various clear finish-coating materials.

considerable material removed. It may not be necessary to fill the pores again. If the surfaces appear porous, apply the paste-like wood filler with a brush. Allow it to remain until the gloss disappears. Then wipe off the excess with a cloth **across the grain** (**15–34**). This will pack it in the pores and cut it off smooth with the surface. Be certain to remove it from all crevices. Allow it to dry for 24 hours.

Woods with a **closed grain**, such as birch or maple, are filled by the sealer coat that is applied after staining.

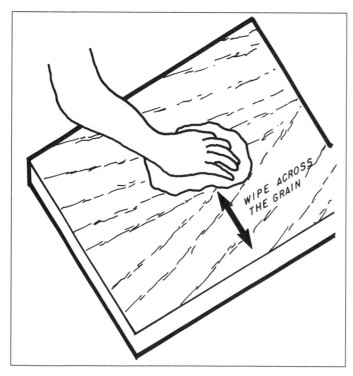

15–34. Wipe off the excess paste wood filler across the grain.

Applying the Finish Coats

The finish-coat materials commonly used are varnish, lacquer, a variety of wipe-on finishes, shellac, and polyurethane.

A **medium-oil varnish** is generally used on furniture. It usually dries in 24 hours. **Synthetic varnishes** are newer and dry by polymerization, a chemical reaction that occurs when they are exposed to air. They are named for the specific plastic they contain. Polyurethane is the most commonly used type. Let each coat dry at least three or four hours. Then sand the surface or lightly go over it with steel wool to increase the bonding of the second coat.

Always use a top-quality chisel-edged **varnish brush**. Hold the brush at the same angle as the chisel edge on the bristles (**15–35**). To be certain the surface is free of dust, wipe it with a tack rag (**15–36**). A **tack rag** is a cloth with a sticky surface to which dust sticks. It is commercially available. Always work in a dust-free room.

Now thin the first coat 25 percent using the thinner recommended on the label. Dip the brush bristles into the varnish about half their length. Load the brush more than when using paint. Lay on each brush load in a single long, smooth stroke. Do not brush in short strokes. Do not overbrush because you will create bubbles on the surface.

The first coat should dry in 24 hours. Allow an additional 24 hours for each succeeding coat. For example, allow 24 hours for the first coat, 48 hours for the second coat, and 72 hours for the third coat.

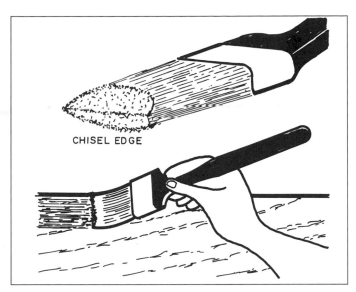

15–35. Place the chisel edge flat on the surface and apply the finish material in long, smooth strokes.

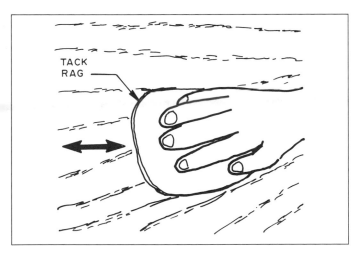

15–36. Wiping the surface with a tack rag to ensure that it is dust free.

Clean the brush with mineral spirits or the solvent recommended on the can.

Lacquer is widely used as a finish coating on furniture. It is available in many degrees of gloss from a flat to a high gloss. Lacquer is never used over other finishes such as varnish or enamel.

Lacquers are best applied with spray equipment. They dry rapidly, and many kinds are difficult to apply with a brush. There is a brushing lacquer which can be applied with a top-quality varnish brush. It dries in about two hours.

To apply lacquer with a brush, hold the brush at about a 45-degree angle and brush it on with the grain (**15–37**). Avoid overlapping the strokes. Do not

rebrush or overbrush because this causes it to build up thicker in places. Work quickly and then allow it to dry. If a place was missed, leave it and cover it with the second coat. You can sand between coats with 320-grit finishing paper.

Clean the brush with lacquer thinner.

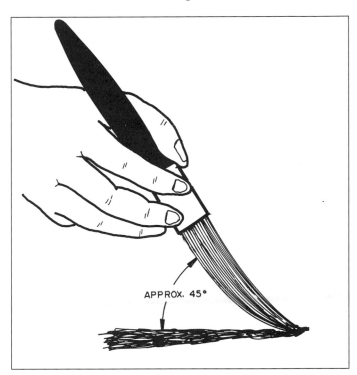

15–37. When you apply lacquer with a brush, hold the brush at about a 45-degree angle.

One-Step Finishes

One-step finishes include a stain and a finish coating in a single application. There are various **penetrating oil finishes** available. **Danish oil** contains a penetrating oil and a resin. The oil penetrates to wood fibers and hardens. If the finish is ever damaged, sand the area lightly and apply another coat of Danish oil. The oil is spread on the surface and smoothed out with a cloth. Let it soak in for about 30 minutes and wipe off the excess. After it has dried for several days, apply a coat of paste furniture wax.

Tung oil is a penetrating oil that is wiped on with a cloth pad. There are several types available. **Pure tung oil** is obtained from the seed of the tung tree. It produces a reasonably durable matte finish. When heated, tung oil is chemically altered into a **polymerized form**. It produces a harder and glossier finish. **Tung oil varnish** does not penetrate the wood as deeply as the others and is more like a surface finish.

Oil-finished interior wood surfaces can be enhanced by rubbing them with a special **liquid solvent-based wax**. It enriches the color, adds a soft luster, and provides additional water resistance. It is available in a natural form for light-colored woods and dark for darker-colored woods.

Polyurethane one-step finishes include a stain and a polyurethane finish coat. They are applied with a brush. Flow these finishes on evenly in long strokes and do not overbrush. These finishes are rather durable and easy to apply.

UPHOLSTERY REPAIRS

Not all damage to upholstery requires a complete reupholstery job. If the webbing is sagging, it may be possible to replace it by turning the chair upside down, removing the cambric dust cover, and sliding in and tacking new pieces of webbing. If a spring becomes loose, it can often be refastened without a major dismantling of the chair. Usually, the furniture frame and springs will outlast several covers.

There are three basic types of upholstered furniture: (1) with pad seats, (2) with sagless springs, and (3) with coil springs.

Chairs with Pad Seats

A **removable pad seat** is held to the chair frame with several wood screws. The base may be a frame with webbing or ¼-inch (13-millimeter) plywood. To reupholster this seat, remove the screws holding it to the frame. Use a screwdriver to remove the tacks holding the fabric to the base. If the pad is in poor condition, replace it with a foam pad. Pads are available in various thicknesses from upholstery supply shops. Usually 1- to 1½-inch (25- to 38-millimeter) foam pads are used on this type of seat.

If the pad needs to be replaced, cut it about ½ inch (13 millimeters) longer and wider than the plywood

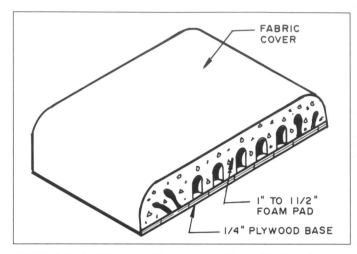

15–38. A typical foam-rubber removable padded seat.

(**15–38**). This will provide some extra material to be squeezed, helping to form a nice edge. The pad can be glued to the plywood with rubber cement, but this is not mandatory.

Next, cut the cover material to size. Save the old cover and use it for a pattern. Cut the new piece slightly larger so you have a little extra material. Lay the material over the cushion and turn it upside down; then tack or staple it in the center of the front and back sides, stretching the material until it forms the corner the way you want it. Next, keeping the cover material tight, drive tacks or staples to the right and left of the center tack on each side. Space them about 2 inches (51 millimeters) apart. Then repeat this for the other two sides (**15–39**). A No. 6 or 8 upholsterer's tack should be used. Finally, cut and fold the corners and tack them to the plywood base (**15–40**).

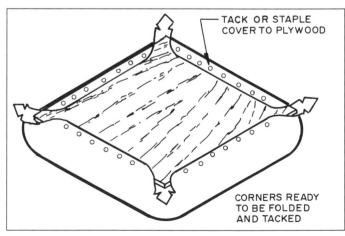

15–39. Keep the cover fabric smooth and pulled tight as you tack or staple it to the plywood base.

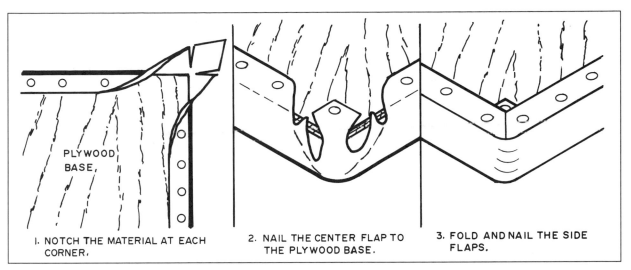

1. NOTCH THE MATERIAL AT EACH CORNER.

2. NAIL THE CENTER FLAP TO THE PLYWOOD BASE.

3. FOLD AND NAIL THE SIDE FLAPS.

15–40. This is how to make the corners so they form a smooth transition as they are nailed to the plywood base.

The pad seat may be used on a chair with a **fixed padded seat** that is secured to the frame and with the upholstery fabric pulled down around the chair frame. The seat base could be plywood, sagless springs, or webbing. The installation of a new pad and cover is about the same as for removable pad seats. The foam pad is secured to the chair frame with tacking tape. The tacking tape is stuck to the foam cushion and nailed to the frame or plywood base (**15–41** and **15–42**). The fabric is cut, folded, and tacked under the frame. When it meets a leg, it is

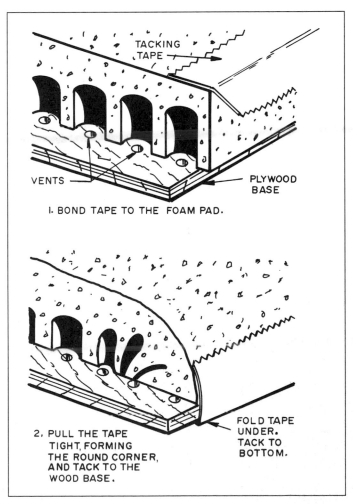

1. BOND TAPE TO THE FOAM PAD.

2. PULL THE TAPE TIGHT, FORMING THE ROUND CORNER, AND TACK TO THE WOOD BASE.

FOLD TAPE UNDER. TACK TO BOTTOM.

15–42. Foam padding for a fixed chair seat can also be installed over a plywood base. This shows a curved, front-edged installation.

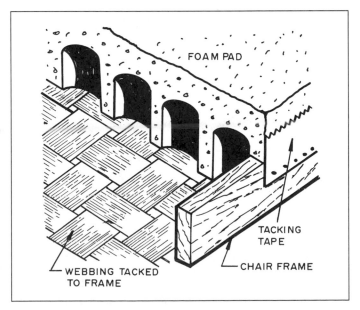

15–41. Foam padding for a fixed chair seat can be placed over webbing and have a square edge.

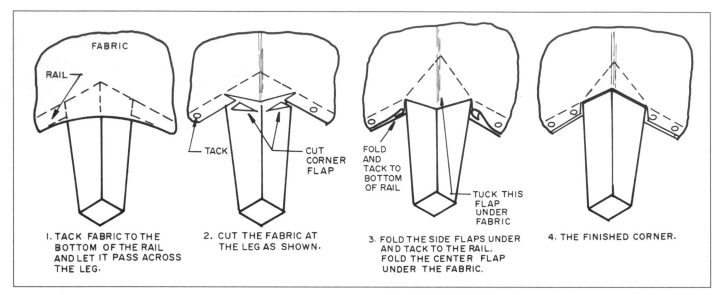

1. TACK FABRIC TO THE BOTTOM OF THE RAIL AND LET IT PASS ACROSS THE LEG.

2. CUT THE FABRIC AT THE LEG AS SHOWN.

3. FOLD THE SIDE FLAPS UNDER AND TACK TO THE RAIL. FOLD THE CENTER FLAP UNDER THE FABRIC.

4. THE FINISHED CORNER.

15–43. This is one way to finish the fabric at a chair leg when the fabric covers the chair rail.

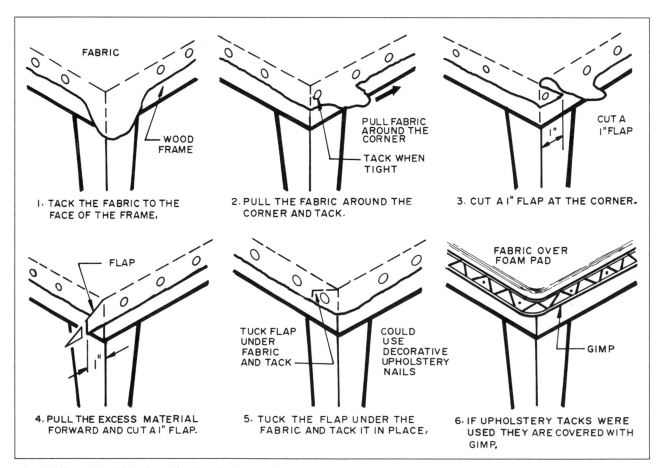

1. TACK THE FABRIC TO THE FACE OF THE FRAME.

2. PULL THE FABRIC AROUND THE CORNER AND TACK.

3. CUT A 1" FLAP AT THE CORNER.

4. PULL THE EXCESS MATERIAL FORWARD AND CUT A 1" FLAP.

5. TUCK THE FLAP UNDER THE FABRIC AND TACK IT IN PLACE.

6. IF UPHOLSTERY TACKS WERE USED THEY ARE COVERED WITH GIMP.

15–44. When the fabric is tacked to the face of the rail, you can secure it with decorative upholstery nails or cover the tacks with gimp.

cut and fit as shown in **15–43**. There are other techniques used by upholsterers to make this corner.

If the fabric is tacked to the face of the seat frame, it is applied as shown in **15–44**. The fabric can be nailed to the frame with decorative head nails that will show. If regular upholsterer's tacks are used, they can be covered with gimp. **Gimp** is a strip of decorative fabric made for this purpose. It is available at upholstery supply shops. Gimp is tacked to the frame with decorative head tacks.

Replacing Webbing

After many years, the webbing stretches and sags and should be replaced. After removing the old webbing, locate the first new piece in the center of the seat. Fold one end over about 1 inch (25 millimeters) and nail one end to the frame with seven 16-ounce upholsterer's tacks as shown in **15–45**. Then pull it tight to the other side with a webbing stretcher and tack it to the other side with three tacks. Cut to length the folded over 1 inch and nail it in place with four tacks spaced between the first three (**15–46**). The rest of the webbing spacing is about ½ inch (13

millimeters) apart. Now run the webbing across from the other direction, weaving it in and out of the first rows. This is illustrated in **15–47**.

Sagless Springs

Some chairs are built with **sagless springs** that are held to the wood frame with metal clips (**15–48**). If a chair is abused, these clips may become bent or pulled loose from the frame. Sometimes they can be replaced with little problem. Other times, it

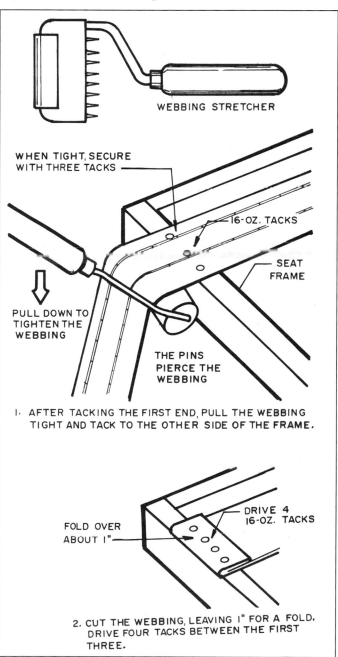

WEBBING STRETCHER

WHEN TIGHT, SECURE WITH THREE TACKS

16-OZ. TACKS

SEAT FRAME

PULL DOWN TO TIGHTEN THE WEBBING

THE PINS PIERCE THE WEBBING

1. AFTER TACKING THE FIRST END, PULL THE WEBBING TIGHT AND TACK TO THE OTHER SIDE OF THE FRAME.

FOLD OVER ABOUT 1"

DRIVE 4 16-OZ. TACKS

2. CUT THE WEBBING, LEAVING 1" FOR A FOLD. DRIVE FOUR TACKS BETWEEN THE FIRST THREE.

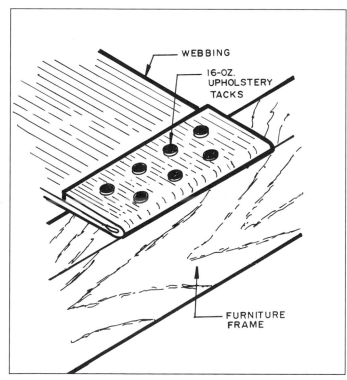

WEBBING

16-OZ. UPHOLSTERY TACKS

FURNITURE FRAME

15–45. When you nail the first end of the webbing to the chair frame, fold it over and drive seven 16-ounce upholstery tacks.

15–46. Pull the webbing tight with a webbing stretcher and secure it to the frame with three 16-ounces tacks. Fold the end over and drive four tacks between the first three.

WEBBING

CENTER OF
THE FRAME

I. CENTER THE STRIP OF WEBBING ON THE FRAME.

2. INSTALL WEBBING ON EACH SIDE OF THE CENTER STRIP.

3. INSTALL A SECOND SET OF WEBBING PERPENDICULAR
TO THE FIRST SET. WEAVE THE ROWS.

15–47. Weave the rows of webbing to get a firmer base for
the foam seat pad.

becomes necessary to remove part of the finished cover and padding to get to the clip. In any case, it can be repaired rather easily. The springs are joined into a unit by metal clips placed between the rows of springs and helical springs that are held to the frame by metal retainer plates (**15–49**).

The springs are covered with heavy burlap. Should you decide to put new upholstery on these springs, consider replacing the pad as well. The upholstery is usually tacked to the bottom of the frame as shown in **15–50**.

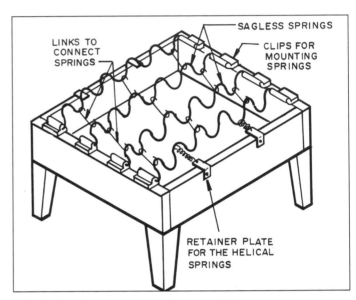

15–48. A typical sagless-spring installation.

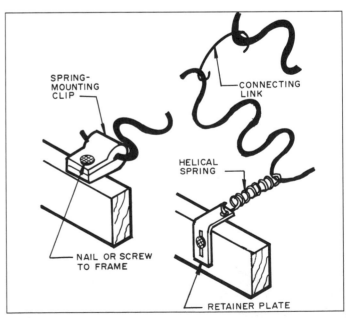

15–49. These are the connectors typically used when installing sagless springs.

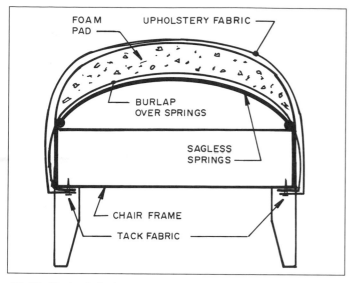

15–50. Typical chair-seat construction when sagless springs are used.

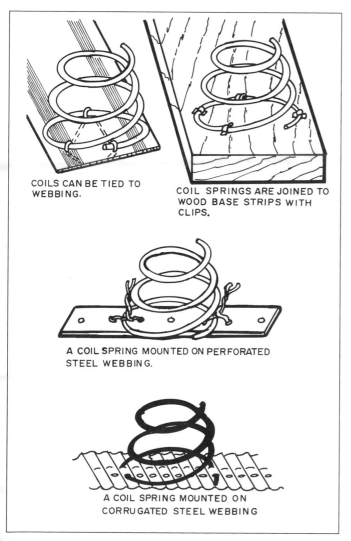

COILS CAN BE TIED TO WEBBING.

COIL SPRINGS ARE JOINED TO WOOD BASE STRIPS WITH CLIPS.

A COIL SPRING MOUNTED ON PERFORATED STEEL WEBBING.

A COIL SPRING MOUNTED ON CORRUGATED STEEL WEBBING

15–51. Coil springs can be mounted on plastic, jute, steel webbing, and wood-base material.

Coil Springs

Coil springs are usually installed by fastening them to jute, plastic, corrugated- or perforated-steel webbing, or to wood cleats that run below the chair frame (**15–51**). Sometimes they come loose and must be refastened. They are sewed to jute and plastic webbing with strong twine. If they come loose from the perforated steel webbing, tighten or replace the tie wires. They may need to be renailed to the wood frame as shown in **15–52**.

If a chair is very old and is to be completely reupholstered, remove the cover material and mark each piece so you know where it belongs. Use these as patterns when cutting the new fabric.

After the cover material is removed, usually the muslin and padding should be replaced. If you strip the chair down to the coil springs, you will notice that they are tied lengthwise, crosswise, and diago-

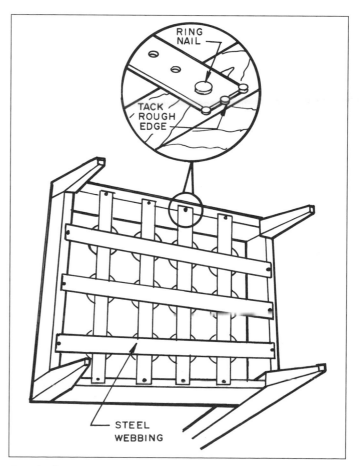

15–52. Steel webbing is nailed to the frame with ring-type nails. Several tacks are nailed on the rough edge to keep it flat to protect the dustcover. Perforated-steel webbing can be woven. However, corrugated steel-webbing is not woven.

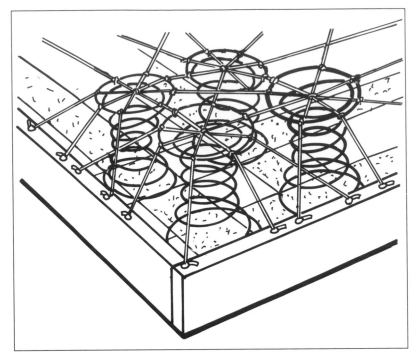

15–53. A typical way to tie coil springs after they are secured to the webbing.

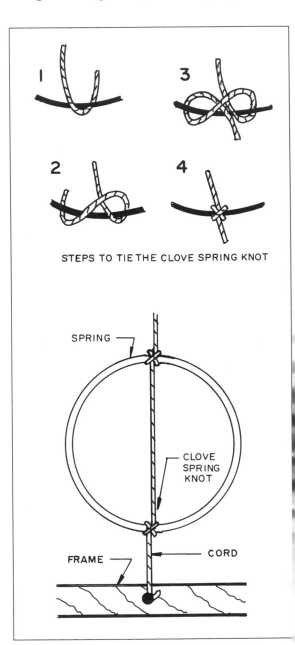

STEPS TO TIE THE CLOVE SPRING KNOT

nally. This joins them into a single unit (**15–53**). If the cord is old, retie the springs with new cord before proceeding. Be certain the cord is nailed firmly to the wood frame.

When you retie the springs, notice if they were tied to produce a crowned or flat base for the padding or cushions (**15–54**).

To retie the springs, begin in the middle of the seat. Nail a cord to the frame and tie it to the outside edge of the first spring. Pull it tight enough to get the spring to the

LOOSE CUSHION

SPRINGS PLACED AND TIED FOR A FLAT BASE OVER WHICH A THICK REMOVABLE CUSHION IS PLACED.

FINISH FABRIC — MUSLIN

BURLAP

FOAM PAD OR RUBBERIZED HAIR

SPRINGS PLACED AND TIED FOR A CROWNED SEAT.

15–54. Springs may be tied to produce a crowned or flat base for the padding or cushions.

SPRING

CLOVE SPRING KNOT

FRAME

CORD

15–55. Tie the springs to the frame and each other.

desired height. Continue tying the string to each side of each spring and fasten it to the frame on the other side. Tie it with a clove spring knot (**15–55**). Be certain to keep the springs equally spaced. Tie each row this way with parallel strings. Then repeat this from the other direction so the cords are perpendicular to those just installed. Finally, tie cords along each of the diagonals. The springs are now ready to be covered with burlap, padding, muslin, cotton, and the final cover as shown in **15–56**.

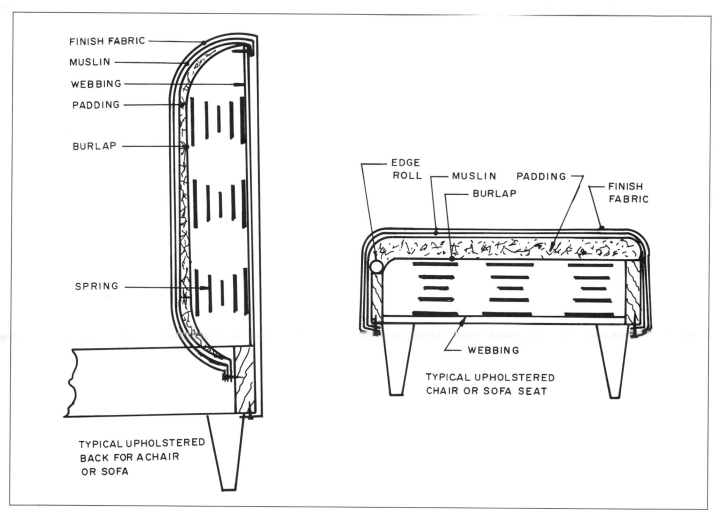

15–56. Typical application of protective fabric, padding, and finish fabric.

CHAPTER SIXTEEN

The Home Workshop

Ohne of the first things to consider when planning to set up a home workshop is the type and extent of work to be undertaken. If the shop is to be used for simple home maintenance chores, it could be simply a small bench in the corner of a room with a few shelves and a tool panel. If it will become the center for a woodworking hobby, considerably more floor space will be needed for the power tools as well as additional lighting, electric power, and a storage area. As a shop is being planned, consider the prospects of future expansion and plans for securing larger and better equipment over a period of years. The expansion should be planned as the original shop is planned (**16–2**).

BASIC PLANNING CONSIDERATIONS

The **location** of the shop depends upon the situation. It could be in the basement, the garage, a spare room, or an outside building. The suitability of the area must be considered, factoring in the need for light, electric power, and space to do the jobs planned. The workshop should have a door large enough to handle sheets of plywood or other large materials and to allow completed projects to be removed from the shop easily. Workshop **noise** should not bother the neighbors. The **space** should be large enough to permit safe use of a circular saw, jointer, or radial arm saw. If only portable power tools are to be used, the shop can be smaller. Portable tools can be stored in cabinets, thus requiring less floor space. Storage of boards and plywood is always a problem. These materials could be stored in another area and rough-cut to size as needed before being brought into the shop.

Ventilation is important to a home shop. In addition to the fresh air needed for comfort, it is necessary to remove dust and other fumes, such as from finishing operations. An open window or two provides good ventilation; however, exhaust fans are usually needed to remove dust and fumes. A small electric fan on the floor or on a bench also helps move air in the shop. Dust in the air can be diminished by installing dust collectors on stationary power machines (**16–1**). A shop vacuum will help remove dust from the bench, floor, and shelves (see **16–3** on page 480). Frequent sweeping, vacuuming, and

16–1. Dust collectors that remove sawdust and chips from individual machines greatly reduce the dust in the air and keep the floor clean. (courtesy Delta International Machinery Corporation).

16–2. A home workshop provides space for home-maintenance activities and hobbies (courtesy Robert L. Blandford, Pinehurst, North Carolina).

16–3. A shop vacuum will speed up the cleaning of the work-bench, floor, and wood chips on your machines (courtesy Robert L. Blandford, Pinehurst, North Carolina).

16–4. The electric oil-filled heater provides a safe heat source because no flame or electric coils are exposed.

trash removal are essential to keeping a safe working environment.

Temperature control provides for a comfortable working situation. A shop need not be kept too warm because the worker will be active and requires a lower room temperature than if inactive. Since a shop provides the ingredients for a fire, the heating unit used should be spark- and flame-resistant. Portable, electric oil-filled heaters are the safest (**16–4**). If you are in the basement, you could extend ducts from the existing hot-air heating system used for the house. In the summer, a small window air conditioner will cool even a large home shop.

Adequate **lighting** is essential for safety and comfort. Working in a semidark or unevenly lighted shop can lead to accidents that need not happen. The lighting should be even over the entire shop area. At least 50 foot-candles of light are needed, while 100 foot-candles are recommended. Some prefer as much as 150 foot-candles. If you can put a paint can on the workbench and it does not cast a shadow, there is enough light.

The lighting should be on separate circuits from the power tools. In this way, if a tool overloads a circuit and the circuit breaker trips, the lights will not go out. An economical light is a two-tube, four-foot-long fluorescent fixture (**16–5**). Natural lighting helps some shops with windows, but it is usually not adequate. Electric lights will most likely be used day or night. Read Chapter 2 for information on wiring lights and switches.

An adequate **electric power supply** is vital. Overloaded circuits trip circuit breakers and can leave a person in the middle of a cut with an unexpected loss of power. This is dangerous to the operator and can damage the job as well.

It is ideal if electricity to the shop can be supplied from the main power panel by a line that feeds the shop circuits from a subpanel (**16–6**). This prevents someone somewhere else in the house from unknowingly overloading a circuit that also runs into the shop. Also, the subpanel box can be turned off and padlocked so no equipment can be used in the absence of the owner. This is especially helpful when there are children in the home. Review Chapter 2 for information on running subpanels and additional circuits.

The number of circuits needed will vary depending

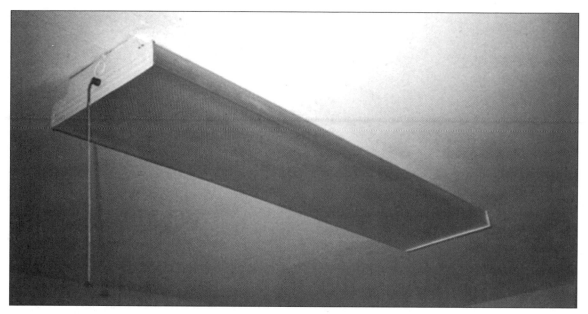

16–5. Fluorescent fixtures are low cost and provide considerable light. They are easy to install.

upon the equipment to be in the shop. If the present and future needs can be established, the loads can be calculated and the wiring provided to handle them. A typical 120-volt circuit could be fused for 30

amps and wired with No. 10 wire. The amperages of the equipment expected to operate on that circuit could be found and the load calculated by adding them.

The circuits in the shop should be protected with **ground-fault circuit interrupters**. These detect minute electrical leakages from a cord or tool that are not strong enough to activate the circuit breaker or blow a fuse. These leakages can cause you to have a severe shock, especially if you are standing on a damp basement or garage floor. Review Chapter 2 for more information.

Noise control must be considered to provide a safe and pleasant atmosphere. Normal speech is rated at 60 decibels. A **decibel** is a unit used to measure intensity (loudness) of sound. It is approximately equal to the smallest difference in intensity that can be detected by the human ear. Sounds greater than 85 decibels can cause hearing damage if a person is exposed for long periods. Temporary hearing loss is not unusual in such situations. If a job creates intense sound, earplugs or sound-resistant muffs should be worn.

Sound can be controlled in a home shop by applying acoustical tile to the ceiling and at least the upper half of the walls. These absorb some of the sound. Machines can be mounted on rubber or fiber pads, which reduce vibration and the trans-

ELECTRIC POWER
FROM POWER COMPANY
TRANSFORMER

MAIN HOUSE
ELECTRIC
PANEL

SUBPANEL IN
WORKSHOP

CIRCUITS FOR SHOP
LIGHTS AND WALL
OUTLETS

16–6. It is best if the lights and outlets in the shop are run off a subpanel taken off the main power panel.

mission of the sound to the floor (**16–7**). They can be bolted to the bench or floor if you want to keep them stationary. Keeping tools sharp greatly reduces noise in the workshop. A dull circular saw or jointer produces much noise.

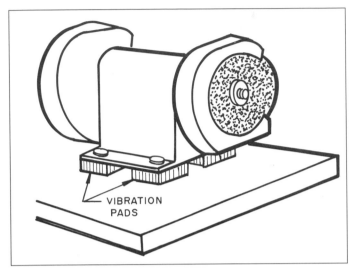

16–7. You can reduce vibration noise by mounting your machines on vibration-dampening pads.

The **floor** should be made slip-resistant. Most home shops will have concrete floors because they are in a basement or the garage. These are strong and satisfactory, but are slippery. Sawdust and other materials make floors even more slippery. Vinyl tiles, while attractive and pleasant to stand on, are also very slippery.

It is important to apply nonskid pads by each machine in the area where the operator stands. These could be fabric pads that are coated with an abrasive material on one side and an adhesive on the other. They are stuck to the floor. Another pad is foam rubber with a skid-resistant back. It has the advantage of being soft and comfortable and reduces operator fatigue.

Concrete floors can be coated with a latex or oil-based concrete paint or epoxy or epoxy-polyurethane paint. Some types are impregnated with abrasive particles. This provides a slip-resistant surface throughout the shop. Consult your local paint dealer for information.

Color can be used for safety and to make the shop a pleasant place to work. All switches should be painted a brilliant orange so they can be quickly spotted. If safety zones around machines are to be used, they should be painted a bright yellow. A white ceiling and light-colored walls help with the lighting because they have high reflection qualities.

FIRE PREVENTION, DETECTION, AND CONTROL

As discussed so far in this chapter, you can help prevent fires by keeping the shop clean. Remove all sawdust from the shop every day. If left in a storage container, it can catch fire by spontaneous combustion. Properly store combustible materials and provide adequate ventilation and a safe form of heat. Store all finishing materials in fire-resistant cabinets and remove soiled rags every day. Do not do any finishing—especially that involving spraying—without adequate ventilation.

Be certain you have an adequate electrical supply. Overloads can cause shorts, which emit sparks. Be certain the wiring is done according to the building code.

Install smoke detectors in several areas around the shop. The battery-operated models are adequate (**16–8**). When the battery is bad, they emit a beep warning you to replace it. Some types are built

16–8. Smoke detectors are an essential safety item in the home workshop.

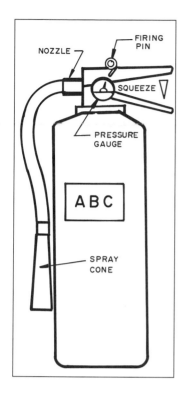

16–9. Keep fire extinguishing equipment capable of putting out Class A, B, and C fires. A multipurpose extinguisher will handle all three types of fires.

into the electrical system, so do not require batteries (**16–8**).

Finally, provide fire extinguishers that can be used on Class A, B, and C fires. Class A fires involve combustible materials such as wood, paper, and textiles. Class B fires include burning gasoline, oil, grease, and fats. Class C fires occur in electrical equipment. There are dry chemical extinguishers that are approved for all three types of fires (**16–9**). This is what you should buy. Get at least a 5-pound extinguisher. Never use a Class A extinguisher on electrical fires. It uses water as the extinguishing agent. Water conducts electricity, so you could be electrocuted.

PLANNING A WORKSHOP

When making the layout for the shop, it is helpful to make a scale drawing of the area. Then make a scale cardboard template of each machine, bench, and storage cabinet or shelf. Move these around on the floor plan until a solution is reached (**16–10**). Apply

16–10 (below). You can make trial shop layouts by laying out the shop on graph paper and using paper templates to represent the equipment.

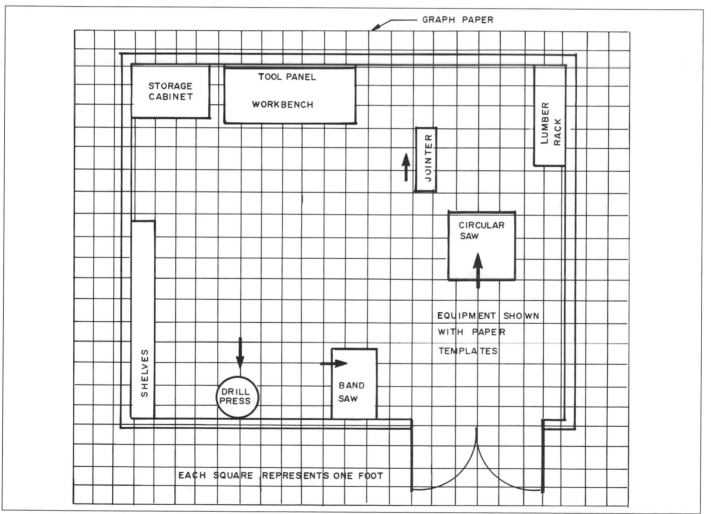

the principles of planning discussed below to each solution until the best plan is developed. While the plan can be made to any scale desired, ¼- or ½-inch (6- or 13-millimeter) squares that represent one foot are two suitable scales.

The first thing to consider is the activity in the shop. Generally, there will be a workbench and near it a tool panel with the hand tools. This is one major work center. The power tools form a second work center, and these need to be considered in relation to each other. Finally, the storage for wood, hardware, and finishing supplies forms a third division of

16-11 (below and pages 485 and 486) Principles to be observed as you locate the power tools in your workshop.

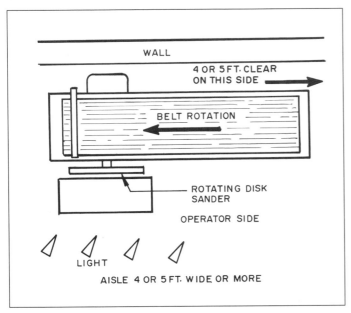

The belt sander needs several feet of clearance on the end so that long boards can be handled. This sander and the disk sander need an aisle on the operator's side around 4 feet wide or wider. Light should come from the left. The belt/disk sander can be placed along a wall or backed up to another machine.

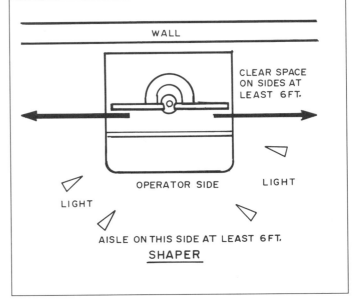

The shaper is one of the most dangerous woodworking machines. It must have considerable clearance on the sides and on the operator's side. The back should be placed next to a wall. Good lighting from the right and left and from the front is important.

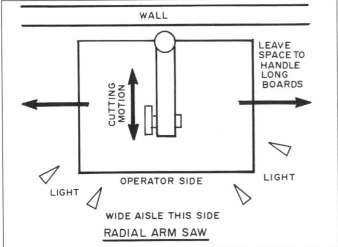

The radial arm saw is best located against a long wall, and a long, empty space should be left on each end so that long boards can be ripped and crosscut. A wide aisle on the operator's side is necessary to protect the operator from an accidental bump by a person passing by the saw.

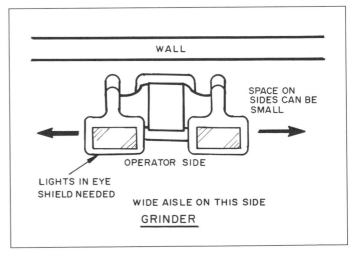

The grinder can be placed next to a wall or backed up to another machine. It does not require much space on the sides. An electric light in the eye shield provides greater safety and is usually required.

the shop. The plan developed should take into account the relation of the supplies to the activities. Wood storage might be near the circular saw and jointer because usually wood is cut to size and smoothed first. Hardware might be near the bench because projects are usually assembled there.

Finishing supplies should be located near the area in which finishing will take place.

The placement of stationary power tools deserves special attention. The planning principles involved are shown in **16–11**. The circular saw requires room for ripping and crosscutting long boards. Since it

16-11 continued.

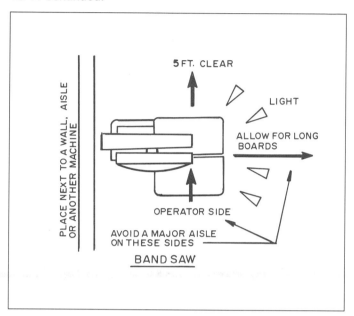

The band saw needs light coming from the right side. A light mounted on the machine is recommended. If there is an aisle on the operator's side and on the end, it should be very wide. Keep the path of cut out of line with other work-stations.

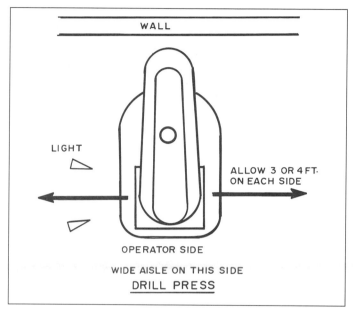

The drill press can be placed against a wall or backed up to another machine. It needs space on each side for long items to be drilled. An individual light on the machine is a big help and is recommended. For the sake of safety, put a 4-or 5-foot wide aisle on the operator's side.

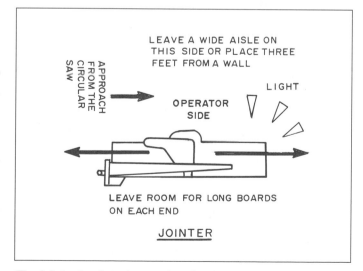

The jointer is placed near the circular saw because stock is usually smoothed after being cut. Light should come from the left and front of the jointer.

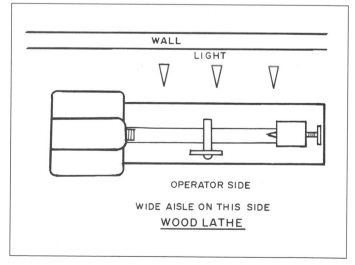

The wood lathe is best placed against a wall. If it throws a piece, it will usually hit the wall. Keep a wide aisle on the operator's side so no one bumps the person at work.

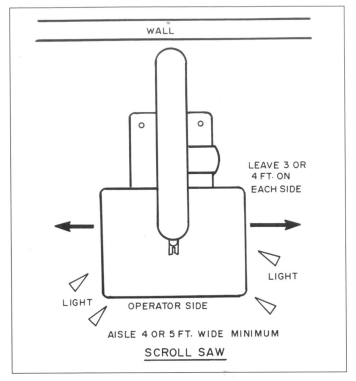

SCROLL SAW

The scroll saw may be placed against a wall or behind another machine. Leave several feet clear on each side and an adequate aisle on the operator side. A light mounted on the scroll saw is a big help.

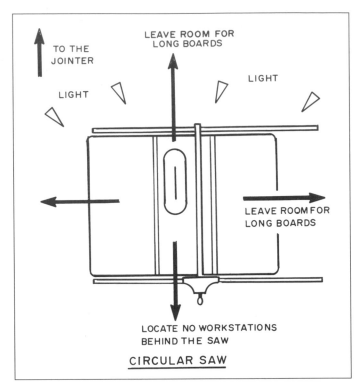

CIRCULAR SAW

The circular saw requires lots of open space on all four sides. Of major importance is to ensure that there are no workstations and other activities behind the saw. Otherwise, if it kicks back a piece of wood, someone could be seriously injured.

will kick back boards improperly fed into it, nothing should be in line with the operator's side. A board kicked back has enough force to go through a frame wall. The jointer should be near the circular saw because the edge of the board should be jointed smooth before it is cut on the circular saw. It is usually in front of it so it is out of the way of kickbacks. The band saw has one side that can be placed next to a wall or aisle. Nothing should crowd the side where the operator stands. The wood lathe can be parallel with a wall, but the light should be between the wall and the lathe.

The belt sander, disk sander, drill press, grinder, shaper, and scroll saw all can be placed against a wall or a post or to the back of another machine. The thing to consider is the length of material to be processed. They are lightweight machines and could be moved if needed. The radial saw can also go against a wall, but special attention should be given to allow sufficient room on each side so long boards can be cut. A wide aisle must be left by all

machines for the operator so no one accidentally bumps him/her while using the machine.

THE WORKBENCH: A BASIC TOOL

The workbench can take many sizes and shapes. Generally, it is rectangular in shape with storage shelves or drawers below. The best height depends upon the height of the person using it, but falls in the range of 32 to 34 inches (813 to 864 millimeters). A top might be from 24 to 30 inches (610 to 762 millimeters) wide and four to six feet (1220 to 1830 millimeters) long. One way to build a bench is to use metal legs available from most hardware stores. The top and shelves are built at home to fit the legs. A sturdy workbench can be built entirely at home. A suggested design is shown in **16–12**.

TOOL AND SUPPLY STORAGE

As you plan the workbench, plan the hand-tool storage. A wall-hung plywood (**16–13**) or pegboard

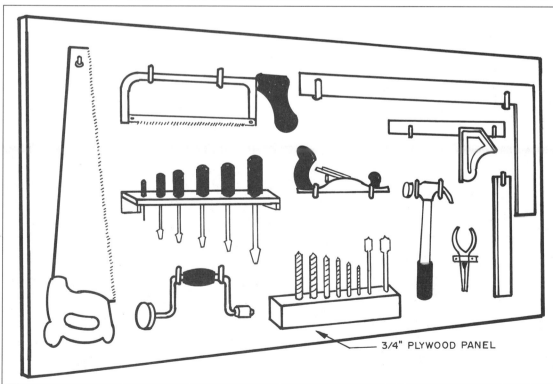

BACK BOARD COULD HOLD SMALL TOOLS

TOP MAY BE ONE OR TWO THICKNESSES
OF 3/4" PLYWOOD OR 2" X 6" KILN-
DRIED LUMBER

4" X 4" LEGS

ALL RAILS
2" X 4"

3/4" PLYWOOD SHELF

6–12. A typical home-built workbench.

16–13. Plywood tool panels use hooks, screw eyes, and homemade wood tool holders.

3/4" PLYWOOD PANEL

Tool and Supply Storage ■ **487**

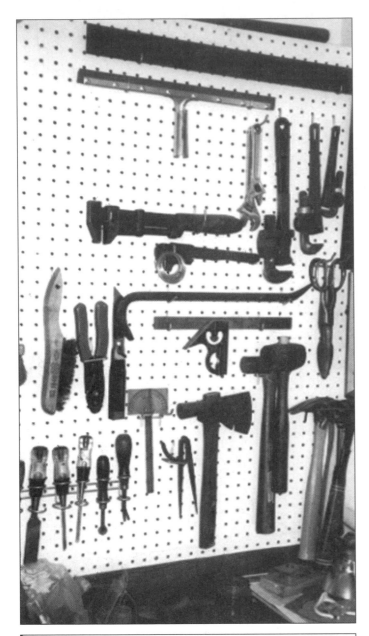

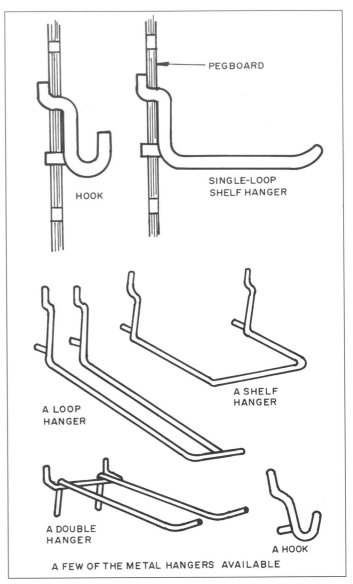

16–15. Tools are hung on pegboard with special clips available at hardware stores. Nails, screws, and holders you make can be used on plywood panels.

16–14. Pegboard is excellent to use for a wall tool panel to hold hand tools. However, plywood may also be used (courtesy Edward Davidheiser, Pinehurst, North Carolina).

panel (**16–14**) is often used. **Pegboard** is perforated tempered hardboard. Tools can be hung by using screw hooks and wood and metal carriers or by buying commercially available metal and plastic racks and clips (**16–15**).

Small hardware items are most easily found if stored in glass jars. This permits a quick visual check to find the screws or nails you want. Build narrow shelves designed to hold the size jars you select (**16–16**).

Special tools used only on a particular machine should be stored on a panel placed near the machine. For example, table-saw blades can be

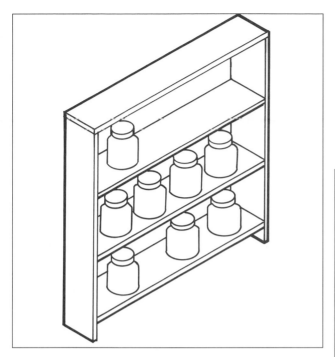

16–16. Narrow shelving designed to hold glass jars will store many small items in one area.

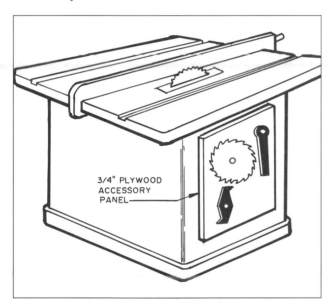

16–17. Special tool panels can be mounted on or near each power tool to hold the cutters and special tools required to adjust it.

16–18. Long pieces of lumber can be stored on horizontal racks. Keep the horizontal supports about 12 inches apart, so the load on any one is not excessive.

stored on the saw (**16–17**). A set of drills can be mounted on or near the drill press.

Cabinets with doors that can be locked are good for storing portable power tools. This keeps them away from children and prevents unauthorized use.

Lumber can be stored on horizontal or vertical racks. Horizontal racks (**16–18**) require a long wall,

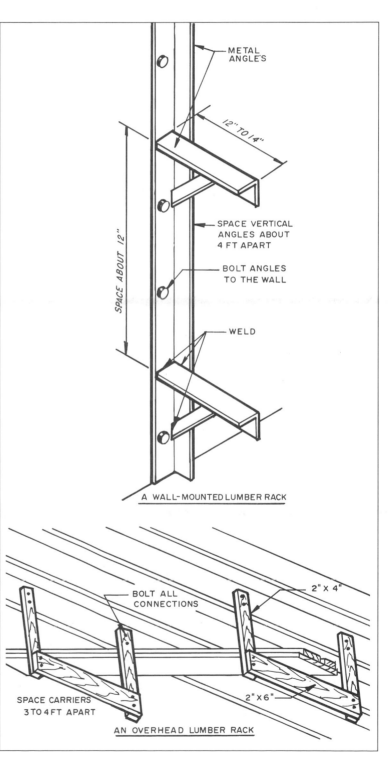

and the larger boards are put on the bottom. To get one, the others have to be unpiled. Vertical racks (**16–19**) permit the storage of more wood per foot of wall. Each board can be easily removed. The length is limited by the ceiling height.

Paints and other finishing materials should be stored in metal fire-resistant cabinets. Soiled rags should be removed from the house immediately after using them. They can be temporarily stored in metal fire-resistant cans.

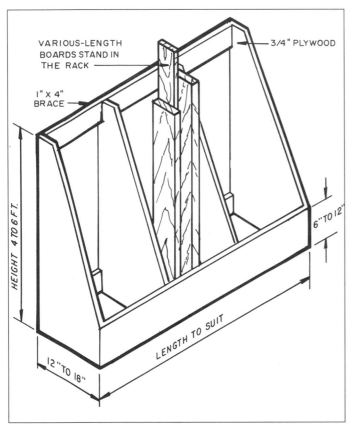

16–19. Short pieces of lumber are conveniently stored using a vertical rack.

GENERAL SAFETY PRECAUTIONS

Everything that is moved into a home shop should be examined from the standpoint of safety. Fire safety demands fireproof storage and the availability of Class A, B, and C fire extinguishers.

A first-aid kit with items needed for immediate treatment should be centrally located. Burns and severe cuts with extensive bleeding are the two major accidents to be handled. Something to re-

vive a person who has lost consciousness is also essential.

All electrical outlets should be grounded, and all power tools should have the third wire necessary to ground them through the outlet. *Never operate power tools when standing on a wet floor or wet ground.* All outlets should have ground-fault circuit-interruption connections.

Keep all tools sharp. A dull tool does not cut properly and requires additional pressure, which often causes a slip and a cut.

Do not use a tool until its safe operation is understood. Manuals with tools plus books on woodworking and metalworking contain complete instructions on safe tool usage. Remember to use clamps to hold parts being worked upon. The human hand is not a satisfactory clamp.

Never operate any tool if the safety guard has been removed or is not operating properly. Also always wear safety glasses (**16–20**). They are invaluable protection when using hand and machine tools. Wear a filter over your nose and mouth when sanding or doing other operations producing noxious fumes (**16–21**).

Safety is a matter of attitude. Accidents are reduced when a person thinks about safety.

16–20. Most operations require that you wear some type of eye protection (courtesy Dalloz Safety).

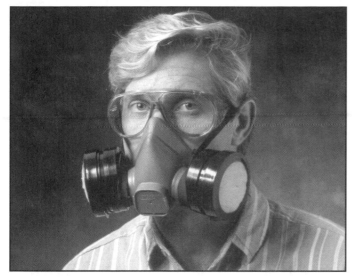

16–21. When working with dust-producing machines, such as sanders, and with materials that produce noxious fumes, such as when finishing, wear a respirator (courtesy Dalloz Safety).

HAND TOOLS

The choice of hand tools in a home workshop varies considerably depending upon the activities that will be undertaken. In all cases, buy quality tools. Cheap tools do not let you produce good work and will usually be replaced with better-quality tools. You can start with a few basic tools and add to them as you gain experience.

Since you have an investment in your hand tools, they should receive the proper care. This will also make them more effective in doing the job. A key to this is proper storage. Do not pile them in drawers. Cutting tools should hang so the cutting edges are protected from damage.

Protect the hand tools from rust. Coat them with a light machine oil or rust inhibitor available at your hardware store. Keep them dry and wipe them clean after using them. If they begin to rust, rub them down with fine steel wool before coating them with a rust inhibitor.

Above all, keep your tools sharp. They do not do a good job if dull and are more likely to slip and cause injury. Add a quality sharpening stone to your shop.

POWER TOOLS

Power tools help make the job easier and faster and produce professional results. However, many home-maintenance jobs can be satisfactorily performed with hand tools. For general home maintenance, the following tools are very often used. An electric drill and saber saw are the two power tools that will be of greatest value. Most saber saws will cut 2-inch (51-millimeter) lumber, which is the thickest size generally used. A grinder will also be of help when sharpening edge tools. If you plan to build furniture and cabinets and do other woodworking projects, additional power tools are necessary. Following are descriptions and some basic safety considerations for these tools. These safety recommendations were developed from the publications of the Power Tool Institute, Inc., 1300 Sumner Ave., Cleveland, Ohio 44115-2851. For additional information and greater detail on the safe operation of power tools, contact the Power Tool Institute, Inc. *The recommendations in this chapter, while important, do not cover all possible situations.*

Portable Electric Drill

The most common sizes of a portable electric drill are ¼, ⅜, and ½ inch (6, 9.5, and 13 millimeters) (**16–22**). The ⅜-inch size is most commonly used.

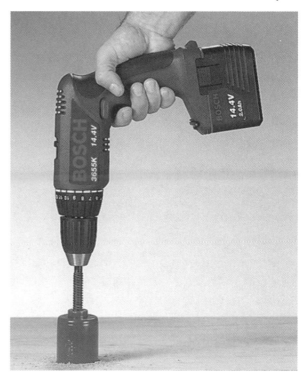

16–22. Portable electric drills are available as battery-operated and 120-volt units. This is a battery-powered unit (courtesy S-B Power Tools).

The size refers to the largest diameter of the shank of a drill that will fit into the chuck. Some have a variable-speed control, and others can reverse the direction of rotation. This is especially helpful when driving and removing screws. Some are battery-operated and are recharged after each use.

Twist drills are most commonly used in portable electric drills. They are available in sets with diameters from ¹⁄₁₆ to ³⁄₈ inch, varying in 64ths of an inch.

There are a variety of accessories for portable electric drills. These include various sanding pads, buffing wheels, wire brushes, grinding wheels, hole saws, masonry drills, and rotary files.

Most drills are now made with a heavy-duty plastic case and are double-insulated, so a ground wire is not necessary.

Electric-Drill Safety Techniques

1. Never use a drill in wet conditions unless it is a battery-operated model.

2. Drills with metal cases must have a ground wire. They must be plugged into extension cords with three wires. The source of electricity must also be grounded. A ground-fault circuit interrupter must be in the circuit.

3. Do not hold small objects in your hand and try to drill holes in them. Clamp them to a workbench.

4. When drilling masonry, grinding, or sanding, wear goggles.

5. Always remove the chuck key before starting the drill. Some drills have keyless chucks.

6. Be certain tools are properly tightened in the chuck.

7. Be careful that your clothing does not get wrapped up in the rotating tool. Beware of loose clothing. Do not wear gloves.

Portable Finishing Sander

These sanders are called finishing sanders because they remove very small amounts of material. There are several types: orbital, random-orbital, vibrating,

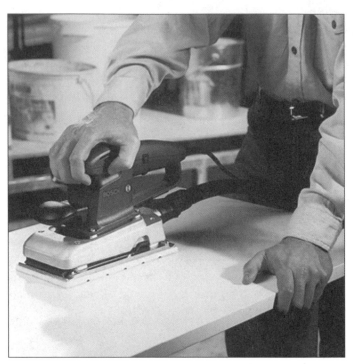

16–23. Finishing sanders produce a fine finish that prepares the surface for painting or staining (courtesy S-B Power Tools).

and straight-line (**16–23**). Orbital and vibrating sanders move across the grain because of their action. The straight-line sander produces the smoothest surface. Some machines can be switched from vibrating to orbital motion. The orbital motion removes material faster.

These sanders have a flat, padded plate on the bottom, over which the abrasive paper is placed. The paper is quickly changed, and standard sheet sizes can be cut to fit the machine. Keep the sander flat on the wood and do not press down. Let it cut at its own speed.

Portable-Finishing-Sander Safety Techniques

1. Be certain the abrasive paper is properly installed.

2. Follow the manufacturer's instructions for using the machine.

3. Wear a respirator or filter over your nose.

4. When sanding small parts, clamp them to the workbench.

5. Be certain the switch is off before you plug in the machine.

16–24. A portable belt sander removes wood much faster than the finishing sanders. Various-grit belts can be used to control the amount removed (courtesy Makita USA).

Portable Belt Sander

A portable belt sander (**16–24**) has an endless abrasive belt running over two cylindrical pulleys. On the bottom is a plate that presses the belt against the work. It removes wood very fast and is used for the first sanding of a board. Finishing sanders are used for the final sanding. Some sanders have a vacuum system that sucks the dust into a bag. This helps reduce the amount of dust in the air.

Sanders are made with 3- and 4-inch (76- and 102-millimeter) -wide belts that run from about 20 to 24 inches (508 to 610 millimeters) in length. The belts are made with emery, garnet, and aluminum-oxide abrasives. When selecting a sander, be certain the motor is strong enough to drive the belt. A 6- to 9-ampere motor is adequate for most work. Be certain the sander has a good tracking adjustment. **Tracking** is the adjustment made to center the belt on the pulleys and keep it there when in use.

If the work to be sanded is rough, start with a coarse belt and switch to a belt with a finer abrasive for the final passes. To start sanding, place the machine flat on the work, hold it by the two handles provided, and turn on the power. Keep it moving or it will sand deeper in the place where it is sitting (**16–25**).

Portable-Belt-Sander Safety Techniques

1. Always hold the sander by both handles and keep it flat on the work.

2. When replacing the belt, be certain it tracks on the pulley. Follow the directions of the manufacturer. Be certain to unplug the machine before changing the belt.

3. Keep the cord clear of the area being sanded.

4. Wear goggles and a respirator.

5. Do not bear down on the machine to try to make it cut faster.

6. Clamp small pieces to the bench or the sander will kick them off.

7. Do not place the machine on the top of the bench with the belt still moving.

8. Be certain the switch is off before you plug in the sander.

Saber Saw

A saber saw (**16–26**) is used to cut curves and straight edges. Since the blade is small and thin, it can cut rather sharp curves but is more difficult to use to cut a straight line. Straight lines can be cut by clamping a board to the surface to be cut and moving the saw along it, touching the board.

Saber saws have motors with ampere ratings of 2.5 to 4. The higher rating provides more power, and the saw will cut thicker wood. A 3.5-ampere saw will cut a 2 x 4 (1½ inches) easily.

There are many types of saber-saw blades available. They can cut wood, metal, plastics, and other materials. Thin materials require a fine-toothed blade.

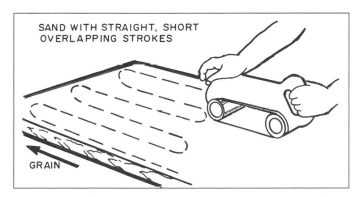

SAND WITH STRAIGHT, SHORT OVERLAPPING STROKES

GRAIN

16–25. Keep the portable belt sander moving or you will get sanding marks and remove more material in one spot than you had planned.

16–26. Saber saws will cut many different materials. They can cut curves and straight edges (courtesy S-B Power Tools).

Saber-Saw Safety Techniques

1. Unplug the saw before replacing the blade.

2. Use the proper blade for the job. Throw away dull or broken blades.

3. Clamp small stock to the bench before cutting it.

4. Be careful not to cut the electrical cord.

5. Keep your hands behind the saw.

6. Remember, the blade protrudes below the work and can hit your hand or items below.

Bench Grinder

An electric bench grinder (**16–27**) is used to sharpen edge tools such as chisels. It is also used to smooth rough edges on metal. Wheels used to sharpen tools have a fine aggregate and should not be used for any other purpose. Wheels are made in various grits. A 60-grit wheel is a medium wheel, and a 120-grit wheel is a fine wheel.

Most bench grinders have two abrasive wheels mounted on the motor shaft. One could have a fine-grit wheel and the other a coarser-grit. Each wheel has a heavy metal guard. This must never be

16–27. Bench grinders are used to sharpen edge tools and remove metal where needed from various objects (courtesy Delta International Machinery Corporation).

removed. If the wheel breaks, the shield will prevent it from flying into your face. Eye shields over each wheel are also absolutely necessary.

Bench grinders are specified by the width and diameter of the wheel and the ampere rating of the motor. A 2.2-amp motor driving a 5-inch-diameter, ½-inch-wide wheel makes a good small unit for general-purpose work (**16–27**). When buying new grinding wheels, be certain to get the correct hole size.

Bench-Grinder Safety Techniques

1. Never operate a grinder unless the wheel and eye-protection guards are in place. Always wear your personal eye-protection devices.

2. Keep the tool rest within ⅛ inch (3 millimeters) of the wheel, as shown in **16–28**. This will require adjusting as the wheel wears and gets smaller.

3. Do not grind on the sides of the wheel.

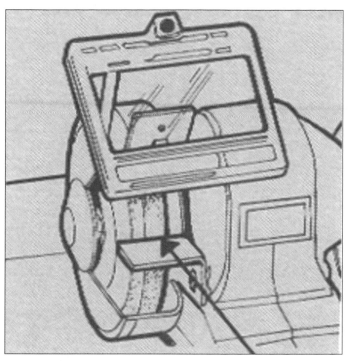

16–28. Keep the tool rest within 1/8 inch of the face of the grinding wheel (courtesy Power Tool Institute, Inc.).

4. Press the metal lightly against the wheel.

5. When the wheel gets clogged and glazed, clean it with a wheel dresser.

6. When a groove develops on the wheel surface, dress it flat with a wheel dresser.

7. If a wheel gets chipped or cracked, replace it.

Router

The router is a portable tool used to shape the edges of stock into decorative profiles. In addition, it can cut various types of grooves and is used extensively to make joints. It is basically a high-speed motor mounted on a base (**16–29**). The motor drives various types of cutters (**16–30**).

Routers have several collet sizes. A **collet** is the chuck-like unit on the end of the motor shaft that holds the cutter. The collet that holds a cutter with a ¼-inch (6-millimeter) shaft is most common. Heavier-duty routers require collets that hold ½-inch (13-millimeter) shafts.

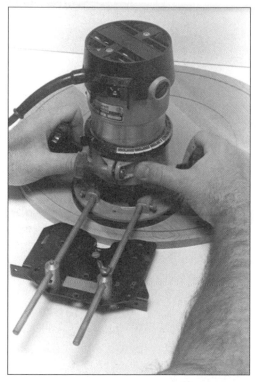

16–29. A portable router is a high-speed machine used to cut grooves and various shaped profiles on the edge of stock (courtesy Makita USA).

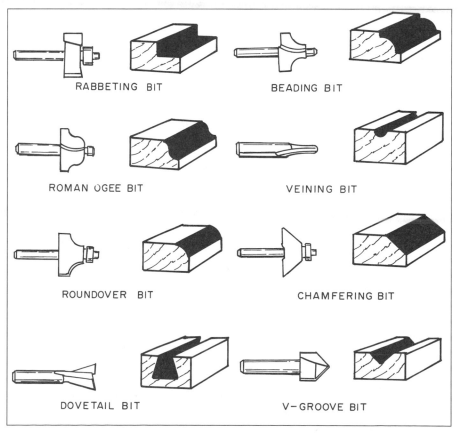

RABBETING BIT

BEADING BIT

ROMAN OGEE BIT

VEINING BIT

ROUNDOVER BIT

CHAMFERING BIT

DOVETAIL BIT

V-GROOVE BIT

16–30. A few of the profiles and the cutters available for use with the portable router.

A small router will have a 6- to 9-ampere electric motor, while a midsize router will have an 8- to 11-ampere motor. They weigh from 6 to 8 pounds.

Router Safety Techniques

1. Since the router operates at high speeds in the range of 20,000 rpm (revolutions per minute), you must be constantly alert and have everything ready for a safe operation.

2. Wear goggles or a face mask and a dust mask.

3. Remove all jewelry and loose clothing, and secure long hair in a hair net.

4. Be certain the router bit is installed as directed by the manufacturer.

5. Keep your hands on both handles at all times so you do not lose control (**16–31**).

6. Unplug the router before you change cutters.

7. Do not reach below the router as it is cutting.

8. Be certain the workpiece is securely clamped to the workbench before routing.

9. Do not take deep cuts. Work in stages as directed by the manufacturer's recommendations in the owner's manual.

10. Do not force the router to cut or try to cut too fast.

Portable Circular Saw

The portable circular saw is used primarily for crosscutting and ripping stock. Since there are a variety of blades available, it can cut hardboard, solid wood, plywood, and plastic laminates. It has a ripping fence that slides along the edge of the board to help guide the saw. The base can be tilted so the saw can cut angles up to 45 degrees. The blade is kept covered with a guard (**16–32**).

Portable circular saws are specified by the diameter of the blade and the ampere rating of the motor. A 7¼-inch (184-millimeter) -diameter blade with a 10- to 12-ampere motor will provide plenty of power and depth of cut.

16–31. Always keep your hands on both handles as you operate the portable router (courtesy Power Tool Institute, Inc.).

16–32. A portable circular saw should have a blade guard that encloses the blade when it is lifted from the work (courtesy S-B Power Tools).

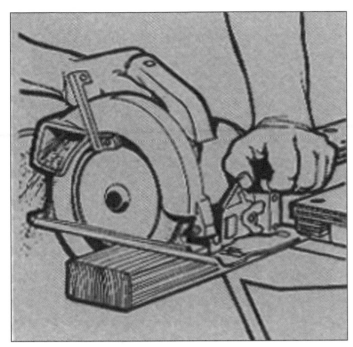

16–33. Keep both hands on the saw and behind the cutting action. Secure the work before cutting so it will not slip (courtesy Power Tool Institute, Inc.).

Portable-Circular-Saw Safety Instructions

1. Unplug the cord before you change the blade.

2. Use only sharp blades.

3. Throw away bent or cracked blades.

4. Clamp small pieces of stock to a bench.
5. Be careful that you do not cut into the electric cord.

6. Secure the piece before cutting so it does not slip and cause the blade to jam.

7. Make certain the area below the board is clear because the blade protrudes below the board.

8. Do not use the saw if the guard is not working properly.

9. Do not stand directly behind the saw as it is cutting.

10. Keep both hands on the saw and above and behind the cutting action (**16–33**).

Table Saw

A table saw, sometimes called a stationary circular saw, has a circular blade mounted on an arbor. It sticks up through a table. It can rip, crosscut, and cut miters, dadoes, grooves, tenons, tapers, and molding. There are a variety of accessories that expand its capabilities.

Table saws are specified by the diameter of the blade. The most common diameters are 8¼ and 10 inches (209 and 254 millimeters). Among the blades available are: crosscut; ripping; combination, for crosscutting and ripping; hollow-ground, for smooth cuts; plywood blades with small teeth, for cutting plywood without splintering the edges; and carbide-tipped blades, for cutting plastic laminates and other composition materials.

The saw will come equipped with a fence for ripping stock. A miter gauge is supplied for crosscutting and cutting miters. Table extensions can be

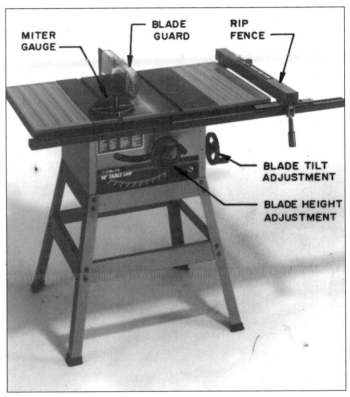

16–34. The table saw is a very versatile machine that enables you to make a wide variety of cuts (courtesy Delta International Machinery Corporation).

added to provide a larger table, making it easier to cut plywood sheets and long boards. A 13- to 15-ampere electric motor will provide adequate power for most operations (**16–34**).

16–35. Never let the blade extend more than ⅛ inch (3 millimeters) above the surface of the work. The guard is not shown in place for illustration purposes only (courtesy Power Tool Institute, Inc.).

Table-Saw Safety Techniques

1. Unplug the machine when replacing the blade.

2. Always use the guard. The only exception is for a few operations where it has to be removed so the wood can pass over the blade.

3. Set the blade to extend not more than ⅛ inch (3 millimeters) above the surface of the wood (**16–35**).

4. Never stand directly behind the saw.

5. Do not cut warped stock.

6. Never cut stock freehand. Always use the fence or miter gauge.

7. Do not cut cylindrical stock.

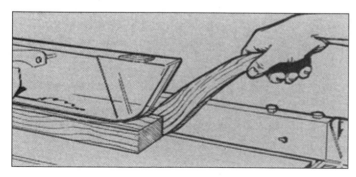

16–36. Use a push stick to move narrow pieces past the saw (courtesy Power Tool Institute, Inc.).

8. Do not reach anywhere near the blade with your fingers. Use a push stick to work narrow boards (**16–36**).

9. Keep the blade free of resin from cutting green woods.

10. Wear eye protection.

11. Use a piece of scrap wood to clear the table while the saw is running.

12. Do not use the rip fence and the miter gauge at the same time.

13. When finished with the saw, lower the blade below the top of the table.

14. Do not wear jewelry or loose clothing.

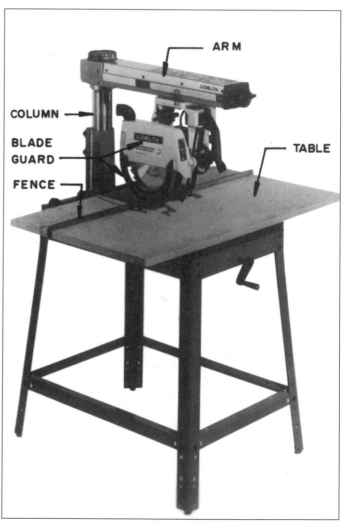

16–37. The radial arm saw is especially good for crosscutting stock (courtesy Delta International Machinery Corporation).

16–38. The radial-arm-saw blade and motor move across the stock that is held securely against a wood fence. Pull the saw out just far enough to complete the cut (courtesy Power Tool Institute, Inc.).

Radial Arm Saw

A radial arm saw has the circular blade mounted on the shaft of the motor (16–37). The work remains in place on the table while the motor and blade are pulled across the board, making the cut (16–38).

The saw can, with the proper accessories, cross-cut, rip, cut grooves, dadoes, and miters, bore holes, sand, and cut molding. A saw with a 10-inch (254-millimeter) blade is adequate. The table should be extended so long boards and plywood sheets can be handled. It uses the same blades as the stationary circular saw.

The motor with the blade can be tilted to cut miters and angles. It can also be raised and lowered to control the depth of cut.

Radial-Arm-Saw Safety Techniques

1. Always keep your hands out of the line of the blade, as shown in 16–38.

2. The guard should always be in place.

3. Cut only stock that is flat and straight.

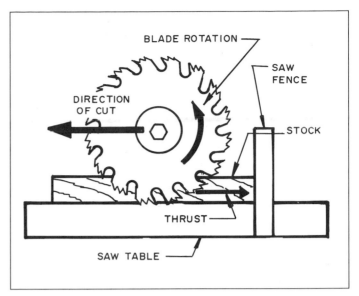

16–39. Be certain the blade is installed so the thrust of cutting presses the stock against the fence.

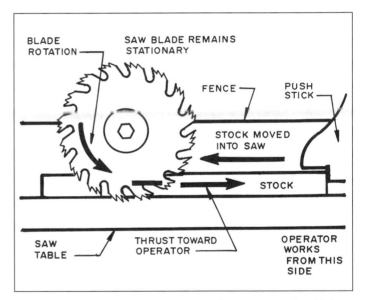

16–40. When ripping stock with a radial-arm-saw, feed it into the rotation of the blade. Install the blade so the teeth cut up into the stock.

4. When crosscutting, be certain the saw blade is installed so the thrust is toward the fence (16–39).

5. When ripping, feed stock into the saw from the correct direction. The teeth of the blade should be cutting up into the stock from the bottom, as shown in 16–40.

6. When ripping, use a push stick to move narrow stock (6 inches or less) between the blade and fence.

7. After completing the cut, always return the saw to the starting position.

8. Disconnect the power before changing a blade.

9. Before starting a cut, allow the saw to reach its full speed.

10. Do not try to cut too fast.

Jointer

A jointer (**16–41**) is used to smooth the faces and edges of boards. It can cut edges straight and at 90 degrees to the face or cut bevels, chamfers, and angles. It can be used to smooth rough boards as well as smooth and adjust the size of surfaced boards.

Jointers are sold in bench-top and stationary floor models. It is best to mount your jointer on a floor

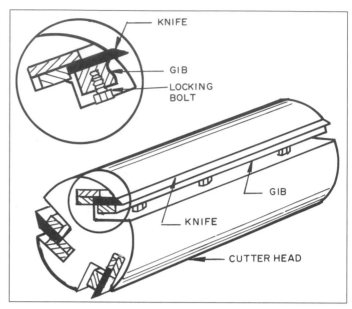

16–42. The jointer cutter head has three knives. They are held in place and adjusted by various methods. This example is typical. However, you should follow the instructions in the owners's manual.

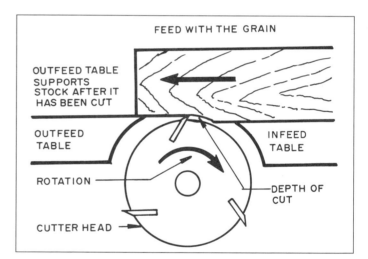

16–43. The outfeed table must be adjusted so the cut stock rests firmly on it. If it is too high, it stops the stock. If it is too low, it will cause a gouge to be cut in the end of the stock.

stand. This makes it easier to use, and you can move it if you need to work extra-long pieces. A typical jointer for a home workshop will have a 6-inch (152-millimeter) cutter width. A ¾- to 1-horsepower electric motor is common on this size jointer. Wider cutting models are available.

The knives are held in a rotating cutter head (**16–42**). They must be kept sharp and carefully installed so they do not come loose. The fence is used to guide the stock over the cutter head. The stock is placed on the infeed table and fed into the

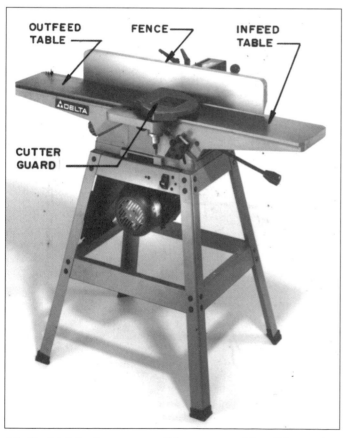

16–41. A jointer is a very useful power machine. It is used to smooth stock and reduce it in thickness (courtesy Delta International Machinery Corporation).

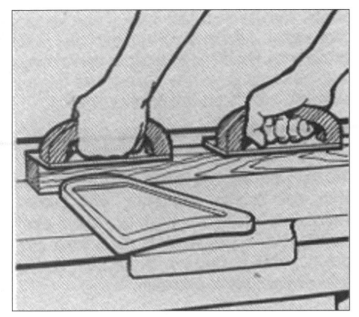

16–44. Always use hold-downs and push blocks when surfacing stock or running small pieces. The guard must be in place (courtesy Power Tool Institute, Inc.).

cutter head. The outfeed table receives the stock after it has been surfaced by the knives in the cutter head, as shown in **16–43**. This is a very dangerous power tool and it must be set up and operated following specific safety procedures.

Jointer Safety Procedures

1. Keep the knives sharp.

2. Always use push blocks and hold-downs (**16–44**).

3. Never use the jointer if the guard is removed or not operating properly.

4. Do not take cuts deeper than recommended by the manufacturer. Usually ⅛ inch (3 millimeters) is maximum. It is better to take several thin cuts than one deep cut.

5. Feed the stock into the cutters so they will remove the wood with the grain (refer to **16–43**).

6. Keep the stock firmly against the fence.

7. Never let either hand actually pass over the cutters.

8. Do not stand directly behind the machine because the stock could kick back and hit you.

9. Wear eye and ear protection.

10. Feed the stock slowly and at an even pace.

11. The stock must be free of nails, dirt, and other debris. Avoid knots whenever possible.

12. After you remove the knives for sharpening, follow the manufacturer's instructions for reinstalling them. A loose knife is a very dangerous projectile.

Wood Lathe

Wood lathes (**16–45**) are used to turn round parts such as furniture legs and bowls. Long, round parts are turned between the spindle and dead center. Objects such as bowls are turned on a faceplate mounted on the headstock.

A typical lathe for use in your workshop will enable you to turn round lengths up to 36 inches

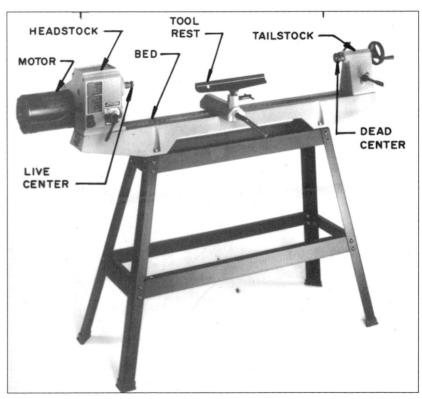

16–45. A wood lathe is used to make round parts (courtesy Delta International Machinery Corporation).

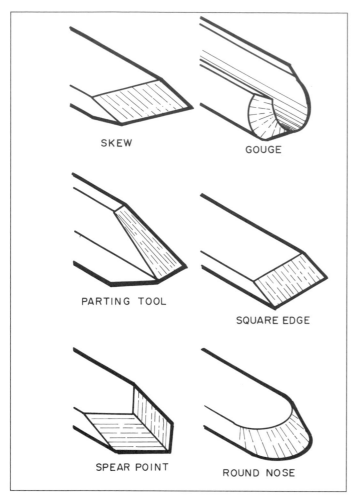

16–46. These are the commonly used wood-turning tools.

(16–46). These have special functions such as roughing a square piece into a round shape and cutting concave and convex shapes.

Wood-Lathe Safety Procedures

1. Always wear a full face shield. A dust mask is recommended.

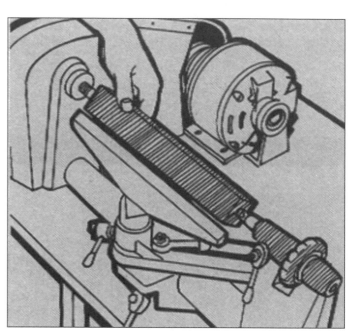

16–47. Before starting the lathe, turn the workpiece by hand to check to see that it clears the tool rest (courtesy Power Tool Institute, Inc.).

(914 millimeters) and bowls up to 12 inches (305 millimeters) in diameter. You can buy models that mount on a workbench or secure a metal stand that makes it easier to use and lets you move it about the shop as needed. A ¾- to 1-horsepower electric motor is typical. The speed of rotation can be varied to suit the job at hand. Speeds from 500 to 3,000 rpm are typical.

The **headstock** (16–45) supports one end of the work with a live center that is driven into the end. This is connected to the motor and supplies the power to rotate the work. The **tailstock** (16–45) has a dead center upon which the other end of the work turns. The wood-turning tools are supported by the tool rest as they are fed into the rotating stock. The headstock, tailstock, and tool rest are mounted on a strong cast-iron **bed**.

A set of wood-turning tools usually consists of five different-shaped cutting edges in several sizes

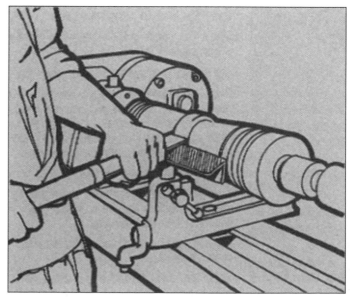

16–48. Keep the tool rest to within ⅛ inch of the work piece. Stop the machine frequently and move the rest closer as the workpiece gets smaller (courtesy Power Tool Institute, Inc.).

2. Remove all jewelry, and don't wear long sleeves and other loose clothing. Long hair should be in a hair net.

3. Double-check to be certain the wood piece is securely installed on the lathe.

4. Do not run the lathe at speeds that exceed the manufacturer's recommendations for the work being performed.

5. Keep the tool rest within ⅛ inch of the rotating work. Rotate the work by hand before starting the lathe to be certain it will clear the tool rest.

6. Never adjust the tool rest with the lathe running. With the power off, rotate the workpiece by hand to make certain it does not hit the tool rest (**16–47**).

7. Do not turn wood with knots, splits, or other defects.

8. Hold the chisel firmly on the tool rest and hold the handle on the end to give you maximum control (**16–48**).

9. Be certain the workpiece is rotating toward you.

Drill Press

A drill press may be designed to mount on a workbench or have a long column and a heavy base that allow it to stand on the floor (**16–49**). While it is used primarily to drill holes, you can get accessories that allow it to cut mortises and plugs, do routing and shaping, and even operate as a small drum sander.

The size is specified by the distance between the column and the center of the spindle that holds the chuck. You will probably want an 8- or 12-inch (203- or 305-millimeter) size. The motors are typically ¼- or ⅓-horsepower. Most drill presses will have some means for changing the speed of rotation.

Drill-Press Safety Procedures

1. Always wear safety goggles.

2. Remove all jewelry and loose clothing. Confine long hair in a hair net.

3. Be certain the chuck key has been removed from the chuck before starting the motor.

4. Never hold the workpiece in your hand. Place long pieces so they are against the left side of the column (**16–50**, on the following page) and clamp short pieces to the table (**16–51**, on the following page).

5. Set the correct speed of rotation for the job at hand.

6. If something goes wrong, do not try to correct it. Shut off the machine.

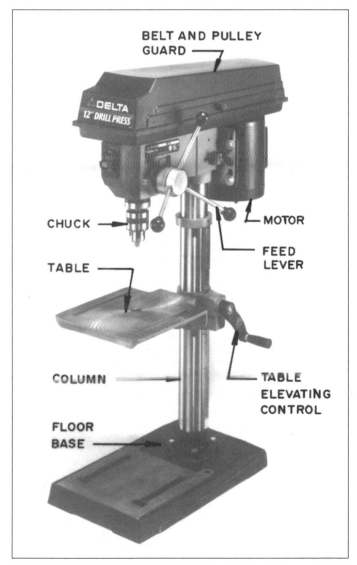

BELT AND PULLEY GUARD

CHUCK

TABLE

COLUMN

FLOOR BASE

MOTOR

FEED LEVER

TABLE ELEVATING CONTROL

16–49. A drill press can drill holes, cut square mortises and round plugs, and serve as a router, shaper, or sander (courtesy Delta International Machinery Corporation).

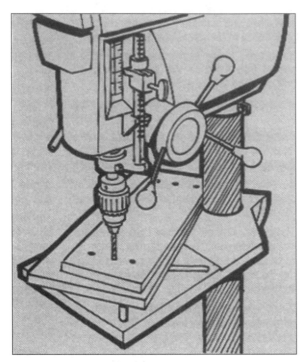

16–50. The drill press will spin the workpiece unless provision is made to secure it. Long pieces should be placed against the left side of the column (courtesy Power Tool Institute, Inc.).

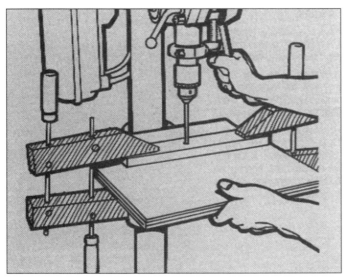

16–51. When drilling into small pieces, clamp them to the table (courtesy Power Tool Institute, Inc.).

Band Saw

The band saw (**16–52**) serves mainly to cut curves. However, with a rip fence installed it can cut stock to width. It also has a miter gauge, so it can crosscut short pieces. The saw has blade-guide mechanisms above and below the table. They keep the blade running true and have a **thrust wheel** (also known as a

bearing) that prevents the blade from being pushed back as a cut is made (**16–53**). The upper guide is lowered to within about ⅛ inch (3 millimeters) of the surface of the wood. This carries the blade guard down so no blade is exposed as you cut the stock.

The size is specified by the distance from the blade to the vertical support for the upper wheel. A 14-inch (356-millimeter) size is frequently chosen. Motors available are typically ½- or ¾-horsepower.

Band-Saw Safety Techniques

1. Wear safety glasses or goggles.

2. Wear a dust mask when dusty work conditions exist.

3. Remove jewelry and loose clothing. Confine long hair in a hair net.

16–52. The band saw is used to make curved cuts, but can also rip and crosscut stock (courtesy Delta International Machinery Corporation).

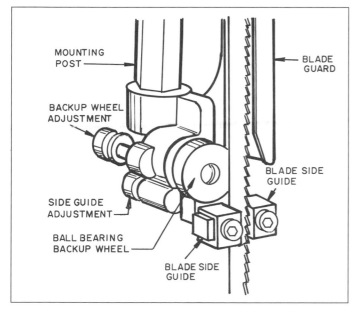

16–53. The band-saw thrust guide keeps the blade running straight and has a backup wheel (sometimes called a thrust bearing) to prevent it from being pushed off the large wheels over which it tracks.

4. Use the proper blade for the work at hand. For example, very small curves require a narrow blade.

5. Before starting, be certain the blade is properly installed.

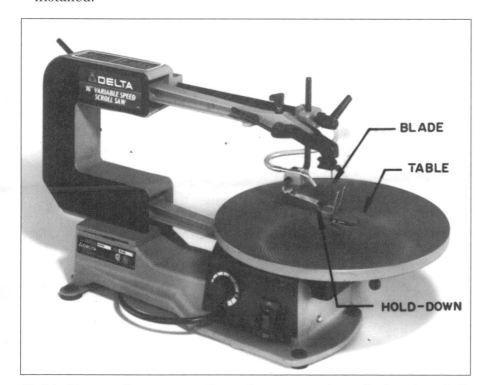

16–54. The scroll saw can cut small curves and scrolls (courtesy Delta International Machinery Corporation).

6. Keep the upper guide as close to the work as possible.

7. Use a stick to remove scraps from the table or allow the blade to come to a complete stop before removing the scraps.

8. If the blade makes a clicking sound as it rotates, it probably has a crack. Replace it immediately.

Scroll Saw

The scroll saw uses very small blades and is able to cut very small curves and shapes. The blade is held in tension between the top and bottom chucks (**16–54**). A variety of blade sizes are available to cut wood, plastic, and metal. The cutting speed can be varied typically from about 50 to 2,000 cutting strokes per minute. Some have a dust blower that keeps the sawdust off the line being cut.

The size is specified by the distance between the blade and support arm at the back of the machine. Sizes from 13 to 20 inches (330 to 508 millimeters) are available. Scroll saws are powered by electric motors ranging from 1.0 to 1.6 amperes.

Scroll Saw Safety Procedures

1. Wear safety glasses or goggles.

2. If dust is bothersome, wear a dust mask.

3. Be certain the blade is properly installed. The teeth should point down toward the table so it cuts on the down stroke.

4. Let the hold-down foot rest lightly on top of the wood (**16–55**, on following page).

5. Keep both hands out of line with the blade. Keep them on one side or the other.

6. Run the scroll saw at a proper speed for the job at hand.

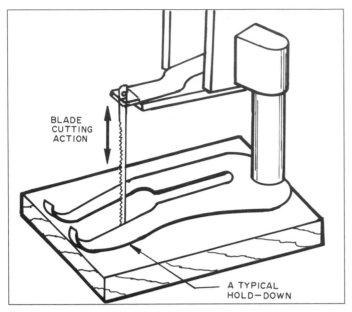

16–55. Scroll saw hold-downs keep the stock tight to the table. Otherwise, it would bounce up as the blade cuts up. There are a number of different hold-down designs.

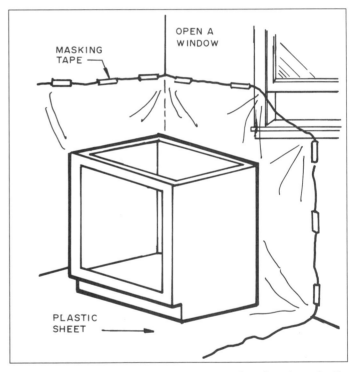

16–56. Small finish-spraying systems are very useful in the home workshop. They provide a means for applying a quality finish.

FINISH-SPRAYING SYSTEM

There are a number of finish-spraying systems available that can be used in the shop for small jobs such as spraying a chair, table, or cabinet (**16–56**). If this will be a very limited activity, you can fix up a temporary spray area by covering the walls and floor with plastic sheets near open windows (**16–57**). Use several fans to pull the air out of the area toward the open window. Since fire is a constant danger, place this area well away from any source of flame (such as a furnace) or sparks. Keep a fire extinguisher handy. Be certain to protect your eyes with goggles and wear a high-quality respirator. When you have finished, clean up the area and remove all soiled plastic, rags, and other materials from the house.

ADDITIONAL REFERENCE SOURCES

Before you use the power tools in your shop, consult various sources for detailed information concerning their safe installation and operation. Following are suggestions:

- Manuals produced by the manufacturers of your power machines.

- Publications of the Power Tool Institute, Inc., 1300 Sumner Ave., Cleveland, Ohio 44115.

16–57. You can build a temporary spray booth using plastic sheeting. Be certain to provide ventilation by opening windows and running fans.

- Spence, William P., and Griffiths, L. Duane, *Woodworking Basics: The Essential Benchtop Reference.* New York: Sterling Publishing Co., 1995.

GLOSSARY

The chapters in this book may contain terms with which the reader is unfamiliar. Below is a chapter-by-chapter clarification of these terms.

CHAPTER ONE: PLUMBING REPAIRS

ABS (Acrylonitrile-butadiene-styrene) A thermoplastic of low chemical resistance used in drain, waste, and vent (DWV) systems.

Accessible As applied to a fitting or valve, this term means being reachable for service, but possibly requiring the removal of an access panel.

Adapter A plumbing fitting that connects one kind of pipe to another.

Air Gap In a water-supply system, the distance between the faucet outlet and the flood rim of the basin it discharges into. "Air gap" is also used to describe a unique fitting installed to prevent back-siphoning in residential dishwasher drain lines.

Anaerobic Existing without free air or oxygen. Anaerobic bacteria found in septic tanks are beneficial in digesting organic matter.

Anti-Siphon A term applied to valves or other devices that eliminate back-siphonage.

Approved Accepted by the plumbing official or other authority given jurisdiction by the code.

Area Drain A receptacle designed to collect surface- or rainwater from an open area.

Backflow The reverse flow of water or other liquids into the distributing pipes of a potable supply of water or into fixtures.

Backflow Preventer A device to prevent backflow into the potable-water system.

Backwater Valve A one-way valve installed in the house drain or sewer that prevents flooding of low-level fixtures from sewer backup.

Ball Cock A toilet-tank-bowl inlet water-supply valve that is controlled by a float ball.

Bell Trap A shallow-water-seal trap used for floor drains. It also is useful because it will catch small objects that might otherwise be lost down a drain.

Blowoff Valve A valve used to relieve high water pressure.

Branch Any part of a piping system other than a riser, main, or stack.

Branch Vent A pipe installed specifically to vent a fixture trap.

Building Drain The lowest house piping that receives discharge from waste and soil stacks and other sanitary drainage pipes and carries it to the building sewer outside the house.

Building Sewer That part of the horizontal piping of a drainage system that connects to the end of the building drain and conveys the waste material to a public sewer or to a septic tank.

Bushing A fitting used inside the socket of another fitting to reduce its size to accept a pipe of a smaller diameter.

Cap A fitting used to seal off the end of a pipe.

Check-Valve A one-way valve controlling water flow. It is used in a sump-pump discharge line to prevent backflow into the sump pit that causes the short-cycling of the sump pump.

Chlorination The application of chlorine to water or treated sewage to disinfect or accomplish other biological or chemical results.

Cistern A small covered tank chiefly used for storing rainwater for domestic use other than drinking. It is usually placed underground.

Cleanout An accessible opening in the drainage system used to provide access for removing obstructions in the pipe.

Code A collection of rules and regulations adopted by authorities having jurisdiction to control the design and construction of buildings and their alteration, repair, materials, use, and occupancy.

Common Vent A vent connecting at the junction of two fixture drains that serves as a vent for both.

Coupling A fitting used to join two lengths of pipe.

CPVC (*Chlorinated Polyvinyl Chloride*) A heat-resistant rigid thermoplastic used for hot- and cold-water pipes and fittings that are joined by solvent welding.

Dead End A branch leading from a soil, waste, or vent pipe, building drain, or building sewer that is terminated by a plug or other closed fitting. A dead end is often used as an extension for future connection, or as an extension of a cleanout for accessibility.

Developed Length The length of a line of pipe measured along the centerline of the pipe and fittings.

Diameter The nominal diameter of a pipe or fitting as designed commercially, unless specifically stated otherwise.

Double Tee A fitting used to bring two branch pipes into a single pipe.

Drain Any pipe that carries wastewater or water-borne wastes in a building drainage system.

Drainage Fitting A fitting with insides designed for smooth flow of waste by gravity. It features obstruction-free passages.

Drainage System All the piping that carries sewage, rainwater, or other liquid wastes to the point of disposal or sewer.

Drum Trap An old-style bathtub or shower trap still found in older buildings.

Dry Vent That portion of a vent system that receives no sewage or waste discharge.

Dry Well An underground excavation used for leaching water but not sewage into the ground.

DWV A term that stands for "Drain, Waste, Vent" system, which collects plumbing-fixture discharges and carries wastes out of the house.

Effluent Liquid Liquid that is discharged as waste, such as that from a septic tank, into the drain field.

Elbow A fitting that changes the angle of two lengths of pipe.

Faucet A fixture valve that opens and closes the flow of water to the fixture.

Faucet Nut A nut that joins a fixture supply tube to the faucet tailpiece.

Female Adapter A fitting with inside pipe threads that permits a connection to male pipe threads.

Finish Plumbing Plumbing done after the building walls have been closed in, such as installing toilets and sinks.

Fixture Branch A drain serving one or more fixtures that discharges to another drain or to a stack.

Fixture Drain The drain from the trap of a fixture that leads to a junction with any other drainpipe.

Fixture Supply A water-supply pipe that connects a fixture to a branch water-supply pipe or directly to a main water-supply pipe.

Fixture Supply Tube A flexible tube that leads from the fixture shutoff up to the faucet tailpiece.

Fixture Supply Valve A valve, located on the wall or floor beneath a fixture, that turns off the hot- or cold-water supply to that fixture.

Fixture Unit A measure of the probable amount of discharge into the drainage system by various plumbing fixtures stated in terms of cubic feet or gallons of water per minute.

Floor Drain A receptacle located at approximately floor level that is connected to a trap. It is designed to receive the discharge from indirect waste and floor drainage.

Flood-Level Rim The edge of a fixture receptacle from which water would overflow.

Floor Strainer A device that prevents debris from entering a drain opening on the floor and fits flush into a fitting hub.

Flush Valve A device, located in a toilet tank and attached to the flush level, that provides the flow of water involved in flushing the toilet.

Grade The forward slope of a line of pipe in comparison to being horizontal. It is usually expressed as a fall in fractions of an inch per foot of pipe length.

Horizontal Branch A drainpipe extending laterally from a soil or waste stack or building drain. It may have vertical sections or branches.

Horizontal Pipe A pipe or fitting that makes an angle of more than 45 degrees with the vertical.

Hub Adapter A device that adapts a cast-iron pipe hub to thermoplastic piping.

Hydrostatic Tests Tests of a drain, waste, vent (DWV) system in which all openings are closed and the system is filled to overflow with water to test for leaks.

Indirect Wastes A waste pipe used to move liquid wastes other than body wastes by discharging them into an open plumbing fixture or receptacle such as a floor drain. The overflow point of the fixture or receptacle must be lower than the item drained.

Individual Vent A pipe installed to vent a fixture drain. It connects the vent system above the fixture to be vented or extends outside the building to the open air.

Insanitary Unclean and unhealthful.

J-Bend The U-shaped portion of a trap.

Liquid Waste The discharge from any fixture or appliance that connects to a plumbing system that does not receive body waste.

Load Factor The percentage of the total flow rate in fixture units likely to occur at any point in the drainage system.

Loop or Circuit Waste and Vent A combination of plumbing fixtures on the same floor level in the same or adjacent rooms connected to a common horizontal branch soil or waste pipe.

Main The principal pipe to which branches are connected.

Main Stack A soil stack running from the building

drain through the roof, having the top end open to the air.

Male Adapter An adapter that contains male pipe threads to fit other pipes into a threaded pipe fitting.

No-Hub Hubless cast-iron pipe that is joined with gasketed sleeve-type connectors rather than caulked joints.

NSF (*National Sanitation Foundation*) An independent third-party certifying agency that assures that products meet nationally recognized standards.

Offset A combination of fittings that makes two changes in direction of a pipe by bringing one section of pipe out of line but into a line parallel with the other section.

PB (*Polybutylene*) A flexible, heat-resistant thermoplastic piping material used for hot-/cold-water supply. It cannot be solvent-welded; therefore, it is joined by mechanical fittings.

PE (*Polyethylene*) A thermoplastic pipe only used for cold water that is out-of-doors and below ground.

Pitch The slope or grade of the pipe.

Plumbing Code A set of rules that govern the installation of plumbing.

Plumbing Fixture A receptacle or device that is connected to the water-supply system. It discharges used water or waste into the drainage system.

Plumbing Official The officer or other designated authority charged with the administration and enforcement of the plumbing code.

Plumbing System A complete system including potable-water supply and distribution pipe; plumbing fixtures and traps; drain, waste, and vent pipe; and building drains, including their joints, connections, devices, and receptacles.

Potable Water Water free from impurities sufficient to cause disease or harmful physiological effects. It conforms to the requirements of the U.S. Public Health Service Drinking Water Standards or the regulations of the public health authority having jurisdiction.

PP (*Polypropylene*) A semi-rigid thermoplastic with high chemical and heat resistance that is ideally suited for use for connecting the sink drain to the waste pipe. Since it cannot be solvent-welded, it must be joined by slip-jam-nut couplings.

Pressure Pipe A cold-water pipe used to carry pressurized water for outdoor and underground uses such as lawn-watering.

Pressure Regulator A device used in water-service-entrance lines to reduce line pressure to that required for household use.

P-Trap A P-shaped trap that forms a water seal to prevent the entry of gases yet lets water flow out of the line.

Public Sewer A common sewer directly controlled by public authority.

PVC (*Polyvinyl Chloride*) Rigid, chemically resistant thermoplastic used for DWV systems and cold-water-only pressurized systems outdoors or in the ground. It is joined by solvent-welding.

PVC-DWV-PVC Pipes and Fittings Pipes and fittings approved for drain, waste, vent use.

Relief Vent A vent whose primary function is to provide circulation of air between the vent stack and the soil stack.

Rim An unobstructed open edge at the overflow point of a fixture.

Riser A vertical pipe in the water-supply system leading from the main to the branches above.

Riser Tube A short, flexible tube that connects the fixture to the water-supply system.

Rough-In The installation of the concealed parts of a plumbing system to the point where fixtures are to be connected. It includes water supply, drainage system, and required supports in the wall.

Septic Tank Watertight, covered receptacle that receives the discharge of waste from the building sewer. It is designed and constructed to separate solids from liquids, digest organic matter through a period of detention, and allow the liquids to discharge into the soil outside the tank through a sub-surface system of open-joint or perforated piping, or other approved methods.

Sewage Any liquid-borne waste containing animal, mineral, or vegetable matter in suspension or solution. May include liquids containing chemicals in solution.

Slope The pitch or grade of a pipe.

Soil Pipe A pipe that conveys the discharge of water closets or fixtures having similar functions, with or without the discharge from other fixtures, to the building drain or building sewer.

Stack Any vertical pipe of a system of soil, waste, or vent piping.

Stack Vent The extension of a soil or waste stack above the highest horizontal drain or fixture branch connected to the stack.

S-Trap An S-shaped trap that forms a water seal to prevent the entrance of gases yet lets water flow out of the line. It is not permitted in new construction.

Styrene (*sometimes called Rubber Styrene [RS] or Styrene Rubber [SR]*). A low-grade thermoplastic sometimes used for sewer and drainage piping, and which is joined by solvent-welding.

Subsoil Drain A drain that collects belowground water, carrying it to a place of disposal such as a drywell.

Sump A tank or pit for sewage or liquid waste, located below the normal grade of the gravity system and emptied by a sump pump.

Sump Pump An automatic water pump powered by an electric motor for the removal of waste from a sump.

Tailpiece The short pipe leading from a faucet or sink drain.

Tee A T-shaped fitting with an outlet at 90 degrees to the main line.

Temperature-and-Pressure Relief Valve A valve installed on a hot-water heater tank to relieve the buildup of dangerous temperatures or pressures inside the tank.

Thermoplastic Plastic that hardens on cooling and softens on heating.

Toilet A bathroom fixture used to dispose of human wastes. Also called a water closet.

Transition Union A special fitting designed to compensate for the difference in expansion between thermoplastic and metal pipe in hot-/cold-water applications.

Trap A fitting used to provide a liquid seal to keep sewer gases out of the house but that does not affect the outflow wastewater through it.

Tubing Pipe that is sized nominally according to copper tubing sizes.

Two-Way Cleanout Fitting A fitting installed in a horizontal drain line that provides cleanout access to the drain in either direction.

Union A fitting that joins pipe disassembly without cutting them apart.

Vacuum Any pressure less than that exerted by the atmosphere.

Vacuum Breaker A device used in a water-supply line to let air in and prevent back-siphonage. Some are designed to operate under line pressure; others are not.

Valve A device that regulates the flow of a liquid.

Vent Pipe A part of the DWV plumbing system that is open to the atmosphere and prevents trap seals from siphonage and back pressure.

Vent System A pipe or pipes connected to a vent stack.

Vertical Pipe Any pipe or fitting installed in a vertical position or making an angle of not more than 45 degrees with the vertical.

Vinyl A generic term used when describing polyvinyl chloride (PVC) or chlorinated polyvinyl chloride (CPVC).

Washbasin A bathroom fixture also known as a lavatory or vanity.

Waste Liquid-borne waste free of fecal matter.

Waste Pipe A pipe that carries drainage from any fixture other than a toilet.

Water Closet A toilet.

Water Distribution Pipe A pipe used to supply water under pressure to fixtures and appliances.

Water Hammer The sound created when water in a supply system comes to an abrupt stop when a valve closes quickly.

Water-Hammer Muffler A shock-absorbing device installed in the hot- and cold-water supplies at fixtures to prevent water hammer.

Water Heater A plumbing appliance used to heat water.

Water Meter A device used to measure the amount of water that flows through it.

Water-Service Pipe The pipe from the water main or other source of water supply to the building served under the jurisdiction of a water company.

Water Softener An appliance that chemically removes calcium and magnesium salts from the water supply, thereby producing soft water.

Water-Supply System A water service-entry pipe; water distribution pipes; and the necessary connecting pipes and fittings, control valves, and appurtenances in or adjacent to a building.

Well A driven, bored, or dug hole in the ground, from which water is pumped.

CHAPTER 2: ELECTRICAL REPAIRS

Adapter Plug, Grounding A plug permitting a three-prong plug to be inserted into a two-slot outlet.

Alternating Current (AC) Electric current that alternates or reverses its direction. Alternating current moves in one direction for a fixed period of time, and then moves in the opposite direction for the same period of time.

Ampacity The maximum current capacity of a wire in amperes.

Ampere A unit of the rate of flow of electric current equal to an electromotive force of one volt acting across a resistance of one ohm. This results in a current flow of one ampere.

Ballast The device in a fluorescent lamp that provides the required starting voltage and operating current.

Bar Hanger Hangers used to mount ceiling outlet boxes.

Branch Circuit A part of an electric wiring system that runs beyond the service panel to lights and outlets.

Bus Bar A rigid metal bar that forms the connection between electric circuits.

Cable An electric conductor made up of small-diameter conductor strands twisted together inside a protective outer sheath.

Cable, Armored An electric conductor protected by a metal sheath.

Cable Connector A device used to secure armored cable or conduit to an outlet box.

Cable, Plastic A conductor sheathed with a heavy plastic covering.

Cartridge Fuse A fuse enclosed in a cylindrical tube that protects an electric circuit from excessive flow of current.

Circuit Breaker An electric device designed to open and close a circuit. Upon an abnormally high current, it will automatically open the circuit. When the flow is corrected, the circuit breaker can be manually reset to close the circuit.

Conduit A rigid metal protective pipe through which conductors are run.

Conduit Bender A tool used to bend conduit.

Continuity Tester A device for checking electric circuits to see if they open or are broken.

Dimmer Switch A light switch that will adjust the brightness of a light and turn it on and off.

Direct Current (DC) Electric current that moves continuously in one direction.

Fish Tape A small-diameter flexible wire used to pull cable through inaccessible areas.

Footcandle A unit of illumination equal to 1 lumen per square foot.

Four-Way Switch A light switch that will control a light from three locations.

Fuse A safety device placed in a circuit to protect it from overloads.

Fuse Puller A tool that looks like pliers, used to remove cartridge fuses.

Ground The connection of an electric circuit and components to the earth. This is a safety feature.

Ground-Fault Circuit Interrupter A device providing protection from minute electric leakage not detectable by circuit breakers. It shuts off the current in a circuit within a fraction of a second.

Hot Wire The wire that carries the voltage in the cable.

Illuminance The density of luminous power in lumens per a specified area.

Incandescence The emission of visible light as a result of heating a filament.

Incandescent Lamp A lamp from which light is emitted when the tungsten filament is heated to incandescence by an electric current passing through it.

Incandescent Lighting Fixture A complete luminaire using incandescent lamps.

Insulator, Electric A nonelectrical conducting material that blocks the flow of electricity.

Junction Box A metal or plastic box in which electric cables are joined.

Kilowatt-Hour A unit of energy, equal to 1000 watt-hours.

Knockout A removable plug on the side of an electric box.

Light Meter A photoelectric device used to measure luminance.

Lumen A unit for measuring the flow of light energy.

Luminaire A complete lighting unit. Also called a lighting fixture.

Luminance The luminous intensity of any surface of a given area as viewed from a given direction.

Meter, Electric An instrument that measures and

records the amount of electricity passing through it in kilowatt-hours.

Neutral Wire A grounded wire in a cable that completes the path of the current and carries no voltage.

Outlet A point at which current is taken to supply electrical appliances and portable electric equipment.
Outlet Box A metal or plastic box into which an electric receptacle is installed.

Panelboard A wall-mounted panel including fuses or circuit breakers used to protect all the circuits in the house.
Plug A device installed on the end of an electric cord that is inserted into a receptacle to tap into the electrical supply.
Power The rate at which work is performed, expressed in horsepower or watts.

Receptacle The device installed in an outlet box into which a plug is inserted to tap into the electrical supply.
Receptacle Plug *See* Plug.
Resistance, Electric The physical property of a conductor to resist the flow of electricity. This reduces the flow of electricity and produces heat.

Service Entrance The panel box to which the electric utility connects the electrical service.
Service Panel *See* Panelboard.
Short Circuit An abnormal electrical connection having low resistance that causes an unusually high current to flow through the connection.
Splicing The joining of the bare ends of wires.
Surface Wiring Electric wiring mounted in metal or plastic channels secured to the wall.
Switch A device to open and close an electric circuit.

Terminal An electrically conductive element on a piece of equipment to which an electrical conduction is connected.
Three-Way Switch An electric switch that allows control of a light from two locations.

Timer Switch A switch with a clock that can be set to start or stop the flow of electric current at the times set on it.
Track Lighting A system of lights that can be moved along a track receptacle.
Transformer A device altering the voltage of the electric current entering it.

Volt A unit of electromotive force often referred to as electrical pressure. One volt when applied across a resistance of one ohm will result in a current flow of one ampere.
Voltmeter An instrument used to measure the voltage drop between two points in an electric circuit.

Watt The unit of electric power. It is the power required to do work at the rate of one joule per second.

CHAPTER THREE: HEATING AND AIR CONDITIONING

Absorbent A solid or liquid that absorbs other substances.
Air Conditioning An engineered system for controlling the temperature, humidity, ventilation, and air purification in an enclosed structure.
Annual Fuel Utilization Efficiency (AFUE) The ratio of the annual fuel output energy to the annual input energy.
Anticipator A part of the thermostat preventing large swings in room temperature.
Automatic Expansion Valve A refrigerant-metering device operated by the low-side pressure of the system. It throttles the liquid line down to a constant pressure on the low side while the compressor is running. Also called pressure valve.

Btu (British Thermal Unit) The heat energy required to raise one pound of water one degree Fahrenheit.

Carbon-Dioxide Analyzer An instrument that measures the chemicals in waste gases as they are vented to check the efficiency of the burner.

Coefficient of Performance (COP) A rating of the amount of heat produced by a heat pump in British thermal units per hour in relation to the total electrical input.

Combustible A substance that will burn.

Compressor A device that pumps or changes the refrigerant vapor from a low pressure to a high pressure.

Condenser Part of a refrigeration mechanism that changes refrigerant vapor back to a liquid.

Conductors Materials that easily release loosely bound electrons.

Convectors Finned tubes used to circulate heat from hot water, which is run through them.

Dampers Moveable metal flaps used to control air flow in ducts and flues.

Dehumidification The process of removing moisture from the air.

Desiccant A drying agent used to remove moisture from refrigerant by absorbing the water until its vapor pressure reaches a balance with the system's vapor pressure.

Dew-Point Temperature The temperature at which vapor, at 100-percent humidity, begins to condense as liquid.

Diffuser Outlet that discharges a widespread, fan-shaped pattern of air.

Draft The flow of gases over a fire and up the chimney.

Dry Bulb A term referring to a normal thermometer.

Dry-Bulb Temperature The air temperature indicated by an ordinary thermometer.

Ductwork Piping that carries air from the warm-air furnace to the conditioned space.

Energy Efficiency Rating (EER) The heat units transferred per hour per watt of power consumed (Btu/h/W).

Evaporator The part of a refrigerator mechanism that vaporizes the refrigerant and absorbs heat.

Expansion Tank A tank used to regulate the pressure within a hot-water heating system.

Feet Per Minute (FPM) The measure of velocity (speed) of an airstream.

Filters Devices that remove dust and other particles from forced-air systems and the fuel oil in oil-fired furnaces.

Flash Point The temperature at which the oil will burst into flame.

Forced-Air System A heating and cooling system in which the tempered air is distributed through ducts to the various rooms.

Fossil Fuels Natural resources, such as coal, oil, and gas, which are used for fuel.

Heat Pump A compression-cycle system that is used to provide heat to a conditioned space. The system also removes heat by reversing the flow of the refrigerant.

Hot-Water System A system for heating a house in which water is heated in a boiler and pumped to radiators in the various rooms through pipes where the heat is disseminated into the space.

Humidifier A device used to add and control the amount of moisture in the air.

Humidistat The electrical control in an air-conditioned space or supply air duct that activates the humidifier.

Humidity A condition pertaining to the percentage of moisture contained in the air.

Hydronic A water system.

Hygrometer The instrument that is used to measure the degree of moisture in the atmosphere.

Infiltration Air leaking into the building through cracks around the outsides of windows and doors.

Latent Heat (*Hidden Heat*) A change of state from a liquid to a solid or vapor that involves latent heat that cannot be measured with a thermometer.

Mean Temperature The average temperature for a given day.

Medium Heat-transfer substance. Air, water, and brine are used as condensing mediums.

Ohm The unit of measurement of electrical resistance. One ohm exists when one volt causes a flow of one ampere.

Ohmmeter An instrument used for measuring resistance in ohms.

Ohm's Law The mathematical relationship between voltage, current, and resistance in an electric circuit: Voltage = Amperes x Ohms.

Oil Burner An oil-fired unit used in furnaces to produce heat for warm-air heating systems.

Passive System A direct-energy transfer system in which the energy flow occurs through natural means.

Plenum A large, major air duct that runs from the warm-air furnace and from which smaller ducts are run to the various rooms.

Radiator A unit that receives hot water from a boiler and transfers heat into a room by radiation and conduction.

Refrigeration The process of transferring or removing heat from a substance in order to lower its temperature.

Register An opening from which warm or cooled air enters the room.

Relative Humidity The difference between the amount of water vapor present in the air at a given time and the greatest amount possible at that temperature.

Risers Vertical water pipes in a hot-water heating system.

R-Value A number that indicates the insulating capacity of a material.

Saturated Pressure Boiling pressure corresponding to surrounding (ambient) temperature.

Saturation Temperature Boiling temperature at surrounding (ambient) pressure.

Seasonal Energy Efficiency Ratio (SEER) The total cooling output of an electric air conditioner in Btu/h divided by the total electric energy input in watt-hours.

Seasonal Heating Performance Factor (SHPF) A ratio of the total heat delivered over the heating season to the total energy input over the season.

Sensible Heat Heat that can be measured with a thermometer.

Solar Heating Heat supplied by radiation from the sun.

Specific Heat The quantity of heat required to raise one pound of a substance one degree Fahrenheit.

Static Pressure The outward force of air within a duct.

Thermal Conductance (C) A measurement used to indicate the amount of heat that will pass through a specified thickness of material. It is the reciprocal of thermal resistance: $C = 1/R$.

Thermal Conductivity (K) A measurement used to indicate the amount of heat that will be conducted through one square foot of a material per a specified unit of thickness.

Thermal Resistance (R) A measurement used to describe thermal resistance of a material. It is the reciprocal of thermal conductance: $R = 1/C$.

Thermal Transmittance (U) A measurement used to describe the ability of a material to transmit heat. It is the reciprocal of thermal conductance: $C = 1/R$.

Thermostat An instrument that controls the operation of a heating/cooling unit by responding to changes in the air temperature.

Total Thermal Resistance (Rt) The resistance to heat flow through an assembly of materials.

Velocity Speed, swiftness, or quickness of motion.

Velocity Pressure Forward-moving force of air within a duct.

Viscosity The measure of flowing quality. A high-viscosity oil is thick and slow-flowing.

Zone Control Independent control of room-air temperature in different areas of a building.

CHAPTER FOUR: ROOF REPAIRS

Asphalt A dark brown cementitious waterproofing material in which the predominating constituents are bitumens. It is applied to roofing materials during their manufacture.

Asphalt Roofing Cement An asphalt-based cement containing a solvent that is used to bond roofing materials.

Blisters Raised areas or bubbles that sometimes appear on the surface of asphalt roofing after installation. They are caused by water trapped below the felt that expands when the roof gets hot.

Buckling The formation of wrinkles across shingles.

Counterflashing Formed metal or elastometric sheet material that is secured to a wall or other vertical surface and covers the top edge of the base flashing.

Course One horizontal row of shingles or roll roofing running across the length of the roof.

Cricket A small inverted projection installed behind a chimney to divert the water around it.

Downspout A pipe that drains water from the roof gutters to the ground. Also called a leader.

Drip Edge A non-rusting material placed along the edges of the eaves and rake to allow the water to drip clear of the fascia.

Felt A flexible sheet made of interlocking fibers (principally glass or organic fibers) and coated with asphalt.

Laminated Shingles Individual shingles containing a second layer of tabs to create extra thickness.

Lap The amount one shingle goes over the surface of the one below.

Leader *See* Downspout.

Mineral-Surfaced Roofing A roofing material in sheet form that has both sides coated with asphalt and one side surfaced with mineral granules.

Ridge Shingles The shingles used to cover the peak formed by the intersection of two sloping roof surfaces.

Roll Roofing Smooth- or mineral-coated felt.

Saturated Felt Asphalt-impregnated felt used as an underlayment over the deck before the shingles are laid.

Self-Sealing Shingles Shingles made with strips of self-sealing adhesive on the inside of the bottom edge. This sticks them to the shingles below.

Soffit The finished underside of the eaves.

Square A unit of measurement used with roofing materials that equals 100 square feet.

Starter Strip The first course of shingles placed along the edge of the roof at the eave.

Underlayment The asphalt-impregnated felt laid on the sheathing before the shingles are installed.

Valley The angle formed by the intersection of two sloping roof surfaces.

Vent A screened opening used to allow water vapor and heat to flow out of the attic.

Woven Valley Valley construction in which shingles from both sides of the valley extend across the valley and are woven together by overlapping alternate courses.

CHAPTER FIVE: EXTERIOR-WALL MAINTENANCE AND REPAIR

Caulking A resilient mastic compound used to fill joints and cracks to make them watertight.

Exterior Insulation and Finish System (EIFS) An exterior-wall finish system composed of an approved water-resistant sheathing and polystyrene insulation board over which a base coat and reinforcing mesh are troweled and covered with a synthetic plaster exterior-finish coat.

Exterior Trim The door and window casing, corner boards, cornice, and rake boards.

Mildew A fungus that forms on exterior siding and roofs due to exposure to moisture.

Plaster, Portland Cement A material composed of portland cement, lime, and gypsum mixed with sand and water. Fiber may be added as a binder. It is applied over lath to finish interior walls.

Stucco, Portland Cement An exterior-wall finish material composed of portland cement, lime, and sand mixed with water. It is applied over lath on the exterior walls.

Stucco, Synthetic *See* Exterior Insulation and Finish System.

Tuck-Pointing The repairing of old masonry joints by removing some of the old mortar and filling the opening with new mortar.

CHAPTER SIX: PAINTING THE EXTERIOR

Adhesion The bonding strength of a coating to a surface.

Air-Dried Coating A coating that dries when the solvent evaporates.

Airless Spray Equipment Spray equipment that uses hydraulic pressure on the liquid paint, forcing it through an orifice that atomizes it.

Alkyd Oil Paint A paint that is a suspension of inorganic pigments in an oil or chemically modified oil and a mineral spirit or turpentine solvent.

Alligatoring Cracks that run across the grain of the wood. They occur after too many layers of paint have been applied over the years.

Back-Priming Priming the back side of wood siding prior to its being installed.

Bleach A liquid applied to wood to produce a weathered appearance.

Bleeding Stains produced by the passing of water-soluble extractives.

Blistering Small bubbles on the surface caused by moisture getting behind the paint coating.

Chalking A stain that occurs when the paint pigment washes down the wall.

Cracking Thin separations in the paint coating.

Enamel A paint made with finely ground pigments and a resin binder that forms a hard, smooth, opaque surface film as it dries.

Feathering The flowing of the edge of a painted area into a thin coating.

Hiding Power The ability of a paint to cover the subsurface.

Knot A place on the wood where a branch grew. It contains resinous material that can bleed through the paint coating.

Latex Paint A paint made with a polyacrylic or polyvinyl acetate mixed with pigments and water.

Masking Tape A pressure-sensitive paper tape that is easily removed after it has protected an area while a nearby surface was being painted.

Mineral Spirits A paint thinner and solvent distilled from petroleum.

Natural Brush Bristles Brush bristles made from natural materials, such as back boar bristles from China.

Opaque Stain A wood stain having a high concentration of pigment and which colors the wood so the grain cannot be seen.

Overspray Paint that is sprayed beyond the sides of the surface being painted.

Peeling A condition in which large pieces of the paint coating come off the surface. This is caused by water getting behind the paint coating.

Pigment Insoluble, finely ground minerals that give the paint its color and hiding power.

Polyurethane An oil-modified urethane that will air dry without the aid of a hardener.

Primer The first coat of paint applied to the surface to seal it and serve as a base upon which the topcoats will be applied.

Putty A mixture of linseed oil and whiting used to set window glass in the frame and fill holes in wood to be painted.

Sealer A special paint that fills the pores of the wood over which a topcoat is applied.

Semigloss Finish A finish that has a hard surface and a low-luster sheen.

Semi-Transparent Stain A finish material with a small amount of pigment, permitting the wood grain to be seen.

Shelf Life The length of time a paint can be stored before it deteriorates.

Shellac A coating made from lac dissolved in alcohol.

Solvent The liquid in which the ingredients of the paint are dissolved and which evaporates from the paint film after the coating has been applied.

Synthetic Brush Bristles Brush bristles made from synthetic materials such as nylon and polyester.

Tack Rag A treated cloth used to pick up the dust on a surface before it is painted.

Thinner A solvent used to thin paint.

Topcoat The final coat of paint or varnish.

Transparent Coating A finish material that seals and protects the wood and allows the grain to be visible.

Turpentine A volatile liquid distilled from the sap of some pine trees. It is used as a solvent for oil-based finishes.

Volatile Organic Compounds (VOC) Volatile compounds in paints such as mineral spirits, which are emitted into the atmosphere as the coating dries.

CHAPTER SEVEN: MISCELLANEOUS EXTERIOR MAINTENANCE AND REPAIRS

Awning Window A window hinged on the top and which swings outside the house.

Bleed The formation of water on the surface of freshly poured concrete.

Casement Window A window hinged on one side and which swings toward the outside of the house.

Compacting Compressing the soil or gravel fill that is to be under a concrete slab.

Concrete Bond Adhesive A product used to help bond concrete to concrete or to a concrete block.

Concrete Liquid Color A product added to the concrete mix as it is being made to give the concrete a permanent color.

Control Joint A groove formed in a concrete slab that controls where the slab will crack if cracking does occur.

Darby A long float tool used to smooth the surface of freshly poured concrete.

Double-Hung Window A window having two sashes that move up and down vertically.

Dry Rot The decay of seasoned wood caused by fungi carrying water into the wood.

Dry Well A lime- or gravel-filled pit into which the surface water is drained and from which the water leaches into the surrounding ground.

Dusting The appearance of a chalky powder on the surface of cured concrete.

Edger A hand tool used to form rounded edges on freshly poured concrete.

Epoxy Patching Material A synthetic, thermosetting resin that produces a tough, hard coating.

Float A concrete finishing tool used to smooth a freshly poured concrete surface.

Glass Cutter A tool with a small wheel that scores the glass, enabling it to be broken along the scored line.

Glazier's Points   Small, flat, triangular three- or four-cornered metal pieces used to hold the glass in wood window frames.

Hopper Window   A window hinged on the bottom and opening into the house.

Isolation Joint   A joint formed by inserting an expansion material between a concrete slab and an adjacent structure such as a foundation wall.

Pop-out   A small opening in finished, cured concrete, caused by aggregates on the surface breaking out.

Replacement Window   A window designed to replace aging existing windows with a minimum of trouble.

Sandy Surface   The appearance of sand granules on the surface of cured concrete.

Scaling   The breaking away of pieces of the surface of cured concrete.

Screed   A long, straight tool used to strike off the surface of poured concrete.

Sliding Window   A window that slides horizontally in a track.

Soldier Termite   A termite that protects the colony from attack from other insects.

Strike Board   A board cut to be used to level gravel fill before the concrete is poured over it.

Winged Termite   A termite that flies from a nest and starts a new colony.

Worker Termite   A termite that bores into wood, destroys it, and builds nests and mud tunnels.

CHAPTER EIGHT: RENOVATING INTERIOR WALLS AND CEILINGS

Adhesive   A glue or mastic used for applying gypsum board to framing or for laminating one or more layers of gypsum board.

Adhesive Nail-On Application   A means of applying gypsum board utilizing adhesives and mechanical fasteners.

All-Purpose Compound   A joint-treatment compound that can be used as a bedding compound for tape, a finishing compound, or for texturing.

Annular Ring Nail   A deformed shank nail with improved holding qualities, used to install gypsum board.

Base Layer   The first layer of gypsum board applied in a multilayer system.

Bed-Coat   The first coat of joint compound over tape, beads, and fastener heads.

Bleeding   A discoloration, usually at a joint, that may occur on a finished wall or ceiling.

Blister   A loose, raised spot on the gypsum-board face or under joint-reinforcing tape.

Blocking   Wood members installed between existing structural wood members to provide reinforcement and a nailing surface.

Brown Coat   The second coat of a plaster wall. It is bonded to the scratch coat.

Buglehead Screw   A specially designed screw that will seat beneath the top of the gypsum-board surface without tearing the paper.

Chalk Line   A straight working line made by snapping a chalked chord between two points.

Cooler Nail   A nail with special size and head configuration for use in gypsum-board applications.

Core   The gypsum structure between the face and back papers of gypsum board.

Corner Bead   A preformed metal or plastic angle to protect the corners of gypsum-board intersections.

Dimple   The depression in the surface of gypsum board caused by a hammer, such as when the nail head is set slightly below the surface.

Double Layer   Two layers of gypsum board combined to improve its fire, sound, or structural characteristics.

Double-Nailing   A method of applying gypsum board by using two nails spaced approximately 2 inches apart in the field along the framing member to ensure firm contact with the framing.

Face The surface of the gypsum-board panel designed to be left exposed to view.

Feathered Edge The thinner outside edge of the joint compound used to conceal a joint.

Finish Coats The final coats of plaster applied over the brown coat.

Fire Resistance The ability of an assembly to maintain structural stability and act as an effective barrier to the transmission of heat for a specified period of time.

Floating Angle A method of applying gypsum board designed to allow structural movement at interior corners.

Furring Wood strips applied to a wall or ceiling upon which a new wall or ceiling-covering material is installed.

Green Board A gypsum board having a tinted face paper that's usually light green. It is a moisture-resistant panel.

Gypsum The mineral consisting of fully hydrated calcium sulfate ($CaSO_4.2H_2O$ [calcium sulfate dihydrate]).

Gypsum Board The generic name for a family of noncombustible sheet products consisting of a core primarily of gypsum and paper surfacing on each side.

Gypsum Lath A gypsum board used as the base for application of gypsum plaster.

Gypsum Sheathing A specially formulated gypsum board for use as an exterior-wall membrane and base for exterior siding and other exterior materials.

Gypsum Wallboard A gypsum board used primarily as interior surfacing material in building structures.

Joint Compound A compound used for taping and finishing gypsum board.

Joint-Reinforcing Mesh A woven fiberglass material used in lieu of joint paper tape.

Joint Tape Paper A special paper tape for use with joint compound to conceal and reinforce the joints.

Metal Lath Expanded metal sheets nailed to the studs upon which the scratch coat of plaster is applied.

Mud A commonly used term for joint compound.

Mud Pan A handheld container for holding a small quantity of joint-compound products.

Nail Pop The protrusion of a nail above the surface of the panel caused by the shrinkage of wood framing.

Plumb In a vertical position perpendicular to the floor.

Predecorated Wallboard A gypsum board with a finished surface that is applied as the panel is manufactured. Gypsum board may be predecorated with paint, texture, or vinyl-film or printed-paper coverings.

Quick-Set Joint Compound A joint treatment that chemically hydrates prior to drying, causing it to set as quickly as 30 minutes.

Ready-Mixed Joint Compound Factory-mixed joint compound in ready-to-use form.

Score To cut the surface of a gypsum panel with a sharp blade before breaking the core.

Scratch Coat The first coat of a plaster-wall finish. It is bonded to the lath.

Screws, Drywall Special fasteners for attachment of gypsum board.

Single Layer One layer of gypsum board used as the finished wall or ceiling.

Suspended Ceiling A ceiling consisting of a metal frame and panels that is hung from the overhead structure on wires.

Tapered Edge The factory edge that is sloped from the face to the outer edge so the joint tape can be hidden.

Topping Compound A specially formulated joint compound designed for the final finishing coat.

Type-X Gypsum Board A specially formulated gypsum board with improved fire resistance.

Vinyl Trim Extruded vinyl molding for concealing edges, ends, joints, and corners.

Wainscoting Paneling that extends up the lower part of the wall.

CHAPTER NINE: INTERIOR PAINTING

Complementary Colors Colors that are opposite each other on the color wheel, such as red and green.
Cool Colors The cool colors are gray, green, blue, and violet.
Intensity of Color The strength of the color.

Lead-based Paint Paint made with lead as one of the ingredients. It is banned from use because it is a health hazard.

Primary Colors The primary colors are red, yellow, and blue.

Secondary Colors Colors made by blending the primary colors. They are violet, orange, and green.
Stencil A device for applying a decorative pattern, consisting of a flat sheet with the design cut out, through which paint is applied to a surface.

Tertiary Colors Colors made by blending a primary and a secondary color, such as blending yellow and green to get yellow-green.

Value of Color The lightness or darkness of a color.

Warm Colors The warm colors are red, orange, and yellow.

CHAPTER TEN: WALL-COVERING MATERIALS AND TECHNIQUES

Adhesive A bonding material applied to the back of the wall covering that causes it to adhere to the wall.

Border A narrow decorative strip that provides accent at ceilings and around doors and windows.
Bubble A pocket of air that has been trapped behind the wall covering, preventing it from bonding flat to the wall surface.

Dry-Strip An attempt to remove an old wall covering by pulling it lose from the wall.

Gel Compound A thick, gel-like compound brushed over old wall covering to soften the paste so it can be stripped.

Liner Paper A black paper product, applied over walls to be covered with a wall-covering material, that is slightly rough to accept the covering directly.

Pasting Applying paste to the back of the sheet of wall-covering material.
Pattern-Matching The process of getting the pattern on the edge and end of a wall-covering roll to match that on the roll already applied to the wall.
Pre-pasted Wall Covering A wall covering manufactured with an adhesive applied to the back. The adhesive is activated by immersing the wall covering in water.

Steamer An electric tool that generates steam which, when used on the old wall covering, tends to soften the paste, thus easing removal.

Wall Covering A general term used to describe all types of flexible wall-decorating material sold in roll form.
Wallpaper A term used to identify a paper-based wall covering.

CHAPTER ELEVEN: CERAMIC WALL-TILE REPAIRS

Cement Board A hard, rigid, water-resistant panel used as a substrate on walls to be tiled, especially in areas of high moisture, such as a shower.

Epoxy Thinset A bonding agent containing sand, cement, a liquid epoxy resin, and a hardener. It is used to adhere ceramic tiles to any wall surface.

File Nippers A tool that looks like pliers but has sharp cutting edges. It is used to take small bits out of a ceramic tile.

Grout A mixture of sand, cement, and coloring materials. It is used to fill the spaces between ceramic wall tiles. Some types contain a latex material.

Mastic A premixed bonding agent used to adhere ceramic wall tiles to the wall surface.

Sealant A silicone-based material that is flexible, waterproof, and mildew-resistant and which is used to seal areas where grout has difficulty staying.

Substrate The base material upon which the tile is bonded.

Thinset A cement-based bonding agent used to adhere ceramic tiles to cement backer board and mortar beds.

Tile Cutter A tool that scores a line on a ceramic tile along which the tile will then snap apart.

CHAPTER TWELVE: FLOORS AND FLOOR COVERINGS

Beam A large structural member running below the floor and upon which the floor joists rest.

Carpet A heavy, durable floor covering made from woven, knitted, or needle-tufted natural or synthetic fibers.

Ceramic Floor Tile A floor covering made from ceramic materials, such as metallic oxide, boride, carbide, nitride, or a mixture of these compounds. It often has a glazed surface.

Concrete Block Piers A series of concrete blocks stacked one on top of the other and bonded together with mortar. They are used to support beams that support floor joists.

Cushion A soft, resilient sheet material placed on the subfloor and over which the carpet is laid. Typically it is made from urethane, rubber, and fibers.

Drum Sander An electric sander that has a large rotating cylinder covered with an abrasive cloth. It is used to sand wood floors.

Flocked Carpet Carpet made by electrostatically spraying short strands of pile yarn onto an adhesive-covered backing.

Fusion-Bonded Carpet Carpet made by bonding pile yarn to sheets of material coated with a vinyl adhesive.

Glaze A ceramic coating, usually thin and with a glass-like gloss, that is formed on the surface of ceramic tiles.

Hardwood Floor A solid-wood floor made from hardwoods such as oak and maple.

Jack Post A metal post with a screw adjustment that allows the length to be changed.

Knitted Carpet Carpet made by looping the stitching, backing, and pile yarns together.

Laminated-Wood Flooring A flooring product made by bonding a high-pressure plastic laminate to a core of medium-density fiberboard with a back covered with another layer of laminate.

Load-Bearing Partition An interior partition (wall)

that carries the weight of ceiling joists or the joists of a second floor.

Parquet Square A square of wood flooring made by gluing up short lengths of strip flooring or laminated blocks.

Penetrating Sealer A wax-based floor-finishing material applied to the wood floor to seal it and prevent it from absorbing liquids.

Plank Flooring Solid-wood or laminated-wood flooring that is wider than strip flooring, typically 4 to 8 inches wide.

Resilient Flooring Floor covering that is flexible and bends and compresses under a load. Vinyl, cork, and rubber are typical types.

Softwood Flooring Solid-wood floors made from yellow pine and Douglas fir.

Stain A finishing material applied to wood flooring to produce the color desired.

Stain-Sealer A floor finishing liquid that stains (colors) the wood floor and seals the wood, providing protection.

Strip Flooring Solid-wood flooring made in soft- and hardwoods. It has tongue-and-groove edges. Typically it is $1^1/_2$ to 3 inches wide.

Subfloor A material, such as plywood or particleboard, that is nailed to the top of floor joists, and upon which the finished floor is laid.

Surface Sealer A liquid floor-finishing material that forms a surface coating on the wood. Polyurethane and urethane are two types.

Tufted Carpet Carpet made by stitching the face pile into a fiber backing material.

Woven Carpet Carpet made by weaving the fibers on a loom.

Cylindrical Lockset A lockset that has a large cylindrical case in which a heavy-duty mechanism is located. It is a secure lock used on exterior doors.

Dead Bolt This security device has a sliding shaft that enters a metal strike plate in the jamb. It is moved with a key or a handle on the inside of the door.

Electric Eye A system that sends a beam across an area to a receiving device. When the beam is broken an alarm is sounded.

Foil Alarm Tape An adhesive-backed metallic tape that is bonded to glass on doors and windows. It activates the alarm if the glass is broken.

Graphite A soft native carbon used to lubricate locks.

Hard-Wired Alarm Systems Systems in which the wires to the door and window switches are placed inside the walls as the house is being built.

Mortise Lock A large rectangular lock set in an opening (a mortise) cut in the edge of a door.

Motion Detector A device that scans an area in the house and sounds an alarm if someone walks into the beam.

Plunger Switch A switch used on doors on hard-wired alarm systems. This switch is like the one for a refrigerator light.

Strike Plate A metal plate secured to the door jamb with openings into which the latch on the lockset enters, keeping the door from being opened.

Tubular Lockset A lockset that has a long, narrow mechanism that enters a hole bored into the edge of the door. It is used on interior doors.

Wireless Alarm System An alarm system using electronic sensors on doors and windows that transmits a signal to the control panel without wires.

CHAPTER FOURTEEN: IMPROVING TEMPERATURE CONTROL

Blanket Insulation Thick, fibrous lengths of insulation, typically fiberglass or rock wool.

Conduction The transference of heat energy by passing through a solid or liquid.

Convection The transference of heat energy by the circulation of heated air or liquids.

Foamed Insulation A plastic mix that is in a creamy form and is pumped into wall cavities and other voids.

Granular Insulation Insulation in the form of small pellets. Perlite, vermiculite, and expanded polystyrene types are available.

Insulating Foams Plastic-foamed sheets commonly made from extruded polystyrene, expanded polystyrene, and polyurethane.

Radiant Insulation Layers of aluminum foil.

Radiation A condition in which heat energy passes through the air between the source of heat and the object heated without heating the intervening air.

R-Value The ability of a material to resist the flow of heat through it. The greater the R-value, the greater the resistance to heat transfer.

Sound-Transmission Class A number indicating the effectiveness of a material or assembly of materials to reduce the transmission of sound through it. The larger the number, the more effective it is in reducing sound transmission.

Storm Door A door installed on the outside of the exterior door. It usually has a glass panel and a screen panel.

Storm Window An aluminum-framed window designed to be installed to the exterior casing of the regular window.

Vapor Retarder A sheet material placed on the inside walls and ceiling to keep moisture generated in the house from penetrating the walls. It may be a polyethylene sheet or treated paper such as that found on the outside of insulation blankets.

Weather-stripping A strip of material placed around the edges of doors and windows to stop the infiltration of air through cracks. Metal, vinyl, and foam materials are available.

CHAPTER FIFTEEN: FURNITURE REPAIR

Anchor Holes Small-diameter holes drilled in wood into which wood screws are driven.

Bleach A liquid applied to stains on wood surfaces to reduce them in color so they are not as noticeable. Household bleach, ammonia, and commercial bleaches are available.

Bonding The process of gluing thin veneer wood strips to the edges of plywood or particleboard to cover the unsightly side grain.

Cleat A wood strip screwed and glued to the bottom of warped tabletops in an attempt to straighten them and hold them flat.

Coil Spring A spring in the shape of a round coil used to support the layers of upholstery material in a chair seat or back.

Corner Block A wood or metal connection secured to the rails at each side of a leg to strengthen the leg-to-rail connection.

Dowel Joint A joint in which round wood pins called dowels are used to secure the abutting pieces.

Lacquer A wood-finishing material consisting of a resin, cellulose ester, or both, dissolved in a volatile solvent such as butyl alcohol or butyl acetate. It sometimes has a pigment added.

Mortise A rectangular opening cut into a wood member to receive a tenon.

Mortise-and-Tenon Joint A joint formed between butting members in which a tenon on one part fits into a mortise in the other piece.

Non-Grain-Raising Stain A rapidly drying stain that does not raise the grain of the wood. It produces a transparent color, allowing the grain to show.

Oil Stain An oil-based liquid coloring agent that is applied to wood surfaces to change the color.

One-Step Finish A wood-finishing material that stains the wood the desired color and contains the finish coating. The one-step finish and the finish coating are applied as a single coating.

Sagless Spring A flat spring placed across the chair frame at the seat and back, and over which the layers of upholstery material are laid.

Stick Shellac Shellac in stick form that is melted into dents in the wood surface to bring the surface flush.

Stripper A liquid or paste applied to old furniture finishes to soften them so they can be removed.

Tenon A projecting end of a wood member reduced in size so it will fit into a mortise in an abutting piece.

Tung Oil A penetrating oil wiped over the surface of wood, producing a hard, glossy finish.

Varnish A protective coating. There are many types of varnishes. One type has a resin dissolved in a quick-drying solvent such as alcohol. Some have drying oils in a base of turpentine.

Veneer A thin piece of wood that has been sliced off a larger wood member. Veneers are typically $1/28$ inch thick.

Warp Distortion in a wood surface, causing it to bend or twist out of a plane.

Webbing A strong woven fabric strip nailed across chair seats and backs to support coil springs, foam-rubber cushions, and layers of upholstery material.

Wood Filler A paste-like material applied to open-grain woods to fill the pore-like openings so the surface is smooth.

CHAPTER SIXTEEN: THE HOME WORKSHOP

Decibel A unit used to measure the intensity (loudness) of sound.

Pegboard Perforated sheets of hardboard.

Portable Power Tools Lightweight electric tools that are carried around to the place where work is to be performed.

Smoke Detectors Sensing devices that sound an alarm when smoke fills an area.

Stationary Power Tools Power tools on stands kept in the same location. The work is brought to them.

Vibration Pads Rubber or fiber pads placed below the legs of power tools to reduce noise transmission.

INDEX